SECOND EDITION

SCALING THE CORPORATE WALL

Readings in Business and Society

S. PRAKASH SETHI

Baruch College, The City University of New York

PAUL STEIDLMEIER

Binghamton University, State University of New York

CECILIA M. FALBE

Albany University, State University of New York

PRENTICE HALL
UPPER SADDLE RIVER, NEW JERSEY 07458

Acquisitions editor: Natalie Anderson
Marketing manager: Sandra Steiner
Managing editor: Carol Burgett
Production editor: Edie Riker
Cover design: Kiwi Design
Manufacturing buyer: Ken Clinton
Editorial assistant: Crissy Statuto

Credits and acknowledgments for materials borrowed from other sources and reproduced, with permission, in this textbook appear on pages iii–vi.

Copyright © 1997, 1991 by Prentice-Hall, Inc.
A Simon & Schuster Company
Upper Saddle River, New Jersey 07458

All rights reserved. No part of this book may be reproduced, in any form or by any means, without permission in writing from the publisher.

Library of Congress Cataloging-in-Publication Data
Scaling the corporate wall : readings in business and society /
   [compiled by] S. Prakash Sethi, Paul Steidlmeier, Cecilia M. Falbe
   — 2nd ed.
      p. cm.
   Rev. ed. of: Scaling the corporate wall / [compiled by] S. Prakash
Sethi. c1991.
   Includes original essays along with articles previously published
in scholarly and professional journals.
   ISBN 0-13-490145-2
   1. Industries—Social aspects—United States. 2. Business ethics—
United States.   I. Sethi, Prakash.   II. Steidlmeier, Paul,
   [date]   III. Falbe, Cecilia M.   IV. Scaling the corporate wall.
HD60.5.U5S33 1996
302.3'5'0973—dc20   96-6795

Prentice-Hall International (UK) Limited, London
Prentice-Hall of Australia Pty. Limited, Sydney
Prentice-Hall Canada Inc., Toronto
Prentice-Hall Hispanoamericana, S.A., Mexico
Prentice-Hall of India Private Limited, New Delhi
Prentice-Hall of Japan, Inc., Tokyo
Simon & Schuster Asia Pte. Ltd., Singapore
Editora Prentice-Hall do Brasil, Ltda., Rio de Janeiro

Printed in the United States of America

10 9 8 7 6 5 4 3 2 1

CONTENTS

I
Competitive Dynamics of Markets and Their impact on Business Activity

THE NATURE OF THE FIRM (1937)   1

R. H. Coase is Professor Emeritus, University of Chicago. This article appeared in *Economica*, Vol. IV, 1937, pp. 386-405. Reprinted with permission from Blackwell Publishers.

THE THEORY OF THE FIRM REVISITED   14

Harold Demsetz is Professor, University of California, Los Angeles. This article appeared in *The Journal of Law, Economics & Organization*, Vol. 4, Spring 1988, pp. 159–178. Reprinted by permission of Oxford University Press.

THE POLITICAL ECONOMY OF REGULATION   31
An Analysis of Market Failures

Robert G. Harris is Professor of Business Administration, Graduate School of Business, University of California at Berkeley. *James M. Carman* is Professor of Business Administration, Graduate School of Business, University of California at Berkeley. An earlier version of this article appeared in the *Journal of Macromarketing*, Spring 1983.

THE POLITICAL ECONOMY OF REGULATION   42
An Analysis of Regulatory Responses

James M. Carman is Professor of Business Administration, Graduate School of Business, University of California at Berkeley. *James M. Carman* is Professor of Business Administration, Graduate School of Business, University of California at Berkeley. An earlier version of this article appeared in the *Journal of Macromarketing*, Spring 1983.

II
Business Ethics

MONEY AND VALUE   62
On the Ethics of Economics and Finance

Amartya Sen is Lamont University Professor in the Department of Economics, Harvard University, Cambridge, Massachusetts. This article is reprinted from *Economics and Philosophy*, Vol. 9, 1993, pp. 203–227, and is the text of the first Baffi Lecture given at the Bank of Italy on April 26, 1991. Reprinted with the permission of Cambridge University Press.

IMPERFECT MARKETS   81
Business Ethics as an Easy Virtue

S. Prakash Sethi is Professor of Management, Baruch College, The City University of New York. This article appeared in *Journal of Business Ethics*. Vol. 13, 1994, pp. 803–815. Reprinted by permission of Kluwer Academic Publishers.

TOWARD A UNIFIED CONCEPTION OF BUSINESS ETHICS   95
Integrative Social Contracts Theory

Thomas Donaldson is the John F. Connelly Professor of Business Ethics, School of Business, Georgetown University, Washington, D.C. *Thomas W. Dunfee* is Professor, University of Pennsylvania. This article appeared in *Academy of Management Review*, Vol. 19, No. 2, pp. 252–284 (1994). Reprinted by permission of *Academy of Management Review*.

BUSINESS ETHICS   119
A Japanese View

Iwao Taka is Assistant Professor, The International School of Economics and Business Administration, Reitaku University, Kashiwa, China.

This article appeared in *Business Ethics Quarterly*, January 1994, Vol. 4, No. 1, pp. 53–78. Reprinted by permission of *The Society for Business Ethics*, copyright 1994.

III
Corporate Governance

THE NEW ECONOMIC THEORY OF THE FIRM   140
Critical Perspectives from History

William W. Bratton, Jr., is the Kaiser Professor of Law, Benjamin N. Cardozo School of Law, Yeshiva University, New York, NY. This article appeared in the *Stanford Law Review*, Vol. 41, No. 1471 (July, 1989). Copyright 1989 by the Board of Trustees of the Leland Stanford Junior University.

ECLIPSE OF THE PUBLIC CORPORATION   167

Michael C. Jensen is the Edsel Bryant Ford Professor of Business Administration at the Harvard Business School, Harvard University, Cambridge, MA. The article is reprinted by permission of *Harvard Business Review,* Sept./Oct. 1989. Copyright © 1989 by the President and Fellows of Harvard College, all rights reserved.

THE EVOLVING CORPORATE BOARD   184

Murray Weidenbaum is Distinguished University Professor and Director of the Center for the Study of American Business, Washington University, St. Louis, MO. This article is an updated version of a paper appearing in *Business and Society* (1987), edited by S. P. Sethi and Cecilia Falbe.

GOLDEN PARACHUTES AND TIN PARACHUTES   195
Top Management Perks, Corporate Governance, and the Public Interest

Philip L. Cochran is Associate Professor of Business Administration, the Mary Jean and Frank P. Smeal College of Business Administration. Pennsylvania State University, College Station, PA. *Steven L.*

Wartick is Associate Professor of Business Administration, University of Missouri at St. Louis. *Bruce C. Skaggs* is a doctoral student at the Mary Jean and Frank P. Smeal College of Business Administration, Pennsylvania State University. This article is an updated version of a paper appearing in *Business and Society* (1987), edited by S.P. Sethi and Cecilia Falbe.

IV
Social Issues in Management

THE NOTION OF THE "GOOD CORPORATION" IN A COMPETITIVE GLOBAL ECONOMY   205
Moving from a Socially Responsible to a Socially Accountable Corporation

S. Prakash Sethi is Professor of Management, Baruch College, The City University of New York. This article was first presented at a conference: "Corporate Social Responsibility in a Global Economy: The Challenge," sponsored by the Center for Ethics and Religious Values in Business and the College of Business Administration, Notre Dame University, April 11–13, 1994. Reprinted with permission.

ADDRESSING A THEORETICAL PROBLEM BY REORIENTING THE CORPORATE SOCIAL PERFORMANCE MODEL   216

Diane L. Swanson is Assistant Professor, Robert Morris College, Pittsburgh, PA. This article is reprinted with permission from *Academy of Management Review*, Vol. 20, No. 1 (January, 1995).

THE STAKEHOLDER THEORY OF THE CORPORATION   233
Concepts, Evidence, and Implications

Thomas Donaldson is the John F. Connelly Professor of Business Ethics, School of Business, Georgetown University, Washington, D.C. *Lee E. Preston* is Professor, College of Business and Management, University of Maryland at College Park, MD. This article is reprinted with permission from *Academy of Management Review*, Vol. 20, No. 1 (January, 1995).

**SOCIETAL PRESSURES
ON BUSINESS   253**
In Whose Interest?

Oliver F. Williams is Professor, School of Business, University of Notre Dame, Notre Dame, IN.

**ECOCENTRIC MANAGEMENT
FOR A RISK SOCIETY   275**
Paul Shrivastava is Howard I. Scott Professor of Management, Bucknell University, Lewisburg, PA. This article is reprinted with permission from *Academy of Management Review*, Vol. 20, No. 1 (January, 1995).

**V
The Impact of News Media
on Business Activities**

TOO CLOSE FOR COMFORT   291
How the Business Press Romances America's Corporate Leaders

Charles A. Riley II is Associate Professor of Business Journalism, Baruch College, The City University of New York, and was a reporter at *Fortune.*

FALLEN HEROES   313
Social Drama on Wall Street

Mitchel Y. Abolafia is a Professor at the State University of New York at Albany. This study is drawn on Chapter 7 of the author's manuscript *Making Markets: Self-Interest and Restraint on Wall Street* (Harvard University Press, forthcoming).

LOSING GROUND   323
In Latest Recession, Only Blacks Suffered Net Employment Loss

Rochelle Sharpe is a reporter. This article appeared in *The Wall Street Journal*, September 14, 1993, p. 1, and is reprinted by permission of *The Wall Street Journal*, 1993, Dow Jones & Company, Inc. All Rights Reserved Worldwide.

**VI
The Role of Corporate Culture and
Corporate Responses to Social Issues**

**HOW AND WHY ORGANIZATIONS
ARE CULTURES   333**
Harrison Trice was Professor, New York State School of Industrial and Labor Relations, Cornell University, Ithaca, NY. *Janice M. Beyer* is the Harkins and Company Centennial Chair in Business Administration, Department of Management, and Professor of Sociology, University of Texas—Austin. This article appeared as Chapter 1 in *The Cultures of Work Organizations*, 1993, Prentice Hall, Englewood Cliffs, NJ. Copyright © 1993, Prentice-Hall Publishers.

**MANAGING CULTURE AS A
COMPETITIVE RESOURCE   365**
An Identity-Based View of Sustainable Competitive Advantage

C. Marlene Fiol is Associate Professor, University of Colorado—Denver. This article appeared in *Journal of Management*, 1991, Vol. 17, No. 1, pp. 191–211. Reprinted by permission.

**WORKING THROUGH DIVERSITY
AS A STRATEGIC IMPERATIVE   383**
Susan E. Jackson is Associate Professor of Psychology, New York University, New York. *Eden B. Alvarez* is a doctoral student in industrial/organizational psychology, New York University, New York. This material is reproduced from *Diversity in the Workplace*, 1992, The Builford Press, New York. Reprinted with permission.

**VII
Corporate Crime**

**CORPORATE AND EXECUTIVE CRIMINAL
LIABILITY   395**
Appropriate Standards, Remedies,
and Managerial Responses

John M. Holcomb is Associate Professor, Department of Legal Studies, College of Business Administration, University of Denver, Colorado.

S. Prakash Sethi is Professor of Management, Baruch College, City University of New York. This article appeared in *Business & the Contemporary World* (Summer 1992), Vol. IV, No. 3, pp. 81–105. Reprinted by permission, copyright Walter de Gruyter & Co., 1992.

CORPORATE CRIME AND CORPORATE SANCTIONS IN JAPAN   419

Williams S. Laufer is Assistant Professor of Legal Studies, Wharton School, University of Pennsylvania, Philadelphia. *Alison J. Cohen* is Research Assistant in the Department of Legal Studies, Wharton School, University of Pennsylvania, Philadelphia. This article appeared in *Business & the Contemporary World* (Summer 1992), Vol. IV, No. 3, pp. 106–125. Reprinted by permission, copyright Walter de Gruyter & Co., 1992.

VIII
International Dimensions of the Business-Society Interface

THE PARADOX OF ECONOMIC GLOBALISM   438
The Myth and Reality of the "Global Village"— The Changing Role of Multinational Corporations

S. Prakash Sethi is Professor of Management, Baruch College, City University of New York. *Joel A. Kurtzman* is an author and former Editor-in-Chief of *Harvard Business Review*. *Bharat B. Bhalla* is Professor of International Business and Finance, Fairfield University, Fairfield, CT. This article originally appeared in *Business & the Contemporary World*, Vol. VI, No. 4, and is reprinted with permission.

POLICY REGIMES IN THE INTERNATIONAL BUSINESS ENVIRONMENT   450

Lee E. Preston. This essay is based on material originally presented in Preston and Windsor. *The Rules of the Game in the Global Economy: Policy Regimes for International Business*, 1992. (Kluwer Academic Publishers, Norwell, MA.)

A NEW PERSPECTIVE ON THE INTERNATIONAL SOCIAL REGULATION OF BUSINESS   464
An Evaluation of the Compliance Status of International Code of Marketing of Breast-Milk Substitutes

S. Prakash Sethi is Professor of Management, Baruch College, City University of New York. *Bharat B. Bhalla* is Associate Professor of International Business and Finance, Fairfield University, Fairfield, CT. This article is reprinted from *The Journal of Socio-Economics*, Vol. 22, No. 2 (1993), pp. 141–158, copyright 1993 JAI Press, Inc., Greenwich, CT.

THE SOCIAL ENVIRONMENT OF BUSINESS IN EUROPE   477

Peter Curwen is Professor, Sheffield Business School, Sheffield, UK. An earlier version of this article appeared in the *European Business Journal*, vol. 4, no. 2, pp. 17–26 as "Social Policy in the European Community in Light of the Maastricht Treaty."

A STAKEHOLDER APPROACH TO THE GLOBALIZATION OF LABOR   489

Richard Morfopoulos is a doctoral student in Organizational Studies and *Cecilia M. Falbe* is Associate Professor of Management and Organizational Studies at State University of New York at Albany.

AMERICAN ACTIVISTS' ATTEMPTS TO REFORM CHINA AND THE PROSPECTS FOR U.S. BUSINESS   501

Paul Steidlmeier is Associate Professor of Management, State University of New York at Binghamton, Binghamton, NY.

PREFACE

This anthology represents a continuity of effort first presented in *Business and Society: Dimensions of Conflict and Cooperation*, edited by S. Prakash Sethi and Cecilia M. Falbe (Lexington Books, 1987), and more recently in *Scaling the Corporate Wall: Readings in Social Issues of the Nineties*, edited by S. Prakash Sethi, Paul Steidlmeier and Cecilia M. Falbe (Prentice Hall, 1991). Our approach in this compendium, as in the previous instances, has been to present a systematic, albeit evolving, framework, encompassing advances in theory development, and various approaches to problem identification, analysis, and issue resolution, in the ever-changing and enlarging domain of the context of business-society interface. The issue-analysis arena draws from a number of fields including management, economics, political science, sociology, philosophy, ethics, and law. Therefore, in search of appropriate materials, we have drawn from professional and scholarly journals covering diverse fields of social enquiry. To these have been added a number of invited original essays by scholars representing distinct points of view and perspectives that provide a newer approach to examining both the existing and emerging issues involving business-society relationships.

The book has been organized in eight major subject areas and includes thirty-one articles. It is by no means a comprehensive collection touching all facets of our enquiry. From some perspectives, it may not even be considered a representative collection. For the selection of articles reflects the preferences and subjective, albeit professional, judgments of the editors in bringing about what is significant and elucidatory in a narrative form. Notwithstanding, we believe that the outcome of these combined judgments should provide the readers with a rich, diverse, and provocative treatment of the subject matter in hand while provoking them with intriguing, and hitherto, unanswered questions and opening up new fields of enquiry for further exploration.

In the opening segment of the book, we address the concept of competitive dynamics and the characteristics of market economies in affecting production and distribution of wealth, the role of the individual entrepreneur, and its organized counterpart, i.e., the firm. The first two papers in this section by Coase and Demsetz have for some time been the bellwether for those who would undertake a more critical analysis of the nature and function of the firm. This reflection is fundamental to the whole of business and society endeavor. It cannot be simply assumed that a firm is merely a "profit maximizer" or that managers are dedicated to "maximizing shareholder return on investment" or, more importantly, that they should somehow ideally attempt to do so. The firm manifests a far more subtle nexus of interrelationships than the canons of economic rationality might suggest.

Along similar lines, the work of Harris and Carman leads us to question our presuppositions concerning the actual nature of markets and regulation. The authors describe the conditions of "ideal markets" that provide the foundation of microeconomics and the economic theory of the firm. This is followed by a discussion of imperfections in the operations of perfect markets leading to "market failures" and creates grounds for market regulation. Even ideal markets, or markets approaching perfection, may not be completely socially acceptable because the market-created income distributions were perceived by large segments of society to be inequitable and unfair. The authors go on to provide an equally insightful discussion to suggest that market failures can have their counterpart in "regulatory failures" and that given a set of circumstances, imperfect markets may be preferable to regulated markets and vice versa.

The section on Business Ethics (Section II) provides a more direct contrast between the logic of economic rationality and the moral basis of human economic behavior. It critically examines both the opportunities and constraints that a market-based competitive economy imposes on individuals and firms in their effort to engage in business and economic activities. The first article by Sen takes the basic lifeblood of the economic system, that is money, and subjects it to an analysis of value. In so doing, he offers a stimulating critique of contemporary financial practices by subjecting the notions of economic use-value to a broader critique of human fulfillment. The next article by Sethi raises the issue of ethics in the marketplace. Sethi demonstrates that, even if the ideal conditions of economic theory were fulfilled, market dynamics do not always tend toward the realization of ethical behavior. These ideas force us back to the question raised earlier by Harris and Carman. To wit, assuming that markets function efficiently, one must ask under what conditions is it possible for the market milieu to create an ethical environment? The article in this section by Donaldson and Dunfee argues in favor of the notion of a "social contract" as the basis for a unified conception of business ethics. They assert that it is the notion of contract that lies at the core of both a market economy and a democratic polity. The social contract itself represents an ideal thought experiment designed to ensure justice and fairness. In its origin, social contract has secular roots recognizing as valid only that authority which is voluntarily conceded by those who would be subjected to it. The final article by Taka presents a Japanese view of business ethics and asks us to consider the cultural limitations (as well of the richness) of our conceptualizations of the business and society interface.

Section III covers one of the thorniest areas of business-society interface by focusing on the legitimacy of the right of managers to control a corporation's resources and how that legitimacy affects the rights of various stakeholders on the one hand and that of social relevance and corporate performance on the other hand. In the lead article, Bratton gives us a tour de force of different theories and rationalizations that have been offered over time to define the scope and justify the authority of corporate management over a corporation's resources. He critically examines the legal dogma of stockholders owning the corporation and managers operating the corporation under the direction of a representative board of directors elected by the corporation's owners. Having demonstrated the fallacy of effective shareholder control and accepting the fact of corporate management as a self-perpetuating oligarchy, he examines various theoretical and practical arguments currently in vogue that justify managerial authority or seek to impose constraints upon its use. In doing so, he offers a succinct description and critical assessment of various theories of corporate governance ranging from managerialism to transaction-contract and from stockholder to stakeholder. Within the same general perspective, but from a management vantage point, Jensen depicts the changing nature of the public corporation in terms of its interactions with its various constituents as well as in terms of its governance structures.

The role of board of directors and how it might be made more effective is the subject of the remaining two articles in this segment. Weidenbaum chronicles the evolving character, nature and function of corporate boards. Cochran, Wartick and Skaggs, on the other hand, underscore the cozy, if not incestuous, relationships that can develop between a corporation's board of directors and its top managers, such that the latter opportunistically serve their own narrow career interests rather than the interests of shareholders, much less those of other stakeholders in society.

The area of Social Issues in Management is explored in Section IV. Whether business creates the issues that society then must cope with, or whether society's ills constrain the activity of the firm, the dynamic of the business-society relationship is certain to exert pressure on a firm's management to examine the values it applies to the firm's decisions, define its relevant constituencies, and account for its social performance. The first two articles appearing in this section present the theoretical underpinnings toward developing a framework for understanding corporate social performance. Sethi advances the concept of social responsibility to one of social accountability by considering those economic and institutional factors that establish the parameters of the corporation's ability to act ethically. He argues for a consideration of these factors both in evaluating corporate performance and in generating programs and creating incentives that will serve to promote positive social behavior. Swanson, in her article, argues in favor of a new normative and operational model for evaluating corporate social performance that synthesizes previously competing orientations to business and society research. In so doing, she reformulates the existing perspectives to arrive at an interactive approach to the business-society relationship, linking individual, institutional and societal ethics in a non-hierarchical configuration.

Moving from the broader theoretical realm to more concrete dilemmas, the next two articles deal with defining who are the stakeholders of the corporation and the extent of their relative stakes. While it is accepted that managers generally must deal with a wide variety of constituents, it is not always so clear why, in a moral sense, they may be obligated to do so nor what is owed each constituent who raises his or her voice. Beginning with a discussion of stakeholder theory, Donaldson and Preston argue that stakeholder claims must rest on a foundation of normative principles. Next, Williams speaks to the specific conflict between corporate and stakeholder interests as characterized by the actions and demands of citizen activist groups. Using illustrative real-world examples, he explains how pressure can be brought to bear on corporations to adopt policies that are in better harmony with societal expectations of good corporate behavior. In the final article, Shrivastava presents a model of ecocentric management in terms of risk and

industrial ecosystems. He views industry in ecological terms and rejects more traditional perspectives that regard the environment as an independent externality.

The collection of four articles in Section V examine the impact of the news media on business activities. In the first article, Riley examines the uncritical way in which major business magazines and newspapers portray corporate leaders arising from their eagerness to please advertisers and upper-level managers who are their audience. In their ambition to pump up circulation and ad revenues, the press has created a cult of the business personality, making journalists into hagiographers and lionizing certain CEOs even in the face of serious problems with their performance or that of their companies. Riley focuses on the way the business press covers AIDS as an example of how the truth is modified to suit the corporate point of view.

The media's capacity for making or breaking reputations and framing public perception is well-depicted in the next article. Abolafia traces the rise and fall of Michael Milken as an illustration of how valiant heroes can be transformed by the press into demonic villains by virtue of their non-conformance to social expectations and lack of restraint. The author exposes the 1980s as a decade of greed and misdeeds during which corporate elites, finding themselves threatened by the unorthodox tactics of Wall Street-backed raiders, sought methods of redress to restore the social balance that had previously favored them. While Americans were held transfixed by the media events swirling around the personages central to this drama, the social fabric of our financial institutions unravelled to reveal motivations and behaviors that belied the public's self-image.

In this section's last article, Sharpe demonstrates how the role of the media can be pivotal in creating public awareness around issues that might otherwise be obscured by corporate public relations efforts. In "Losing Ground," the plight of Blacks in their attempt to climb the corporate ladder is unfolded, disclosing the numbers that argue against company claims of minority empowerment. Here, the media is wielded as a tool for prying open the doors of prejudice that seal off opportunities for Blacks in American society, and unlock the myth of minority advancement at the expense of the majority.

The role of organizational culture in explaining corporate social performance (Section VI) adds another important dimension to this anthology. A great variety of corporate accomplishments—as well as corporate sins of omission and commission—are attributed to corporate culture. Notwithstanding the importance of the association between culture and corporate social performance, the phenomenon is poorly understood and has suffered from a lack of systematic research. In part, this neglect can be attributed to the fact that culture-related research has been carried out in a number of disciplines whose connection to the study of business and management was at best tenuous, and at worst, nonexistent. As a result, there was little useful material available on how organizational culture affects business activity and corporate social performance, and how (or even whether) organizational culture can be managed. In the absence of sound knowledge of how an institution's culture is developed and maintained, and the roles culture can play in an organization, it is difficult to understand the relationship between corporate culture and performance. Fortunately, a number of important integrative theoretical and empirical pieces have appeared recently that have meaningful implications for managers that offer useful insights.

The paper by Trice and Beyer provides us with an overview of the most important issues in culture research. It sorts out some of the major disagreements regarding the characteristics of culture including whether there are single or multiple cultures in an organization, the extent to which we can generalize about cultural elements across organizations, and the extent to which cultures are malleable or rigid. In the next article, Fiol writes from the resource-based perspective of the firm. The author is critical of the two tradi-

tional approaches to culture —deep level assumptions and surface level behavioral manifestations—noting that neither contributes much to the study of competitive analysis. She reframes the concept of culture and introduces the notion of contextual identities to link behaviors and their social meaning in organizations. Managing the cognitive aspect of distinctive competency is to manage the linkages between identities and abstract cultural values and identities and behavioral expressions of these values. Applying Fiol's framework to corporate social performance shows promise for explaining the persistence of types of corporate behavior.

The article by Jackson and Alvarez discusses managing diversity in light of the recent increase in service businesses, global competition and the resulting restructuring of organizations. It includes an overview of the types of diversity that reflect changes in the labor force including cultural, gender and age diversity as well as diversity in corporate cultures as a result of mergers and alliances. The authors note that in a recent major survey of business managers, the most frequently cited problem in managing customer and client alliances was differences in corporate cultures.

As recent news events relate, the image of the corporation as good citizen has been sorely challenged if not shattered by the line of corporate executives in the docket. Part of the business-society landscape depicts corporate illegal behavior, and this is the subject of Section VII. The focus of this section is to define the scope of corporate behavior that is deemed illegal and socially unacceptable; various mechanisms developed by society to detect corporate illegal behavior and measures that might be used to seek restitution for the victim, and punish the culprit; and, even more important, deter future illegal behavior on the part of the corporations and individuals within corporations.

In the first article, authors Holcomb and Sethi examine the effectiveness of existing systems of punishment for corporate crime in actually deterring recidivism, controlling excesses, and in appropriately addressing the scope of the problem. They argue for a more comprehensive understanding of the conditions that enable criminal activity, both internal and external to the organization, in order to arrive at legal remediation that serves the twin objectives of deterrence and economic survival of the firm. Too often, the current legal standards neglect the complexities of organizational life contributing to corporate misdeeds, such as political power, decision-making patterns, and competitive pressures. Lack of identifiable individual accountability for corporate misdeeds renders the process of criminal punishment less than equitable from the viewpoint of all concerned parties. The authors recommend the development of a new model of corporate liability whereby deterrents to crime that simultaneously permit the firm to meet its objectives be constructed with an eye to benefiting social welfare.

An interesting comparison between the effectiveness of the American and the Japanese legal systems in curtailing corporate crime in their respective societies is brought forth by Laufer and Cohen. The authors point to cultural determinants of the relative ability of each society to control deviance and suggest that reliance on social control in Japan over more formal, legal mechanisms for deterrence, has been relatively effective. However, as the borders between Japan and the West become more indistinct, the call for more rigorous regulation of Japanese corporate activity intensifies. In the final analysis, both societies are cautioned against an overreliance on either borrowed principles from a distant culture, or on tradition-bound rituals that serve expediency at the expense of uprightness.

The final section (Section VIII) of the anthology addresses a number of issues pertaining to the international dimension of business-society interface. It is well-nigh impossible to treat this subject with any degree of completeness in this book given the enormity of the subject matter and its complexity.

Therefore, we have confined ourselves to addressing the issues along those dimensions that we feel are of particular importance to corporate executives and students concerned with business-society issues within an international context.

The first article by Sethi, Kurtzman, and Bhalla challenges the notion of "global village" which has become the defining rhetoric in the supposedly ever-increasing interdependence of nations in international trade and investments; its implications in terms of globalization of our concerns in business behavior; and, the role of national governments and regional bodies in creating both generalized and country-specific conditions for acceptable corporate behavior. This article suggests that while there may indeed be a "global village," it is confined to a small part of the globe and a small minority of the world's population living in the First World. The vast majority of the world's people live under conditions best described as the Third and the Fourth Worlds. These people have no concept of the First World, do not share in its economic largesse and are not privileged to live under enlightened social organizations and democratic political systems. And yet, this other "global village" cannot be ignored without imperiling the progress made in the First World.

The next two articles by Preston, and Sethi and Bhalla, address the issue of new policy regimes that define and create order for conducting international economic relations on the one hand and business-government relations on the other hand. Preston's paper provides a theoretical framework describing various types of international policy regimes and how they operate to facilitate international economic relations at the international, regional and national levels. In particular, he describes the new international (supranational) organizations, created by the United Nations and other regional political systems to address emerging issues in international economic relations. Sethi and Bhalla report on the working of one such regime where an international body, that is, the World Health

Organization, created an international code to regulate and guide the marketing and promotional activities of multinational corporations in the sale of infant formula products. Unfortunately, the prognosis of the two authors as to the working of the new policy regimes, at least in this case, was not very encouraging. Notwithstanding the fact that the code was enacted with an almost unanimous consent by the voting member nations and was urged upon by the Third World countries, these countries have been singularly remiss in creating the implementing mechanisms to put the code into practice in their home countries.

Another approach to policy regimes is suggested by Curwen wherein he discusses the new European Community Charter of the Fundamental Social Rights of Workers, usually known as the European Charter. The Charter was enacted in May 1990. Although, as yet it does not have a legal force, it contains a mandate allowing the European Commission to set out detailed proposals on workers' rights in twelve areas, including employment and remuneration; improvement of living and working conditions; rights to social protection, freedom of association and collective bargaining, vocational training, equal treatment of men and women, information, consultation, workers' participation, health protection, workplace safety, and, protection of children and adolescents, elderly, and the disabled.

The last two articles by Morfopoulos and Falbe, and Steidlmeier examine the influence of U.S.-based social activists on the behavior of U.S. multinational corporations (MNCs) in their overseas operations. Morfopoulos and Falbe examine the phenomenon of labor practices in plants in Third World countries whose product is sold primarily, if not, exclusively to the First World multinational corporations. The contentious issue in this case is the often abysmal work conditions and low wages of the workers and the extent to which MNCs

should be held responsible for the actions of these subcontractors who are independent businesses and are invariably acting within the framework of local laws and customs. They analyze two instances where U.S. companies, namely, Nike and Levi Strauss, have been subjected to criticism and pressure by U.S. activist groups for their actions, or lack thereof, with regard to working conditions in the plants of their subcontractors in developing countries. At a more macro level, Steidlmeier examines the attempt by U.S.-based social activists in bringing pressure on the U.S. companies with investments in China in order to improve that country's human rights record and workers' rights. His analysis shows that such actions are, at best, of limited value where the country involved offers highly attractive investment opportunities; enterprises from other industrially advanced nations are not compelled to follow similar policies; and political and national security considerations severely limit the ability and desire of the governments of industrially advanced nations of the West to force the issue.

ACKNOWLEDGMENTS

We wish to acknowledge with thanks the capable and energetic research assistance of Linda M. Sama, a doctoral student in corporate strategy and public policy at Baruch College, CUNY. Her assistance was invaluable in tracking down references and citations from otherwise intractable library sources and from databases whose insatiable desire to hoard information under various obscure and obfuscating subject categories was only exceeded by her determination not to be outwitted by "dumb" machines.

S. Prakash Sethi
Paul Steidlmeier
Cecilia M. Falbe

THE NATURE OF THE FIRM (1937)

R.H. Coase

Economic theory has suffered in the past from a failure to state clearly its assumptions. Economists in building up a theory have often omitted to examine the foundations on which it was erected. This examination is, however, essential not only to prevent the misunderstanding and needless controversy which arise from a lack of knowledge of the assumptions on which a theory is based, but also because of the extreme importance for economics of good judgment in choosing between rival sets of assumptions. For instance, it is suggested that the use of the word "firm" in economics may be different from the use of the term by the "plain man."[1] Since there is apparently a trend in economic theory towards starting analysis with the individual firm and not with the industry,[2] it is all the more necessary not only that a clear definition of the word "firm" should be given but that its difference from a firm in the "real world," if it exists, should be made clear. Mrs. Robinson has said that "the two questions to be asked of a set of assumptions in economics are: Are they tractable? and: Do they correspond with the real world?"[3] Though, as Mrs. Robinson points out, "More often one set will be manageable and the other realistic," yet there may well be branches of theory where assumptions may be both manageable and realistic. It is hoped to show in the following paper that a definition of a firm may be obtained which is not only realistic in that it corresponds to what is meant by a firm in the real world, but is tractable by two of the most powerful instruments of economic analysis developed by Marshall, the idea of the margin and that of substitution, together giving the idea of substitution at the margin.[4] Our definition must, of course, "relate to formal relations which are capable of being *conceived* exactly."[5]

I

It is convenient if, in searching for a definition of a firm, we first consider the economic system as it is normally treated by the economist. Let us consider the description of the economic system given by Sir Arthur Salter.[6] "The normal economic system works itself. For its current operation it is under no central control, it needs no central survey. Over the whole range of human activity and human need, supply is adjusted to demand, and production to consumption, by a process that is automatic, elastic and responsive." An economist thinks of the economic system as being co-ordinated by the price mechanism and society becomes not an organization but an organism.[7] The economic system "works itself." This does not mean that there is no planning by individuals. These exercise foresight and choose between alternatives. This is necessarily so if there is to be order in the system. But this theory assumes that the direction of resources is dependent directly on the price mechanism. Indeed, it is often considered to be an objection to economic planning that it merely tries to do what is already done by the price mechanism.[8] Sir Arthur Salter's description, however, gives a very incomplete picture of our economic system. Within a firm, the description does not fit at all. For instance, in economic theory we find that the allocation of factors of production between different uses is determined by the price mechanism. The price of factor A becomes higher in X than in Y. As a result, A moves from Y to X until the difference between the prices of X and Y, except in so far as it compensates for other differential advantages, disappears. Yet in the real world, we find that there are many areas where this does not apply. If a workman moves from department Y to department X, he does not go because of a change in relative prices, but because he is ordered to do so. Those who object to economic planning on the grounds that the problem is solved by price movements can be answered by pointing out that there is planning within our economic system which is quite different from the individual planning mentioned above and which is akin to what is normally called economic planning. The example given above is typical of a large sphere in our modern economic system. Of course, this fact has not been ignored by economists. Marshall introduces organization as a fourth factor of production; J.B. Clark gives the co-ordinating function to the entrepreneur; Professor Knight introduces managers who co-ordinate. As D.H. Robertson points out, we find "islands of conscious power in this ocean of unconscious co-operation like lumps of butter coagulating in a pail of buttermilk."[9] But in view of the fact that it is usually argued that co-ordination will be done by the price mechanism, why is such organization necessary? Why are there these "islands of conscious power"? Outside the firm, price movements direct production, which is co-ordinated through a series of exchange transactions on the market. Within a firm, these market transactions are eliminated and in place of the complicated market structure

with exchange transactions is substituted the entrepreneur co-ordinator, who directs production.[10] It is clear that these are alternative methods of co-ordinating production. Yet, having regard to the fact that if production is regulated by price movements, production could be carried on without any organization at all, well might we ask, why is there any organization?

Of course, the degree to which the price mechanism is superseded varies greatly. In a department store, the allocation of the different sections to the various locations in the building may be done by the controlling authority or it may be the result of competitive price bidding for space. In the Lancashire cotton industry, a weaver can rent power and shop-room and can obtain looms and yarn on credit.[11] This co-ordination of the various factors of production is, however, normally carried out without the intervention of the price mechanism. As is evident, the amount of "vertical" integration, involving as it does the supersession of the price mechanism, varies greatly from industry to industry and from firm to firm.

It can, I think, be assumed that the distinguishing mark of the firm is the supersession of the price mechanism. It is, of course, as Professor Robbins points out, "related to an outside network of relative prices and costs,"[12] but it is important to discover the exact nature of this relationship. This distinction between the allocation of resources in a firm and the allocation in the economic system has been very vividly described by Mr. Maurice Dobb when discussing Adam Smith's conception of the capitalist: "It began to be seen that there was something more important than the relations inside each factory or unit captained by an undertaker; there were the relations of the undertaker with the rest of the economic world outside his immediate sphere . . . the undertaker busies himself with the division of labour inside each firm and he plans and organises consciously," but "he is related to the much larger economic specialisation, of which he himself is merely one specialised unit. Here, he plays his part as a single cell in a larger organism, mainly unconscious of the wider role he fills."[13]

In view of the fact that while economists treat the price mechanism as a co-ordinating instrument, they also admit the co-ordinating function of the "entrepreneur," it is surely important to enquire why co-ordination is the work of the price mechanism in one case and of the entrepreneur in another. The purpose of this paper is to bridge what appears to be a gap in economic theory between the assumption (made for some purposes) that resources are allocated by means of the price mechanism and the assumption (made for other purposes) that this allocation is dependent on the entrepreneur-co-ordinator. We have to explain the basis on which, in practice, this choice between alternatives is effected.[14]

II

Our task is to attempt to discover why a firm emerges at all in a specialized exchange economy. The price mechanism (considered purely from the side of the direction of resources) might be superseded if the relationship which replaced it was desired for its own sake. This would be the case, for example, if some people preferred to work under the direction of some other person. Such individuals would accept less in order to work under someone, and firms would arise naturally from this. But it would appear that this cannot be a very important reason, for it would rather seem that the opposite tendency is operating if one judges from the stress normally laid on the advantage of "being one's own master."[15] Of course, if the desire was not to be controlled but to control, to exercise power over others, then people might be willing to give up something in order to direct others; that is, they would be willing to pay others more than they could get under the price mechanism in order to be able to direct them. But this implies that those who direct pay in order to be able to do this and

are not paid to direct, which is clearly not true in the majority of cases.[16] Firms might also exist if purchasers preferred commodities which are produced by firms to those not so produced; but even in spheres where one would expect such preferences (if they exist) to be of negligible importance, firms are to be found in the real world.[17] Therefore there must be other elements involved.

The main reason why it is profitable to establish a firm would seem to be that there is a cost of using the price mechanism. The most obvious cost of "organizing" production through the price mechanism is that of discovering what the relevant prices are.[18] This cost may be reduced but it will not be eliminated by the emergence of specialists who will sell this information. The costs of negotiating and concluding a separate contract for each exchange transaction which takes place on a market must also be taken into account.[19] Again, in certain markets, e.g., produce exchanges, a technique is devised for minimizing these contract costs; but they are not eliminated. It is true that contracts are not eliminated when there is a firm but they are greatly reduced. A factor of production (or the owner thereof) does not have to make a series of contracts with the factors with whom he is co-operating within the firm, as would be necessary, of course, if this co-operation were as a direct result of the working of the price mechanism. For this series of contracts is substituted one. At this stage, it is important to note the character of the contract into which a factor enters that is employed with a firm. The contract is one whereby the factor, for a certain remuneration (which may be fixed or fluctuating), agrees to obey the directions of an entrepreneur *within certain limits*.[20] The essence of the contract is that it should only state the limits to the powers of the entrepreneur. Within these limits, he can therefore direct the other factors of production.

There are, however, other disadvantages—or costs—of using the price mechanism. It may be desired to make a long-term contract for the supply of some article or service. This may be due to the fact that if one contract is made for a longer period, instead of several shorter ones, then certain costs of making each contract will be avoided. or, owing to the risk attitude of the people concerned, they may prefer to make a long rather than a short-term contract. Now, owing to the difficulty of forecasting, the longer the period of the contract is for the supply of the commodity or service, the less possible, and indeed, the less desirable it is for the person purchasing to specify what the other contracting party is expected to do. It may well be a matter of indifference to the person supplying the service or commodity which of several courses of action is taken, but not to the purchaser of that service or commodity. But the purchaser will not know which of these several courses he will want the supplier to take. Therefore, the service which is being provided is expressed in general terms, the exact details being left until a later date. All that is stated in the contract is the limits to what the persons supplying the commodity or service is expected to do. The details of what the supplier is expected to do is not stated in the contract but is decided later by the purchaser. When the direction of resources (within the limits of the contract) becomes dependent on the buyer in this way, that relationship which I term a "firm" may be obtained.[21] A firm is likely therefore to emerge in those cases where a very short-term contract would be unsatisfactory. It is obviously of more importance in the case of services—labor—than it is in the case of the buying of commodities. In the case of commodities, the main items can be stated in advance and the details which will be decided later will be of minor significance.

We may sum up this section of the argument by saying that the operation of a market costs something and by forming an organization and allowing some authority (an "entrepreneur") to direct the resources, certain marketing costs are saved. The entrepreneur has to carry out his function at less cost, taking into account the fact that he may get factors of production at a lower price than the market transactions which he supersedes, because it is always possible to revert to the open market if he fails to do this.

The question of uncertainty is one which is often considered to be very relevant to the study of the equilibrium of the firm. It seems improbable that a firm would emerge without the existence of uncertainty. But those, for instance, Professor Knight, who make the *mode of payment* (the distinguishing mark of the firm—fixed incomes being guaranteed to some of those engaged in production by a person who takes the residual, and fluctuating, income—would appear to be introducing a point which is irrelevant to the problem we are considering. One entrepreneur may sell his services to another for a certain sum of money, while the payment to his employees may be mainly or wholly a share in profits.[22] The significant question would appear to be why the allocation of resources is not done directly by the price mechanism.

Another factor that should be noted is that exchange transactions on a market and the same transactions organized within a firm are often treated differently by Governments or other bodies with regulatory powers. If we consider the operation of a sales tax, it is clear that it is a tax on market transactions and not on the same transactions organized within the firm. Now since these are alternative methods of "organization"—by the price mechanism or by the entrepreneur—such a regulation would bring into existence firms which otherwise would have no *raison d'etre*. It would furnish a reason for the emergence of a firm in a specialized exchange economy. Of course, to the extent that firms already exist, such a measure as a sales tax would merely tend to make them larger than they would otherwise be. Similarly, quota schemes, and methods of price control which imply that there is rationing, and which do not apply to firms producing such products for themselves, by allowing advantages to those who organize within the firm and not through the market, necessarily encourage the growth of firms. But it is difficult to believe that it is measures such as have been mentioned in this paragraph which have brought firms into existence. Such measures would, however, tend to have this result if they did not exist for other reasons.

These, then, are the reasons why organizations such as firms exist in a specialized exchange economy in which it is generally assumed that the distribution of resources is "organized" by the price mechanism. A firm, therefore, consists of the system of relationships which comes into existence when the direction of resources is dependent on an entrepreneur.

The approach which has just been sketched would appear to offer an advantage in that it is possible to give a scientific meaning to what is meant by saying that a firm gets larger or smaller. A firm becomes larger as additional transactions (which could be exchange transactions co-ordinated through the price mechanism) are organized by the entrepreneur and becomes smaller as he abandons the organization of such transactions. The question which arises is whether it is possible to study the forces which determine the size of the firm. Why does the entrepreneur not organize one less transaction or one more? It is interesting to note that Professor Knight considers that:

> the relation between efficiency and size is one of the most serious problems of theory, being, in contrast with relation for a plant, largely a matter of personality and historical accident rather than of intelligible general principles. But the question is peculiarly vital because the possibility of monopoly gain offers a powerful incentive to *continuous and unlimited* expansion of the firm, which force must be offset by some equally powerful one making for decreased efficiency (in the production of money income) with growth in size, if even boundary competition is to exist.[23]

Professor Knight would appear to consider that it is impossible to treat scientifically the

determinants of the size of the firm. On the basis of the concept of the firm developed above, this task will now be attempted.

It was suggested that the introduction of the firm was due primarily to the existence of marketing costs. A pertinent question to ask would appear to be (quite apart from the monopoly considerations raised by Professor Knight), why, if by organizing one can eliminate certain costs and in fact reduce the cost of production, are there any market transactions at all?[24] Why is not all production carried on by one big firm? There would appear to be certain possible explanations.

First, as a firm gets larger, there may be decreasing returns to the entrepreneur function, that is, the costs of organizing additional transactions within the firm may rise.[25] Naturally, a point must be reached where the costs of organizing an extra transaction within the firm are equal to the costs involved in carrying out the transaction in the open market, or, to the costs of organizing by another entrepreneur. Secondly, it may be that as the transactions which are organized increase, the entrepreneur fails to place the factors of production in the uses where their value is greatest, that is, fails to make the best use of the factors of production. Again, a point must be reached where the loss through the waste of resources is equal to the marketing costs of the exchange transaction in the open market or to the loss if the transaction was organized by another entrepreneur. Finally, the supply price of one or more of the factors of production may rise, because the "other advantages" of a small firm are greater than those of a large firm.[26] Of course, the actual point where the expansion of the firm ceases might be determined by a combination of the factors mentioned above. The first two reasons given most probably correspond to the economists' phrase of "diminishing returns to management."[27]

The point has been made in the previous paragraph that a firm will tend to expand until the costs of organizing an extra transaction within the firm become equal to the costs of carrying out the same transaction by means of an exchange on the open market or the costs of organizing in another firm. But if the firm stops its expansion at a point below the costs of marketing in the open market and at a point equal to the costs of organizing in another firm, in most cases (excluding the case of "combination"[28]), this will imply that there is a market transaction between these two procedures, each of whom could organize it at less than the actual marketing costs. How is the paradox to be resolved? If we consider an example the reason for this will become clear. Suppose A is buying a product from B and that both A and B could organize this marketing transaction at less than its present cost. B, we can assume, is not organizing one process or stage of production, but several. If A therefore wishes to avoid a market transaction, he will have to take over all the processes of production controlled by B. Unless A takes over all the processes of production, a market transaction will still remain, although it is a different product that is bought. But we have previously assumed that as each producer expands he becomes less efficient; the additional costs of organizing extra transactions increase. It is probable that A's cost of organizing the transactions previously organized by B will be greater than B's costs of doing the same thing. A therefore will take over the whole of B's organization only if his cost of organizing B's work is not greater than B's cost by an amount equal to the costs of carrying out an exchange transaction on the open market. But once it becomes economical to have a market transaction, it also pays to divide production in such a way that the cost of organizing an extra transaction in each firm is the same.

Up to now it has been assumed that the exchange transactions which take place through the price mechanism are homogeneous. In fact, nothing could be more diverse than the actual transactions which take place in our modern world. This would seem to imply that the costs of carrying out exchange transactions through the price mechanism will vary considerably as will also the costs of organizing these transactions within the firm. It seems therefore possible that quite apart from the question of diminishing returns the costs of organizing certain transactions within the firm may be greater than the costs of carrying out the exchange transactions in the open market. This would necessarily imply that there were exchange transactions carried out through the price mechanism, but would it mean that there would have to be more than one firm? Clearly not, for all those areas in the economic system where the direction of resources was not dependent directly on the price mechanism could be organized with one firm. The factors which were discussed earlier would seem to be the important ones, though it is difficult to say whether "diminishing returns to management" or the rising supply price of factors is likely to be the more important.

Other things being equal, therefore, a firm will tend to be larger:

a. the less the costs of organizing and the slower these costs rise with an increase in the transactions organized.
b. the less likely the entrepreneur is to make mistakes and the smaller the increase in mistakes with an increase in the transactions organized.
c. the greater the lowering (or the less the rise) in the supply price of factors of production to firms of larger size.

Apart from variations in the supply price of factors of production to firms of different sized, it would appear that the costs of organizing and the losses through mistakes will increase with an increase in the spatial distribution of the transactions organized, in the dissimilarity of the transactions, and in the probability of changes in the relevant prices.[29] As more transactions are organized by an entrepreneur, it would appear that the transactions would tend to be either different in kind or in different places. This furnishes an additional reason why efficiency will tend to decrease as the firm gets larger. Inventions which tend to bring factors of production nearer together, by lessening spatial distribution, tend to increase the size of the firm.[30] Changes like the telephone and telegraph which tend to reduce the cost of organizing spatially will tend to increase the size of the firm. All changes which improve managerial technique will tend to increase the size of the firm.[31/32]

It should be noted that the definition of a firm which was given above can be used to give more precise meanings to the terms "combination" and "integration."[33] There is a combination when transactions which were previously organized by two or more entrepreneurs become organized by one. This becomes integration when it involves the organization of transactions which were previously carried out between the entrepreneurs on a market. A firm can expand in either or both of these two ways. The whole of the "structure of competitive industry" becomes tractable by the ordinary technique of economic analysis.

III

The problem which has been investigated in the previous section has not been entirely neglected by economists and it is now necessary to consider why the reasons given above for the emergence of a firm in a specialized exchange economy are to be preferred to the other explanations which have been offered.

It is sometimes said that the reason for the existence of a firm is to be found in the division of labor. This is the view of Professor Usher, a view which has been adopted and expanded by Mr. Maurice Dobb. The firm becomes "the result of an increasing complexity of the division of labour. . . . The growth of this economic differentiation creates the need for some integrating force without which differentiation would collapse into chaos; and it is as the integrating force in a differentiated economy that industrial forms are chiefly significant."[34] The answer to this

argument is an obvious one. The "integrating force in a differentiated economy" aready exists in the form of the price mechanism. It is perhaps the main achievement of economic science that it has shown that there is no reason to suppose that specialization must lead to chaos.[35] The reason given by Mr. Maurice Dobb is therefore inadmissible. What has to be explained is why one integrating force (the entrepreneur) should be substituted for another integrating force (the price mechanism).

The most interesting reasons (and probably the most widely accepted) which have been given to explain this fact are those to be found in Professor Knight's *Risk, Uncertainty and Profit*. His views will be examined in some detail.

Professor Knight starts with a system in which there is no uncertainty:

> acting as individuals under absolute freedom but without collusion men are supposed to have organised economic life with the primary and secondary division of labour, the use of capital, etc., developed to the point familiar in present-day America. The principal fact which calls for the exercise of the imagination is the internal organisation of the productive groups or establishments. With uncertainty entirely absent, every individual being in possession of perfect knowledge of the situation, there would be no occasion for anything of the nature of responsible management or control of productive activity. Even marketing transactions in any realistic sense would not be found. The flow of raw materials and productive services to the consumer would be entirely automatic.[36]

Professor Knight says that we can imagine this adjustment as being "the result of a long process of experimentation worked out by trial-and-error methods alone," while it is not necessary "to imagine every worker doing exactly the right thing at the right time in a sort of 'pre-established harmony' with the work of others. There might be managers, superintendents, etc., for the purpose of co-ordinating the activities of individuals," though these managers would be performing a purely routine function, "without responsibility of any sort."[37]

> With the introduction of uncertainty—the fact of ignorance and the necessity of acting upon opinion rather than knowledge—into this Eden-like situation, its character is entirely changed. . . . With uncertainty present doing things, the actual execution of activity, becomes in a real sense a secondary part of life; the primary problem or function is deciding what to do and how to do it.[38]

This fact of uncertainty brings about the two most important characteristics of social organization.

> In the first place, goods are produced for a market, on the basis of entirely impersonal prediction of wants, not for the satisfaction of the wants of the producers themselves. The producer takes the responsibility of forecasting the consumers' wants. In the second place, the work of forecasting and at the same time a large part of the technological direction and control of production are still further concentrated upon a very narrow class of the producers, and we meet with a new economic functionary, the entrepreneur. . . . When uncertainty is present and the task of deciding what to do and how to do it takes the ascendancy over that of execution the internal organisation of the productive groups is no longer a matter of indifference or a mechanical detail. Centralisation of this deciding and controlling function is imperative, a process of "cephalisation" is inevitable.[39]

The most fundamental change is:

> the system under which the confident and venturesome assume the risk or insure the doubtful and timid by guaranteeing to the latter a specified income in return for an assignment of the actual results. . . . With human nature as we know it it would be impracticable or very unusual for one man to guarantee to another a definite result of the latter's actions without being given power to direct his work. And on the other hand the second party would not place himself under the direction of the first without such a guarantee. . . . The result of this manifold specialisation of function is the enterprise and wage system of industry. Its existence in the world is the direct result of the fact of uncertainty.[40]

These quotations give the essence of Professor Knight's theory. The fact of uncertainty means that people have to forecast future wants. Therefore, you get a special class springing up who direct the activities of others to whom they give guaranteed wages. It acts because good judgment is generally associated with confidence in one's judgment.[41]

Professor Knight would appear to leave himself open to criticism on several grounds. First of all, as he himself points out, the fact that certain people have better judgment or better knowledge does not mean that they can only get an income from it by themselves actively taking part in production. They can sell advice or knowledge. Every business buys the services of a host of advisers. We can imagine a system where all advice or knowledge was bought as required. Again, it is possible to get a reward from better knowledge or judgment not by actively taking part in production but by making contracts with people who are producing. A merchant buying for future delivery represents an example of this. But this merely illustrates the point that it is quite possible to give a guaranteed reward providing that certain acts are performed without directing the performance of those acts. Professor Knight says that "with human nature as we know it, it would be impracticable or very unusual for one man to guarantee to another a definite result of the latter's actions without being given power to direct his work." This is surely incorrect. A large proportion of jobs are done to contract, that is, the contractor is guaranteed a certain sum providing he performs certain acts. But this does not involve any direction. It does mean, however, that the system of relative prices has been changed and that there will be a new arrangement of the factors of production.[42] The fact that Professor Knight mentions that the "second party would not place himself under the direction of the first without such a guarantee" is irrelevant to the problem we are considering. Finally, it seems important to notice that even in the case of an economic system where there is no uncertainty Professor Knight considers that there would be co-ordinators, though they would perform only a routine function. He immediately adds that they would be "without responsibility of any sort," which raises the question by whom are they paid and why? It seems that nowhere does Professor Knight give a reason why the price mechanism should be superseded.

IV

It would seem important to examine one further point and that is to consider the relevance of this discussion to the general question of the "cost-curve of the firm."

It has sometimes been assumed that a firm is limited in size under perfect competition if its cost curve slopes upward,[43] while under imperfect competition, it is limited in size because it will not pay to produce more than the output at which marginal cost is equal to marginal revenue.[44] But it is clear that a firm may produce more than one product and, therefore, there appears to be no prima facie reason why this upward slope of the cost curve in the case of perfect competition or the fact that marginal cost will not always be below marginal revenue in the case of imperfect competition should limit the size of the firm.[45] Mrs. Robinson[46] makes the simplifying assumption that only one product is being produced. But it is clearly important to investigate how the number of products produced by a firm is determined, while no theory which assumes that only one product is in fact produced can have very great practical significance.

It might be replied that under perfect competition, since everything that is produced can be sold at the prevailing price, then there is no need for any other product to

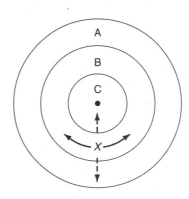

be produced. But this argument ignores the fact that there may be a point where it is less costly to organize the exchange transactions of a new product than to organize further exchange transactions of the old product. This point can be illustrated in the following way. Imagine, following von Thunen, that there is a town, the consuming center, and that industries are located around this central point in rings. These conditions are illustrated in the diagram above in which A, B, and C represent different industries.

Imagine an entrepreneur who starts controlling exchange transactions from X. Now as he extends his activities in the same produce (B), the cost of organizing increases until at some point it becomes equal to that of a dissimilar product which is nearer. As the firm expands, it will therefore from this point include more than one product (A and C). This treatment of the problem is obviously incomplete,[47] but it is necessary to show that merely proving that the cost curve turns upwards does not give a limitation to the size of the firm. So far we have only considered the case of perfect competition; the case of imperfect competition would appear to be obvious.

To determine the size of the firm, we have to consider the marketing costs (that is, the costs of using the price mechanism), and the costs of organizing the different entrepreneurs and then we can determine how many products will be produced by each firm and how much of each it will produce. It would, therefore, appear that Mr. Shove[48] in his article on "Imperfect Competition" was asking questions which Mrs. Robinson's cost curve apparatus cannot answer. The factors mentioned above would seem to be the relevant ones.

V

Only one task now remains; and that is, to see whether the concept of a firm which has been developed fits in with that existing in the real world. We can best approach the question of what constitutes a firm in practice by considering the legal relationship normally called that of "master and servant" or "employer and employee."[49] The essentials of this relationship have been given as follows:

(1) the servant must be under the duty of rendering personal services to the master or to others on behalf of the master, otherwise the contract is a contract for sale of goods or the like.
(2) The master must have the right to control the servant's work, either personally or by another servant or agent. It is this right of control or interference, of being entitled to tell the servant when to work (within the hours of service) and when not to work, and what work to do and how to do it (within the terms of such service) which is the dominant characteristic in this relation and marks off the servant from an independent contractor, or from one employed merely to give to his employer the fruits of his labour. In the latter case, the contractor or performer is not under the employer's control in doing the work or effecting the service; he has to shape and manage his work so as to give the result he has contracted to effect.[50]

We thus see that it is the fact of direction which is the essence of the legal concept of "employer and employee," just as it was in the economic concept which was developed above. It is interesting to note that Professor Batt says further:

That which distinguishes an agent from a servant is not the absence or presence of a fixed wage or the payment only of commission on business done, but rather the freedom with which an agent may carry out his employment.[51]

We can therefore conclude that the definition we have given is one which approximates closely to the firm as it is considered in the real world.

Our definition is, therefore, realistic. Is it manageable? This ought to be clear. When we are considering how large a firm will be the principle of marginalism works smoothly. The question always is, will it pay to bring an extra exchange transaction under the organizing authority? At the margin, the costs of organizing within the firm will be equal either to the costs of organizing in another firm or to the costs involved in leaving the transaction to be "organized" by the price mechanism. Business men will be constantly experimenting, controlling more or less, and in this way, equilibrium will be maintained. This gives the position of equilibrium for static analysis. But it is clear that the dynamic factors are also of considerable importance, and an investigation of the effect changes have on the cost or organizing within the firm and on marketing costs generally will enable one to explain why firms get larger and smaller. We thus have a theory of moving equilibrium. The above analysis would also appear to have clarified the relationship between initiative or enterprise and management. Initiative means forecasting and operates through the price mechanism by the making of new contracts. Management proper merely reacts to price changes, rearranging the factors of production under its control. That the business man normally combines both functions is an obvious result of the marketing costs which were discussed above. Finally, this analysis enables us to state more exactly what is meant by the "marginal product" of the entrepreneur. But an elaboration of this point would take us far from our comparatively simple task of definition and clarification.

NOTES

1. Joan Robinson, *Economics Is a Serious Subject* (1932), 12.
2. See N. Kaldor, "The Equilibrium of the Firm," 44 *The Economic Journal* (1934) 60-76.
3. Op. cit., 6.
4. J.M. Keynes, *Essays in Biography* J(1933), 223-24.
5. L. Robbins, *Nature and Significance of Economic Science* (1935), 63.
6. This description is quoted with approval by D.H. Robertson, *Control of Industry* (1923), 85, and by Professor Arnold Plant, "Trends in Business Administration," 12 *Economica* (1932) 45-62. It appears in *Allied Shipping Control*, pp. 16-17.
7. See F.A. Hayek, "The Trend of Economic Thinking," 13 *Economica* (1933) 121-37.
8. See F.A. Hayek, op cit.
9. Op. cit., 85.
10. In the rest of this paper I shall use the term entrepreneur to refer to the person or persons who, in a competitive system, take the place of the price mechanism in the direction of resources.
11. *Survey of Textile Industries*, 26.
12. Op. cit., 71.
13. *Capitalist Enterprise and Social Progress* 1925, 20. Cf., also, Henderson, *Supply and Demand* (1932), 3-5.
14. It is easy to see when the State takes over the direction of an industry that, in planning it, it is doing something which was previously done by the price mechanism. What is usually not realized is that any business man in organizing the relations between his departments is also doing something which could be organized through the price mechanism. There is therefore point in Mr. Durbin's answer to those who emphasize the problems involved in economic planning that the same problems have to be solved by business men in the competitive system. (See "Economic Calculus in a Planned Economy," 46 *The Economic Journal* [1936] 676-90.) The important difference between these two cases is that economic planning is imposed on industry while firms arise voluntarily because they represent a more efficient method of organizing production. In a competitive system, there is an "optimum" amount of planning!

15. Cf. Harry Dawes, "Labour Mobility in the Steel Industry," 44 *The Economic Journal* (1934) 84-94, who instances "the trek to retail shopkeeping and insurance work by the better paid of skilled men due to the desire (often the main aim in life of a worker) to be independent" (86).
16. None the less, this is not altogether fanciful. Some small shopkeepers are said to earn less than their assistants.
17. G.F. Shove, "The Imperfection of the Market: a Further Note," 44 *The Economic Journal* (1933) 113-24, n. 1, points out that such preferences may exist, although the example he gives is almost the reverse of the instance given in the text.
18. According to N. Kaldor, "A Classificatory Note of the Determinanteness of Equilibrium," 1 *The Review of Economic Studies* (1934) 122-36, it is one of the assumptions of static theory that "All the relevant prices are known to all individuals." But this is clearly not true of the real world.
19. This influence was noted by Professor Usher when discussing the development of capitalism. He says: "The successive buying and selling of partly finished products were sheer waste of energy." (*Introduction to the Industrial History of England* (1920), 13.) But he does not develop the idea nor consider why it is that buying and selling operations still exist.
20. It would be possible for no limits to the powers of the entrepreneur to be fixed. This would be voluntary slavery. According to Professor Batt, *The Law of Master and Servant* (1933), 18, such a contract would be void and unenforceable.
21. Of course, it is not possible to draw a hard and fast line which determines whether there is a firm or not. There may be more or less direction. It is similar to the legal question whether there is the relationship of master and servant or principal and agent. See the discussion of this problem below.
22. The views of Professor Knight are examined below in more detail.
23. *Risk, Uncertainty and Profit*, Preface to the Reissue, London School of Economics Series of Reprints, No. 16 (1933).

24. There are certain marketing costs which could only be eliminated by the abolition of "consumers' choice" and these are the costs of retailing. It is conceivable that these costs might be so high that people would be willing to accept rations because the extra product obtained was worth the loss of their choice.

25. This argument assumes that exchange transactions on a market can be considered as homogeneous; which is clearly untrue in fact. This complication is taken into account below.

26. For a discussion of the variation of the supply price of factors and production firms of varying size, see E.A.G. Robinson, *The Structure of Competitive Industry* (1932). It is sometimes said that the supply price of organizing ability increases as the size of the firm increases because men prefer to be the heads of small independent businesses rather than the heads of departments in a large business. See Jones, *The Trust Problem* (1921), 531, and Macgregor, *Industrial Combination* (1935), 63. This is a common argument of those who advocate Rationalization. It is said that larger units would be more efficient, but owing to the individualistic spirit of the small entrepreneurs, they prefer to remain independent, apparently in spite of the higher income which their increased efficiency under Rationalization makes possible.

27. This discussion is, of course, brief and incomplete. For a more thorough discussion of this particular problem, see N. Kaldor, "The Equilibrium of the Firm," 44 *The Economic Journal* (1934) 60-76, and E.A.G. Robinson, "The Problem of Management and the Size of the Firm," 44 *The Economic Journal* (1934) 242-57.

28. A definition of this term is given below.

29. This aspect of the problem is emphasized by N. Kaldor, op. cit. Its importance in this connection had been previously noted by E.A.G. Robinson, *The Structure of Competitive Industry* (1932), 83-106. This assumes that an increase in the probability of price movements increases the costs of organizing within a firm more than it increases the cost of carry out an exchange transaction on the market—which is probable.

30. This would appear to be the importance of the treatment of the technical unit by E.A.G. Robinson, op. cit., 27-33. The larger the technical unit, the greater the concentration of factors and therefore the firm is likely to be larger.

31. It should be noted that most inventions will change both the costs of organizing and the costs of using the price mechanism. In such cases, whether the invention tends to make firms larger or smaller will depend on the relative effect on these two sets of costs. For instance, if the telephone reduces the costs of using the price mechanism more than it reduces the costs of organizing, then it will have the effect of reducing the size of the firm.

32. An illustration of these dynamic forces is furnished by Maurice Dobb, *Russian Economic Development* (1928), 68. "With the passing of bonded labour the factory, as an establishment where work was organised under the whip of the overseer, lost its raison d'etre until this was restored to it with the introduction of power machinery after 1846." It seems important to realize that the passage from the domestic system to the factory system is not a mere historical accident, but is conditioned by economic forces. This is shown by the fact that it is possible to move from the factory system to the domestic system, as in the Russian example, as well as vice versa. It is the essence of serfdom that the price mechanism is not allowed to operate. Therefore, there has to be direction from some organizer. When, however, serfdom passed, the price mechanism was allowed to operate. It was not until machinery drew workers into one locality that it paid to supersede the price mechanism and the firm again emerged.

33. This is often called "vertical integration," combination being termed "lateral integration."

34. Op. cit., 10. Professor Usher's views are to be found in his *Introduction to the Industrial History of England* (1920), 1-18.

35. Cf. J.B. Clark, *Distribution of Wealth* (1899), 19, who speaks of the theory of exchange as being the "theory of the organisation of industrial society."

36. *Risk, Uncertainty and Profit*, 267.

37. Op. cit., 267-68.

38. Op. cit., 268.

39. Op. cit., 268-95.

40. Op. cit., 269-70

41. Op. cit., 270.

42. This shows that it is possible to have a private enterprise system without the existence of firms. Though, in practice, the two functions of enterprise, which actually influences the system of relative prices by forecasting wants and acting in accordance with such forecasts, and management, which accepts the system of relative prices as being given, are normally carried out by the same persons, yet it seems important to keep them separate in theory. This point is further discussed below.

43. See Kaldor, op. cit., and Robinson, *The Problem of Management and the Size of the Firm.*

44. Mr. Robinson calls this the Imperfect Competition solution for the survival of the small firm.

45. Mr. Robinson's conclusion, op. cit., 249, n. 1, would appear to be definitely wrong. He is followed by Horace J. White, Jr., "Monopolistic and Perfect Competition," 26 *The American Economic Review* (1936) 645, n. 27. Mr. White states "It is obvious that the size of the firm is limited in conditions of monopolistic competition."

46. *Economics of Imperfect Competition* (1934).

47. As has been shown above, location is only one of the factors influencing the cost of organizing.

48. G.F. Shove, "The Imperfection of the Market," 43 *The Economic Journal* (1933), 115. In connection with an increase in demand in the suburbs and the effect on the price charged by suppliers, Mr. Shove asks ". . . why do not the old firms open branches in the suburbs?" If the argument in the text is correct, this is a question which Mrs. Robinson's apparatus cannot answer.

49. The legal concept of "employer and employee" and the economic concept of a firm are not identical, in that the firm may imply control over another person's property as well as over their labor. But the identity of these two concepts is sufficiently close for an examination of the legal concept to be of value in appraising the worth of the economic concept.

50. Batt, *The Law of Master and Servant*, 6.

51. Op. cit., 7.

THE THEORY OF THE FIRM REVISITED

Harold Demsetz

From the birth of modern economics in 1776 to 1970, a span of almost 200 years, only two works seem to have been written about the theory of the firm that have altered the perspectives of the profession—Knight's *Risk, Uncertainty, and Profit* (1921) and Coase's "The Nature of the Firm" (1937). This neglect is attributable fundamentally to the preoccupation of economists with the price system; the study of the price system, characterized as it is by Marshall's representative firm and Walras's auctioneer, undermines serious consideration of the firm as a problem solving institution.

Coase's contribution is seminal for several reasons, but certainly for calling attention to the absence of a theory of the existence of the firm and to the importance (to this theory) of the fact that markets do not operate costlessly. Nonetheless, the theory of the firm is still incomplete and unclear in ways that are discussed in the middle part of this paper. A more complete theory of the firm must give greater weight to information cost than is given either in Coase's theory or in theories based on shirking and opportunism. This is discussed in the last part of this paper. Information cost figures importantly in transaction cost theory because information cost is an important component of transaction cost. It also figures importantly in Knight's risk-sharing and in agency theories of the firm. Its

importance, however, is more fundamental than even these theories contemplate. It is useful therefore to begin this paper with a discussion of why the costless information that is assumed in the perfect competition model renders the model ineffective for studying the firm.

1. PERFECT DECENTRALIZATION

What parades as perfect competition is a model that has much to say about the price system, but little to say about competition or the organization of firms. This probably is due to its intellectual origins in the eighteenth-century debate between mercantilists and free traders. The debate was not about competition per se, and it certainly was not about the organization of the firm. It was about the proper scope of government in the economic affairs of England and Europe. Is central economic planning necessary to avoid chaotic economic conditions? Smith's answer, though preserving a limited role for the state, was persuasively in the negative. The subsequent conflict between "Smithian" and dissenting views led to a closer examination of the conditions necessary for the price system to function in a manner that substantiates Smith's arguments. Almost 200 years later, these conditions became formalized in the perfect competition model.

The intellectual achievement of this model is its complete abstraction from centralized control of the economy (Demsetz, 1982). What is modeled is not competition but extreme decentralization, and one can assess through its use whether extreme decentralization leads to chaotic resource allocation. The actors in this model maximize utility or wealth, and they do so in complete disregard of the decisions of others or, indeed, of even the existence of others. The same decisions follow from the same prices (and technology) whether or not anyone else is "out there" reacting to these parameters. If such impersonal maximizing behavior is competition, it is a very restricted variety. As Knight points out, doing better than others is not involved. No small amount of mischief has resulted from identifying this model with competition. Its appropriate name is perfect *decentralization*.

Perfect decentralization is realized theoretically through assumptions guaranteeing that authority, or command, plays no role in coordinating resources. The only parameters guiding choice are those that are given—tastes and technologies—and those that are determined impersonally on markets—prices. All parameters are beyond the control of any of the model's actors or institutions, so these assumptions effectively deprive authority of any role in allocation. they are fully justified by the theory's remarkable yield—a compact, coherent, subtle yet simple model for deducing the equilibrium consequences of extreme decentralization of resource ownership. The model is not only a powerful tool for understanding how prices guide decisions in a decentralized economy, but also for assessing the impact of exogenous changes in the parameters that are taken as given by the model. The impact of changes in tax rates or tariffs,or the consequences of price supports, can be deduced with comparative ease.

The model contributes little to our understanding of the workings of a command economy or of political processes that might be structured around authority. Its use in public finance, for example, is to understand how the price system "digests" taxes, not to understand the behavior of political parties. The model also casts little light on legal institutions. Exchange is viewed as taking place without regard to problems of theft or fraud. The property right system, so important to the functioning of the price system, is implicitly assumed to operate costlessly in matters of exchange. These abstractions are defensible because the real objective of the model is to study allocation in the absence of authority.

More to the point of this paper, the model sets the maximizing tasks of the firm in a context in which decisions are made with full and free knowledge of production possibilities and to control resources consciously, where owners of resources have a penchant for pursuing their own interests, are not easily analyzed in a model in which knowledge is full and free. "Firm" in the theory of price is simply a rhetorical device adopted to facilitate discussion of the price system. Tasks normally to be expected of management are given only the most superficial, formal discussion; they are performed without error and costlessly, as if by a free and perfect computer. The real tasks of management, to devise or discover markets, products, and production techniques, and actively to manage the actions of employees, have no place in the perfect decentralization model because it assumes that all products, markets, production techniques, and prices are fully known at zero cost.

The only management task that seems to remain, and which is the focus of attention in the firm of traditional price theory, is the selection of profit-maximizing quantities of outputs and inputs. But, since the required information for doing this is also freely in hand, and the required calculations are costless to make, the model strips management of any meaningful productivity in the performance of even these tasks. The *cost of maximizing* is ignored or implicitly assumed to be zero. De facto, the resources that might be required to make maximizing decisions are treated as if they are not scarce.[1]

The sole (seeming) exception to this generalization is the rationale sometimes adopted to justify U-shaped average cost curves—diminishing returns to "entrepreneurial capacity." Entrepreneurial decision capacity is assumed to be limited and, therefore, costly. Because this capacity cannot be increased in proportion to increases in other inputs, cost curves ultimately turn up. However, this rationale is inconsistent with the model's assumptions, and it must be thought of as ad-hoc and exogenous. The model assumes free and full information about technical relationships and prices, thus making it difficult to rationalize why size of the firm should affect the owner/entrepreneur's decision making capacities.[2]

The absence of substantive managed coordination is the sine qua non of the perfect decentralization model. This is its intellectual achievement and its source of strength in providing an understanding of the price system in a situation of extreme decentralization. It is its source of weakness in analyzing managed coordination. Clearly our understanding of firms can be improved by recognizing that management is a scarce resource employed in a world in which knowledge is incomplete and costly to obtain. This is explicitly recognized by Knight and Coase, and it is an important component of theories based on monitoring cost. Knight's analysis of the firm as an institution for efficient risk-sharing is based on risk aversion and costly knowledge; Coase's theory, known as the transaction cost theory of the firm, has as its central theme the relevance of costly managing and exchanging, which certainly contain important components of information cost.

2. THE TRANSACTION COST THEORY OF THE FIRM: SOME PROBLEMS

Before turning to a discussion of transaction cost theory, it is desirable to clarify terminology. Throughout this paper, I use transaction cost and management cost to refer to the costs of organizing resources, respectively, across markets and within firms. This accords with Coase's terminology. Recent writings on the theory of the firm sometimes use transaction cost to refer indiscriminately to organizational costs whether these arise from within the firm or across the market. This rather inept language forces textual discussion to make distinctions that would be better left to single-word labels. For example, Williamson frequently is forced to use phrases such as "the governance costs of internal organization exceed those of market organization." If the reader feels more comfortable with the newer terminology, although I cannot see why he should, he may translate my use of management and transaction costs for the governance costs, respectively, of organization achieved through firms and organization achieved across markets.

The early development of the transaction cost paradigm deals with the question of the existence of firms. Why do firms emerge as viable institutions when the perfect decentralization model amply demonstrates the allocative proficiency of the prices that emerge from impersonal markets? The question is asked and answered by Coase. Profit maximization (or efficiency) requires the substitution of firms for markets if the cost of using markets becomes large relative to the cost of managing. With compelling skill, he plays transaction cost against management cost to arrive at the formal condition that defines the extent of the firm. Equality between the marginal values of these costs, with respect to extending the tasks undertaken by the firm, defines a boundary on one side of which resources are managed within the firm and on the other side of which they are price-directed across markets. This comparison of transaction and management costs has become the focusing conceptualization of the transaction cost theory in all applications to the theory of the firm of which I am aware. Difficulties with it have gone unrecognized. Some of these are discussed next.

It is not so easy to distinguish purchase across a market from in-house production because in-house production involves the use of inputs that are *purchased*. Purchasing inputs (across markets) is substituted for purchasing goods that are more nearly complete (across markets). Hence, in-house production does not constitute a clear elimination of transaction cost. Similarly, purchasing goods from another firm, rather than producing these in-house, involves an implicit purchase of the management services undertaken by the other firm, so management cost is not eliminated by purchasing more nearly complete goods across markets. The correct question to ask if we remain within the Coasian framework is not whether management cost is more or less than transaction cost, but whether the sum of management and transaction cost incurred through in-house production is more or less than the sum of management and transaction cost incurred through purchase across markets, since either option entails expenditures on both cost categories.

This problem can be considered from a slightly different angle. If transaction cost is zero, yet management cost is positive, the transaction cost theory predicts the demise of the firm. But what can this mean? It can mean only that each individual acts as a firm, selling the output of his efforts to other individuals acting in similar fashion. But it is a mistaken belief of the transaction cost theory that this organization of production eliminates management cost. Management is not eliminated except, perhaps, by definition. It is functioning in more diffuse fashion across very many firms since management cost is incurred by each such individual as he plans and executes his production activities unless the meaning of management is restricted to dealing with others.

Moreover, the inference drawn, that all production is individualized if transaction cost is zero, is wrong. Whether individuals act independently, as just described, or cooperate through a multiperson firm, depends on the extent of scale economies to management. Multiperson firms are fully consistent with zero transaction cost if management is subject to scale economies. Zero transaction cost informs us only that these cooperating efforts will be organized with greater reliance on explicit negotiations than would be true if transaction cost were positive. Greater reliance on explicit negotiations may be of importance in some contexts, but not others. The difference between these organizing techniques does not carry substantive consequences if the cooperating individuals would perform essentially the same actions, with the same continuity of association over time, when they rely on a series of explicit transitory negotiations as when they rely on an "employment contract," In either case, the substance of the firm is reflected in the style of cooperative behavior that obtains. This may be the same with both organizing techniques.

Another informative way to view the problem is to recognize that the output of another firm can be purchased, or, in substitution for this, the other firm can be purchased. Purchasing the other firm is in-house production because it amounts to the purchase of the inputs required to produce the good. If transaction cost is assumed to be zero, while management cost is assumed to be positive, the answer given by transaction cost theory is to purchase the good, for it will cost something to manage in-house production. But there is a cost to managing the other firm when it stands independently, and this cost must factor into the price of the good that is to be purchased. This implicit management cost must be paid whether the firm or its output is purchased. Hence, the decision rests on a traditional consideration—is management subject to economies of scale? And, in the more realistic context in which management, transaction, and production costs are all assumed to be positive, the correct decision is reached by assessing whether merger or independent production yields the lowest unit cost, taking all these costs into account, over the relevant range of output.

Transaction cost is relevant to this judgment, but so are the other costs.

The degree to which coordination is vertically decentralized is no longer simply a matter of transaction cost, or even of transaction cost relative to management cost. Firms purchase inputs when they can secure them more cheaply than by producing them. The cost of transacting is one element of the cost of purchasing from others, but only one. There are a variety of others, including what we ordinarily call production costs. A firm purchases an input if the price asked for the input, which reflects the production cost of prospective sellers, when added to the costs of transacting and transporting, comes to less than the cost of making the input in-house. Thus, to say that firms produce their own inputs when it is cheaper to do so is *not* equivalent to saying that firms will purchase from others if the cost of transacting is less than the cost of managing. The decision also hinges on the internal costs of production that burden the potential purchaser and supplier. Quite simply, it depends on a comparison of *all* the gains and losses that attach to external procurement relative to in-house production. Indeed, an increase in the cost of transacting leads not to a substitution of managed coordination for market coordination, as users of the transaction cost theory assert, but to a substitution of managed coordination within fewer, larger firms for managed coordination in more numerous, smaller firms. *Managed* transfer of inputs between the departments of (a now larger) firm is substituted for *managed* buying and selling. One type of management substitutes for another.

It is with respect to the above points that new terminology is especially confusing. By using governance or transaction costs to refer to all costs, whether they be within the firm or across markets, it is easy to assert that the newer writings utilizing transaction cost theory refer to the necessity for taking account of all costs (at least of all costs of organizing). If so, have we come to the point of saying that firms are used when they are cheaper, all

costs considered, but not when markets are cheaper? I am quite prepared to accept this position for what it is worth, but my point is that it deprives transaction cost theory of any predictive content. Moreover, the broader considerations that occupy some of the newer writings about the firm put them at some distance from the transaction cost theory being discussed here. For example, Williamson uses the first part of his book about the institutions of capitalism to claim that its foundation lies in transaction cost considerations, but he fails to make substantive use of transaction cost throughout the remainder of the book. The only link to predictive content that remains is to be found in asset specificity, which he interprets to imply higher cost of using market governance of activities. But, as I argue later, and as Coase himself argues in the present lectures, the linkage is weak.

The emphasis that has been given to transaction cost (or that has been claimed to be given) dims our view of the full picture by implicitly assuming that all firms can produce goods or services equally well. "Implicitly," because the "other" firm is represented by the "market," and the market is treated as a perfect substitute in production for a firm. The only comparison sought is between the cost of transacting across this market and the cost of in-house managing. Since firms may not be perfect substitutes in the production of goods and services, and since they generally will not be if information cost is positive, it might be in the interest of a firm to produce its own inputs even if transaction costs were zero and management costs were positive. The production cost of other firms might simply be so high as to make in-house production superior to relying on these other firms. Or, if the production cost incurred by other firms is sufficiently los, it might serve the firm to purchase its inputs even though the cost of managing in-house production is zero.[3]

The confusion that exists in the literature derives from a hidden presumption that we are still guided by the perfect decentraliza-tion model, and that, in some respects, infor-mation remains full and free. Although infor-mation is treated as being costly for transaction or management control purpos-es, it is implicitly presumed to be free for pro-duction purposes. What one firm can pro-duce, another can produce equally well, so the make-or-buy decision is not allowed to turn on differences in production cost. The only choice criterion that remains is that which compares transaction and in-house management costs, or, more correctly, the sum of these costs in each alternative offered by the make-or-buy choice. In this manner, the transaction cost theory of the firm ignores differences between firms when these lie out-side the control function and discourages a search for such differences. Merged firms may be unable to duplicate the sum of what independently standing firms can accom-plish for a variety of reasons, and many of these may be resistant to an analysis that is guided by the management and transaction cost categories. Productivity may be affected by considerations that are not plausibly included in these cost categories. Each firm is a bundle of commitments to technology, per-sonnel, and methods, all contained and con-strained by an insulating layer of information that is specific to the firm, and this bundle cannot be altered or imitated easily or quick-ly. The components of this bundle that are emphasized by transaction cost theory are important, but not exclusively so.

In a brief general critique of transaction cost theory, such as this, there is bound to be some oversimplification and some neglect of more subtle uses of the theory. Justice cannot be done to everyone who has used the theory in a broader sense than the interpretation given to it here. Nonetheless, the main emphasis and usage of transaction cost theo-ry surely is to compare transaction and man-agement costs so that conclusions may be drawn about organization. This emphasis has led to the neglect of other determinants of economic organization (one of which is dis-

cussed below) even though some of these are mentioned in passing, as it were, by those who make (or claim to make) transaction cost theory their paradigm of institutional organi-zation. It is the paradigmatic use of transac-tion cost theory that is at issue here.[4]

Beyond considerations of production functions and the total cost of organization, the power of transaction cost theory turns on our ability to make it operational and to bring it to bear on substantive issues. This is not so easily done. It is difficult to discuss the rele-vance of transaction, management, and pro-duction costs without a clear distinction between these, and none is provided. One person phones another and directs him to purchase specific assets by a certain time if they can be acquired for less than a stipulat-ed price. Is this activity transacting or man-aging? Knowing the answer would allow us to determine if an increase in the cost of this activity is expected to lead to the substitution of one firm for two or two for one. Since the call might be from an owner/manager of a firm to his employee in the purchasing department or from a customer/investor to the brokerage house whose services he pur-chases, it is hard to know whether we are dealing with a transaction or management cost until we *already know* whether we are discussing a firm or a market. This is true for the general case even though it might be possible in a specific instance, such as in the case of a tax on transactions, to be certain that we are dealing with only one of these costs. This makes it difficult to use the mag-nitude of "transaction" cost relative to "management" cost to predict how changed circumstances affect economic organization. The inherent difficulty is that the same orga-nizing activities often characterize exchange and management.

Assuming that the problem of disentan-gling these costs is somehow resolved, there is still the problem of being able to stipulate the conditions that tend to make the relative magnitude of these costs high or low. This is necessary if we are to apply the theory of transacting positively to explain the structure of economic organization. Does an increase in the size of the market decrease transaction cost relative to management cost? Does dealing in services rather than products? Does dealing across national boundaries? Questions such as these must have answers about which we are confident if the transaction cost theory of the firm is to be applicable to the study of firms. As of now, we know very little about the forces that might influence the relative magnitude of these costs.

Klein, Crawford, and Alchian (1978), Riodan and Williamson (1985), and Williamson (1985) adopt the view that asset specificity is one such force. Asset specificity raises the prospect for opportunism. This heightened prospect is presumed to raise the cost of transacting. I am not sure that it costs (much) more to detail the terms of a contract when asset specificity is involved than when it is not. Even if it does, the change in the cost of contracting is unlikely to be very great. Asset specificity problems may be almost as easy to resolve through contract as through vertical integration, the latter being the option preferred by these authors. Truth is, it is not a predictably significant variation in transaction cost that motivates the vertical integration solution offered by these authors. It is the presumption that losses are greater if an agreement fails when asset specificity is involved than when it is not. This can be the case (although I am not sure that it is) even if transaction cost is unaffected by the presence or absence of asset specificity. It is simpler and less misleading to state that asset specificity increases the loss attendant on failure of agreement than that it increases the cost of transacting.

If we suppose that activities which increase transaction cost are distinguishable from those that increase management cost, there remains a problem of understanding just which issues are illuminated by using transaction cost theory. Consider the long-term contract that Coase identifies with the employment relationship. From Coase's perspective, costly transactions lead to greater reliance on longer term contracts. The firm hires an employee for a duration rather than for each day or for each instant. There is much truth to this but, in principle at least, since employees can quit at any instant, or be fired, we have a long-term arrangement only because it is in the interest of both parties to continue in association. The avoidance of costly transacting is part of the motivation for this interest, but our focus on this has led us to ignore other, possibly more important, reasons for continued association. If these other reasons exist, and some are discussed below, then a durable association replicating that achievable through a long-term contract would be sought even if transaction cost were zero. A series of costless transitory market negotiations would bring the same employers and employees together, so that, de facto, the firm that is characterized in terms of employment contracts would be achieved through repeated market negotiations. The same behavioral interrelationship might arise when transaction cost is zero as when it is positive. If we conceive of "the" firm as a set of particular behavioral interactions guided by agreements of one sort or another, transaction cost would then determine only how the firm is achieved, not whether it exists. How the firm is achieved is of interest in some contexts, but the behavior that characterizes the firm, which may be achieved through a variety of contractual arrangements, would seem to be a substantive issue determined by considerations that go beyond those highlighted by the transaction cost theory of the firm.

3. MORAL HAZARD, SHIRKING, AND OPPORTUNISM

Writings about the theory of the firm began to diverge from the simple transaction cost format during the decade of the 1970s. Increasing attention was given to the problem of achieving incentive alignment. Attention began turning toward the issue raised by Berle and Means in *The Modern Corporation and Private Property* (1932)—the alleged separation between ownership and control—with the important difference that, unlike Berle and Means, the task became one of understanding how firms organize to resolve the problem. The recent investigation of the ownership structure of the firm undertaken by Ken Lehn and myself (1985) is a continuation of this line of development.

This issue does not permit one to ignore the task of understanding the inner organization of the firm, whereas the transaction cost approach encourages one to dwell on questions like "Why do firms exist?" or "Why is there vertical integration?" Moral hazard analysis, shirking, and opportunism—the problems of incentive compatibility—yield explanations of the internal organization of the firm that are difficult to derive from only transaction cost considerations. It is true that transaction cost is involved in the existence of these problems, at least for a (too) broad definition of transaction cost.[5] They presuppose a positive cost of negotiating them completely out of existence. However, the role of transaction cost in explaining the manner in which organization responds to these problems is like the role of gravity in explaining chemical reactions; gravity influences chemical reactions, but seldom is it the key variable whose behavior importantly explains variations in the reactions observed.

Thus, Alchian and Demsetz (1972) rely on differences in shirking opportunities to understand the organization of the firm, not differences in transaction cost. Their focus is on how the organization of the firm can be accounted for by the differences in the monitoring needs that result.[6] Similarly, as discussed above, the literature on opportunism really relies on a presumed correlation between asset specificity and the loss to be expected from contract failure, and not on variations in transaction cost. The organizations selected and the incentive systems brought into play to moderate incentive incompatibilities are analyzed through vari-

ations in the nature of the monitoring problem that is faced, not through variations in the cost of transacting. It is because of this that incentive incompatibilities offer an alternative to transaction cost analysis in the developing theory of the firm, even though transaction cost is embedded in the organization problem. However, the shirking-opportunism alternative has shortcomings of its own. These are now outlined briefly.

Alchian and Demsetz view shirking as an activity to which firm-like organization (to be discussed more fully below) is particularly susceptible. This is because the revenues of the firm must be shared by the various owners of inputs used by the firm without the full guidance or protection normally offered by intervening competitive markets. These markets would exist if the firm purchased goods from other firms rather than producing them in-house. The centralization of production in firm-like (team) organization therefore is more productive under particular conditions if it survives in the face of the greater shirking costs it must bear. The reason for firm-like production is to be found in the special productivity it offers in some circumstances. Alas, although Alchian and Demsetz make this clear, they fail to discuss the sources of this special productivity. Abating the cost of shirking helps explain the firm's inner organization but provides no rationale for the firm's existence. The extension of this analysis to general agency problems (Jensen and Meckling) fails to remedy this defect.

The literature on post-contractual opportunistic behavior extends the notion of shirking to contractual exchange, but it takes a position that is different than, and possibly contrary to, Alchian and Demsetz. Thus, Klein, Crawford, and Alchian (and Riordan and Williamson also) lean toward a position in which firm-like production, through vertical integration, reduces the severity of opportunism in the presence of asset specificity. This position implicitly views market contracting as bearing the special costs of opportunism (shirking across markets), but then an explanation is needed as to why markets exist if firm-like organization reduces the cost of opportunism more than does the market. The existence of markets is rationalized by the belief that they offer "high-powered" incentives not provided by the firm, but Alchian and Demsetz view the keener incentives offered by the market as a reason why firms are subject to more shirking than are markets! This brings us to the awkward position of stating that firm-like organization is preferred when the advantages of managing opportunism internally outweigh the advantages of managing them through markets, that is, firm organization is preferred when it is superior.

This awkwardness is alleviated somewhat by the fact that Alchian and Demsetz stress team production without special reference to vertical relationships; their emphasis is on the problem of free-riding when production is joint, event when this "jointedness" occurs within a single "horizontal" activity level. The literature on opportunism stresses vertical relationships, and the emphasis is on reneging or guile. It may well be that firm-like organization raises the cost of dealing with free-riding while lowering the cost of dealing with guile. Awkwardness might also be alleviated by asset specificity considerations, for asset specificity can be used to index those situations in which firm-like organization has more of an advantage (but, as Coase points out in these lectures, possibly not enough of an advantage). As of now, this is a frail reed upon which to build a theory of the firm. It is silent in regard to the survivability of firm-like organization in the absence of asset specificity, and it is directed primarily at explaining the vertical depth of firms rather than the existence of firms or other aspects of their internal organization. Moreover (as Coase also points out in the present lectures), the opportunism that is associated with asset specificity may be easier to resolve through contract stipulation.

Perhaps more important, asset specificity may reduce the non-opportunistic costs of maintaining vertically separated organizations. There is less need to manage (through vertical integration) the coordination of assets when the are "dedicated" to specific uses, as they are likely to be under conditions of asset specificity. In such a case, if the legal system is a sufficiently good enforcer of contracts, asset specificity may give rise to vertical disintegration.

The major use to which asset specificity has been put is to make the predictive statement that vertical integration is more likely when assets are specific, vertical integration being presumed to circumvent the opportunistic problems caused by asset specificity. Riordan and Williamson adopt this position in their commendable attempt to make predictive statements about vertical integration. Their claim is that when conditions are such as to require asset specificity to achieve low-cost production, vertical integration is more likely.

But there is more to asset specificity than what is contemplated in their paper (and in the important paper by Klein, Crawford, and Alchian). Owners and management make commitments to each other in order to solicit many years of devoted service; human capital specificity arises as a result of long tenure (and this specificity may be exacerbated by the use of physical assets that are highly specific). Conditions change, requiring these commitments to be broken if the firm is to survive. Unlike the claim made by the literature on opportunism, owners or top management do not rush out to break these commitments. They seek to keep them, both for reasons of personal honor and for reasons of continuing to solicit devoted duty from other employees. This is one reason mergers or takeovers occur. A new broom sweeps clean, and these commitments give way to the exigencies of economic conditions.[7] Such is the claim of much of the writings about takeovers. Here we find mergers (initially) taking place to facilitate opportunism toward those who have invested in human capital. Behavior that is opportunistic toward employees is facilitated through mergers, possibly vertical, by bringing in new owners and management that are personally free of these past commitments.

There is much more to the problem of economic organization than is plausibly subsumed under transaction and monitoring cost. Perhaps the transaction and monitoring approaches to the theory of the firm have confined our search too much. Firms would exist in a world in which transaction and monitoring costs are zero, although their organization might be considered different. In the space that remains, I consider an alternative approach, one based on aspects of information cost considerations that are different than those captured by transaction and monitoring costs. No well-developed model is offered. My intent is only to illustrate one way in which we have ignored considerations that seem important to a theory of the firm. It is desirable first to give some notion of what it is that we wish to explain with a theory of the firm.

4. FIRM-LIKE ORGANIZATION

The firm properly viewed is a "nexus" of contracts. Our interest might center on explaining (1) the persistence of certain types of contracts that are found in this nexus, (2) the variation observed in other types of contracts that are "more or less" included in this nexus, and (3) the (horizontal and vertical) scope of activities covered by these contracts. No doubt this list can be extended greatly. For example, we might want to understand the relationship between the existence of firm-like contracts and problems of unemployment and politics. Past and current interest in the existence, the internal organization, and the vertical and horizontal scope of "the firm" fit comfortably into the three areas of inquiry listed above, and it is in these that I wish to show that information cost has relevance that extends beyond its significance in transaction cost and moral hazard problems.

The defining content of the nexus of contracts referred to above remains rather vague in literature on the theory of the firm.[8] We may as well recognize that we have no clear notion of firm-like contractual arrangements, especially since we now recognize the difficulty of distinguishing between coordination achieved "across markets" and coordination achieved "within firms." It might be useful to adopt legal notions of what a firm is and what it is not, for there do arise cases in which this determination has been called forth because of the important impact it has on which body of law determines the liabilities of the parties involved. I prefer instead to identify three aspects of the nexus of contracts that plausibly influence firm-like coordination. (At least two of them receive mention in case law.) These aspects of firm-like contractual arrangements brush aside the question of absolutes—"When is a nexus of contracts *a firm*?"—and substitute instead a question of relatives—"When is a nexus of contracts *more firm-like*?"

A common feature of corporate charters is a statement about the business of the firm. While this may change over time, one aspect that persists is that the firm produces goods that are to be sold. This implies an agreement to *specialize*, by which I mean to produce mainly for persons who are not members of the firm's team. The complement to this is self-sufficiency or production by and *for* the same persons, which, in the limit, is one person doing for himself without the cooperation of others. Specialization, which can differ in degree between firm-like institutions, is adopted as a characteristic of firm-like contracts in order to maintain compatibility with the theory of price. The firm in the theory of price does not consume what it produces, it sells to others.[9]

The second aspect of the nexus of contracts is the expected length of time of association between the same input owners. Do the contractual agreements entered into contemplate mainly transitory, short-term association, which in the extreme would be characterized by spot market exchanges, or do these agreements contemplate a high probability of continuing association between the same parties? The firm viewed as team production exhibits significant reassociation of the same input owners. The third facet is the degree of conscious direction that is used to guide the uses to which resources are to be put; this is minimal in spot market transactions, but more important in a context in which continuity of association is relied upon. The direction of some by others catches the spirit of managed coordination.

Our interest centers mainly on the cooperative efforts of more than one person, but the one-person firm is not ruled out by these characteristics. The financial advisor, working alone, offers specialized services. Continuity of association and directability of behavior would seem more difficult to imagine in the case of a one-person firm. Still, a person must deal with himself in a relationship that is continuous over a lifetime, and conflicts do arise between the capabilities and tastes of a person today, or in one set of circumstances, and the "same" person tomorrow, or in a different set of circumstances. Because of these conflicts, a person sometimes finds it desirable to restrict his activities by entering into binding precommitments that control his future behavior (Thaler and Shefrin). Deadlines are often accepted as a self-enforcing device and costs are imposed on future errant (from today's perspective) behavior (as when Christmas savings clubs are joined). The agency problem resides within each of us as well as in interactions between us.

Specialization, continuity of association, and reliance on direction are characteristics of firm-like coordination. They substitute for self-sufficiency and spot markets. These are frequently found characteristics of firm-like organization because they are productive in many circumstances. This productivity derives in part from transaction and monitoring cost considerations, but it also depends on other conditions. Particularly important

are the conditions that underlie the acquisition and use of knowledge.

5. KNOWLEDGE AND THE ORGANIZATION OF SPECIALIZATION

Smith has enshrined forever the idea that specialization is productive, but Smith's focus is on the changes wrought in the individual worker. The problem of how the activities of cooperating specialists are organized so as to mesh better is largely ignored. He ascribes the productivity gains achieved through specialization to three aspects of the division of labor—improvement in dexterity realized by each workman, time saved by avoiding switching from one task to another, and ease with which workmen conceive of innovating improvements when they are steadily occupied in a single task. He writes as if the examples of specialization that he discusses take place with different departments of a firm, but they could also take place across different firms. Indeed, this is the interpretation adopted by Stigler (1951) in his discussion of the impact of market size on vertical integration. It is safe to ignore the organization problem only if the gains achievable through specialization are independent of the way in which specialization is achieved. This seem implausible, and surely would be thought so by Smith who saw in natural liberty an organizing principle vastly superior to central planning. Even if the details of this organization are best left to the invisible hand of natural liberty, its broad outline is important to the theory of the firm.

Information is also a subject upon which much has been written, at least since Stigler's "The Economics of Information" (1961). It is a subject that has obvious connections to moral hazards and transactions, but here I want to emphasize other, neglected connections to the theory of the firm. Economic organization, including the firm, must reflect the fact that knowledge is costly to produce, maintain, and use. In all these respects there are economies to be achieved through specialization. Although the true conglomerate firm is a puzzle, we generally identify industries, and firms in these industries, as repositories of specialized knowledge and of the specialized inputs required to put this knowledge to work. Steel firms specialize in different stocks of knowledge and equipment than do firms in investment banking or industrial chemicals, and even firms in the same industry differ somewhat in the knowledge and equipment upon which they rely.

Knowledge does not directly convert to utility or living standards. If each of us specialize in a single branch of knowledge but attempt to use this knowledge without relying on others, the standard of living achievable would be less than if everyone had become a jack-of-all-trades. Although knowledge can be learned more effectively in specialized fashion, its use to achieve high living standards requires that a specialist somehow use the knowledge of other specialists. This cannot be done only by *learning* what others know, for that would undermine gains from specialized learning. It cannot be done only by *purchasing* information in the form of facts, for in many cases the theory that links facts must be mastered if facts are to be put to work.

This difference between the economics of acquiring and using knowledge has profound implications for social organization. "Common knowledge," particularly of language and arithmetic, is useful because its possession allows *greater* specialization. There must be a low-cost method of communicating between specialists and the large number of persons who either are non-specialists or who are specialists in other fields. Since this communication cannot consist of extensive education in this knowledge without losing the gains from specialized learning, and since the bare facts contained in this knowledge are often uninterpretable, much communication must consist in the giving of *directions*. These directions may pertain to product use or to work activity. The large cost

borne to educate masses of persons in language and calculating skills is worth bearing because it facilitates the giving and taking of directions.

Firms and industries must form a pattern of economic organization that takes account of the need for acquiring knowledge in a more specialized fashion than the manner in which it will be used. Those who are to produce on the basis of this knowledge, but not be possessed of it themselves, must have their activities *directed* by those who possess (more of) the knowledge. Direction substitutes for education (that is, for the transfer of the knowledge itself). Direction may be purchased through short- or long-run commitments, depending partly on the cost of transacting. In either case, direction is involved, and direction is an important dimension of managed coordination. A second way to put information to work without sacrificing specialization in knowledge is to produce and sell goods that require less information to use than is required to produce them: *direction*, in the form of instructions, is involved but, unlike the direction of employees, who are expected to respond in details of timing and execution of their assigned tasks, the users of purchased goods have greater discretion about the timing and application of the instructions that accompany purchased goods. The larger the number of different bodies of knowledge that are required to produce a good, or the more specialized the knowledge that is required, the greater the reliance that must be placed on the direction of some by others. The division of this direction between the direction of employees and the direction of buyers of the good is relevant to the issue of vertical integration. The vertical depth of the firm may be considered from the perspective of the need for conserving on information costs. Other costs matter also, but I wish to focus attention on the consequences of costly knowledge, and I wish to do so without reference to the information costs inherent in transaction and moral hazard problems.

Because it is uneconomical to educate persons in one industry in the detailed knowledge used in another, recourse is had to developing or encapsulating this knowledge into products or services that can be transferred between firms cheaply because the instructions needed to use them do not require in-depth knowledge about how they are produced (and because of transport considerations). The economical use of industrial chemicals by steel firms does not generally require knowledge of how these chemicals are produced; similarly, the use of steel by industrial chemical firms does not require transfer of knowledge of how the steel is produced. A production process reaches the stage of yielding a saleable product when downstream users can work with, or can consume, the "product" without themselves being knowledgeable about its production. Short of this point, it would be necessary to educate downstream users more fully, and this would sacrifice the gains from specialized learning.

However, "products" could continue to be processed into downstream derivatives that are even easier to use. Steel could be set into its structural places by producers rather than by construction companies; this would reduce the need for construction companies to learn the properties of steel that are relevant to riveting and integrating the structure. Steel could be driven for its buyers when they use it in the form of an automobile. The process of further product refinement is halted when the next version of the product will be put to many multiple uses downstream that rely on different bodies of knowledge. A single firm if it was vertically integrated would have difficulty acquiring and maintaining the stocks of knowledge necessary to control cost and quality and to make good managerial decisions when downstream uses are multiple in this sense.

The many uses that are made of steel generally require knowledge that is substantially different from that which is required to produce steel. It is therefore costly to house production of steel in the same firm that is to produce many of these downstream products. Instead, steel is sold. Title passes to others who are masters of the knowledge required to use steel to produce derivative products and services.

Roughly speaking (since other things also matter), the vertical boundaries of a firm are determined by the economics of conservation of expenditures on knowledge. A single firm works a product into new, simpler-to-use (on the basis of directions) products until the diversity of uses further downstream is so great as to require this firm, if it is to continue developing product lines, to bear greater costs of information acquisition and maintenance than are avoided by potential users when there is additional simplification of each product line. Title to "the" product is likely to change hands when this point in the development of product lines is reached, but even if title does not change, further work on derivative products is likely to become the task of other firms. The boundary defining degree of vertical integration will have been established.

It will normally be the case that the boundary suitable for changing title is not coterminous with the point at which one person can economically possess the knowledge required to bring the process to this boundary. Still, the firm that is owned, managed, and operated by a single person is more common than might be supposed. It exists when a person's capacity to absorb knowledge, and to become expert in its use, is great enough for him to learn and use those skills required to bring a product to the boundary at which title is likely to change. The town baker may find it expedient to master knowledge of kitchen chemistry, recipes, and cash accounting himself, and to purchase only products from others. In the more important case, however, the capacity of an individual to acquire and use knowledge is too limited to allow this boundary to be reached without requiring the services of several people each of whom is occupied in a different vertical stage of production.

Economies of scale with respect to number of persons optimally linked to the use of other inputs at any given horizontal level of economic activity may also call for many more than just one person at each stage of production. Information cost may play a role here also. The giving of directions (in substitution for educating) to others may be subject to scale economies of a limited sort. The utilization of the services of a "direction giver" may demand the presence of several "direction receivers" if these services are to be used efficiently.

This brings us to the question of how these services are secured, and to the issue of continuity of association. In many cases it is not practical to purchase the knowledge itself unless someone is to become expert in it; hence, in one way or another a growing reliance on additional knowledge requires securing the services of additional persons. Such services can be secured through short-term transitory purchases or through long-term, less frequently repeated purchases. Transaction cost will influence this decision, but it is not the only important consideration. The decision also turns on the productivity *benefits* derivable from different arrangements. Two firms facing the same labor transaction costs may choose different employment arrangements because the benefits they derive from these arrangements differ. Particularly important in determining these benefits are knowledge-based considerations. Continuing association of the same persons makes it easier for firm-specific and person-specific information to be accumulated (see the large literature on specificity of human capital). Knowledge about the objectives and organization of the firm is learned "cheaply" through continuing association, and so is knowledge about the capabilities and limitations of the persons involved in this association. Continuing association, however, implies commitment, and commitment has the disadvantage of inflexibility. The benefits to be derived from continuing association must be set against the cost of inflexibility in determining the best manner in which to acquire the talents and services of many persons.

Short-term arrangements become more favorable when firms are more likely to change what they are doing in the important respects of objectives, locations, tasks, and style. Long-term arrangements are more suitable when the conditions under which a firm operates are stable. The considerable changes in quantities and types of labor services required by firms who have been forced to shift from a relatively stable regulated environment to a more volatile unregulated environment reflects these considerations, and my guess is that deregulated firms choose an average continuity of association with the typical employee that is shorter than they choose in a regulated environment.

The complete absence of variability in the tasks that are likely to be required by a firm is an incentive to substitute machinery for personnel. Machinery, being very durable, can be thought of as used on a continuing basis by the firm. As task variability increases, the inflexibility of machines exacts a toll. Labor services increase in relative productivity. Great variability in the likely uses to which an employee is to be put creates an even stronger need for flexibility, and long-term employment tends to give way to short-term. Thus, while long-term employment relies on the direction of employees in a changing pattern of tasks, great variability in such tasks makes any one employee less suitable than a series of employees each better suited to the immediate requirements of the job. The resulting variation in continuity of association is affected by transaction cost, but it is also affected (more importantly, I believe) by how the relative productivities of tenure change when the stability of the knowledge requirements of an employee changes.

Theories of transaction cost and agency have greatly enriched our understanding of the nature of firm-like organization. Coase's insight into the importance of the cost of using markets helped to stimulate much of the work that has been done on this topic during the last two decades. My concern is that our thinking may be too constrained by our past successes. Some important problems are amenable to solution by application of the logic of both transaction cost theory and agency theory, but other problems, equally important, are not. Coase's work is best honored by using it as the foundation upon which to build a still richer set of tools. One step in this construction has already been added—the theory of agency relationships. In the present effort to encourage the taking of additional steps, I have found it necessary to outline some of the weaknesses in what has already been accomplished, while suggesting a new direction of inquiry. This would not be needed except for the fact that the work that Coase has done, and that which he has prompted other to do, remains so compelling.

NOTES

I wish to thank Rebecca Demsetz, Kevin James, Ben Klein, George Stigler, Mike Waldman, and Rupert Windisch for useful comments and questions.

1. Free information about production and prices may be contrasted with information about consumption. Knowledge about production and prices is assumed to be *universally* knowable at zero cost. With no one privy to this information, there is no role for a specialized input called management. Knowledge about personal tastes is freely knowable only *to the person* whose tastes they are; hence, individuals as consumers must manage their own affairs, including the hiring of experts, but this requirement for personalized decisions is also satisfied costlessly.

   It is this asymmetric theoretical treatment of knowledge—universally knowable in the case of production, only personally knowable in the case of consumption—that makes socialism appear appealing. The state is viewed by intellectuals as capable when it comes to production, where it is presumed to possess knowledge as good as anyone else's, but incapable when it comes to psychological tradeoffs between consumption goods and between work and leisure. The policy that flows quite naturally from such assumed asymmetry in knowledge is nationalization of industry combined with privatization of consumption and work.

2. If free and full information about technical relationships and prices make it difficult to cap the size of firms in the model of perfect decentralization, they also make it difficult to develop a theory of market concentration. Short of making information costly, the only way out of these dilemmas is to conjure other sources of diseconomies of scale. Conjuring is necessary, because economic theory makes no pretension at knowing these sources or when they will be more and less operative.

3. This analysis of the make-or-buy decision is inframarginal in nature. If the problem of make-or-buy is viewed in the context of completely divisible adjustments, it must be that on the margin all firms are indifferent between making inputs or buying them. The fact that some firms make considerable quantities of their inputs, even while they purchase the same inputs from others, simply reveals that inframarginal comparisons show that over some range of output the sum of these costs is lower in inputs are produced in-house.

4. Williamson may be cited again. In *Economic Institutions of Capitalism*, he does discuss in three pages (92-94) the role of scale economies in raising the cost of enlarging the scope of activities included within a single firm, and he discusses different ways of organizing work later in the book. It would be wrong to claim that he has completely ignored production cost. Yet, his discussion of these does not emphasize the *differences* that may exist between firms within the same industry. His discussion of scale economies is confined to the problem of where on a given production function, available to all firms, the firm functions (similarly with regard to choice of method of organizing work). That the history of a firm may impose constraints on its knowledge about and its ability to alter the way it functions plays no key role in his

discussions. Indeed, preceding his discussion of scale economies, in another short section (86-90), he rejects the importance of technological conditions to economic organization. With respect to asset specificity (which he fails to recognize as at least partly technical), it is not with technology that he is concerned but with the (asserted) fact that asset specificity raises the cost of governance through market arrangements. Even "bounded rationality" is not used to emphasize the *differences in the content of the information* that may be possessed by the personnel and traditions of different firms. It is used to limit the span of control that may be exercised by one person over others, and, thereby, to create a monitoring problem.

5. The question of how transaction cost is to be defined is raised in my 1964 paper, "The Exchange and Enforcement of Property Rights." The questions raised are of two sorts. Should the cost of enforcing agreements be a transaction cost? Should the cost of avoiding the "under revelation" of demand (as when collective goods are purchased) be a transaction cost? My preference is for a more restricted definition, dealing with the cost of negotiating. Otherwise, we come seriously close to a definition of transaction cost that amounts to "the cost of solving a problem."

6. Recognition of the relevance of moral hazard for the theory of the firm both precedes and follows Coase's seminal work on transaction cost. Many writers using the moral hazard theme take the discussion of shirking in Alchian and Demsetz as a starting reference, but Knight, in his classic *Risk, Uncertainty, and Profit*, anticipates much of what they say. Knight clearly understands the shirking problem, which he calls moral hazard; he also recognizes its relationship to the organization of the firm. The failure to appreciate his contribution fully is mainly due to Knight himself, and this for two reasons. First, his interest really is not in the firm, but in the enterprise *system*, so he does not bring his ideas about the inner workings of the firm to center stage or to full maturity. Second, his theoretical perspective is overwhelmed by his belief in the importance of allocating risk (of compensation loss) efficiently, and this leads him to make the existence of risk his dominant and pervasive explanation for the existence and organization of firms. He views the separation of claims on the firm's revenues into a stable component, the wage that is received by employees, and a less stable component, the profit that is received by owner/entrepreneurs, as reflecting different degrees of aversion to and competence in handling risk. It is this theme that attracts the criticism of Alchian and Demsetz, Coase, and other writers too, and that diverts them from Knight's discussion of the relationship between economic organization and moral hazard. Just as there can be little doubt that transaction cost is relevant to the existence of the firm, and to the existence of moral hazard problems, so there cannot be much doubt that moral hazard problems influence the internal organization of the firm.

7. This role of mergers was brought to my attention by an unpublished econometric exercise of my research assistant, John Simpson.

8. Alchian and Demsetz define the firm implicit in classical economics by the bundle of rights that determines the permissible actions of the owner-monitor. He has the right (1) to be a residual claimant; (2) to observe input behavior; (3) to be the central party common to all contracts with input owners; (4) to alter the membership of the team; and (5) to sell these rights.

9. The large number of activities carried on in specialized fashion is too broad to meet the needs of an inquiry seeking to explain firms as these are commonly identified. Every person who acts as a specialist, and every combination of such persons who act as a team of specialists, can be considered a firm, and in many respects they are different firms. The calculus of choice that motivates a person who provides engineering service to GM is not much different if he functions as an "independent" consultant or as an "employee." Nonetheless, a particular combination of the above dimensions may define a firm that is of special interest and importance. This combination is likely to be a *multiperson* team involving a *central contracting agent* operated mainly for *profit*, whose members associate together on a *continuing* basis and have their actions coordinated in large part by *direction*.

REFERENCES

Alchian, Armen A., and H. Demsetz. 1972. "Production, Information Costs, and Economic Organization," 62 *American Economic Review* 777-95.

Berle, A.A., and G.C. Means. 1932. *The Modern Corporation and Private Property*. New York:Macmillan.

Coase, R.H. 1937. "The Nature of the Firm," 4 *Economica* n.s. 386-405.

Demsetz, H. 1964. "The Exchange and Enforcement of Property Rights," 7 *Journal of Law and Economics* 11-26.

———. 1982. *Economic, Legal and Political Dimensions of Competition*. Amsterdam: North-Holland.

———., and K. Lehn. 1985. "The Structure of Corporate Ownership: Causes and Consequences," 93 *Journal of Political Economy* 1155-77.

Jensen, M.C., and W.H. Meckling. 1976. "Theory of the Firm: Management Behavior, Agency Costs and Ownership Structure," 3 *Journal of Financial Economics* 305-60.

Klein, B., R.G. Crawford, and A.A. Alchian. 1978. "Vertical Integration, Appropriable Rents and the Competitive Contracting Process," 21 *Journal of Law and Economics* 297-336.

Knight, Frank H. 1921. *Risk, Uncertainty, and Profit*. New York: Hart, Schaffner, and Marx; repr. (1965) New York: Harper and Row.

Riordan, M.H., and O.E. Williamson. 1985. "Asset Specificity and Economic Organization," 3 *International Journal of Industrial Organization* 365-78.

Stigler, G.J. 1951. "The Division of Labor Is Limited by the Extent of the Market," 59 *Journal of Political Economy* 185-93.

———. 1961. "The Economics of Information," 69 *Journal of Political Economy* 213-25.

Thaler, R.H., and H.M. Shefrin. 1981. "An Economic Theory of Self-Control," 89 *Journal of Political Economy* 392-405.

Williamson, Oliver E. 1985. *The Economic Institutions of Capitalism*. New York: Free Press: New York: Macmillan.

THE POLITICAL ECONOMY OF REGULATION

An analysis of market failures

Robert G. Harris
James M. Carman

This article is concerned with the social control of business in a predominantly market economy. Charles Lindblom (1977) has identified five major methods of social control: authority, exchange, persuasion, morality, and tradition (custom). Authority, (that is, most of what we call public policy) is difficult to establish and expensive to administer. Furthermore, in societies that value the rights and freedoms of individuals, there are strong preferences for restricting the use of authority. A central postulate of democratic theory, therefore, is that authority ought to be employed only when other methods of social control fail. Therein lies the logic of this article.

Of the five types of social control, we are concerned primarily with the interaction between authority and market exchange. It is our view that the relationship between public policy and markets (that is, between authority and exchange in Lindblom's terms) can be characterized in the following way. In a market economy, the authority of the state is employed to create and protect the property and other rights requisite to market exchange. Individuals, acting alone or in voluntary association, produce, exchange, and consume goods and services. As long as these private actions are consistent with social values and goals, there is a strong argument against public intervention. If failures occur, however, authority is employed to correct them (by modifying existing markets, creating new markets, or substituting authority for markets). But as markets sometimes fail, so too do political remedies. We must choose, then, among highly imperfect institutions; we make these choices in the belief that, in any particular set of circumstances, one method of control may produce better results than another.

Here and in the succeeding article in this book we present a conceptual scheme for identifying and classifying the effects and interactions between exchange and authority as methods of social control. Our approach in this endeavor is institutional (see Arndt 1981) and can be illustrated as follows:

Although the linear representation here is simple, it represents a highly complex, interactive process, providing a general framework for analyzing the ways in which society makes trade-offs between two allocative mechanisms: market exchange and political authority. We do not mean to imply, however, that the scheme presented here actually describes that process.

Although democratic societies may have a strong value preference for relying on private exchange as a method of social control, markets do not exist in a state of nature; they must be created. Unless there is a system for creating and protecting property rights, one has nothing to exchange (or at least one is constantly threatened by involuntary loss of the potential objects of exchange).[1] Furthermore, in a developed economy, where exchange is seldom extemporaneous and often complex, the state must provide a set of contractual rights and a system for enforcing them. Even the most extreme libertarian grants these as legitimate functions of the state. What is important to our argument is that these political acts are inherently regulatory in function, if not in intent; that is, the way in which property and contract rights are (or are not) defined has enormous consequences for the actions of market agents and outcomes of market transactions.

The role of the state in creating markets is critical to our understanding of market failures. In many cases, failures result not because a market is working improperly, but because the market does not exist,is incomplete, or is presently constrained by regulation. Thus, we need to distinguish between the inherent limits of markets and the failures of existing markets. If the failures are inherent in market exchange as a method of control, that suggests using a nonmarket solution. If the failure is one of existing markets, one option is to extend, or modify, existing property, contract, or liability rights.

TYPES OF MARKETS

Before proceeding to market failures, it may be helpful to present a very brief classification of types of market linkages. David Revzan was fond of defining a market as a "meeting of minds." But in advanced societies these meetings occur in an extraordinary number and complexity of ways. Although highly simplified, this myriad of market types can be categorized as follows:[2]

- *Auction markets*: in the ideal case, the identities of the buyer and seller are unknown to each other; a disinterested auctioneer simply matches up buy and sell orders; terms of trade do not take account of past or future transactions (for example, commodities, securities markets).
- *Bidding markets*: like auction markets in some respects, but with one crucial difference—the auction is conducted by either the buyer or the seller, who is therefore not a disinterested intermediary (for example, oil leasing, government procurement).
- *Relational markets*: there is a personal (though not intimate) relationship between the buyer and seller, who meet by phone or by mail; furthermore, by relational, we mean that the terms and conditions of any single transaction are influenced by prior or potential transactions between the same parties (for example, retail goods and services markets).
- *Contractual markets*: there is a contractual relationship between buyer and seller that transcends a single transaction and covers a wide range of goods and/or services, including supplies, advertising, architectural services, financing, management services (for example, retail franchises).
- *Obligational markets*: there is a contractual relationship between buyer and seller spanning a period of time; the conditions of exchange include provisions that shift the locus of control over, but not ownership of, the object exchange to the buyer (for example, employment contracts, which give the employer authority over the employee; equity investment, in which the shareholder gives to managers control over the use of the capital).[3]

There is one other characteristic of markets that is critical to our analysis of the authority-exchange relationship, namely their interconnectedness. Each market has its own institutional characteristics, rich and complex, changing and developing over time. Markets are also connected to many other markets, some in a direct fashion, more in indirect ways. Just as the intended, beneficial consequences of market outcomes are transmitted across markets, so too are market failures. Accordingly, in analyzing and deciding public policies toward markets, we must take explicit account of these interdependencies. These intermarket effects may be classified as horizontal or vertical. For example, undue bargaining power in a labor market clearly affects the prices of the products of the producers, and thereby the sales of complementary and substitute goods and services. Thus, public policies can, and often do, attempt to remedy failures in one market by modifying outcomes in related markets. By the same measure, public policies directed at correcting a failure in one market will have side effects in other markets.

THE IDEAL MARKET

As there are strong value preferences for one method of social control over another, so there are value preferences and differences in perceptions about how each of these control methods does or ought to work. There are norms about what constitutes a fair exchange and a recognition that certain conditions must apply, more or less, in order for a control method to work the way it is supposed to. In the case of market exchange classical political economy defines this ideal type as the perfectly competitive market, and specifies the following conditions for market success:

- *Perfect competition*: subjects to the exchange should have relatively equal bargaining positions (that is, neither should have power over the other).
- *Perfect information*: subjects should be fully informed about the object of exchange and about other exchange possibilities (for example, the prices and product attributes of substitutes).
- *Absence of externalities*: all of the consequences of the exchange process (including pre-exchange production and post-exchange consumption or use) should be internalized in the exchange.
- *Divisibility*: the object of exchange must be divisible into exchangeable units.
- *Excludability*: the subjects of exchange can exclude nonsubjects from the benefits of the exchange.

- *Zero transactions costs*: there are no barriers to exchange, so that the market instantaneously clears at a price the equilibrates current supply and demand conditions.
- *Zero entry barriers*: there are no long-run supply constraints that inhibit additional production when demand exceeds supply in the short-run.
- *Economic rationality*: subjects to the exchange act to maximize their individual self-interest, as measured in materialistic terms (that is, utility maximization by consumers, profit maximization by producers).
- *Fir distribution of wealth and income*: distribution of economic resources available for exchange is consistent with social consensus of fairness; in a market economy, that means that each individual has wealth and income corresponding to his production of economic goods and services.

These are ideal conditions that never literally hold true in any market; there is considerable controversy regarding the extent to which these conditions typically hold true in markets. Indeed, this difference in opinion is a major component of political ideology: the libertarian believes markets to be almost always nearly perfect (at least if given sufficient time to reach equilibrium), whereas the liberal (as the term is presently employed) believes that markets are often fundamentally flawed. Hence, the libertarian favors exchange over authority as a control mechanism, while the liberal often favors authority over markets.

TYPES OF MARKET FAILURES

Although ideological differences involved in this debate often color perceptions of what is actually happening, the measurement problem of determining when a market should be considered a failure may be a more serious impediment to public choice between exchange and authority than are ideological differences. While we will expand on this point now, the typology of market failure should be free of value considerations. By market failure (the reader might prefer to

TABLE 1. Types of Market Failures

Type of Failure	Nature of Failure	Examples of Failure
Imperfect competition		
Natural monopoly	Economies of scale	Electric utilities
Monopoly(sony)	Bargaining power	Standard Oil(pre-1912)
Oligopoly(sony)	Interdependent conduct	Tobacco
Monopol(son)istic competition	Transaction costs; excess capacity	Retail sale of convenience goods
Excessive competition	Fluctuating supply/demand	Trucking
Anticompetitive conduct	Collusion; predation	OPEC cartel; AT&T; MCI
Imperfect information		
Bounded rationality	Uninformed exchange	Professional services
Information costs	Uninformed exchange	Life insurance
Asymmetric information	Unequal bargaining	"Lemons"
Misinformation	Misinformed exchange	Wonder bread
Lack of information	Uninformed exchange	New therapeutic drugs
Side effects		
Internalities	Transmittal of costs to nonsubjects	Health effects of tobacco
Negative externalities	Overconsumption; costs imposed on nonsubjects	Air pollution; communicable diseases
Positive externalities	Underconsumption; benefits accrue to nonsubjects	Inoculations against communicable diseases
Public goods	Indivisibility; nonexcludability; zero MC	Street lighting;parks; national defense
(De)merit goods	Divergence of private wants, social values	Education; (gambling)
Income maldistribution		
Factor market failures	Any of above	Employee discrimination
Economic vs. social value	Earned income not equal to social worth	Children; disabled; "superstars"
Intergenerational transfers	Inconsistency with value that income be "earned"	Inheritances; socially advantaged upbringing

SOURCE: From *Journal of Macromarketing*, vol. 3, no. 1 (Spring 1983), p. 53.

substitute market imperfections), we mean to identify those possible instances in which the ideal conditions for a market success do not hold. We do not mean to suggest that in each instance a regulatory response is desirable.

In our typology, we specify the nature of the failures as they relate to the classical ideal conditions for market exchange. This is a descriptive, not normative, statement. Although we have attempted to develop a descriptive typology that is unambiguous, inclusive, and mutually exclusive, we readily acknowledge that any particular attribute or outcome of market exchange could be classified in a number of other ways.[4]

Because of their classical roots, the ideal conditions overemphasize static, structural market attributes and underemphasize dynamic and functional considerations. It is not our intent to champion that perspective; we recognize, for example, that the dynamic benefits of economic profits flowing to research and development and thence to product improvements, or products and services, are real. The question is, How imperfect can markets be before they become socially undesirable? In attempting to answer that question, scholars have attempted to define a concept of workable or effective competition in a market, then to address the measurement suggested by that definition. One definition that is useful for present purposes (but certainly not easy to make operational) is that competitive market exchange is workable when there is no regulatory response that would result in greater social gains than social losses (Markham 1950).

Such a rule could be applied in deciding whether to intervene in a given market, and in choosing among regulatory responses. In response to dangerous drugs, for example, we might prohibit their exchange, require sellers to disclose information regarding the dangers of consuming their products, or leave the market alone. The choice among these options depends on the perceived harms of the market solution, as compared to the costs of exercising authority to modify market outcomes. We address regulatory failures, and the implications of those failures for public policies toward markets, in the succeeding article. The typology of market failures is presented in Table 1. The remainder of this section is a discussion of the elements of the type typology, and illustrative examples of each type.

Imperfect Competition

In order for market exchange to function well as a method of social control, subjects of exchange cannot have unequal bargaining positions (since we assume that self-interest would cause them to exploit that bargaining advantage, resulting in unfair terms of exchange). Although we might measure bargaining position or power directly, we can more easily infer it from the structure of the market, that is, the number and size distribution of buyers and sellers in the market, and the conditions of entry into and exit from the market. The classical definitions of industrial organization identifies those market structures in which market failures are most likely.

Natural Monopoly. Natural monopoly is due to economics of scale (or scope in a multiproduct producer) relative to total market demand, which only one (or a few) producer(s) can produce at minimum cost. When these economies are of dominating importance, markets fail because too many firms will produce at costs exceeding the minimum achievable (technical inefficiency), or too few firms will exist in the market (so each seller will market power). Examples are electric utilities, postal services, and highway systems.

Monopoly (sony). Although a monopoly is not achieved by economies of scale, one seller (buyer) has power in the exchange because it is the sole available subject to exchange. Libertarians argue that the only monopolies are created by government. Liberals argue that there are no monopolies only because the antitrust laws have prohibited them. In any event, we cannot think of any clear cases of monopoly that are not based on economies of scale.

Oligopoly (sony). Whether natural (economies of scale) or not, sellers (buyers) have power in the market because there are too few sellers (buyers). Thus, while there may be some gains from economies of scale, there will be a concomitant increase in the market power of the oligopolists. Examples of oligopoly are tobacco, cement, and paper carton markets. Examples of oligopsony are labor markets in which a few employers account for a large share of total employment.

Monopolistic (sonistic) Competition. Even though there are a large number of sellers (buyers), they have some power over buyers (sellers) because transactions costs inhibit competition. Examples are retail markets in which shopping costs are high relative to the total transaction value (for example, convenience goods).

Excessive Competition

If supply or demand fluctuates unpredictably over time, there may be excessive entry by producers during peak demand, resulting in excess capacity during off-peak demand. Furthermore, if capital is specialized, supply adjustments may take longer than the duration of the fluctuation and prices will be driven below long-run average costs. In addition to the instability in supply and loss of income by producers, excessive competition may induce producers to reduce the quality of their services, perhaps with jeopardy to consumers. Examples are agricultural markets (for example, the hog cycle) and trucking and airline (pre-regulation) companies.

Anticompetitive Conduct

Because of the potential economic gains, sellers (buyers) may commit acts in concert with (collusion) or against (predation) other sellers in order to enhance their position in the market. In the short run these acts may raise (collusion) or lower (predation) prices and correspondingly reduce or increase output relative to the competitive levels. By modifying the market structure, both collusion and predation raise prices and reduce output in the long run. There are numerous examples in both product and service markets. There is one other class of anticompetitive behavior, unfair trade practices (for example, misleading advertising), which we treat as an informational failure rather than as a competitive failure.

Imperfect Information

In order for markets to work well, subjects to exchange must be fully informed about the object of exchange and about conditions and objects in other markets; ideally, information is perfect and costless. In highly localized, premodern economies, buyers and sellers may have had something approaching perfect information. But in developed economies, with geographically dispersed markets, complex goods and services produced by very large, anonymous organizations, and many available substitutes and complements, information is highly imperfect and very costly. There are several distinct types of information failures:

Bounded Rationality. Even if information was costless, it would not be perfect, in that information has value only if the subject has the knowledge needed to use the information. Given the limits of individuals to analyze, store, and retrieve information, we can predict that many exchange transactions will not be fully informed. An example is the prescription of surgical services by the doctor (seller) when the patient (buyer) lacks knowledge (and often the emotional or physical stamina to procure it) required to assess needs for, or benefits of, those services. Closely related to bounded rationality is the problem of cognitive dissonance, which causes individuals to fail to acknowledge (or even receive) information even when it is presented to them. An example is the consumers who will not accept scientific evidence of the health effects of smoking.

Information Costs. Even when information is readily available, it is seldom costless. Because of the money and opportunity costs of obtaining information, subjects to exchange often act without full information. The problem is most serious when: (1) the product or service is purchased infrequently; (2) performance characteristics are difficult to evaluate either before or soon after purchase; (3) the rate of technological change is rapid relative to the interval between purchases; and (4) the terms of exchange change rapidly relative to the purchase interval. Examples are life insurance and automobile tires (Holton 1978, 1981).

Asymmetric Information. Because there are economies of scale in the collection, storage, retrieval, and analysis of information, subjects who engage in many exchanges involving the same object will typically have an information advantage. Thus, because a producer typically sells more of a given object than a consumer buys, there often exists an asymmetry between producers and consumers. Moreover, self-interest causes producers to exploit this information advantage in the exchange process. Note two important exceptions to this rule of asymmetry. In industrial markets, purchasing agents specialize in particular goods or services, so the buyer may have better (or at least as good as) information than the seller. In factor markets, buyers may have considerably better information about working conditions (for example, toxic fumes or hazardous machinery) than the seller of labor services, or better information about the financial condition and prospects of the company than the seller of capital.

Misinformation. Because information is costly but often essential to exchange, subjects have economic incentives to provide information to other potential subjects to exchange. Sellers advertise and promote their products by providing information about the attributes of their products, and the ways in which they satisfy buyer's needs or wants. Sellers also provide information about the offerings of other sellers, either explicitly (as in comparative advertising) or implicitly (as in persuading consumers to buy one class of objects rather than another). Unfortunately, sellers also have economic incentives to misinform potential buyers about their products or the products of others. For the very reason that buyers lack information about the relative merits of available products, they are often unable to distinguish good information from bad information. Examples of misinformation are when sellers use advertising to create the impression of product differentiation (and a corresponding willingness to pay higher prices) for homogeneous products; when professionals advise clients to purchase services not needed by the buyer; when employers mislead workers about the health effects of workplace pollution; when managers mislead shareholders about the terms of an acquisition offer.

Lack of information. As human knowledge is limited, important information about a product does not exist. The fact that both seller and buyer are equally ignorant is of no relief in such cases. This problem is especially relevant to the negative attributes (or side effects) of objects of exchange. Examples are when long-term effects of therapeutic drugs and effects of asbestos on workers' health are not known.

Information as Object of Exchange. When information is itself the object of exchange, there are severe limits as to what information about the product can be revealed without revealing the product itself. Furthermore, once revealed, the cost of reproducing information is often so low that the producer of the information has difficulty internalizing the value of his product. We will discuss this issue further under the section entitled "Public Goods."

Side Effects

All goods have their bads, in their production, their consumption, or both. Sometimes those side effects accrue to subjects of the exchange (internalities); often they accrue to individuals who are not subjects to the exchange (externalities). In either case, market exchange is often imperfect because the terms of exchange will probably not incorporate all of the consequences of the production and consumption of the object of exchange.

Internalities. If the side effects are borne by a subject of exchange (for example, the consumer of the product or the provider of labor services), and there is no information failure (that is, the subject is aware of the side effect and incorporates that information in the exchange terms), then there is no immediate market failure. But side effects can be transmitted through other markets; if, for example, the side effect raises health care costs but insurance premiums are not sensitive to the higher risk, then the internality is externalized in the form of higher premiums to other individuals.

Another type of internality imposes negative side effects on other users (whether as producers or consumers) when too many users attempt to consume a service at the same time. This congestion effect is not really an externality, since the costs are borne by those involved in the exchange process. Examples of internalities are waiting lines at banks and highway congestion.

Negative Externalities.   When negative side effects of production or consumption are borne by nonsubjects, resource allocation will be distorted by overproduction and overconsumption. Examples are pollution by manufacturing plants, automobiles, or smokers; reckless driving; transmitting contagious diseases due to improper sanitation by providers of personal care services.

Positive Externalities.   When some of the positive effects of production or consumption are realized by nonsubjects, underproduction and underconsumption result. Examples are inoculation against contagious disease reduce the probability of incidence to the uninoculated as well as the inoculated; education (presumably) benefits all members of society, in addition to the person receiving the education.

Public Goods

In order for exchange to function well, the objects of exchange must be private, in the sense that they are divisible into exchangeable units and that nonsubjects can be excluded from the benefits of exchange. By public goods, we mean economically valuable goods or services that are characterized by indivisibility and nonexcludability. When goods cannot be privatized for these reasons, exchange fails because of the free-rider problem. Although individuals would benefit from the provision of the good, none has an adequate incentive to purchase the good; no one individual can afford to purchase the entire (indivisible good, but if enough others purchase the good, the nonpurchasers can still enjoy the benefits. Examples are street lighting, urban "green space," and national defense.

As already noted, information is a most important class of public goods. Intellectual products (for example, books), inventions, and production know-how (that is, trade secrets) are all instances of public goods that are characterized by indivisibility and nonexcludability. When information is an important attribute of an object of exchange, markets fail because free-riders can obtain the value of the product without buying from the seller. Brand names and corporate good will are instances of public goods from which markets cannot exclude other subjects (for example, competitors) from realizing the benefits.

Two additional features of public goods should be noted. First, there is seldom an absolute barrier to excludability; rather there would be a waste of economic resources in excluding on-purchasers (for example, shading, directing or placing street lighting to privatize the benefits). Second, by definition of indivisibility, the marginal costs of providing the goods to consumers is (until a congestion point) near zero. So, although we could use pricing to limit entry to parks, it would violate one norm of competitive markets: that price reflect the marginal social cost of production.

(De)Merit Goods

The normative theory of exchange assumes that individuals are economically rational: that individuals are capable of knowing what is good for them (or bad for them) and acting accordingly. on this premise are based the principles of individual freedom and consumer sovereignty. In all societies, however, value conflicts exist between individual and social preferences about economic goods and services, often because the production or consumption of economic goods runs counter to noneconomic (for example, religious or ethical) social values.[5] Markets are not capable of providing optimal allocation of resources if social, rather than personal, values are used as the welfare criterion. So, although black markets may work exceedingly well for some products and services, they fail as a means of social control by providing too many demerit goods and too few merit goods. Examples of demerit goods are gambling, prostitution, alcohol, tobacco, and recreational drugs. An example of merit goods is education (even if there are no externalities, society believes that individuals are better off with an education, whether or not the individual is of the same opinion).

Rents

While exchange is premised on the existence of scarcity (if all goods were limitless, there would be no need for private property and no need to exchange), that normative theory of exchange assumes that, over the long run, there are no inherent limits to the production of any particular object of exchange. Indeed, one chief attribute of markets is that prices send signals to potential producers indicating the need for additional production, inducing entry, capacity, and returning the market to equilibrium. Markets fail when there exists a long-run inelasticity of supply, preventing production from expanding sufficiently, so that existing producers realize prices exceeding the competitive level. Whereas monopoly profits result from an inelastic demand curve (which by definition indicates that the market is not perfectly competitive), rents are attributable to an inelastic supply curve. Examples are petroleum, natural gas extraction, and urban land markets.

We should note here that scarcity-induced rents are very often generated by authority, rather than by market failures. In these instances, there are no natural limits on the factors of production (or at least those limits would be reached at a higher level of output). Rather, there are regulatory constraints that prohibit or inhibit access to, or use of, the factors required to increase production and eliminate rents. Examples are housing rents due to zoning laws that restrict the density of housing units, and petroleum extraction rents due to limiting access to oil reserves.

Maldistribution of Income and Wealth

Exchange is a method of allocating and distributing resources: how much of which goods get produced and by whom are they consumed. Allocation is the domain of intermediate and final goods and services markets, whereas distribution is principally controlled in factor markets. In a market system, society believes that income—personal control of exchangeable goods and services—ought to be a function of the individual's economic contribution to society. But our ethical system also believes that each person has an inherent value, quite apart from his or her economic worth. Thus, markets fail when there is an incongruence between economic and social value, or when income does not reflect true economic value. Aid to Dependent Children, for example, is a social program predicated on the belief that a child's value is not reflected in the low income of his or her parent(s).

Failures in Factor Markets. As already noted, all the market failures just classified exist in factor markets. When they occur, there is a misallocation of resources (too many objects will be produced in the workers are underpaid; or, fixed factors will be underutilized if workers are paid more than their production justifies). Moreover, imperfections in factor markets will affect the distribution of wealth and income among factors.

Discrimination. One particular factor market failure is discrimination, which violates the normative standards that subjects are economically rational (that is, personal attributes of subjects should have no effect on the terms of exchange). When discrimination occurs, individuals may be unable to see their labor services, or may have to sell them at a less than fair price. Discrimination also occurs in labor-related consumer markets, such as schools and universities. When the sellers of educational services discriminate against potential consumers on noneconomic grounds, there is a misallocation of educational resources and the possibility of losses in income-earning potential by those discriminated against.

Social versus Economic Value. Even is factor markets were perfect, individuals might not possess sufficient economically valuable resources to earn an income that is consistent with social values. There are three main classes of individuals for whom this is likely to be true: children, who have not yet attained economic value; disabled, who for reasons of physical or mental impairment have limited economic value; and elderly, whose economic value has declined due to age. There may also be cases where individuals earn more than what society deems the individuals are worth. An example is highly paid celebrities.

Intergenerational Transfers. One other source of distributional market failures is attributable to differences in interpersonal transfers of wealth. Here there is a conflict between the norm of individual freedom (control over the use of resources includes the right to give them to others) and the norm that individuals' income should reflect their own economic contribution to society. Hence, one rationale for inheritance taxes (quite apart from raising revenues) is to prevent individuals from receiving substantial unearned income. Note that these transfers include services (for example, a good upbringing, which enhances income-earning potential) as well as tangible assets (for example, a money inheritance).

NOTES

An earlier version of this article was published in the *Journal of Macromarketing* in Spring 1983.

1. For a more thorough discussion of the relationship between property rights and marketing systems, see Carman (1982).
2. This system of classification is consistent with the types of marketing channels identified in Carman (1982), page 206.
3. According to Williamson's view (1975), this amounts to a substitution of hierarchy for

market as the means of control (as in the distinction between MacDonald's franchised outlets and their company-owned outlets). Because there is a market for employees to manage and staff company-owned, we view hierarchy and market as complementary means of control.
4. For the classic typology of market failures, see Bator (1958).
5. For an excellent review of sumptuary laws, see Hollander (1982).

BIBLIOGRAPHY

Arndt, Johan, "The Political Economy of Marketing Systems: Reviving the Institutional Approach," *Journal of Macromarketing*, Fall 1981.

Bator, Francis E., "Anatomy of Market Failure," *Quarterly Journal of Economics*, August 1958, pp. 351–379.

Breyer, Stephen, *Regulation and Its Reform.* Harvard University Press, Cambridge, Mass., 1982.

Carman, James M., "Private Property and the Regulation of Vertical Channel Systems," *Journal of Macromarketing*, Spring 1982.

Caves, Richard E., and Marc J. Roberts, eds. *Regulating the Product: Quality and Variety.* Ballinger, Cambridge, Mass., 1975.

Coase, R.H., "The Problem of Social Cost," *Journal of Law and Economics* 3 (October 1960):1–44.

Commons, John R., *Legal Foundations of Capitalism.* University of Wisconsin Press, Madison, 1959.

Crozier, Michel, *The Bureaucratic Phenomenon.* University of Chicago Press, Chicago, 1964.

Fritschler, A. Lee, and Bernard H. Ross, *Business Regulation and Government Decision Making.* Winthrop Press, Cambridge, Mass., 1980.

Hawley, Ellis, "Three Facets of Hooverian Associationalism," in *Regulation in Perspective*, Thomas K. McCraw, ed. Harvard University Press, Cambridge, Mass., 1981.

Hemenway, David, *Industrywide Voluntary Product Standards*. Ballinger, Cambridge, Mass., 1975.

Hollander, Stanley C., "Sumptuary Legislation—Demarketing by Edict," presented to the Seventh Annual Macromarketing Seminar, Boulder, Colo., 1982.

Holton, Richard H., "advances in the Backward Art of Spending Money," in *Regulating Business: The Search for an Optimum*. Institute for Contemporary Studies, San Francisco, 1978.

Holton, Richard H., "Public Regulation of Consumer Information: The Life Insurance Case," in *Regulation of Marketing and the Public Interest*, P.E. Balderston, J.M. Carman and F.N. Nicosia, eds. Pergamon Press, New York, 1981.

Lindblom, Charles E., *Politics and Markets*. Basic Books, New York, 1977.

Markham, J.N., "An Alternative Approach to the Concept of Workable Competition," *American Economic Review* 40 (June 1950): 349–361.

McGraw, Thomas K. (ed.), *Regulation in Perspective: Historical Essay*. Harvard Business School Press, Boston, 1981.

Mueller, Dennis C., *Public Choice*. Cambridge University Press, Cambridge, 1979.

Olson, Mancur, *The Logic of Collective Action*. Harvard University Press, Cambridge, Mass., 1965.

Samuels, Warren, *The Classical Theory of Economic Policy*. World Publishing Company, New York, 1966.

Schelling, Thomas C., "On the Ecology of Micromotives," *The Public Interest*, Fall 1971, pp. 59–98.

Schmalansee, Richard, *The Control of Natural Monopolies*. Lexington Books, Lexington, Mass., 1979.

Schultze, Charles, L., *The Public Use of Private Interest*. Brookings Institution, Washington, D.C., 1977.

Weidenbaum, Murray L. *Business, Government and the Public*. Prentice Hall, Englewood Cliffs, N.J, 1981.

Williamson Oliver E., *Markets and Hierarchies: Analysis and Antitrust Implications*. Free Press, New York, 1975.

Wilson, James Q. (ed.), *The Politics of Regulation*. Basic Books, New York, 1980.

Wolf, Charles, Jr., "A Theory of Nonmarket Failure: Framework for Implementation Analysis," *The Journal of Law and Economics*, October 1978, pp. 107–139.

THE POLITICAL ECONOMY OF REGULATION

An analysis of regulatory responses

James M. Carman
Robert G. Harris

Since markets cannot function without a system of property and contract rights, there are no pure market economies.[1] What we mean by a market economy is that society has a strong value preference for using exchange as the method of resource allocation, distribution, and social control, and markets are in fact the predominant means of social control. Conversely, there is no economy without markets, but nonmarket economies are those in which there is a normative preference for using authority, tradition,or persuasion, rather than exchange, as the primary means of social control.

We have already assumed that the United States is a market society in that there is a preference for market solutions. However, that leaves an enormous range of differences over the extent to which, and the actual cases in which, authority will be used to create, modify, or substitute for markets. As markets are exceedingly varied and complex, so too are the instruments of authority. Furthermore, there are few cases in which a single type of authority is employed; regulations come in bunches. In any particular market there is a nexus of rights and regulations that affect the subjects, objects, and medium or terms of exchange.

As background to our discussion of the types of regulation, there are several important dimensions of authority worth delineat-ing. The first dimension is a continuum from private to public exercise of authority. Perhaps the most private of political institutions is the family in which certain individuals have authority over other individuals, as a consequence of public policy and private economic power. Next, there are private associations, to which the members contract certain elements of authority, but only under the auspices of a more general social contract (for example, rights of religious association, labor unions, or private property associations). In some cases, however, the state can make membership in these private associations mandatory (that is, as a condition of having an exchange relationship) as in closed shops in labor markets, or membership in professional societies as a condition for selling the corresponding professional services. In some cases, private associations are assigned regulatory functions by the state, giving them a quasipublic character (professional licensing bodies). Finally, even at the public level of authority, one can distinguish regulations by the scope of the political authority (as in city, county, state, regional, and national governments). In some cases, political jurisdiction has inherent rights under the prevailing social contract (the national and state governments). Other units of government do not have sovereignty, but have been delegated their authority by some higher level of government (for example, city charters granted by states).

Along a second dimension of political authority are regulatory instruments that are more or less compatible with exchange. Although continuous, we can distinguish five discrete categories:

1. *Market creating*: public policies designed to create markets by establishing rights, incentives, and opportunities for exchange (for example, creating a market for air pollution rights).
2. *Market facilitating*: policies that promote or improve the operation of markets by reducing transactions costs, enhancing incentives, or internalizing benefits and costs (for example, public investment in transportation to expand the geographic scope of markets by reducing transport costs).
3. *Market modifying*: regulations that attempt to change the conduct of the subjects, objects, medium or terms of exchange, in order to produce outcomes different from those the market would otherwise produce (for example, agricultural marketing orders).
4. *Market substituting*: policies that create substitutes for markets; instruments of political authority are used to allocate or distribute resources or control conduct of individuals or organizations; outcomes are achieved by the exercise of authority rather than by exchange, (for example, the provision of public school education through rationing rather than through market exchange).
5. *Market proscribing*: policies that attempt to prohibit exchanges by particular subjects or of particular objects, with no attempt to use authority as a substitute method for achieving a given outcome; rather, authority is used in an effort to prevent that outcome from occurring (for example, laws prohibiting the sale of dangerous drugs).

A third dimension along which policies differ is their respective degree of coercion or compulsion. At one extreme, there are laws or policies carrying virtually no compulsion, because they are superfluous (that is, people would have acted in the legally prescribed way with or without the law); unenforced (for lack of adequate enforcement capacity, prosecutorial discretion or social consensus that it is a bad law); or though enforced, the sanctions imposed are not sufficiently severe to have much effect on conduct. At the other extreme, policies can be extremely coercive, when enforcement and sanctions are highly effective and the conduct prescribed or proscribed by the law is greatly different from individual preferences. Most laws, of course, lie in the middle ground in which individuals' conduct is modified, but with no great sense of loss of personal freedom due to a high degree of compulsion. When categorizing policies with respect to coerciveness, it should be noted that laws often require us to do what is good for us and others; we are happy to comply with the law, and happy to have the law so that others will comply as well (for example, traffic laws).[2]

These three dimensions of authority—the degree of publicness, the degree of compatibility with exchange, and the degree of compulsion—explain much of the ideological battle over the use of authority in general, or the selection of public policies in particular. Libertarians prefer instruments of authority that are more private and less public, most compatible with markets, and least coercive. Conservatives tend to prefer policies that protect prevailing property interests (whether compatible with markets or not) and that are coercive (for example, heavy penalties for socially unacceptable behavior). Liberals tend to favor public authority instruments that constrain, replace, or limit the scope of exchange. One might characterize the recent wave of neoliberalism as a shift in liberal thought toward public policies more compatible with, rather than hostile toward, market exchange and private incentives.

TYPES OF REGULATIONS

We have attempted to order out typology of regulations along these three dimensions. Thus, we have arranged policy instruments from most to least compatible with markets, from most private to most public, and from least to most cohesive. This is done for the sake of logical organization, not necessarily as a reflection of our own ideological preferences.

One is tempted to argue that a particular type of regulatory response is most appropriate to deal with a particular type of market failure; certainly there are those who offer specific responses as a panacea. If this were so, then we could map the responses onto the failures and provide a guide as to what kind of response to use on any particular problem. But political reality is quite the contrary:

there is no one-to-one correspondence between each respective type of market failure and regulatory response. Although certain responses may be recognized as more appropriate, and hence more often used in response to particular market failures, public policy makers have historically applied almost every type of response to each type of market failure. Table 1 summarizes the types and categories of regulatory responses to market failures.

Legal Rights

In a market-oriented economy, legal rights are essential to the creation and functioning of

TABLE 1. Types of Regulations.

Type of Response	Variations	Examples
Legal rights	Property rights	Land ownership
	Contracts rights	Compliance enforcement
	Associated rights	Public utility franchises
	Procedural rights	Rule-making participation
	Due process	Corporation as "person"
Information responses		
Promoting markets	Protection from liability	Consumer reports
	Allowing cooperative action	Better Business Bureau
Disclosure	Available on request	Worker health records
	Public reporting	SEC Financial reports
	Provision in exchange	Labeling laws
Content	Specific	Sugar content of food
	Comprehensive	Therapeutic drug insert
Protection	Privacy rights	Confidential records
	Accuracy of information	Credit reporting
	Agreement of owner	Patents, trademarks
Public provision	Available on request	Consumer buying guides
	General dissemination	Auto safety records
	Mandatory consumption	Public health education
Standards		
Compliance	Voluntary	Uniform package sizes
	Mandatory	Milk processing
Object of standard	Producers	Occupational licensing
	Production process	Food processing
	Product	Auto safety standards
	Consumption process	Speed limits
	Consumer	Drivers' licensing
Source of standard	Market incentives	CP/M° operating system
	Private provision	Underwriter's laboratory
	Exchange transactions	Procurement standards
	Private collective action	FASB account principles
	Public agencies	Restaurant sanitation
Nature of standard	Performance	Allowable emissions
	Design	Catalytic converters

TABLE 1.   *(cont'd.)*

Type of Response	Variations	Examples
Taxes/subsidies		
Form of transfer	Money payments	Income tax, Soc. Security
	Stamps, coupons	Food stamps
	Discounts	Senior citizens/transit
	Services in kind	Indigent medical services
Method of transfer	Incentive for private action	Charitable deductions
	Internal cross-subsidies	Regulated prices
	Rationing	Import quotas
	Direct	Income tax, Soc. Security
Object of transfer	Exchanged objects	Sales, excise taxes
	Production process	Effluent charges/subsidies
	Factors of production	Personal income tax
	Ownership	Property tax
		Corporate income tax
Controls on collective action		
Horizontal structure	Prohibiting mergers	Sherman Act
	Public franchise	"Regulated" industries
Vertical structure	Prohibiting mergers	Clayton Act
Horizontal conduct	Limits on investment	Joint venture restrictions
	Limits on private restraint	Resale price maintenance
	Exemption from limits	Agricultural cooperatives
Vertical conduct	Limits on cooperation	Boycotts
	Limits on private restraints	Resale price maintenance
	Limits on differences in terms of trade	Price discrimination; exclusive dealing
Price controls		
Compliance	Voluntary	Wage, price guidelines
	Incentives	"Tax Incentive Plan"
	Mandatory	Published tariffs
Source of controls	Contractual	Uranium contract use
	Private cooperation	Food marketing coops
	Public sanction of associational control	State liquor boards
	Public agencies	Public utility commissions
Nature of controls	Price information	Posting, public provision
	Allowable price range	ICC zone of reasonableness
	Public approval of prices	Public utility commissions
	Price setting	Postal rates
Applicability	Seller-specific	Electricity rates
	Class of sellers	Truck rates; minimum wage
	General	Wage/price freeze
Allocative controls	Price subsidies	Food stamps
	Mandate exchange	Common carrier obligation
	Restricting exchange	Rationing coupons
	Proscribing exchange	Cocaine, child labor
Public provision	Quasipublic enterprise	ComSat
	Public enterprise/prices	TVA
	Public agency/user charges	Highways, universities
	Public agency/rationing	Social service agencies

SOURCE: From *Journal of Macromarketing*, vol. 4, no. 1 (Spring 1984), pp. 50-51.

markets. The definitions of these rights sometimes determine whether exchange will even
occur; more often, they affect the terms of
exchange. They do so by designating property
that can be exchanged (property rights) and
are protected (criminal law); assigning transactions and compliance costs (contract rights);
defining liability for intended or unintended

consequences of exchange (liability rights); allowing, facilitating, or denying associational rights (corporate law, collective bargaining rights); delineating the range of applicability of the rights; and establishing the rules of evidence,proof, proceeding, and standing (civil and administrative procedural rights and due process rights).

In the U.S. legal system, these rights are defined and protected through a hierarchy of common, administrative, statutory, and constitutional laws. All of these evolve historically, which is to say that precedence and tradition are powerful determinants of legal policies and their interpretation by legislative, judicial, executive, and administrative agencies. The continual redefinition, expansion, or contraction of legal rights reflects prevailing social consensus, legal and political theory, and the perceived effects of current and potential definitions. Although legal instruments of authority are seldom selected solely on the basis of their effects on exchange relations, it is undeniable that they have important exchange-regulatory intent and consequences.

Information Responses

Authority can be used in a variety of ways to generate and disseminate information. Within this category, there is a hierarchy of responses that merely create or extend markets to those that inhibit markets in information, and to those that substitute public for private provision of information.

Information Markets. By means of property rights (or exemptions from liability), authority can be used to facilitate private markets for information, in which individuals exchange for the information needed to make rational decisions in exchange transactions (consumer reports). Policies can also facilitate the voluntary, private provision and production of information by exempting such activities from general proscriptions against cooperation among competitors (Better Business Bureau).

Disclosure. Authority can require disclosure of information by the possessor of the information. This typically means that subjects to exchange must provide information regarding the object or terms of exchange. Variants of disclosure requirements include: making information available on demand (allowing workers to inspect health and safety records), public reporting (filing 10-K financial statements), and providing specific disclosure (packaging or labeling laws). The required content of disclosure may range from very narrow (salt content of foods) to very broad (all known attributes and side effects of a therapeutic drug). Authority can also be used to prevent private associations from inhibiting the flow of information (for example, recent Federal Trade Commission rulings prevent professional societies from banning price advertising in their professional codes of ethics).

Protection of Information. Because of the public good aspects of information, authority can be used to prevent the collection or dissemination of information. These remedies include protection against unwarranted intrusions into personal affairs (rights of privacy, confidential records); proscriptions about the accuracy of information content (personal or corporate credit reports); or use of the information without the agreement of the owner of the information (patents, trademarks, copyrights, trade secrets).

Public Provision of Information. Political authority can also be used to actually provide information about the subjects, objects, or terms of exchange to the general public or to specific audiences. The public provision of information can take the form of general distribution through public media (automobile safety records and crash test results); distribution of materials on request by individuals (agricultural market-information services); or mandatory consumption of information by individuals in government institutions (public-health information in public schools).

Production of Information. Government can regulate information by requiring private parties to produce (or government can produce) information that might not otherwise exist. Required product testing by private parties or government agencies is the most prominent instance of information production by exercise of authority.

Standards Remedies

Even if information were free, human rationality is limited, so more information is not necessarily better. In complex market economies, the frequency and complexity of exchange generates information overload. In recognition of these limits, authority is employed to reduce the need for information by creating standards applicable to exchange relations. By indicating that the object of the standard meets or exceeds some threshold level on one (or more) attribute(s), subjects of exchange need less or no information about that attribute. Unfortunately, standards are so varied and complex that they cannot be reduced to a linear hierarchy of types. Rather, we identify the several dimensions on which standards differ and discrete categories of standards.

Compliance. Standards can range from purely voluntary (uniform package sizes) to highly mandatory, meaning that products failing to meet the standard are excluded from legal markets (for example, milk standards).

Object of the Standard. Standards can be applied to the producers (professional certification or licensing), the production process (workplace safety standards), the product (auto safety standards)[3] the consumption process (highway speed limits), the consumers (driver's licensing), and the complementary goods and services (highway safety standards, lead content of gasoline). The oldest use of standards regulates the quantities, rather than qualities, of goods exchanged (standard weights and measures). In traditional regulation (the regulated industries in transportation, communications, energy distribution, and financial services), authority is used to comprehensively regulate the production and provision of goods and services, although we sometimes separate responsibility for quality regulation from quantity and price regulation between agencies (Federal Aviation Administration regulates airline safety, whereas the Civil Aeronautics Board regulates entry, exit, quantity, and price of service).

Source of Standards. We can also distinguish standards by the process by which standards are developed, promulgated, and/or enforced. Standards are regularly generated by market processes, of course, when firms have incentives to standardize product attributes even though no authority requires them to do so (as in the adoption of PC-DOS operating systems for sixteen-bit microprocessors). Authority can be used to promote private contractual standards (legally enforceable exchange terms, as in procurement contracts or collective bargaining agreements) and private associational standards (promulgated by industry trade association, privately or publicly enforced, as in SEC-encouraged standards generated by the Financial Standards Accounting Board).[4] Standards are promulgated and enforced by public agencies (usually with private participation), as in public health and sanitation standards for restaurant and personal care establishments.

Nature of Standards. We can also categorize standards as performance-oriented, design-oriented, or ingredient-oriented. Performance standards establish threshold levels for outcomes, while leaving producers or consumers discretion as to the method of achieving the specified performance (for example, specifying the units of emitants allowed from a factory). Design standards require that the object of the standard be manufactured or operate in a specific way (for example, requiring manufacturers to install catalytic converters to control emissions). Ingredient standards specify actual, minimum, and/or maximum ingredients required in order for the product to be sold, or in order to be designated by a commonly accepted name (for example, mayonnaise).

Taxes and Subsidies

There are three general purposes served by government fiscal policies and operations: allocation, distribution, and stabilization. Government collects revenues to cover the costs of government; to redistribute income among individuals; and to stabilize prices, reach full employment, and reach full economic growth. Our concern here is with the use of taxes or subsidies as the means of correcting market failures, that is, with the regulatory functions of fiscal policies. In thereby limiting the discussion, we do not mean to suggest that there are not other important functions of taxes and subsidies.

Taxes and subsidies are logically similar, although of opposite sign. The one logical difference between them as instruments of authority is that, in any given instance, there is almost always a higher degree of coercion attached to taxes than to subsidies. Someone eligible for Social Security payments can simply not request them, or refuse them if offered, with no legal sanction. One does not have the same option with respect to payment of Social Security taxes, however. Having acknowledged this distinction, it will greatly expedite the discussion to treat taxes and subsidies as roughly equivalent instruments of public policy, except that in one case the transfer of resources is negative, in the other, positive.

Form of Transfer.   Taxes or subsidies can take one of several forms. The most commonly used means of transfer is money (or near-money) payments (as in Social Security). The second form of transfers is stamps or coupons, which can be spent like money, but only for the purchase of specified goods or services (food stamps, educational vouchers). The third form of transfer is through the price mechanism, that is, modifying the terms of exchange so that the subjects pay (receive) less (more) than the market-determined price (senior citizen discounts). If these exchanges are made at a zero price, we can classify them as a fourth form of transfers, namely the direct provision of goods and services (indigent medical services, urban playgrounds).

Method of Transfer.   Authority can be used directly or indirectly to tax and subsidize. Indirect methods include creating incentives for private, voluntary transfers among individuals and associations (charitable giving promoted by tax deductibility). Transfers can also be achieved by regulating the prices of goods and services (long distance telephone users being taxed to subsidize local telephone users). Another indirect public method of transfer is to ration or restrict markets, so as to affect the income of factors in the market (subsidizing the domestic auto producers, shareholders, and employees by import quotas on Japanese autos). Finally, transfers can be made directly (income taxes, Social Security payments).

Object of Transfer.   Transfers vary in the object and range of their applicability. One generic class of transfers is directed toward objects transferred in exchange; goods and services are taxed or subsidized, either in general (sales tax) or specific (excise tax). Taxes or subsidies can be applied to the side effects of production, consumption or exchange (effluent taxes, emission-control subsidies). Another category of transfers is tied to the ownership (rather than transfer) of goods (property taxes). Another generic class of transfers is related to the earnings of factors of production (personal income, capital gains taxes). Finally, transfers can be directed at producing agencies (corporate income taxes, subsidies to mass transit agencies or universities).

Controls on Collective Action

Given the nature of the consumption, production, and exchange processes, collective organizations are a virtual necessity in modern economies. Collective action has three main purposes: (1) to realize economies of scale in production, (2) to internalize the benefits of productive actions, and (3) to change the balance of power between participants in the exchange process. The state allows and encourages collective action by a variety of regulatory instruments already covered, including associational rights.[5] Surely the most important of these are the rights of incorporation granted to companies and labor unions (including limited liability and equity ownership and transfer rights in the first case, collective bargaining and grievance procedural rights in the second). Authority also promotes collective action by use of taxes and subsidies: by granting subsidies to collective agents (government grants to private social service agencies or research institutes), by exempting contributions to collective from taxation (contributions to charitable agencies are tax deductible, whereas contributions made directly to needy individuals are not), and by exempting collective agencies from taxation (tax exempt status of nonprofit organizations). In addition to these regulatory instruments, authority is used to control markets and market failures by directly shaping the structure of markets and controlling the conduct of organizations in the following ways.

Horizontal Structure. In order to affect bargaining positions in the exchange process, authority shapes the structure of competitors (buyers or sellers). While property rights and the rights of incorporation create a presumption that organizations may grow and expand without further approval, authority can be used to specifically deny such expansion when it threatens the competitive process (antitrust laws on mergers and acquisitions). A more restrictive class of structural controls are entry and exit regulation, which strictly limit the opportunity of producers to enter a market, or to exit from it (public franchises in transportation, communications, and financial services).[6] Although authority primarily has been concerned with power within a given market, there are also controls that span markets, since power in one market might give an unequal bargaining position in another market (restrictions on conglomerate mergers, restrictions on the activities of bankholding companies).

Vertical Structure. All markets exhibit a high degree of vertical interdependence, with goods moving through many successive transactions from the original source to the final consumer. Accordingly, authority can be employed to regulate the vertical structure of markets especially those involving economic organizations on both sides of exchange. Structural controls may specify the conditions under which firms will be allowed to vertically integrate across channel levels, or actually prohibit such vertical integration (statutes on vertical mergers).

Horizontal Conduct Controls. In order to shape market structure, authority allows, encourages, and prohibits competitors from cooperating in various ways. To promote the flow of information and the establishment of standards, competitors are usually allowed to cooperate in those areas. Cooperation in research and development, investments in productive capacity, and marketing activities may be allowed or denied (joint-venture regulations). Because of its onerous effects on bargaining, cooperation on the design of the product or on the terms of exchange (especially price) is often prohibited (Sherman and Clayton proscriptions against restraints in trade). In cases where there is a perceived imbalance in bargaining positions, however, cooperation among competitors is allowed, usually by exemption from laws prohibiting such cooperation (antitrust exemptions granted to agricultural marketing cooperatives, the rationale for which is the market failure of excessive competition; buying cooperatives).

Vertical Conduct Controls.   In recognition of the complexity of channels of distribution, the state regulates relations among members of the channel, by allowing acts of cooperation (cooperative advertising), denying other acts of cooperation (boycotts), prohibiting certain restrictions in the terms of trade (resale price maintenance), and setting limits on discriminatory treatment in the terms of trade (Robinson-Patman proscriptions on price discrimination, provisions in the proposed AT&T consent decree requiring local operating companies to provide equal access to competing long-distance signal carriers).

Price Controls

Because prices are so central to the allocative functioning of markets, and so critical to the distributional consequences of exchange, authority is used to influence or determine the prices at which exchanges occur. As already noted, prices may be influences by the imposition of taxes or granting of subsidies, and by controls on the structure of markets and the conduct of subjects in markets. In addition, there are class-of-authority instruments aimed more or less directly at prices themselves, either because other forms of control have failed to produce the desired result or because price controls are preferred to alternative forms of control.

There are a number of dimensions on which price controls vary, and the number of permutations across dimensions is very large. Rather than identifying discrete types of price controls, we will discuss the dimensions that characterize any particular control instrument, and attempt to identify the variants on each dimension.

Compliance.   Price controls range from purely voluntary (wage and price guidelines), to quasi-voluntary (use of economic incentives to induce particular pricing behavior, the Tax Incentive Plan for restricting wage increases in labor markets), to mandatory (published tariffs in regulated industries).

Source of Controls.   As with standards, prices can be established, and compliance enforced, in a number of ways. The most private method of price control is private exchange, as enforced by contractual rights (long-term supply contracts). Prices also can be established by private agreement among competitors (producer cartels), although this form of price control is often precluded by controls of collective action. Authority can be used to establish or sanction price controls (fee schedules established by professional societies), which means that public authority is employed to enforce compliance with the controls. Price controls can be established by private agencies or associations, but submitted to public authority for approval and implementation (state liquor control boards). Finally, price controls can be generated and enforced by public agencies, although usually with procedural rights assuring private participation.

Nature of Controls.   Although price controls are always directed at the price terms of exchange, they vary in the manner by which the intended results are achieved. The most marketlike forms of price control are related to price information: requiring disclosure (price posting of wholesale liquor prices to dealers or posting of gasoline prices at the pump); precluding private control on disclosure (banning professional code limits on price advertising); and public provision (comparative price studies published by government agencies). Direct intervention in the pricing process includes establishing a zone within which private parties can set prices (the zone of reasonableness recently adopted by the Interstate Commerce Commission); requiring specific approval of privately set prices (most administrative agencies only approve prices, not actually set them); and establishing the price at which goods or services will be exchanged (postal rates, minimum wages).

Applicability of Controls. Price controls can be applied very narrowly to a specific transaction, or to all transactions between a particular seller (buyer) and its buyers (local telephone rates are seller-specific). More generally, price controls can be applied to all sellers (buyers) in a broad class (motor carrier rates). The most general type of price controls applies to whole sectors of the economy, or even, hypothetically to all prices in the economy (general price freeze). While price controls are most often applied to goods and services in intermediate and final markets, they can also be used in factor markets (minimum wage laws, interest rate ceilings).

Direct Allocative Controls

Prices and rationing are alternative means of allocating or distributing resources. Although rationed goods often carry prices, the defining characteristic of rationing is that exchange is no longer a purely voluntary act by the parties to the exchange: there is some compulsion (in addition to economic incentives) at work on either or both sides of the transaction. Rationing can be implemented directly by public agency or through private exchange transaction channels (public schools versus educational vouchers for private schools). Furthermore, rationing can be positive or negative: it can be used to facilitate the transfer of resources or restrict exchange transactions. We can distinguish the following type of allocative controls.

Price Subsidies. As we indicated previously, subsidies can be granted in the form of stamps or coupons, which can be used along with money in the purchase of specified goods or services. The function of the subsidies in these cases is to increase the ration of those goods to the recipients of the coupons (that is, relative to their ration under market prices). This form of rationing is not intended to limit or restrict the allocation of goods to nonrecipients of the subsidies, although it may have that affect (by increasing the de-

mand for, and therefore market-equilibrating price of, the subsidized goods). It should be noted that this form of rationing may actually be intended to subsidize the producers of the goods, rather than the consumers (hence the support of agricultural lobbies for the food stamp program).

Mandating Exchange. Goods and services also can be positively rationed by requiring sellers to exchange with specified buyers (either at a privately negotiated price or at a regulated price). This form of rationing is commonly employed in public utilities and common carriers, wherein franchised producers are required to provide services on demand to all potential buyers within their franchise area, and at published tariffs. As in price subsidies, the intent of this rationing is to increase, rather than decrease, the volume of exchange; it may also have the effect of restricting exchange (some classes of buyers usually pay implicit taxes in order to subsidize the provision of services to customers whose revenues do not cover the cost of service).

Restricting Exchange. In the event of excess demand for goods, allocative controls can be used to restrict production, exchange, and/or consumption of certain goods and services. Under these controls, money alone is an insufficient means of payment; stamps, coupons, or some other evidence of authority is also required (ration coupons during World War II). Allocative controls also can be applied to factor markets, as in laws regulating hours of employment, or credit allocation.

Proscribing Exchange. The most market-delimiting form of allocative controls is the prohibition of (legal) exchange of goods and services. This form of control is typically directed at those instances in which there is a substantial conflict between market outcomes (in the absence of controls) and prevailing social values (that is, demerit goods). The most emphatic application of this form of control is embodied in the Emancipation Proclamation, which forbade exchange of human beings, and in the labor laws designed to protect children from exploitation in labor markets. As applied to consumer markets, proscriptive controls apply to goods (dangerous drugs) and services (prostitution). We might add that market responses to these prohibitions is a rather striking example of the limits of enforcement and level of compliance with acts of authority.

Government Provision of Goods and Services

As has been noted in the previous sections on regulatory responses authority can be exercised by allowing encouraging, or requiring specified conducts or outcomes of private parties, or it can be implemented by the state itself. Depending on the actual configuration of public action, then, authority is more or less consistent with market exchange. When the government is merely providing information that facilitates and improves the operation of markets, there is no conflict between politics and markets. The government can also influence market outcomes by its own actions in the marketplace, as in the use of procurement standards to influence product design (for example, purchasing government auto fleets with air bags to help auto makers on the scale necessary to economically offer them as an option to other customers).

Beyond these market facilitating acts, though, government can be directly involved in markets by substituting for them. Through the use of public enterprise, for example, the government grants to itself the franchise necessary for transacting in the market (postal services). By holding the rights of ownership to itself, government can more or less exclude the enterprise from capital markets and substitute public authority for market control of the firm; along this dimension are quasipublic enterprises (ConRail, ComSat) and government enterprises (U.S. Postal Service). Having established agencies of government as the provider of goods and services, these agencies differ in whether their output is exchanged through markets with prices (public universities), quasiprices (user charges such as gasoline excise taxes), or rations (social services).

TYPES OF REGULATORY FAILURES

This section presents a typology of regulatory failures—that is, how and why public actions intended to correct market failures (at last purportedly) fail to achieve their goals. This section provides guidelines for deciding when regulatory action may be justified and for choosing among alternative regulatory responses.

To set the state for this typology, we provide a summary of regulatory responses and market failures. While we would expect fundamental rights and the common law to affect virtually all types of market failures, it would seem logical that other regulatory responses would be used to solve specific types of market failures. Table 2 shows quite a different picture. It is possible to cite instances in which each type of regulation is being used in response to each type of market failure.

Thus, while we will say something about the design of regulatory responses and their likelihood of success, it is not possible to specify a single kind of remedy that should be applied to each particular type of market failure: the uses of regulatory instruments are more pervasive, and their success or failure more complicated. Key questions that should be addressed in evaluating regulatory responses are:

- Are the consequences of a market failure sufficient to justify the cost of the regulation and the performance that it can reasonably be expected to achieve?
- Do the apparent shortcomings of a given regulation stem from its design or implementation, or are they inherent in the nature of the original market failure?

TABLE 2. Typology of Market Failures and Regulatory Responses.

TYPES OF MARKET FAILURES

Regulatory Responses	Monopoly Power	Anticompetitive Conduct	Excessive Competition	Imperfect Information	Externalities/ Side Effects	Public Goods	(De)Merit Goods	Income Distribution
Legal rights and liabilities	Unenforceable contracts (e.g., cartels)	Criminal antitrust statutes	Bankruptcy laws	Product liability; commercial libel limits	Nonsmoking workplace rights	Anti-discrimination laws	Controlled substance criminal liabilities	Limits on right-to-fire employment-at-will
Information	Line-of-business reporting	Ban of professional advertising restrictions	Licensing boards' information services	Cigarette packaging/advertising warnings	Toxic waste "sight right-to-know" ordinances	Public health information	Ratings of movies	State employment agencies
Standards	Electric utility service reliability	Fair trade laws	Aircraft maintenance standards	Funeral industry disclosure requirements	Automobiles catalytic converters	Federal highway design standards	State accreditation of schools	Equal opportunity employment standards
Taxes/subsidies	Excess profits tax (WWII)	Antitrust civil fines	Local air service subsidies	FDA's "failure-to-disclose" fines	Fines for air-water effluent violations	Tax exemption of non-profit schools	National endowments for arts-humanities	A.I.D., Medicare
Controls on/ rights of collective action	Antitrust/restraint of trade	Boycott restrictions	Legal cartels (agricultural marketing boards)	Class action product liability	Class action environmental suits	Permit control on parades/demonstrations in public places	Antitrust exemption for newspapers	Labor union organizing. collective bargaining
Price controls	Utility rate regulation	Predatory pricing limits	Minimum rate regulation	State insurance regulation	Peacetime price/wage controls	Deposit bottle bills to combat litter	State liquor price controls	Lifeline utility rates
Allocative controls	Equal carrier access (telephone)	Antidumping provisions	Entry controls (taxi, motor carrier permits)	Prescription drugs	Offshore drilling rights	Allocation of radio and TV broadcast license	Public school attendance requirements	Import preferences to Third World countries
Public provision	Highways; municipal electric utilities	Law concerning political debates on TV	Depository insurance; crop loans	Consumer buying guides	Public schools and higher education	National parks and forests	Public schools and higher education	Social welfare services

- Are there other regulatory responses that would be more likely to achieve better performance or be more cost effective?
- Will a regulatory response that is successful in the short term prove to be a failure over the longer term?
- Are there secondary or aggregate effects of a regulation on the marketing system or other social systems that outweigh the direct or immediate effects of the regulation?

Public Choice Failures

While most public-policy analyses are typically cast in terms of economic efficiency, fairness, freedom, and equity are criteria that are more basic to a democratic society. Indeed, the most fundamental basis for a market economy is that only a free-market system is consistent with political freedom and individual liberty. Moreover, democratic societies regularly use methods of organization and control that are not efficient in the narrow sense of the term. Perhaps the best example of inefficiency in a democratic society is an election. Imagine bearing the costs of having millions of people go to the polls when a small random sample of the population could produce the same result at a fraction of the cost, although with some small margin of sampling error. In democratic societies, we do use representational methods to increase efficiency over ongoing town meetings. In addition to elections, our primary institutions of public choice are legislatures, judiciaries, and executive agencies. As with markets, we can identify the ideal character of these institutions, but we use those ideals as standards against which to measure or compare realities. As markets fail, so do the institutions and instruments of authority. Some failures are inherent in the public-choice process itself.[7]

Transaction Costs.   Public choice is a costly proposition, regardless of the method or object of choice. For this reason, public choices have a natural longevity, the duration of which is determined by a subsequent act of public choice that eliminates, modifies, or substitutes for prior choice. While in markets we often make frequent, periodic choices (which store to shop at, which brand of soft drink to buy), we make public choices much less frequently. By and large, prevailing policies are the accumulation of prior public choices. As circumstances change over time, we should expect that, even if the policy were once appropriate, it will become less so over time. But because of the transactions costs of public choice, we do not spontaneously change policies in accord with changing circumstances.

Electoral Failures.   Elections play three different roles in public choice: (1) by referenda, voters actually decide public policy; (2) by electing legislators, voters decide who will make policy decisions; and (3) by electing executives, voters decide who will make and/or implement policy decisions. Although there are some similarities between markets and elections (enough so that modern political economists refer to the supply of and demand for political services and the marketing of candidates), there are some fundamental differences.

The most critical difference between markets and politics is that there can be no exchange; candidates for elected office can promise to support certain policies or promote certain values if elected, but they cannot offer anything specific in exchange for someone's vote. Even if such a promise were made, it would be an unenforceable contract between the parties (which is not to deny that such promises have been made, and parties have attempted to enforce such contracts, albeit in violation of the law). In short, elections lack the reciprocity essential to exchange.

Elections differ most from markets in their inherently collective nature. Whereas market exchanges are acts of private individual choice, elections must necessarily be acts of public, collective choice (Olson, 1971). Unless we impose a rule of unanimity (which would make public choice impossible in most electorates), election results will favor some individuals over others. Indeed, a central feature of the social contract in democratic societies is that individuals agree to accept the results of elections, even when they lose.

As a consequence of majority rule, the result of an election is a public good in that an individual voter can neither determine the outcome not be excluded from incurring the benefits or costs of the outcome. As a public good, the electoral process suffers from the problem of free riders. No matter how or even whether one individual votes, the outcome will be the same. So even though elections may have very important consequences for individuals, they have little incentive to become well informed, or even participate in the process.

Even when citizens do vote, elections suffer from a number of problems not unlike market failures. There are very serious information failures: compared to most economic products and services, public choices are exceedingly more complex. In order for elections to work well, voters must understand the nature and consequences of alternative votes; such information is always costly, time-consuming to process, often unavailable, and sometimes misleading. Issues of public choice are on occasion so complex that not even the experts fully understand the alternatives, much less the electorate.

Another electoral failure relates to the bundling of issues. Although market goods are a bundle of desired attributes, we typically have considerable choice among bundles. Indeed, some tied sales are illegal. In elections, we are usually limited to two (or other small number) of choices: yes or no on referenda, Democratic or Republican representation. Because an elected official will represent his/her constituency on countless issues of public choice, it is a certainty that there will be differences between the votes of the legislator (or the acts of an executive or judge) and the preferences of any given voter. Thus, bundling forces individuals to make difficult trade-offs among issues; they may favor one

candidate's stand on transportation policy, another on energy policies.

Alternatively, some voters may use a choice process that places such importance on a particular high saliency issue that the candidates' positions on that single issue may determine their vote. The result may be that the winning candidate, while favoring the right position on the single issue, may have positions on other issues that are at odds with the majority of the electorate.

Legislative Failures. Once elected, legislators ideally act in the interests of a majority of their constituency, although that necessarily means action against the interests of some constituents on any given issue. Moreover, we assume that legislators are not fundamentally different from other individuals, so we expect them to behave (if sometimes opportunistically) in their own self-interest. Given the costs of conducting electoral campaigns, and the need for organized support to overcome information failures, one significant failure is the influence of resourceful, vocal, well-organized citizens in the legislative process. Legislators also suffer from information failures, in that the issues they decide are extremely complex individually, and usually bundled together in legislative acts.

Other legislative failures relate to their representation and organizational structure. These structural failures include: (1) the overrepresentation of rural interests in the U.S. Senate or state senates (that is, citizens in jurisdiction with small populations have far more senators per capita than those in populous jurisdictions); (2) the committee and seniority systems concentrate power in the hands of a minority of representatives, whose interests (or even whose constituents' interests) are not necessarily those of a majority of the electorate; and (3) the complexity and number of issues is such that elected representatives increasingly depend on staff whose private interests (for example, future employment with lobbying organizations) may differ from constituents' interests.

Jurisdictional Failures. Whether public choice is made directly through elections or through representation, it can create externalities not dissimilar to those found in market systems. Externalities occur because public policies of a given jurisdiction can have effects on citizens or activities in other jurisdictions. Examples of these externalities include air or water pollution moving across state lines, liberal corporate charter provisions causing companies to incorporate in a state other than the one in which they principally do business, and interstate differences in taxes or subsidies causing personal movement to lower tax or higher welfare states. At the highest level, jurisdictional failures arise among nation states, where the consequences of regulatory or market failures of one country may fall on the populace of other countries. Indeed, nationalistic self-interest might seek such results, especially when reciprocity or retaliation is improbable.

Design Failures

As we have shown in Table 2, many different types of regulation are used to prevent, modify, and shift the costs/benefits of each type of market failure. Regardless of the type of the intent or method of regulation, policies fail in part because policy makers often lack the information needed to (1) correctly assess the nature and extent of the market failure, (2) evaluate the direct effects of alternative responses, (3) evaluate the side effects of alternative responses, (4) correctly predict the incidence of costs and benefits of the regulation, or (5) simply design a regulatory response that will solve the market failure. In some cases, the necessary information is simply not available (that is, it lies beyond the limits of human knowledge or is prohibitively expensive to obtain). In other cases, the problem is one of information asymmetry: the parties to be regulated have, or control access to, the information needed for the policy design, but the public policy makers do not. Participants in the policy design process will exploit this asymmetry to gain strategic

advantage. These information failures, combined with the legislative failures just described, lead to, ex post, poorly designed regulation.

A special kind of information failure concerns external and side effects. Efforts to regulate one market or product almost inevitably affect other goods or markets. Regulating auto emissions by requiring the installation of catalytic converters dramatically shifts the demand for converters while decreasing the demand for research and development into superior methods of emission control. There is virtually no limit to these side effects, as they are transmitted, like ripples, from one market to another. In the worst cases, negative effects are amplified in magnitude; in such cases, regulation may be successful where it was intended, but still is a failure overall because the indirect effects outweigh the direct benefits.

Even where there are discernible benefits of regulation, there are always costs as well. The self-evident costs are those incurred by the government in implementing a policy, but these are sometimes small relative to the total costs, which include the costs of complying with the regulations by private parties. Because the costs and benefits of a regulation are seldom, if ever, borne by the same parties in the same proportions, there are inevitably distributional consequences of regulation, whatever their primary purpose may be.[8]

Implementation Failures

Once policies are selected, through the democratic public-choice process (either in the present or very distant past), they must be implemented to have an effect on private conduct or market outcomes. The legislature delegates responsibility for implementation to an agency of the government, a quasipublic agency (one with legal powers granted by the state), or a voluntary association of individuals. Although legislative enactments sometimes contain specific provisions regarding delegation, more often acts are implicitly delegated on the basis of general principles (or laws) of delegation. Thus, the implementation of contract compliance provisions falls to the judicial system as a matter of constitutional principle. Sometimes legislative acts create new agencies for implementation of the policies in the act, although even then legislatures are constrained by legal separation of power, jurisdictional rights among units of government, and the organization of those units.

Although there are a large variety of institutional mechanisms for implementing public policies, we will concentrate our attention by grouping into four classes: judicial agencies, bureaucratic agencies, public boards, and private associations. While all of these suffer from more or less the same generical institutional failures (mainly, information failures, transactions costs, free riders and agent-principal problems), the manifestations of these failures differ across institutional types. It is because of these differences that we choose one agency of implementation over another in order to minimize the failures and improve performance and outcomes.

Judicial Failures. The distinguishing characteristic of judicial agencies is that they implement policies by deciding whether parties have, in a given instance, complied with prevailing policies (constitutional, statutory, administrative, or common law). The parties engaged in the process can be individuals, associations, or other public agencies. Typically, these decisions are made in an adversarial process, which has a number of institutional implications.

First, principals in the dispute (plaintiff, prosecutor, or defendant) are represented by agents (lawyers) who receive income for their services. Self-interested behavior of agents often conflicts with the interests of the principals (for example, expending resources to appeal a decision that will surely be upheld).

Second, the adversaries in the dispute represent only two of the interests affected by the decision; there are externalities of judicial

acts both positive and negative (for example, establishing a precedent that will be used in future cases). One of the most frequently cited failures of regulatory agencies is of this sort: the tendency of agencies to be captured by well-organized interested parties, to the exclusion of other interests.

Third, the information available to the decision maker (judge, jury, or regulatory commission) will depend in large part on the evidentiary submissions of the parties, with consequent information failures. Information needed for a good decision may not exist, or it may be concealed. The quality of the information presented is dependent on the representational abilities of the agents and the resources of the principals; if there is an imbalance in abilities or resources, the decision process may not be fair.

Finally, there are inherent limits of judicial decisions (as opposed to executive actions); courts have very limited enforcement capabilities. Though actions can be prevented (injunctions), courts are generally limited to punishing or compensating for acts that have already occurred. When those acts have irreversible, irreparable, or otherwise noncompensable consequences, courts cannot remedy them.

Bureaucratic Failures. Responsibility for interpretation and implementation of public policies are commonly assigned to agencies of government. The standard organizational form of these agencies is bureaucratic, hence the classification of the failures associated with implementation by public agencies. Because individuals in bureaucracies are self-interested, a most significant class of bureaucratic failure is the pursuit of organizational objectives contrary to objectives of the public policies (Crozer 1963). One prominent instance of such behavior is budget-maximization, but there are many others as well: promoting policies that will further the career objectives of agency employees, acting favorably toward parties for financial gain or future employment prospects, or interpreting policies in a manner consistent with personal values, but inconsistent with the social values on which the policies are premised (Fritschler and Ross 1980; Wilson 1980).

Bureaucracies also fail due to information failures. As they often are dependent on regulated industries for date and analysis, they are subject to opportunistic behavior by those parties. In any case, the issues they must decide and the actions they must take to successfully implement policies are complex, sometimes beyond the limits of bounded rationality.[9]

The most widely noted failure of bureaucracies is their cost, which is indeed staggering (add up the combined expenditures of all levels of government). But as recent studies have shown (Weidenbaum 1981), the costs of bureaucracy are quite small compared to the costs of compliance with the regulations they impose. Even so, these costs must be measured in relative terms, since alternative institutional forms are not costless.

Finally, there are bureaucratic failures of a jurisdictional kind, due to overlapping jurisdictions across agencies or levels of government (for example, attempts by the CAB, FAA, and OSHA to regulate airline working conditions; or the myriad of environmental reports and approvals required for new factory construction). Although many of these are instances of turf protection by agencies, they also result from the inherent structure of governmental authority in a society that values separation of powers and checks and balances. Even in societies of this persuasion, however, there are organizational alternatives. In the United States, the checks are principally through a congressional committee; in the United Kingdom, the checks are principally through the Exchequer; in India, the checks are principally through purposely given overlapping authority to agencies in other ministries.

Quasipublic Agency Failures.   One common technique to get around the suboptimization, information failures, and high cost of bureaucracies is the public board. In this structure, private citizens are appointed to sit on a regulatory board. In some cases they serve for only expenses; in other cases they may receive a fee. However, they are not career civil servants. These appointments should reduce costs. The citizens are appointed because, when viewed as a whole, they represent the broad interests of the society, and therefore, are unlikely to seek objectives other than those of society. They are also selected because they have some expert knowledge in the field they are appointed to regulate. Thus, they should overcome some informational failures, and if provided with some agency staff support, they should at least be able to ask the right questions.

Unfortunately, such boards can exhibit failures on all counts. First, since they are expert, active citizens, they are busy. They may not always have the motivation to prepare their positions and decisions as carefully as the society would like. Thus, the staff involvement and costs are as great or greater than if the board were not there. Second, how does an executive branch select a board that represents society, is motivated to serve, and is expert in the special field (as well as active in the right political faction)? The answer is often to pick persons from the field being regulated. Even if true public members are on such boards, they often defer to the expertness of the industry members. Thus, such boards often use their additional information to serve the special interests of the regulated rather than the interests of the society.

Private Association and Self-Regulation Failures.   The problems just cited may not be serious if the regulation is concerned with efficacy, internal equity, health, and safety with regard to the practice of a particular profession. In such cases, responsibility for implementing public policies is often granted to private associations in such professions. Normally, these delegations of authority involve individuals or organizations with economic interests affected by the policy, for example, professional licensing boards and agricultural marketing boards. Here, one of the failures of public boards becomes far more serious in such attempts at self-regulation. Clearly, the association's authority can be used in the self-interest of the members of the association without regard to unrepresented interests. This problem is exacerbated by the problems of bounded rationality and asymmetric information. The costs or benefits of authority are usually distributed very unevenly, for example, the benefits of milk price-supports accrue mainly to a few thousand producers, while the costs are borne by tens of millions of consumers. In these circumstances, it is quite rational for the producer group of individuals to devote their time, energy, and resources to the formation and implementation of authority, while the rest of society ignores the situation.

Another class of failures of self-regulation relates to the appointed citizens' limited authority. When we delegate authority to private associations, we specifically limit that grant, either in the terms of the act authorizing the delegation or by more general legal principles. Thus, private remedies sometimes fail because the private association lacks the authority to obtain a sufficient degree of compliance for its policies. This is especially true when there are public goods at issue, as when the benefits or costs of labor organizing for collective bargaining accrue to all employees, whether or not they participate in the organizing and bargaining process.

Finally, policy implementation by a private association often fails due to agent-principal problems. Authority is seldom exercised directly by the members of an association. Having received a grant of authority from the state, they in turn delegate the responsibility for implementation to administrators or representatives, who may or may not be members of the class of recipients of authority (staff members of professional licensing boards or trade associations). As self-interested individuals, these agents may behave opportunistically to advance their own interests at the expense of the association members.

IMPLICATIONS FOR PUBLIC POLICY

During the mid-1960s to the mid-1980s, public policies in the United States have undergone historic changes. We have witnessed, on the one hand, an enormous increase in the degree and extent of social regulation such as equal employment, environmental and consumer protection, occupational and product safety, financial disclosure, and civil rights. On the other hand, deregulation of whole industries has occurred in trucking, airlines, telephone equipment, intercity telecommunications, and securities brokerage. What accounts for these seemingly contradictory trends, and what do they tell us about public policies toward business and business-government relations?

There seem to be four general forces at work. First, as the structure of markets changes, so does the structure of regulation. Regulations that were once wellsuited for a given market failure no longer fit the situation well. This clearly happened in the deregulation of airlines, trucking, and intercity telecommunications. Airlines and trucking were, when first regulated, infant industries subject to problems of excessive competition. By the 1970s, though, both were mature industries with well-developed route systems serving every corner of the nation. The costs of price controls far exceed the benefits, as the results of deregulation have demonstrated. When telecommunications was first regulated, the basic technology was wire and poles, with substantial economies of scale, making the industry a natural monopoly. With the development of microwave communications in the 1950s, and its widespread adoption by the 1970s, the industry was no longer a natural monopoly. Again, a change in economic conditions justified a shift in public policy. The same is true of social regulation, but with a resulting increase, rather than decrease, in regulation.

A second force underlying regulatory change is changing public attitudes about what constitutes market failures. Neither environmental pollution nor racial employment discrimination were new problems in the 1960s, yet neither had occupied prominent positions on the public-policy agenda. Led perhaps by populist journalism and mass communications media, public perceptions of the social harms caused by these and other market failures increased dramatically. Legislative hearings shed the search light of political attention and public opinion on these problems, new laws were enacted, and whole new regulatory agencies created. It may well be that, as a body politic, we over-reacted to the problems, weighing the costs of market failures while discounting the costs of regulatory intervention. But the point here is that changing public values and attitudes do cause changes in public policies toward business.

The third force affecting regulatory change is the growth of knowledge regarding the consequences of production and consumption activities. There have been many cases of externalities, for example, that simply were not known, sometimes for decades. The long-term health effects of workplace environments and consumer products have become much better understood with recent advances in medical knowledge. We did not regulate in the past because we literally did not know of, or understand the sources of, harms to public health and safety. As our knowledge improves, we can change the mix of markets and regulations to better achieve efficiency and equity objectives Many changes in occupational safety, product safety, and related regulations exemplify the application of new knowledge in the policy-making process.

Increasing knowledge of political, social, and economic institutions, and their consequences represents a fourth major factor affecting regulatory change. As we learn more about regulation and markets and the costs and benefits of using these institutions as methods of economic organization, we use that knowledge to increase, decrease, or modify regulation to improve social performance. Many of the important regulatory changes of the past few years embody innovative techniques or institutional forms. As with all forms of innovation, the development of better ways of regulating can reduce the costs, and increase the effectiveness of regulation.

Finally, regulatory change is driven by shifts in the general conditions of the economy. While market failures can be costly in human terms, regulation can be costly in economic terms. As a society, we are continually confronted with the choice of whether to regulate, but, more fundamentally, how much can we afford to regulate. As the United States has declined from its former position of a dominant world economic power, we have had to confront the ultimate economic choice: of deciding how much public provision of goods, and how much public protection from bads, we are willing to pay for. That is a central source of the tension and the vitality of a democratic society.

NOTES

1. For this view of the legal framework of markets we owe intellectual debts to Commons (1959) and Samuels (1966). For full bibliographic references, see the bibliography of the preceding article in this book.
2. Schelling (1971) presents an insightful analysis of the use of laws or other instruments of authority in cases involving congestion or free riders.
3. For an excellent set of essays on product quality regulation, see Caves and Roberts (1975).
4. Hemenway (1975) is a thorough analysis of voluntary product standards, with several case studies.
5. Hawley (1981) presents a very interesting discussion of associationalism: the use of public authority to promote social control by private associations.

6. Schmalansee (1979) offers a comprehensive review of the rationale for, and implementation of natural monopoly regulation, and an excellent bibliography of recent theoretical and empirical research in that field.
7. For an excellent synthesis and survey of the public choice literature, see Mueller (1979).
8. Weidenbaum (1981) has estimated compliance costs to be a large multiple of government expenditures on regulation.
9. For a discussion of the role of information and knowledge in regulation, see Hays, Samuel P., "Political Choice in Regulatory Administration," in McCraw (1981).

MONEY AND VALUE

On the ethics and economics of finance

Amartya Sen

I feel deeply honored and privileged to have the opportunity of giving the first Baffi Lecture at the Bank of Italy. Paolo Baffi was not only a distinguished banker and financial expert, he was also a remarkable economist and a visionary social thinker. He had outstanding technical expertise in many different fields, but combined his intellectual eminence with a profound sense of values. As Governor Ciampi put it at the general meeting of the Bank of Italy last May, Paolo Baffi represented "an extraordinary combination of penetrating logic, erudition, and moral strength . . . [he was] not only a gifted student of economics, he had a deep-seated commitment to act for the common good."[1] In remembering Baffi today, we must keep in mind both his intellectual contributions and his general evaluative concerns.

1. DUTIES AND CONSEQUENCES

Ethical reasoning about what should or should not be done often involves various notions of *duty*. This applies to the ethics of financial activities as well. Conventional ideas of duty are often based on dissociating the duties that we must perform (so-called "deontological obligations") from their consequences. There have, in fact, been various proposals in formal ethics as well as in common sense morality that suggest that duties could be seen in consequence-independent terms. I have tried to argue elsewhere that such dissociation would be a mistake and that it is hard to reconcile such disconnection with the demands of the discipline of ethical reasoning.[2] In the present context, that is, in analyzing the ethics and economics of finance, the connections can be particularly crucial. The interrelation between *duties* and *consequences* is, in fact, deeply relevant to financial ethics, and it is important to examine how the connections operate.

Finance is a subject on which ethical precepts have been critically examined over thousands of years. I shall examine some aspects of traditional analyses of financial ethics and economics, varying from Kautilya and Aristotle in the fourth century B.C. to Adam Smith in the eighteenth century. It will be argued that the principles and concerns that emerge from these analyses remain deeply relevant to current issues of financial organization and help us to confront contemporary problems. I shall illustrate this with some interrelated problems of financial and business ethics dealing with the duties of the financial agents, such as managers and other administrators of financial institutions and business firms.

One issue I will examine relates to the *objectives* to be pursued by the firm—in particular the role of *profit maximization*. The priority of profits could be advocated on two *very different* grounds: (1) that this is the way to some social optimum; (2) that the fiduciary responsibility to the shareholders implies a duty to maximize profits on their behalf. The connection between the two arguments is also of considerable interest.

A second issue concerns the *instrumental constraints* that should limit the firm in the pursuit of its chosen objectives (such as profit maximization). Particular business or financial actions may be ruled out as inadmissible even though they might have enhanced the promotion of those objectives. For example, does the pursuit of the objective of profit maximization admit the instrument of influencing public policy in its direction? To take a different type of issue, should there be some constraints on handling ill-gotten fortunes, or on "laundering" money, even when the financial institution itself is not involved in anything directly illegal?

The third issue concern the *behavioral constraints* that may fittingly restrict the pursuit of private profits by individual financial agents. The quest for personal gains by the agents themselves may conflict with the interests of the shareholders, or with those of the community at large. How might we assess the *legitimacy* of different types of personal pursuits within business firms? The big question of "insider trading" is an interesting and important one to look into in this context.

These issues may be readily recognized as problems that have attracted attention in recent years. Some have led to animated debates, and it may be helpful to examine some of those debates.

2. A PUZZLING CONTRAST?

I turn now to the traditional approaches to the ethics of finance and begin by posing what seems to me to be an interesting contrast—a dissonance between the low image of the practice of finance and the high social contribution it undoubtedly makes. In Polonius's advice to his son, "Neither a borrower nor a lender be," there is perhaps more pragmatic caution than moral rejection, but the profession of lending money has been chastised in no uncertain terms over thousands of years. Jesus drove the moneylenders out of the temple; the injunctions of the prophets and the Jewish rules of conduct denounced the charging of interest; Islam proceeded to forbid usury.

Similarly, secular thinkers did not generally view living on interest with great favor. Solon canceled most debts and forbade many types of lending altogether in his laws, which were emulated by Julius Caesar five centuries later. Aristotle remarked that interest was unnatural and unjustified breeding of money from money, and his criticisms have influenced scholars and ethicists of many centuries. Cicero mentions that when Cato [the Elder] was asked what he thought of usury, Cato responded by asking the inquirer what he thought of murder.

The social acceptability of those who had become rich by lending money remained a deeply problematic issue until recent times. In Britain, in particular, banking activities were frequently shunned by the English upper classes, leaving such transactions to foreigners and Jews, and to this day the location of the Bank on England on Lombard Street bears testimony to the crucial role of foreigners in English finance until recent times.[3] Shakespeare's portrayal of Shylock brings out some features of prevailing social attitudes regarding financiers in Elizabethan England.

I can go on with other examples, but perhaps the point is clear enough. Finance has been traditionally subjected to much moral criticism. And yet it is also widely acknowledged that finance plays an important part in the prosperity and well-being of nations. Much of today's affluence would have been impossible if the world had followed Polonius's advice. In matters of culture and science, too, the creative role of finance is powerful. Historically, not merely the Industrial Revolution but even the

Renaissance would have been deeply problematic—perhaps impossible—without the helping hand of finance.[4]

So the first question is simply this: How is it possible that an activity that is so useful has been viewed as being morally so dubious?

3 DEONTOLOGY, CONSEQUENTIALISM AND USURY

In modern ethics, the distinction between "deontological" and "consequentialist" approaches is frequently made. Deontological approaches give the concept of duty a primary and dominant position. In contrast, consequentialist approaches derive duty and right actions on the basis of their respective consequences. They start off by asking what our goals are, what makes the outcomes good, and so on, and then go on to derive our duties from the goal-based evaluation of consequences.[5]

Deontology can take different forms—some less sensitive to consequences than others. Broad deontological approaches advanced by such philosophers as Immanuel Kant (1788) do not de-link the idea of duty from the consequences of the actions related to that duty and explore consequential features quite extensively. On the other hand, the gap could be very substantial when consequence sensitivity is denied, as is the case in more "purist" deontological structures. For example in *Bhagavadgita*, Krishna takes an explicitly anti-consequentialist view of one's duty in advising the sensitive hero Arjuna on his duty to fight for the right cause, despite Arjuna's argument that it cannot be right to fight even a just war that would cause so much suffering of both friends and foes. As summarized by T.S. Eliot, with evident sympathy, Krishna's position takes the form of the admonishment: "And do not think of the fruit of action. / Fare forward." Eliot concludes: "Not fare well,/ But fare forward, voyagers."[6]

The activities of a usurer in charging high interest might appear, in some perspective, as a violation of the obligation to treat other human beings in a humane way. No humane approach—consequentialist or deontological—can escape taking some note of this aspect of the problem, along with other consequences. But in some "purist" deontological frameworks, this recognition, in itself, might be taken to be an adequate basis for making usury morally or legally inadmissible. This could be so even if it turns out to be the case that things would be *even worse* for the would-be borrowers in the absence of those lendings.[7]

Thus, in a "purist" (that is, consequence-insensitive) deontological framework, there need be no conflict between condemning the lending of money at an interest and at the same time agreeing that the practice of lending can be conducive of many good results (for example, facilitating trade, employment, and income). The apparent dissonance can easily arise from seeing right conduct in a consequence-independent way.

Traditional scrutinies of financial ethics, however, did not always take the form of "purist" deontology. Indeed, the more weighty condemnations of finance and usury have tended to come from those who have taken careful note of their unfortunate consequences in the examined circumstances.[8] As was mentioned earlier, consequence sensitivity is consistent with broad deontological approaches as well as fully consequentialist analysis.

I turn now to four particular critical approaches to usury and finance, those of Kautilya, Aristotle, interpreters of Biblical Deuteronomy, and finally, Adam Smith.

4. KAUTILYA'S *ARTHASASTRA*

Kautilya, who lived in India in late fourth century B.C. (and was, thus, a contemporary of Aristotle), wrote a famous treatise on statecraft and on economic and political policy called *Arthasastra* (translated from Sanskrit, it would mean something like "instructions on material prosperity," or simply "political economy"). Kautilya had no intrinsic criticism to make of the charging of interest for loans, and he did not suggest that anyone had any duty to make interest-free loans to anyone else. He started from the proposition that "the welfare of the kingdom depends" on "the nature of the transactions between creditors and debtors," and he saw the need for "scrutiny" of financial activities in that perspective (Kautilya, *Arthasastra* II. 11.174, p. 200; Shamasastry's (1967) translation).

Kautilya's approach to finance, like his approach to many other activities, was centered on the consequences of actions and rules. The determination of right activities and duties depends on their consequences. For example, the king, who is charged *inter alia* with adjudicating disputes in finance, is asked to accept the priority of the goal of "the happiness of his subjects," and to "be active and discharge his duties." "In the absence of activity, present and future acquisitions will perish; by activity he can achieve both his desired ends and abundance of wealth."[9]

Kautilya wanted the state to scrutinize financial transactions thoroughly, to specify maximal rates of interest, and to punish money-lenders if they were to charge rates higher than the stipulated maximum. Maximum rates were to be varied according to various criteria related to the use of the loans and their respective burdens. For example, the rates suggested by Kautilya were especially low for normal household use, quite a bit higher for commercial loans, and very much higher for such risky activities as lending to sea-traders. Note had also to be taken of changes of prices and commodities over time, in some approximate manner.[10]

Aside from illustrating the fact that not all ancient approaches to finance were hostile to the taking of interest, Kautilya's *Arthasastra* also indicates that it is not necessary to regard interest-charging to be intrinsically evil (or finance to be a generally inferior form of activity) in order to arrive at the recommendation that it be extensively regulated through laws geared to normative objectives. The issue of consequential badness has to be distinguished from intrinsic wickedness. It is a general position that, as we shall presently see, is powerfully developed and used by Adam Smith, and this elementary distinction remains relevant today.

5. ARISTOTLE'S POLITICS AND ETHICS

I turn now to Aristotle's writings. As was mentioned earlier, Aristotle's condemnation of usury had an extraordinary influence on European thought over a couple of thousand years. It was particularly powerful in affecting the medieval scholastic traditions, including the works of St. Albert the Great, St. Thomas Aquinas, Johannes Andreae, John Buridan, Nicholas of Oresme, and a great many others, as well as the Franciscan School, with such critical commentators as Alexander Lombard, William of Ockham, Giovanni Olivi, and others.[11]

It is important to see the many-sided nature of Aristotle's treatment of finance and usury. He discussed a number of related issues together, including the following: the distinction between making profits from production of output (at constant prices) and making profits by arbitrage (with constant quantities); the lower level of art involved in making financial gains in comparison with the science of commodity production; the evil effects—in generating monopoly and inequality—of the relentless search for profits; the difficulty in giving any really productive role to money in an economy that can be understood in terms of real production, distribution and exchange (*Politics* I. 9-11).

I believe the main focus of Aristotle's attack on usury has been thoroughly misunderstood in the centuries of commentaries that have followed. From the chapters relating to usury in Book I of Aristotle's *Politics*, the following passage has been singled out again and again, and taken to represent his reasons for rejecting the legitimacy of interest and the activity of finance in general:

> [Money] came into being for the sake of exchange, but interest (*tokos*) actually creates more of it. And it is from this that it gets its name: offsprings are similar to those who give birth to them, and interest is money born of money. So of the sorts of business this is the most contrary to nature.[12]

The Greek word *tokos* does mean both usury and offspring, and the whole passage has the air of looking like a play on words. But the more serious claim that is being made in this and the proximate passages—a claim that Karl Marx pursues and develops in the first volume of *Capital*[13]—is that it is unnatural to get a reward for *lending* money, for lending is not in itself a creative activity, even though creative things can be done with resources that can be bought *with* money. It is not this probing distinction, however, but the simpler theme that "usury is unnatural breeding of money from money," that has been repeated again and again in allegedly Aristotelian analyses of usury.[14]

It was in that simple form, too, that the Aristotelian critique was attacked by various authors defending finance, varying from Gerardo of Siena[15] in the fourteenth century (himself an Augustinian but influenced by the Franciscan School) to Jeremy Bentham (1790) in the eighteenth, who provided a classic consequentialist rationalization of financial activities in his forcefully argued pamphlet, *Defence of Usury*. Bentham ridiculed Aristotle for (allegedly) attaching great significance to the barrenness of money, suggesting that Aristotle had looked for genitalia in coins and found none: he "had never been able to discover, in any one piece of money, any organs for generating any other such piece. . . . Emboldened by so strong a body of negative proof, he ventured at last to usher into the world the results of his observations, in the form of a universal proposition, *that all money is in its nature barren.*"[16]

Aristotle's assertion on the unproductive nature of lending money has nothing much to do with the barrenness of coins. In the discussion from which the much-quoted brief passage is selected. Aristotle contrasts the profits made by exchange through the use of *price variations* over time or space (and in particular by lending and the repossessing of money) with increases in the *quantity of outputs* brought about by household management and commodity creation, such as

weaving (*Politics* I. 10. 1258b). Aristotle's rejection of the legitimacy of income earned by the use of price variations may or may not be accepted, and it could also be argued that lending and trading are, in fact, services that must be considered in the accounting, but there is no difficulty in understanding the distinction that is being presented by Aristotle and to see that the fecundity of coins is *not* the issue.

Nor is there much difficulty in appreciating Aristotle's concern that in a model of production, distribution, and exchange of commodities, it is not easy to accommodate some essential role of money, which (as Aristotle put it) "seems to be something nonsensical and [to exist] altogether [by] law."[17] While this is not the occasion to pursue that foundational issue of economic modelling, making room for money in a "real" model is one of continuing challenge in modern economic theory.[18]

The legitimacy of earnings from financial activities can be defended by pointing to its consequential merits. If Aristotle is to be criticized, that is a natural direction to go, arguing that Aristotle's accounting of the consequences of financial activities is very limited. In the chapter that immediately follows the often-quoted passage on interest being "money born of money," Aristotle does go into the practical effects of financial activities, beginning the chapter with the remark that "since we have discussed adequately what relates to knowledge, what relates to practice must be treated." He proceeds to point toward some *bad* consequences of the search for financial profits, especially the creation of monopoly to further gains. "In Sicily," says Aristotle, "a man used some money deposited with him to buy all the iron from iron foundries, and when traders came from their trading places he alone had it to sell; and though he did not greatly increase the price, he made a hundred talents' profit out of an original fifty" (*Politics* I. 1259, 51).

It is clear that Aristotle is much concerned that in some types of financial or business activities, there may be little social gain—in fact considerable social loss—even though the activities yield handsome private profits.[19] He did not accept that financial activities required unusual talents: "this piece of business expertise is universal, if someone is able to establish a monopoly for himself."[20]

Aristotle's criticism of finance and trade also related to the accentuation of inequality resulting from them: "in one way it appears necessary that there be a limit to all wealth; yet if we look at what actually occurs we see that the opposite happens—all who engage in business increase their money without limit" (*Politics* I. 1258a. 30-35, p. 48). In the *Nicomachean Ethics*. Aristotle is concerned about the exploitative aspects of usury:

> Others again exceed in respect of taking by taking anything and from any source, e.g., those who ply sordid trades, pimps and all such people, and those who lend small sums and at high rates. For all these take more than they ought and from wrong sources. (*Nicomachean Ethics* IV. 2. 1121, p. 85; Ross's (1980) translation)

Here as well as elsewhere, Aristotle points to considerations underlying the need for behavioral constraints in dealing with acceptable business and financial activities.

While a modern assessment of finance can scarcely rely exclusively on Aristotelian ethical analysis, nor can it dismiss out of hand Aristotle's concerns (1) about the moral legitimacy of effortless fortunes, or (2) about the consequential harms of (2.1) monopolistic gain-seeking, or (2.2) the accentuation of inequality, or (2.3) the exploitation of the vulnerability of the needy.

6. DEUTERONOMIC ANALYSIS

The basic prohibition on usury in the Jewish faith goes back to Deuteronomy, the fifth and the last book of the Pentateuch in the Old Testament, and is by tradition ascribed to Moses. The injunctions take the form of demanding: "Thou shalt not lend upon usury (*neshek*) to thy brother (*l'ahika*)" (23: 19), but: "Unto a stranger (*nokri*) thou mayest lend upon usury" (23: 20).[21] Since any lending at interest is identified with usury in standard Jewish interpretation,[22] the prohibition of usury among Jews is an exacting one. It is made more exacting by the requirement of support for poorer members of the community, making it an obligation to help others in need by lending free of interest (*The Code of Maimonides* I. 1, p. 78).

The conception of duty involved in these injunctions is clearly tribal in origin, and it is not hard to see that the codes are so formulated as to benefit other members of the tribe. The interpretation of the rules (for example, in *The Code of Maimonides*) has tended to use the underlying consequential reasoning to draw the dividing line between charging interest, on the one hand, and renting property, sharing profits, using time-related pricing, and so on, on the other.

For example, while it is permissible to invest in a joint venture sharing both the profit and the loss, "a man is forbidden to give his money to another for the purpose of engaging in a joint venture on condition that he share in the profit but not in the loss" (*The Code of Maimonides* XIII. V. 8, p. 95). This is seen as "quasi usury," because it has the effect of lending without taking on the full risk of equity investment. The dividing line in the case of other disputed territories is similarly drawn on the basis of checking whether the consequence would be similar to lending at an interest (for example, the prohibition of sales at parametric prices that go up at specified times in the future). Thus, an element of consequential evaluation is incorporated in the nature of the duties specified.

An amusing example of a thoroughly consequential reasoning in Maimonides deals with the distinction between *lending to* and *borrowing from* heathens. Maimonides notes that the sages discouraged *lending* to heathens precisely because an Israelite lender could pick up the bad customs of the heathens by consorting with them frequently. "It is therefore permissible," Maimonides assures us, "to *borrow* at interest from a heathen, since the Israelite borrower is more likely to *avoid* the lender than to associate with him" (*The Code of Maimonides* XIII. V. 2, p. 93; italics added).

The ethical status of the distinction between Jews and non-Jews raises interesting questions. The dual standards involved have been a matter of considerable discussion in Christian as well as Jewish literature. In Christian interpretation of the distinction, the tendency has been to see it as having some positive role at the time of its origin, but as St. Thomas Aquinas put it to the inquiring Duchess of Brabant, the permission to take usury from strangers has "long elapsed."[23] Indeed, one way of universalizing the prohibition of usurious lending to other Jews would be simply to prohibit usurious lending to anyone whosoever—the direction in which Islam went and so did many Christian theologians.

It is, however, possible to universalize the injunction in a different way, that is to say, by prohibiting interest-taking between different members of the same group for *every* group. There are many rules of conduct that require a sense of solidarity with a group with which one identifies (for instance, accepting obligations toward other family members), and it may be a mistake to seek universalization directly in the form of having the same obligations toward everyone everywhere. Such an ethical analysis builds group-solidarity into a universalist framework, which can take a broadly consequentialist form, treating group loyalty as an instrument.[24]

Some rabbinical interpretations of the apparently dual standards have tended to go in that direction. For example, in the *Torah Temimah* it has been argued:

> Our refraining from taking interest from one another is similar to the regulations of many trade and other associations in which the members provide each other with special

benefits. Such benefits are not available to outsiders. Yet there is nothing to prevent others from establishing similar associations and providing the same help.[25]

When we take up contemporary issues of financial ethics, the question of consequential analysis of group solidarity would have to be considered.

7. ADAM SMITH, THE INTERVENTIONIST

Adam Smith is often thought of as the classic advocate of pure reliance on the market. He did certainly do a lot to bring out the logic of the market mechanism, but he also analyzed some of its more important limitations.[26] As far the charging of interest is concerned, while Smith was opposed to banning it,[27] he was supportive of legal restrictions imposed by the state on the maximum rates that could be charged:

> In countries where interest is permitted, the law, in order to prevent the extortion of usury, generally fixes the highest rate which can be taken without incurring a penalty. . . .

> The legal rate, it is to be observed, though it ought to be somewhat above, ought not to be much above the lowest market rate. If the legal rate of interest in Great Britain, for example, was fixed so high as eight or ten per cent, the greater part of the money which was to be lent, would be lent to prodigals and projectors, who alone would be willing to give this high interest. Sober people, who will give for the use of money no more than a part of what they are likely to make by the use of it, would not venture into the competition. A great part of the capital of the country would thus be kept out of the hands which were most likely to make a profitable and advantageous use of it, and thrown into those which were most likely to waste and destroy it.[28]

Underlying Smith's interventionist logic is the argument that market signals can be misleading and the consequences of the free market may be much waste of capital, resulting from private pursuit of projects promising quick profits.

Taking Adam Smith to task in a long letter he wrote to Smith in March 1787, Jeremy Bentham argued for leaving the market alone (Bentham, 1790, letter XIII, "To Dr. Smith"). It is an odd episode in the history of economic thought, with the utilitarian interventionist and public reformer lecturing on the virtues of market allocation to the pioneering guru of market economics.[29] Smith and Bentham both shared a primarily consequentialist approach to the assessment of business and finance, but Bentham disputed Smith's claim that at high rates of interest, "prodigals and projectors" would lead to social waste, by competing out more productive users of capital. Regarding "prodigals" or extravagant spenders, Bentham thought that "it is not among them we are to look for the natural customers for money at high rates of interest" (*Ibid.*, p. 39). And he argued at length that those whom Smith saw as "projectors"—with various projects of making quick money—were also the innovators and pioneers of change and progress (*Ibid.*, pp. 40-46).

The issue of a legally imposed maximum interest rate is not of immediate relevance in contemporary debates (in this respect Bentham has clearly won over Smith), but it is important to see why Smith took such a negative view of the impact of "prodigals and projectors" on the economy. He was deeply concerned with the problem of social waste and the loss of productive capital. And he discussed in some detail how this could come about (Book II, Chap. 3). For example, Smith saw in "prodigals" a great potential for social waste, driven as they are "with the passion for present enjoyment." So it is that "every prodigal appears to be a publick enemy." In regard to "projectors," Smith's worries related again to social waste:

> The effects of misconduct are often the same as those of prodigality. Every injudicious and unsuccessful project in agriculture, mines, fisheries, trade, or manufactures, tends in the same manner to diminish the funds destined for the maintenance of productive labour. In every such project, . . . there must always be some diminution in what would otherwise have been the productive funds of the society. (Smith, 1776/1976, I. II. 3. 25-26, pp. 340-341)

In seeing the relevance of Smith's interventionism to contemporary financial issues, it is this aspect of Smith's analysis—the possibility of social loss in pursuit of quick private gains—that deserves particular attention. I shall come back to this issue presently.

8. PROFITS AND MANAGERIAL RESPONSIBILITY

"The smell of profit is clean/And sweet, whatever the source," wrote Juvenal, in one of his satirical poems about Roman life around 100 A.D. (*Satires* 14. 204; translated by Hubert Creekmore). That skeptical view of profit-seeking has not been proved entirely erroneous in any country or age, but the role of profit is seen quite differently in the modern world that dynamic capitalism has successfully created. The search for profit is now seen, with considerable justice, as the force that creates economic opportunities and leads to their utilization. As John Maynard Keynes (1930)—no uncritical admirer of capitalism—put it: "The engine which drives Enterprise is not Thrift, but Profit."

In discussing the relation between duty and consequences, in the context of historical treatments of financial ethics, we had the occasion to note the elementary point that actions that are not intrinsically attractive can nevertheless be productive of good results. That perspective is quite central to assessing the role of profit maximization in economics that make substantial use of the market mechanism. The two aspects of profit-seeking, to wit, (1) the search for selfish gain, and (2) its role in providing incentive for yielding efficiency and good results, may be distinct and distant, but a good deal of modern economics (including substantial parts of general equilibrium theory) has been concerned with showing their interconnections (taking off from Adam Smith's *The Wealth of Nations*).

The basic result that modern general equilibrium theory has presented (sometimes called "the fundamental theorem of welfare economics") is that, with certain specified assumptions (for example, the absence of externalities in the form of interdependences working outside the market), profit-maximizing competitive equilibria correspond exactly to the achievement of Pareto efficiency, in the sense that no one can be made better off without making someone else worse off.[30] Also, any Pareto efficient outcome—no matter how egalitarian—can be achieved through *some* competitive equilibrium by making the initial distribution of resources and endowments appropriate for it. But this may well require a thoroughly radical redistribution of ownerships, and, thus, the full use of this result belongs distinctly to the "revolutionary's handbook" (see Sen., 1987, chap. 2).

The less ambitious part of the result, that no matter what the initial distribution of endowments is, every profit-maximizing competitive equilibrium must be Pareto efficient is more generally available. In assessing it, however, we have to bear in mind that Pareto efficiency in itself need not be a tremendous achievement, and in particular, is consistent with much inequality and poverty. Thus, the Aristotelian concerns about inequalities being associated with a successful business economy are not fully assuaged by the more practical part of the "the fundamental theorem." Furthermore, Aristotle would not have been much satisfied by a result that explicitly restricts itself to competitive equilibria, since his criticism of profit-seeking was also concerned with profits that could be made if a person "is able to establish a monopoly for himself" (*Politics* I. 1259).

The unequivocal recommendation that business enterprises must maximize profits for the sake of generating good economic consequences is also hampered by the restrictive nature of the underlying assumptions. Here, Adam Smith's concern that market signals can be misleading becomes relevant. Given Smith's tendency to focus on the preservation and expansion of what he called "the productive funds of the society," he would have been particularly concerned with the environmental impact of many business decisions,on which the signalling of the market is clearly defective. The modern-day "prodigals and projectors" can play havoc with the air we breathe, the water we drink, and the screening of harmful rays which we take for granted.

I have tried to argue elsewhere that as far as the consequential evaluation of profit-seeking market mechanism is concerned, there is "a case for faint praise—not any less, nor much more" (Sen, 1985b, p. 19). I see no reason to revise that judgment now. But there is a different type of defense of profit maximization that has recently been much discussed, particularly in the context of practical political debates. This does not appeal to any central result in economic theory (such as the so-called "fundamental theorem"), but to the fiduciary responsibility of the managers to maximize profits because that is what is owed to the owners of capital. The point has been forcefully made, not least here in Italy, that business managers are responsible for the exclusive pursuit of interests of shareholders and as such are duty-bound to maximize profits. A departure from that objective might *look* ethical, but in this view, it would amount to an abandonment of the moral responsibilities of trust and guardianship.

This line of approach to business and financial ethics does have a clear-cut and forceful rationale, and also has the distinct advantage of not being dependent on the validity and relevance of some particular piece of economic theory. It simply turns on the immediate responsibility that the managers and other administrators are seen as having—to do what they have been trusted to do. The idea of fiduciary responsibility is undoubtedly appealing. The failure of the managers of many business and financial enterprises to look after the interests of those who trusted them (for example, the irresponsible behavior of managers of savings-and-loans establishments in the United States) has made us particularly willing to listen to this approach to business and finance.

The distinction, from the point of view of the managers' responsibility, between the shareholders and owners, on one side, and the rest of the world, on the other, has certain Deuteronomic features—some Old Testament characteristics. Responsibility is made to turn on a distinction between one special group and all others. But the question can be raised as to why responsibility should be based on that particular distinction? The fortunes of many different types of people are involved in a business enterprise, and many people—workers for example—may put their trust on the management, no less than shareholders do.[31] If a business goes bust, that is not only a tragedy for the owners of capital, but also for others—particularly the labor force.

In the context of financial enterprises, such as the savings-and-loans institutions, it cannot be easily argued that the fiduciary responsibility of the managers covers the shareholders but not the millions of trusting *depositors* who put their money into such establishments. Financial institutions operate on a particularly diverse pattern of trust and custodianship, and the domain of the "fiduciary obligation" can scarcely be confined to the earning of profits for shareholders only.

In general, even for nonfinancial institutions, it is not at all clear why shareholders's interests should be taken to be so dominant in determining the responsibility of the managers of enterprises, given the importance of the cooperation of different groups for the success of the enterprise. A different line of defense, however, could be to see the fiduciary responsibility of the managers as being restricted to the shareholders only. In discussing Deuteronomic distinctions, it was argued earlier that assuming special responsibility to a group need not be based only on intrinsic grounds, and may well be justified on the basis on consequential analysis of the combination of respective group responsibilities. It could be proposed that the dominance of the shareholders' interests in the decisions of the firm might be seen as a *part* of such a larger schema of group responsibilities. It could be that if the managers look after profits of the shareholders, the trade unions take care of the interests of workers, and so on, the overall result may be just fine. On this view, managers commit themselves implicitly to act in the interests of shareholders only ("as if" they are the shareholders themselves), and the justification for that way of interpreting an "incomplete" contract may be sought in the consequences of such a practice, in particular its efficiency advantages.

Such a proposal would merit serious examination, though I doubt that it would pass it. For one thing, the exclusion of the interests of the others involved in the enterprise affirms a divisiveness that could well be consequentially counterproductive. Indeed, it could even be argued that it is precisely the *denial* of this distinction between shareholders and others involved in the firm, and the adoption of a more integrated view of the enterprise as "a large family," that has been a major force in the cooperative efficiency that Japanese industry has tended to achieve.[32] That consequential argument for taking a less narrow view of responsibility may be seen as reinforcing—rather than contradicting—the intrinsic argument.

While the narrowly defined "fiduciary responsibility" view of managerial responsibility (that is, managers being responsible only for the fortunes of the shareholders) appears to be consequentially unsound, it does not, of course, follow that the best consequences would invariably be obtained by the managers constantly aiming their actions at the maximization of some measure of total social goodness. There may well be good consequential argument for some narrowing of focus, if only on grounds of economy of information and of the viability of the proposed incentive structure. The main point here is the limitation of the extremely narrow "fiduciary responsibility" view of managerial agency, rather than a defense of "the other extreme" of demanding the broadest "social goodness" motivation for all agents. There is a need to examine the consequential merits of different decision procedures and distinctive incentive structures in the light of their broad consequences, but that does not, of curse, entail that those broad consequences are necessarily best pursued through every agent invoking them in every decision problem.[33]

Ultimately, the case for any view of business responsibility has to be linked up with the consequences of behavior based on that view. This brings the merits of managerial maximization of profits back to "the faint praise"—accepting its positive and important role in generating economic efficiency, but acknowledging its limitations as well. The alternative of giving it total support on the ground of fiduciary responsibility based on consequence-independent deontology raises too many unanswered questions. It is not easy to accept Krishna's and Eliot's uncompromising advice: "And do not think of the fruit of action./Fare forward."

9. INSTRUMENTAL CONSTRAINTS FOR FIRMS

No matter how defective the criterion of profit maximization may be from the point of view of consequential analysis, it is, of course, unlikely that the behavior of firms would not be, at least partly, based on profit maximization. One way of bringing in some of the other considerations that should sway decisions—when the market signals mislead—is to insist on a class of constraints that must be met. For example, fulfilling some environmental criteria may help to moderate profit maximization in the appropriate direction. Some of these constraints can be imposed through public regulations, and it is possible,

in this way, to find some room for many of the considerations not capturable by the profit calculus.[34]

Influencing financial behavior through regulations is not a new procedure.[35] However, the scope of effective regulation is often substantially limited by problems of enforceability, and this is where an important part could be played by self-regulating rules and behavioral ethics. For example, one of the problems faced by present day banks and financial institutions is the treatment of illegal profits deposited by shady firms or individuals, sometimes accompanied by proposals that would amount to "laundering" those ill-gotten gains. In many instances, such operations would, in fact, be illegal, in which case the behavioral dilemma is reduced by the incentive of the big stick. Often there may be no illegality involved in such operations, however, and the possibility of getting away without any prosecution can be extremely good. The question may be asked as to how the ethics of decisions facing these financial institutions should be assessed.

It might be argued that the illegality in question is something that was committed by the other firm or business, and dealing with their money in the same way as any other deposit is not in itself inappropriate. Furthermore, if the fiduciary responsibility to pursue profits (discussed earlier) is given priority by the financial institution, then collaboration might clearly be the right course of action.

That conclusion can be resisted on two quite different grounds, corresponding respectively to considerations of "intrinsic wickedness" and "consequential badness." In the first case, participation in the use of the proceeds of illegal operations might well be considered to be wicked behavior in itself. This is where we come closest to the old-fashioned—but nonnegligible—pressure of "purist" deontology (similar to the non-consequentialist banning of usury). I don't have a great deal to say on this subject, though I see it as among the possibly relevant considerations.

Turning to the second argument, if duty is to be determined through consequential analysis, then the argument that somebody else committed the illegality in question is not in itself decisive. It becomes, then, necessary to examine the consequences of the particular acts, and also the likely results of following *rules of behavior* permitting such actions, and here financial ethics comes straight into line with standard consequential analysis. Depending on the nature of the "ill" in the ill-gotten gains, consequential analyses of the appropriate rules for treating such gains may be far from permissive.

Similar observations can be made about other problems of debatable financial behavior. One particular question concerns the possibility of using political influences that may be exercised by the private sector and that could alter public policy dealing with economic or monetary matters or sway the operative decisions of the public sector. This particular ethical problem, that of using *public* policy for the pursuit of *private* gains was one of the issues that evidently disturbed the late Paolo Baffi.[36]

The problem is not, of course, a new one, and Adam Smith discussed this issue extensively in *The Wealth of Nations*.

> To expect, indeed, that the freedom of trade should ever be entirely restored in Great Britain, is as absurd as to expect that an Oceana or Utopia should ever be established in it. Not only the prejudices of the publick, but what is much more unconquerable, the private interests of many individuals irresistibly oppose it. . . . The member of Parliament who supports every proposal for strengthening this monopoly [of manufacturers], is sure to acquire not only the reputation of understanding trade, but great popularity and influence with an order of men whose numbers and wealth render them of great importance. If he opposes them, on the contrary, and still more if he has authority enough to be able to thwart them, neither the most acknowledged probity, nor the highest rank, nor the greatest publick services can protect him from the most infamous abuse

> and detraction, from personal insults, nor sometimes from real danger, arising from the insolent outrage of furious and disappointed monopolists. (Smith 1776/1976, I. IV. 2. 43, p. 471; see also I. II.)

The use of political influence cannot be easily defended by invoking the fiduciary responsibility to maximize profits *through every available instrument* (for reasons I have already discussed). Nor can it be generally fitted into consequentially justified behavior. Indeed, the presumption of ill effects from such behavior is based on its role in creating various distortions (including some that both Aristotle and Smith had discussed), for example, by securing monopoly advantages.

In judging the consequential merits and demerits of such behavior, and of the related behavioral constraints, the common sense presumption of ill effects may well have much plausibility. One general point is particularly worth emphasizing in this context. The instrumental success of profit maximization in achieving efficiency and other good results (as outlined in general equilibrium theory, for example, in "the Fundamental Theorem") is thoroughly dependent on the fulfillment of an exacting set of conditions. For instance, a competitive market requires that transactions must take place at *given prices* that the firms cannot influence. When business tactics in promoting profits take the form of influencing prices or reducing competition, and so on, little of the standard theory of market-based efficiency remains available to be invoked in support of no-nonsense profit maximization.

10. INSIDER INFORMATION AND TRADING

I turn, finally, to a brief examination of the vexed issue of the acceptability of realizing personal gain through "insider trading." Members of the managerial or administrative team of a firm are often in a much better position to make profits from market transactions related to the firm because of the "insider information" they have. Large fortunes have frequently been amassed on the basis of trading according to such information, for instance, buying up shares of a firm just before they go up in price (because of, say, an impending take-over bid—known to insiders but not to others).

Insider trading has drawn moral disapproval and also, in some countries, is subject to explicit legal restrictions, for example, in the United Kingdom and in the United States.[37] Similar regulations are now being introduced in Italy. On the other hand, the situation is much less restrictive in, say, Japan or Switzerland. Making personal gains from "insider information"—by abusing the confidence of others—is by no means attractive behavior, and in an obvious sense, there is some "wickedness" involved in this. But as we have discussed earlier in this paper, the consequential badness of a practice has to be distinguished from its intrinsic unattractiveness. How do we go about assessing the consequential harm done by insider trading?

It is certainly true that the insider who benefits from the privileged information he or she happens to have has, in some sense, an unfair advantage over others who also buy and sell stocks. But, it has been argued (in particular by John Kay, 1988) that insider trading does not really harm people other than "market professionals." If, for example, a stock is about to go up in price from 100 to 180, and the insider buys up some for, say, 120, just before this happens, he is, obviously, not harming the *continuing* holders of the stocks in any direct way. Nor is he harming those who *independently decide* to sell just as the insider is making his purchase. If anything, they can get a higher price (120) from the insider than they would have got otherwise (100).

That leaves the person who was not planning to sell but is *persuaded* to do so by the offer of the insider. Such a person unloads his stocks for the lesser price of 120, when he could have got 180 immediately

after. Since such a person is likely to be a "market professional" (buying and selling stocks), Kay's contention is that the entire exercise of preventing insider trading is aimed at safeguarding the interests of the market professionals and at giving them "fair odds" against insiders armed with their privileged information. These rather narrow concerns are pursued at the cost of increasing the distance between those who finance industry and those who manage it, and this can be a seriously bad consequence of *preventing* insider trading, argues Kay. Hence his opposition to the banning of insider trading.

The consequential focus of Kay's *defense* of insider trading fits in well with what has already been discussed in the earlier parts of this paper. In the absence of something like a Deuteronomic distinction focussing on the interests of one specific group, that is, the market professionals, this would seem like an oddly arbitrary objective, based on a rather narrow conception of group responsibility. It is reinforced only by a righteous dislike of "greedy" insiders, with an implicit appeal for the penalty of "the morally wicked."

However, the question that does arise is whether all the relevant consequences have, in fact, been counted. King and Roell (1988) have pointed out that insider trading has other costs. First, the presence of asymmetric information tends to increase the "bid-ask spreads" as market makers fear that they might be dealing with insiders. This cost acts like a tax on trading as such. Second, because of the possibility of gains based on insider information, a good deal of effort and resources are expended on making such quick money. Since there is no obvious *social* benefit from these operations, there is a net social loss, corresponding to the costs incurred.

We can, in fact, supplement King and Roell's analysis by considering the possibility that an insider might even influence the timing and articulation of the announcements made by the firm to enhance the opportunity of insiders to make quick gains. This, too, would involve social costs and thus a social loss. The consequential picture can also take into account the discouraging effect that insider trading may have on the confidence in the stock market, and this could quite possibly be an important ill-effect to be included in the consequential accounting, especially in a country in which the stock market is in need of further extension.

Adam Smith's concern about considerable social loss being generated by the private pursuit of quick profits can be particularly relevant here. There are also some similarities between inside traders and Aristotle's "seekers of monopoly gains." That Aristotelian issue is particularly important to bear in mind since the banning "insider trading" has the odd effect of keeping out precisely those who have *more* information, rather than less, and it might well be puzzling, at least at first sight, as to how the cause of efficiency could possibly be well served by keeping out precisely the well informed in favor of those with less information. One of the main sources of problems lies in the monopoly of information that some of the operators (the "inside" ones) have vis-á-vis the others, and the gains that are made through maintaining that monopoly advantage. Since the participation of "the others" (including the general public) is important for the success of business finance, the problem of informational asymmetry cannot be dealt with simply by "weeding out" the others, through some process of natural selection. Furthermore, the possibility that the "insiders" can deliberately increase the gap between their own information and what outsiders know through the insider's *own* actions, by manipulating the company's articulations and other moves, makes the prospects of distortion that much more serious.

These are, ultimately, the appropriate grounds for discouraging and regulating insider trading. Insider trading does cause moral indignation, but that, I have tried to argue is not in itself a good basis for banning or regulating that practice. While in some cases, moral indignation might well reflect an underlying reasoned criticism, that is not necessarily the case. Ultimately, the assessment of insider trading and other disputable practices must turn on careful consequential analysis of direct and indirect effects. There *is* a consequential case against insider trading, but the grounds for that must be clearly distinguished from our simple propensity to dislike profits based on privileged information, or to disapprove of personal gain from social trust.

11. A CONCLUDING REMARK

I have argued here that the central issue in financial ethics is the relationship between duties and consequences. The temptation to see finance in terms of its immediate appeal—or its proximate *un*attractiveness—is strong and has influenced the assessment of financial ethics in the past, as it does at the present time. But the serious treatments of finance in the past have rightly resisted that simple route. This applies not only to such authors as Kautilya and Smith, but also to Aristotle's famous critique of usury (even though persistent misunderstandings of the nature of Aristotle's arguments have tended to hide that important fact). The issues that consequential analyses of finance in the past have tended to isolate remain relevant today.

I have examined some issues of modern financial ethics to illustrate the nature of the consequential concerns and the pitfalls of "purist" deontology. For example, the pursuit of profit maximization as an overriding commitment (irrespective of its social consequences) is often defended, in contemporary arguments, on the simple ground of the "fiduciary responsibility" to the shareholders. This approach remains deeply defective both because of the consequential harm that such behavior may cause to the public at large (for example, through environmental waste or monopolistic distortions), and also because of the need to consider duties to the others involved in the business. For a partial justification of profit maximization, we have to see the role that profits can play as incentives in generating economic efficiency, and that acknowledgment has to be supplemented by a firm recognition of the social losses and inequities to which it could, in many circumstances, also contribute.

Similarly, the choice of instruments that business firms could use in pursuit of their objectives (including financial profits) is another subject in which "purist" deontology can be misleading. This has bearing on the relation between public policy and private interests, and also on developing rules and norms of behavior to constrain the handling (for example, "laundering") of financial gains that may have been "ill-gotten" elsewhere.

Another example concerns the behavioral constraints that may apply to managers and administrators who have "inside" information. It is tempting to rule out so-called "insider trading" simply on grounds of apparent "wickedness" or alleged "unfairness," but such criticisms remain foundationally weak. The more serious objections relate to the extensive social harm that may result from insider trading through increases in costs and distortions of incentives.

Careful assessment of consequences is central to financial ethics and cannot be replaced by appeals to consequence-independent "duties." I have argued, giving particular illustrations, that rules and regulations as well as codes of conduct may be seriously misdirected by the attempt to base public decisions or private behavior on the simple deontology of immediate concerns and obligations. In financial matters, no less than in other economic fields, the significant goes well beyond the proximate.

NOTES

The text of the first Baffi Lecture, given at the Bank of Italy on April 26, 1991. My greatest debt is to Tommaso Padoa-Schioppa for his helpful advice at every stage of the preparation of this lecture. For many useful suggestions, I am also most grateful to Fabrizio Barca, Sissela Bok, Moshe Halbertal, John Kay, Mervyn King, Franco Modigliani, Emma Rothschild, Ignazio Visco, and Stefano Zamagni. I have also profited from the comments of Ignazio Angeloni, Chitrita Banerji, Giorgio Basevi, Robert Dorfman, Gianni Fodella, Eugenio Gaiotti, Charles Goodhart, Frank Hahn, Albert Hirschman, Eric Hobsbawm, Alexandre Lamfalussy, David Landes, Siro Lombardini, Mario Monti, and Luigi Spaventa.

1. The Governor's Concluding Remarks at the Ordinary General Meeting of Shareholders of the Bank of Italy on 31 May 1990. In Baffi's conception of duty, there was a firm commitment to economic and social advance, combined with much sympathy for the predicament of those unfavorably placed. For example, in writing about his visit to the London School of Economics in 1931, he not only talks about the lectures he heard, but also about "the sight of Welsh miners tramping in single file along the edge of the sidewalk singing mournful dirges and begging pennies, and of the laid-up ships and stilled cranes in the port" (Baffi, 1985, p. 2).

2. See Sen (1982b, 1985a). See also Stefano Zamagni's "Introduzione" to the Italian translation of Sen (1982a).

3. Kindleberger (1984) notes that the involvement of people outside the mainstream is a more general phenomenon: "In many societies money-lenders belong to a different religion, and hence are not bound by the ethical standards of the community" (p. 41). For an interesting study of the clash of the cultures involved—in this case—in European banking in Egypt, see Landes (1958).

4. It has also been argued that even the emergence of writing and the development of mathematics were closely linked with financial activities in the early history of the world. On this see Bernal (1954, chap. 3).

5. The nature and relevance of this and related distinctions have been discussed in Smart and Williams (1973), Nagel (1979), and Sen (1987), among others.

6. T.S. Eliot's "The Dry Savages" in *Four Quartets* (1944, p. 31).

7. There can indeed be a general conflict between (1) the intrinsically *inappropriate* nature of some acts, and (2) the *improvement* that those acts may in fact bring about in the state of affairs that comes to pass. In a more

general context (not specifically related to finance), such conflicts have, in fact, been much discussed in modern deontological critiques of consequentialism in general. See, for example, Bernard Williams (1973), Robert Nozick (1974), Thomas Nagel (1980), and Derek Parfit (1984). None of them has, however, argued in favor of ignoring consequences altogether in assessing the rightness of acts, that is, they have not taken the "purist" deontological position (advocated by, say, Krishna and Eliot).

8. This applies even to many of the medieval scholastic—including Franciscan—treatments of usury. For example, St. Thomas Aquinas, William of Ockham, Nicholas of Oresme, and others used extensive analyses of the practical consequences of usury (useful introductions to their reasonings can be found in Nelson, 1949, and Noonan, 1957). The Islamic assessment of usury was explicitly based on the bad effects of the practice, and that foundational concern has been revived in the modern interpretations of Islam, arguing in particular that the ban is not meant to apply to the charging of interest as such, but only to the taking of usurious interest—a subject of considerable importance to the legal framework of contemporary Islamic countries (on this, see Naqvi and Qadir, 1986, and Ali Khan, 1990).

9. Kautilya, *Arthasastra* I. 19. 39, p. 39. I have changed the translation from "acquisitions present and to come" to "present and future acquisitions."

10. For example, if the borrowing and lending are both in the form of food grains, rather than cash, then "interest in grains in seasons of good harvest shall not exceed more than half when valued in money" (Kautilya, *Arthasastra* II. 11. 174, p. 200).

11. See Nelson (1949), Noonan (1957), Barker (1959), and Langholm (1984).

12. Aristotle, *Politics* I. 1258b, p. 49-50; Lord's (1984) translation. See also the freer translation presented by Langholm (1984), p. 56.

13. Marx (1887, chap. V, 141-45). On the issues of "value" involved in this assessment, see Dobb (1937).

14. See Noonan (1957, p. 47). The quoted sentence is from a discussion by St. Albert in the thirteenth century, but that remark is repeated again and again by a great many commentators.

15. On this see Langholm (1984, p. 61).

16. Bentham (1790, p. 100). Bentham is eloquent on this subject: "A consideration that did not happen to present itself to that great philosopher, but which, had it happened to present itself, might not have been altogether unworthy of his notice, is, that though a *daric* would not beget another daric, any more than a ram, or a ewe, yet for a daric which a man borrowed, he might get a ram and a couple of ewes, and that the ewes, were the ram left with them a certain time, would probably not be barren" (p. 101). He goes on to say more on what he takes to be a stupid mistake of Aristotle.

17. *Politics* I. 1257b. 10, p. 47.

18. On this see Hahn (1982, 1985).

19. Nor did he think that making money from trade and finance was a very good life to lead, even for the person who gets rich thus.

20. *Politics* I. 1259a 20. Aristotle defends his position by citing the case of Thales of Miletus, who—despite being a philosopher—made money with ease, by establishing a monopoly on olive presses, correctly anticipating a bumper harvest of olives (*Politics* I. 1259a 5-8, p. 51).

21. See Nelson (1949), pages xv-xvi, who also goes into interpretational issues.

22. On this, see *The Code of Maimonides: The Book of Civil Laws, Laws Concerning Creditor and Debtor VI*: 1, p. 88 in Rabinowitz's (1949) translation.

23. See Nelson (1949), p. 14. Aquinas argued that the intention of the injunction was really to indicate that "to take usury from any man is simply evil, because we ought to treat every man as our neighbor and brother, especially in the state of the Gospel, whereto all are called." He went on, oddly enough, to contend that the special exemption to take usury from foreigners was granted to the Jews "to avoid a greater evil, lest, to wit, through avarice, to which they were prone, according to Is. lvi:11, they should take usury from Jews, who were worshipers of God" (quoted in Nelson, 1949, p. 14).

24. For some technical aspects of the consistency of consequentialism with agent-relative moralities, see Sen (1982b, 1983, 1987). On different roles of loyalty, see Akerlof (1983, 1984).

25. Quoted in Tamari (1987, p: 182). *Torah Temimah* is an influential twentieth-century commentary by Rabbi B. Epstein.

26. On this see Sen (1987), Werhane (1991), and Rothschild (1992).

27. "In some countries the interest of money has been prohibited by law. But as something can every where be made by the use of money, something ought every where to be paid for the use of it. This regulation, instead of preventing, has been found from experience to increase the evil of usury; the debtor being obliged to pay, not only for the use of money, but for the risk which the creditor runs by accepting a compensation for that use" (Smith, 1776.1976, I. II. 4. 13, p. 356).

28. Smith (1776/1976, I. II. 4. 14-15, pp. 356-57). The term "projector" is used by Smith not in the neutral sense of "one who forms a project," but in the pejorative sense, apparently common from 1616 (according to *The Shorter Oxford English Dictionary*), meaning, among other things, "a promoter of bubble companies; a speculator; a cheat." Giorgio Basevi has drawn my attention to some interesting parallels between Smith's criticism and Jonathan Swift's unflattering portrayal of "projectors" in *Gulliver's Travels*, published in 1726, half a century before *The Wealth of Nations*.

29. Smith did not take much public notice of Bentham's criticism, and in the subsequent editions of *The Wealth of Nations*, did not revise, in any way, the passage that Bentham had criticized. But he was good humored about the critique, made favorable references to it—even to the extent that Bentham felt that he had indirect evidence that Smith's "sentiments with respect to the points of difference are at present the same as mine" (on this see Campbell and Skinner, 1976, pp. 357-58, n. 19, and Spiegel, 1987, p. 770).

30. On this see Debreu (1959) and Arrow and Hahn (1971). Koopmans (1957) presents a lucid introductory account.

31. Adam Smith, in his time, took a particularly critical view of the neglect of the interests of the workers in articulating demands and grievances: "there is no order that suffers so cruelly from its [the productive society's] decline. . . . In the publick deliberations, therefore, his voice is little heard and less regarded, except upon some particular occasions, when his clamour is animated, set on,

and supported by his employers, not for his, but their own particular purposes" (Smith, 1776/1976, I. I. 11.9, p. 266).

32. On this and associated matters concerning the experience of Japan and its interpretations, see Morishima (1982), Dore (1987), Aoki (1989). On related matters, see also Akerlof (1983, 1984). The "large family" view may well have exploitative effects on some groups vis-á-vis others, but that is a further issue that need not affect the efficiency disadvantages of the divisive view.

33. See Sen (1987) for this and related issues.

34. One of the interesting recent developments in the world of business behavior is the support that some private firms seem to give to stiff anti-pollution laws. Indeed, as *The Economist* points out, when a substantial private firm decides to become "eco-friendly" ("for public relations, staff morale and other reasons"), they "are not willing to put themselves at a disadvantage by allowing their competitors to get away with environmental scruffiness" ("Prosecuting Polluters: Dishing the Dirt," *The Economist*, 9-15 February, 1991, pp. 70-71). The general case for appropriate regulations as a supplement to private profit motive seen from the enlightened perspective of private enterprise itself has been well presented by Fumagalli (1990).

35. While I have not taken up, in this paper, the problem of macro-financial management, regulations may be related also to the demands of such management. For example, the rate of interest does have a major influence on the operation of the economy, and could be an important instrumental variable in employment policy and in fostering economic growth (on this see Robinson, 1952). in practice, the level of interest rates is fairly extensively controlled by the policies of the central bank in most countries in the world, and that control is based on regulations as well as other channels of influence. In the present context, however, I am concerned with regulations relating to the acceptability of individual financial behavior, rather than with the demands of macro-management.

36. Baffi's call for a "moral regeneration" had much to do with his reading of contemporary affairs in Italy in this respect. What may be thought of as "the message of Baffi" is closely related to this concern.

37. In Britain the simpler kinds of "insider dealings" are prohibited through "the Core Rules" enunciated by the Securities and Investment Board. See SIB, *Principles and Core Rules for the Conduct of Investment Business* (London, 1991).

REFERENCES

Akerlof, G. 1983. "Loyalty Filters," *American Economic Review* 73:54-63.

———. 1984. *An Economic Theorist's Book of Tales.* Cambridge: Cambridge University Press.

Ali Khan, M. 1990. "Distributive Justice and Need Fulfillment in an Islamic Economy: A Review." Johns Hopkins University, Baltimore, MD, mimeograph.

Aoki, M. 1989. *Information, Incentive and Bargaining in the Japanese Economy.* Cambridge: Cambridge University Press.

Aristotle. *The Nicomachean Ethics.* Translated by W.D. Ross. Oxford: Oxford University Press, 1980.

Aristotle. *The Politics.* Translated by C. Lord. Chicago: Chicago University Press, 1984.

Arrow, K.J., and F.H. Hahn. 1971. *General Competitive Analysis.* San Francisco: Holden-Day. Amsterdam: North Holland, 1979.

Baffi, P. 1985. "The Bank of Italy and Foreign Economists 1944-53: A Personal Memoir." *Rivista di Storia Economica* 2:1-40.

Barker, E. 1959. *The Political Thought of Plato and Aristotle.* New York: Dover.

Bentham, J. 1789. *An Introduction to the Principles of Morals and Legislation.* London: Payne. Oxford: Blackwell, 1948.

———. 1790. *Defense of Usury.* London: Payne.

Bernal, J.D. 1954. *Science in History*, Vol 1. Harmondsworth: Penguin.

Campbell, R.H., and A.S. Skinner, eds. (1976). *Adam Smith: An Inquiry into the Nature and Causes of the Wealth of Nations.* Oxford: Clarendon Press.

Clark, R.C. 1986. *Corporate Law.* Boston: Little, Brown.

Debreu, G. 1959. *Theory of Value.* New York: Wiley.

Dobb, M.H. 1937. "The Requirements of a Theory of Value." In *Political Economy and Capitalism.* London: Routledge.

Dore, R. 1987. *Taking Japan Seriously: A Confucian Perspective on Leading Economic Issues.* Stanford: Stanford University Press.

Fumagalli, A. 1990. "State and Market: What Rules?" Presidential Address to the Young Entrepreneurs, Capri, September 21-22.

Hahn, F.H. 1982. *Money and Inflation.* Oxford: Blackwell.

———. 1985. *Money, Growth and Stability.* Cambridge: MIT Press.

Kant, I. 1788. *Kritik der Praktischen Vernunft.* Translated into English by T.K. Abbott under the title *Kant's Critic of Practical Reason.* London: Longmans, 1909.

Kautilya. *Arthasastra.* Translated by R. Shama Sastry. Mysore: Mysore Printing and Publishing House, 1967.

Kay, J. 1988. "Discussion." *Economic Policy.* April.

Keynes, J.M. 1930. *A Treatise on Money.* London: Macmillan.

Kindleberger, C.P. 1984. *A Financial History of Western Europe.* London: Allen & Unwin.

King, M., and A. Roell. 1988. "Insider Trading." *Economic Policy.* April.

Koopmans, T.C. 1957. *Three Essays on the State of Economic Science.* New York: McGraw-Hill.

Landes, D.S. 1958. *Bankers and Pashas.* Cambridge, MA: Harvard University Press.

Langholm, O. 1984. *The Aristotelian Analysis of Usury.* Bergen: Universitetsforlaget As.

Lord, C. 1984. *Aristotle: The Politics.* Chicago: Chicago University Press.

Maimonides, M. *Code of Maimonides.* Book 13: *Book of Civil Laws.* Translated by J.J. Rabinowitz, New Haven: Yale University Press.

Marx, K. 1887. *Capital*, Vol. 1. Translated by S. Moore and E. Aveling. London: Sonnenschein.

Morishima, M. 1982. *Why Has Japan "Succeeded"?: Western Technology and Japanese Ethos.* Cambridge: Cambridge University Press.

Nagel T. 1979. *Mortal Questions.* Cambridge: Cambridge University Press.

———. 1980. "The Limits of Objectivity." In *Tanner Lectures on Human Values*, Vol 1., edited by S. McMurrin. Cambridge: Cambridge University Press.

Naqvi, S.N.H., and A. Qadir. 1986. *A Model of a*

Dynamic Islamic Economy and the Institution of Interest. Islamabad: Pakistan Institute of Development Economics.

Nelson, B.N. 1949. *The Idea of Usury*. Princeton: Princeton University Press.

Noonan, J.T., Jr. 1957. *Scholastic Analysis of Usury*. Cambridge, MA: Harvard University Press.

Nozick, R. 1974. *Anarchy, State and Utopia*. New York: Basic Books.

Parfit, D. 1984. *Reasons and Persons*. Oxford: Clarendon Press.

Rabinowitz, J.J. (translator). 1949. *The Code of Maimonides: Book Thirteen. The Book of Civil Laws*. New Haven: Yale University Press.

Robinson, J. 1952. *The Rate of Interest and Other Essays*. London: Macmillan.

Ross, D. 1980. *Aristotle: The Nicomachean Ethics*. The World's Classics. Oxford: Oxford University Press.

Rothschild, E. 1992. "Adam Smith and Conservative Economics." *The Economic History Review* 45:74-96.

Sen, A.K. 1982a. *Choice, Welfare and Measurement*. Oxford: Blackwell. Italian translation with Introduction by S. Zamagni under the title *Scelta, benesse, equita*. Boglona: Il Mulino, 1986.

———. 1982b. "Rights and Agency." *Philosophy and Public Affairs*. 11:3-39; reprinted in S. Scheffler, ed., *Consequentialism and Its Critics: Oxford Readings in Philosophy*. Oxford: Oxford University Press.

———. 1983. "Evaluator Relativity and Consequential Evaluation." *Philosophy and Public Affairs* 12:113-132.

———. 1985a. "Well-being, Agency and Freedom: The Dewey Lectures 1984." *Journal of Philosophy* 82:169-221.

———. 1985b. "The Moral Standing of the Market." *Social Philosophy and Policy* 2:1-19.

———. 1987. *On Ethics and Economics*. Oxford: Blackwell.

Shama Sastry, R. (translator). 1967. *Kautilya's Arthasastra*. Mysore: Mysore Printing and Publishing House.

Smart, J.J.C., and B.A.O. Williams. 1973. *Utilitarianism: For and Against*. Cambridge: Cambridge University Press.

Spiegel, H.W. 1987. "Usury." In *The New Palgrave: A Dictionary of Economics*, Vol 4, edited by J. Eatwell, M. Milgate, and P. Newman. London: Macmillan.

Tamari, M. 1987. *"With All Your Possessions": Jewish Ethics and Economic Life*. New York: Free Press.

Werhane, P.H. 1991. *Adam Smith and His Legacy for Modern Capitalism*. New York: Oxford University Press.

Williams, B.A.O. 1973. "A Critique of Utilitarianism." In Smart and Williams (1973).

IMPERFECT MARKETS

Business ethics as an easy virtue

S. Prakash Sethi

ABSTRACT: This paper marks a radical diversion from the large body of prevailing literature in business ethics which primarily views the issue in individual-personal terms, i.e., corporate executive and employee, and suggests that making corporations more ethical would primarily come through changes in executive behavior. While this approach has strong intellectual roots in moral philosophy and religion, it fails in explaining the persistence of unethical and illegal behavior among corporations of all sizes, financial health, competitive market conditions, and, level of individual executive compensation. This paper argues for a fundamentally different approach to understanding ethical behavior, or lack thereof, among corporations and their executives. It is asserted that an overwhelmingly large rationale and/or inducement for proactive ethical business behavior is rooted in competitive aspects of particular markets, and industry structures prevailing in those markets. Furthermore, while highly competitive markets may promote efficiency, they do not guarantee ethical behavior and may indeed provide greater opportunities and incentives for unethical business behavior. Thus, by following the current prognosis, we could be wasting enormous resources in terms of teaching business ethics, and creating and imposing corporate codes of conduct. We assert that these approaches would at best make a marginal improvement in the ethical performance of corporations while at the same time exacerbate the problem by ignoring more fundamental, structural issues.

Imperfect markets, with their above-market profits, are a necessary but insufficient condition for corporations to behave ethically. It is only under conditions of imperfect markets that individual executives can play an important role in guiding their corporations toward greater ethical norms. These are undertaken for a variety of reasons, including, protecting a corporation's good name, public expectations, competitive norms, and, corporate culture and individual executive's predilections, to name a few.

The institutional context of business ethics has become an increasing concern of enquiry among management scholars, other social scientists, corporate executives and political leaders. To wit, what are the conditions, i.e., external sociopolitical and competitive structures, and intrainstitutional frameworks, that propel and instigate corporations and their executives to indulge in unethical and even illegal actions that they would otherwise condemn when undertaken by others. The point is not merely rhetorical, it raises important issues of public policy and social organization. At the micro level, it is the individual conduct acting in a business context that gets reflected in the adverse social impact of the business institution. Philosophers and ethicists have almost invariably referred to this aspect of business behavior contending that moral values find their expression only through human beings acting either individually or collectively. The macro or the structural context of business ethics is even more important. As economic activity increases in complexity and technological orientation,it is unhinged from the mooring of individual actions. Large scale economic activity,ironically, calls for collective action where each individual contributes but a tiny fraction to the whole and where individual acts are rewarded and punished not so much for their ethical content, but on the notion of one's loyalty to the institution where individual morality and institutional welfare, however defined, are perceived to be in conflict.

The paramount question for us to examine involves the circumstances, individual and contextual, that make business people and business institutions act in socially harmful ways. We must ask whether there are levels of unethical activity and immoral behavior that would persist under different types of economic conditions and individual proclivities regardless of a society's efforts to curb such behavior and which, therefore, must be accepted as the necessary cost of doing business. Market systems with their self-correcting discipline and competitive forces, however, are presumed to keep such behavior at a minimum compared to alternative mechanisms for organizing economic activity, i.e., state control of production and distribution systems. Therefore, among a constellation of imperfect worlds, a market economy with individuals exercising their free will to make choices, is said to offer the least repugnant of alternatives and the one with the greatest susceptibility toward responding to corrective mechanisms. It is this proposition which is the subject of our enquiry and to which we now turn our attention.

BUSINESS ETHICS IN A HISTORICAL CONTEXT

Concern about business ethics, or lack thereof, seems to be a historical phenomenon which appears with remarkable regularity through periods of economic prosperity and hard times. One can easily recall significant periods in American history, and for that matter in the history of most capitalistic nations, when major business scandals assaulted the nation's moral psyche and its denizens' pocketbooks. Witness the price-rigging conspiracy among such electrical giants as GE and Westinghouse in the 1950s which led to a flurry of lawsuits, swindled the nation's economy in an enormous way, and sent many senior corporate executives to jail (Cook, 1966; Fuller, 1962; Herling, 1962). The Electrical Conspiracy is not an isolated historical example of ethical drama unfolding within the walls of corporate America. Scandals like The Tea Pot Dome and robber barons of yesteryear have easily been relegated to the status of historical anachronisms by the sheer audacity, greed, and a callous disregard for society's standards of their latter-day peers. The eighties will be remembered in the United States as much for "Reaganomics" and "get-the-government-off people's backs," as for the decade of greed personified by such luminaries as Ivan Boesky, Mike Milken and Charles Keating, to name a few (Binstein and Bowden, 1993; Burrough and Helyar, 1990; Day, 1993; Lewis, 1989; Lorsch, 1989; Stewart, 1991; Vise and Coll, 1991).

We are never tired of being told that a majority of business institutions and executives are honest, ethical and law-abiding. It is only the deviant few from whom the business system and society needs to be protected. This statement, however, begs the question rather than answers it. Majorities are always honest, caring and suffused with intrinsic humanistic values. They are also largely law-abiding and operate according to society's standards of acceptable behavior whether driven by an innate sense of good conduct or fear of social reprobation. Otherwise social organizations could not survive and civilized societies would cease to exist.

LACK OF BUSINESS ETHICS— IT'S THE ADVERSITY, STUPID!

Ethical lapses and illegal behavior are not the domain of some sleazy firms operating at the fringes of otherwise respectable and responsible companies. On the contrary, they are to be found in every segment of business activity, afflicting corporations large and small, and regardless of their financial and market circumstances. While a large majority of all business operates within the socially and legally acceptable standards of corporate behavior, the deviant corporations and executives do not necessarily display structural, institutional, or even personal characteristics that are different from their more ethical counterparts. In many cases, it is the same corporation that receives public accolades for exemplary behavior in one aspect of its business while at the same time being hauled into the court of public opinion and the judicial arena for acts of moral reprobation and illegal behavior.

We have insider trading, money laundering, brokerage account churning and saving and loan scandals in the banking and finance industry. The wilful violence against our environment can be traced to major firms in chemical, forestry and other heavy industries. Food companies are not averse to selling adulterated foods and resort to bid rigging and price fixing in feeding programs for the poor. Pricing for what the market will bear—regardless of how it might affect the most vulnerable amongst us—is not confined to the pharmaceutical industry. Even companies engaged in the national defense effort are not averse to using unethical means to secure business. Bidding for inside information, cost inflation through account padding, inadequate product testing and shoddy manufacturing practices are all part of a day's work and are not confined to a deviant few, but have been found to be widely practiced behaviors (Holcomb and Sethi, 1992; Sethi, 1981). In marketing abroad, multinational corporations (MNCs) are equally indiscriminate in selling products, e.g., infant formula, cigarettes, chemicals and pesticides, prescription and over-the-counter drugs, in a manner that would be considered unethical and illegal at home, with nary a work of caution or disclosure, to a set of customers who are even less equipped to make informed choices. In their overseas operations, MNCs search for ever lower costs and, in the process, they become deliberately ignorant, or at best indifferent, to the hazardous working conditions, starvation level wages, and environmental degradation that inflict many Third World countries as these countries constantly compete with each other for the privilege of serving the economically powerful multinational behemoths (Donaldson, 1989; Guyon, 1992; Sethi and Steidlmeier, 1991; Shrivastava, 1987).

PERFECT COMPETITION AND BUSINESS ETHICS

Competition keeps businesses honest. It should, therefore, follow that firms would act more ethically, even in the economic sense of maximizing social welfare, as markets approximate the ideal conditions of perfect competition. Competitive markets strive for productivity and allocative efficiency and thereby serve the general welfare even when the business person is pursuing his/her own self-interest and is not concerned about promoting general welfare. Unfortunately, this is not the case when applied to business morality. While efficient markets may prompt firms to act ethically, "'perfect' markets are highly imperfect in their enforcement of business morality" (Baumol, 1991, p. 24). Indeed, a counter-intuitive argument could be made to suggest that perfect competition creates the conditions that are ripe for unethical behavior.

Briefly described, the conditions of ideal markets include the existence of a large number of buyers and sellers none of whom is able to influence total supply or demand; all buyers and sellers are fully informed; the objects of exchange are completely divisible into exchangeable units, and the parties who are not subject to the transaction can be excluded from the benefits of the exchange; there are no externalities, i.e., spill-over benefits or costs going to non-exchange parties; and, exchange transactions incur no costs and there are no entry barriers (Harris and Carman, 1991).

The absolute discipline of ideal markets leaves little room for the individual firm to undertake voluntary activities that go beyond what is legally required and which all other parties are obligated to perform. To do so otherwise would incur additional costs that a firm could not absorb since buyers, being perfectly informed, would refuse to pay higher prices for products that could be bought more cheaply elsewhere. The requirements of perfect competition, and its concomitant condition of a large number of minuscule and homogeneous firms with no individual distinguishing features with which the consumers may identify, are by themselves

> enough to undermine the working of the market mechanism . . . An anonymous supplier who looks like every other supplier to potential customers will risk little or no loss of reputation by product degradation . . . These are precisely the conditions that lead to repeated games of market reality to be populated by transient players . . . because of the implied or explicit assumption that sunk costs are absent firms lose nothing by entering a market, milking any profits it has to offer to those prepared to use fair means or foul, and then exiting it in haste if and when past misconduct makes their continuing presence uncomfortable (Baumol, 1991, p. 9).

One of the most notable exceptions to this behavior pattern should occur when firms are deemed to gain competitive advantage by hiring members of minority groups at lower wages because they are being discriminated against by other companies. Thus it would seem that competitive markets should induce more ethical non-discriminatory behavior in the market place. However in practice this does not happen even where such discrimination is widely applied. In such cases, society enforces discriminating behavior uniformly, through a web of social coercions, both legal and extra legal, which prevent individual firms from exercising free choice under the threat of communal boycott of its products and services and social ostracism of the offending firms. We have only to look in our own backyards to realize the potency of collective exploitation on the part of those who possess power against those who do not. The cases in point range all over the world from the Blacks of South Africa, the untouchables of India, native pre-colonial populations in scores of Latin American countries, and minorities of all ilks and persuasions in the United States, Europe, Japan, the Far East, and the Middle-East.

LACK OF BUSINESS ETHICS— THE DEVIL MADE ME DO IT!

A related explanation for unethical business practices can be found in the "deviant executive" syndrome. This explanation, however, is grossly inadequate given the systematic pattern of illegal and unethical behavior that persists in all industrial and corporate sectors and where the executives involved—like their companies—exhibit no differences in their socio-economic and other discernible characteristics. Business people are no more immune to illicit temptations and unethical behavior than other mortals. They are also equally capable of acts of high moral courage and personal integrity. An executive's financial circumstances also do not appear to be related to his/her unethical behavior. Nor is it a particular trait of the entrepreneurial empire builder as against the corporate mogul in the pin-stripe suit. Money has no conscience and no memory. Some of the most egregious white collar crimes of the eighties were committed by executives who would be comfortable in every type of business situation and whose financial wealth would be the envy of most earthlings.

An alternative, and more logical, proposition might be found in the argument that these executives are driven by rational calculations in enhancing their personal and corporate wealth where the opportunity for gain far exceeds the risk of being caught and punished. Even in the event of being apprehended, the legal guilt rarely gets transferred into social ostracism. Propelled by their competitive urges to do one better than one's peers, ethical and moral concerns get pushed lower on one's value hierarchy. Acts of executive unethical behavior are not confined to a company's external constituencies. They also manifest themselves in dealing with a company's legal owners, i.e., stockholders. Through their control of corporate boards, executives successfully manage to increase their incomes while delivering less than stellar performance to the stockholders, consistently keeping them in the dark as to the size and scope of their compensation beyond legally mandated disclosure requirements (Roberts, 1992; Sethi and Namiki, 1987).

Corporate decision-making processes also mitigate against individual employees or managers to pursue ethical standards similar to those they would apply in their personal conduct outside the corporate context. Group norms, and pressure to conform, exert strong influence on individuals to yield to demands for lower ethical standards when they are seen to be protecting the group at the cost of potential harm to "outsiders." Corporate decisions, from conception to implementation, involve hundreds and often thousands of individuals, each contributing an infinitesimal amount, and often with little or no understanding and appreciation as to its potential impact on the overall decision. Thus divorced from the consequences of collective outcome, the employee focuses on the cost/benefit analysis of his/her decision primarily in personal terms where the collective harm of an anti-social choice is rarely apparent. We become hostage to the tyranny of small decisions. The group orientation of corporate unethical behavior depersonalizes business leadership. Thus, while the impact of an unethical or anti-social act may be more serious for the society when compared with a multiplicity of personal unethical acts committed by individuals in their private capacity, the corporate personality diffuses the individual burden of guilt.

IMPERFECT MARKETS: OPPORTUNITIES FOR BEING VIRTUOUS

From the foregoing discussion, we must conclude that prevailing conventional explanations of why corporations and managers behave unethically, and how they might be induced to do otherwise, are inconsistent with available evidence. Instead, we must look for those structural, institutional, and individual attributes that explain ethical business behavior under normal operating conditions, and relate to the overwhelming majority of business actions in the marketplace.

There are two conditions—given the competitive nature of markets—that must exist in order to create a potentially conducive environment for businesses to behave ethically: (1) there must be some imperfections in the marketplace that the firm can exploit to generate "above normal" profits, i.e., strategic slack; (2) the firm must be assured of garnering both economic and non-economic benefits from such ethical conduct in terms of greater customer loyalty, public goodwill and trust, employee satisfaction, and, reduced government regulation and oversight, to name a few. A part of these profits could then be used by the firm to go beyond what is minimally or legally required to sustain one's competitive position.

Existence of strategic slack is a necessary but not a sufficient condition for companies to act more ethically than their competitors in the marketplace. Although it provides the resources to enhance managerial discretion, it does not direct it. A company's management may use its "slack" resources to enhance its ethical posture. It could just as easily use them to defy societal expectations and resist external demands for changes in its goals and operational strategies (Falbe and Sethi, 1989). For example, even a cursory examination of business practices prevailing in large market segments all over the world would suggest that under conditions of oligopoly and market concentration firms invariably resort to non-price competition, suppressing information that would allow customers to make informed choices and providing only that information which would lead customers to choose a particular firm's products; and, create spurious product differentiation which customers would find difficult to evaluate, thereby allowing the firm to charge premium prices for little or no added value.

The second necessary condition, i.e., market reward for a firm's enhanced ethical and socially desirable behavior, is also rooted in market imperfections especially as they relate to market concentration. Contrary to the conditions of ideal markets, the long-term prosperity and growth of a company depends on its ability to make those very conditions inoperable, i.e., the firm must: become known to the customer; seek customers' loyalty and repeat business through offering them quality products, adequate information as to their appropriate use, and at competitive prices; deal with its stockholders, employees and suppliers in a fair and equitable manner to ensure their continuous support and inflow of resource inputs; treat the community-at-large fairly so as to maintain a high level of socio-political trust; and, nurture a corporate culture that puts high value on ethical and socially responsible behavior as an integral part of doing business and corporate ethos (Baumol, 1991; Heal, 1976, Sethi, 1994). A reputable firm inspires trust and confidence. This reduces the customers' cost of learning as they accept the company's claims and assurances as to product quality and service and thereby reduce the latter's transaction costs. Thus it behooves the firm to sacrifice at least some of its short-term profits arising out of market imperfections and use them to build greater entry barriers against its competitors and thereby insure long-term, above-normal profitability for the enterprise.

Notwithstanding, a firm does not have to use its strategic slack in an ethically proactive and socially responsible manner. Market conditions may induce the firm to maximize short-term profits because it does not see long-term advantage in such a trade-off. The ideological orientation of management may influence its behavior by disregarding the needs of the general community and those stakeholders who cannot directly impact its operations. On a more personal level, top managers may also choose to use strategic slack-based discretion in philanthropic and other activities that give them personal pleasure and a sense of power although these activities might be inappropriate or have low priority for the community-at-large. Thus, "management uniqueness" or the sum total of all those factors that define the corporate personality, plays an important part in the use of strategic slack in influencing a company's ethical posture (Baumol, 1991; Sethi, 1994; Sethi and Steidlmeier, 1991). Strategic slack affords management the arrogance of power to respond negatively to external forces of change. A self-assured and self-righteous management may be willing to tolerate a high degree of mis-match between corporate behavior and external environmental expectations thereby causing a higher level and an extended period of dissonance between the corporation and its adversaries (Nystrom and Starbuck, 1984; Pettigrew, 1973; Sethi, 1994). Alternately, strategic slack may provide corporate management with an opportunity to experiment, fashion innovative solutions, and respond proactively to external forces of change. A self-assured and yet tolerant management, when cushioned with a high level of current profits, may be willing to take a longer term perspective of the situation and move more rapidly to reduce the level of mismatch in adapting to changes in its external environment.

IMPERFECT MARKETS AND IMPEDIMENTS TO BEING VIRTUOUS

A large part of business activity in most industrialized countries is accounted for by industries that are oligopolistic in character. Moreover, as new technologies grow and mature, and new markets are discovered and nurtured, they invariably acquire the characteristics of oligopolistic structures. Imperfect markets have become a dominant condition of capitalistic societies and are likely to remain so for the foreseeable future. It is also not clear whether perfect competition, or conditions approaching it, is indeed feasible or desirable for the efficient working of large and complex industrialized market economies.

This raises an important question. To wit, under a persistent condition of imperfect markets,how can the large corporation be induced to act ethically and socially-proactively, without the burden of onerous governmental regulation and oversight, and thereby minimize the cost of regulatory failures?

At one rational level,industries and companies should strive to act ethically so as to maintain the viability and social acquiescence of imperfect markets and preserve their franchises. There is enough rhetoric and some action to suggest that business recognizes the essentiality of this argument. In practice,however, this condition is more often violated even when it is apparent that observance of higher ethical standards would best serve not only the community's interest but also that of the businesses involved. There are two possible explanations for this anomalous behavior. The first one has to do with the character of public and private goods in society and the social means of distributing public goods, and social criteria of converting public goods into private goods. The second one pertains to the nature of the intellectual core and value set of the business institution, industry structure, and, value orientation and reward framework of top corporate managers.

The endemic character of business-society conflicts in market economies and democratic societies has to do with the nature of public-collective goods and private goods. The former are viewed as society's endowments to be shared by all of its members without regard to one's ability to pay for them. The distributive criteria are those of need, social relevance and collective enjoyment. Private goods are for the exclusive enjoyment of their owners and, within broad limits, to be bought, sold and exchanged at their owners' discretion. In general, market institutions are not equipped to deliver collective goods and may fail completely at the collective provision of social norms. Expansion of market activities, by its very nature, creates more private goods, often contracting the supply of public goods. While business institutions are applauded for their production of private goods and services, they also take the major blame for depleting the stock of public goods.

In one sense, society's moral and ethical values are public goods. All members of a society stand to benefit from an enhancement of these values regardless of their individual contribution to such enhancement. Here the nature of corporate mission and goals and those of private voluntary organizations (PVOs) stand in sharp contrast. It may partially explain the inherent discrepancy in public trust and goodwill enjoyed by public interest groups against that of the business community (Granovetter, 1985; Hirsch, 1976; McNutt, 1988; Sen, 1973, 1985, 1987; Yaari, 1981). The *intellectual core* and *value set* of the corporate entity are rooted in the premise that individuals and groups have the right to produce and exchange goods and services which the society needs and at prices which are competitively determined in the marketplace. The success of a corporation is determined in direct proportion to its ability to serve public needs. Profits are one measure of a corporation's reward for doing its job well. In the strict sense of the word, the most profitable corporation is also the most socially responsible corporation because it has satisfied the needs of a large segment of society.

Unfortunately, this state of affairs creates real problems for those firms that wish to act ethically and thereby increase the common stock of society's moral values. In the case of other social institutions, i.e., PVOs, e.g., churches, universities, and charitable institutions, there is a presumption of altruism which is further strengthened by their espoused mission and goals. Even where one of these institutions acts in a manner which could be construed to be antisocial in some quarters, it is still viewed as only acting for some larger social good. The problems of the free rider, i.e., one who takes a greater share of public-collective goods without adequately contributing to the enhancement of their stock or being concerned about depriving others of similar enjoyment, are not applicable. PVOs are expected to behave in the public interest. It is their raison d'etre. Ergo, there is no free rider (Sethi, 1994).

Private firms face exactly the opposite problem. They must always try to maximize private gains by internalizing all possible profits and externalizing all possible costs. Even under conditions of imperfect markets, dominant firms cannot always control—for legal and other reasons—the behavior of rogue firms wishing to exploit an industry's stock of public trust for their own gain, i.e., become a free rider. This condition is likely to exacerbate where public trust in an industry or a firm's integrity is quite high; the offending firm stands to garner significant financial reward for being a free rider; and especially where retaliation by the industry or society is likely to be too late or too little and would cause the offending firm proportionately less harm because of its smaller market stake.

Industry members, therefore, must assume that other companies would follow suit and behave equally aggressively as free riders since they have more to lose from contributing to general public trust and moral and ethical values and everything to gain from being a free rider. Conversely, while dominant firms stand to lose through the actions of the free rider, they also stand to gain by acting in concert and maintaining industry cohesiveness which provides some restraints to constantly lowering standards by industry members. On the other hand, where industry standards of ethical norms are low, and so perceived by the public-at-large, a deviance by an industry member to raise ethical standards and undermine industry's public stance would be severely resisted by the rest of the industry with the deviant member subjected to intense public and private pressure to fall in line.

The one exception to this rule would take place where a firm's market position and resultant non-market rent are so strong that it must protect them at all costs by courting the goodwill of its customers, government regulators and public-at-large (Hirsch, 1976; Schelling, 1971, 1978). The incentive to do so, however, is not altruism but a desire to preserve the firm's extra profits. The benefit of public goodwill is measured in terms of potential profits. This condition tends to undermine the value of a firm's contribution to enhancing society's stock of ethical and moral values because companies are viewed to be primarily acting in self-interest thereby discounting their claims of being disinterested public citizens. Even when corporations engage in philanthropic activities that are not designed solely to ameliorate the second-order effects of their normal business activities, they dilute their social import and the altruistic character of their "public or collective goods" by linking them to those groups and activities that further a corporation's commercial goals by labelling them "strategic giving."

A third problem pertaining to companies' reluctance to pursue higher ethical standards is related to the authority and power of top managers within a company's organization structure; the nature of their rewards, financial and non-financial, private and social; the reference group to which these managers view themselves and are in turn viewed by society. Received legal theory and corporate hyperbole suggest that a company's managers work primarily to enhance the best interests of the firm's owners, i.e., stockholders, commensurate with some measure of acceptable risk. Where interests of other stakeholders, e.g., employees, customers, are considered, they are balanced within the framework of a corporation's long-term survival and growth and not in terms of their inherent benefit to these stakeholders. However, in practice this is far from true.

While corporate managers may perpetuate such a myth in order to protect their authority and power, there is ample evidence to suggest that managers do not always act in the best interest of stockholders. The rapid turnover in stockholders, and the increasingly institutional character of stockholdings, make stockholder governance less than effective. Top managers hold most of the cards in controlling the destiny of the corporation and, except in dire circumstances, are hard to replace by discontented stockholders. Furthermore, this situation is unlikely to change in the foreseeable future despite some recent, widely publicized examples of boardroom revolt resulting in the ouster of CEOs in companies like American Express, General Motors, IBM and Sears, Roebuck (Bolton, 1993; Dobrzynski, 1993; Loomis, 1993; Magnet, 1992, 1993; Monks and Minow, 1991; Pulliam, 1993; Pulliam and Patterson, 1993; Rowe, 1993; Saporito, 1993; Stewart, 1993). In the absence of fundamental changes in incorporation laws, SEC oversight, management control of board election processes, and shareholder activism, these examples would remain what they are, i.e., aberrations that show the magnitude of the problem rather than avenues of solution. Studies also suggest that there is little correlation between top management compensation and corporate performance either in the short or in the long run (Byrne, 1993; Crystal, 1992; Drucker, 1984; Leonard, 1990; Longnecker *et al.*, 1992; Murphy, 1985; Redling, 1981; Sethi and Namiki, 1987; Wilson *et al.*, 1992).

The self-interest orientation of the corporation; the arbitrary character and self-perpetuating nature of managerial authority; and, public perception of top management's pursuit of self-interest at the expense of a company's legitimate owners, other significant stakeholders, and society-at-large; all combine to create an aura of low public legitimacy and esteem for corporate managers, especially those of large, publicly held enterprises. Devoid of public accolades and respect given almost automatically to the leaders of most other major social institutions, corporate managers turn to their own peer group, i.e., other business leaders, for legitimization of their behavior, perquisites, and social raison d'etre. Thus individual corporate ethical standards mimic closely those of the industry, business in general, and the reference group of a company's top managers, i.e., to managers of other companies.

Top managers as a group, therefore, seek legitimacy of their authority and power in reference to those objects and activities that command high value and prestige within their reference group. These include, among others: the absolute size of the corporation, assets and resources that they control; their financial compensation and perquisites of office; board membership of other large corporations; and, trusteeships and board positions among a select group of highly prestigious cultural, educational and philanthropic organizations, that lend further credence to their sense of self-esteem within a particular reference group. Since cries of lowered ethical standards and a declining sense of social responsibility are invariably made by individuals and groups outside their milieu and are considered hostile to private enterprise, these views are tolerated by the corporate managers only to the minimum extent necessary. Similarly, political/legislative initiatives to improve corporate morality are viewed with disdain since they are seen to be originating from politicians whose own moral standards are even more suspect and whose initiatives can be modified through pro-business advocacy and other means of political representation.

MAKING ETHICAL BEHAVIOR AN ATTRACTIVE OPTION FOR MANAGERS AND CORPORATIONS

It would seem almost counter-intuitive to suggest that economic institutions could ever be made to seek altruistic goals as an end in themselves, or at least, as an integral part of their overall objectives. And yet, this is precisely what needs to be done if we are to achieve an ascension in the ethical norms of corporate institutional behavior. We also contend that the ethical behavior of individual managers and employees, acting either in their personal or institutional capacities, but within the corporate institutional framework, would similarly be improved to a great extent by the existence of supportive institutional and social incentives rather than merely proscriptive exhortations or punishments. While exemplary and extraordinary altruistic individual behavior might give us our heroes, they would certainly not be the heroes that ordinary mortals could emulate in the routines of their everyday lives. Nor do these heroes, and villains, provide us with an adequate basis for structural analysis of social institutions. The emphasis in our effort, therefore, must be on those social-structural underpinnings and institutional frameworks that are necessary for improving the ethical norms of corporate behavior.

American society, hitherto, has largely resorted to the use of legally imposed proscriptive measures where the focus of regulatory behavior is on controlling *negative* deviation from *a base level* of social norms of ethical conduct leaving *positive* deviation largely to the discretion and individual proclivities of corporations and managers involved. It is also apparent that legal approaches to inducing more ethically responsive corporate behavior, while necessary, will at best provide a minimal level of a commonly accepted standard—a standard which the organized business groups constantly attempt to erode and evade. The critical need, therefore, is to create a proper balance between regulatory proscriptions and means of social persuasion for proactive ethical behavior. Our challenge is to seek ways and means by which economic institutions and their leaders are induced to act in a more ethical and socially proactive manner and with minimal resort to mandated governmental controls and their concomitant cost of policing and enforcement.

SOCIAL MEANS FOR ENHANCING PROACTIVE CORPORATE ETHICAL BEHAVIOR

The intensity of prevailing ethical norms in a society provides a good framework to create social carrots for inducing enhanced ethical standards of institutional behavior. To act ethically is less onerous in a social environment where mutual interdependence is strong and where social acquiescence is necessary for the realization of individual goals. It is not surprising, therefore, that variance from group norms is minimal under conditions of cultural homogeneity, shared values and group orientation in social organization. Thus ethical standards of behavior can be collectively raised without incurring excessive costs of policing and regulation on the one hand and leakages from the free rider problem on the other hand.

The role of a company's top managers is extremely important in influencing a corporation's norms of ethical conduct within the parameters outlined in the earlier part of this paper. While public exposure of the damage to society as a whole will help promote a social ethos, it will not be sufficient to secure it so long as individualistic behavior retains its legitimacy over large areas of collective action (Hirsch, 1976). According to Erich Fromm (1949),

> It is the function of the social character to shape the energies of the members in such a way that their behavior is not left to conscious decisions whether or not to follow the social pattern but that people want to act and at the same time find gratification in acting according to the requirements of the culture. In other words, the social character has the function of molding human energy for the purpose of the functioning of a given society.

Nowhere is this concept more relevant than in the role and actions of corporate chief executive officers (CEOs) and other top managers. Studies show that most corporate CEOs are appointed from within their own companies, consider their first loyalty to their firms, and tend to have fewer interests outside the affairs of the companies they manage and CEOs of other companies with whom they interact. Corporate managers, like most professionals seek peer group approval. Unfortunately, their peer group is extremely narrowly based and consists primarily of other CEOs or senior corporate managers. This narrow peer group seeks and measures "power and prestige . . . very largely in direct proportion to status in the corporate community acquired during a career. Conspicuous consumption and overt signs of wealth are used as class symbols in the fashion of Veblen's 'leisure class'" (Sethi *et al.* 1984, pp. 119-120). Conversely, a significant deviation from the prevailing norms of acceptable *within group conduct* exposes the CEO to peer group contempt, injures his/her self-esteem, and risks his/her financial well-being by curtailing job mobility and other opportunities for income generation and wealth enhancement.

ALTRUISM AS A DESIRABLE INSTITUTIONAL AND PERSONAL GOAL

An important characteristic of the American socio-political system, unlike many other societies, is that most corporate leaders do not come from established social elites. Nor do they have recognized symbols of social class such as titles. Moreover, they are grossly under-represented in peak social institutions of status or considered social elites and positive role modes, e.g., scientists and educators, representing society's higher moral and aesthetic values. The public-at-large has little familiarity with their individual personalities and character, and colors them with the same brush as the corporations they manage. Devoid of mutual trust, people use political processes to impose rigid conditions on corporate behavior. Managers respond in kind by satisfying the form of the law and legal requirements without concerning themselves with the substance or objectives for which those requirements were imposed.

Where offending behavior is within acceptable norms of general business practice—whether or not it is illegal and punishable when found—its impact on the executive involved is limited and short-lived. Individuals do not see their unethical actions as causing great social harm when they form part of a larger common pattern whose pervasive collective impact they all abhor. The unethical behavior of the CEO—conveniently defined as allegedly small variations from socio-ethical norms—is often judged leniently within the reference-peer group whose loyalty and support is more important than that of the public-at-large for legitimizing his/her self-worth and within-group status.

For corporate managers to act beyond the minimally prescribed and legally enforced norms of social conduct, it would be important to foster mechanisms for generating a higher threshold level of trust between business leaders and leaders of other socio-political institutions on the one hand and business leaders and the public-at-large on the other hand. An important element of this approach would necessitate a redefinition of the nature of the "business game," moving away from its predominantly zero-sum character of gains and losses in dealing with one or more elements of society. One of the ways to develop "cultural isomorphism" would be through conscious imitation and adaptation of *symbols of social success* that have worked well within and between the context of other social institutions. This would not necessarily call for a diminution of competitive spirit. Instead, it would enforce those social conditions that would foster a more proactive corporate ethical behavior in the firm's dealings with other social institutions and individuals.

One of the important ways in which we might improve corporate ethical conduct and accountability would be to encourage in the CEOs a broader vision of their role—and those of the companies they manage—in society. This could be accomplished by elevating the corporate chief executive by endowing him/her with the stature of an important public figure. To this end, it is suggested that:

(a) the selection of a CEO of a major corporation should be considered an important social decision requiring significant public discussion and exposure;

(b) the installation of the CEO of a major corporation should be invested with great pomp and ceremony, i.e., investiture that such an office should command given the importance of that institution to the welfare of the nation. This would be akin to the investiture of the high office of the presidents of major universities and other important social and political institutions;

(c) such a selection process would not constitute a democratic process in the appointment of a CEO. Nor would it mean that a CEO so selected would necessarily be incompetent or unacceptable to the board of directors. However, by investing the job with a greater sense of social recognition, we would give the occupant a better self-image and encourage him/her to assume a broader perspective of his/her function and role at the helm of a major corporation;

(d) at the time of assumption of office, the CEO would announce to the public what specific policies he/she would pursue to improve the quality of the company's operations, its other stakeholders, the communities where the company has major operations, and society-at-large. The CEO would also make specific pledges that could be monitored through independent oversight—as to the norms of ethical conduct the company would apply in its operations and in dealing with its internal and external stakeholders;

(e) there would be a systematic and regular process—akin to that currently applied to financial disclosures and reporting—for the companies to report on its activities not covered in its financial reports.

In theory, all corporations could follow this course. However, in reality, it is likely to be confined to the top 50-100 companies because of the public attention that such an activity must command in order to be meaningful. Over time, suitable traditions would develop. There is no reason to believe that these ceremonies would not be conducted with the same degree of restraint and dignity as those of the investiture of a university president.

We must not reject this exercise as mere frivolity and an attempt at self-aggrandizement and propaganda. Those who are constantly berated as unworthy tend to see the world in a similarly unfavorable light as they try to eliminate dissonance by coloring the world in the very image fostered upon them by society. The process in the end is self-defeating, as both the individual and the institution involved try to destroy each other. The sole purpose of this exercise would be to set a moral tone for the CEO and corporate management. Philosopher kings are not unknown in history. Philosopher scientists are commonplace today. Isn't it time that we asked for philosopher managers to run our major economic institutions? (Votaw and Sethi, 1973).

The arena of social conflict between business and society are not those between right and wrong, or between guilty and innocent, but between one type of inequity and another, between giving one group more while taking some from another group, between the virtue of frugality and the sin of accumulation, and between morality of principle and morality of situations. In an unjust world, the distinctions between the guilty and innocent have become ambiguous. What we are confronted with is the realization that we live in an increasingly interdependent society where individual good is not possible outside the context of common good. It makes no sense to separate moral principles from institutional behavior, political power from material rewards. To do so is to divorce the social system from its basic element, the human being, who does not behave in a fragmented manner.

ACKNOWLEDGEMENT

The author is grateful for the research support in the preparation of this article provided by Ms. Linda M. Sama, a doctoral student at Baruch College.

REFERENCES

Baumol, W.J.: 1991, *Perfect Markets and Easy Virtue: Business Ethics and the Invisible Hand* (Blackwell, Cambridge, MA).

Binstein, M., and C. Bowden: 1993, *Trust Me: Charles Keating and the Missing Billions* (Random House, New York).

Bolton, J.R.: 1993, "A Second Look at Boardroom Reform," *The Wall Street Journal*, June 2, A14.

Burrough, B. and J. Helyar: 1990, *Barbarians at the Gate: The Fall of RJR Nabisco* (Harper & Row, New York).

Byrne, J.A.: 1993, "Executive Pay: The Party Ain't Over Yet," *Business Week*, April 26, 56–79.

Cook, F.J.: 1966, *The Corrupted Land: The Social Morality of Modern America* (The Macmillan Company, New York).

Crystal, G.S.: 1992, "Dubious Connection of Pay to Performance," *Pensions and Investments* **20**, 14.

Day, K.: 1993, *S&L Hell: The People and the Politics Behind the $1 Trillion Savings and Loan Scandal* (Norton, New York).

Dobrzynski, J.H.: 1993, "Relationship Investing," *Business Week*, March 15, 68–75.

Donaldson, T.: 1989, *The Ethics of International Business* (Oxford University Press, New York).

Drucker, P.F.: 1984, "Reform Executive Pay or Congress Will," *The Wall Street Journal*, April 24, 34.

Falbe, C.M., and S.P. Sethi: 1989, "The Concept of Strategic Slack: Implications for the Choice of Public Policy Strategies by Corporations," Paper presented at the *Ninth Annual Strategic Management Conference 'Strategies for Innovation'* (San Francisco, CA), Oct. 11–14, 1989.

Fromm, E.: 1949, "Psychoanalytic Characterology and its Application to the Understanding of Culture," in S.S. Sargent and M.W. Smith (eds.), *Culture and Personality*: 5 (Viking Fund, Wenner-Wenner-Gren Foundation for Anthropological Research: 5, New York).

Fuller, J.G.: 1962, *The Gentlemen Conspirators: The Story of the Price-fixers in the Electrical Industry* (Grove Press, New York).

Granovetter, M.: 1985, "Economic Action and Social Structure: The Problem of Embeddedness," *American Journal of Sociology* **91**, 481–510.

Guyon, J.: 1992, "Tobacco Companies Race for Advantage in Eastern Europe While Critics Fume," *The Wall Street Journal*, Dec. 28, B1.

Harris, R.G. and J.M. Carman: 1991, "The Political Economy of Regulation: An Analysis of Market Failures," in S.P. Sethi, P. Steidlmeier and C.M. Falbe (eds.), *Scaling the Corporate Wall* (Prentice Hall, Englewood Cliffs, NJ), pp. 24–35.

Heal, G.: 1976, "Do Bad Products Drive Out Good?", *Quarterly Journal of Economics* **90**, 499–503.

Herling, J.: 1962, *The Great Price Conspiracy: The Story of the Antitrust Violations in the Electrical Industry* (Robert B. Luce, Inc., Washington).

Hirsch, F.: 1976, *Social Limits to Growth* (Harvard University Press, Cambridge, MA).

Holcomb, J. and S.P. Sethi: 1992, "Corporate Executive Liability for Law Violations: Appropriate Standards, Remedies, and Managerial Responses," *Business and the Contemporary World* **Summer**, 81–105.

Leonard, J.S.: 1990, "Executive Pay and Firm Performance," *Industrial and Labor Relations Review* **43**, 135–295.

Lewis, M.: 1989, *Liar's Poker: Rising Through the Wreckage on Wall Street* (Norton, New York).

Longnecker, B.M., S.L. Cross and C.L. Wood: 1992, "High Executive Pay Meets Tough Scrutiny," *Journal of Compensation & Benefits* **7**(4), 13–17.

Loomis, C.J.: 1993, "King John Wears an Uneasy Crown," *Fortune*, January 11, 44–48.

Lorsch, J.W., with MacIver, E.: 1989, *Pawns or Potentates: The Reality of America's Corporate Boards* (Harvard Business School Press, Boston, MA).

Magnet, M.: 1992, "Directors, Wake Up," *Fortune*, June 15, 85–92.

Magnet, M.: 1993, "What Activist Investors Want," *Fortune*, March 8, 59–63.

McNutt, P.A.: 1988, " Note on Altruism," *International Journal of Social Economics* **15**(9), 62–64.

Monks, R. and N. Minow: 1991, *Power and Accountability* (Harper Business, New York).

Murphy, K.J.: 1985, "Corporate Performance and Managerial Remuneration: An Empirical Analysis," *Journal of Accounting and Economics*, 11–42.

Nystrom, P.C. and W.H. Starbuck: 1984, "To Avoid Organizational Crisis, Unlearn," *Organizational Dynamics* **12**(4), 53–65.

Pettigrew, A.: 1973, *The Politics of Organizational Decision-Making* (Tavistock, London).

Pulliam, S.: 1993, "Calpers Goes Over CEOs' Heads in its Quest for Higher Returns," *The Wall Street Journal*, Jan. 22, C1, C10.

Pulliam, S. and G.A. Patterson: 1993, "Sears is Target of Holder Group Urging Chairman to Give Up One of Two Titles," *The Wall Street Journal*, Feb. 4, A1.

Redling, E.T.: 1981, "Myths vs. Reality: The Relationship Between Top Executive Pay and Corporate Performance," *Compensation Review*, 16–24.

Roberts, R.W.: 1992, "Determinants of Corporate Social Responsibility Disclosure: An Application of Stakeholders Theory," *Accounting, Organization and Society* **17**(6), 595–612.

Rowe, F.E., Jr.: 1993, "Hurrah for October 15," *Forbes*, Feb. 15, 234.

Saporito, B.: 1993, "The Toppling of King James III," *Fortune*, Jan. 11, 42–43.

Schelling, T.C.: 1971, "On the Ecology of Micromotives," *The Public Interest*, **25**, 59–98.

Schelling, T.C.: 1978, *Micromotives and Macrobehavior* (W.W. Norton & Company, New York).

Sen, A.: 1973, "Behavior and the Concept of Preference," *Economica* **August**.

Sen, A.: 1985, "The Moral Standing of the Market," *Social Philosophy and Policy* 2, 1–19.

Sen, A.: 1987, *On Ethics and Economics* (Basil Blackwell, Oxford, England).

Sethi, S.P.: 1981, "The Expanding Scope of Executive Liability (Criminal and Civil) for Corporate Law Violation," in S.P. Sethi and C.L. Swanson (eds.), *Private Enterprise and Public Purpose* (John Wiley & Sons, New York), pp. 245–274.

Sethi, S.P.: 1994, *Multinational Corporations and the Impact of Public Advocacy on Corporate Strategy: Nestle and the Infant Formula Controversy* (Kluwer Academic Publishers, Boston).

Sethi, S.P. and N. Namiki: 1987, "Top Management Compensation and Corporate Performance," *The Journal of Business Strategy* 7(4), 37–43.

Sethi, S.P., N. Namiki and C.L. Swanson: 1984, *The False Promise of the Japanese Miracle* (Pitman Publishing, Boston).

Sethi, S.P. and P. Steidlmeier: 1991, *Up Against the Corporate Wall: Modern Corporations and Social Issues of the Nineties*, 5th edition (Prentice Hall, Englewood Cliffs, NJ).

Shrivastava, P.: 1987, *Bhopal: Anatomy of a Crisis* (Ballinger Publishing Company, Cambridge, MA).

Stewart, J.B.: 1991, *Den of Thieves* (Simon & Schuster, New York).

Stewart, T.A.: 1993, "The King is Dead," *Fortune*, Jan. 11, 34–40.

Vise, D.A. and S. Coll: 1991, *Eagle on the Street* (Scribners, New York).

Votaw, D. and S.P. Sethi: 1973, *The Corporate Dilemma: Traditional Values Versus Contemporary Problems* (Prentice Hall, Englewood Cliffs, NJ), pp. 173–175.

Wilson, M.A., T.I. Chacko, C.B. Shrader and E. Mullen: 1992, "Top Executive Pay and Firm Performance," *Journal of Business and Psychology* 6, 495–-501.

Yaari, M.E.: 1981, "Rawls, Edgeworth, Shapley, Nash: Theories of Distributive Justice Reexamined," *Journal of Economic Theory* 24, 1–39.

TOWARD A UNIFIED CONCEPTION OF BUSINESS ETHICS

Integrative social contracts theory

Thomas Donaldson
Thomas W. Dunfee

"Would you tell me, please, which way I ought to go from here?" Alice asked the Cheshire Cat. "That depends a good deal on where you want to get to," said the Cat. "I don't much care where . . . " said Alice. Then it doesn't matter which way you go," said the Cat. (Carroll, 1983:72)

Throughout its meteoric rise over the last two decades, the field of business ethics has been troubled by a lack of direction and has become, like Alice, entangled in its own logic. Its problem stems from the discordant research methods used to explore ethics. On the one hand, business ethics research can be informed by empirical ideas, that is, by concepts that describe and explain factual states, relationships between ethical behavior, and financial performance. In other words, it canbe informed by the "is" of economic affairs

We thank the following people for their helpful comments on successive drafts of this article: Anita Cava, Dennis Collins, Phil Cochran, Henri Claude DeBettignies, Wanda Foglia, Bill Frederick, Ed Freeman, David Fritzche, Paul Hodapp, Michael Keeley, Eric Orts, Diana Robertson, Bill Shaw, Richard Shell, and Iwao Taka. We also benefitted from the comments of workshop/conference participants at the Association for Practical and Professional Ethics, Copenhagen Business School, the European Business Ethics Network, Georgetown University, INSEAD, Notre Dame, St. John's Law School, University of Michigan, University of North Carolina, University of Texas at Austin, Wake Forest University, Western Michigan University, and the Wharton School.

On the other hand, business ethics research can be informed by normative[1] concepts, that is, by ideas which, although not necessarily grounded in existing business practices and structures, are what ethicists call *prescriptive*. They guide us to what we *should* do. In this vein, most philosophers remind us that no amount of empirical accuracy, including an infinite array of facts, can ever by itself add up to an "ought" (Sorley, 1904/1969). To suppose that one can deduce an "ought" from an "is," or, what amounts to the same thing, that one can deduce a normative ethical conclusion from empirical research, is to commit a logical mistake some dub the "naturalistic fallacy" (Moore, 1903/1951: 10–14).

These two approaches to business ethics, which we shall call the *empirical* and the *normative*, have produced two powerful streams of business research. During the last 15 years, researchers with philosophical training have introduced purely normative, nonempirical methods to the study of business ethics, just as they introduced them earlier to the fields of legal and medical ethics. In this way, the philosophical tradition of ethical theory has contributed rigor to ongoing discussions of business ethics (Barry, 1982; Bowie, 1988; Donaldson, 1982; Freeman & Gilbert, 1988; French, 1979; Gauthier, 1986; Ladd, 1970; May, 1987; Nickel, 1974; Sen, 1985; Shue, 1981).

Meanwhile, using the alternative perspective, business school researchers with training in empirical methods have applied their techniques (often adapted from existing approaches in marketing, finance, and elsewhere) to study important issues in corporate and organizational ethics (Akaah & Riordan, 1989; Cochran & Wood, 1984; Fritzsche & Becker, 1984; Hunt, Wood, & Chonko, 1989; Trevino & Youngblood, 1990; see particularly Randall & Gibson, 1990, and sources cited therein for an extensive overview of this literature). This research has been extended by the development of frameworks suggesting relationships among key behavior variables and interconnections between the two divergent streams of research (Ferrell & Gresham, 1985; Hunt & Vitell, 1986; Jones, 1991; Trevino, 1986). These frameworks focus on predicting or understanding ethical behavior, and they have generally incorporated either broad statements of ethical theories, such as utilitarianism and rights and justice (Ferrell & Gresham, 1985), or they have relied upon concepts from moral psychology (Jones, 1991; Trevino, 1986).[2,3]

Yet despite these preliminary efforts at reconciling the two disparate viewpoints, the two worlds of empirical and normative research in business ethics remain at a respectful distance from each other. Trevino and Weaver (1993) articulate clearly the contrasts between the two approaches, noting that the sharpest differences lie between the methods used by empirical researchers and philosophical ethicists in their discovery and analysis of information.

In this article, we seek to advance the interconnection between empirical and normative research in business ethics by presenting a normative theory, called integrative social contracts theory (ISCT), which incorporates empirical findings as part of a contractarian process of making normative judgments. Derived from roots in classical and social contract theory, this integrative theory recognizes ethical obligations based upon two levels of consent: first, to a theoretical "macrosocial" contract appealing to all rational contractors and second, to real "microsocial" contracts by members of numerous localized communities. Through this process, we seek to put the "is" and the "ought" in symbiotic harmony, requiring the cooperation of both empirical and normative research in rendering ultimate value judgments. In order to render normative judgments under the contractarian framework presented, it is necessary first to make accurate empirical findings concerning the ethical attitudes and behaviors of members of relevant communities. The emphasis on the role of communities in generating moral norms characterizes this approach as communitarian. The primary focus of this article is on the exposition of the overall integrated theory and on identifying implications for further empirical and normative research.

INTEGRATIVE SOCIAL CONTRACTS THEORY

We label the theory we are proposing *integrative social contracts theory* (ISCT) because it integrates two distinct kinds of contracts. The first is a normative and hypothetical contract among economic participants, a social contract similar to the classical contraction theories in philosophy and political economy. This general contract, in turn, defines the normative ground rules for creating the second kind of contract. The second is an existing (extant) implicit contract that can occur among members of specific communities, including firms, departments within firms, informal subgroups within departments, national economic organizations, international economic organizations, professional associations, industries, and so on. The aggregate of these extant social contracts contains much of the substance of business ethics. We believe that this way of conceiving business ethics no only helps one in understanding the normative justification for business decisions, but it also helps one in reaching such decisions.

Existing normative theories and concepts, such as stakeholder approaches (Carroll, 1989; Freeman, 1984; Hosseini & Brenner, 1992; Meznar, Chrisman, & Carroll, 1990;

Preston & Sapienza, 1990:362–67) or philosophical "Deontology" (Kant, 1785/1959) and "Utilitarianism" (Mill, 1965), provide general guidance but fail to reflect the context-specific complexity of business situations. Consider, for example, three kinds of ethical problems often confronted by multinational managers. In the first, the manager worries about giving and accepting gifts and entertainment; in the second, she or he wonders about the ethics of certain negotiation practices; and in the third, she or he wonders about the propriety of compensating employees not with money, but with personal benefits such as housing and guarantees of employment for their children. Now in all three of these contexts the advice given by each traditional theory is suitable, but frustratingly vague. Stakeholder approaches are merely able to advise this manager to consider both the interests of stockholders and other "stakeholders," (i.e., employees, community residents, customers, etc.). Kantian Deontology is only able to advise the manager to search for the general principle that she or he could follow in that particular case and which, furthermore, satisfies the test that she or he could will *all other managers to follow* the same principle under relevantly similar circumstances. Finally, Utilitarianism merely advises the manager to choose the action from among alternative courses of action that will maximize the future welfare of the most people. Even though each recommendation offers a broad-brushed guide to action, none speaks directly to the relevant ethical expectations or shared understandings of the participants.

None of the general ethical theories reflects directly the cultural patterns of business and friendship in gift giving, the culture-specific or industry-specific expectations surrounding negotiation practices, and/or the differences between cultures with a traditional acceptance of corporate paternalism and ones with highly individualistic nonpaternalistic beliefs. Each can handle the obvious situations well enough: If gift giving includes blatant fraud, if negotiations involve physical coercion, and if nonmonetary employee compensation serves to make economic prisoners of employees, then stakeholder approaches, Kantian Deontology, and Utilitarianism offer univocal advice. But most business situations involving community values are neither so stark nor so well defined. In short, each of the three recommendations is helpful—but only up to a point. For the purpose of illustrating different aspects of ISCT, we will return from time to time to these three issues (i.e., gift giving and receiving, questionable negotiation practices, and nonmonetary employee compensation).

The key to understanding ISCT, and, in turn, dealing with one aspect of the "is"/ "ought" problem, lies in understanding two concepts that we intend to explore in some detail, namely, *bounded moral rationality* and *social contracts*.

Bounded Moral Rationality

Imagine that you are a master of moral theory. You have read and absorbed the moral theories from Aristotle's Eudaemonism and Spinoza's Rationalism to Kant's Categorical Imperative and Sidgewick's Methods of Ethics. Imagine further that you have either determined which one of these traditional theories is best or have constructed a wholly new "best" theory using parts of existing theories. Now imagine that someone asks you to define *unethical employee compensation*. Will you be able to provide a satisfactory answer based upon your extensive knowledge and your new moral theory? Will you be able to know the correct course of action in all contexts where employee compensation is at issue? For example, is it appropriate to pay employees the average wage rate in developing countries when that rate is far lower than wages paid for similar work in developed countries?

So long as the only thing you knew was "the best moral theory," you would be hard pressed to produce a satisfactory definition of unethical employee compensation or to know the correct course of action in all circumstances. The reason is that moral rationality in economic contexts is *strongly bounded*.

In using the term *moral rationality* we presume what is granted by all major contemporary and traditional moral theorists, namely, that moral concepts are proper objects of rational analysis and that they possess at least minimal objectivity. Extreme moral or culture relativism is ruled out; (Donaldson, 1989:10–29; Stace, 1937; Wellman, 1963). We also assert that moral rationality is *bounded*, by which we mean that otherwise rational moral agents, when applying moral theory to actual situations, confront confining limits. First, they confront their own finite capacity to comprehend and absorb all details relevant to ethical contexts. Consider a contemporary ethical issue debated in many developed countries, namely, the morality of takeovers, acquisitions, and mergers (Hoffman, Frederick, & Petry, 1989). To assess the morality of corporate acquisitions, whether in general or in a specific instance, one must reference a maze of complex facts. This is true even if one believes oneself to be reasonably clear about the normative or ethical concepts at stake. It is also true whether one is a committed Rawlsian, believing that systemic inequalities are unjust unless they work to the advantage of everyone, including the least well off, or if one is a Hayakian or Friedmanite, believing that liberty is the linchpin of market morality. One needs to have a grasp of the consequences of acquisitions for the stockholders of the acquired firm, for the stockholders of the firm doing the acquiring, for any bondholders and other creditors, and for the managers and employees, among many others. One must have some view as to the long-term social consequences of accumulated debt, or of the tendencies toward increased or decreased efficiency of corporations under new management. This aspect of the boundedness of moral rationality is similar to Herbert Simon's concept of the same name. Human beings have finite intellectual resources and will inevitably "satisfice" in both economic and moral decision making.

But rational moral agents confront another kind of limit, different from that popularized by Simon. Their moral rationality is bounded by the limited ability of moral theory to account for commonsense moral convictions and preferences. Contemporary discussions reveal instances of slippage between what common sense asserts is morally correct and what moral theory dictates. For example, common sense will hold that family members should be preferred over strangers, and if a total stranger were drowning alongside one's spouse, and only one could be saved, common sense dictates saving one's spouse. But significant familial partiality is difficult to reconcile with traditional moral theory (Donaldson, 1990). (See also, Symposium on Impartiality and Ethical Theory, in *Ethics*, special edition, July 1991.) Certainly no one has argued that moral theory should be tested entirely by reference to settled moral conviction; indeed, it is because people often want to do the reverse (i.e., to test common conviction by theory) that theories are developed. Yet most moral theorists find it hard to imagine that a correct theory would fly in the fact of some of the most universally held, firmly believed moral convictions.

One disturbing result of what we are calling bounded moral rationality is moral uncertainty. For insofar as the correctness of each moral decision must be referenced to an infinite array of facts, or subject to theories that clash with key moral convictions, people are doomed to confront moral risk. Life is more confusing than one might hope.

Methods exist to deal with such confusion, as we will explain, but for the time being it is crucial to notice that moral life in economic affairs is not only bounded, but *strongly* bounded. It is this final aspect of the boundedness of moral rationality in economic life that makes business ethics even less determinant from the standpoint of general moral theory than ethics in, say, family or political life. We begin by noting that economic systems are not products of nature. In contrast, some human associations may be considered in large part products of nature. The family no doubt fits this description. But economic systems are products of artifice, not nature, and their structures can and do vary immensely. Such systems (which include the laws, practices, and value systems that inform economic practices) are, in a word, *artifacts*. People create them. People make them what they are, and people might have chosen to make them differently.

An analogy will help. Because they are artifacts, economic systems share important characteristics with games. Just as people can change the rules of games or invent entirely new games, so too can they change the rules of economic practices. The evolution of the corporation and of market economics from 1800 to the present are striking examples of the plasticity of the corporate form and of capitalism (Chandler, 1977), as is the collapse of the managed economies in the former Soviet Union and Eastern Europe. The definitions of economic practices are *stipulated* rather than given by nature.

Yet this amazing plasticity creates problems for the moral analysis of economic systems. For, in the same way that it would be impossible to create a general theory of the ethics of games without knowing in advance *which* game was under consideration, so too it is impossible to create a general theory of the ethics of economics without knowing at least the general shape of the economic system under consideration. The ethics of basketball, or of soccer or squash, must be contoured somewhat to the rules of these particular games. Similarly, the ethics of client entertainment, negotiation, and employee compensation must be contoured somewhat to the rules of particular economic systems in which they occur.

In an analogous way, knowing all the moral theory in the world does not equip a person to specify in advance the moral norms of business ethics, much less the norms for the specific contexts of gift giving, negotiation, and employee compensation. In each, the ethical norms must be contoured to the rules of the specific economic practices and the notions of fairness of the participants. This is not to deny that some extremely general moral prescriptions hold for all economic practices and, for that matter, for all eco-

nomic systems. For example, refraining from flagrant dishonesty, torture, and intentional killing are required in all human activities. Nor is it to deny that economic systems, unlike games of pick-up basketball, have dramatic implications for people who are not directly a part of the rule-formation process.

It is, however, to deny that a person can know in advance what the correct rules of business ethics are for a specific system without knowing more about the system and its participants. It is to deny, for example, the possibility of knowing in advance whether ethics requires that a high company official from an airline visit the surviving relatives of an airplane crash and present them with money (as Japanese airline officials do), in contrast to, say, merely offering sympathy and minor assistance. To know what ethics requires here, a person must know both what local custom encourages and also something about the system of compensation in the economic system. In the United States, a well-developed adversarial system exists for delivering compensation to victims. It is cumbersome and expensive, but relatively reliable. In Japan and elsewhere, the legal system for delivering compensation is less developed and less reliable. Thus, it would be reasonable to place greater moral burdens on the shoulders of Japanese corporate officials, than on those of U.S. corporate officials, for compensating and helping the families of victims.

In sum, rationality in economic ethics is bounded in three ways: by a finite human capacity to assess facts, by a limited capacity of ethical theory to capture moral truth, and by the plastic or *artifactual* nature of economic systems and practices.

In addition to the arguments already offered for bounded moral rationality, one can evaluate the claim of boundedness by looking for the consequences one should expect to follow if the claims were true. Were moral rationality bounded, one should expect to find that moral norms governing socioeconomic interaction vary widely from system to system and that they shift significantly over time. One also should expect that using abstract, universal concepts of ethics to solve specific ethical dilemmas in business would be extremely difficult. Finally, one should expect to find frequent appeals to system-specific or culture-specific practices in justifying ethical behavior.

All three predictions are fulfilled and are familiar features of the economic landscape. Concepts of business ethics vary significantly from culture to culture,as well as from time period to time period. What counts, for example, as "usury" varies dramatically from Western to Moslem culture, and, indeed, has changed radically over time, even in Western culture, from the Middle Ages, when all lending at interest was prohibited, to today, when all but the highest levels of interest are allowed with proper disclosure (Cameron, 1989:48–92, 322–344). It is also true that using abstract, universal concepts of ethics to solve specific ethical dilemmas is notoriously difficult, and as business ethics instructors frequently remark, the course that never moves beyond a discussion of Utilitarian or Kantian ethics (with appeals to "apply" them to business problems) is doomed to disaster. Finally, the claim that a particular practice may be ethically permissible because "everyone is doing it" is nowhere more common than in business ethics (Green, 1991). This is not necessarily because people in business have a lower ethical standard than those in other walks of life, but because business people exist in an artifactual context where institutions are sometimes *created* by common practice. The rules concerning proper disclosures and behaviors in negotiations (e.g., revelations about the condition of real estate in a commercial transaction), for example, often arise out of a history of common practice. Although never a sufficient condition for ethical justification, the claim that "everybody's doing something" can have some moral force in business contexts.

A Macrosocial Contract

The methodology of social contact is found in a well-respected stream of normative philos-

ophy stretching from Greek origins in Plato's *Republic* (1968) through the political philosophy of Hobbes (1651/1946), Locke (1690/1948), and Rousseau (1792/1959–1969), and, in the 20th century, John Rawls's (1971) celebrated theory of justice. The method has been applied directly to economic matters in the last decade in the work of theorists such as Donaldson (1982: 36–58), Dunfee (1991), Gauthier (1986), and Keeley (1988). Although each social contract practitioner tends to adjust the method to his or her own purposes, the central idea involves a manipulation of moral variables in the context of a thought experiment designed to ensure procedural fairness in setting the terms of the contract. So, for example, in order to ensure impartiality in the selection of principles of justice, John Rawls asks the reader to imagine rational persons choosing such principles behind a "veil of ignorance" that blinds the choosers to knowledge of their own characteristics, such as wealth, age, ability, and gender. In turn, choosers are blinded to how to ensure their own particular advantage. The principles that people would choose behind such a veil of ignorance are in this way presumed to be fair (i.e., morally objective and unbiased). In other instances of social-contract reasoning, fairness is secured simply by including among the contractors *all* persons whose interests are affected and by requiring consensus in the adoption of the terms of the contract—without the additional device of a veil of ignorance. It is this second strategy that we adopt.

The central social contract question we frame fits within the tradition of social contract thinking. It is focused, however, on principles of economic morality:

> What general principles, if any, would contractors who are aware of the strongly bounded nature of moral rationality in economic affairs choose to govern economic morality?

Let us call the set of principles regarding economic morality to which contractors would agree the *macrosocial contract*.

Moral Free Space

Rational contractors would desire the freedom to specify more precisely the norms of economic interaction as a response to the opaque world of strongly bounded moral rationality. Their first reason for doing so is economic efficiency. As has been mentioned, a key feature of *boundedness* in economic contexts is uncertainty. Without norms to govern, say, the giving of business-related gifts, the use of intellectual property, and the meaning of verbal commitments, the ensuing uncertainty becomes costly. Consider business negotiation. Negotiation by definition occurs prior to reaching an agreement or contract; it is, in short, a process of attempting to come to, or exploring the possibility of, reaching agreement. It occurs among strangers as well as friends and can reflect parties' naked self-interest (Shell, 1991a), yet in order to be efficient, even this suspect and uncertain process must occur against a backdrop of moral norms (Shell, 1991b). To the extent that negotiating information is systematically unreliable, the process becomes clumsy and time consuming. Of course, efficiency does not require that all relevant information be disclosed, or even disclosed accurately. Shrewd negotiators refuse to show all their cards, and they may sometimes bluff about their intentions. Hence, misinformation in the form of incomplete disclosure can figure in efficient negotiations, but when it does, it is crucial for purposes of efficiency that certain rules about possible misinformation be understood by all parties. In one context, bluffing about intent may be expected, so that the expression "I couldn't take less than . . ." is not taken at face value. In another context, less than complete disclosure about the subject of exchange may be expected. Again, it does not follow that there is only one set of efficient ethical rules for all systems of negotiation. If it is clearly understood within the international rice market that bulk rice sellers do not expect to provide an exhaustive list of the rice's defects to purchasing agents, then purchasing agents know either to prod the sellers or to check the rice themselves. In contrast if international rubber buyers expect sellers to acquire information about defects and then voluntarily to disclose those defects, they may not check the rubber themselves (Kollack, 1992:1–29). In the instance of the rubber market, failure of full disclosure would be unethical, but in the rice market, it would not. It is important that there be an ethical framework as a background condition for efficient negotiation. There must be some set of ethical rules. In many situations the particular rules chosen will not matter, because the existence of any reasonable set of rules will reduce uncertainty and enhance efficiency.[4]

The second reason for contractors of the macrosocial contract to retain the freedom to specify more precisely norms of economic interaction may be cultural, ideological, or religious. Contractors will wish to maintain their freedom as groups or communities to make specific interpretations of what *bounded* moral rationality requires in economic transactions. In some instances this freedom of interpretation will be connected to their desire to maintain their cultural distinctiveness, in other instances, it is connected to their desire to reflect their ideological beliefs, and in still other instances, it is connected to their desire to maintain their religious values. Muslim managers may wish to participate in systems of economic ethics compatible with the teachings of Mohammed (Esposito, 1988:116–202), European and American managers may wish to participate in systems of economic ethics giving due respect to individual liberty, and Japanese managers may prefer systems showing respect for the value of the collective (San, 1987). Individual corporations also may have value preferences. IBM traditionally prided itself on a buttoned-down, well-controlled culture, even as Hewlett Packard thrived on creative chaos (Kotter & Heskett, 1992:58–67).

Both these considerations of the desire (a) to enhance efficiency by reducing uncertainty and (b) to maintain freedom of cultural, ideological, or religious interpretation imply that contractors will choose terms of the macrosocial contract that allow the generation of specific community-level moral norms regulating economic activity. In effect, the contractors in the *macrocontract* will adopt a principle allowing the existence of community-specific *microcontracts* that serve to reduce the moral opaqueness left by the bounded nature of moral rationality. Thus, the term *microcontracts* represents agreement or shared understandings about the moral norms relevant to specific economic interactions. Moreover, we may call the freedom represented by the ability to endorse microsocial contracts *moral free space.* Thus, by allowing communities or other groups to define moral norms for themselves, the macrocontractors are affirming the existence of moral free space. In turn, the first principle of the macrocontract is:

1. Local economic communities may specify ethical norms for their members through microsocial contracts.

By the word *community*, we mean a self-defined, self-circumscribed group of people who interact in the context of shared tasks, values, or goals and who are capable of establishing norms of ethical behavior for themselves.

Consent and Exit

Choice entails freedom, and freedom in a community entails the right to leave or exit the community. Choice also entails knowledge, for surely the person who chooses in ignorance cannot be said to choose meaningfully. "Illusions," as the saying goes, "are not liberties." Hence, because they are rational, macrosocial contract participants will recognize that because people are entitled to be parties to microsocial contracts in specific communities, they must be entitled to exit from those communities, and further that their consent to the microsocial contract is binding only when it is informed. This, in turn, constitutes the second principle of the macrosocial contract, namely:

2. Norm-specifying microsocial contracts must be grounded in informed consent buttressed by a right of exit.

To illustrate: the right of a labor union or bar association to define ethical principles would, in light of Principle 2, be dependent upon the right of each individual member to quit the union or to resign from the bar association.

Consent need not be expressed. Often, engaging in a practice is sufficient to imply consent, as when a person who engages in an auction thereby commits herself or himself to abiding by the rules of the auction. Consider, again, the issue of compensating employees with nonmonetary benefits. Suppose a manager living in a Third World country is employed by a paternalistic company that provides housing and other personal benefits in lieu of a portion of salary, but which allows employees little choice regarding the kind of housing and benefits offered. The manager, in turn, is required to act in accordance with this practice of paternalism whether he or she personally approves or disapproves. The manager has signaled consent, according to the present theory, through failure to leave the company and seek alternative employment. The manager may, of course, speak out against the ethics of the practice but so long as he or she fails to exercise the right of exit, he or she is bound ethically to live by the standards in place.[5]

Coercion invalidates implied consent. An employee subject to indentured servitude or commercial slavery lacks freedom and, hence, cannot be inferred to have "consented" to existing norms. Even though coercive restraint of the right of exit is common in political contexts (e.g., in Nazi Germany or in pre-Peristroika Soviet Union), it is relatively uncommon in commerce. Instances such as the infamous porcelain factories of Germany in the 19th century (Bok, 1983:138–150), the company towns of coal miners in West Virginia (immortalized in Tennessee Ernie Ford's song, "Sixteen Tons" in the refrain, "I owe my soul to the company store"), or the modern brick factories of Pakistan, are increasingly rare. Hard-to-classify cases include those in which physical coercion is not at issue, but in which moral agents nonetheless appear to have no choice. Can poor employees living in areas of extremely high unemployment, with no alternate sources of work or food, be said to have "consented" to the terms of their employment through their failure to exit (Nickel, 1987)? Could, for example, a subsistence-level employee in the Third World—where unemployment averages 40 percent—be said to have "consented" to a highly paternalistic compensation system through his or her refusal to exit? We note, without attempting to resolve, this difficult issue.

Authentic Norms

When Principle 2 has been fully satisfied, that is to say, when a microcontract for a given community has been grounded in informed consent and buttressed by the right to exit, then we shall call its norms *authentic*. Again, the term *communities* includes firms, departments within firms, informal subgroups within departments, national economic organizations, international economic organizations, professional associations, industries, and so on.

Determining when a business community in fact subscribes to a particular norm is a difficult task. Drawing on related work concerning conventions and norms (Lewis, 1969; Pettit, 1990), we suggest the following empirical rules of thumb for identifying authentic norms in particular communities:

A norm (N) constitutes an authentic ethical norm for recurrent situation (S) for members of community (C) if and only if:

1. Compliance with N in S is approved by most members of C.
2. Deviance from N in S is disapproved by most members of C.
3. A substantial percentage (well over 50%) of members of C when encountering S, act in compliance with N.

The existence of authentic ethical norms can be determined by empirical tests of ethical attitudes and behaviors in particular communities. It also sometimes can be confirmed by amassing a significant amount of indirect empirical evidence. The use of empirical research in identifying authentic norms is discussed in detail in the final section of this article entitled "Implications for Research."

Legitimacy and Hypernorms

Yet authenticity, although extremely important, lacks moral authority. Were macrocontractors to end their process after formulating these two principles, they would have established a contract endorsing moral free space but lacking any limits. The theory would be reduced to cone capable of countenancing any norm affirmed by a group of economic actors. If the securities industry wished to define norms of acceptable communication so that gross puffery, lies, and broken promises were acceptable, no exogenous moral complaints would be relevant. If the association of professional architects wished to declare unethical any attempt by a rival architecture firm to woo a customer away from a competing firm (something actually attempted years ago), then no external observer could cry "foul." A view limited to these two principles would be a version of what philosophers call *cultural relativism*, or in other words, the view that all ethics is reduced to cultural tastes (Brandt, 1983:40–43). In business, such relativism would endorse a confusing and corrupt array of incommensurate moral systems and principles. As noted previously, our definition of moral rationality rules out such relativism. Belief in *moral rationality* presumes minimal objectivity and, in turn, rules out thoroughgoing moral incommensurability among communities. This, as we noted, is not a controversial definition, but it is in step with the conclusions of virtually every past and present moral theorist. The point is simply that moral free space cannot be unlimited: Macrocontractors will not wish to authorize a moral free-for-all at the microlevel.

The question, then, becomes what principle, if any, macrocontractors would consent to as limiting the "free space" of microcontractors' deliberations? We may presume that whatever limits the microcontractors wish to impose would need to be limits that were not *microcommunity relative*. That is to say, they would need to be limits that did not depend upon a particular community's endorsement but applied, rather, to *all* communities. Using the philosopher Charles Taylor's (1989) expression, they would need to be analogous to *hypergoods*, or goods sufficiently fundamental to serve as a source of evaluation and criticism of community-generated norms. Drawing on Taylor's basic concept, let us call the principles that would limit the moral free space of microcontractors *hypernorms*.

Hypernorms, by definition, entail principles so fundamental to human existence that they serve as a guide in evaluating lower level moral norms. As such, we would expect them to be reflected in a convergence of religious, philosophical, and cultural beliefs, and, indeed, such convergence is a handy clue to use in attempting to specify hypernorms. Substantial evidence from a variety of perspectives and sources would be required to establish a hypernorm. We would caution that particular philosophies or evidence of widespread practices or attitudes cannot be projected, ipso facto, into hypernorms. The moral philosophy of the Marquis de Sade or the broad acceptance of slavery in the ancient world are cases in point.

The search for hypernorms is basically a search to validate statements such as Taylor's (1989:64) that "many accept as their highest good . . . a notion of universal justice and/or benevolence," and Walzer's (1992:9) that "perhaps the end product of this effort will be a set of standards to which all societies can be held—negative injunctions, most likely, rules against murder, deceit, torture, oppression and tyranny." Hypernorms do not settle the question of whether Utilitarianism, Kantian Deontology, or Aristotelian Eudiamonism is the best theory, but rather provide room for and presume support for any or all acceptable theories of morality.

Hence, for example, contractors would not permit microsocial contracts, even when produced under conditions of unanimous consent, that condoned murder as a method of enforcing contracts, nor would they tolerate subjecting employees to physical coercion. This constitutes the third principle to which macrocontractors would agree, namely:

3. In order to be obligatory, a microsocial contract norm must be compatible with hypernorms.

Practically speaking, how are people to isolate and identify hypernorms? We do not take a position concerning whether hypernorms have a purely rational basis, as Kant argued (Kant, 1788/1956), or a partly empirical and historical basis, as Hegel argued (Hegel, 1807/1977), nor do we think resolving such a venerable and fundamental epistemological question is necessary to the process of identifying hypernorms. We propose to use the existence of the convergence of religious, cultural, and philosophical beliefs around certain core principles merely as a *clue* to the identification of hypernorms. For even if hypernorms could be certified solely through the light of reason, we should expect to encounter patterns of the acceptance of hypernorms among people around the world. Hence, patterns of religious, cultural, and philosophical belief can serve as a clue, even if not as total validation, for the identification of hypernorms.

Interestingly enough, a consensus appears to be growing among scholars that such a convergence exists. Anthropologists, political scientists, and philosophers continue to articulate principles of global relevance. Even though they speak with something less than a univocal voice, their concepts reflect a broad commonality of opinion. Clyde Kluckhorn, anthropologist, identified a uniformity of needs and psychic mechanisms among all humans (1955:673). Political scientist Terry Nardin identified a core list of moral notions undergirding international law, including:

legal equality among states, the right to national self-defense, the duties to observe treaties and to respect human rights, the concepts of state sovereignty and nonintervention, and the duty to cooperate in the peaceful settlement of disputes (1983:233). International theorist Ethan Nadelmann identified specific activities that are globally proscribed, among which are "piracy, slavery, trafficking in slaves, counterfeiting of national currencies, hijacking of aircraft, trafficking in women and children for purposes of prostitution, and trafficking in controlled psychoactive substances" (1990:479). Business theorist William Frederick identified a series of *normative corporate guidelines* that emerged from a careful analysis of six intergovernmental compacts (including e.g., the "OECD Guidelines for Multinational Enterprises," the "Helsinki Final Act," and the "ILO Tripartite Declaration of Principles Concerning Multinational Enterprises and Social Policy"). In this synthesis of international corporate norms, Frederick develops a wide array of principles, including:

- MNCs should adopt adequate health and safety standards for employees and grant them the right to know about job-related health hazards.
- MNCs should respect the rights of all persons to life, liberty, security of person, and privacy.
- MNCs should control specific operations that contribute to pollution of air, water, and soils. (Frederick, 1991:166–167)

Lee Preston and Duane Windsor (1991) have identified these and other emerging sets of global norms and subsumed them all under the label of international public policy. In Japan, the Institute of Moralogy has sought to define transcultural morality in the context of five universally applicable principles. These are: self-renunciation, realization of benevolence, precedence of duty over personal rights, respect for ortholinons (benefactors who contributed to the development and happiness of humankind), and enlightenment/salvation. Other groups, such as the

United Nations Commission on Transnational Corporations and the International Organization of Securities Commissions, have engaged in quests to define key principles of ethical behavior in business which transcend the biases of localized perspectives.[6]

The best accepted and most widely promulgated candidates for universal norms today are those cast in the language of rights. Many theorists treat rights as hypernorms. Henry Shue, in his book, *Basic Rights*, articulated a list of four basic rights, including the right to subsistence and the freedom of physical movement, security, and political participation. For Shue, a basic right is one so important that its deprivation, "is one standard threat to rights generally" (Shue, 1980:34). Donaldson (1989:65–94) argued that on the basis of three accepted rights-generating criteria a list of 10 fundamental international rights can be construed.[7] In England, the international political theorist, R.J. Vincent, argued persuasively that a single cosmopolitan culture is emerging worldwide "which is spread across all indigenous cultures, and which carries to each of them what are, in some at least geographical sense, global human rights" (Vincent, 1986:50). Perhaps the best known international rights document is the Universal Declaration of Human Rights (1948). Endorsed by virtually every nation in the world, this document specifies over 20 principles that secure rights for all nations. We agree with Walzer (1992:9) that although a "moral equivalent of Esperanto is probably impossible," the vocabulary of rights "is not a bad way of talking about injuries and wrongs that no one should have to endure." The idiom may vary when the concepts are expressed in the terminology of duty-oriented philosophies (as much of Eastern philosophy is), but the basic ideas remain the same (Tomasi, 1991).

The task of identifying and interpreting a comprehensive list of hypernorms is immense and falls well beyond the scope of this article. Furthermore, the task is an open-ended one because no criterion exists for determining when a proposed list of hyper-norms is complete. In fact, it seems quite plausible that our understanding of hyper-norms can change over time so that any list will continuously evolve. For present purposes we assume only that some hypernorms exist and that an initial list of hypernorms should include, at a minimum, the following two concepts:

> Core human rights, including those to personal freedom, physical security and well-being, political participation, informed consent, the ownership of property, the right to subsistence; and
> The obligation to respect the dignity of each human person[8].

To understand how even an authentic norm (i.e., one passing Principles 1 and 2) could fail to be obligatory because it failed Principle 3 (i.e., the hypernorm test) consider again gift giving in business. It is well known that ethical custom varies widely from culture to culture on the propriety of gifts (Lane & Simpson, 1984:35–42). In some cultures, business gift giving is mandatory; in others it is routinely condemned. Integrative social contracts theory stops short of requiring that all cultures establish the same ethical norms regarding gift giving: Macrocontractors agree that cultures may define the limits on such practices for themselves. But, again, they may do so only up to a point, because at some point the practice will come in conflict with norms valid in all business contexts (i.e., hypernorms). To take an extreme case, imagine a business culture in a mature democratic society that condoned the systemic practice of making judgment-warping gifts to elected government officials. Imagine, in other words, a business culture systematically condoning the kind of bribe represented by Lockheed's $13 million payment to Japanese Prime Minister Tanaka in the 1970s. Such a bribe, representing a distortion of democratic process and the undermining of the trust of a publicly elected official, can be seen to violate the fundamental right to political participa-

tion (Donaldson, 1989:88–89) and, hence, to fail the hypernorm test. A business community, whether industry centered, nation centered, or corporation centered, endorsing such a practice, would be endorsing an authentic but nonobligatory norm.

Priority Rules

Finally, world-level rational contractors, recognizing both their strongly bounded rationality and the frequency of conflicts occurring among norms in various economic communities, would want a means to arbitrate and resolve such conflicts. Sometimes conflicts will be easy to resolve because the norm that conflicts with one's own community norm will also conflict with a hypernorm. For example, if a German company were asked by Iraq to sell equipment for the production of biological weapons, the conflict between its abhorrence of biological weapons and Iraq's tolerance of them is easily resolved if one believes that biological weapons violate a hypernorm proscribing the indiscriminate killing of the innocent. At other times the resolution will be more difficult, especially in instances where conflict occurs between two legitimate norms emanating from two separate communities. For example, in Jamshedpur, India, the Tata Steel Company has for years guaranteed employees that it will provide a job at the Tata Company to at least one of the employee's children. This practice is extremely popular among Tata workers, as it also is among members of the Jamshedpur business community. The practice does not obviously conflict with any hypernorm; nonetheless, it would be regarded as nepotistic in many Western countries. Would it be permissible, then, for a Western company with a subsidiary in Jamshedpur to replicate the job guarantees of the Tata company?

Clearly, the design of any priority rules for arbitrating such conflicts must reflect and be consistent with the terms of the macrosocial contract. The macrocontract emphasizes the freedom of individual communities to develop ethical norms. For this reason, attention should be given to norms that do not adversely have an impact on the freedom of other economic communities to create and support their own norms. In contrast, when norms have an impact solely within their community of origin (i.e., when they have no impact on outsiders) they should, celeris paribus, be allowed to stand, even in instances where they are inconsistent with the norms of other communities. If the rules of a pubic auction are different in New Zealand from Lithuania, the Lithuanian manager should follow New Zealand auction norms so long as doing so has consequences entirely confined to New Zealand.

Sometimes economic communities anticipate the possibility of conflict with the norms of other communities and in response develop formal preference rules for their members to follow in cross-cultural transactions. The Foreign Corrupt Practices Act (FCPA) in the United States is an example. Assuming that the FCPA constitutes an authentic norm for the United States (a proposition that some people would challenge), it thereby represents a local community-based standard for resolving conflicts between U.S. norms and another country's norms of bribery But suppose that another country has a local norm of preference inconsistent with the principles of the FCPA. In this circumstance, there is a need for an overarching set of priority rules to determine which local preference rule should dominate in a cross-cultural transaction.

Thus, the fourth and final principle of the macrosocial contract is as follows:

4. In case of conflicts among norms satisfying Principles 1–3, priority must be established through the application of rules consistent with the spirit and letter of the macrosocial contract.

Although many alternatives could be followed in developing priority rules (Dunfee, 1991:43–44), the following six principles seem consistent with the spirit and letter of the macrosocial contract. They are meant not as theoretically precise principles but as rules of thumb.

1. Transactions solely within a single community, which do not have significant adverse effects on other humans or communities, should be governed by the host community's norms.
2. Community norms indicating a preference for how conflict-of-norms situations should be resolved should be applied, so long as they do not have significant adverse effects on other humans or communities.
3. The more extensive or more global the community which is the source of the norm, the greater the priority which should be given to the norm.
4. Norms essential to the maintenance of the economic environment in which the transaction occurs should have priority over norms potentially damaging to that environment.
5. Where multiple conflicting norms are involved, patterns of consistency among the alternative norms provide a basis for prioritization.
6. Well-defined norms should ordinarily have priority over more general, less precise norms.

For purposes of illustration, let us return to the hypothetical case of a Western company's subsidiary in India considering adopting the practice of guaranteeing employment for the children of existing workers. In this case, some of the priority rules are inappropriate. Rules 2, 4, and 6, which speak to the issues of existing local community preference rules, the maintenance of the economic environment, and the degree of precision of definition in the norm, have no direct relevance to the issue. On the other hand, Rules 1, 3, and 5 have some, albeit limited, relevance. In particular, Rules 3 and 5 may appear to speak against following the Indian practice insofar as the norms against nepotism seem both more broadly accepted and more consistent with other norms (such as the norm favoring qualifications as a decisive criterion in hiring). However, if two key points were established, these rules lose their relevance and another (Rule 1) would be invoked. Suppose, for example, it could be shown that the practice of promising employment is consistent with other widely held moral beliefs. Suppose it were demonstrated that the very principle supporting the concept of private property—which allows, among other things, the son of a rich property owner to benefit by receiving a large money inheritance, or even a job, from his parent—is the same principle at stake when an employee receives (as a part of his compensation) the guarantee of a job for his child. Suppose also that it could be shown that virtually no impact will occur for persons outside the Jamshedpur economic community (such as for better qualified potential job applicants) and that, in turn, priority Rule 1 applied. If such points were established, the priority rules would endorse the permissibility of the practice for the Western company's subsidiary in India.

As the example makes evident, the six priority rules have a *celeris paribus* condition and must be weighed and applied in combination. The proposed priority rules find significant support in the jurisprudence of conflicts of law principles. As is true of the process of statutory interpretation, the application of the priority rules should eschew a precise hierarchy for the six rules and, instead, emphasize factors such as the fit of the particular ethical decision with one or two of the principles or with a convergence of the rules toward a particular result.

To summarize, the general principles that contractors, aware of the strongly bounded nature of moral rationality in economic affairs, would choose and which therefore define the *macrosocial contract* of economic morality, are:

1. Local economic communities may specify ethical norms for their members through microsocial contracts.
2. Norm-specifying microsocial contracts must be grounded in informed consent buttressed by a right of exit.
3. In order to be obligatory, a microsocial contract norm must be compatible with hypernorms.

4. In case of conflicts among norms satisfying Principles 1–3, priority must be established through the application of rules consistent with the spirit and letter of the macrosocial contract. (See also Donaldson & Dunfee, 1993.)

When a norm has been generated by a community in accordance with Principles 1 and 2 (thereby constituting an authentic norm) and then satisfies the requirements of Principle 3, we refer to it as a legitimate norm. Subject to the application of the priority rules, legitimate norms are morally binding for members of the norm-generating community.

IMPLICATIONS FOR RESEARCH

ISCT is replete with empirical and theoretical research implications. Initially, there is the core question of whether the assumptions of the macrosocial contract are consistent with current social belief and practice. Even though ISCT is offered as purely a normative theory, and therefore does not require descriptive validation, a variety of interesting research questions exists concerning its acceptance in the real world.

ISCT is dependent upon background empirical findings to help it render specific normative judgments about particular cases. For example, the attitudinal and behavioral elements of the authenticity test must be empirically established. Empirical work also may be necessary to apply the priority rules in cases involving clashing authentic norms. In addition, there are a host of background issues raised by ISCT, including the precise nature and source of hypernorms, how these norms may be identified with precision, whether these norms may evolve or instead are unchanging, whether the priority rules should be themselves prioritized, and so on.

In this section we briefly highlight the research implications of ISCT and note how it provides a lens through which existing empirical research can be evaluated for its normative implications ISCT represents an opportunity for empirical researchers to provide business ethics decision making with much needed substance and context. The contractarian foundation of ISCT provides a theoretical mortar for normative structures for business ethics built upon the bricks and stones put in place by empiricist artisans. In order to provide normative guidance in this context, empirical research must be consistent with the assumptions and definitions of ISCT.[9]

A. Research Issues Concerning the Descriptive Validity of ISCT

ISCT is presented as a normative theory. It is responsive to the ultimate questions: "By what criterion?" or "Says who?" in judging whether a given action is right or wrong. ISCT is not intended to represent the sole source of ethical obligation for societies generally, or even for business managers in all contexts. Instead, ISCT is offered as a useful, pragmatic, communitarian-based theoretical framework setting forth a process for making certain normative judgments in business ethics.

As a normative theory, ISCT is not set forth as necessarily descriptive of current reality. However, some researchers may wish to raise the issue of whether, and to what extent, people act in accordance with the procedural norms of ISCT.[10] Doing so would involve ascertaining the extent to which individuals think that a macrosocial contract exists along the general lines suggested by ISCT and the extent to which they recognize and act upon community-based contractual/promissory obligations in their normative judgments in business.

The extent of acceptance of ISCT could be tested in part by adapting from the eight-item multidimensional scale proposed by Reidenbach and Robin (1990) as a means for measuring the ethical decision-making process of individuals. Two of the items in the scale are explicitly contractual: violate/does not violate an unspoken promise, violates/does not violate an unwritten contract. Tot he extent that these factors help explain beliefs among members of a recognized community concerning whether practices are ethical, they support the claims of ISCT. Interestingly,

in their test of the scale, Reidenbach and Robin retained the contractarian factors while purging references to utilitarianism and egoism. They explained this by noting that "in debriefing analyses it was obvious that respondents had a difficult time in understanding and applying the concepts inherent in utilitarian thinking" (1990:647). If individuals intuitively understand that they confront obligatory, yet implicit contractual obligations as a result of membership in communities, then there is some support for the acceptance of ISCT. This is particularly the case if they find these concepts more meaningful and useful than utilitarianism.

B. Research Issues Pertaining to the Empirical Dimensions of ISCT

The primary intersection between ISCT as a framework for making normative judgments and empirical research in business ethics concerns the identification and specification of ethical norms at the community level, designated as *authentic* norms. The claim that community ethical norms can be identified with some precision is consistent with similar claims in reference to business norms more generally (Thomas & Soldow, 1988). Empirical research will also be required to apply the priority rules in certain contexts. Priority-rule issues such as whether or not particular norms may have significant adverse effects on other humans or communities or may be damaging to a particular transaction environment will often require empirical analysis. Finally, empirical research may constitute one method for parsing out the parameters of the limiting hypernorms of ISCT.

B1. Definition of an ISCT-Relevant Community

A key issue under ISCT is delineation of the boundaries of a community in which a particular norm may be considered obligatory. ISCT defines *community as a self-defined, self-circumscribed group of people who interact in the context of shared tasks, values, or goals and who are capable of establishing norms of ethical behav-*

ior for themselves. Importantly, a particular business practice may have an impact on multiple communities, so that the process of judging the rightness/wrongness of the practice may require identification of several community-based norms. The need to consider the norms of several discrete communities is particularly likely in evaluating global business practices.

Practically, how are the boundaries of communities to be determined? Reference to formal groupings or structures such as corporations, departments, trade associations, generally recognized business functions, and professional bodies may serve as a starting point for identifying relevant communities. Thus, employees of a specific drug company, corporate attorney, attorneys generally, and consumers of dialysis equipment may be relevant communities in determining whether it is appropriate to fire a corporate attorney who disclosed information to government officials about defective dialysis equipment being sold by the company.[11] Identification of a community may be supported by a group-awareness test whereby members of the putative community recognize their association with the group and view it as a source of obligatory ethical norms. Once the rough boundaries of the community(ies) are determined, then standard sampling techniques can be employed to obtain ISCT-relevant information representative of the population of the community as a whole.

Convenience samples, particularly those using students, may fail to provide an adequate context for obtaining representative attitudes and behaviors of ISCT-relevant communities. Students may not identify with the communities to which their attitudes are being projected, and, most important, they may lack knowledge concerning the extant norms in those communities. Thus, student samples would appear to have limited value in the context of ISCT, relevant only to issues within the community of students (e.g., cheating) (McCabe, Dukerich & Dutton, 1991) or to the circumstance, probably quite

limited, in which their views may be projected fairly as representative of business or the nation as a whole, in a context in which such broadly defined communities may be considered relevant. Similarly, where norms vary across industries, a sample taken of marketing managers generally may not provide adequate insights regarding the substance of professional norms, such as those pertaining to whether or not an agent should disclose that his or her commission rate varies among the supplies she or he can recommend. Marketing managers working for travel agencies may be responding to quite different community norms concerning commission disclosures than those working for financial consulting firms. Large samples of salespeople, which cross many different business communities, may produce opaque outcomes concerning projected behaviors or normative judgments due to the diversity of context which the respondents bring to otherwise very carefully crafted projective vignettes (Robertson & Anderson, In press).

The selection of the community(ies) most relevant to a particular normative judgment is critically important and will influence the types of authentic norms that are recognized. For example, it may be asserted that "bribery is endemic to nation X." However, it may turn out that accepting bribes is authentic only to a small group of bribe-taking government officials within nation X, whereas the larger business and social communities of nation X reject the practice. This would explain why bribery is generally conducted in secrecy and would render inappropriate the claim that bribery is endemic to nation X.[12] The search for relevant communities required in applying ISCT should often produce a more accurate understanding of the scope of actual practice and, as a consequence, result in fairer ethical judgments.

B2. Identifying ISCT-Relevant Ethical Attitudes

Authentic norms are evidenced in part by the uncoerced, genuine attitudes of the community membership concerning the rightness/wrongness of a particular standard of behavior. The focus of the attitudinal research in ISCT is on individuals' perceptions concerning the existence of ethically appropriate and obligatory norms or rules in their communities.

The authenticity test under ISCT concerns attitudes about norms of appropriate behavior in the community. This requirement is distinct from the projected behaviors of the community members, or their estimates of existing behavior patterns in the community. Assumptions concerning extant behavior are not sufficient because the existing behaviors may be viewed as neutral or even as immoral by members of the community and therefore could not serve as the basis for authentic ethical norms.

Care must be used in measuring ISCT-relevant attitudes. In stressing the assumption of bounded moral rationality in business affairs, we emphasize that individuals may only be capable of knowing their genuine moral preferences when confronted with the full environment of a decision. Generic values-based approaches, or broad-based non-contextual inquiries (e.g., asking respondents whether they agree that "a corporation's primary responsibility is to stockholders" [Monippallil, Kathawala, Hattwick, Wall, & Shin, 1990]) would have limited value under ISCT. In contrast, research based on detailed, context-rich scenarios or vignettes requiring subjects to respond to precisely delineated dilemmas is more consistent with the requirements of ISCT. (See, e.g., Akaah & Riordan, 1989, and Norris & Gifford, 1988). If they have properly defined communities and focused questions of belief, researchers may be able to avoid the confounding results often obtained in prior empirical work.[13]

B3. Identifying ISCT-Relevant Ethical Behaviors

Once it is determined that most members of a given community agree about the rightness/wrongness dimension of a particular norm, it is then necessary to determine whether sufficient compliance exists within the community to constitute the putative norm as authentic. Although studies of actual behaviors would be direct evidence, they are notoriously difficult, particularly in the domain of deviant behavior. It is not surprising, therefore, that the dominant research paradigm to date "proceeds mainly from the cognitive component to *inferred* behavior" (Frederick, 1992:93).

The central question under ISCT is determining actual behaviors of the community members. In many studies, researchers ask respondents to project how they would act in a given contest. These studies that ask respondents to estimate how others behave are valid for ISCT purposes only if they constitute accurate representations of community behaviors. Projected behaviors may be problematic. This is an important dimension of the ISCT foundational assumption of bounded moral rationality. Ethical behavior in business may invoke ardent emotional responses (Jones & Verstegen, 1992), making it difficult for an individual to predict accurately how he or she would respond. As dramatized by Crane's *The Red Badge of Courage*, in ethics as in war, one may never know how one will react until one is on the spot.

The relationship between projected behaviors and actual behaviors is critical for ISCT usage. Any means that is used to infer behavior must be an accurate indicator of actual behaviors. Empirically tested constructs such as Fishbein's and Ajzen's (1975) theory of reasoned action (see Randall, 1989) suggest that there is a close relationship between intention and action and that intention is influenced by attitudes toward the behavior and recognition of subjective norms (Dunfee & Robertson, 1984). Such theories may lead to the establishment of valid proxies of behavior relevant to the test of authenticity under ISCT.

In attempting to ascertain community behaviors through surveys based upon self-reporting, the long-standing, thorny problem of respondents giving socially desirable answers or acting to be "good" interview subjects must be considered (Fernandes & Randall, 1992).[14] When deviant behaviors are at issue, individuals may be suspicious of claims of confidentiality or nontraceability and they may, for a variety of reasons, fail to accurately report their own behaviors. Methodologies such as the randomized response technique have been advocated (Dalton & Metzger, 1992) as a means of mitigating bias.[15] Although some research has focused on the reasons given by managers in support of projected behaviors, the forms of reasoning used within communities for the adoption of norms do not directly influence the determination of authentic norms under ISCT. Communities are entitled to adopt their own processes for the generation of norms; they are not limited to particular "correct" forms of reasoning. The reasoning used may be important in one sense external to the normative judgment process of ISCT. If one seeks to bring about changes in norms with a community, then knowledge about the reasoning favored with a community is critical. ISCT recognizes that norms will constantly change at the community level and that members will exercise voice and exit in response to the evolution of norms.

B4. Priority Rules, Hypernorms, and International Dimensions of ISCT

In cases where multiple community norms in opposition to each other survive the hypernorm test, the process of normative judgment will require application of the priority rules. This is likely to be a common occurrence in the normative judgment process of ISCT. The priority rules are a critical feature of ISCT. Several of the priority rules require estimates of the impact of contemplated actions which may require empirical analysis. Aspects of the priority rules requiring empirical elaboration include whether or not a questioned transaction may have an impact outside of the community in which the action occurs (Rules 1 and 2) and whether a norm is essen-

tial to the maintenance of the transaction environment, or to the contrary, is likely to be damaging to that environment. In addition, the suggested priority rules require determination of the existence of community norms indicating local preferences for resolving priority (Rule 2). Even though these often may be reflected in law or formal codes, as is the case of the example of the Foreign Corrupt Practices Act, they also may be found in more informal norms.

As explained earlier, we would expect genuine hypernorms to be reflected at the convergence of global beliefs and, as such, observable indirectly through empirical research. Skeptics may note the failure of the U.N. Commission on Transnational Corporations to obtain a consensus concerning a U.N.-sponsored code of behavior and the limited impact of The Guidelines for Multinational Enterprises adopted by the OECD countries in 1976. Nonetheless, as we documented previously, a substantial search is under way to identify universal norms. Empirical research can contribute to this search by focusing on representative samples of international communities and seeking to identify areas of convergence of belief concerning universal standards so fundamental to humanity that they cannot be abrogated by local communities. Hypernorms may be either negative or affirmative in nature. Many hypernorms would be negative prohibitions, similar in nature to the global prohibition regimes identified by Nadelmann (1990), which prohibit or restrict certain practices. Others would impose affirmative obligations either to act in a certain manner (taking certain active steps to protect human health or protect the physical environment) or would impose duties upon those undertaking certain activities (drug manufacturers must restrict sales to those not competent to use the product safely).

We stress the particular relevance of ISCT for global business ethics. Research comparing business practices among different countries can provide a basis for the application of

ISCT by identifying authentic norms for different international communities. Once that is done accurately, the framework of ISCT can be used to sort out, through the application of priority rules and hypernorms, the relative importance of the various norms in a particular boundary-spanning transaction.

C. Implication for Theoretical Research Extending ISCT

The basic summary of ISCT still leaves many questions to be resolved at the theoretical level. For example, the concept of hypernorms encompasses many as yet unresolved issues. We expect that a great deal of work will be required to develop a prima facie list of hypernorms capable of serving as the basis for extended theoretical scrutiny. Implicit within this question is the issue of selection of the best methodologies for identifying hypernorms. Is it sufficient as a first step to look for convergence among the reports of scholars seeking convergence? Are global surveys of values, attitudes, and beliefs appropriate for providing clues as to the nature of specific hypernorms? If so, are they scientifically feasible? If convergence can serve as a clue to the nature of hypernorms, then how much convergence should be required?

Again, we explicitly leave open the question of the epistemological nature of hypernorms. Are they primarily rational, or instead empirical, or some hybrid of the two? Can they evolve over time, or are they set in some natural law sense?

Similar questions may be raised concerning other aspects of ISCT. Should the priority rules themselves be prioritized, or is it better to leave them to a more open-ended process of application? We argue that they all derive from the assumptions of the macrosocial contract. But are those arguments sufficient? Are there additional priority rules that should be added to the list?

How relativistic is ISCT? In our judgment, commentators tend to overemphasize the role of moral free space in characterizing ISCT. As argued elsewhere, the seemingly relativistic nature of this moral free space is limited in three distinct ways by the terms of the macrosocial contract: first,through a requirement of consent at the level of the microsocial contracts; second, through the application of independently authoritative *hypernorms*; and, third, through the operation of a st of priority rules designed to determine which norms generated by communities become obligatory in cases of directly conflicting norms.

Finally, there are many questions concerning how these concepts might be translated for managers. Can, for example, the foundational assumptions and implications of ISCT be reduced to a meaningful set of rule-of-thumb principles capable of providing realistic guidance for managers? Ultimately, what are the most effective ways of translating these ideas for managers?

An enormous research agenda, both empirical and theoretical, is generated by the basic conceptual framework of integrative social contracts theory.

CONCLUSION

The tension between empirically based and normatively based methods currently frustrating business ethics research will persist.[16] Nonetheless, in this article we hope we have shown that an ISCT is capable of providing a schema that allows both normative and empirical factors to harmonize. The theory we have defended does not presume to eradicate differences between the "is" and the "ought." It also does not presume to pull normative rabbits from empirical hats and to derive prescriptive from description. Yet it establishes a means for displaying the ethical relevance of existing norms in industries, corporations, and other economic communities, even as it limits the acceptable range of such norms. It attempts to reach beyond the generality of Kantian Deontology and Utilitarianism to allow a more detailed normative assessment of particular ethical problems in economic life—in a world of transactions that we have shown to be peculiarly susceptible to bounded moral rationality. Finally, by revealing the normative relevance of existing cultural and economic norms, the theory identifies pockets of inadequacy in existing empirical business ethics research. In this way, as we previously explained, the theory entails an agenda for empirical research. It is an agenda that authorizes the search for authentic ethical norms in industries, corporations, alliances, and regional economic systems. It is an agenda that advocates much closer scrutiny of existing ethical beliefs and practices in institutions as dissimilar as the EC, the Sony Corporation, the international rubber market, and Muslim banking. Notably, it is an agenda that emphasizes more than any other contemporary theory the ethical import of empirical research.

For this reason, ISCT will no doubt provoke cries of "ethical relativism" from some quarters, but, as we have taken pains to explain, the theory not only sanctions moral free space for economic communities, it also establishes unequivocal boundaries on free space. The claim that moral free space, though limited, nonetheless exists is unremarkable. The belief that ethical problems in business can be resolved entirely without appeal to the shared convictions of living people has never been popular among anyone except modern ethical theoreticians.

NOTES

1. We use the term *normative* in the philosophic sense; it is a prescriptive rather than descriptive term. It provides *guidance* about actions or policies instead of describing them. Yet, unlike the sense of the word sometimes used in management literature, our use of the term excludes prescriptive but merely instrumental uses. The instrumental sense of "normative" is hypothetical; it says, in effect, "If you want to achieve X, then do Y." For example, "If you want lower per-unit cost, expand market share." In contrast, the philosophical sense is not hypothetical but "categorical"; it says, in effect, "Do this because it is the right thing to do." We also contrast our use of the term *normative* from the way it is often used in the social sciences to denote typical or average behavior. For a useful discussion of the philosophical versus social science use of the term normative, see Waterman, 1988.

2. Even though none of these frameworks attempts to develop an explicitly normative or contractarian perspective.[3] Jones's framework has some important parallels with the approach introduced in this article. Jones's emphasis (1991) on the context of ethical decision making and his stressing that "human beings may respond differentially to moral issues in a way that is systematically related to characteristics of the issue itself" (1991:372) is consistent with our own claim that normative and empirical factors can influence one another, and his incorporation of the factor of social consensus with its emphasis on implied social agreement is implicitly contractarian.

3. One exception is Reidenbach and Robin (1990), whose multidimensional scale for evaluating perceptions of ethical content incorporates two contractarian factors recognizing unspoken promises and unwritten agreements.

4. The norms of behavior evolving out of the marketplace are likely to track preferred economic factors. Thus, societies preferring lowest cost outcomes may place the ethical burden of disclosure on the lowest cost discloser. Societies preferring producer welfare to consumer welfare may prefer to have consumers always incur the obligations of disclosure.

5. We use an unsettled issue to emphasize our point. A noncontentious example would be that of a racially prejudiced manager who personally objects to the norm of equal opportunity followed by the firm, but who, nevertheless, is ethically bound to follow the norm.

6. The basis for attributing universal responsibilities to multinational corporations varies. For example, Manuel Velasquez (1992) has argued that even the rational pursuit of its self-interest by a multinational corporation entails accepting specific moral responsibilities.

7. These rights are to freedom of physical movement, ownership of property, freedom from torture, a fair trial, nondiscriminatory treatment (i.e., freedom from discrimination on the basis of such characteristics as race or sex), physical security, freedom of speech and association, minimal education, political participation, and subsistence (Donaldson, 1989:81).

8. There is substantial support for this initial list of hypernorms. For example, the proposed text of the draft United Nations Code of Conduct of Transnational Corporations provides in paragraph 14 that "Transnational corporations shall respect human rights and fundamental freedoms in the countries in which they operate. In their social and industrial relations, transnational corporations shall not discriminate on the basis of race, color, sex, religion . . ." (United Nations, 1990).

9. There is an enormous published literature of empirical work in business ethics. For the most comprehensive summaries and critiques of this extensive body of empirical literature, see Randall and Gibson (1990), Tsalikis and Fritzsche (1989), and Weber (1992). The quality of the research has been subjected to considerable criticism particularly due to recurring failure to employ a theoretical foundation or to use testable hypotheses.

10. Some empirical testing of general ethical theories has already been initiated. For example, Greenberg and Bies (1992) review some of the core assumptions of utilitarianism against the existing empirical literature on organizational justice.

11. See *Bala* v. *Gambro*, 584 N.E. 2d., 104(III. Sup. Ct. 1991).

12. In this case of conflicting norms, assuming that none of the norms violate hypernorms, the ultimate normative judgment would depend on the operation of the priority rules. Consider a case where a Dutch corporation is asked to pay a bribe to government official in Indonesia. Assume that "bribe taking is o.k." is an authentic norm among the Indonesian government officials and that "bribe taking is wrong" is an authentic norm among the broader Indonesian business community and for the Dutch corporation. In such a circumstance, under the priority rules, the norm of "bribe taking is wrong" would dominate, and payment of the bribe would be found to be unethical under ISCT.

13. Hunt, Wood, and Chonko have noted that one somewhat defeatist reaction to the confusing pattern of results has been that "researchers frequently have been encouraged to measure the broad principles underlying ethical values rather than the domain-specific ethical issues" (1989:82).

14. There could even be a related phenomenon, a social norm denial bias, concerning the attitudinal requirement of authentic norms. Subjects might misrepresent their attitude about whether a certain community norm exists because they know their own behavior does not measure up to that standard.

15. Dalton and Metzger (1992) provide examples of the use of unrelated questions in which respondents are asked to flip a coin and then to answer questions truthfully only if the coin is "heads," or to answer truthfully only if their last phone digit is an even number. All others are answer each question "no" or in some other mandatory manner. The results are adjusted statistically for the probability associated with the unrelated question.

16. A special symposium on the possibility of reconciling normative and empirical methodologies, entitled "An Integrated Business Ethics: Multiple Perspectives," was convened at the 1992 Academy of Management Meeting in Las Vegas, Nevada. See also the special issue of the *Business Ethics Quarterly* on "The Empirical Quest for Normative Meaning: Empirical Methodologies for the Study of Business Ethics," Vol. 2, No. 2, April 1992.

REFERENCES

Akaah, I.P., & Riordan, E.A. 1989. Judgments of marketing professionals about ethical issues in marketing research: A replication and extension. *Journal of Marketing Research*, 26:112–120.

Barry, B. 1982. The case for a new international economic order. In J.R. Pennock & J.W. Chapman (Eds.), *Ethics, economics, and the law; Nomos*, vol. 24, New York: New York University Press.

Bok, S. 1983. Trade and corporate secrecy. In *Secrets*: 136–152. New York: Vintage Books.

Bowie, N. 1988. The moral obligations of multinational corporations. In S. Luper-Foy (Ed.), *Problems of international justice*: 97–113. Boulder, CO: Westview Press.

Brandt, R. 1983. Ethical relativism. In T. Donaldson & P. Werhane (Eds.J), *Ethical issues in business* (2nd ed.): 40–46. Englewood Cliffs, NJ: Prentice Hall.

Business Ethics Quarterly. 1992. The empirical quest for normative meaning: Empirical methodologies for the study of business ethics. (Special Issue #1).

Cameron, R. 1989. *A concise economic history of the world*. Oxford, England: Oxford University Press.

Carroll, A.B. 1989. *Business and society: Ethics and stakeholder management*. Cincinnati: South-Western Publishing Company.

Carroll, L. 1983. *Alice's adventures in wonderland*. New York: Knopf

Chandler, A.D. 1977. *The visible hand: The managerial revolution in American business*. Cambridge, MA:Belnap Press.

Cochran, P.L., & Wood, R.A. 1984. Corporate social responsibility and financial performance. *Academy of Management Journal*, 27:42–56.

Dalton, D.R., & Metzger, M.B. 1992. Towards candor, cooperation, and privacy in applied business ethics research: The randomized response technique (RRT). *Business Ethics Quarterly*, 2:207–221.

Donaldson, T. 1982. *Corporations and morality*. Englewood Cliffs, NJ: Prentice Hall. (Korean translation of *Corporations and Morality*, 1985).

Donaldson, T. 1989. *The ethics of international business*. New York: Oxford University Press.

Donaldson, T. 1990. Morally privileged relationships. *Journal of Value Inquiry*, 24:1–15.

Donaldson, T., & Dunfee, T.W. 1993. Integrative social contracts theory: A communitarian conception of economic ethics. *Economics and Philosophy*.

Dunfee, T.W. 1991. Business ethics and extant social contracts. *Business Ethics Quarterly*, 1:23–51.

Dunfee, T.W., & Robertson, D.C. 1984. Work-related ethical attitudes: Impact on business profitability. *Business and Professional Ethics Journal*, 3(2):25–40.

Esposito, J.L. 1988. *Islam: The straight path*. New York: Oxford University Press.

Fernandes, M.F., & Randall, D.M. 1992. The nature of social desirability response effects in ethics research. *Business Ethics Quarterly*, 2:183–195.

Ferrell, O.C., & Gresham, L.G. 1985. A contingency framework for understanding ethical decision making in marketing. *Journal of Marketing*, 49:87–96.

Fishbein, M., & Ajzen, I. 1975. *Belief, attitude, intention: An introduction to theory and research*. Reading, PA: Addison Wesley.

Frederick, W.C. 1991. The moral authority of transnational corporate codes. *Journal of Business Ethics*, 10(30):165–177.

Frederick, W.C. 1992. The empirical quest for normative meaning: Introduction and overview. *Business Ethics Quarterly*, 2:91–98.

Freeman, R.E. 1984. *Strategic management: A stakeholder approach*. Boston: Pitman/Ballinger.

Freeman, R.E., & Gilbert, D.R., Jr. 1988. *Corporate strategy and the search for ethics*. Englewood Cliffs, NJ: Prentice Hall.

French, P. 1979. The corporation as a moral person. *American Philosophical Quarterly*, 16: 207–215.

Fritzsche, D.J., & Becker, H. 1984. Linking management behavior to ethical philosophy—An empirical investigation. *Academy of Management Journal*, 27:166–175.

Gauthier, D. 1986. *Morals by agreement*. Oxford, England: Oxford University Press.

Green, R.M. 1991. When is "everyone's doing it" a moral justification? *Business Ethics Quarterly*, 1:75–93

Greenberg, J., & Bies, R.J. 1992. Establishing the role of empirical studies of organizational justice in philosophical inquiries into business ethics. *Journal of Business Ethics*. 11(5/6): 433–444.

Hegel, G.W.F. 1807/1977. *Phenomenology of spirit*. (A.V. Miller, Trans.). Oxford, England: Clarendon Press.

Hobbes, T. 1651/1946. *Leviathan; or, The matter, forme and power of a commonwealth, ecclesiastical and civil*. (M. Oakeshott, Ed.). Oxford, England: Blackwell.

Hoffman, W.M., Frederick, R., & Petry, E.S., Jr. (Eds.). 1989. *The ethics of organizational transformation*. New York: Quorum Books.

Hosseini, J.C., & Brenner, S.N. 1992. The stakeholder theory of the firm: A methodology to generate value matrix weights. *Business Ethics Quarterly*, 2:99–119.

Hunt, S.D., & Vitell, S. 1986. A general theory of marketing ethics. *Journal of Macromarketing*, 6(1):5–16.

Hunt, S.D., Wood, V. R., & Chonko, L.B. 1989. Corporate ethical values and organizational commitment in marketing. *Journal of Marketing*, 53(3):79–90.

Jones, T., & Verstegen, L.J. 192. *A moral approbation model of ethical decision making in organizations.* Paper presented at the annual meeting of the Society for Socioeconomics, Irvine, CA.

Jones, T.M. 1991. Ethical decision making by individuals in organizations: An issue-contingent model. *Academy of Management Review*, 16: 366–395.

Kant, I. 1788/1956. *Critique of practical reason* (L.W. Beck, Trans.). New York:Library of Liberal Arts.

Kant, I. 1785/1959. *Foundations of the metaphysics of morals.* (L.W. Beck, Trans.). New York: Liberal Arts Press.

Keeley, M. 1988. *A social contract theory of organizations.* Notre Dame, IN: University of Notre Dame Press.

Kluckhorn, C. 1955. Ethical relativity: Sic et non. *Journal of Philosophy*, 52:663–677.

Kollack, P. 1992. *The emergence of markets and networks: An experimental study of uncertainty, commitment, and trust.* Paper presented at the SASE Conference, Irvine, CA.

Kotter, J.P., & Heskett, J.L. 1992. *Corporate culture and performance.* New York: Free Press.

Ladd, J. 1970. Morality and the ideal of rationality in corporate organizations. In T. Donaldson & P. Werhane (Eds.), *Ethical issues in business* (2nd ed.):110–122. Englewood Cliffs, NJ: Prentice Hall.

Lane, H.W., & Simpson, D.G. 1984. Bribery in international business: Whose problem is it? *Journal of Business Ethics*, 3:35–42.

Lewis, D.K. 1969. *Convention.* Cambridge, MA: Harvard University Press.

Locke, J. 1690/1948. *The second treatise of civil government and a letter concerning toleration.* (J.W. Gough, Ed.). Oxford, England: Blackwell.

May, L. 1987. *The morality of groups: Collective responsibility, group-based harm, and corporate rights.* Notre Dame, IN: University of Notre Dame Press.

McCabe, D.L., Dukerich, J.M., & Dutton, J.E. 1991. Context, values and moral dilemmas: Comparing the choices of business and law school students. *Journal of Business Ethics*, 10:951–960.

Meznar, M., Chrisman, J.J., & Carroll, A.B. 1990. Social responsibility and strategic management: Toward an enterprise strategy classification. *Academy of Management Best Papers Proceedings*: 332–336.

Mill, J.S. 1965. *Mill's ethical writings.* (J.B. Schneewind, Ed.). New York: Collier.

Monippallil, M., Kathawala, Y., Hattwick, R., Wall, L., & Shin, B.P. 1990. Business ethics in America: A view from the classroom. *Journal of Behavioral Economics*, 19:125–140.

Moore, G.E. 1903/1951. *Principia ethica.* Cambridge, England: Cambridge University Press.

Moralogy, Institute of. 1987. *An outline of moralogy*, (English, ed.). Kashiwa-Shi, Japan: Institute of Moralogy.

Nadelmann, E.A. 1990. Global prohibition regimes: The evolution of norms in international society. *International Organization*, 44: 479–526.

Nardin, T. 1983. *Law, morality, and the relations of states.* Princeton, NJ: Princeton University Press.

Nickel, J.W. 1974. Classifications by race in compensatory programs. *Ethics*, 84(2): 146–150.

Nickel, J.W. 1987. *Making sense of human rights: Philosophical reflections on the universal declaration of human rights.* Berkeley: University of California Press.

Norris, D.G., & Gifford, J.B. 1988. Retail store managers' and students' perceptions of ethical retain practices: A comparative and longitudinal analysis (1976–1986). *Journal of Business Ethics*, 7:515–524.

Pettit, P. 1990. Virtus normativa: Rational choice perspectives. *Ethics*, 100:725–755.

Plato. 1968. *The republic*: Book I (A. Bloom, Trans.). New York:Basic Books.

Preston, L.E., & Sapienza, H.J. 1990. Stakeholder management and corporate performance. *The Journal of Behavioral Economics*, 19:361–375.

Preston, L.E., & Windsor, D. 1991. *The rules of the game in the global economy: Policy regimes for international business.* Norwell, MA: Kluwer Academic Publishers.

Randall, D.M. 1989. Taking stock: Can the theory of reasoned action explain unethical conduct? *Journal of Business Ethics*, 8:873–882.

Randall, D.M., & Gibson, A.M. 1990. Methodology in business ethics research: A review and critical assessment. *Journal of Business Ethics*, 9:457–471.

Rawls, J. 1971. *A theory of justice*. Cambridge, MA: Harvard University Press.

Reidenbach, R.E., & Robin, D.P. 1990. Toward the development of a multidimensional scale for improving evaluations of business ethics. *Journal of Business Ethics*, 9:639–653.

Robertson, D.C., & Anderson, E. In press. Control system and task environment effects on ethical judgment: An exploratory study of industrial salespeople. *Organization Science*.

Rousseau, J.J. 1762/1959–1969. *Oeuvres completes*. (Vols. 1–4). Editions de la Pleiade. Paris: Librarie Gallimard.

San, Z.F. 1987. Traditional Western value from Asian perspective. *Dialectics and Humanism*, 14(3/4):57–64.

Sen, A. 1985. The moral standing of the market. *Social Philosophy & Policy*, 3:1–19.

Shell, G.R. 1991a. Opportunism and trust in the negotiation of commercial contracts: Toward a new cause of action. *Vanderbilt Law Review*, 44:221–282.

Shell, G.R. 1991b. When is it legal to lie in negotiations? *Sloan Management Review*, 32(3):93–101.

Shue, H. 1980. *Basic rights: Subsistence, affluence, and U.S. foreign policy*. Princeton, NJ: Princeton University Press.

Shue, H. 1981. Exporting hazards. *Ethics*, 91:579–580.

Sorley, W.R. 1904/1969. *The ethics of naturalism* (2nd ed.). Freeport, NY: Books for Libraries Press.

Stace, W. 1937. *The concept of morals*. New York: Macmillan.

Symposium on Impartiality and Ethical Theory. 1991. *Ethics* (Special ed.), 101:698–864.

Taylor, C. 1989. *Sources of the self*. Cambridge, MA: Harvard University Press.

Thomas, G.P., & Soldow, G.F. 1988. A rules-based approach to competitive interaction. *Journal of Marketing*, 52:63–74.

Tomasi, J. 1991. Individual rights and community virtues. *Ethics* 101:521–536.

Treviño, L.K. 1986. Ethical decision making in organizations: A person-situation interactionist model. *Academy of Management Review*. 11: 601–617.

Treviño, L.K., & Weaver, G.R. 1993. In press. Business ethics/business ethics: One field or two? *Business Ethics Quarterly*.

Treviño, L.K., & Youngblood, S.A. 1990. Bad apples in bad barrels: A casual analysis of ethical decision-making behavior. *Journal of Applied Psychology*, 75:378–385.

Tsalikis, J., & Fritzsche, D.J. 1989. Business ethics: A literature review with a focus on marketing ethics. *Journal of Business Ethics*, 8:695–743.

United Nations. 1990.Letter dated 31 May 1990 from Chairman of Commission on Transnational Corporations to the President of the Economic and Social Council.

Universal Declaration of Human Rights. 1948. G.A. RES. 217. In L. Henkin, R.C. Pugh, O. Schacter, & H. Smit (Eds.). *Basic documents supplement to international law cases and materials:* 381–386. St. Paul, MN: West.

Velasquez, M. 1992. International business, morality, and the common good. *Business Ethics Quarterly*, 2:27–40

Vincent, R.J. 1986. *Human rights and international relations*. Cambridge, England: Cambridge University Press.

Walzer, M. 1992. Moral minimalism. In W.R. Shea & G. A. Spadafora (Eds.). *The twilight of probability: Ethics and politics*. Canton, MA: Science History Publications.

Waterman, A.S. 1988. On the uses of psychological theory and research in the process of ethical inquiry. *Psychological Bulletin*, 103:283–298.

Weber, J. 1992. Scenarios in business ethics research: Review, critical assessment, and recommendations. *Business Ethics Quarterly*, 2:137–160.

Wellman, C. 1963. The ethical implications of cultural relativity. *Journal of Philosophy*, 60:169–184.

BUSINESS ETHICS

A Japanese view

Iwao Taka

Abstract: Although "fairness" and "social responsibilities" form part of the business ethics agenda of Japanese corporations, the meaning of these terms must be understood in the context of the distinctive Japanese approach to ethics. In Japan, ethics is inextricably bound up with religious dimension (two normative environments) and social dimension (framework of concentric circles). The normative environments, influenced by Confucianism, Buddhism, and other traditional and modern Japanese religions, emphasize that not only individuals but also groups have their own spirit (numen) which is connected to the ultimate reality. The framework of concentric circles lets moral agents apply different ethical rules to the respective circles. The dynamics of these religious and social dimensions lead to a different view of both individuals and corporations from that dominant in the West.

I. BUSINESS ETHICS IN JAPAN

What are considered to be ethical issues by the Japanese business community? The easiest way to answer this question is to look at the annual reports of major Japanese business associations. Although there are several business associations in Japan, I will rely on the recent annual report of *Keizai Doyukai* (Japan Association of Corporate Executives), partly because this association is seen as being in the forefront of business ethics in

Japan, and partly because the other influential business associations such as *Keidenren* (Japan Federation of Economic Organizations) are developing similar ideas about business ethics.[1]

In the 1989 report of *Doyukai*, chairman Takashi Ishihara placed emphasis on "fairness," saying "Fairness is an important standard in solving international conflicts in which Japan gets involved. Japan, because of its economic power, is required to be 'fair' with increasing severity. On account of this, both corporations and their executives have to consider more seriously what is fair and unfair in a business context."[2]

Based on the concept of fairness, he pointed out two types of responsibilities that corporations and corporate executives must fulfill. The first type includes basic responsibilities such as fulfilling duties for customers, employees, and stockholders, contributing to the community, and making the corporations useful and meaningful in society.[3]

The second type consists of pressing responsibilities that corporations have to recognize. As for this type, he identified the following five responsibilities.

First, for the purpose of developing a free society, we should behave in an orderly manner and in a fair way, taking into consideration not only legal but also moral aspects of behavior. . . . Second, we have to clarify corporate philosophies and purposes, formulate norms of business practices with as little delay as possible, and follow them faithfully. . . . Third, it is imperative for us to moderate the aggressiveness that has been thought of as usual in business activities. Corporations, especially big ones, should absolutely refrain from doing anything which is against good sense and common interests. . . . Fourth, we should contribute to a formation of a better society as its members. . . . Corporations are obliged to contribute positively to the better welfare and cultural development of society. This is now regarded as a proper responsibility of corporations. Fifth, we must consider more seriously our ways of business from the international point of view, as long as we do business in the international arena. For example, Japanese transnational corporations should understand real needs of host countries, and take carefully-thought-out measures for social contribution to them. We are strongly expected to show the credos which the international society can understand and support, and it is obligatory for us to create a new corporate philosophy which declares the international contribution in a clear-cut manner.[4]

With these remarks regarding "fairness" and "social responsibilities" (especially the emphasis placed on "fairness") in mind, one might conclude that ethical standards of the Japanese business community are almost the same as those of western countries. Before jumping to this conclusion, however, I shall consider traditional ethical standards of the Japanese business community. From the viewpoint of these standards, I intend to discuss how the Japanese business community conceives American business practices, and finally to show what ethical issues face the Japanese community.

II. TWO NORMATIVE ENVIRONMENTS —RELIGIOUS DIMENSION

In order to evaluate the traditional ethical standards of the Japanese business community, it is necessary to describe the Japanese cultural context or background. When it comes to cultural or ethical background, we can classify Japanese conscious and unconscious beliefs into a "religious dimension" and a "social dimension," in that Japanese culture cannot be understood well in terms of only one of the two dimensions. While the former is closely combined with a metaphysical concept or an idea of human salvation, the latter is based on how Japanese observe or conceive their social environment. Stated otherwise, while the former is "ideal-oriented," the latter is "real-oriented."

First, the religious dimension. This dimension supplies a variety of concrete norms of behavior to the Japanese in relation to the ultimate reality. As a consequence, I shall call this dimension the "normative environment."

By this I mean the environment in which most events and things acquire their own meanings pertaining to something beyond the tangible or secular world.[5] Following this definition, there are mainly two influential normative environments in Japan: the "transcendental normative environment" and the "group normative environment."[6]

1. Transcendental Normative Environment

One of the famous Japanese didactic poems says, "Although there are many paths at the foot of a mountain, they all lead us in the direction of the same moon seen at the top of the mountain." This poem gives us an ontological equivalent of "variety equals one." To put it in another way, though there are innumerable phenomena in this tangible world, each individual phenomenon has its own "numen" (soul, spirit, *raison d'être*, or spiritual energy), and its numen is ultimately connected with the unique numen of the universe. In Japan, this ultimate reality is often called "natural life force," "great life force of the universe," "*michi*" (path of righteousness), "*ri*" (justice), "*ho*" (dharma, laws), and the like.[7]

"Transcendentalism" is the philosophy that every phenomenon is an expression of the great life force and is ultimately connected with the numen of the universe. It follows that the environment where various concrete norms come to exist may be called the "transcendental normative environment." What is more, the set of these norms is simply called "transcendental logic."[8]

In this transcendental environment, everyone has an equal personal numen. This idea has been philosophically supported or strengthened by Confucianism and Buddhism. That is to say, in the case of neo-Confucianism,[9] people are assumed to have a microcosm within themselves, and are considered condensed expressions of the universe (macrocosm). Their inner universe is expected to be able to connect with the outer universe.[10]

In the case of Buddhism, every living creature is said to have an equal Buddhahood, a Buddhahood which is very similar with the idea of numen and microcosm. Buddhism has long taught, "Although there are difference among living creatures, there is no difference among human beings. What makes human beings different is only their name."[11]

In addition, however, under the transcendental normative environment, not only individuals but also jobs, positions,organizations, rituals, and other events and things incorporate their own "numina." Needless to say, these numina are also expected to be associated with the numen of the universe.

Deities of Shintoism, Buddhism, and the Japanese new religions, which have long been considered objects of worship, are often called the "great force of the universe," or regarded as expressions of that force. In this respect, the life force can be sacred and religious. On the other hand, however, many Japanese people have unconsciously accepted this way of thinking without belonging to any specific religious sect. In this case, it is rather secular, non-religious, and atheistic. Whether it is holy or secular, the significant feature of Japan is that this transcendental normative environment has been influential and has been shared by Japanese people.[12]

2. Meaning of Work in the Transcendental Environment

Inasmuch as Japanese people live in such a normative environment, the meaning of work for them becomes unique. That is to say, work is understood to be a self-expression of the great life force. Work is believed to have its own numen so that work is one of the ways to reach something beyond the secular world or the ultimate reality. Accordingly, Japanese people unconsciously and sometimes consciously try to unify themselves with the great life force by concentrating on their own work.[13]

This propensity can be found vividly in the Japanese tendency to view seemingly trivial activities—such as arranging flowers, making tea, practicing martial arts, or studying calligraphy—as ideal ways to complete their personality (or the ideal way to go beyond the tangible world). Becoming an expert in a field is likely to be thought of as reaching the stage of *kami* (a godlike state). Whatever job people take, if they reach the *kami* stage or even if they make a strong effort to reach it, they will be respected by others.

M. Imai has concluded that whereas Western managers place priority on innovation, Japanese managers and workers put emphasis on *Kaizen* (continuous improvement of products, of ways to work, and of decision-making processes). While innovation can be done intermittently only by a mere handful of elites in a society, *Kaizen* can be carried on continuously by almost every person.

Technological breakthroughs in the West are generally thought to take a Ph.D., but there are only three Ph.D.s on the engineering staff at one of Japan's most successfully innovative companies—Honda Motor. One is founder Soichiro Honda, whose Ph.D. is an honorary degree, and the other two are no longer active within the company. At Honda, technological improvement does not seem to require a Ph.D.[14]

The transcendental normative environment has contributed to the formation of this Japanese propensity to place emphasis on *Kaizen*. Work has been an important path for Japanese people to reach the numen of the universe. Thus, they dislike skimping on their work, and instead love to improve their products, ways of working, or the decision-making processes. These Japanese attitudes are closely linked with the work ethics in the transcendental normative environment. Kyogoku describes this as follows:

> In marked contrast with an occidental behavioral principle of "Pray to God, and work!" at the cloister in Japan, "Work, that is a prayer!" became a principle. In this context, devotion of one's time and energy to work, concentration on work to such a degree that one is absorbed in the improvement of work without sparing oneself, and perfectionism of "a demon for work," became institutional traditions of Japan.[15]

In this way, the transcendental environment has supplied many hard workers to the Japanese labor market, providing an ethical basis for "diligence." Nonetheless, it has not created extremely individualistic people who pursue only their own short-term interests. Because they have hoped for job security and life security in the secular world, they have subjectively tried to coordinate their behavior so as to keep harmonious relations with others in the group. Within this subjective coordination, and having the long-term perspective in mind, they pursue their own purposes.

3. Group Normative Environment

The second or group normative environment necessarily derives from this transcendental normative environment, insofar as the latter gives special *raisons d'être* not only to individuals and their work, but also to their groups. As a result of the transcendental environment, every group holds its own numen. The group acquires this *raison d'être*, as long as it guarantees the life of its members and helps them fulfill their potentials.

But once a group acquires its *raison d'être*, it insists upon its survival. An environment in which norms regarding the existence and prosperity of the group appear and affect its members is called the "group normative environment," and the set of the norms in this environment is called "group logic."

In Japan, the typical groups have been: *ie* (family), *mura* (local community), and *kuni* (nation). After World War II, although the influence of *ie* and *kuni* on their members has been radically weakened one cannot completely ignore their influence. *Mura* has also lost much power over its members, but *kaisha* (business organization) has taken over many functions of *mura*, in addition to some functions of *ie*. These groups are assumed to have their own numen: *ie* holds the souls of one's ancestors, *mural* relates to *genius loci* (tutelary deity), *kaisha* keeps its corporate tradition (or culture), and *kuni* has Imperial Ancestor's soul.

Pre-World War II, when Japanese leaders made a mistake in politics, business, military, etc., they used to say, "I don't know how to apologize to my nation." Even today, Japanese are likely to say, "I don't know how to apologize to my parents and ancestors," or "I don't know what excuse to make for my corporation and society," when they make trouble for others or society. These facts strongly suggest that Japanese people unconsciously hold the belief that the groups have their own *raison d'être* (numen) beyond that of the individual members.

Groupism and a group-oriented propensity, which have often been pointed out as Japanese characteristics, stem from this group normative environment.

III. ETHICAL DILEMMA AND THE IMPLICATIONS OF ISHIHARA'S REMARKS

Japanese often face an ethical dilemma arising from the fact that they live simultaneously in the two different influential normative environments. In the transcendental environment, groups and individuals are regarded as equal humina and equal expressions of the great life force. In the group environment, however, a group (and its representatives) is considered to be superior to its ordinary members, mainly because while the group is expected to be able to connect with the numen of the universe in a direct way, the members are not related to the force in the same way. The only way for the members to connect with the life force is through the activities of their group.

1. The Ethical Dilemma of Living between Two Environments

Depending on which normative environment is more relevant in a given context, the group stands either above or on an equal footing with its members. Generally speaking, as long as harmonious human relations within a group can be maintained, discretion is allowed to individuals. In this situation, the transcendental logic is dominant.

But once an individual begins asking for much more discretion than the group can allow, or the group starts requiring of individuals much more selfless devotion than they are willing to give, ethical tension arises between the two environments. In most cases, the members are expected to follow the requirements of the group, justified by the group logic. An alternative, although this rarely happens, is for an individual to leave the group, a behavior which may be justified by the transcendental logic.[16]

The assertion or gesture by a group leader to persuade subordinate members to follow, is called *tatemae* (formal rule). *Tatemae* chiefly arises from the need of the group to adapt itself to its external environment. In order to adjust itself, the group asks its members to accept changes necessary for the group's survival. In this moment, the group insists upon *tatemae*. On the other hand, the assertion or gesture by the members to refuse *tatemae*, is called *honne* (real motive). *Honne* mainly comes from a desire to let the subordinates' numen express itself in a free way.

Usually, a serious confrontation between *tatemae* and *honne* is avoided, because both the leader and subordinates dislike face-to-face discussions or antagonistic relations.[17] Stated otherwise, the members (the leader and the subordinates) tend to give great weight to harmonious relations within the group. Because of this, the leader might change his or her expectation toward the subordinates, or the subordinates might refrain from pursuing their direct self-interest. In either case, the final decision-maker is unlikely to identify whose assertion was adopted, or who was right in the decision-making, since an emphasis on who was correct or right in the group often disturbs its harmony.[18]

Simply described, this ambiguous decision-making is done in the following way. The group lets the subordinates confirm a priority of group-centeredness, and requires their selfless devotion. This requirement is generally accepted without reserve in the group normative environment. But if the subordinate individuals do not really want to follow the group orders, they "make a wry face," "look displeased," "become sulky," or the like, instead of revealing their opinions clearly. These attitudes are fundamentally different from formal decision-making procedures. In this case, taking efficiency and the harmonious relation of the group into consideration, the group "gives up compelling," "relaxes discipline," or "allows *amae*" of the subordinates.[19]

If the failure to follow the norms endangers the survival of the group, the leader repeatedly asks the members to follow the order. In this case, at first, the leader says "I really understand your feeling," in order to show that he or she truly sympathizes with the members. And then he or she adds, "This is not for the sake of me, but for the sake of our group." Such persuasion tends to be accepted, because almost everybody implicitly believes that the group has its own numen and the group survival will bring benefits to all of them in the long run.[20]

2. Ishihara's Remarks as *Tatemae*

On the basis of this understanding, if we look back at the remarks by the Japanese business association, we can easily understand that the remarks bear the characteristics of *tatemae*. This is due tot he fact that they are made in relation to foreign countries or to the "outer world." Once the remarks have taken a status of *tatemae*, to wit, acquired numen in the transcendental normative environment, they begin to exert enormous influence on each member of the business community.

Of course, as long as *tatemae* of the business community is not in accord with *honne* (real motives) of the individual corporations (or individuals), *tatemae* of the business association can hardly be practiced by the individual corporations on an everyday basis. Nonetheless, when a serious ethical dilemma comes out in the international business context or in relations between the "inner world" and the "outer world," *tatemae* plays an important role in solving the dilemma. Thus, this *tatemae* stands above *honne* of the individual corporations in the group normative environment.

For these reasons, Ishihara's remarks mentioned at the beginning of this paper have a substantial implication for business ethics in Japan. Especially, because he (or *Doyukai* regards "fairness" as an important standard in solving international conflicts, the member corporations are required to follow positively the spirit of "fairness" in business.

But even if the Japanese business community admits that "fairness" is the most important ethical standard, and even if the member corporations try to follow it, if the concept of "fairness" is different from that of Western countries or the United States, this standard might not solve the international conflicts so efficiently as the Japanese business community expects.

Before considering this point, however, I would like to look at the other dimension, namely "the social dimension," because "the religious dimension" cannot produce a complete picture of the Japanese ethical background. By describing how the Japanese actually conceive of their social environment and how they attach the traditional ethics to this conceived environment, I will complement the picture of the ethical background. By describing how the Japanese actually conceive of their social environment and how they attach the traditional ethics to this conceived environment, I will complement the picture of the ethical background drawn from the religious perspective.

IV. ETHICS OF CONCENTRIC CIRCLES—SOCIAL DIMENSION

Due to human bounded cognitive rationality or cultural heritage, Japanese moral agents, whether individuals or corporations, tend to conceptualize the social environment in a centrifugal order similar to a water ring.Although there are many individuals, groups, and organizations which taken together constitute the overall social environment, the Japanese are likely to categorize them into four concentric circles: family, fellows, Japan, and the world.[21] On the basis of this way of thinking, Japanese people and organizations are likely to attribute different ethics or moral practices to each circle. Let us look at the concentric circles of individuals and of corporations respectively.

1. The Concentric Circles of Individuals

First, the family circle is basically composed of the parent-child relationship, sometimes including close and intimate relatives such as grandparents, grandchildren, uncles, or aunts. The prototype of this circle is a relation between benevolence by a mother to accept almost all behaviors of her children, and excessive dependence of the children on their mother. Because of this, reserved attitudes are not expected in this circle.[22] In addition, the cannon of this circle is "harmonious unity," so that when some confrontations appear in this circle, in the end every member is apt to follow the opinion of the head of the family, even if that opinion seems to be irrational at first glance. As the other members think that following the opinion will bring them benefits in the long run, they will follow the family leader's opinion.

In the first circle, members are expected to practice the virtue of filial piety, since filial piety is viewed either as the ideal way to satisfy the generous self-devotion of parents (and ancestors) to their descendants, or as a form of repayment of ethical debts to parents.[23]

Second is the fellow circle, which includes friends, colleagues, distant relatives and the like. This circle for the ordinary Japanese is likely to be composed of the superiors and colleagues of his or her workplace. In this circle, material or spiritual benefits and debts are balanced in various ways in the long run. "Long-term reciprocal relations" are dominant. Reserved attitudes are required here. R. Benedict characterized this trait as "shame culture."[24]

Third, is the Japan circle called "the wide society." In this third circle, people become strangers so that they neither care about their appearance in others' eyes nor do they criticize others' behaviors. Because they do not have close relationships with one another, reserved attitudes are not expected in this circle either. Although agents behave more freely and aggressively here than in the fellow circle, they do acknowledge that a "long-term reciprocal ethics" is important in Japanese society.

Last, the international society surrounds the three circles mentioned above. This largest circle means "a wide world," overseas, or foreign countries. For the ordinary Japanese, this is thought of as a chaotic sphere, which threatens the cosmos of the inner circles. Because of its chaos or difference, however, the world circle makes people take contradictory attitudes: closing attitudes and opening attitudes.

If people regard the chaos as something risky, they will try to close the door of the inner circles against the world; if it is seen as a source of civilization or a focus of admiration, they will open the doors of the inner circles to the world. The main reason why studying aborad has long been considered an important step to climb the career ladder in Japan is closely related to the opening attitudes.

2. The Concentric Circles of Corporations

Just as individuals understand their social environment as concentric circles, so groups such as corporations have a similar tendency to characterize their environment. For the sake of simplicity, I shall classify the corporate environment into four circles: quasi-family, fellows, Japan, and the world.

First, corporations have a quasi-family circle. Of course, though corporations do not have any blood relationships, they might still have closely related business partners. For example, parent, sister, or affiliated companies can be those partners. "Vertical *keiretsu* (vertically integrated industrial groups like Toyota, Hitachi, or Matsushita groups) might be a typical example of the quasi-family circle. In this circle we find something similar to the parent-child relationship.[25]

The main corporate members (about 20 to 30 companies in each group) of "horizontal *keiretsu*" (industrial groups such as Mitsubishi, Mitsui, Sumitomo, Dai Ichi Kangyo, Fuyo and Sanwa groups) might be viewed as quasi-family members. Nonetheless, most of the cross-shareholding corporations in the horizontal *keiretsu* should be placed in the second circle, because their relations are less intimate than commonly understood.

In the second circle, each corporation has its own main bank, fellow traders, distant affiliated firms, employees, steady customers, and the like. If the corporation or its executives belong to some outside associations like *Nihon Jidousha Kogyo Kai* (Japanese Auto Manufacturers Association), *Doyukai* (Japan Association of Corporate Executives), *Keidanren* (Japan Federation of Economic Organizations), etc., the other members of such outside associations might constitute part of the second circle of the corporation. And if the corporation is influential enough to affect Japanese politics or administration, the Japanese governmental agencies or ministries, and political parties might constitute part of this circle.[26]

Recognition within the fellow circle requires that there must be a balance between benefits and debts in the long run. On account of this, if a corporation does not offer enough benefits to counterbalance its debts to others in this circle, the corporation will be expelled from the circle, being criticized for neither understanding nor appreciating the benefits given it by others. On the other hand, if the corporation can successfully balance benefits and debts or keep the balance in the black, it will preferentially receive many favorable opportunities from other companies or interest groups. For these reasons, every corporation worries about the balance sheet of benefits and debts in the fellow circle.

This way of recognizing the business context is closely related to original Confucianism, in the Confucianism allows people to treat others in proportion to the intimacy of their relations. Unlike Christianity, Confucianism does not encourage people to love one another equally. It rather inspires people to love or treat others differently on the grounds that, if people try to treat everybody equally in a social context, they will often face various conflicts among interests. This does not mean that Confucianism asserts that people should deny love to unacquainted people. The main point of this idea is that, although people have to treat all others as human beings, they should love intensely those with whom they are most intimate; those who cannot love this way cannot love strangers either. I can call this "the differential principle" in Confucianism.[27] Influenced or justified by this differential principle, Japanese corporations also classify their business environment in this way.

In the Japan circle, the fellow circle ethics is substantially replaced by "the principle of free competition." Competitors, unrelated-corporations, ordinary stockholders, consumers, (for ordinary corporations, the Japanese government constitutes part of this circle) and so forth, all fall within this circle.

Yet almost all corporations in this circle know well that the long-term reciprocal ethics is extremely important in constructing and maintaining their business relations, because of their similar cultural background. This point makes the third circle different from the world circle.

In the fourth or world circle, corporations positively follow "the principle of free competition," subject to the judicial system, with less worrying about their traditional reputations. Roughly speaking, the behavioral imperatives for corporations turn out to be producing or supplying high quality and low price products, dominating much more market share, and using the law to resolve serious contractual problems.

As in the case of the individuals, the world circle is conceived as a relatively chaotic sphere causing attitudes to become contradictory. On the one hand, Japanese corporations tend to exclude foreign counterparts that do not understand the extant Japanese business practices, hoping to maintain the normative order of its own business community. Notwithstanding these closing attitudes, on the other hand, they yearn after foreign technologies, know-how, products, and services which are expected to help corporations to be successful and competitive in the Japanese and world market. In particular, western technologies have long been objects of admiration for Japanese companies. This tendency vividly shows their global attitudes.[28]

3. Dynamics of the Concentric Circles

Now that I have roughly described the static relations among the concentric circles (of individuals and of corporations), I need to show the dynamic relations among these circles, that is to say, how these circles are interrelated. Generally speaking, the relations are similar to those of "operation base and battlefield."

For example, when the second circle of an individual is recognized as a battlefield, the first circle takes on the role of operation base.

When there is severe competition among the members of the second circle, individuals look for peace of mind from their first circle. I cannot show the same picture in relations between the first and second circles of corporations as clearly as in those of individuals, due to the fact that a corporation does not have similar feelings toward its quasi-family members as does an individual.

But when it comes to Japan as a whole, I can draw almost the same picture between the first/second and third circles of corporations as in those of individuals. At this level, while Japan is viewed as a battlefield, an individual person or an individual corporation expects that both the first and second circles of each of them will serve the role of an operation base. These multilayered inner circles can be called "multiple operation bases." When the fourth is understood as a battlefield, however, this third circle also turns into one of the multiple operation bases (conversely, I can postulate the existence of "the multiple battlefields").

In order to describe these complicated relations in a parsimonious light, I shall limit my discussion to the relations between the members of an "ideal big Japanese corporation" and its business environment. By a "big Japanese corporation," I mean the "idealized very influential organization" in an industry that places priority on the interests of employees, and holds a long-term strategic perspective. By "operation base" in this context, I mean the place where the members can relax, charge their energy, and develop action programs to be applied to the business environment. Whether the corporation can be such a base or not heavily depends on its members' abilities with respect to human relations: their ability to sympathize or understand other members' feelings, their ability to put themselves in the others' position, their ability to internalize other members' expectations toward them, and the like.

It has been said that in Japanese corporations, many people have such abilities. For instance, E. Hamaguchi has called people with these abilities "the contextuals" in contrast with "the individuals."

> An "individual" is not a simple unit or element of a society, but a positive and subjective member. This so-called "individual-centered model of man" is the typical human model of the western society.
>
> This model, however, is clearly different from the Japanese model. The Japanese human model is a "being between people" or an internalized being in its relations. This can be called "the contextual" in contrast with the individual.[29]

To be sure, these abilities have also positively contributed to the performance of Japanese corporations. The corporations have not rigidly divided work into pieces and distributed them to each employee so as to clarify the responsibilities each has to take. The corporations have rather let employees work together so that the contextual members make up for the deficiencies of one another allowing the quality of products and efficiency of performance to be surprisingly improved.[30]

On the contrary, the business environment as a "battlefield" is reckoned to be a strenuous sphere, where "the law of the jungle" is the dominant ethical principle.[31] In the market, the principle of free competition replaces the ethics expected in an operation base (quasi-family and fellow circles). What is more, this principle of free competition is justified by the transcendental logic, because, as I have described earlier, in the transcendental environment, work is one of the most important "ways" or "paths" to reach something sacred or the ultimate reality. In this way, "the principle of free competition" in the battlefield and "the transcendental logic" are coincidentally combined to encourage people to work hard, an encouragement which results in survival and the development of the corporation.

Wealth, power, market share, competitive advantage, or other results acquired in this business context become important scales to measure the degree of the members' efforts to proceed on the "path" to the ultimate stage. And based on these scales, contributors are praised within the operation base, namely in a corporation, in an industrial group, or in Japan.

For example, the Japanese government, administrative agencies, or ministries have so far endorsed the efforts of corporations under the present *Tenno* system (the Emperor System of Japan). The decoration and the Order of Precedence at the Imperial Court have been given to corporate executives who have contributed to the development of the Japanese economy.

Theoretically speaking, it is very hard to compare the performance of various corporations in different industries of a nation, simply because each industry has its own scale or own philosophy to measure performance. In the case of Japan, however, the annual decoration and attendance at the Imperial Court plays the role of a unitary ranking scale, applied to every industry as well as non-business-related fields. Since the Japanese mass-media makes the annual decoration and attendance public, the Japanese people know well who or which corporations are praiseworthy winners.[32]

4. The Group Environment and the Concentric Circles

Now that I have explained both the group normative environment and the concentric circles of corporations, I should make clear the relationship between the group normative environment and the concentric circles. According to the group logic, each group has its own numen and has different social status. For example, even if the R&D unit of corporation A has its own numen, the status of the unit is lower than that of A itself. The status of A is also lower than that of the leading company B in the same industry. The status of B is lower than that of the Japanese government. But if I observe their relations from the viewpoint of concentric circles, these groups can be members of the same fellow circle of corporation C. Namely, the R&D unit of corporation A, company B, and the government can constitute part of the fellow circle of C. Therefore, even if they are in the same fellow circle, it does not mean that all members have equal status in the group normative environment.

For these reasons, reciprocal relations within the fellow circle are varied according to the members' status in the group normative environment. For instance, because, in most cases, the Japanese government is regarded as a powerful agent in the fellow circle of large corporation C, C makes efforts to maintain its good relations with the government and is likely to depend on the government.

The main reason why *gyosei-shido* (administrative guidance) has so far worked well in Japan comes from this dependent trait of the corporation and from the fact that the administrative agencies or ministries have a very important status in the second circle of the large Japanese corporations.

Each Japanese corporation also maintains relations with the business associations such as *Keidanren* and *Doyukai*. Once an authoritative business association declares *tatemae*, the member corporations make efforts to follow the formal rules, even though they might have some doubts about *tatemae*, simply because those associations hold socially or politically higher status in the group normative environment.

V. JAPANESE RECOGNITION OF THE AMERICAN BUSINESS COMMUNITY

Because Japanese follow the transcendental logic, group logic, and concentric circles' ethics, their way of observing business societies might appear to be idiosyncratic. And this idiosyncrasy might bring serious misunderstanding to trading partners such as the United States, European industrialized countries, Asian NIEs, and the other developing countries.

Because of this, I would like to clarify how Japanese conceive the American business community: how the American business community is seen in the eyes of the Japanese business people who adopt the two normative logics and the concentric circles' ethics.

1. Job Discrimination and the Transcendental Logic

First, as noted earlier, in the transcendental normative environment, whatever job people take, they are believed to reach the same goal or the same level of human development. Because of this logic, Japanese are unlikely to evaluate others in terms of their "job" (specialty). They would rather evaluate one another in terms of their "attitudes" toward work.

To be concrete, it is not important for Japanese to maintain the principle of the division of labor. Of importance is the process and the result of work. If people cannot attain goals in the existing framework of the division of labor, they are likely to try other alternatives which have not been clearly defined in the existing framework. This kind of positive attitude toward work is highly appreciated in Japan.

On the contrary, a society such as the United States, where jobs are strictly divided, is perceived as not only inefficient but also discriminatory in Japanese eyes. To be sure, this society might hold a belief that the division of labor makes itself efficient or makes it possible for diverse people to utilize their own abilities. The Japanese business community, however, is likely to assume that people's reluctance to help others' work in the same group is based on job discrimination.

In America, in a large retail shop, for instance, often those who sell a heavy consumer product are reluctant to carry it for the customer. They have a specific person, whose job is just to carry goods, do so. If the person is busy with other goods, the salesperson will ask the customer to wait until the person is finished carrying the other goods.

Similarly, those who manage a large shop typically do not clean up the street in front of their shop. They let a janitor do so. Even if

they find garbage there, when the janitor has not come yet, they are likely to wait for the janitor. This kind of attitude of salespeople or managers is regarded as inefficient and discriminatory by Japanese.[33]

2. Employees' Interest and the Group Logic

Second, in the group normative environment, the group is believed to hold its own numen and expected to guarantee the members' life. That is to say, a corporation is thought to exist for its employees rather than for its shareholders.[34]

Because of this logic, the Japanese business community ethically questions American general attitudes toward the company where many accept the ideas that 1) a company is owned by its shareholders, 2) executives should lay off the employees whenever the layoff brings benefits to the shareholders, 3) executives should buy other companies and sell part of their own company whenever such a strategy brings benefits to the shareholders, etc.

Of course, even in Japan, shareholders are legal owners of a company so that the shareholders might use their legal power to change the company in a favorable way for themselves. Therefore, many Japanese corporations have invented a legitimate way to exclude the legal rights of shareholders, i.e. "cross-shareholding." This is the practice in which a corporation allows trusted companies to hold its own shares, and in return the corporation holds their shares. By holding shares of one another and refraining from appealing to the shareholders' rights, they make it possible to manage the companies for the sake of the employees.[35] Because this cross-shareholding is based on mutual acceptance, any attempts to break this corporate consortium from the outside, whether Japanese or foreigners, are often stymied by the consortium of the member corporations.

For example, in April 1989, Boone Company, controlled by T. Boone Pickens, bought a 20 percent stake in Koito Manufacturing,

Japanese auto parts maker. In 1990, Pickens increased it to 25 percent, becoming Koito's largest single shareholder.[36] But because Pickens asked for seats on Koito's board for himself as well as three Boone Company associates, and requested an increase in Koito's annual dividend, he was labeled as a "greenmailer" in the Japanese business community. As a result, the other consortium members cooperatively protected Koito from the Pickens' attack.[37]

Although Pickens claimed that his exclusion epitomized unfair Japanese corporate tactics, his behavior was no doubt seen as unethical in the eyes of the Japanese business community, because of the group normative logic. In addition, the layoff of employees and the high salaries of American executives are also regarded as unethical by the Japanese business community. It is well known that President Bush's trip to Japan in early 1992 exacerbated the issue of executive pay in America.[38]

In Japan, when executives face serious difficulties, they first reduce their own benefits, then dividends and other costs, and, after that, employees' salary or wage.[39] If the situation is extremely hard to overcome with these measures, they sell assets and only as a last resort do they lay off workers. Even in this case, the executives often find and offer new job opportunities for those who are laid off, taking care of their family's life.[40]

Because of this, Japanese executives criticize the American business climate in which only salaries of executives keep rising, even while they lay off employees (especially in the 1980s). This criticism is also based on the Japanese group normative logic.

3. Claims Against the Japanese Market and the Concentric Circles' Ethics

As I have noted above, because of the framework of concentric circles, especially of the ethics of the fellow circle, foreign corporations often face difficulties entering the Japanese market. Although Japanese admit that the market is very hard to enter, a majority of them believe that it is still possible to accomplish entry.[41]

Even if the Japanese market has many business-related practices such as semi-annual gifts, entertainment, cross-share holding, "triangular relationship" among business, bureaucracy, and the Liberal Democratic Party, the long-term relationship is formed mainly through a series of business transactions.

That is to say, the most important factor in doing business is whether suppliers can respond to the assemblers' requests for quality, cost, the date of delivery, and the like, or on how producers can respond to the retailers' or wholesalers' expectations.[42]

In the case of consumer electronics (a typical example of the vertical *keiretsu*), if the existing suppliers cannot respond to the requests sufficiently, the assemblers are likely to reduce the amount of the order to the suppliers, while starting new transactions with new part makers. In this case, the assemblers might help the suppliers improve the designing or manufacturing processes several times. But when the suppliers still cannot meet the expectations about the product the assemblers terminate the business relationship with them.[43] The same goes for the suppliers. Suppliers often belong to various cooperative associations of different assemblers which might be competing against one another.[44]

Even relations within the horizontal *keiretsu* are not absolute obstacles for outsiders. For example, the latest Japanese Fair Trade Commission's survey shows that ratio of cross-shareholding of the six *keiretsu* has declined consistently from 25.48 percent to 21.61 percent (from 1981 to 1988).[45] In addition to this, the ratio of transactions among the member corporations has clearly declined,[46] and the ratio of common directors has been on the decline too.[47] Just as corporate survival is important for ordinary companies, it is also important for the horizontal *keiretsu*. Whenever new transactions will clearly contribute to the corporate development, the corporation is willing to find new business partners.

In fact, the ratio of capital concentrated on the top 100 Japanese corporations has been decreasing. In 1967, the degree of the concentration was 25.6 percent (the ratio of the top 100 corporations' total assets against the total assets of all the Japanese corporations except for financial institutions). Since then, it has declined to 21.4 percent in 1980, to 19.8 percent in 1985, and to 18.3 percent in 1988. This implies that the Japanese market is still dynamic, and suggests that possibilities still remain for economic agents located outside the fellow circle to enter the existing business relationships.[48]

Foreign corporations might claim that because they are located outside Japan, they cannot enter even the Japan circle. On this claim, the Japanese business community is likely to insist that if they understand the "long-term reciprocal ethics," they can enter the Japan circle; and what is more, might be fellows of Japanese influential corporations. As I have described, what makes the Japan circle different from the world circle is that people in the Japan circle know well the importance of this ethics. In fact, successfully enjoying the Japanese market are foreign corporations such as IBM, Johnson & Johnson, McDonald, Apple, and General Mills which have understood well this ethics.[49]

In this respect, realistically, the Japanese business community interprets the criticism by the American counterpart of the Japanese market as unfair and unethical. To put it differently, Japanese believe that if foreign corporations understand the long-term ethics, they will easily be real members of the Japanese business community.

VI. ETHICAL ISSUES OF THE JAPANESE BUSINESS COMMUNITY

I have shown how Japanese people conceive the American business society and its business-related practices from the viewpoint of the two normative environments and the concentric circles. Yet this does not mean that the Japanese business community has no ethical problems. On the contrary, there are many issues it has to solve. What are the ethical issues of the Japanese business community?

In order to reveal some of the issues, I shall confine my interest to the concept of "fairness," mainly because Mr. Ishihara, Chairman of *Doyukai*, placed emphasis on fairness in its report.[50] When it comes to "fairness," I hypothetically interpret it as "openness" since "fairness" generally implies "treating every agent equally according to the same rule," or "opening the market or organization for every agent who is willing to follow the same rule." On the basis of this simplified definition, I will cover two levels of ethical issues: "opening the Japanese organizations" and "opening the Japanese market."

Moreover, I will identify three ethical "prime values," which I will use to discuss the issues and possible solutions. By "prime values" I mean the core concepts of the transcendental logic, group logic, and fellow circle's ethics. The main reason why I extract the core concepts is based on a hypothesis that the more generalized the philosophical concepts are, the more internationally or cross-culturally acceptable they are.

1. Discrimination and the Transcendental Logic

I will shed light on the organizational issues (opening the Japanese organizations) from the prime value of transcendental logic. The prime value here is "everybody has an equal microcosm." Whether men or women, Japanese or foreigners, hard workers on non-hard workers, everybody has to be treated equally as a person. When I observe the organizational phenomena from the viewpoint of this value, there are at least the following two discriminatory issues.

First, the transcendental logic has worked favorably only for male society. That is, in this normative environment, Japanese women have been expected to actualize their potentials through their household tasks. Those tasks have ben regarded as their path toward the goal. Of course, insofar as women voluntarily agree with this thinking, there seems to be no ethical problem. And in fact, a majority of women have accepted this way of living to date. Nonetheless, now that an increasing number of women work at companies and hope to get beyond such chores as making tea to more challenging jobs, the Japanese corporations have no longer been allowed to treat women unequally.[51]

Second, the transcendental normative logic itself has often been used to accuse certain workers of laziness. As far as a worker voluntarily strives to fulfill his or her own potential according to the transcendental logic, this presents no ethical problems. Nevertheless, once a person begins to apply the logic to others and evaluate them in terms of their performance, the transcendental logic easily becomes the basis for severe accusations against certain workers.

For example, even if a man really wants to change his job or company, his relatives, colleagues, or acquaintances are unlikely to let him do so, because they unconsciously believe that any job or any company can lead him to the same high stage of human development, if he makes efforts to reach it. Put in a different way, it is believed that despite the differences between the jobs or companies, he can attain the same purpose in either. On account of this, many Japanese say, "once you have decided and started something by yourself, you should not give up until reaching your goal." This is likely to end up justifying a teaching that "enough is as good as a feast."

If the person does not follow this teaching, thereby refusing overtime or transfers, he will jeopardize his promotion and be alienated from his colleagues and bosses, since he is not regarded as a praiseworthy diligent worker. Even if he is making efforts to fulfill his potential in work-unrelated fields, he is not highly appreciated, simply because what he is doing is not related to the company's work.

Analyzing those practices from the viewpoint of the prime value (everybody has equal microcosm), I cannot help concluding that the Japanese business community should alter its organizational climate.

2. Employees' Dependency and the Group Logic

In the group normative environment, groups are regarded as having a higher status than their individual members. Because the members are inclined to take this hierarchical order for granted, they come to be dependent on the groups. And their groups also come to be dependent on the next higher groups.[52] This dependency of the agents, whether of individuals or groups, brings the following two problems into the Japanese business community. Because of the dependent trait 1) the individual members of the group refrain from expressing their opinions about ethical issues, and 2) they tend to obey the organizational orders, even if they disagree with them. The first tendency is related to decision-making, while the second affects policy-implementation.

The prime value of the group logic, as I noted earlier, is "As long as a group guarantees the life of its members and helps them fulfill their potentials, the group acquires its *raison d'être*." Conversely, unless the group meets these conditions, it cannot assert its superiority over its members. Of importance are the conditional clauses so that both "guaranteeing members' life" and "helping members to fulfill their potentials" are understood as the prime value of the group logic.

When I look at the two tendencies mentioned above from the viewpoint of this prime value, they will be translated into the following two ethical issues respectively: 1) Japanese corporations are likely to exclude the employees' participation in ethical decision-making, and 2) in some cases, they might not guarantee the employees' right to life.

The first issue is that the dependent trait ends up excluding different opinions or ideas.[53] *A fortiori*, in exchange for job security, the rank and file rarely raise questions about the decisions made by management, even if the decisions are against their sense of righteousness. In this respect, the rank and file are likely to take no ethical responsibility for the decisions.

What is more, because both authority and responsibility of the individuals are not clearly defined in the Japanese organizations, the individual employees do not regard involvement in wrongdoing as their own responsibility, but rather as the responsibility of the middle management. Even in middle management however, it is not clear who will take responsibility for wrongdoing. The top management quite often does not know exactly what the employees or middle management are doing in daily business.

Because of this, in the worst case, Japanese corporations might be involved in an unimaginable scale of scandals. One of the latest examples is the compensation by the Japanese securities houses for the losses of their major institutional clients. Most employees of the brokerages (even the major clients) had known well that such a practice was against the spirit of "fairness." Notwithstanding this, they had never expressed their opinions about such compensation and never practiced justice, before the mass-media made the scandals public.[54] As a result, this dependent trait had lead the Japanese securities industry into a vicious cycle, and brought the Japanese economy into the recession of the early 1990s. This interrelated depression of the securities industry and Japanese economy, in turn, caused the deterioration of employees' working and living conditions.[55]

Second, the dependent trait is inclined to force individual members to devote their time and energy to work. To be sure, the dependency might encourage the individual employees to behave ethically, if the higher groups such as *Doyukai, Keidanren*, or the board of directors, seriously proclaim the necessity of business ethics.

At the same time, however, the group normative logic tends to be used to force the individual members to obey their group's orders. That is to say, the prime value, "a group has to guarantee the life of its members and help them fulfill their potentials" will be changed into the following two sentences: "Because a group holds its own *raison d'être*, its members have to obey the orders." "Only when members follow the orders, can the group guarantee the members' life and the fulfillment of their potential."

As described earlier, if a confrontation appears between the group (*tatemae*) and its members (*honne*), the leader will repeatedly ask the members to follow the group orders. In most cases, this kind of persuasion ends up being accepted, mainly because almost everybody implicitly believes that the group has its own numen.

Even if they acknowledge the conditional clause (to guarantee the life of its members and help them fulfill their potentials), the interest of each member is rarely the same. Namely, if a member pursues his own interest in the company, this behavior often hurts the interests of other members. In this case, the other members exert social pressures on the member to comply with the group's aggregate interest. For this reason, in the end, in the group normative environment, the member is likely to give up his own interest and obey the group orders.[56]

One of the typical examples which show this tendency of members to waive their basic rights is *karoshi* (death caused by overwork). In 1991, the Japanese Labor Ministry awarded 33 claims for *karoshi*.[57] Since it is very hard to prove a direct and quantifiable link between overwork and death, this number is not large enough to clarify the actual working condition, but is certainly large enough to show that there is a possibility of turning the group logic into unconditional obedience.

This corporate climate not only jeopardizes the employees' right to life, but also hampers the healthy human development of the individual members. Because of this, the Japanese business community has to alter this group-centered climate into a democratic ground on which the individuals can express their opinions more frankly than before.

3. Exclusiveness of the Concentric Circles

The Japanese conceptualization of the social environment in a centrifugal framework is closely connected with Confucianism (the differential principle): it allows people to treat others in proportion to the intimacy of their relationships. As I touched upon before, however, the main point of this principle is not that people should deny love to strangers, but rather that those who cannot love their most intimate relatives intensely are surely incapable of loving strangers. Stated otherwise, even if the way to achieve a goal is to love differentially, the goal itself is to love everybody. Therefore, "to love everybody" should be regarded as the prime value of the concentric circles' ethics.

If I look at the Japanese market (opening the Japanese market) from the viewpoint of this prime value, there appear to be at least the following two issues. 1) The Japanese business community has to make an effort to help foreigners understand the concept of long-term ethics. This effort will bring moral agents of the world circle into the Japan circle. 2) The Japanese community has to give business opportunities to as many newcomers as possible. This effort will bring the newcomers into the fellow circles.

The first issue is how to transfer foreign corporations from the world circle to the Japan circle. As noted, Ishihara recommends that Japanese corporations follow the spirit of "fairness." This "fairness" implies that they treat foreign companies the same as they treat other Japanese firms. To put it differently, the concept of "fairness" encourages the Japanese corporations to apply the same ethical standard to all companies.

Although this is a very important point of "fairness," there is a more crucial problem involved in opening the market. That is how to let newcomers know what the rules are and how the Japanese business community applies the rules. As mentioned before, for the purpose of constructing and maintaining business relationships with a Japanese company (a core company) a foreign firm has to be a fellow of the company. In this fellow circle, every fellow makes efforts to balance benefits and debts with the core company in material and spiritual

terms in the long run, since making a long-term balance is the most important ethics. Yet balancing them is too complicated to be attained for the foreign corporation, as long as benefits and debts are rather subjective concepts.

For example, in Japan, if company A trusts the executive of company B and helps B, when B is in the midst of serious financial difficulties, then B will give the most preferential trade status to A after overcoming its difficulties. B will rarely change this policy, even if B finishes repaying its monetary debts to A. Moreover, even if A's products are relatively expensive, as long as the price is not extraordinarily unreasonable, B will continue to purchase A's output. If A's products are not sophisticated enough to meet B's standard, B will often help A to improve A's products in various ways.

If A's help is understood only as financial aid, this close relationship between A and B will not appear reasonable. In Japan, in most cases, B is deeply impressed by the fact that A has trusted B (even if B is in serious difficulties) so that B continues to repay its spiritual debts to A as long as possible. Yet if B were to change this policy soon after repaying the borrowed capital to A, and if it began buying the same but cheaper products from company C, not only A but also other corporations which have been aware of this process from the beginning will regard B as an untrustworthy company in their business community.

"Fairness," in a Japanese sense might involve asking foreign companies to follow the former way of doing business. Nonetheless, foreign companies, especially Americans, do not understand "fairness" this way. Their understanding is rather similar to the latter behavior of B: switching from A to C. This difference of understanding "fairness" between Americans and Japanese undoubtedly causes a series of accusations against each other.

The Japanese business community should not let this happen over and over again. If the community takes the prime value seriously, as the first duty, it has to explain the long-term reciprocal ethics to foreign counterparts in an understandable way. This effort will help the foreigners enter the Japan circle.

But even if they can enter the Japan circle successfully, there still remains another problem. That is how those foreigners, which have been already in the Japan circle, enter the fellow circles of influential Japanese corporations. This is related to the second issue of opening the Japanese market.

Even when foreign companies understand and adopt long-term reciprocal ethics, they might not be able to enter those fellow circles, if they rarely have the chance to show their competitive products or services to the influential corporations. On account of this, as an ethical responsibility, the Japanese corporations should have "access channels" through which every newcomer can equally approach.[58]

To be sure, the "mutual trust" found in the fellow circle should not be blamed for everything. But if the trust-based business relation is tightly combined among a few influential corporations, it tends to exclude newcomers. As long as such a relation is not against the Japanese Antimonopoly Law, it is safe to say that efforts to maintain the relationship are not problematic, because most of the corporations do so according to their free will.[59] Despite that, if I look at the exclusive tendency of a fellow circle like that of the Japanese distribution system, I cannot help saying that the trust-based relation is a critical obstacle for newcomers.[60]

If the Japanese business community follows the prime value (to love everybody) of the concentric circles' ethics, it has to make an effort to remove the obstacles to entry. One of the ideal ways to do so is to give newcomers more competitive bids than before. Of course, it is not obligatory for Japanese corporations to accept every bidder as a fellow after the tender. If a bidder is not qualified as an ideal business partner in terms of its products or services, Japanese corporations do not need

to start transactions with the bidder. But as a minimum ethical requirement, Japanese corporations should have access channels through which every newcomer can equally approach them.

CONCLUSION

For the purpose of clarifying the fundamental ethical issues of the Japanese business community, I have examined its cultural context or background from the religious and social dimensions. The religious background is composed of the transcendental and group normative environments. The social one consists of the four concentric circles.

After looking at the static and dynamic relations between normative environments and concentric circles, I have shown how the American business community is seen in the eyes of the Japanese business people with the two normative logics and concentric circles' ethics. And I have indicated why some American business practices are regarded as unethical by the Japanese business community.

Finally, I have focused upon the ethical issues rooted in Japan. In order to suggest the ethical directions in which the Japanese business community should proceed, I have extracted the "prime values" of the normative logics and concentric circles' ethics.

I conclude that: 1) From the transcendental prime value, the Japanese business community has to change its discriminatory organizational climate. 2) From the group prime value, it has to alter the group-centered climate into a democratic ground. 3) From the prime value of the concentric circles' ethics, it has to have access channels open to every newcomer.

As is often pointed out, these ethical suggestions might hurt the efficiency or competitiveness of Japanese corporations. Because of this, I have to discuss them in relation to those economic factors, too. What is more, in order to proceed in the direction of the suggestions, each corporation will have to establish its own concrete code of business ethics.

NOTES

I wish to thank Prof. Thomas W. Dunfee and Prof. Richard T. DeGeorge, Prof. Thomas Donaldson, and Prof. Norman E. Bowie, for their valuable comments and advice with business ethics and my terminology. I also extend my heartfelt thanks to Miss Mollie B. Zion for her many useful suggestions.

1. The present Chairman of *Doyukai* is Takashi Ishihara (Chairman of Nissan Motor). It is composed of about 1500 executives and a Subcommittee on "Corporate Citizenship" was established in April, 1990. The present Chairman of *Keidanren* is Gaishi Hiraiwa (Chairman of Tokyo Electric Power). It is composed of about 940 corporate executives and it established a "Committee on Corporate Philanthropy" in February, 1991. The other business associations in Japan have not yet created specialized committees of business ethics.

2. Keizai Doyukai, *Heisei Gannendo Teigen Ikensho Shu (Annual Report of 1989: Proposals and Opinions)*, (Tokyo: 1990), p. 91.

3. Ibid., p. 92.

4. Ibid., p. 92–93.

5. The original idea of the "normative environment" is the "semantic cosmos" proposed by J. Kyogoku. J. Kyogoku, *Nihon no Seiji (Politics of Japan)* (Tokyo: Tokyo University Press, 1983).

6. J. Kyogoku, ibid.,pp. 139–88. H. Abe, M. Shindo and S. Kawato, *Gendai Nihon no Seiji (Politics of Modern Japan)* (Tokyo: Tokyo University Press, 1990), pp. 235–39.

7. J. Kyogoku, op. cit., pp. 137–38. The philosophy of the great life force is explained in detail in M. Tsushima, et al., "*Shinshukyo niokeru Seimeishugiteki Kyusaikan*" (Life-oriented Salvation in the Japanese New Religions), *Shiso (Thoughts)* (Nov., 1979), pp. 92–115.

8. The closest translation of the Japanese term is "uni-variety normative environment." The concept, a difficult one even for the Japanese, does not translate easily into English. I am using the term, "transcendental" in its sense of placing emphasis on "the primacy of the spiritual and intuitive over the material and empirical" from the definition of "transcendentalism" in *Webster III New International Dictionary*. Prof. Thomas W. Dunfee kindly suggested to me the term, "transcendental normative environment."

9. Taoism criticized Confucianism, saying that Confucianism had constructed an artificial society. For Taoism, formulating manners and requiring people to learn them meant making an artificial society. Taoism regarded this society as immoral. Buddhism also exerted its influence on ordinary people, establishing its own cosmology and metaphysics which Confucianism lacked. Confucians, therefore, aiming at strengthening its influence on common people, developed an elaborated its cosmology and metaphysics in 11th century. It was "neo-Confucianism" or the doctrines of Chu-tzu (1130–1200) that underwent these philosophical changes. K. Miura, *Shushi (Chu-tzu)* (Tokyo: Kodansha, 1979), pp. 35–263. N. Kaji, *Jukyo towa Nanika (What Is Confucianism?)* (Tokyo: Chuo-koronsha, 1990), pp. 170–217.

10. K. Miura, op. cit., p. 28.

11. K. Fujita, *Jinsei to Bukkyo (Life and Buddhism)* (Tokyo: Kosei Shuppansha, 1970), p. 54.

12. J. Kyogoku, op. cit., p. 164.

13. S. Yamamoto found a prototype of the spirit of Japanese capitalism in the Buddhism of Seisan Suzuki (1579–1620). Yet, the logic is almost the same. That is, all people, whether peasants, merchants, priests, or warriors, can enter Nirvana, if they concentrate on their own calling with sincerity an faithfulness. S. Yamamoto, *Nihon Shihonshugi no Seishin (Spirit of the Japanese Capitalism)* (Tokyo: Kobunsha, 1979), pp. 118–41.

14. M. Imai, *Kaizen* (New York: McGraw-Hill Publishing Company, 1986), p. 34.

15. J. Kyogoku, op. cit., pp. 182–83.

16. In 1991 (from March, 1991 to February, 1992), 2.77 million Japanese changed jobs. Although this figure is the highest since 1984, the figure accounts for only 4.4 percent of the labor force. *The Philadelphia Inquirer* (July 25, 1992).

17. One of the typical ways to avoid face-to-face confrontation is "*Nemawashi*." This is taken by those who want to propose some new ideas to the group. They explain the content of the ideas in detail and in advance to the conservatives, for the purpose of both eliminating their doubt and anxiety about the new proposal, and also to get the conservatives' understanding, compliance, and support.

18. According to Nihon Minzoku to *Nihon Bunka (Japanese People and Culture)*, the origin of this

propensity is found in *Kojiki (The Legendary Stories of Old Japan)* as follows: "Compared with Christian mythology, Japanese mythology shows its vivid characteristic. In Christianity, the world is completely synthesized with the absolute God who sands at the central point. A standard of good and evil is made clear there. On the contrary, in Japanese mythology, although *Amaterasu* and *Susanou* (Japanese ancient goddess and god) are opposing each other, Kojiki did not show the absolute standard (central position) of good and evil. After all, opposition between them comes to balance. If we call the structure of Christian mythology a centrally-unified-type, we can call that of the Japanese chuku kinko (balanced-vacuum) type." N. Egami, *Nihon Minzoku to Nihon Bunka* (Tokyo: Yamakawa Shuppansha, 1989), pp. 430–31.

19. J. Kyogoku, op. cit., p. 161.
20. Ibid., pp. 161–62.
21. Ibid., pp. 191–94. This kind of framework of social conception is also used by T. Doi. T. Doi, *Amae no Kozo (Structure of Amae)* (Tokyo: Kobundo, 1971), pp. 33–37.
22. T. Doi, ibid., pp. 38–43.
23. It is said that the original idea of this philosophy came from Confucianism, because Confucianism placed emphasis on a virtue of filial piety. But the virtue of filial piety has long been extended and made sophisticated in such a way as to include various virtues not only toward parents and ancestors but also toward nature, social benefactors, descendants, and so forth. Namely, neo-Confucianism has considered that the universe, the natural environment, ancestors, and the community allow a person to live on this earth. The person can never enjoy innumerable favors unless they support his or her existence and life. Therefore the person has to give benefits willingly to society, offspring, and others as a token of his or her gratitude to nature and benefactors. N.Kaji, op. cit., pp. 51–86, and pp. 185–210. This ethical idea is also said to have been nurtured or strengthened by Buddhism. Buddhism says that what makes it possible for a person to live is not due to his or her own power, but due to others' support and sacrifice. If we look back to the past, we can say that every person's life depends on his or her parents, grandparents and other ancestors. If we look around our society, we cannot help admitting that not only other people surrounding the person but also many animals and plants support his or her life. Buddhism regards these benefits as ethical debts the person owes, and therefore insists on the necessity to repay these debts to nature, society, descendants, and the like. K. Fujita, op. cit., pp. 84–112.
24. R. Benedict, *The Chrysanthemum and the Sword: Patterns of Japanese Culture* (New York: Meridian, 1946).
25. K. Imai, and R. Komiya, *Nihon no Kigyo (Japanese Corporations)* (Tokyo: Tokyo University Press, 1989), pp. 131–58.
26. As for the triangular relationship among Japanese business leaders, bureaucrats Liberal Democrats, see F.K. Upham, *Law and Social Change in Postwar Japan* (Harvard University Press, 1987), pp. 14–16.
27. N. Kaji, op. cit., pp. 70–77. Y Yuasa, "*Shakai Seiji Shiso (Chinese Philosophy of Social Politics), Shiso Gairon (Summary of Chinese Philosophy)*", edited by Akatsuka, Kanaya, Fukunaga, and Yamanoi (Tokyo: Taishukan Shoten, 1968), p. 307.
28. When Sony, Kyocera, or other newcomers faced difficulties in entering an existing Japanese market, they tried to succeed in doing business in the international market, especially in the American market. Once they succeeded in that market, they were highly appreciated and welcomed by big companies at home in Japan. These historical facts show vivid examples of opening attitudes of Japanese corporations. I. Taka, "*Kigyoka no Shinnen Taikei to Soshiki no Kyuseicho (Belief System of Entrepreneurs and Rapid Growth of Organizations),*" *Waseda University Shokei Ronshu* (No. 44, 1983), pp. 1–24.
29. E. Hamaguchi, *"Nihon Rashisa" no Saihakken (Rediscovery of Japaneseness)* (Tokyo: Kodansha, 1988), pp. 66–67.
30. Hamaguchi calls this trait "outside-in." Hamaguchi, E., ibid., pp. 305–16. And Imai calls it "market-in." M. Imai, op. cit., pp. 52–54.
31. J. Kyogoku, op. cit., 218.
32. Ibid., p. 222.
33. Although I do not deny that there is also a discrimination based on specialty in the Japanese society, the discrimination in Japan seems to be less serious than that in America.

34. According to a survey, 80 percent of respondents (104 employees of publicly traded companies) think that a corporation should be for its employees, and 77 percent think that a corporation actually exists for its employees (multiple answers). *Nikkei Sangyo Shinbun* (April 23, 1990).

35. This practice was basically formed for a purpose of defending Japanese industries from foreign threats. But at the same time, Japanese people thought this threat might destroy the employee-centered management. T. Tsuruta, *Sengo Nihon no Sangyo Seisaku (Industrial Policies of Post-War Japan)* (Nihon Keizai Shinbunsha, 1982), pp. 121–30.

36. W.C. Kester, *Japanese Takeovers: The Global Contest for Corporate Control* (Cambridge: Harvard Business School Press, 1991), pp. 258–59.

37. *Mainichi Daily News* (May 15, 1990).

38. According to the United Shareholders Association, in 1991, corporate profits fell by 7 percent, while pay of chief executives advanced an average 7 percent. *The Philadelphia Inquirer* (February 16, 1992).

39. R. Iwata has pointed out that when Japanese corporations face radical increases or decreases of the work load, they have coordinated 1) the amount of overtime work, 2) the number of the orders to their subcontractors, and 3) the number of their reserved employees such as female and part-time work force. R. Iwata, *Nihon no Keiei Soshiki (Japanese Management Organizations)* (Tokyo: Koudansha, 1985), pp. 62–68.

40. The income gap between executives and employees has been relatively narrow. For example, in 1988, the average president's annual salary of the main Japanese corporations was about $230,000 which was only 7 times as much as that of the new employee. *Nihon Keizai Shinbunsha*, op. cit., pp. 190-191.

41. The Japanese Fair Trade Commission, "*Kigyokan Torihiki ni kansuru* (Research on Corporate Transactions)" (Tokyo: JFTC, June 1991). The Japanese Fair Trade Commission, "*Kigyo Shudan no Jittai nituite* (Research on Corporate Groups)" (Tokyo: JFTC, Feb. 1992). These latest reports conclude that Japanese business practices and corporate groups are not monopolistic.

42. According to a FTC report, most of the foreign electronic part makers give up too easily in their attempts to start a new business with the Japanese assemblers, once they are rejected. They are reluctant to ask the assemblers about the problems their products have. In the case of Japanese part makers, they ask many times about it, and make efforts to improve their products: Through this interaction, they become trustworthy partners of the assemblers. The Japanese Fair Trade Commission, "*Kigyokan Torihiki ni kansuru Chosa* (Research on Corporate Transactions)" (June 1991), p. 44.

43. Not only in consumer electronics, but also in ship-buildings, synthetic textiles, and gas, continuous transactions can be found as a characteristic. But this does not mean that newcomers are excluded. If they are excellent at product quality or cost, they can be new contractors. The Japanese Fair Trade Commission, *Annual Report of the Japanese Fair Trade Commission: White Paper of Antimonopoly* (Tokyo: JFTC, 1991), pp. 88–92.

44. The Japanese Fair Trade Commission, "*Kigyokan Torihiki ni kansuru Chosa* (Research on Corporate Transactions)" (June 1991), pp. 36–41.

45. Ibid., p. 15. This ratio is "the total of the ratios of the number of issued stocks owned by the group corporations against the total number of the issued stocks divided by the number of group corporations."

46. From 1981 to 1988, the ratio of sales for the same group corporations declined from 10.8 percent to 7.28 percent, the ratio of purchases from the same group corporations declined from 11.7 percent to 8.10 percent, respectively. The Japanese Fair Trade Commission, "*Kigyo Shudan no Jittai Nituite* (Research on Corporate Groups)" (Feb. 1992), p. 31.

47. Ibid., p. 93. From 1981 to 1988, the ratio of group corporations which accept directors from the rest of the same group of corporations declined from 69.79 percent to 62.26 percent.

48. The Japanese Fair Trade Commission, *Annual Report of the Japanese Fair Trade Commission: White Paper of Antimonopoly* (1991), pp. 76–85. As for the American market, on the contrary, it is said that the capital concentration on the top 100 has been stable. I. Taka, and W. Laufer, "Japan and Social Control: New Perspectives on Trade with a Mediator-Centered Society," *International Association for Business and Society: 1993 Proceedings* (San Diego: March 1993), p. 146. T. Nanbu, "*Nichibei Sangyo Soshiki no Dotai Hikaku* (Dynamic Comparison of the Japanese and American Industries)," *Nihon Kigyo no Datnamizum*

(Dynamism of Japanese Corporations), ed. by H. Uzawa (Tokyo University Press, 1991), pp. 19–23.

49. Recently IBM, Toshiba, and Siemens announced a three-way collaboration to develop a memory chip. Challenging this alliance, Advanced Micro Devices and Fujitsu announced a joint venture to develop a new type of chip. They can be regarded as latest examples of foreign companies' efforts to enter Japanese fellow circles. *The New York Times* (July 14, 1992). And also 30 percent of foreign interest groups such as corporations in Japan hold retired Japanese bureaucrats and give them high positions. In contrast only 19 percent of Japanese counterparts employ them. Y. Tsujinaka, *Rieki Shudan* (Interest Group) (Tokyo: Tokyo University Press, 1988), pp. 196–97.

50. Not only *Doyukai*, but also *Keidanren* places emphasis on "fairness." Mr. Gaishi Hiraiwa, chairman of *Keidanren*, insists that "it is essential that we establish fair rules and systems of the kind that can be understood by everyone." *Keidanren Review on Japanese Economy* (No. 131, Oct. 1991), p. 2.

51. This logic also seems to be applied to only the Japanese people. In the recession of the early 1900s, the Japanese major companies, which once employed many Japanese South Americans (e.g., Brazilians) in the time of economic boom, have begun laying them off. To be sure, since most of them are part-time workers, the Japanese corporations might be able to treat them as a buffer against the business cycle. But if I look at this practice from the viewpoint of the transcendental prime value, this appears discriminatory.

52. Nonetheless, this dependent trait does not mean the complete dependence of Japanese corporations on the Japanese government. Just as individuals live in the transcendental normative environment, so corporations live in the transcendental environment. Therefore, if agencies act excessively to require the corporations to follow administrative orders, relations between the agencies and corporations come into conflict. T. Tsuruta, op. cit., pp. 201–10.

53. In fact, in the same annual report, in the light of this trait, *Doyukai* proposed the following three reforms to Japanese corporations. 1) "We should contribute to the world with the spirit of noblesse oblige." 2) "We have to be able to express our way of thinking in an adequate and easily understandable manner." 3) "We must understand and accept a variety of values and behavioral manners of other people." Keizai Doyukai, op. cit., pp. 156–57.

54. H. Okumura, "Shoken Sukyandaru de Towareteirumono (What are Real Problems in the Securities Scandals)," *The Keizai Seminar* (No. 443, Dec. 1991), pp. 17–22.

55. Of course, it is often said that Japanese workers or employees more positively participate in the corporate decision-making than the counterparts of the other countries. But what the Japanese can suggest is limited to the routine work.

56. According to a *Keidanren's* survey 96.8 percent of respondents (managers) say "Efforts should be made to reduce working hours and respect personal freedom in light of the growing tendency to seek leisure and comfort." *Keidanren Review on Japanese Economy*, op. cit., p. 3.

57. *The Philadelphia Inquirer* (Jan. 16, 1992).

58. In fact, G. Hiraiwa has suggested "economic activities based not on fair rules but on Japanese customs and practices that emphasize interpersonal relationship, such as unspoken communication and tacit mutual understanding, no longer hold water even in Japan." *Keidanren Review on Japanese Economy*, op. cit., p. 2.

59. A. Negishi, "*Kigyo Keiretsu no Ho Kozo* (Legal Structure of Industrial Groups)," *Kigyo Keiretsu to Ho (Industrial Groups and Law)*, A. Negishi, Y. Tsuji, K. Yokokawa, & M. Kishida (Tokyo: *Sanseido*, 1990), pp. 1–68.

60. We should not forget that the trust-based relation sometimes tends to be illegal. For example, recently a Japanese parcel-delivery firm, Sagawa Kyubin, through its Tokyo subsidiary, gave about $4 billion in loans and guarantees to several corporations, without receiving interest payments, for the purpose of establishing and maintaining a favorable fellow circle. Unquestionably, this is illegal. Moreover, Sagawa Kyubin is believed to have given more than 100 politicians (one in seven members of the Diet) some handouts, in order to make political friends in the fellow circle, expecting that the political friends would help Sagawa to expand its business in the long run. This case also shows that the tendency to construct and maintain long-term reciprocal relations could be illegal. *The Economist* (Feb. 1–7, 1992), p. 38.

THE NEW ECONOMIC THEORY OF THE FIRM

Critical perspectives from history

*William W. Bratton, Jr.**

Theories of the firm inform and undergird corporate law, but they only intermittently appear as principal points in corporate law discourse. They stayed in the background during the half century ending in 1980, while a conception of the firm as a management power structure prevailed unchallenged in legal theory. The situation changed around 1980, when a new theory of the firm appeared, imported from economics. According to the theory, corporate relationships and structures could be explained in terms of contracting parties and transaction costs. This "new economic theory of the firm" asserted a contractual conception. The firm, said its leading text, is a legal fiction that serves as a nexus for a set of contractual relationships among individual factors of production.[1]

Law and economics writers restated corporate law in the new theory's terms and successfully reoriented legal discourse on corporations. The new theory already has sunk into the fabric of academic corporate law (Gordon and Kornhauser, 1986). Now we have two paradigms, one managerialist, the other contractual.

The new theory's proponents made strong claims on its behalf. The economists who originated it proclaimed a major discovery: Professor Michael Jensen, for example, predicted that this infant "science of organizations" will produce a "revolution . . . in our knowledge about organizations" during "the next decade or two . . ." (Jensen, 1983). In the law schools, its enthusiasts moved aggressively for equal academic status. Even outside observers expressed enthusiasm about the new perspective's potential (Ackerman, 1984).

Employing historical analysis, this article disputes these claims. History contains essential information about theories of the firm: Lawyers and economists have formulated principles to describe and regulate the relationship between individuals and producing institutions on repeated past occasions. Once seen in historical context, the theory loses the revolutionary impact claimed by its proponents. Although it constitutes a significant innovation in neoclassical microeconomic theory, outside that limited methodological context, it is merely the latest in a long series of attempts to describe and justify the phenomenon of collective production in individualist terms. Such theories have followed from and responded to economic practice; they have not dominated and determined it.

*Professor of Law, Benjamin Cardozo School of Law, Yeshiva University, New York. This paper is an edited and condensed version of an article which was originally published in *Stanford Law Review* vol. 41 (July 1989): 1471–1527.

I. LEGAL THEORIES OF THE CORPORATE FIRM AND THE NEW ECONOMIC THEORY

A. Traditional Legal Theories of the Corporate Firm

Traditional legal theories of the corporation pursue an essentialist inquiry into the corporation's nature and origins (Horwitz, 1985). One set of questions asks about the corporation's beings. Here one line of responses holds the corporation to be at most a reification—a construction of the minds of the persons connected with the firm and those who deal with them and their products. A conflicting line holds the corporate firm to be a real thing having an existence, like a spiritual being, apart from the separate existences of the persons connected with it. A related set of questions looks into distinctions between the corporate entity (whether real or reified) and the aggregate of separate individuals and transactions in and around it. It concerns the placement of emphasis between the group and the individual. If the corporate entity has a cognizable existence, questions arise about the nature and origins of its separate characteristics. Here personification—the attribution of human characteristics—provides a metaphorical mode of isolating components of the entity's essence. On the other hand, if the notion of an entity lacks meaning, the nature and origins of the corporation are determined by the relationship of its aggregate parts. Historically, observers taking this latter view characterize corporate life as contractual. There also is a political version of this essentialist inquiry into the corporation's nature and origins; to wit, whether the corporation must derive positive authority from the state. The statist response is called concession theory; the contrary view is called contractual. A strong version of concession theory attributes the corporation's very existence to state sponsorship. A weaker version sets up state permission as a regulatory prerequisite to doing business. The contractual response locates the source of all firms' economic energy in individuals. Stated most strongly, this view holds that the individuals' freedom of contract implies a right to do business as a corporation without state interference (Bratton, 1989a).

B. Managerialism

Speculation about the reality of corporations, their entity and aggregate characteristics, and their origins in concession or contract was commonplace in legal theory until around 1930. At that time, discourse in these terms largely ceased as the management-centered conception of large corporate entities took hold. The managerialist picture put corporate management groups at the large corporation's strategic center. Management possessed hierarchical power. This structural power, stemming from their expertise in organizing resources, had three aspects. First, management determined the processes of production and distribution. Second, management dominated enormous bureaucracies and exercised authority over the lives of all those lower down on the ladder. Third, management-dominated firms imposed externalities (Berle, 1954; Nader, Green, and Seligman, 1976). The managerialist consensus recently disappeared, due in part to the successful emergence of the new economic theory in the legal literature beginning around 1980. The accuracy of the concept was not an issue in corporate law. All participants, pro- or anti-managerialist, saw the firm as a "structure"; that the structure gave rise to power relationships, and that management dominated the structure. The issue was whether management held and exercised the power legitimately. Anti-managerialists charged that management exercised its power without accountability. Although, legal doctrine vested governing power of the corporate entity in the board of directors subject to shareholder vote, management in fact controlled the board aided and abetted. And third, by the financial community which supported management. Therefore, management groups were unaccountable to higher authority. Management's defenders countered with the assertion that utility-expertise legitimized management authority which was followed by assurances of social responsibility, i.e., that managers were capable of statesmanship (Frug, 1984).

C. The New Economic Theory of the Firm

Economists devised the new economic theory during the 1970s. It appeared in corporate legal theory, achieving wide currency and acceptance, after 1980.[2] The theory challenged the managerialist picture of the corporation and prompted renewed concern about the nature of the corporation among legal academics. The new economic theory has two variants. One variant has antecedents in neoclassical economic; the other has closer ties to institutional economics.

The institutional variant appeared first. Its earliest antecedent is an essay by Ronald Coase (1937). Coase explained firms and markets as alternative forms of contracting, identifying transaction costs as the determinants of the choice between the two. This work, while seminal, had no noticeable influence among neoclassical economists until after 1970 (Coase, 1972, 1988). Even then, Coase's distinction between markets and firm hierarchies only influenced the institutionalists, who restate the received managerialist picture in contractual terms.

The advent of neoclassical variant can be precisely dated to the publication of a paper by Alchian and Demsetz (1972) which was followed by Jensen and Meckling's analysis of the firm which appeared in 1976.

1. The Neoclassical Variant
The neoclassical variant reconceives management as a continuous process of negotiation of successive contracts. Its central point is that the firm is a legal fiction that serves as a nexus for a set of contracting relations among individual factors of production. Applied to corporations, this assertion displaces the management cen-

tered conception. The firm, taken as a neoclassical contracting nexus, is not necessarily a hierarchy in which authority determines terms by fiat. "No power of fiat, no authority, no disciplinary action." They do not differ "in the slightest degree from ordinary market contracting between any two people." (Alchian and Demsetz, 1972:794; and Demsetz, 1982). The dissatisfied party always can terminate its dealings with the firm.

From this starting point, the neoclassical theorists construct a model of the management corporation. They find parties and terms for their firm of contracts by drawing on economists' basic assumptions about the behavior of marketplace actors and the nature of marketplace contracts. The actors are rational economic actors—self-interested individuals with divergent interests. The contracts are the equilibrium contracts that rational economic actors enter into whe dealing in markets—instantaneous exchanges between maximizing parties. The parties make complete choices, dealing with unknown factors in the exchange price. The theorists further assume that effective competition exists among the contracting parties. They also apply the principle of natural selection. That is, rational economic actors, consciously or not, solve problems in the process of pursuing wealth maximization. Given the actors' capabilities and intense competition, only optimal contracting strategies survive (Fama, 1980; Jensen, 1983; Meckling, 1976; and Macneil, 1981).

Within this framework, firm contracts take forms determined by the now well known imperative of agency cost reduction. The process works as follows. Risk-allocating contracts have winners and losers. Maximizing losers tend to "shirk"—that is, take actions to avoid having to perform their promises fully. Agency costs are the costs of shirking. Since rational economic actors know about shirking, they charge agency costs against their contracting partners ahead of time. Given competition, the party who most reduces agency costs has the edge. Again, applying the principle of natural selection, the lowest cost contract forms survive.

With this model the theorists have rationalized, *inter alia*, the positive law of relations among shareholders, boards of directors, and officers; the internal decisionmaking structures, policies, and procedures of corporate bureaucracies; and the contracts firms make with employees, suppliers, and creditors. Managers act as agents to shareholder principals. When securities are sold publicly by management groups to outside shareholder principals, the purchasing shareholders assume that the managers will maximize their own welfare; the purchasers, therefore, bid down the price of the securities accordingly. Management thereby bears the costs of its own misconduct and has an incentive to control its own behavior. It achieves self-control, increasing the selling price of its securities by offering monitoring devices. These include common features of the corporate landscape such as independent directors and accountants, and legal rules against self-dealing. Pressures from the management labor market and the market for corporate control also impel management to reduce agency costs.[3] The received division of authority between officers and board is explained in terms of low-cost information flow (Jensen and Meckling, 1976:326–339).

This picture's implications become apparent if we contrast it with the earlier managerialist picture. The managerialist picture set out a structure and placed management at the top in a position of power. Pro-managerialists asserted that expertise necessitated it while anti-managerialists asserted that the power arose due to the absence of market constraints. The neoclassical new economic theory brings market constraints back into the picture. The discipline of price competition in the product market is accompanied by pricing disciplines from the markets for corporate securities and the markets for managers and other labor. The firm springs out of contracts in all of these markets. Since the contracts are bilateral, management power and corporate

hierarchy, as previously conceived, disappear. In a firm of bilateral contracts between free market actors, both parties possess equal power to contract someplace else. The neoclassical picture also implies a limited role for corporate law. Corporate law does not invest and legitimize power in hierarchical superiors; indeed, it appears as just another term of the contract governing equity capital input. Given the model's basic assumption that the fittest arrangements survive, the contract presumably effects an optimal sharing of risk. The model, then, affords no basis for intervention by government for the protection of shareholders.

2. The Institutional Variant The institutional variant also treats the firm as a series of contracts with some noteworthy difference, however. First, the institutionalists grant that the firm exists as a single maximizing unit, not simply as an artifact of transactions among maximizing individuals. While comprised of contracts, this firm entity amounts to a hierarchy. It is a "governance structure," distinguishable in a meaningful way from market contracting (Klein, 1983: 370; Macneil, 1981:1022–23; and Williamson, 1981:1537; 1983: 210–214). Second, the institutionalists assume an economic actor possessing a wider repertoire of human traits than does neoclassical economic man. Specifically, the institutional contracting party suffers from "bounded rationality" and engages in "opportunistic conduct." (Williamson, 1981: 1357; 1983:210–214). The former refers to an actor's limited ability to solve problems and process information. Bounded rationality prevents the institutionalist actor from achieving the neoclassical actor's concrete risk analysis and from making complete choices. Opportunistic conduct goes beyond the neoclassical actor's self-interested maximization to "guile"—behavior a lawyer would term "culpable."

These human failings inform the institutionalist picture of the firm contracting process. The parties know that they cannot achieve complete exchanges in all situations. They, therefore, leave terms open and consent to structures and processes to govern the relationship's future. Parties choose these "governance structures" over market exchanges where, for example, one or both parties' performance requires a transaction-specific investment susceptible to appropriation by the other. The parties design a transactional structure to prevent appropriation. Firm organization, along with most other forms of long-term contracting, is one of these transactional structures. Many other matters affect the institutionalists' transaction structures, e.g., the free rider problem and agency costs. But the institutionalists also mention nonrational phenomena, such as human attitudes. Authority and relational values also enter into the parties' transactional solutions. For example, fiat may be the cheapest way to solve problems; cooperation and reciprocity may reduce uncertainties, and hence costs, by causing expectations to converge (Williamson, 1981: 1547-1548; 1975: 30-40, 256-257).

Difference between the neoclassical and institutional pictures should not be emphasized too much, however. If we view both variants of the new economic theory together against the universe of alternative possible explanations of the firm, they represent a common point of view for many purposes. The institutional theorists, like the neoclassicists, view the firm as a contract and explain its structural features as the cost-saving devices of transacting parties. They share with neoclassicists a noninterventionist political perspective. Since their firm "is contract," and since private actors do a better job at making contracts than do government officials, they see little constructive role for public policy. In addition, the institutionalists, like the neoclassicists, employ a methodology that delimits the scope of their inquiry and analysis. This approach assumes that transaction cost reduction best explains private contracting patterns, and they explain firm phenomena only as means to that end. When their inquiry does not lead to an explanation within this functional paradigm, both institutionalists and neoclassicists either try again or abandon the search; neither looks to the world of political, social, and economic behavior outside.

II. THE HISTORICAL EVOLUTION OF LEGAL THEORIES OF THE CORPORATE FIRM

This part recounts the evolution of theory of the firm concepts in American corporate law history. The story has a constant theme: The corporate entity rises, posing challenges to both economic and legal theory. Both types of theory are based on individualism. They employ models of economic life based on visions of production by individual producers and transactions between individuals, all of whom bear responsibility for their own actions. These models must be adjusted to account for group production. In the case of economic theory, with its construct of entrepreneurial, profit-maximizing behavior by rational economic actors the adjustment requires that the individuals' entrepreneurial behavior patterns be reconstructed or replaced somewhere in the collective producing institution. In the case of legal theory, the corporate unit must be integrated with a wider legal fabric that assumes individual actors, makes them responsible, and seeks to facilitate their development (Dan-Cohen, 1986).

A. The Early Nineteenth Century to 1850

Very little tension arose between economic practice and individualist economic and legal theory in the early nineteenth century.[4] The economy closely resembled the atomistic type described in Adam Smith's classical theory. Economic units tended to be individual rather than collective. Individuals produced goods for sale in the market. Individuals bought goods for consumption in the market. To the extent production was organized, the market did the organizing by coordinating prices. This individual perspective undergirded business law. Actors in the economic system received legal support from a regime of individual possessory property rights (Berle, 1961:1954). People did not yet associate the corporate form with general business, and, in fact, few businesses took the corporate form. This was corporate law history's "special charter" phase (Hurst, 1970).

The prevailing legal theories described the corporation as a legal fiction and an artificial entity (Dewey, 1926; Vinogradoff, 1924). Rephrased in modern terms, this meant that the corporation was an entity, and that the entity was a state-created reification. This operative "concession" notion had been received from British law. With the special charter as the dominant mode of corporate creation, this concession-based corporate theory accurately described American corporate practice. Corporations were "artificial" and "fictive" in part because observers looked to the conduct of individuals for the economic substance of businesses.[5] Thus, American legal theory fastened the classical conception of the economy as a system of transactions among individuals onto a legal foundation of individual property rights.

B. The Middle Period—The 1850s to the 1880s

This was a transitional period in corporate history. Increased production by incorporated businesses ended the harmony between economic practice and individualist modes of thinking. A factory economy developed during this period, as entrepreneurs launched the first manufacturing corporations. The corporation became a common legal form for doing business, including manufacturing and selling. The first great management hierarchies also appeared during this period, but these governed only the railroads. Manufacturing, while now corporate, continued under simple governance structures; substantial identity still existed between owners and managers (Clark, 1981; George, 1982; Chandler, 1977).

The states enacted "general corporation laws" to assure equal access to the corporate form. These laws emerged in a relatively set pattern, including provisions respecting corporate purposes, directors' powers, capital structure, dividends, amendments, and mergers (Hurst, 1970; Mark, 1987). The proliferation of general corporation laws necessitated adjustments in the underlying theory of the firm. The "legal fiction" and "artificial entity" notions were questioned because new statutes impaired their base in concession theory. Widespread use of the corporate form also aroused individualist criticism. Individual economic power seemed to decline as corporate manufacturing expanded. As separate economic entities, corporations diluted individual moral and legal responsibility among groups of business people. Commentators charged that corporations subverted market control of private economic power.

The management structures of the mid-century railroads presented the most striking departures from the classical economic model. Like later management corporations, these corporations had large managerial hierarchies and were financed by outside equity holders. But unlike later management corporations, which had large numbers of outside stockholders holding small blocks of stock, these railroads had small numbers of outside stockholders holding large blocks of stock. These outside equity investors sought an active role in corporate internal affairs. Outside investment bankers sat on the boards and exercised vetoes against management. Conflicts of interest arose because the financial interests wanted short-term profits while the managers took a long-term perspective (Chandler, 1977; Hurst, 1970).

The classical economic model did not offer a solution for this conflict. It assumed that profit-maximizing, individual entrepreneurs both owned the means of production and directed production. With the railroads, this basic assumption no longer obtained. To address individualist concerns, corporate doctrine developed restraints against corporate and managerial power. To keep managers under control, the doctrine confined corporate activities within the parameters of a stated purpose. To keep corporations small, the doctrine limited their capital (Hurst, 1970; Stevens, 1949; Horwitz, 1985). Nevertheless, like the preceding and subsequent periods of corporate legal history, this one was kind to management. General corporation laws effectively defused egalitarian objections to the corporation. Corporate law also legitimized broad authority to officers while it kept stockholders out of direct participation in the decisionmaking process (Hurst, 1970: 45–57). Corporate doctrine did facilitate some self-protection by stockholders through proportional voting rules and proportional rights to subscribe to new issues of stock. On the other hand, mismanagement was not actionable without a showing of gross negligence. Although a corporate law of investor protection developed during this period, its beneficiaries were corporate creditors.

C. From the 1880s through the Turn of the Century—the Appearance of the Management Corporation

Management corporations appeared around 1890.[6] Hierarchies of salaried executives dominated these new corporations. Successful mass production required long-term policy commitments and substantial investment; professional, salaried managers were designated to make these formulations and to direct production. Actors on the capital markets withdrew from active participation in corporate management because they saw themselves as lacking in necessary expertise. The split in the classical entrepreneurial function, presaged by the experience of the mid-century railroad companies, widened: Ownership of capital and control of the firm became completely separate (Berle and Means, 1968). Management corporations rapidly came to dominate the economy.[7] Their dominance occasioned a substantial relocation and reformulation of economic power. Corporate control of production partially displaced market control, causing power to flow from individuals to groups. with management corporations dominant, entities, rather than transactions between individuals, guided the flow of goods through the processes of production and distribution. Some of this management power was effectively unilateral—hierarchical superiors directed subordinates in the production and marketing processes. As to other economic actors-investors, suppliers, and consumers-management groups exercised varying degrees of dominance in the context of bilaterally structured relations.

Different explanations have been advanced for the management corporation's displacement of the market-controlled economy. Chandler (1977) offers an explanation from the perspective of cost economics. In his view, administrative coordination permitted greater productivity by lowering costs; corporations thus won out in the competitive marketplace. The internalization of units of production lowered transaction and information costs, and permitted more intensive use of resources. Internalization required management. Piore and Sabel (1984) offer a contrasting explanation centered on production. In their view, coordination of resources by the price system became impossible as industrial resources became highly specialized in the late nineteenth century. The new production technologies had high fixed costs, the recovery of which necessitated high levels of capacity utilization. To justify high utilization, markets had to be created. The price system could not, by itself, coordinate mass production and mass marketing, so the management corporation was devised to perform the task.

The legal theory of the firm became a topic of debate just at the time management corporations appeared. Both sides of the debate rejected the earlier doctrinal notions of the corporation as "legal fiction" and "artificial entity." But they diverged in their responses to the management corporation. One side was individualist and hostile, hewing closely to classical economic notions. The other side abandoned individualism for "corporate realism," a metaphysical theory that proved congenial to management interests.

D. The Twentieth Century to 1980

Management corporations continued their rise during the first half of the twentieth century. The image of the corporation as an entity rose with them. During this period, internal changes in corporate structure enhanced management discretion. Early management corporations had been single hierarchical units following a "line and organization" structure.[8] After the First World War, a new structure composed of multiple divisions appeared in a few leading corporations. The multidivisional corporation contained more than one operating unit and had a top management group responsible for all the units. Top management became separate from operations management. This permitted long-term policy to be formulated more effectively as decisionmakers were freed from localized biases stemming from ties to operating units. This form of organization became widespread after the Second World War, reaching maturity with the conglomerate corporations of the late 1960s (Chandler, 1977; Temin, 1964).

Investment patterns also enhanced management discretion during this period. Shareholders became widely dispersed as small investors joined the full-time capitalists as equity investors in management corporations. Widespread public purchases of shares provided the heavy capitalization required by the firm that appeared at the turn of the century (Temin, 1964). By the 1920s and 1930s, management and these widespread equity investors reached an unspoken, working understanding about power and money. Managers of large firms "agreed" to maintain stable dividends in return for the freedom to pursue a "growth" strategy. A growth strategy would permit management to raise equity capital internally, thereby avoiding new issues of equity securities and accompanying market judgments about management performance. The capital markets, valuing corporate "growth," went along (Berle, 1954).

Corporate law also continued to support management. The model of state corporate law originated by New Jersey and Delaware at the turn of the century became the national norm. In the 1930s, the federal government supplemented state law with the federal securities laws. These required public disclosure of material information for the benefit of investors and the securities markets. In contrast to state corporate law, the securities laws operated as a moderate constraint on management discretion. Legal theories respecting the management corporation changed substantially around 1930. Berle and Means (1968) marked the beginning of the new era and set out a paradigm based on managerialist concepts drawn from economics. Berle and Means recognized that shares of stock no longer carried the traditional shareholder/corporate relations built around intermediate securities markets. This was a contractual concept: Shareholders supplied capital and took risks, but then looked to the securities markets for fulfillment of their essential expectations of liquidity and appraisal. Failures in the operations of the marketplace required legislative intervention. But, even assuming successful technical correction of these failures, the shareholder interest could not be said contractually to control management.[9]

1. Managerialist Economics   Given this picture, which locates corporate power in hands of management, management legitimacy became an issue. Berle and Means's book popularized the basic points of institutional economics. It analyzed the firm from outside of the assumptions and methodology of classical and neoclassical economics and concluded that the classical model of efficient production, in which production occurs at prices tending toward producers' marginal costs, did not apply to corporate productive processes. Furthermore, market forces controlled neither the structure, the organization, nor the performance of management corporations. Within the management corporation, profit no longer was a motivating force. With the separation of ownership and control, the entrepreneurial drive assumed in classical economics had become split between management and capital. Management, the group controlling the means of production, was not motivated primarily by profit-seeking, but by drives for power, prestige, and job security.

The question was, absent behavior in the classical profit-maximizing mode, what behavior patterns and objectives characterized the management corporation? Institutionalists made many suggestions. The most famous replaced profit with "growth" as the objective (Baumol, 1962), and maximizing with "satisficing" as the behavior pattern (Cyert and March, 1963). While in some respects critical of management, institutionalist literature had a supportive aspect. It afforded a cost justification: The management corporation produced goods more cheaply than could disaggregated producers in a classical economic universe; management corporations produced and competed effectively, if not efficiently in the narrow sense. The lack of direct controls on management, either by the price system or by the capital markets, did not necessarily present a serious problem. Growth was the mark of successful enterprise and successful managing. Managers sought it, and strong institutional pressures from investors and peers encouraged them to do so. This "growth bias" left managers close enough to classical profit maximizers (Herman, 1981: 106–13; Chandler, 1977; Baumol, 1959; Marris, 1964; and, Buxbaum, 1984).

Economic theory also explained why the investment community view management's pursuit of the growth objective with equanimity by bringing it into balance. It aligned management's long-term investment perspectives with capital's often short-term investment perspectives. Since growth ultimately raised the level of dividend return, it manifested itself in present capital appreciation, that is, a higher stock price, or so it seemed, the long-term industrial stability and short-term profit.

Meanwhile, a separate discipline within economics—neoclassical economics—contin-

ued to operate in the classical tradition. Prior to the appearance of the new economic theory of the firm in the 1970s, however, neoclassical microeconomists declined to theorize about the internal operations of the management corporation, restricting their attention to the market (Jensen, 1983; Rosenberg, 1983; Hessen, 1979). Their models explained coordination of the use of resources and distribution of income by the price system. They employed the received model of the single-product firm operating in a static but highly competitive environment. This approach reduced the firm to a "black box"—a "production function" deemed to follow profit considerations exclusively and behave as an entity in rational patterns no different from those of human actors. Managerial power, if it existed at all, was assumed to be effectively controlled by market forces.[10]

In the age of the management corporation, this limited inquiry made neoclassical microeconomics a discipline of obviously limited explanatory capabilities. Yet microeconomists did not perceive a debilitating problem and rush to expand their models. They thought of actions inside firms as "engineering"—functions of hierarchical structures—and, therefore, not a subject matter suited to a discipline that studies markets. The neoclassicists' hierarchical conception of internal firm affairs signified concurrence in the managerialist conception prevalent among the institutionalists and academic lawyers.

2. Managerialist Law   The debate over management legitimacy included one issue stated in terms of traditional legal theory. This issue—whether the corporation was public or private—addressed the validity of government regulation. A century earlier, concession theory would have justified regulation. But concession had fallen out of currency; its imagery no longer made sense. Accordingly, advocates of regulation reformulated the political assertions bound up in concession theory. They abandoned the sovereign creation story and accepted the primacy of individual creativity and energy in corporate life. But they characterized the product of all this individual activity as "public" in nature. This characterization supported the position that uncontrolled management wielded its power illegitimately and should be subjected to additional legal controls.

Anti-managerialists demonstrated the firm's public nature by analogizing managerial power to governmental power. Like government, large corporations took actions important to those outside of the organization. Like government authorities, managers exercised their power by means of a rationalized system of control and administration. Like the government, the "public" firm was a "political" entity.[11] Political theories respecting government, such as interest group pluralism, therefore should be applied to it.[12]

The "public" theme also figured into doctrinal fairness jurisprudence. Corporate doctrine follows the trust model in name only. In practice, it leaves substantial room for self-interested conduct by corporate managers. Anti-managerialists drew on the analogy to government in their criticism of the doctrine's managerialist bias. Our system normally treats public offices as trusts. We require public officers to show respect for others, even-handedness, and selflessness in situations in which we leave private persons unregulated. Given these assumptions, a "public" model of corporations implies strict scrutiny of the managerial actions affecting the interests of investors.

E. The Contemporary Debate—
The New Economic Theory
versus Managerialism

With the new economic theory, neoclassical microeconomists surmounted the conceptual barriers that prevented them from elaborating a modern theory of corporate structure (Jensen, 1983; Rosenberg, 1983; Cheung, 1983; Blaug, 1980; Friedman, 1962; and, McNulty, 1984). The solution was simple. The new theory avoided direct consideration of hierarchies in management corporations, setting out a picture in which corporate entity and hierarchy were irrelevant. By describing all internal relationships as market transactions, the theory permitted large organizations to be discussed within the traditions of neoclassical microeconomic. No acknowledgement of "engineering" sullied the theorists' hands.

The neoclassical new economic theory pronounced a new solution to the problem of the split entrepreneurial function. Where turn-of-the-century corporate realism patched over the split with a unified, real corporate being, the new economic theory offered the converse solution of a completely deconstructed corporate entity. Since no cognizable corporate collectivity appears amidst the nexus of contracts, no tension arises between collective and individual interests. The new theory does not look for corporate replication of individual profit-maximizing. The entrepreneurial function emerges in separate but unified pieces among the aggregated individuals. Ironically, this solution draws on the same classical tradition that originally stated the problem.

With this market-based solution, the neoclassicists rebutted both the managerialists' statement of the corporate problem and their regulatory solutions. The managerialist corporate entity almost disappears, dissolving into disaggregated but interworking transactions among the participating actors. The "separation of ownership and control," on which the managerialist picture based management power, no longer matters. "Ownership" becomes as irrelevant a concept as "firm entity." The "firm" is only a series of contracts covering inputs being joined so as to become output. "Capital," and thus the traditional legal situs of ownership, devolves into one of the many types of inputs (Alchian and Demsetz, 1972: 781-89).

Though the neoclassicists nominally made these moves for the purpose of explanation, their operative assumptions gave the theory a normative aspect. Treating hierarchy as if it does not exist offers wonderful support to those at the top of the hierarchy, so long as the treatment implies no concomitant recording of the status quo. Moreover, by challenging the anti-managerialist critique of corporate law, the neoclassicists in some respects challenge the status quo in management's favor. They rebut the anti-managerialists' "public" characterization with a model of "private" contracts among successfully contracting market actors. "Concessions" of sovereign authority have no place in this picture of free contract.

By stripping the content from the firm entity and introducing the self-interested rational economic actor, the new theory also rebuts the concept of fiduciary duty. Legal duties of selflessness do not figure into the neoclassicists' conception of bilateral contract relations (Bratton, 1989). These market contracts implicitly justify what they depict: Since they are priced to take management self-interest into account, extant customs of managerial self-dealing therefore must be all right, or cost competition would have caused them to disappear long ago. None of this was lost on participants in the corporate governance debates of the late 1970s and early 1980s. To one anti-managerialist observer, the new economic theory completes the twentieth century trend toward loosened fiduciary restraints and enhanced management discretion (Brudney, 1985). It legitimizes the received hierarchical picture of the management corporation as a contractual arrangement which minimizes transaction costs. This picture also makes the corporation a "private" phenomenon. It affirms the corporate structure and management's place in it, even as it admits the possibility of contract failure. Some of the new economic theory's initial success in the legal academy may be attributable to this support of management. The new economic theory brought academic theory into line with the practices of corporate doctrine. The academic line had stressed managerial public duty and legal constraint. Corporate doctrine equivocated; it repeated the fiduciary principle and maintained a governmental presence even as it steadfastly protected the management corporation's private

law bases and the discretionary authority of managers.

F. Summary

In the classical world of the early nineteenth century, economic practice and theory coexisted in peace. Corporate production was an anomalous feature of the economic landscape. The corporation was integrated into the classical picture by a limiting theory—it was a legal institution only. But as the century proceeded and corporate production became the norm, it became clear that the corporate firm was more than a legal institution. The entrepreneurial function became split in economic practice, and the classical peace ended. Legal theory offered two opposing solutions. One, contractualism, sought to minimize the split and protect the individual by suppressing the corporation. The other, realism, made the split irrelevant by transcending the individual interest with a spiritual firm entity. Neither solution wore well in the twentieth century.

In the twentieth century, the management corporation became a normal institution. But the classical reproach continued to influence theoretical perspectives. With managerialism, the split entrepreneurial function became the base point of both economic and legal theory. Nineteenth century individualism, however, did not dominate managerialist responses to the classically stated problem. In the ongoing discourse of legitimization, individual, bilateral relations within corporate entities were obscured amidst the concepts and habits of social policy-making. In legal theory, the individualist impulse remained largely subordinated until the appearance of the new economic theory. With this new theory, twentieth century individualists integrated classical theory and twentieth century practice. This theory offered a return to a world of classical peace: It healed the split entrepreneurial function and returned the corporate entity to limited life as a legal institution.

III. THE NONEVOLUTIONARY HISTORY OF THE DOCTRINAL THEORY OF THE CORPORATE FIRM

A second, nonevolutionary history of the theory of the corporate firm parallels the foregoing evolutionary account. This account looks only to corporate doctrine, drawing on the definitions of the firm operative in treatises and other doctrinal work from the mid-nineteenth to the mid-twentieth century. This account shows that as the focus of attention shifts from theory to practice, historical tensions between individualism and the demands of collective enterprise ease. The doctrine mediated the tensions. It amalgamates the theoretical alternatives, averting controversy by balancing the variant points of view advanced in more purely theoretical contexts. Thus, the doctrinal theory of the firm is capacious. And it appears to have performed a useful function: As a base of agreement on basic conceptions, it has permitted corporate law decisionmakers to subordinate theoretical concerns and look to the particulars of situations in deciding cases (Blaug, 1980).

A. The Angell and Ames Definition

The doctrinal theory of the firm may be traced, in America, to Angell and Ames (1871), the leading antebellum corporate law treatise. Angell and Ames dealt with the problem of devising a theoretical characterization of the corporation by drawing on definitions from three prominent works. One definition came from Kent's *Commentaries* (1866), but had origins going as far back as the writings of Pope Innocent IV. The second came from Kyd's late eighteenth century British treatise on corporate law (1793). The third was the famous description of the corporation in Chief Justice Marshall's opinion in the *Dartmouth College* case (1819).

First, the definition Angell and Ames drew from Chancellor Kent:

> A corporation is [an artificial and fictitious] body, created by law, composed of individu-

als united under a common name, the members of which succeed each other, so that the body continues the same, notwithstanding the change of individuals who compose it, and is, for certain purposes, considered as a natural person. (Angell and Ames, 1871: 150)

Second, the Kyd definition:

> A corporation, or a body politic, or body incorporate, is a collection of many individuals, united into one body, under a special denomination, having perpetual succession under an artificial form, and vested, by the policy of law, with the capacity of acting, in several respects, as an individual, particularly of taking and granting property, if contracting obligations, of suing and being sued, of enjoying privileges immunities in common, and of exercising a variety of political rights more or less extensive, according to the design of its institution, or the powers conferred upon it, either at the time of its creation, or at any subsequent period of its existence. (Kyd, 1793)

Finally, Chief Justice Marshall's discussion:

> A corporation is an artificial being, invisible, intangible, and existing only in contemplation of law. Being the mere creature of law, it possesses only those properties which the charter of its creation confers upon it, either expressly, or as incidental to its very existence. These are such as are supposed best calculated to effect the object for which it was created. Among the most important are immortality, and, if the expression may be allowed, individuality. . . . Its immortality no more confers on it political power, or a political character, than immortality would confer such power or character on a natural person. It is no more a state instrument, than a natural person exercising the same powers would be. (*Dartmouth* v. *Woodward*, 1819: 636)

Significant commonalities tie the three definitions together, despite their variant vocabularies and emphases. Each definition conceives of the corporation as a reification, finding reality in the actions of individual participants. Each simultaneously recognizes entity and aggregate characteristics, concession and contractual origins, and public and private aspects. Which aspect proves relevant in a given situation depends on the facts and the particular observer's perspective. Kent and Chief Justice Marshall may be distinguished from Kyd for stronger emphasis on the entity. Kyd permits virtually nothing in the way of determinate thought structures inside his corporate entity, and Kyd's lesser emphasis on concession follows from his treatment of the entity: The less content in the entity, the less practical significance attaches to the state's act of creating it.

B. Usage of the Angell and Ames Definition Prior to 1930

The Angell and Ames definition, or in some cases one or two of its three components became standard matter. The definition even can be found, stated as living legal doctrine, in a treatise published in 1958 (Oleck, 1958). The definition therefore may be taken as a constant doctrinal theory of the corporate firm. The writers adjusted the Angell and Ames formula as corporate doctrine changed. For example, the late nineteenth century texts tended to drop the immortality point. Unlimited corporate life, presumably, had become an unremarkable doctrinal assumption. The late nineteenth century texts also mentioned the decline of concession theory and the passing of the fiction notion. Late nineteenth century writers also took the trouble to note explicitly that the received definition renders the corporation as an entity and an aggregate both. Modifications continued after the turn of the century. Writers included the governance model of the liberal incorporation statutes next to the historical definitions. This move provided the reified entity with some additional substance, but otherwise left the Angell and Ames conceptions unchanged.

After the turn of the century, writers began to lose confidence in the Angell and Ames definition's effectiveness. The nine-teenth century emphases on fiction and concession had disappeared, but no new concepts came in to replace them and limit the definition's capacity. Rather than reformulate from the ground up on some new theoretical basis, writers supplemented the definition with a practical admonition. As one writer said, "A full and complete definition of a corporation can only be given by telling what are its rights, powers, duties, and relations, and the legal and equitable principles which control it in all its parts and functions and how they operate" (Spelling, 1982: 4). These practical definitions, by referring inquiries to particulars of corporate law, said in effect that the legal corporation is the sum of the laws, and that the received theoretical characterizations of the whole lack something in meaning.

C. The Doctrinal Theory of the Corporate Firm after 1930

Theory of the firm had a bad reputation after the realist/anti-realist debate terminated in the late 1920s. By 1976, traditional theory of the firm concepts had fallen so far from view that theoretically ambitious works on corporate structure omitted any mention of them. Discussion shifted to policy inquiries into management performance. Commercial images of the corporation had overshadowed the concept of the corporation; corporate law's underlying intellectual construct had rotted away (Manning, 1962; Eisenberg, 1976; Knauss, 1981).

The twentieth century writers, freed from transcendental "corporate realism," practiced the very different lessons of "conceptual approaches" to policy problems (Conard, 1976: 419–20). Instead, they employed various substitute concepts to describe the reality of corporation, as "more nearly a method than a thing" (Anderson, 1931; Ballantine, 1946)—a "technique" for organizing relationships among individuals (Ratner, 1980–81). This approach stripped the fixed content from the entity concept, causing the entity to devolve into a rope tying together the bundle of relationships. Under this approach, each corporate relationship, whether a contract, or performance of a duty stemming from positive law, was analyzed separately according to its own circumstances. The corporation emerged with a variable meaning.

A second substitute was Wormser's "legal unit." Here again, the corporation was described as a device—the means to the end of distinguishing corporate rights and liabilities from those of associated individuals. A third substitute was the "group interest." Here the corporation appeared as a "body of [individual] bodies" in which group and individual interests were to be distinguished (Henn, 1961). This conception replaced the "entity" with the "group." One writer claimed that this replacement caused all the conceptual difficulties presented by the corporation's nonphysical qualities to disappear (Stevens, 1949: 51).

The twentieth century writers' various characterizations of the firm entity—group interests, binding methods, and legal units—give us more or less the corporate entity envisioned by Kyd and respected in the treatises for a century (Anderson, 1931). Even Chief Justice Marshall can be read back into the modern writers. When they pointed out that corporations are merely means to an end, they only repeated one of the Chief Justice's points. Putting aside the concession notions peculiar to his time, Chief Justice Marshall's legal fiction is difficult to distinguish from the legal unit of the Ballantine treatise (Ballantine, 1946). Both existed for the conduct of business; both were private; both were reified; and both gained meaning in the wider context of corporate doctrine.

IV. COMMENTS FROM THE HISTORY

Drawing on the foregoing historical accounts, this part comments critically on the principal contemporary assertions about the legal theory of the firm. Horwitz's proposition that corporate realism was a determinative force in legitimizing the management

corporation is addressed first. Horwitz does not take into account the doctrinal theory of the firm emphasized in this article. Second, attention turns to the new economic theorists' assertion that the corporation "is contract." The discussion suggests that the point is unsuited to literal transfer from the narrow context of economic theory to the wider, more complex context of legal doctrine.

A. Horwitz's Proposition

According to Horwitz, corporate realism and the management corporation rose together. Corporate realism offered collectivist justification for the new mass producing entities. Moreover it appeared just as these entities worked past the hostile implications of classical economic concepts to secure a safe place in the harbor of corporate law. But Horwitz's point that corporate realism caused the management corporation's success can be turned around—the practice could have aided the theory more than the theory aided the practice.

First consider the relationship between the doctrinal theory of the firm and the development of the management corporation. The management corporation changed the landscape that the corporate treatises described. The definitions reflected the change, albeit indirectly. The late nineteenth century writers omitted the legal fiction concept. This omission had a doctrinal cause—the appearance of general incorporation laws—but it also may be inferred that the management corporation made the theory untenable. Given the management corporation, more in the way of social reality had to be conceded to the firm. The historical definitions made this concession by dropping the limiting concept.

Next consider the relationship between the doctrinal theory of the firm and the debate over corporate realism and contractualism. Here the treatise-writers made a significant move. As the concession and fiction notions dropped out, the contractual and realist schools invited the doctrine in different directions. One offered contract and pure liberal individualism; the other offered realism and European organicism. The doctrinalists refused both invitations, choosing instead, as their predecessors had done, to balance the metapolitical alternatives. The doctrinal theory only changed in appearance when the writers abandoned the historical vocabulary around 1930.

Thus, when the managerialist era arrived, neither corporate realism nor contractualism had achieved a sufficiently deep level of acceptance to become the generally accepted basis for everyday corporate doctrine. Realism and contractualism were events of primarily academic interest. When academic theory changed course around 1930, corporate realism disappeared with hardly a trace.

The fragility of theory of the firm concepts permits the inference that practice had the primary causative role. The new management corporation necessitated considerable adjustment to ways of thinking about economic life (Piore and Sabel, 1984:49-51). It took some time before a settle bundle of concepts achieved general currency. The corporate realism debates occurred during the period of adjustment. Observers were generally favorable to the management corporation because of its apparent economic success, but lacked present explanatory and legitimizing theories. This uncertainty made corporate realism plausible for a time, but the realist explanation proved tentative. As the management corporation matured, a more suitable set of concepts achieved general currency. As a result, corporate realism fell out of currency rather abruptly.

The supplanting and enduring ideas came from contemporary American economics rather than from nineteenth-century European jurisprudence. These ideas were practical: Management possessed expertise and performed its job effectively; therefore, it had the law's support. To the extent management's performance failed to fit whatever scheme of social, political, or economic guidelines the particular observer applied, then some economic or legal adjustment was required. As this practical picture of the management corporation was drawn, and pro- and anti-managerial positions staked out within its framework, corporate realism's basis in European speculation about group imperatives must have come to seem out of touch with practice.

Ever-present American individualism provides a deeper explanation for the change. Americans historically tend to be uncomfortable with theories—here termed "organicist"—that accord the group intrinsic primacy over the individual (Romano, 1984). Corporate realism was organicist; managerialism was not, even though it tended to socialize individual interests. Managerialism internalized individualism by conditioning its legitimization of collective corporate life on management performance. It acknowledged a significant,if not dominant, place for contract in the structure of the management corporation. And it offered a firm conception consonant with the political alignment sought by both sides of the debate: With managerialism, individualists could be pro-managerialist at the same time that collectivists could be anti-managerialist.

B. The New Economic Theory of the Firm

The new economic theory presented something new to the world of neoclassical microeconomics when its neoclassical variant appeared in the 1970s. Its nexus of contracts assertion solved a century-old problem by offering a way around the conceptual barriers to a neoclassical theory of corporate structure. But transposed to a legal context, the assertion was less new than it looked. Contract always has figured into the legal theory of the firm. The new economic theory confirms and repeats legal history when it asserts that the corporation "is contract." It joins a tradition when it offers to resolve the tension between the ideals of classical economics and the institution of the management corporation. But the new theory also breaks with historical pattern: It is absolutely contractual, while contract never has dominated legal theory.

Significantly, modern academic theory reflected the doctrinal theory less clearly before the new economic theory appeared. The managerialist picture understated the presence of contract, particularly arms length contract, in corporate arrangements. For decades, anti-managerialist commentators criticized corporate doctrine for insufficient recognition of fiduciary constraints. Not all observers shared this anti-managerialism, but supporters of managerial discretion had no well-articulated theoretical response. The new economic theory's contractualism gave them an answer, explaining and justifying the doctrine's pro-management recalcitrance. It thereby brought academic theory back into alignment with the doctrinal theory and its enduring base point of individualism.

The new theory also resonated well because it drew on elements already present in and around corporate doctrine. Twentieth-century corporations and corporate doctrine offered plenty of contracts around which to base a theory. The case law alternated between an entity-based structural conception in which the entity employs management, and a contractually based structural conception, in which management acts as the shareholders' agent.

Thus, the new theory articulated points and values already embedded in the doctrine but only faintly recognized in earlier academic theory. But the new theory broke sharply with another, equally significant strand of historical precedent: the relegation of contract to a supporting role in corporate legal theory and practice. Absolutely asserted contractual theories had appeared before—one during the late nineteenth century and a second with Coase's essay of 1937. Nineteenth-century contract theory failed to garner general acceptance and Coase's 1937 discussion of the firm as a product of cost-effective contracting had limited influence, even among economists, for more than thirty years.

The new economic theory descends directly from Coase. It has a more collateral relation with the contractualism of nineteenth-century legal theory, but a cognizable tie binds the two. Fixing the new theory's relations with earlier corporate theory, and explaining the earlier theory's failure to achieve general acceptance, demonstrates limitations on the new theory's potential practical influence.

Despite these similarities, the two approaches have materially different goals. The nineteenth century contractualists sought to protect a disaggregated economic system from the constraints of corporate hierarchies. The new economic theory abandons their goal even as it revives their concepts. The new theory accepts the management corporation and employs classical economic ideas—ideas originally derived from observation of a disaggregated economy—to justify its continuing presence.

This is a significant turn in the history of relations between corporate enterprise and American individualism. Before the turn of the century, individualists held to an atomistic social ideal and attacked all big organizations, public and private. Next came an uneasy coexistence, manifested in the neoclassicists' limited consideration of the firm. Finally, with the new economic theory, the heirs of the classical tradition surrender to the corporate hierarchy and embrace it. In so doing, the new theorists announce that corporate hierarchies had been composed of bilateral market contract all along. But theirs is a different, more rearguard political action than that of their nineteenth-century predecessors. Today's contractualists limit their critique to the largest hierarchical institution, the government. To bolster opposition, they legitimize nongovernmental institutions with a diluted version of the atomistic social ideal.[13]

To explain contracts's long absence from academic theories of the corporate firm, we look to the appearance of power relationships in practice. Before the 1970s, legal academics and institutional economists emphasized hierarchies, while neoclassical economists turned a blind eye to the firm's interior, because contract, and particularly the discrete contract of academic contract law of this century's early decades,[14] did not seem to capture the institution's essence. The contracting process had a quiet dynamic; it did not appear actively to govern. Management seemed to be the catalyst that made the factors of production work successfully in the management corporation, and this catalytic capability stemmed from structural position. Management appeared to possess unilateral power—it directed production. The obvious complex of bilateral contracts in and around the firm failed to comprise the center of gravity in the theory because they did not seem to affect the distribution of power in practice.

Had actors in the capital markets chosen to exercise a governance role, as they did during the middle period of the nineteenth-century, the complex of contracts respecting stocks and bonds might have prompted formulation of a different, more contractual theory of the firm. Instead, a contractual event in practice—the implicit agreement between management and the financial community—kept investors and their stock and bond sales contracts from figuring actively in the power picture. Given this background, the anti-managerialists quite sensibly looked to public sources—the force of public opinion (Berle, 1954: 54) or legal reform (Cary, 1974; Nader, Green & Seligman, 1976)—for controls on management discretion.

Recent practical changes, subsumed under the heading "market for corporate control," have changed the corporate power picture. Stockholders and their contracts have taken a prominent place. But the changes have not been sufficiently revolutionary to create a practice that mirrors the absolute contractualism held out by the new economic theory.

Anything being possible, the new theory's absolutist contractualism could find its way into corporate doctrine and effect a break with the historical pattern. But given past experience, such a fundamental change seems unlikely. In the past, theories that would close off the capacity of corporate law to facilitate transactions or their regulation

have not made the transfer from commentary into doctrine. Singleminded adherence to the new economic theory is as out of touch with the values historically undergirding corporate law as some of the singleminded anti-managerialism of the 1970s was in its time.

To sum up, the doctrinal theory of the corporate firm refutes the assertion that the corporation "is contract." History tells us that the corporation "is contract, and always has been contract and other things besides." While the doctrinal theory always takes cognizance of contractual elements, it never makes contract the essence. The doctrinal theory balances contract against the corporate entity and a sovereign presence. If, as seems probable, corporate law continues to evolve in accordance with the historical pattern, decisionmaking will proceed with reference to the particulars of the corporate relationship in question. Selection of the applicable theoretical paradigm—managerialist or contractual—will occur in the particular context as a quasi-political decision. Contractual notions will be entertained, but any move to foreclose wider discussion by the assertion that contract should govern as a function of the intrinsic nature of the corporation will fail.

V. CONTEMPORARY HISTORY— THE MARKET FOR CORPORATE CONTROL, THE MANAGEMENT CORPORATION, AND THE NEW ECONOMIC THEORY

The preceding discussion focused on recent changes in the theories describing power relationships in management corporations. Practical changes in these power relationships also have occurred recently. After 1960, corporate control became a more and more aggressively traded commodity. After 1980, trading became so extensive that it precipitated a widespread restructuring of management corporations. The following discussion connects the theory and the practice on a different level. It considers the practice, in history, as an explanation for the existence of the theory, and the theory, in history, as an explanation for changes in the practice.

A. The Early Market for Corporate Control and the Appearance of the New Economic Theory

As discussed in part IV, practical appearances of hierarchical power kept contract in a supporting role in corporate theory during most of this century. The market for corporate control has changed the practical picture materially. The hostile takeover makes it possible to remove corporate superiors by the exercise of stock market purchasing power. As takeovers have proliferated, changes have followed in the structure and internal affairs of management hierarchies. In effect, discrete contracts among stockholders take a significant place in the governance of the management corporation for the first time. The new economic theory parallels this practical change: It brings discrete contracting to a significant theoretical place in the governance of the management corporation for the first time. The histories of the theory and the practice invite interrelation.

Here is the proposition: The appearance of this aggressive model of discrete contracting was necessary to make a contractual picture of the management corporation plausible. Although the new economic theory, particularly its neoclassical variant, tends to be stated ahistorically, its success, and possibly its very existence, meaningfully can be accounted for historically. Had the practical changes not occurred, the new theory probably never would have appeared, and it certainly would not have achieved general currency in the legal academy.[15]

The chronology of the market for corporate control supports the proposition. Tender offers have a long history as a corporate tool, but prior to the 1950s they were used internally as a mode of stock repurchase. The earliest hostile uses of the tender offer came in the 1950s, and this usage matured in the 1960s. The first intensive year was 1963, in

which twenty-three hostile tender offers were made; eighty-six tender offers were made in 1967. Most of these early hostile tender offers were successful (Austin, 1973, 1975). Neoclassical observers saw the tie to their methodology right away. Henry Manne made the first theoretical assertion that the takeover phenomenon constituted market control of management conduct in an article published in 1965 (Manne, 1965). He introduced the phrase "market for corporate control" and asserted that the market accorded shareholders practical power commensurate with their interests in the corporation.

Manne's neoclassical interpretation was not the only plausible view of the takeover phenomenon during the early period. Indeed, prior to 1980, Manne's probably was not the most widely accepted view. The early takeovers also fit into the institutional economists' picture. In their view, the takeover enhanced managerial power. The paradigm hostile takeover during the 1960s and 1970s was an aggressive act by the managers of a large corporation against the managers of a smaller corporation. This paradigm takeover was one of several means employed in building conglomerate corporations. Such takeovers served the managerialist growth objective. Although the managers of the losing target corporation lost their jobs, their removal came at the initiative of a more powerful, similarly situated group. Management's image of structural empowerment therefore remained in place even as some insecurity of tenure came into the picture.[16]

Williamson, writing in accord with this perspective, explained the appearance of takeovers after 1960 as a product of the spread of the multidivisional corporate structure. This new structure redirected management attention from running production lines to the collection of conglomerate portfolios of operating units. Takeovers then arose to facilitate portfolio construction.[17]

During the early takeover period, lawyers and legal academics, like most economists, continued to operate under the managerialist picture. Anti-managerialists viewed management growth by acquisition with suspicion. Most of this suspicion manifested itself in antitrust objections, but corporate law reasons for caution also existed. Anti-managerialists sought application of fiduciary duty concepts to restrain the conduct of management in defending against tender offers, and to protect the interests of minority shareholders after takeover.[18] Furthermore, hostile takeovers tended to depress the price of the stock of the successful offeror, showing a market judgment that the takeovers aggrandized the managers of offeror corporations, and enriched target shareholders at the expense of the offeror's shareholders (Herman, 1984:537; Malatesta, 1983; Jensen and Ruback, 1983).

B. The Contemporary Market for Corporate Control and the New Economic Theory

The new economic theory does not unequivocally support management interests. The theory's denial of hierarchy strengthens management's position, but only as long as it does not support any serious challenges to that position. During the 1980s, the market for corporate control created such challenges. Just as the new economic theory's contractualism supports management against statist challenges from the corporate governance movement, its contractualism also supports corporate control transactions against management objections.[19]

In the more aggressive market for corporate control that appeared after 1980, almost all corporations became potential subjects for attack. Trading extended to corporation reconstruction as well as corporate control. Even middle management began to suffer. In this new cast, the takeover challenged not only management's security of position, but also its discretionary power.

New actors and financing devices carried the market to this more aggressive posture. Independent financial entrepreneurs entered the market as hostile offerors (Coffee, 1986). The new entrepreneurs played a different game. Unlike the conglomerate-building managers of the earlier period, they did not use the devices of the corporate control market to enhance operational power positions. They simply sought to force large payments to equity holders.

Funds for the big premiums came through aggressive use of the oldest financing tool, debt. The target's assets supplied the borrowing base. Once target-based debt financing became a critical component in a tender offer's success, a structural position atop a corporate hierarchy ceased to be a prerequisite for participation in the market. An actor taking an aggressive posture needed only credibility in the capital markets.

"Bust up" takeovers commenced in 1984. These opened up a second source of finance —sale of the target company's assets. Big payments to equity holders came from the proceeds of a subsequent dismantling of the target corporation as well as from borrowing. With these takeovers, actors on the corporate control market began to deconstruct the conglomerate corporations that the early control market helped construct. Reconstruction also was pursued defensively, through leveraged buyouts and stock repurchases. These defensive payouts to equity holders utilized the same financing tools of borrowing and asset sales.[20]

Although the full implications of this corporate restructuring remain unclear, a few generalizations can be made. The restructurings materially alter the old managerialist picture of structural empowerment. First, their quantity, scope, and frequency has made management tenure generally insecure. Second, the longstanding implicit agreement between management and capital has dissolved. The investment community no longer passively accepts the growth objective. Thus, restructurings may be viewed as the capital markets' successful demand for the return of capital suboptimally invested in pursuit of growth. By forcing the return of this capital, the investment community indirectly, but strongly, influences the shaping of investment policy. Because investment policy is the central discretionary function of the multidivisional corporate management group, capital's refusal to comply and cooperate denudes management of significant power.

For the first time since the brief appearance of finance capitalism in the nineteenth-century, then, actors in the capital markets critically influence investment policy. Capital's perspective still tends toward the short term. As a result, conflicts between the short- and long-term investment perspectives of investors and managers have become a problem once again (Lowenstein, 1988). Legal policy discussions have adjusted in response. Emphasis has shifted from management's abuse of power acquired by structural default, to management's inability to invest with a long view because of capital's power to terminate management at will.[21]

The restructurings also require conforming adjustments in the existing body of work under the new economic theory. The institutionalists explained the conglomerate corporation as a product of a contracting process driven by the competitive need to decrease costs (Chandler, 1977: 462-63, 482). The restructurings undo conglomerate combinations, eliminating layers of multidivisional form diversification and firing layers of management staff.[22] In effect, the financial community repudiates the proposition that conglomerates are cost effective.

The neoclassical model also must be adjusted (Coffee, 1986: 25-28). The model assumed that contracting actors adopted structures capable of bringing agency costs down to a competitive minimum. It then explained existing arrangements, including the relative passivity of capital markets and the dominance of management, in those terms. When historical forces suddenly and materially rewrote the contracts, doubts arose about the validity of this ahistorical picture, and of the methodology that created it. The restructurings manifest the capital markets' judgment that previous market arrangements did not effectively minimize management agency costs. In response, Jensen has modified his picture of the firm to explain the massive replacement of equity by debt in terms of an efficient contracting device: Management borrows at a high fixed rate to "bond" its future performance (Jensen, 1986). But, as Coffee has pointed out, this prospective and ahistorical adjustment does not erase the model's previous failure to accommodate history (Coffee, 1986: 28).

Despite these difficulties with particulars, the new economic theory may be connected with the appearance of the market for corporate reconstruction. To see the connection one must take a broad view. The new theory's contractual perspective assumes that people look closely and act firmly when money is at stake. It depicts a corporate structure in which rational investors work hard to circumvent managerial claims to nonreviewability due to differential expertise (Coffee, 1986; Levmore, 1982). This approach consigns management to a reduced status.

The neoclassical picture contains additional, strong negative implications for management. The theory's minimal firm entity remove management from its former position as the essence of the firm. Management emerges in the picture as but one of many factors of production (Fama, 1980). In the neoclassical world of discrete contracts, factors of production come and go as contracts continually are made, performed and remade, or are made and broken. No relational values afford management a defense against attack by investors seeking to rewrite the next generation of contracts. No entity notions, no notion of professionalism, and no sense of the necessity of tenure protection enter into the picture.

Even the institutional variant implicitly recognizes managerial vulnerability. Its description of multidivisional structure demystifies the management process. Hands-on production skills no longer figure into management's strategic position. The multidivisional architect of a portfolio of operating divisions has no skills not possessed in rudimentary form by the latest crop of business school graduates. Like the neoclassicists' factors of production, the institutionalists' portfolio manager is replaceable in the active search for a higher return.

Thus, the market practice of corporate restructuring generated by contract—sales of stock on or off the trading markets, and arms-length debt contracts—demonstrates the theory's dynamic, if not every point of the extant models. The market practice follows the theory in time: In the 1970s, the theory asserted that the managerialist picture of unilateral power was inaccurate; in the 1980s, the marketplace changed the picture and used the theory's primary tool, the discrete, bilateral contract, as the means of shifting power. Today's popular conception of the powerful business figure is not the managerialist chief executive officer but the capitalist deal maker—the financial entrepreneur or the investment banker. Characterized in the vocabulary of the new economic theory, these figures acquire power as transaction cost engineers. They conceive and initiate transactions, depriving the managerial beneficiaries of the more costly existing contracts of power and wealth.

Can we ascribe to the antecedent theory a causative role in the subsequent practice? Paraphrasing Horwitz's conclusions on the turn-of-the-century interplay between theory of the firm and corporate practice, the causation assertion would be that the rise of the new economic theory was a "major factor" in legitimizing the market restructuring of the management corporation and that "none of the theoretical alternatives could provide as much sustenance" (Horwitz, 1985) to the new anti-management utilization of the market for corporate control.

This causation assertion overstates the theory's role. Conceptual associations between the theory and the practice are easy to make; articulating a precise causative role for the theory in recent movements of millions of dollars of capital is more difficult. Models in

the *Journal of Financial Economics* do not become business plans for the new financial entrepreneurs. Moreover, practice offers alternative, plausible determinative antecedents. Two decades of managerialist use of the takeover account for the presence of the devices used. The contemporary structure of the institutional investment community accounts for the disappearance of the Wall Street rule and for more aggressive shareholder postures. The competitive failures of American management in international markets during the last two decades (Piore and Sabel, 1984: 184-202), and the disappointing returns on common stock during the decade prior to 1984, account for a general consensus on the need to restructure.

Even so, the new economic theory has a place in all this. The restructuring takeover has met little effective opposition, and any number of legislative moves might have deterred it (Nash, 1987). The theory persuasively manifests the wider antiregulatory and contractualist environment in a respectable academic form specific to the context. The neoclassical variant, with its roots in classical economic theory, comes particularly well-made to support moneymaking by independent entrepreneurs through bilateral contracting.

Significantly, corporate legal doctrine performs a similar legitimizing role. The doctrine, despite its close association with managerialism throughout this century, has accommodated the resurgent capitalists without significant alteration. The received structure incorporates bilateral contracting and aggregate interests. The doctrine made available all of the contractual devices employed in the restructuring market, and the longstanding conceptual association of management and the corporate entity did not prevent their use. Even as the restructuring takeover brought the continued validity of reams of managerialist literature into question, it left the doctrine nearly untouched. The historical doctrinal theory of the firm and its facilitative and capacious qualities come to mind, providing the new economic theory with a "place" in the legitimization of the recent restructuring.

C. Comments

The restructuring takeover does not return us to the world of Adam Smith. The number of managerial personnel may have declined; their identities may have changed; and conglomerate corporations may have become less bloated. But they still exist. Management retains a position of "power by default." Its basic operational authority over resources and people in the organization remains largely intact.[23] Restructuring takeovers do not threaten the hierarchy; they only replace one set of managers with another. And aside from single rounds of cost cutting, no creative interplay between the restructuring takeover and the production operations of the firm has appeared.

Assume that a chastened and more heavily monitored management emerges with its position otherwise left intact. It can, ironically, turn to contractualism to reconstruct a theory of the firm protective of its position. Legal theory offers more than one model of contract. Theories more relational than that employed by the neoclassical new theorists offer values protective of individuals who invest their labor and energies in business enterprises, including firms.

CONCLUSION

This article's historical perspectives do not deny the legitimacy of the new economic theory's approach to corporations. Nor do these perspectives deny that contract holds a constitutive place in firm life or that the new economic theory isolates significant aspects of corporate relationships. By contextualizing this theory of the firm discourse in time, however, these perspectives do facilitate a more accurate appraisal of the new economic theory's contribution. The history prompts doubts as to the theorists' extreme essentialist claims:

Their new corporate contract becomes hard to accept either as an evolutionary climax or as an objectively correct edifice standing outside of time. Instead, the theory appears as an edifice partly built on enduring ontology, partly prompted by recent,perhaps transitory, trends in corporate practice, and partly shaped by the theorists' political dispositions.

These historical perspectives, it should be noted, do not support discrimination among theories of the firm. They do not single out the new economic theory for critical questioning. Instead, they counsel wariness of essentialist claims made for any academic theory of the firm. The history shows us that the pairs of opposing concepts that make up theories of the firm—entity and aggregate, contract and concession, public and private, discrete contract and relational contract—endure in opposition over time. Academic firm theories and corporate legal doctrine tend to handle these internal conflicts differently. Doctrinal firm theory lacks analytical integrity; the opposing concepts are synchronized as decisionmakers make normative responses to unfolding events in business practice. If recognition of one of these contradictions results in analytical paralysis in a specific case, the doctrinalists deny the contradiction, mentioning one side only. Despite this lack of integrity, the doctrinal theory works well as it operates at close quarters with economic practice. Rather than trying to privilege one or another contradictory element, it builds the contradictions into a capacious structure that loosely contains real-world producing organizations. This legal structure accommodates economic change easily.

Practice also drives academic firm theory. But in an academic context, a theory that follows the doctrine and merely synchronizes contradictions in particular situations probably falls short of prevailing standards. Academics, free of the immediate problem of deciding cases, try to achieve analytical consistency; they attempt to transcend the contradictions. Academic theory of the firm, created in pursuit of this objective, has a more volatile, evolutionary pattern than does doctrinal theory. One tends to have to overstate things in order to achieve consistency and at the same time remain in touch with practice in a complex world. Wariness therefore is appropriate in considering new academic theories that purport to explain existing doctrine and at the same time satisfy academic standards. Such theories may have more reconstructive potential than their progenitors admit.

The new economic theory falls into this historical pattern of academic/doctrinal interplay. Introduced in the law as a critical supplement to managerialist theory, it succeeded because it recognized discrete contract as a constitutive part of firms. The recent appearance of discrete contract as an important corporate power tool made the theory especially welcome: It brought academic theory closer both to business practice and to legal doctrine. But the theorists, driven by the

academic need to universalize, outstripped this ontological base by privileging narrow notions of contract.

Pressure builds up as the new theory's paradigm approaches hegemony in legal academic discussion. Some structure of thought will have to change. Two possible scenarios present themselves. Under one, the doctrine is reconstructed. The theory's influence causes the doctrine to be reformulated to eradicate strains that contradict the theory. Under the other scenario, the theory adapts. The contract paradigm expands to encompass the range of conflicting firm components. Given the history, the second scenario seems the more likely to occur. Doctrinal reconstruction tends to occur in response to practical, not theoretical, developments, legitimizing or inhibiting them as the case may be. Actors who create corporate law have shown little disposition to reconstitute it as a means to the end of recognition of the latest academic theory.

NOTES

1. Jensen and Meckling, 1976; Hessen, 1979; Kraakman, 1984; Scott, 1983.
2. See Baysinger & Butler, 1984; Bebchuk, 1989; Easterbrook & Fischel, 1986, 1985, 1983, 1982; Fischel, 1983, 1982; Gilson, 1987; Kraakman, 1984; Macey, 1984.
3. For the suggestion that management labor markets provide the primary discipline, see Fama, 1980: 294–295. This is disputed in Benjamin Klein (1983), which takes the position that wage discounts cannot be taken into account in wage contracts ex ante. For criticism of Fama's point that junior managers can be expected to monitor senior managers, see Eisenberg, 1984:584.
4. This was true at least once the Jeffersonian and Jacksonian adherents of classical, political economy eliminated Federalist mercantilist policies (Hovernkamp, 1988: 1605–1612).
5. Chief Justice Marshall's opinion in the most famous corporate law case of the early period demonstrates this. The *Dartmouth College* case held that a "corporation is an artificial being, invisible, intangible, and existing only

in contemplation of law." *Trustees of Dartmouth College* v. *Woodward*, 17 U.S. (4 Wheat.) 518, 636 (1819).
6. Means, 1962: 50-51. Means uses the term "collective capitalism." I use "management corporation" to avoid the particular political implications of Means's phrase.
7. For the view that the management corporation need not dominate production in the future, see Piore and Sabel (1984).
8. The central office of United States Steel, a complex of many firms that merged over a short period in the late 1890s, did little more than collect accounting information for the company's first decade. Central office expansion occurred after 1910. (Temin, 1964:192)
9. Berle and Means thus combined a contractual conception of the corporation with a Weberian bureaucratic conception: Corporations in part were management controlled bureaucratic entities vested with power by positive law, and in part were the contractual arrangements of economic actors. (Dan-Cohen, 1986: 17–20)

10. Friedman, M. 1962. Capitalism and freedom, 121, 135; see also Jensen & Meckling, 1976: 306; Williamson, 1984: 1220–21. Neoclassical models avoided taking entrepreneurship and its concomitant, profit, into account through single-minded adherence to the concept of marginal productivity. In perfect conditions, entrepreneurs theoretically have no function and receive no income. Profits thus were conceived in terms of imperfect competition and disequilibrium conditions, and explained either as payment for the assumption of uninsurable risks or as temporary windfalls. See McNulty, P.J. 1984. On the nature and theory of economic organization: The role of the firm reconsidered, 16 Hist. Pol. Econ. 240–41.

11. Latham, E. 1966: The body politic of the coporation, the corporation in modern society 218 (E. Mason, ed.); Nader, Green & Seligman, 1976: 33, 36–37. Anti-managerialist commentary written instead in the post-realist proceduralist tradition declines to make the "public" and "political" assertion. See Eisenberg, M.A. 1976: The structure of the corporation 16 (corporate law is "constitutional"—that is, it "regulates the manner in which the corporate institution is constituted").

12. The analytical framework of interest group pluralism prevalent during the post-war period was so applied. Cf. Horwit, M. 1982: The history of the public/private distinction, 130 U. Pa. L. Rev. 1423, 1427 (describing changing views of the public interest).

13. Anti-individualist perspectives have gone through twists of their own during this century in their application to corporations. At the turn of the century, the theorists concentrating on group existence were the realists, and their work favored management. In today's corporate law discussions, anti-managerialists take entities most seriously. See Aoki, 1984; Frug, 1984. Actually, the point is more complex. Early twentieth-century Progressives also took group existence seriously, and they opposed the corporate realists. See Horwitz, 1985. Post-war institutional economists take corporate entities very seriously on management's behalf. See Baumol, 1962; Herman, 1984, 1981. The institutionalist new theorists also take group existence seriously, even though they privilege the individual participant's role.

14. This is the formal, objectified contract law of Williston and the first *Restatement of Contracts* (1932).

15. One caveat should be entered here. While practice in this context facilitated the emergence of new theory by raising practical questions about the accuracy of the received managerialist picture, the theorists did not necessarily make primary reference to the practice. The neoclassical variant of the new economic theory draws heavily on neoclassical microeconomic assumptions. The classical market ideal from which these assumptions are drawn has been largely superseded in history. The theory's adherence to these assumptions attenuates its connection to practice.

16. The takeover "threat" also was considered a market mechanism for discipline of management conduct. It accordingly provided a response to the anti-managerialists' legitimacy point. Aoki, 1984.

17. Focusing on multidivisional structure reconstituted the firm as a governance structure rather than a production function. Williamson, 1983, 1981.

18. Heavily criticized decisions permitting defensive tactics include: *Panter* v. *Marshall Field & Co.*, 646 F.2d 271 (7th Cir. 1981); *Moran* v. *Household Int'l. Inc.*, 500 A.2s 1346 (Del. 1985); *Cheff* v. *Mathes*, 41 Del. Ch. 494, 199 A.2d 548 (1964). Recently, the courts have begun to scrutinize more closely management decisions regarding the control market. See *Revlon, Inc.* v. *MacAndrews & Forbes Holdings, Inc.*, 506 A.2d 173 (Del. 1983); *Hanson Trust PLC* v. *ML SCM Acquisition, Inc.*, 781 F.2d 264 (2d Cir. 1986).

    In cases concerning the treatment of minority shareholder interests remaining in the acquired corporation after a takeover, the Delaware courts have made some famous anti-managerial rulings. See *Weinberger* v. *UOP, Inc.*, 457 A.2d 701 (Del. 1983); *Singer* v. *Magnavox Co.*, 380 A.2d 969 (Del. 1977).

19. The theory's agency cost line comes to bear against management here. The tender offer is conceived as a traditional form of market control. It encourages devotion to the principal's interest in the agent. This idea can be traced to Manne, 1965, and it reappears frequently in the contemporary literature on takeovers. See Bebchuck, 1982; Easterbrook and Fischel, 1981; Gilson, 1981.

20. Of the 850 largest American corporations, 398 undertook voluntary restructurings between the beginning of 1984 and the middle of 1985. See Gordon and Kornhauser, 1986; Macey and McChesney, 1985.
21. The contemporary discussions are well summarized in several articles in a *Business Week* special report entitled Deal Mania. See Jonas and Berger, 1986; Dobrzynski, 1986.

22. This is Coffee's critique of Williamson. See Coffee, 1986: 31-35; Williamson, 1988: 86-87.
23. Changes are beginning to appear also, as management organization structures become looser and more flexible in emerging industries. See Piore, 1986.

REFERENCES

Ackerman, B.A. 1984. Reconstructing American law, 62.

Alchian, A.A. & Demsetz, H. 1972. Production, information costs, and economic organization, 62 *American Economic Review*, 777.

Anderson, W.H. 1931. Limitations of the corporate entity, 7.

Angell, J. & Ames, S. 1871. Treatise on the law of private corporations aggregate (9th ed.).

Aoki, M. 1984. The co-operative game theory of the firm, 34–37.

Austin, D.V. 1975. Tender offer statistics: New strategies are paying off, 10 *Mergers & Acquisitions*, fall 1975, at 9, 10–11.

Austin, D.V. 1973. Comparison with the past and future trends, 8 *Mergers & Acquisitions*, fall 1973, at 16.

Ballantine, H.W. 1946. Ballantine on corporations, 2 (rev. ed.).

Baumol, W.J. 1962. On the theory of the expansion of the firm, 52 *American Economic Review*, 1078.

Baumol, W.J. 1959. Business behavior, value and growth.

Baysinger, B.D. & Butler, H.N. 1984. Revolution *versus* evolution in corporation law: The ALI's project and the independent director, 52 *George Washington Law Review*, 557.

Bebchuk, L.A. 1982. The case for facilitating competing tender offers, 95 *Harvard Law Review* 1028, 1030–31.

Bebchuk, L.A. 1989. Limiting contractual freedom in corporate law: The desirable constraints on charter amendments, 102 *Harvard Law Review*, 1820.

Berle, A.A. Jr. 1954. The 20th century capitalist revolution, 32–39.

Berle, A.A. Jr. 1961. Coherency and the Social Sciences, in *People, Power and Politics*, 6, 10 (L.J. Gould & E.W. Steele eds.)

Berle, A.A & Means, G.C. 1968. The modern corporation and private property, 121.

Blaug, M. 1980. The methodology of economics, 175–86.

Bratton, W.W. 1989. The Nexus of contracts: corporation: a critical appraisal, 74 *Cornell Law Review* (forthcoming).

Brudney, V. 1985. Corporate governance, agency costs, and the rehetoric of contract, 85 *Columbia Law Review*, 1403.

Buxbaum, R.M. 1984. Corporate legitimacy, economic theory, and legal doctrine, 45 *Ohio State Law Journal*, 515.

Cary, W.L. 1974. Federalism and corporate law: reflections upon Delaware, 83 *Yale Law Journal*, 663.

Chandler, A.D. Jr. 1977. The visible hand: The managerial revolution in American business, 15–28.

Cheung, N.S. 1983. The contractual nature of the firm, 26 *Journal of Law & Economics*, 1, 18.

Clark, R.C. 1981. The four stages of capitalism: Reflections on investment management treatises, 94 *Harvard Law Review*, 561, 562.

Coase, R.H. 1937. The nature of the firm, 4 *Economica* 386, 390–94.

Coase, R.H. 1988. The nature of the firm: Meaning, 4 *Journal of Law Economics & Organization*, 19, 23.

Coase, R.H. 1972. Industrial organization: A proposal for research, 3 *Economic Research: Retrospect and Prospect* 59, 62–63 (V. Fuchs ed.)

Coffee, J.C. Jr. 1986. Shareholders versus managers: The strain in the corporate web, 85 *Mich. Law Review*, 1, 2–3.

Conrad, A. 1976. Corporations in perspective, 417 & n. 5.

Cyert and March, 1963. A behavioral theory of the firm.

Dan-Cohen, M. 1986. Rights, persons and organizations: A legal theory for a bureaucratic society.

Dartmouth College v. *Woodward*, 1819, 7 U.S. (4 wheat.) 518, 636.

Demsetz, H. 1982. Professor Micheman's unnecessary and futile search for the philosopher's touchstone, in 24 *Nomos: Ethics, Economics and the Law* 41, 44.

Dewey, J. 1926. The historic background of corporate legal personality, 35 *Yale Law Journal*, 655, 667–78.

Dobrzynski, J.H. 1986. More than ever, it's management for the short term, *Business Week*, Nov. 24, 1986, 92–93.

Easterbrook, F.H. & Fischel, D.R. 1986. Close corporations and agency costs, 38 *Stanford Law Review*, 271.

Easterbrook, F.H. & Fischel, D.R. 1985. Limited liability and the corporation, 52 *University of Chicago Law Review*, 89.

Easterbrook, F.H. & Fishcel, D.R. 1983. Voting in corporate law, 26 *Journal of Law & Economics*, 395.

Easterbrook, F.H. & Fischel, D.R. 1982. Corporate control transactions, 91 *Yale Law Journal*, 698.

Easterbrook, F.H. & Fischel, D.R. 1981. The proper role of a target's management in responding to a tender offer, 94 *Harvard Law Review*, 1161, 1169–74.

Eisenberg, M.A. 1976. The structure of the corporation, 16.

Eisenberg, M.A. 1984. New modes of discourse in the corporate law literature, 52 *George Washington Law Review*, 582.

Fama, E.F. 1980. Agency problems and the theory of the firm, 88 *Journal of Political Economics*, 288, 289.

Fischel, D.R. 1983. The appraisal remedy in corporate law, 1983 *American Business Found Res. Journal*, 875.

Fischel, D.R. 1982. The corporate governance movement, 35 *Vand. Law Review* 1259.

Friedman, M. 1962. Capitalism and freedom, 121, 135.

Frug, G.E. 1984. The ideology of bureaucracy in American law, 97 *Harvard Law Review*, 1276, 1328–34.

George R.J. 1982. The emergence of industrial America, 79.

Gilson, R.J. 1987. Evaluating dual class common stock: The relevance of substitutes, 73 *Va. Law Review*, 807, 808–11.

Gilson, R.J. 1981. A structural approach to corporations: The case against defensive tactics in tender offers, 33 *Stanford Law Review*, 819, 841.

Gordon, J.N. & Kornhauser, L.A. 1986. Takeover defense tactics: A comment on two models, 96 *Yale Law Journal*, 295.

Gordon, J.N. & Kornhauser, L.A. 1985. A recent round of discussion on takeovers demonstrates this, assuming contractualism without applying the theory formally.

Henn, H.G. 1961. Handbook of the law of corporations, 88.

Herman, E.S. 1984. The limits of the market as a discipline in corporate governance, 9 *Delaware Journal of Corporate Law*, 530, 533–34.

Herman, E.S. 1981. Corporate control, corporate power, 5–9, 106–13.

Hessen, R. 1979. A new concept of corporations: A contractual and private property model, 30 *Hastings Law Journal*, 1327, 1330.

Hovernkamp, H. 1988. The classical corporation in American legal thought, 76 *CEO. Law Journal*, 1593, 1605–12.

Horwitz, M.J. 1985. Santa Clara revisited: The development of corporate theory, 88 W. *Va. Law Review*, 173, 176.

Hurst, J. W. 1970. The legitimacy of the business corporation in the law of the United States, 1780–1970, at 82.

Jensen, M. C. 1986. Agency costs of free cash flow, corporate finance and takeovers, 76 *American Economcs Review*, 323, 324–26.

Jensen, M. C. 1983. Organization theory and methodology, 58 *Accounting Review*, 319, 324.

Jensen, M. C. & Meckling, W. H. 1976. Theory of the firm: Managerial behavior, agency costs and ownership structure, 3 *Journal of Fin. Econ.* 305, 310.

Kent, 2 J. 1866. Commentaries on American law, 303 (11th ed).

Klein, B. 1983. Contracting costs and residual claims: The separation of ownership and control, 26 *Journal of Law & Economics*, 367, 368.

Knauss, R.I. 1981. Corporate governance—a moving target, 79 *Michigan Law Review*, 478, 487.

Kraakman, R.H. 1982. Corporate liability strategies and the costs of legal controls, 93 *Yale Law Journal*, 857, 862.

Kyd, 1. S. 1793. A treatise on the law of corporations, 13.

Levmore, S. 1982. Monitors and free rides in commercial and corporate setting, 92 *Yale Law Journal*, 49.

Lowentein, L. 1988. What's wrong with Wall St.?

Macey, J.R. 1984. From fairness to contract: the new direction of the rules against insider trading, 13 *Hofstra Law Review,* 9, 39–47.

Macey, J.R. & McChesney, F.S. 1985. A theoretical analysis of corporate greenmail, 95 *Yale Law Journal,* 13.

Macneil, J.R. 1981. Economic analysis of contractual relations: Its shortfalls and the need for a "rich classifactory apparatus," 75 *Nw. U.L. Rev.* 1018, 1022–23, 1039–40.

Malatesta, P.H. 1983. The wealth effects of merger activity and the objective functions of merging firms, 11 *Journal of Fin. Econ.* 155, 177.

Manne, H.G. 1965. Mergers and the market for corporate control, 73 *Journal of Political Econ.* 110–113.

Manning, B. 1962. The shareholders' appraisal remedy: An essay for Frank Coker, 72 *Yale Law Journal,* 223, 245.

Mark, G.A. 1987. The personification of the business corporation in American Law, 54 *University of Chicago Law Review,* 1441–55.

Marris, R. 1964. The economic theory of "Managerial" capitalism.

McNulty, P.J. 1984. On the nature and theory of economic organization: The role of the firm reconsidered, 16 *His. Pol. Econ.* 240–41.

Means, G.C. 1962. The corporate revolution in America 50–51.

Meckling, W.H. 1976. Values and the choice of method in the social sciences, 112 Schweizerische Zeitschrift Fuer Volkwirtschaft und Statistik, 545, 548–49.

Nader, R. Green, M. & Seligman, J. 1976. Taming the giant corporation, 62–65.

Nash, N. 1987. A hands-off takeover stance, *New York Times,* July 23, 1987, D1, Col. 3.

Oleck, H. 1958. Modern corporation law.

Piore, M.J. 1986. Corporate reform in American manufacturing and the challenge to economic theory (paper presented at the Conference on Economics of Organization at the Yale School of Organization and Management, October 24–25).

Piore M. J. & Sabel, C. F. 1984. The second industrial divide 72.

Ratner, D. L. 1980–81. Corporations and the constitution, 15 *U.S. F.L. Review,* 11, 12.

Romano, R. 1984. Metapolitics and corporate law reform, 26 *Stanford Law Review,* 923, 929–30.

Rosenberg, N. 1983. Comments on Robert Hessen. "The modern corporation and private property: A reappraisal, 26 *Journal of Law & Economics,* 291, 295.

Scott, K.E. 1983. Corporation law and the American Law Institute Corporate Governance Project, 35 *Stanford Law Review,* 927, 930.

Spelling, C. 1892. Law of private corporations.

Stevens, R.S. 1949. *Handbook on the law of private corporations,* 224–27, 331–36, 2nd Ed.

Temin, P. 1964. Iron and steel in nineteenth-century America , 190–93.

Vinogradoff, P. 1924. Judicial Persons, 24 *Columbia Law Review,* 594, 601.

Williamson, O.E. 1988. The logic of economic organization, 4 *Journal of Law, Economics, & Organization,* 65, 68.

Williamson, O.E. 1983. Intellectual foundations: The need for a broader view, 33 *Journal of Legal Education,* 210, 214.

Williamson., O.E. 1981. The modern corporation: Origins, evolution, attributes, 19 *Journal of Econ. Lit erature,* 1544–1545.

Williamson, O.E. 1975. Markets and hierarchies: Analysis and antitrust implications, 30–40, 256–257.

ECLIPSE OF THE PUBLIC CORPORATION

Michael C. Jensen

The publicly held corporation, the main engine of economic progress in the United States for a century, has outlived its usefulness in many sectors of the economy and is being eclipsed.

New organizations are emerging in its place —organizations that are corporate in form but have no public shareholders and are not listed or traded on organized exchanges. These organizations use public and private debt, rather than public equity, as their major source of capital. Their primary owners are not households but large institutions and entrepreneurs that designate agents to manage and monitor on their behalf and bind those agents with large equity interests and contracts governing the use and distribution of cash.

Takeovers, corporate breakups, divisional spinoffs leveraged buyouts, and going-private transactions, are the most visible manifestations of a massive organizational change in the economy. These transactions have inspired criticism, even outrage, among many business leaders and government officials, who have called for regulatory and legislative restrictions. The backlash is understandable. Change is threatening; in this case,the threat is aimed at the senior executives of many of our largest companies.

Despite the protests, this organizational innovation should be encouraged. By resolving the central weakness of the public corpo-ration—the conflict between owners and managers over the control and use of corporate resources—these new organizations are making remarkable gains in operating efficiency, employee productivity, and shareholder value. Over the long term, they will enhance U.S. economic performance relative to our most formidable international competitor, Japan, whose companies are moving in the opposite direction. The governance and financial structures of Japan's public companies increasingly resemble U.S. companies of the mid-1960s and early 1970s—an era of gross corporate waste management that triggered the organizational transformation now under way in the United States.

THE PRIVATIZATION OF EQUITY

The last share of publicly traded common stock owned by an individual will be sold in the year 2003, if current trends persist. This forecast may be fanciful (short-term trends never persist), but the basic direction is clear. By the turn of the century, the primacy of public stock ownership in the United States may have all but disappeared.

Households have been liquidating their direct holdings and indirect positions (through channels like mutual funds) at an unprecedented rate. Over the last five years, they have been net sellers of more than $500 billion

167

of common stock, 38% of their holdings at the beginning of 1984.

Why have stock prices risen sharply despite this massive sell-off? Because there has been one huge buyer—corporations themselves. LBOs, MBOs, share re-purchasers, leveraged mergers and acquisitions, and takeovers have been contracting the supply of publicly held equity. In 1988, 5% of the market value of public equity (more than $130 billion) disappeared through these kinds of transactions, even after adding back all of the new issues brought to market during the year.

Of course, the risks and returns from the underlying corporate assets have not disappeared. To some extent they now reside in quasi-equity debt instruments like high-yield bonds, whose total market value exceeds $200 billion. But many of the risks and returns still exist as equity; they just take the form of large positions of privately held equity. The "privatization of equity" is now a central feature of corporate ownership in the United States.

Historically, public stock markets dominated by individual investors developed to a greater extent in the United States than in any other country. Broad public ownership offered managers a reasonably priced source of more or less permanent equity capital that could buffer the company against adversity in a way debt could not. Share ownership allowed individual investors to participate in equity returns and get the benefits of liquidity (because they could see their shares) and diversification (because they could hold a small number of shares from many corporations).

The virtues of broad public ownership are not what they used to be, for managers or investors. One important factor is the emergence of an active market for corporate control. A capital structure consisting mostly of equity still offers managers protection against the risks of economic downturn. But it also carries substantial risks of inviting a hostile takeover or other threats to management control.

The role of the public market has also changed because investors themselves have changed. For decades, stock ownership has been migrating from direct holdings by millions of individuals to indirect beneficial ownership through large pools of capital—in particular, the huge corporate and governmental pension funds whose total value exceeded $1.5 trillion in 1988. These institutional funds, which now comprise more than 40% of total stock ownership, used to behave like large public investors. They kept diversified by retaining many different investment managers, each of whom traded an array of highly liquid public securities. But their investment philosophy has been evolving in recent years to include participation in a select number of private illiquid investments and private pools of equity capital. This new investment philosophy makes broad public markets less essential for institutions.

Large pools of capital such as pension funds and endowments don't really need the liquidity the public market offers. Liquidity serves two basic purposes. It allows investors to meet unexpected cash needs and to trade their stocks. Unlike individuals, the large funds can project their cash needs well into the future based on predictable factors such as employee demographics, life expectancies, and health trends. So they can take a long-term view of investment returns and keep their holdings in illiquid assets.

Fund managers are also realizing that trading is a tough discipline in which they hold little comparative advantage. Trading is a zero-sum game played in a fairly efficient market against equally talented rivals. Worse still, large funds face dis-economies of scale when executing trades. The larger a fund, the more difficult it is to trade quickly, based on transient information advantages. The very act of trading moves markets.

Still, these managers remain charged with generating returns in excess of passive benchmarks. Enter the market for private assets such as real estate, venture capital, and, more recently, the market for corporate control and restructurings. Instead of trading a large number of small, liquid positions, the funds can buy and own smaller numbers of large, illiquid positions in a form where they (or, more likely, their agents) participate more actively with management in the control of the assets.

This alternative can be a positive-sum game; real changes in corporate policies can be a route to enhanced value. The very large funds also have a competitive advantage here. The larger their positions, the more actively they can participate in the ownership and management of the underlying assets. In the extreme, as with LBO funds,these changes can be dramatic. The LBO fund itself becomes the managing owner in partnership with company managers. In short, large institutional funds can behave more like owners and less like traders.

The same basic changes are at work in a wide variety of corporate recapitalizations where outside (or related) parties acquire large, relatively nontraded equity positions. Large pools of capital can participate in these private equity positions yet remain diversified by virtue of their own enormous size. Smaller funds and households cannot.

In the short run, this new investment philosophy has been, in the aggregate, a great success. Without the sobering influence of an economic contraction, the returns from these private investments have been very attractive. In the long run, the institutions' new philosophy is ushering in a system of equity ownership dominated by "private positions" that resembles ownership systems in Germany and Japan. Individual investors in this system will increasingly be free riders on the coattails of a small number of very large private investors rather than the central feature of the financial markets.

Jay O. Light

Consider these developments in the 1980s:

The capital markets are in transition. The total market value of equity in publicly held companies has tripled over the past decade—from $1 trillion in 1979 to more than $3 trillion in 1989. But newly acquired capital comes increasingly from private placements, which have expanded more than ten times since 1980, to a rate of $200 billion in 1988. Private placements of debt and equity now account for more than 40% of annual corporate financ-

ings. Meanwhile,in every year since 1983, at least 5% of the outstanding value of corporate equity has disappeared through stock repurchases, takeovers, and going-private transactions. Finally, households are sharply reducing their stock holdings.[1] (See the insert, "The Privatization of Equity.")

The most widespread going-private transaction, the leveraged buyout, is becoming larger and more frequent. In 1988, the total value of the 214 public-company and divisional buyouts exceeded $77 billion—nearly one-third of the value of all mergers and acquisitions. The total value of the 75 buyouts in 1979 was only $1.3 billion (in constant 1988 dollars), while the 175 buyouts completed in 1983 had a total value of $16.6 billion. This process is just getting started; the $77 billion of LBOs in 1988 represented only 2.5% of outstanding public company equity. (See the table, "Rise of the LBO."

Entire industries are being reshaped. Just five years ago, the leading U.S. truck and automobile tire manufacturers were independent and diversified public companies. Today each is a vastly different enterprise. Uniroyal went private in 1985 and later merged its tire-making operations with those of B.F. Goodrich to form a new private company called Uniroyal Goodrich. In late 1986, Goodyear borrowed $2.6 billion and repurchased nearly half its outstanding shares to fend off a hostile tender offer by Sir James Goldsmith. It retained its core tire and rubber business while moving to divest an array of unrelated operations, including its Celeron oil and gas subsidiary, California-to-Texas oil pipeline, aerospace operation, and Arizona resort hotel. In 1987, GenCorp issued $1.75 billion of debt to repurchase more than half its outstanding shares. It divested several operations, including it General Tire subsidiary, to pay down the debt and focus on aerospace and defense. Last year, Firestone was sold to Bridgestone, Japan's largest tire maker, for $2.6 billion, a transaction that created shareholder gains of $1.6 billion.

Developments as striking as the restructuring of our financial markets and major industries reflect underlying economic forces

Rise of the LBO

Year	Public-Company Buyouts		Divisional Buyouts		Total Value of Buyouts (In billions of 1988 dollars)
	Number	Average Value (In millions of 1988 dollars)	Number	Average Value (In millions of 1988 dollars)	
1979	16	$ 64.9	59	$ 5.4	$ 1.4
1980	13	106.0	47	34.5	3.0
1981	17	179.1	83	21.0	4.8
1982	31	112.2	115	40.7	8.2
1983	36	235.8	139	58.2	16.6
1984	57	473.6	122	104.0	39.7
1985	76	349.4	132	110.1	41.0
1986	76	303.3	144	180.7	49.0
1987	47	488.7	90	144.2	36.0
1988	125	487.4	89	181.3	77.0

SOURCE: George P. Baker, "Management Compensation and Divisional Leveraged Buyouts," unpublished dissertation, Harvard Business School, 1986. Updates from W.T. Grimm, *Mergerstat Review 1988*. Transactions with no public data are valued at the average price of public transaction.

more fundamental and powerful than financial manipulation, management greed, reckless speculation, and the other colorful epithets used by defenders of the corporate status quo. The forces behind the decline of the public corporation differ from industry to industry. But its decline is real, enduring, and highly productive. It is not merely a function of the tax deductibility of interest. Nor does it reflect a transitory LBO phase through which companies pass before investment bankers and managers cash out by taking them public again. Nor, finally, is it premised on a systematic fleecing of shareholders and bondholders by managers and other insiders with superior information about the true value of corporate assets.

The current trends do not imply that the public corporation has no future. The conventional twentieth-century model of corporate governance—dispersed public ownership, professional managers without substantial equity holdings, a board of directors dominated by management-appointed outsiders—remain a viable option in some areas of the economy, particularly for growth companies whose profitable investment opportunities exceed the cash they generate internally. Such companies can be found in industries like computers and electronics, biotechnology, pharmaceuticals, and financial services. Com-

panies choosing among a surplus of profitable projects are unlikely to invest systematically in unprofitable ones, especially when they must regularly turn to the capital markets to raise investment funds.

The public corporation is not suitable in industries where long-term growth is slow, where internally generated funds outstrip the opportunities to invest them profitably,or where downsizing is the most productive long-term strategy. In the tire industry, the shift to radials, which last three times longer than bias-ply tires, meant that manufacturers needed less capacity to meet world demand. Overcapacity inevitably forced a restructuring. The tenfold increase in oil prices form 1973 to 1981, which triggered worldwide conservation measures, forced oil producers into a similar retrenchment.[2]

Industries under similar pressure today include steel, chemicals, brewing, tobacco, television and radio broadcasting, wood and paper products. In these and other cash-rich, low-growth or declining sectors, the pressures on management to waste cash flow through organizational slack or investment in unsound projects is often irresistible. It is in precisely these sectors that the publicly held corporation has declined most rapidly. Barring regulatory interference, the public corporation is also likely to decline in industries such as aerospace, automobiles and auto parts, banking, electric power generation, food processing, industrial and farm implements and transportation equipment.

The public corporation is a social invention of vast historical importance. Its genius is rooted in its capacity to spread financial risk over the diversified portfolios of millions of individuals and institutions and to allow investors to customize risk to their unique circumstances and predilections. By diversifying risks that would otherwise be borne by owner-entrepreneurs and by facilitating the creation of a liquid market for exchanging risk, the public corporation lowered the cost of capital. The tradable claims on corporate ownership (common stock) also allowed risk to be borne by investors best able to bear it, without requiring them to manage the corporations they owned.

From the beginning, though, these risk-bearing benefits came at a cost. Tradable ownership claims create fundamental conflicts of interest between those who bear risk (the shareholder) and those who manage risk (the executives). The genius of the new organizations is that they eliminate much of the loss created by conflict between owners and managers, without eliminating the vital functions of risk diversification and liquidity once performed exclusively by the public entity markets.

In theory, these new organizations should not be necessary. Three major forces are said to control management in the public corporation: the product markets, internal control systems led by the board of directors, and the capital markets. But product markets often have not played a disciplining role. For most of the last 60 years, a large and vibrant domestic market created for U.S. companies economies of scale and significant cost advantages over foreign rivals. Recent reversals at the hands of the Japanese and others have not been severe enough to sap most companies of their financial independence. The idea that outside directors with little or no equity stake in the company could effectively monitor and discipline the managers who selected

them has proven hollow at best. In practice, only the capital markets have played much of a control function—and for a long time they were hampered by legal constraints.

Indeed, the fact that takeover and LBO premiums average 50% above market price illustrates how much value public-company managers can destroy before they face a serious threat of disturbance. Takeovers and buyouts both create new value and unlock value destroyed by management through misguided policies. I estimate that transactions associated with the market for corporate control unlocked shareholder gains (in target companies alone) of more than $500 billion between 1977 and 1988—more than 50% of the cash dividends paid by the entire corporate sector over this same period.

The widespread waste and inefficiency of the public corporation and its inability to adapt to changing economic circumstances have generated a wave of organizational innovation over the last 15 years—innovation driven by the rebirth of "active investors." By active investors I mean investors who hold large equity or debt positions, sit on boards of directors, monitor and sometimes dismiss management, are involved with the long-term strategic direction of the companies they invest in, and sometimes manage the companies themselves.

Active investors are creating a new model of general management. These investor include LBO partnerships such as Kohlberg Krevis Roberts and Clayton & Dubilier; entrepreneurs such as Carl Icahn, Ronald Perelman, Laurence Tisch, Robert Bass, William Simon, Irwin Jacobs, and Warren Buffet; the merchant banking arms of Wall Street houses such as Morgan Stanley, Lazard Frères, and Merrill Lynch; and family funds such as those controlled by the Pritzkers and the Bronfmans. Their model is built around highly leveraged financial structure, pay-for-performance compensation systems, substantial equity ownership by managers and directors, and contracts with owners and creditors that limit both cross-subsidization among business units and the waste of free cash flow. Consistent with modern finance theory, these organizations are not managed to maximize earnings per share but rather to maximize *value*, with a strong emphasis on cash flow.

More than any other factor, these organizations' resolution of the owner-manager conflict explains how they can motivate the same people, managing the same resources, to perform so much more effectively under private ownership than in the publicly held corporate form.

In effect, LBO partnerships and the merchant banks are rediscovering the role played by active investors prior to 1940, when Wall Street banks such as J.P. Morgan & Company were directly involved in the strategy and governance of the public companies they helped create. At the height of his prominence, Morgan and his small group of partners served on the boards of U.S. Steel, International Harvester, First National Bank of New York, and a host of railroads, and were a powerful management force in these and other companies.

Morgan's model of investor activism disappeared largely as a result of populist laws and regulations approved in the wake of the Great Depression. These laws and regulations—including the Glass-Steagall Banking Act of 1933, the Securities Act of 1933, the Securities and Exchange Act of 1934, the Chandler Bankruptcy Revision Act of 1938, and the Investment Company Act of 1940—may have once had their place. But they also created an intricate web of restrictions on company "insiders" (corporate officers, directors, or investors with more than a 10% ownership interest), restrictions on bank involvement in corporate reorganizations, court precedents, and business practices that raised the cost of being an active investor. Their long-term effect has been to insulate management from effective monitoring and to set the stage for the eclipse of the public corporation.

Indeed, the high cost of being an active investor has left financial institutions and money management firms, which control more than 40% of all corporate equity in the United States, almost completely uninvolved in the major decisions and long-term strategies of the companies their clients own. They are almost never represented on corporate boards. They use the proxy mechanism rarely and usually ineffectively, notwithstanding recent efforts by the Council of Institutional Investors and other shareholder activists to gain a larger voice in corporate affairs.

All told, institutional investors are remarkably powerless; they have few options to express dissatisfaction with management other than to sell their shares and vote with their feet. Corporate managers criticize institutional sell-offs as examples of portfolio churning and short-term investor horizons. One guesses these same managers much prefer churning to a system in which large investors on the boards of their companies have direct power to monitor and correct mistakes. Managers really want passive investors who can't sell their shares.

The absence of effective monitoring led to such large inefficiencies that the new generation of active investors arose to recapture the lost value. These investors overcome the costs of the outmoded legal constraints by purchasing entire companies—and using debt and high equity ownership to force effective self-monitoring.

A central weakness and source of waste in the public corporation is the conflict between shareholders and managers over the payout of free cash flow—that is, cash flow in excess of that required to fund all investment projects with positive new present values when discounted at the relevant cost of capital. For a company to operate efficiently and maximize value, free cash flow must be distributed to shareholders rather than retained. But this happens infrequently; senior management has few incentives to distribute the funds, and there exist few mechanism to compel distribution.

A vivid example is the senior management of Ford Motor Company, which sits on nearly $15 billion in cash and marketable securities in an industry with excess capacity. Ford's management has been deliberating about acquiring financial service companies, aerospace companies, or making some other multibillion-dollar diversification move—rather than deliberating about effectively distributing Ford's excess cash to its owners so they can decide how to reinvest it.

Ford is not alone. Corporate managers generally don't disgorge cash unless they are forced to do so. In 1988, the 1,000 largest public companies (by sales) generated total funds of $1.6 trillion. Yet they distributed only $108 billion as dividends and another $51 billion through share repurchases.[3]

Managers have incentives to retain cash in part because cash reserves increase their autonomy, vis-à-vis the capital markets. Large cash balances (and independence from the capital markets) can serve a competitive purpose, but they often lead to waste and inefficiency. Consider a hypothetical world in which companies distribute excess cash to shareholders and then must convince the capital markets to supply funds as sound economic projects arise. Shareholders are at a great advantage in this world, where management's plans are subject to enhanced monitoring by the capital markets. Wall Street's analytical, due diligence, and pricing disciplines give shareholders more power to quash wasteful projects.

Managers also resist distributing cash to shareholders because retaining cash increases the size of the companies they run—and managers have many incentives to expand company size beyond that which maximizes shareholder wealth, compensation is one of the most important incentives. Many studies document that increases in executive pay are strongly related to increases in corporate size rather than value.[4]

The tendency of companies to reward middle managers through promotions rather than annual performance bonuses also creates a cultural bias toward growth. Organizations must grow in order to generate new positions to feed their promotion-based reward systems.

Finally, corporate growth enhances the social prominence, public prestige, and political power of senior executives. Rare is the CEO who wants to be remembered as presiding over an enterprise that makes fewer products in fewer plants in fewer countries than when he or she took office—even when such a course increases productivity and adds hundreds of millions of dollars of shareholder value. The perquisites of executive suite can be substantial, and they usually increase with company size.

The struggle over free cash flow is at the heart of the role of debt in the decline of the public corporation. Bank loans, mezzanine securities, and high-yield bonds have fueled the wave of takeovers, restructurings, and going-private transactions. The combined borrowings of all nonfinancial corporations in the United States approached $2 trillion in 1988, up from $835 billion in 1979. The interest charges on these borrowings represent more than 20% of corporate cash flows, high by historical standards.[5]

This perceived "leveraging of corporate America" is perhaps the central source of anxiety among defenders of the public corporation and critics of the new organizational forms. But most critics miss three important points. First, the trebling of the market value of public-company equity over the last decade means that corporate borrowing had to increase to avoid a major *de*leveraging.

Second, debt creation *without retention of the proceeds of the issue* helps limit the waste of free cash flow by compelling managers to pay out funds they would otherwise retain. Debt is in effect a substitute for dividends—a mechanism to force managers to disgorge cash rather than spend it on empire-building projects with low or negative returns, bloated staffs, indulgent perquisites, and organizational inefficiencies.

By issuing debt in exchange for stock, companies bond their managers' promise to pay out future cash flows in a way that simple dividend increases do not. "Permanent" dividend increases or multiyear share repurchase programs (two ways public companies can distribute excess cash to shareholders) involve no contractual commitments by managers to owners. It's easy for managers to cut dividends or scale back share repurchases.

Take the case of General Motors. On March 3, 1987, several months after the departure of GM's only active investor, H. Ross Perot, the company announced a program to repurchase up to 20% of its common stock by the end of 1990. As of mid-1989, GM had purchased only 5% of its outstanding common shares, even though its $6.8 billion cash balance was more than enough to complete the program. Given the management's poor performance over the past decade, shareholders would be better off making their own investment decisions with the cash GM is retaining. From 1977 to 1987, the company made capital expenditures of $77.5 billion while its U.S. market share declined by 10 points.

Borrowing allows for no such managerial discretion. Companies whose managers fail to make promised interest and principal payments can be declared insolvent and possibly hauled into bankruptcy court. In the imagery of G. Bennett Stewart and David M. Glassman, "Equity is soft, debt hard. Equity if forgiving, debt insistent. Equity is a pillow, debt a sword."[6] Some may find it curious that a company's creditors wield far more power over managers than its public shareholders, but it is also undeniable.

Third, debt is a powerful agent for change. For all the deeply felt anxiety about excessive borrowing, "overleveraging" can be desirable and effective when it makes economic sense to break up a company, sell off parts of the business, and refocus its energies on a few core operations. Companies that assume so much debt they cannot meet the debt service payments out of operating cash flow force themselves to rethink their entire strategy and structure. Overleveraging creates the crisis atmosphere managers require to slash unsound investment programs, shrink over-head, and dispose of assets that are more valuable outside the company. The proceeds generated by these overdue restructurings can then be used to reduce debt to more sustainable levels,creating a leaner, more efficient and competitive organization.

In other circumstances, the violation of debt covenants creates a board-level crisis that brings new actors onto the scene, motivates a fresh review of top management and strategy, and accelerates response. The case of Revco D.S., Inc., one of the handful of leveraged buyouts to reach formal bankruptcy, makes the point well.

Critics cite Revco's bankruptcy petition, filed in July 1988, as an example of the financial perils associated with LBO debt. I take a different view. The $1.25 billion buyout, announced in December, 1986, did dramatically increase Revco's annual interest charges. But several other factors contributed to its troubles,including management's decision to overhaul pricing, stocking, and merchandise layout in the company's drugstore chain. This mistaken strategic redirection left customers confused and dissatisfied, and Revco's performance suffered. Before the buyout, and without the burden of interest payments, management could have pursued these policies for a long period of time, destroying much of the company's value in the process. Within six months, however, debt served as a brake on management's mistakes, motivating the board and creditors to reorganize the company before even more value was lost.[7]

Developments at Goodyear also illustrate how debt can force managers to adopt value-creating policies they would otherwise resist. Soon after his company warded off Sir James Goldsmith's tender offer, Goodyear chairman Robert Mercer offered his version of the raiders' creed: "Give me your undervalued assets, your plants, your expenditures for technology, research and development, the hopes and aspirations of your people, your stake with your customers, your pension funds, and I will enhance myself and the dealmakers."[8]

What Mr. Mercer failed to note is that Goodyear's forced restructuring dramatically increased the company's value to shareholders by compelling him to disgorge cash and shed unproductive assets. Two years after this bitter complaint, Tom Barrett, who succeeded Mercer as Goodyear's CEO, was asked whether the company's restructuring had hurt the quality of its tires or the efficiency of its plants. "No," he replied. "We've been able to invest and continue to invest and do the things we've needed to do to be competitive."[9]

Robert Mercer's harsh words are characteristic of the business establishment's response to the eclipse of the public corporation. What explains such vehement opposition to a trend that clearly benefits shareholders and the economy? One important factor, as my Harvard Business School colleague Amar Bhide suggests, is that Wall Street now competes directly with senior management as a steward of shareholder wealth. With its vast increases in data, talent, and technology, Wall Street can allocate capital among competing businesses and monitor and discipline management more effectively than the CEO and headquarters staff of the typical diversified company. KKR's New York offices and Irwin Jacobs' Minneapolis base are direct substitutes for corporate headquarters in Akron or Peoria. CEOs worry that they and their staffs will lose lucrative jobs in favor of competing organizations. Many are right to worry; the performance of active investors versus the public corporation leaves little doubt as to which is superior.

Active investors are creating new models of general management, the most widespread of which I call the LBO Association. A typical LBO Association consists of three main constituencies: an LBO partnership that sponsors going-private transactions and counsels and monitors management in an ongoing cooperative relationship; company managers who hold substantial equity stakes in an LBO division and stay on after the buyout; and the institutional investors (insurance companies, pension funds, and money management

firms) that fund the limited partnerships that purchase equity and lend money (along with banks) to finance the transactions.

Much like a traditional conglomerate, LBO Associations have many divisions or business units, companies they have taken private at different points in time. KKR, for example, controls a diverse collection of 19 businesses including all or part of Beatrice, Duracell, Motel 6, Owens-Illinois, RJR Nabisco, and Safeway. But LBO Associations differ from publicly held conglomerates in at least four important respects. (See the illustration, "Public Company vs. LBO Association.")

Management Incentives Are Built Around a Strong Relationship between Pay and Performance. Compensation systems in LBO Associations usually have higher upper bounds than do public companies (or no upper bounds at all), tie bonuses much more closely to cash flow and debt retirement than to accounting earnings, and otherwise closely link management pay to divisional performance. Unfortunately, because these companies are private, little data are available on salaries and bonuses.

Public data are available on stock ownership, however, and equity holdings are a vital part of the reward system in LBO Associations. The University of Chicago's Steven Kaplan studied all public-company buyouts from 1979 through 1985 with a purchase price of at least $50 million.[10] Business-unit chiefs hold a median equity position of 6.4% in their unit. Even without considering bonus and incentive plans, a $1,000 increase in shareholder value triggers a $64 increase in the personal wealth of business-unit chiefs. The median public-company CEO holds only .25% of the company's equity. Counting *all* sources of compensation—including salary, bonus, deferred compensation, stock options, and dismissal penalties—the personal wealth of the median public-company CEO increases by only $3.25 for a $1,000 increase in shareholder value.[11]

Thus the salary of the typical LBO business-unit manager is almost 20 times more

Public Company vs. LBO Association

Typical Public Company

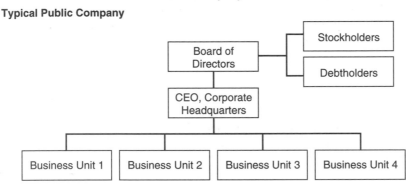

Typical LBO Association

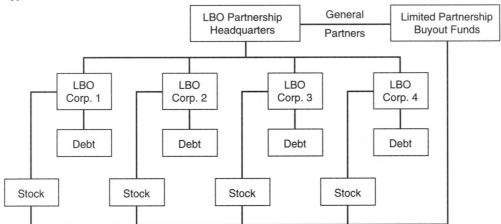

sensitive to performance than that of the typical public-company manager. This comparison understates the true differences in compensation. The personal wealth of managing partners in an LBO partnership (in effect, the CEOs of the LBO Associations) is tied almost exclusively to the performance of the companies they control. The general partners in an LBO Association typically receive (through overrides and direct equity holdings) 20% or more of the gains in the value of the divisions they help manage. This implies a pay-for-performance sensitivity of $200 for every $1,000

in added shareholder value. It's not hard to understand why an executive who receives $200 for every $1,000 increase in shareholder value will unlock more value than an executive who receives $3.25.

LBO Associations Are More Decentralized than Publicly Held Conglomerates. The LBO Association substitutes compensation incentives and ownership for direct monitoring by headquarters. The headquarters of KKR, the worlds's largest LBO partnership, has only 16 professionals and 44 additional employees. In contrast, Atlanta headquarters of RJR Nabisco employed 470 people when KKR took it private last year in a $25 billion transaction. At the time of the Goldsmith tender offer for Goodyear, the company's Akron headquarters had more than 5,000 people on its salaried payroll.

It is physically impossible for KKR and other LBO partnerships to become intimately involved in the day-to-day decisions of their operating units. They rely instead on stock ownership, incentive pay that rewards cash flow, and other compensation techniques to motivate managers to maximize value without bureaucratic oversight. My survey of 7 LBO partnerships found an average headquarters staff of 13 professional and 19 nonprofessionals that oversees almost 24 business units with total annual sales of more than $11 billion. (See the table, "LBO Partnerships Keep Staff Lean.")

LBO Associations Rely Heavily on Leverage. The average debt ratio (long-term debt as a percentage of debt plus equity) for public companies prior to buyout is about 20%. The Kaplan study shows the average debt ratio for an LBO is 85% on completion of the buyout.

Intensive use of debt dramatically shrinks the amount of equity in a company. This allows the LBO general partners and divisional managers to control a large fraction of the total ownership without requiring huge investments they would be unable to make or

large grants of free equity. For example, in a company with $1 billion in assets and a debt ratio of 20%, management would have to raise $80 million to buy 10% of the equity. If that same company had a debt ratio of 90%, management would have to raise only $10 million to control a 10% stake. By concentrating equity holdings among managers and LBO partners, debt intensifies the ownership incentives that are so important to efficiency.

High debt also allows LBO Associations and other private organizations to tap the benefits of risk diversification once provided only by the public equity market. Intensive use of debt means much of it must be in the form of public, high-yield, noninvestment-grade securities, better know as junk bonds. This debt, which was pioneered by Drexel Burnham Lambert, reflects more of the risk borne by shareholders in the typical public company. Placing this public debt in the well-diversified portfolios of large financial institutions spreads equitylike risk among millions of investors, who are the ultimate beneficiaries of mutual funds and pension funds —without requiring those risks to be held as equity. Indeed, high-yield debt is probably the most important and productive capital market innovation in the last 40 years.

LBO Associations Have Well-Defined Obligations to Their Creditors and Residual Claimants. Most buyout funds are organized as limited partnerships in which the

LBO Partnerships Keep Staff Lean

LBO Partnership	Year Started	Number of Professionals	Number of Nonprofessionals	Number of Business Units	Combined Annual Revenues (In billions of dollars)
Berkshire Partners	1986	14	6	15	$ 1
Butler Capital	1979	8	14	33	2.3
Clayon & Dubilier	1976	10	11	8	4.8
Gibbons Green van Amerongen	1969	6	7	12	5.3
Kohlberg Kravis Roberts	1976	16	44	19	58.7
Thomas H. Lee Company	1974	15	12	25	8
Odyssey Partners	1950	19	39	53	N.A.

partners of the sponsoring LBO firm serve as general partners. The buyout fund purchases most of the equity and sometimes provides debt financing. The limited partnership agreement denies the general partner the right to transfer cash or other resources from one LBO division to another. That is, all returns from a business must be distributed to the limited partners and other equity holders of that business. Such binding agreements reduce the risk of unproductive reinvestment by prohibiting cross-subsidization among LBO units. In effect, the LBO sponsor must ask its institutional investors for permission to reinvest funds, a striking difference from the power of public-company managers to freely shift resources among business units.

The management, compensation, and financial structures of the LBO Association square neatly with the rebirth of active investors. Institutional investors delegate the job of being active monitors to agents best qualified to play the role. The LBO partnerships bond their performance by investing their own resources and reputations in the transaction and taking the bulk of their compensation as a share in the companies' increased value.

To be sure, this delegation is not without its tensions. The fact that LBO partnerships and divisional managers control the LBO Association's small equity base but hold little of the debt creates incentives for them to take high-risk management gambles. If their gambles succeed, they reap large rewards by increasing their equity value; if their gambles fail, creditors bear much of the cost. But the reputational consequences of such reckless behavior can be large. As long as creditors behave rationally, an LBO partnership that tries to profit at the expense of its creditors or walks away from a deal gone sour will not be able to raise funds for future investments.

To date, the performance of LBO Associations has been remarkable. Indeed,it is difficult to find any systematic losers in these transactions, and almost all of the gains appear to come from real increases in produc-

tivity. The best studies of LBO performance reach the following conclusions:

LBOs create large gains for shareholders. Studies estimate that the average total premium to public shareholders ranges from 40% to 56%.[12] Kaplan finds that in buyouts that go public again or are otherwise sold (which occurs on average 2.7 years after the original transaction), total shareholder value increases by an average of 235%, or nearly 100% above market-adjusted returns over the same period.[13] These returns are distributed about equally between prebuyout shareholders and the suppliers of debt and equity to transaction. Prebuyout shareholders earn average market-adjusted premiums of 38%, while the total return to capital (debt plus equity) for buyout investors is 42%. This return to buyout investors is measured on the total purchase price of the LBO, not the buyout equity. Because equity returns are almost a pure risk premium, and therefore independent of the amount invested, they are very high. The median market-adjusted return on buyout equity is 785%, or 125% per year.

Value gains do not come at the expense of other financial constituencies. Some critics argue that buyout investors, especially managers, earn excessive returns by using inside information to exploit public shareholders. Managers do face severe conflicts of interest in these transactions; they cannot simultaneously act as buyer and agent for the seller. But equity-opening managers who are not part of post-buyout management teams systematically sell their shares into LBOs. This would be foolish if the buyout were significantly underpriced in light of inside information, assuming that these non-participating insiders have the same inside information as the continuing management team. Moreover, LBO auctions are becoming common; underpriced buyout proposals (including those initiated by management) quickly generate competing bids.

No doubt some bondholders have lost value through going-private transactions. By my estimate, RJR Nabisco's prebuyout bondholders lost almost $300 million through the downgrading of their claims on the newly leveraged company. This is a small sum in comparison to the $12 billion in total gains the transaction produced. As yet, there is no evidence that bondholders lose on average from LBOs. Evidence on LBOs completed through 1986 does show that holders of convertible bonds and preferred stock gain a statistically significant amount and that straight bondholders suffer no significant gains or losses.[14]

New data may document losses for bondholders in recent transactions. But the expropriation of wealth from bondholders should not be a continuing problem. The financial community id perfecting many techniques, including poison puts and repurchase provisions, to protect bondholders in the event of substantial restructurings. In fact, versions of these loss-prevention techniques have been available for some time. In the past, bondholders such as Metropolitan Life, which sued RJR Nabisco over the declining value of the company's bonds, chose not to pay the premium for protection.

LBOs increase operating efficiency without massive layoffs or big cuts in research and development. Kaplan finds that average operating earnings increase by 42% from the year prior to the buyout to the third year after the buyout. Cash flows increase by 96% over this same period. Other studies document significant improvements in profit margins, sales per employee, working capital, inventories, and receivables.[15] Those who doubt these findings might take a moment to scan the business press, which has chronicled the impressive postbuyout performance of companies such as Levi Strauss, A.O. Scott, Safeway, and Weirton Steel.

Importantly, employment does not fall systematically after buyouts, although it does not grow as quickly as in comparable companies. Median employment for all companies in the Kaplan study, including those engaged in substantial divestitures, increased by nearly 1%. Companies without significant divestitures increased employment by 5%.

Moreover, the great concern about the effect of buyouts on R&D and capital investment is unwarranted. The low-growth companies that make the best candidates for LBOs don't invest heavily in R&D to begin with. Of the 76 companies in the Kaplan study, only 7 spent more than 1% of sales on R&D before the buyout. Another recent study shows that R&D as a fraction of sales grows at the same rate in LBOs as in comparable public companies.[16] According to Kaplan's study, capital expenditures are 20% lower in LBOs than in comparable non-LBO companies. Because these cuts are taking place in low-growth or declining industries and are accompanied by a doubling of market-adjusted value, they appear to be coming from reductions in low-return projects rather than productive investments.

Taxpayers do not subsidize going-private transactions. Much has been made of the charge that large increases in debt virtually eliminate the tax obligations of an LBO. This argument overlooks five sources of additional tax revenues generated by buyouts: capital gains taxes paid by pre-buyout shareholders; capital gains taxes paid on postbuyout asset sales; tax payments on the large increases in operating earnings generated by efficiency gains; tax payments by creditors who receive interest payments on the LBO debt; and taxes generated by more efficient use of the company's total capital.

Overall, the U.S. Treasury collects an estimated 230% more revenues in the year after a buyout than it would have otherwise and 61% more in long-term present value. The $12 billion gain associated with the RJR Nabisco buyout will generate net tax revenues of $3.3 billion in the first year of the buyout; the company paid $370 million in federal taxes in the year before the buyout. In the long term, the transaction will generate total taxes with an estimated present value of $3.8 billion.[17]

LBO sponsors do not have to take their companies public for them to succeed. Most LBO transactions are completed with a goal of returning the reconfigured company to the public market within three to five years. But recent evidence indicates that LBO sponsors are keeping their companies under private ownership. Huge efficiency gains and high-return asset sales produce enough cash to pay down debt and allow LBOs to generate handsome returns as going concerns. The very proliferation of these transactions has helped create a more efficient infrastructure and liquid market for buying and selling divisions and companies. Thus LBO investors can "cash out" in a secondary LBO or private sale without recourse to a public offering. One recent study finds that only 5% of the more than 1,300 LBOs between 1981 and 1986 have gone public again.[18]

Public companies can learn from LBO Associations and emulate many of their characteristics. But this requires major changes in corporate structure, philosophy, and focus. They can reduce the waste of free cash flow by borrowing to repurchase stock or pay large dividends. They can alter their charters to encourage large investors or experiment with alliances with active investors such as Lazard Frères' Corporate Partners fund. They can increase equity ownership by directors, managers, and employees. They can enhance incentives through pay-for-performance systems based on cash flow and value rather than accounting earnings. They can decentralize management by rethinking the role of corporate headquarters and shrinking their staffs.

Some corporations are experimenting with such changes—FMC, Holiday, Owens-Corning—and the results have been impressive. But only a coordinated attack on the status quo will halt the eclipse of the public company. It is unlikely such an attack will proceed fast enough or go far enough.

Who can argue with a new model of enterprise that aligns the interests of owners and managers, improves efficiency and productivity, and unlocks hundreds of billions of dollars of shareholder value? Many people, it seems, mainly because these organizations rely so heavily on debt. As I've discussed, debt is crucial to management discipline and resolving the conflict over free cash flow. But critics, even some who concede the control function of debt, argue that the costs of leverage outweigh the benefits.

Wall Street economist Henry Kaufman, a prominent critic of the going-private trend, issued a typical warning earlier this year: "Any severe shock—a sharp increase in inter-est rates in response to Federal Reserve credit restraint, or an outright recession that makes the whole stock market vulnerable, or some breakdown in the ability of foreign firms to bid for pieces of U.S. companies—will drive debt-burdened companies to the government's doorstep to plead for special assistance."[19]

The relationship between debt and insolvency is perhaps the least understood aspect of the entire organizational evolution. New hedging techniques mean the risk associated with a given level of corporate debt is lower today than it was five years ago. Much of the bank debt associated with LBOs (which typically represents about half of the total debt) is done through floating-rate instruments. But few LBOs accept unlimited exposure to interest rate fluctuations. They purchase caps to set a ceiling on interest charges or use swaps to convert floating-rate debt into fixed-rate debt. In fact, most banks require such risk management techniques as a condition of lending.

Critics of leverage also fail to appreciate that insolvency in and of itself is not always something to avoid—and that the costs of becoming insolvent are likely to be much smaller in the new world of high leverage than in the old world of equity-dominated balance sheets. The proliferation of takeovers, LBOs, and other going-private transactions has inspired innovations in the reorganization and workout process. I refer to these innovations as "the privatization of bankruptcy." LBOs *do* get in financial trouble more frequently than public companies do. But few LBOs ever enter formal bankruptcy. They are reorganized quickly (a few months is common), often under new management, and at much lower costs than under a court-supervised process.

How can insolvency be less costly in a world of high leverage? Consider an oversimplified example. Companies A and B are identical in every respect except for their financial structures. Each has a going-concern value of $100 million (the discounted value of its expected future cash flows) and a liquidation or salvage value of $10 million. Company A has an equity-dominated balance sheet with a debt ratio of 20%, common for large public companies. Highly leveraged Company B has a debt ratio of 85%, common for LBOs. (See the illustration, "The Privatization of Bankruptcy.")

Now both companies experience business reversals. What happens? Company B will get in trouble with its creditors much sooner than Company A. After all, Company B's going-concern value doesn't have to shrink very much for it to be unable to meet its payments on $85 million of debt. But when it does run into trouble, its going-concern value will be nowhere near its liquidation value. If the going-concern value shrinks to $80 million, there remains $70 million of value to preserve by avoiding liquidation. So Company B's creditors have strong incentives to preserve the remaining value by quickly and efficiently reorganizing their claims outside the courtroom.

No such incentives operate on Company A. Its going-concern value can fall dramatically before creditors worry about their $20 million of debt. By the time creditors do intervene, Company A's going-concern value will have plummeted. And if Company A's value falls to under $20 million, it is much more likely than Company B to be worth less than its $20 million salvage value. Liquidation in this situation is the likely and rational outcome, with all its attendant conflicts, dislocations, and costs.

The evolving U.S. system of corporate governance and finance exhibits many characteristics of the postwar Japanese system. LBO partnerships act much like the main banks (the real power center) in Japan's *keiretsu* business groupings. The keiretsu make extensive use of leverage and intercorporate holdings of debt and equity. Banks commonly hold substantial equity in their client companies and have their own executives help them out of difficulty. (For years, Nissan has

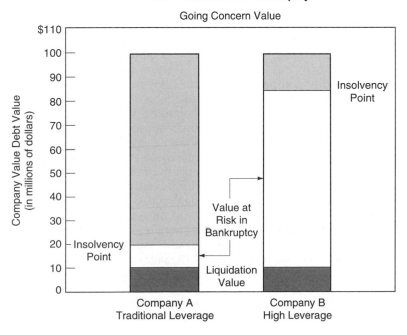

The Privatization of Bankruptcy

Going Concern Value

been run by an alumnus of the Industrial Bank of Japan, who became CEO as part of the bank's effort to keep the company out of bankruptcy.) Other personnel, including CEOs, move frequently between banks and companies as part of an ongoing relationship that involves training, consulting, and monitoring. Japanese banks allow companies to enter formal bankruptcy only when liquidation makes economic sense—that is, when a company is worth more dead than alive. Japanese corporate boards are composed almost exclusively of insiders.

Ironically, even as more U.S. companies come to resemble Japanese companies, Japan's public companies are becoming more like U.S. companies of 15 years ago. Japanese shareholders have seldom had any power. The banks' chief disciplinary tool, their power to withhold capital from high-growth, cash starved companies, has been vastly reduced as a result of several factors. Japan's victories in world product markets have left its companies awash in profits. The development of domestic and international capital markets has created ready alternatives to bank loans, while deregulation has liberalized corporate access to these funds. Finally, new legal constraints prevent banks from holding more than 5% of the equity of any company, which reduces their incentive to engage in active monitoring.

Many of Japan's public companies are flooded with free cash flow far in excess of their opportunities to invest in profitable internal growth. In 1987, more than 40% of Japan's large public companies had no net bank borrowings—that is, cash balances larger than their short- and long-term borrowings. Toyota, with a cash hoard of $10.4 billion, more than 25% of its total assets is commonly referred to as the Toyota Bank.[20]

In short, Japanese managers are increasingly unconstrained and unmonitored. They face no effective internal controls, little control from the product markets their companies already dominate, and fewer controls from the banking system because of self-financing, direct access to capital markets, and lower debt ratios. Unless shareholders and creditors discover ways to prohibit their managers from behaving like U.S. managers, Japanese companies will make uneconomic acquisition and diversification moves, generate internal waste, and engage in other value-destroying activities. The long-term result will be the growth of bureaucracy and inefficiency and the demise of product quality and organizational responsiveness—until the waste becomes so severe it triggers a market for corporate control to remedy the excesses.

The Japanese remedy will reflect that country's unique legal system and cultural practices. But just as hostile takeovers, LBOs, and other control transactions went from unacceptable behavior in the United States to a driving force in corporate restructuring, so too will they take hold in Japan—once the potential returns outweigh the costs and risks of challenging the corporate status quo.

Meanwhile, in the United States, the organizational changes revitalizing the corporate sector will create more nimble enterprises and help reverse our losses in world product markets. As this profound innovation continues, however, people will make mistakes. To learn, we have to push new policies to the margin. It will be natural to see more failed deals.

There are already some worrisome structural issues. I look with discomfort on the dangerous tendency of LBO partnerships, bolstered by their success, to take more of their compensation in front-end fees rather than in back-end profits earned through increased equity value. As management fees and the fees for completing deals get larger, the incentives to do deals, rather than good deals, also increases. Institutional investors (and the economy as a whole) are best served when the LBO partnership is the last member of LBO Association to get paid and when the LBO partnership gets paid as a fraction of the back-end value of the deals, including losses.

Moreover, we have yet to fully understand the limitations on the size of this new organizational form. LBO partnerships are understandably tempted to increase the reach of their talented monitors by reconfiguring divisions as acquisition vehicles. This will be difficult to accomplish successfully. It is likely to require bigger staffs, greater centralization of decision rights, and dilution of the high pay-for-performance sensitivity that is so crucial to success. As LBO Associations expand, they run the risk of recreating the bureaucratic waste of the diversified public corporation.

These and other problems should not cloud the marketable benefits associated with the eclipse of the large public corporation. What surprises me is how few mistakes have occurred thus far in an organizational change as profound as any since World War II.

NOTES

1. Equity values based on trends in the Wilshire index. Private-placement data from IDD Information Services as published in Sarah Bartlett, "Private Market's Growing Edge," *New York Times*, June 20, 1989.
2. For more analysis of the oil industry, see my article, "The Takeover controversy: Analysis and Evidence," in *Corporate Restructuring and Executive Compensation* (Cambridge, Mass: Ballinger, 1989).
3. Calculated from Standard & Poor's Compustat file.
4. Kevin J. Murphy, "Corporate Performance and Managerial Remuneration," *Journal of Accounting and Economics*, 1985, vol. 7, no. 1–3.
5. Federal Reserve Board, Balance Sheets of U.S. Economy.
6. G. Bennett Stewart III and David M. Glassman, "The Motives and Methods of Corporate Restructuring: Part II," *Journal of Applied Corporate Finance*, Summer 1988.
7. Stephen Phillips, "Revco: Anatomy of an LBO that Failed," *Business Week*, October 3, 1988.
8. "A Hollow Victory for Bob Mercer," *Industry Week*, February 23, 1987.
9. Jonathan P. Hicks, "The Importance of Being Biggest," *New York Times*, June 20, 1989.
10. Steven Kaplan, "Sources of Value in Management Buyouts," *Journal of Financial Economics*, forthcoming.
11. Michael C. Jensen and Kevin J. Murphy, "Performance Pay and Top Management Incentives," *Journal of Political Economy*, forthcoming.
12. Yakov Amihuc, "Leveraged Management Buyouts and Shareholders' Wealth," in *Leveraged Management Buyouts: Causes and Conse-*

quences (Homewood, Ill. Dow Jones-Irwin, 1989).
13. That is, returns net of the returns that would normally be earned on these securities, given their level of systematic risk (beta) and general market returns.
14. L. Marais, K. Schipper, and A. Smith, "Wealth Effects of Going Private for Senior Securities," *Journal of Financial Economics*, 1989, vol. 23, no. 1.
15. In addition to Kaplan, see Abbie Smith, "Corporate Ownership Structure and Performance," unpublished paper, University of Chicago, 1989. See also Frank R. Lichtenberg and Donald Siegel, "The Effects of Leveraged Buyouts on Productivity and Related Aspects of Firm Behavior," *National Bureau of Economic Research*, 1989.
16. Lichtenberg and Siegel, NBER, 1989.
17. Michael C. Jensen, Robert Kaplan, and Laura Stiglin, "Effects of LBOs on Tax Revenues of the U.S. Treasury," *Tax Notes*, February 6, 1989.
18. Chris Muscarella and Michael Vetsuypens, "Efficiency and Organizational Structure: A Study of Reverse LBOs," unpublished paper, Southern Methodist University, April 1989.
19. Henry Kaufman, "Bush's First Priority: Stopping the Buyout Mania," *Washington Post*, January 1, 1989.
20. Average (book value) debt ratios fell from 77% in 1976 to 68% in 1987. Given the 390% increase in stock prices over this period, market-value debt ratios fell even more dramatically. Figures calculated from the NEEDS Nikkei Financials file for all companies on the First Section of the Tokyo Stock Exchange.

THE EVOLVING CORPORATE BOARD

Murray Weidenbaum

In a period of takeover battles and dramatic replacements of top managements, the role of the corporate board of directors is rapidly evolving into a major strategic force in American business.

Some companies have enacted "poison pill" provisions which put the board of directors squarely in the middle of merger and acquisition battles. The directors adopt such a measure to discourage unwanted takeovers. The "pill" is in the form of new rights to shareholders to acquire, at a marked discount, a large equity stake in any successful suitor whose offer has not been approved by the company's board. The new activism on the part of corporate directors rose in 1993 to include replacing CEOs for such industrial giants as American Express, Eastman Kodak, General Motors, and IBM.

The new burst of public attention to the corporate board, from friend and foe alike, is matched by widespread ignorance—both of how that important economic institution functions and how it has been changing in re-

cent years. Thus, it is appropriate to examine the evolving role of boards of directors, with special attention to the strengthening of the board at a time when it is often the focal point of corporate response to external threats. Although I present my own viewpoint, developed in part from my service as a corporate director, much of the material is a distillation of many studies in law, economics, and business administration.

CRITICISMS OF THE BOARD

Three major criticisms have been leveled at the institution of the corporate board of directors.

"The Board Is a Rubber Stamp"

One retired board chairman of a successful company describes the board of directors as the "Achilles heel of the American corporation."[1] A leading scholar refers to the corporate board as an "impotent legal fiction."[2]

The most frequently made criticism of the corporate board of directors is that it is ceremonial, rubber-stamping the views of management. This belief comes from many sources. In his 1948 classic study of large companies, R.A. Gordon concluded that directors are closer to top management than to the stockholders, and that ratification of management proposals by the board is large-

This draws heavily on the author's study *Strengthening the Corporate Board* (St. Louis: Washington University, Center for the Study of American Business, 1985), and on his textbook *Business and Government in the Global Marketplace*, 5th edition (Englewood Cliffs, N.J.: Prentice Hall, 1955). Samuel Hughes provided helpful research assistance.

ly a formality.[3] He also reported that, as a result of its control of the proxy machinery, it is more common for management to select directors than vice versa.

Myles L. Mace, in his authoritative study of corporate boards in the late 1960s, reported that the role of directors is largely advisory and not of a decision-making nature. He quotes one company president as saying, "The board of directors serves as a sounding board. . . . The decision is not made by the board.[4]

An account of the bankruptcy of the Penn Central reached an even stronger conclusion:

> Penn Central's directors seem to have done very little to earn the $200 each received each time he attended a board meeting. . . . With few exceptions, they appeared to be blind to the on-rushing events that sent the Penn Central hurtling off the tracks.[5]

Robert H. Malott, an experienced corporate director and retired CEO, identifies the biggest barrier to effective outside directorship as the "old boy" network that dominates some boards. This makes it personally unpleasant for directors to question the performance of their peers "and often their friends."[6]

"The Board Is Dominated by the CEO"

A closely related criticism is that the board's deliberations are dominated by the CEO, who typically also serves as chairman. When the same person controls the agenda and conduct of boardroom proceedings as well as the day-to-day performance of the company, the power of the individual director may indeed become attenuated. Despite the rising number of outside directors and special committees of corporate boards, in most cases the center of power remains with the management. CEOs serve as chairman of the board in 80 percent of the larger corporations.

Management consultants report that many directors act as part of top management, rather than as monitors able and willing to reward and penalize management's performance.[7] A long-time board member states that the ambiguity of the role of the corporate board begins with the prevailing combination of management leadership and board leadership in the same person.[8]

"The Board Is Plagued with Conflicts of Interest"

Corporate directors often are criticized for conflicts of interest and for showing greater concern for the welfare of other companies. Many outside directors of corporations do business with the companies on whose board they serve. The literature contains a number of cases of apparent wrongdoing on the part of outside directors who were also officers of companies that supplied services to the corporation or who benefitted unfairly from company operations.[9]

An analysis of 286 banks that failed in 1990 and 1991 revealed that, in 74 cases, the main cause of the failure was fraud and other abuses by directors and officers, such as receiving loans at very low rates. In 101 other instances, insider abuses contributed to the bank's insolvency.[10]

In the case of the Penn Central, a staff report of the Committee on Banking Currency of the U.S. House of Representatives censured the company's board members for their excessive involvement in other corporate boards. The Committee staff noted the subservience of many of the outside directors to the interests of the financial institutions of which they were officers. As corporate boards shift to a larger percentage of outside directors, the likelihood of such corporate "interlocks" could increase.[11]

In the case of the larger firms, a problem is emerging in the form of opportunity for "backscratching" when setting management compensation. The board's compensation committee is typically a group dominated by outside directors. What's wrong with that? Frequently, those outside directors are senior officers of other firms, who are very sympathetic to motions for generous treatment of their counterparts. Aside from the intrinsic merits of the matter, their self-interest dictates such a stand. After all, the compensation committees of their own boards are often similarly composed of CEOs of peer firms. Moreover, the management consultants advising those committees take full account of such peer-group action by the other boards. The ratchet effect that results is quite obvious.

Other nominally independent outside directors, in practice, may represent another set of special interest—those of the local community. Senior officers of local firms that primarily sell goods and services to the surrounding area may see great value in the company donating lavishly to local causes, even if its markets are national or international. Another serious concern is the relationship of the inside directors to the chairman CEO. After all, he is their day-to-day supervisor, usually with the effective authority to radically change the directors' role in the company and even to fire or demote them. It is rare to see a subordinate officer serving on a board dissent from the position taken by the CEO.

THE PUSH FOR REFORM

These criticisms have let to a variety of proposals to reform corporate governance.

Ralph Nader's Proposals

Over the years, Ralph Nader and his colleagues have developed numerous ambitious and far-reaching proposals to restructure the corporation. To give "all stockholders in corporate decision-making a real voice in corporate governance," he advocates a Corporate Democracy Act. Under this proposal, the federal government would assume the chartering power now residing in the individual states. Nader wants to install full-time outside directors who would take an active role in the governance of the corporation.[12]

It is interesting to note that the charter of the Equitable Life Insurance Company requires the Chief Justice of New Jersey to appoint several outside directors. Over the years, these appointees have included women civic leaders and physicians, who are far from typical corporate directors. Under the Nader approach, individual directors would be assigned responsibility for specific areas of concern, such as the environment or employee relations. In his concept, federal chartering would develop a "constitutionalism" for corporate employees and provide various protections for whistle blowers who object to specific company activities. He also urges a mandatory mail plebiscite of shareholders on all "fundamental" transactions.

The intent of his reforms, according to Nader, is to address a concept of "social bankruptcy" whereby a company would be thrown into receivership if it failed to meet its "social" obligations.

The Geneen-Williams Proposals

More modest—yet quite substantial—suggestions for change in the structure of the American corporation have come from several outspoken former corporate CEOs. The two that have received most attention are Harold Geneen, retired CEO of ITT, and Harold Williams, former chairman of the Securities and Exchange Commission and former CEO of Norton Simon. Williams contends that the ideal board of directors would include only one company officer, the chief executive. All other board members, including the chairman, would be chosen from outside the company. William's concept of outside directors excludes bankers, lawyers, or anyone else having business dealings with the company. In his view, outside-dominated boards could do a better job of representing the stockholders' long-term interests than executives who are responsible for day-to-day management.

There is considerable precedent for an outside director chairing the board meetings. That is the standard procedure at non-profit institutions such as hospitals, museums, and universities, many of which rival in size and complexity all but the largest for-profit corporations. Also, many Western European companies normally follow this practice, as do many American companies with concentrated ownership on the part of venture capitalists and other outside investors.

Williams, unlike Nader, would not allocate individual directorships to representatives of employees, consumers, minorities, or other groups. "It would be disastrous. . . . Constituency representative . . . makes the board a political body," according to Williams. Does his proposal infringe on private property rights? The former SEC chairman states that corporations are more than economic institutions owned by shareholders: "Corporate America is too important, and perceived as too powerful, to fail to address the kinds of issues that are noneconomic."[13]

Geneen would go further than Williams, barring all members of management from serving on the board of the corporation for which they work. The CEO and other members of management would continue to attend board meetings, but they would be there to report to the board and to explain their actions.[14]

In a variation of this approach, Walter J. Salmon, of the Harvard Business School and a veteran board member, suggests that the boards of larger corporations be limited to three inside directors—the chief executive (CEO), the chief operating officer (COO), and the chief financial officer (CFO). As the current leaders of the corporation, the CEO and COO are there to communicate, explain, and justify strategic direction to the outside directors. Because CFOs share fiduciary responsibility with the directors for the financial conduct of the corporation, they should also have a seat on the board.[15]

A more modest variation on the theme of strengthening the role of the outside directors in the American Law Institute's draft *Principles of Corporate Governance and Structure*. The ALI draft proposes to replace the now voluntary arrangements on corporate governance, as interpreted by the courts, with legislative statutes and administrative regulations. For example, the ALI draft proposes that, as a matter of law, a majority of the board members of each large publicly held corporation (those with at least 2,000 shareholders and $100 million in total assets) must be outside directors. Following substantial criticism from the business community, the ALI draft has remained merely a basis for discussion.[16]

It does not seem likely that any of these sets of detailed proposals for the reform of corporate governance will be adopted on a compulsory basis. Yet, legislators continue to introduce proposals for legislating some of these changes. In 1993, Representative Ed Markey (D-Mass.) urged that the federal government require that all board chairmen be outside directors. He would also limit the number of boards that a director can serve on. In the United Kingdom, the Cadbury Committee on Financial Aspects of Corporate Governance has urged that non-management (outside) directors serve on only one board.

Voluntary Changes in the Boardroom

While the criticism on corporate governance continues unabated, important changes in the boardroom are being made on a voluntary basis. These adaptive adjustments have resulted from significant shifts in the environment in which corporations and their boards function. First is increased government regulation and the threat of further intervention. The second influence is active concern with corporate governance by some large institutional investors (especially state and local government employee pension funds). Other factors include greater foreign competition, rising levels of litigation by shareholders, and criticism from the press. In part, these changes deflect or reduce the pressures for new statutes or regulations requiring compulsory modifications in corporate governance. Also, the increased liability of corporate directors for their actions is reinforcing the trend toward their greater involvement in company decision-making.

According to the head of a major consulting firm, "Passive ceremonial directors are fast becoming an endangered species." A recent survey of the boards of directors of large U.S. corporations concluded that "the days of the 'rubber stamp' board are over." Clearly, many boards are taking on a more active role. Eight basic voluntary changes in the boardroom can be identified.

1. Outside Directors Have Become a Majority of Most Boards of Large Companies in the United States, and the Move toward More Outside Directors Continues.

In 1938, only one-half of industrial corporations had majorities of outsiders on their boards. By 1992, the average corporate board had nine outside directors and three inside directors. Also, board size has declined somewhat, reflecting in part the reduced role of inside directors. In 1992, the typical board had 14 directors, down from 16 in 1982.

Some movement is also being made voluntarily toward the Geneen-Williams view on board composition. Of the 100 large corporations analyzed in 1992 by Spencer Stuart, the executive search firm, eleven were comprised entirely of outside directors except for the chairman/CEO. In 1987, this condition was true in only 3 of the 100 firms. Simultaneously, the prevalence of "dependent" outside directors (those who also provide services to the company) has diminished. In the 1970s, the average board included a commercial banker and/or an attorney. That is true in only a small minority of instances in the 1990s.[17]

2. A Broader Diversity of Backgrounds is Evident in the Type of Persons Serving on Corporate Boards.

Increased numbers of directors have public service, academic, and scientific experience. Boards also include rising percentages of women and minorities. A survey of top company board placements in 1992 indicated that approximately 30 percent were women or blacks.[18] During the same period, the percentage of boards with ethnic minority members rose from 11 percent to 26 percent, those with academics from 36 percent to 52 percent, and those with former government officials from 12 percent to 31 percent.

Another trend in the composition of U.S. boards of directors is the rising number of directors from other countries. In 1992, 22 of the 100 large corporations surveyed by Spencer Stuart had a total of 27 international outside directors.

3. Auditing Committees Have Become a Nearly Universal Phenomenon.

Typically, these financial oversight bodies are composed entirely of independent outside directors (an absolute requirement for firms listed on the New York Stock Exchange). The audit committees have direct access to both outside and inside auditors and usually review the financial aspects of company operations in great detail. As recently as 1973, only one-half of large U.S. corporations had auditing committees. Currently, the proportion is 99 percent.

4. In Many Companies, Nominating Committees Propose Both Candidates for the Board and Senior Officers.

These committees usually have a strong majority of outside directors (typically, four out of five). However, these statistics do little to illuminate the continuing powerful role of the CEO in initiating or approving committee selections. In practice, most outside directors are selected by the chairman/CEO and in virtually all cases, he or she must be agreeable to their appointment.

5. In Most Large Companies, Compensation Committees Evaluate the Performance of Top Executives and Determine the Terms and Conditions of Their Employment.

These committees are composed largely or entirely of outside directors. In practice, many of these committees rely extensively on outside consultants whose compensation surveys often set the framework for committee deliberations.

6. On Average, about One Out of Five of the Larger Companies Have Established Public-Policy Committees on Their Boards. These committees give board-level attention to company policies and performance on subjects of special public concern. Topics with which public-policy committees often deal include affirmative action and equal employment opportunity, employee health and safety, company impact on the environment, corporate political activities, consumer affairs, and ethics.

Pfizer, the large pharmaceutical firm, has appointed a new vice president for corporate governance. The company's expectation is that this officer will be proactive in responding to legislation and regulations in the field of corporate governance and will advise the top management on the latest thinking on corporate structure and shareholder relations.[19]

7. Internal Management and Accounting Control Systems Have Been Strengthened. In part, the impetus has come from the need to comply with the provisions of the Foreign Corrupt Practices Act. The activities of the audit committees surely are a reinforcing factor. As a result, the flow of information to board members has been upgraded and expanded.

8. Recruiting Directors Has Become More Difficult. Increasing the role and the remuneration of directors have helped make board service more attractive. However, these positive factors are on occasion offset by a change in the narrow, technical area of directors' liability insurance. In recent years, courts have narrowed the scope of the business judgment rule, which provides board discretion to board members in carrying out their functions. The resultant acceleration of lawsuits against corporate boards has increased the costs of the insurance companies that have previously covered the bulk of such expenses. In turn, this has led to a marked decline in the willingness of carriers to write directors' and officers' liability insurance policies. As a consequence, some directors have reduced the number of boards on which they serve in order to concentrate on their responsibilities on the remaining boards.

Boards have traditionally responded strongly when corporations have faced real crises. In the early 1990s, outside directors began taking a more active stance in reacting to poor performance on the part of the managements reporting to them and thus to avoid the development of crisis situations. In 1992, the General Motors board, led by outside directors, replaced the CEO and designated an outside director (a recently retired CEO of another major enterprise) as nonexecutive chairman.

In 1993, IBM, after replacing its CEO, created a new committee of outside directors to focus on corporate governance. The function of the new committee is to nominate new directors, handle proposals from shareholders, and oversee the functioning of the board. In the same year, Eastman Kodak replaced its CEO and formed a corporate directors committee of outside directors to oversee its basic strategy.

An important and voluntary institutional change occurred in 1984 when the board of directors of General Motors issued 28 "guidelines on significant corporate governance issues." The GM guidelines formalize the stronger control over management that the board had moved to in 1992. Specifics include designating a "lead" outside director to chair three meetings of independent directors a year, giving the board rather than the CEO real authority to select new members, and a new director affairs committee. The duties of that new committee include assigning members to board committees and evaluating the board's performance each year.[20]

As a result of the financial difficulties encountered by many companies during the 1980s and early 1990s, some labor unions were given the authority to designate one or more members of the firm's board of directors as part of an overall package that contained reductions from customary wage increases and often outright cuts in labor compensation. In 1980, Chrysler Corporation became the first major company in the United States to elect a union leader to its board. That was done in connection with a package of union concessions to help the company to continue operating during a very difficult period.

In 1983, the Teamsters Union agreed to a substantial lowering of wage and benefit levels at Commercial Lovelace Motor Freight, Inc., a company hard hit by competition from nonunion truckers. In return, workers were given just over 50 percent of the stock and the right to elect three of the seven members of the board. At five other trucking firms, the Union agreed to a similar package, but worker ownership was kept to less than 50 percent. In some instances, the union-designated board members have been retired executives from business and government, avoiding conflicts of interest.

In 1993, several steel companies—Bethlehem, Wheeling-Pittsburgh, and LTV—agreed to having a representative of the United Steelworkers Union serve on their boards. At about the same time, Northwest Airlines and TWA both agreed to give their employees a major share of the corporation's ownership. As part of a move out of bankruptcy, TWA gave its employees a 45 percent ownership of the company plus four board seats. Northwest provided three board seats plus 37.5 percent of the company's stock. Both airlines received several hundred million dollars of concessions in labor costs.

Union memberships on corporate boards are still isolated examples, and the entire subject remains extremely controversial. Although the concept of employee representation on the board is common in Western Europe, it is not a generally accepted notion in the United States. In Germany, codetermination laws have required worker representation on the boards of larger companies since 1951. However, the nation has a long tradition of labor-management cooperation. The fact that German worker compensation averages higher than other industrialized nations is not an inducement to U.S. firms to copy the example.

Such actions, although few, provide a powerful signal to top management that inadequate performance can result in their replacement by a hitherto supportive board of directors. It is especially noteworthy that these changes in management did not require a formal takeover ("change of control") with its ancillary legion of expensive investment bankers, attorneys, and accountants.

Recommendations for Strengthening the Board[21]

Despite the progress that has been made in recent years, most writers on the role of the corporate board reach some variation of the same dual conclusion: the board of directors is a vital part of the business firm, but it often does an inadequate job of carrying out its responsibility to represent the shareholders.

The result can be a policy vacuum, which provides opportunity for those outside of the corporation. Dramatic moves have been made to take advantage of the fundamental shortcoming of corporate boards. These responses have come from the so-called predatory raiders who attempt to take advantage of the latent support of shareholders for changes in the status quo.

Of course, corporate managements view this phenomenon differently. A spokesman for the Business Roundtable describes the strategy of "professional raiders" as waging "blitzkrieg warfare" devised to "outflank the corporate board of directors and stampede the stockholders." There is no need to glamorize the activities or the motives of the raiders while noting the positive contributions they make. One of the most successful takeover specialists describes his efforts as "acting in pursuit of personal financial gain and not out of altruism. . . . I do it to make money."

The following suggestions are offered in the spirit of strengthening the corporate board without setting up a mechanism competitive with the company management.

We Must Recognize the Extent to Which Takeover Battles Have Occurred Because of the Cumulative Inaction of Some Boards of Directors. It is easy enough to denounce financial entrepreneurs who have little interest in the production of goods and services, but who profit—often in the form of "greenmail"—merely from making unsolicited take-over bids. But if they are opportunists, we must ask whether existing board and management practices have created these opportunities. A clue is given, perhaps inadvertently, by the Roundtable's lament that a successful corporate defense may involve drastic restructuring to maximize share value in the short run. Without endorsing the desirability of such a change, we can wonder whether it does reflect the true desires of many shareholders who indeed want to maximize share value in the short run.

"Despite their attraction to defending managements, legislative proposals to make unfriendly takeovers more difficult do not deal with the fundamental need to respond to the desires of the shareholders. That is both the basic responsibility of the board and the key to its potential power. Corporate officials, both board members and officers, may forget that shareholders continually vote with their dollars. The less frequently key issues are presented to the shareholders, the more likely they are to resort to their ultimate weapon —selling their holdings in a company whose policies they disagree with.

It Is Ironic That Some of the Problems of the Takeover Targets May Have Arisen from the Desire to Be More Socially Responsible. Examples include Cummins Engine and Control Data Corporation, both of which suffered under management with an unusual interest in broad social problems. Much of the modern management literature refers to the need for top management to balance the desires of employees, customers, suppliers, public-interest groups, and shareholders. For example, the Committee for Economic Development, in its widely circulated report on the

social responsibility of business, stated that the modern professional manager is regarded as a trustee balancing the interests of many diverse participants and constituents in the enterprise (shareholders are only listed as one among many worthy groups).

> The chief executive of a large corporation has the problem of reconciling the demands of employees for more wages and improved benefit plans, customers for lower prices and greater values, vendors for higher prices, government for more taxes, stockholders for higher dividends and greater capital appreciation.[22]

In the case of Control Data, after an annual loss of $680 million, a new CEO replaced his predecessor who had stressed corporate social responsibility. The new CEO bluntly stated that the previous management had not always "thought in terms of building shareholder value" and had not built a culture of controlling costs.[23]

The Heart of a Positive Response to the Dissatisfaction with Corporate Performance Is for Directors to Act More Fully as Fiduciaries of the Shareholders, as the Law Requires. The same authorities who are almost universally critical of the way in which corporate boards operate are unanimous in their belief that a well-functioning governing board is essential to the future of the modern corporation. Virtually no one has concluded that the board of directors has outlived its usefulness. Even such business critics as Ralph Nader would lodge majority responsibility for governing the corporation in a revitalized board of directors.

The Most Fundamental Need in Corporate Governance Is Educational—To Get Senior Corporate Officers to Understand Their High Stake in Enhancing the Role of the Board of Directors. There would be fewer challenges to the existing managements of their companies if more boards acted from a day-to-day concern with the interests of their shareholders. The benefits of a more active board will not be attained without costs. Achieving a stronger and more effective board means sharing the authority now lodged in the CEO—and at times reaching somewhat different decisions. But that does not require the establishment of a competitive power center. It does mean being more conscious of the desires of shareholders, and of the need to keep them more fully informed. Only one person—the chief executive—can guide the corporation's day-to-day activities. That function cannot be performed by a committee.

Successful directors learn to monitor and question while creating an atmosphere of confidence in the management. Simultaneously, a truly secure CEO will not attempt to stifle criticism by individual directors. The legendary Alfred P. Sloan reportedly made the following statement at a General Motors board meeting:

> Gentlemen, I take it we are all in complete agreement on the decision here. . . . Then I propose we postpone further discussion of this matter until our next meeting to give ourselves time to develop disagreement and perhaps gain some understanding of what the decision is all about.[24]

What about the composition of the board? Experience teaches us to be leery of simple solutions. An example is the popular proposition that only outside directors should serve on a corporate board, with the possible exception of the CEO. Diversity of talent is a strength in the management of an economic organization.

Corporate Boards Should Consist Primarily of Independent Outsiders. Outside directors should not represent banks, law firms, customers, or the community in which the corporation happens to have its headquarters. Such actual or potential conflicts should be avoided.

A Strong but Minority Representation of Knowledgeable Insiders Should Continue. Nominating committees would do well to bear in mind the advice of management scholar S. Prakash Sethi that a board of directors is not a debating society: "While it is normal to have different viewpoints and expertise represented on the board, it is illogical to represent special interests on the board."[25]

Retired Officers of a Company Do Not Belong on Its Board. It is enough to have independent outside directors looking over the shoulders of the management, without the previous generation of management also doing so. The outsiders have less stake in defending the status quo than do the retirees who may have created existing conditions. There are advantages in retired corporate officers serving as directors of other companies, so long as they are not competitors of or suppliers to the company from which they have retired.

Opinions differ sharply on whether the CEO should also serve as chairman of the board. *In my personal view, the board chairman should usually be an outside director in order to assure the independence of the board.* Much depends on the attitude of the CEO to the board and to the specific challenges facing the company. There is no compelling need to modify the traditional arrangement in the case of a well-functioning company whose CEO also maintains an open, healthy relation with the board. In such circumstances, it would be silly to change merely for the sake of change.

However, when the company is not performing well or when the CEO regards the board as merely a legal necessity, then a departure from the status quo is warranted. Under such circumstances, it would be helpful if the presiding officer had relevant experience—the recently retired CEO of another firm or of a large non-profit institution, for instance. A few other senior members of the management also can be useful board members. The chief operating officer would be appropriate. His or her presence on the board does not give rise to the problems that occur when operating officials are made board members—when they participate in reviewing their own operations and those of their colleagues. Because of the crucial relationship of financial reporting to the monitoring function, the chief financial officer probably also should be a board member. None of these inside directors can be expected to differ frequently with the CEO, thus emphasizing the need for a substantial representation of outside, independent directors.

Where the board chairmanship is filled by an outside director, the position should be a private role whereas the CEO should represent the firm to the public. Only the CEO and his or her subordinates can truly represent the firm in public arenas since they bear the responsibility and possess the authority to conduct the business of the company. This approach requires a high degree of good will on the part of both outside directors and corporate officers. The indispensable factor in ensuring an effective board is that directors and management be committed to making the board work. A great deal of effort and discretion is required on the part of outside directors to carry on an active and constructive role that is simultaneously probing and supportive.

The points just made for board service apply with equal force to committee work. Compared to board meetings, directors are more likely to take the initiative in committees. Some institutional protections of the independence of board committees are necessary and are now often in place. Specifically, the audit committee—even if the corporation is not listed on the New York Stock Exchange—should consist entirely of independent outside directors. The compensation committee, which passes on the pay and fringe benefits of top management, should be similarly constituted. Also, the nominating committee, with a key role in selecting directors and senior executives, should be comprised of independent outside members.

In contrast, the finance and public-policy committees can benefit from a balance between insiders and outsiders. The management directors bring a special institutional knowledge, while the outside directors hopefully operate

with a wider framework. Another reason for the mixed finance committee is that it provides a built-in opportunity to balance the pressures for dividends and retained earnings. Often many shareholders emphasize the short-run benefits of increased income, whereas management is more concerned about investing in the company's future growth. Also, the officers may simply find it easier or at least more satisfactory to use retained earnings rather than going to the credit markets. For the typical business firm, this is not an either-or choice, but a case of balancing two important and basic considerations.

The subject of board turnover is often a painful matter. A directorship is not a type of civil-service appointment, but it is not easy to dislodge a long-term director. Long-term directors become so accustomed to the existing way of doing business that they viscerally oppose innovation on the oldest bureaucratic grounds: "We have never done it that way."

CEOs and other busy professionals are rationing more carefully than in the past the number of boards on which they serve. Likewise, boards are more selective in their new appointments. Outside directors should be truly independent. They should not also simultaneously be paid consultants or advisors to the management. They should not have their own interests in mind, be it supporting the local community or advocating more generous treatment of corporate executives generally. Outside directors need to bear in mind that, in a very special way, the future of the corporation is in their hands—so long as they serve the desires of the shareholders.

A Look to the Future

A growing array of external forces impinges on the contemporary corporation. Some of these factors are financial and economic, focusing on the traditional functions of business enterprise. Others are social and political, dealing with business responses to other issues. Together, these influences will likely produce significant further changes in the composition of corporate boards of directors and in the conduct of the boardroom.

Looking ahead, researchers and practitioners alike in the twenty-first century will probably still be speculating about the needed changes in the roles and activities of corporate directors. Fundamentally, this will reflect the fact that the corporation is a continually evolving institution in the U.S. economy and, as external requirements change, key elements such as the board of directors continue to adapt and modify their actions. These factors help to explain the fundamental strength and long-term resiliency of private enterprise institutions in the United States.

NOTES

1. Kenneth N. Dayton, "Corporate Governance: The Other Side of the Coin," *Harvard Business Review*, January/February 1984, p. 34.
2. Peter Drucker, "The Bored Board," *Wharton Magazine*, Fall 1976, p. 19.
3. R.A. Gordon, *Business Leadership in the Large Corporation* (Berkeley: University of California Press, 1948), pp. viii, 131.
4. Myles L. Mace, *Directors: Myth and Reality* (Boston: Harvard University, Graduate School of Business Administration, 1971), p. 13.
5. J.R. Daughen and P. Binzel, *The Wreck of the Penn Central* (Boston: Little, Brown, 1971), p. 12.
6. Robert H. Malott, "Directors: Step Up to Your Responsibilities," *Directors & Boards*, Summer 1992, p. 69.
7. Arch Patton, "Why Corporations Overpay Their Underachieving Bosses," *Washington Post*, March 3, 1985, p. C-2.
8. Courtney C. Brown, *Putting the Corporate Board to Work* (New York: Macmillan, 1976), p. 15.
9. Edward S. Herman, *Corporate Control, Corporate Power* (New York: Cambridge University Press, 1981), pp. 41, 136.
10. "GAO Report Finds Insider Problems At Banks Often Contribute to Failure," *Wall Street Journal*, March 31, 1994, p. B4.
11. S. Prakash Sethi, Bernard Cunningham, and Carl Swanson, "The Catch-22 in Reform Proposals for Restructuring Corporate Boards," *Management Review*, January 1979, p. 28.
12. Ralph Nader, "Democratic Revolution in an Age of Autocracy," *Boston Review*, March/April 1993, pp. 3–6.
13. Harold M. Williams, "Corporate Accountability," address to the Fifth Annual Securities Regulation Institute, San Diego, Calif., January 18, 1978.
14. Harold S. Geneen, "Why Directors Can't Protect the Shareholders," *Fortune*, September 17, 1984, p. 31.
15. Walter J. Salmon, "Crisis Prevention? How to Gear Up Your Board," *Harvard Business Review*, January-February 1993, p. 69.
16. Steve Pejovich, *Corporate Democracy* (Washington, D.C.: Washington Legal Foundation, 1984), pp. 2–3.
17. *Spencer Stuart Board Index, 1992 Proxy Report* (New York: Spencer Stuart, 1992).
18. "Boardroom Composition," *The Corporate Board*, July/August 1993, p. 26.
19. Robert W. Lear, "The Decade of Corporate Governance," *Chief Executive*, June 1993, p. 10.
20. Judith Dobrzynski, "At GM, A Magna Carta for Directors," *Business Week*, April 4, 1994, p. 37.
21. For a thoughtful set of proposals, see *TIAA-CREF Policy Statement on Corporate Governance* (New York: Teachers Insurance Annuity Association, 1993).
22. *Social Responsibilities of Business Corporations* (New York: Committee for Economic Development, 1971), p. 22.
23. Richard Gibson, "Control Data Head Offers An Apology for Prodigal Past," *Wall Street Journal*, May 3, 1990, p. B5.
24. Quoted in Robert J. Haft, "Business Decisions by the New Board," *Michigan Law Review*, November 1981, p. 35.
25. Sethi et al., "The Catch-22," p. 39.

GOLDEN PARACHUTES AND TIN PARACHUTES

*Top management perks, corporate governance,
and the public interest*

Philip L. Cochran
Steven L. Wartick
Bruce K. Skaggs

Over the last two decades a wide range of special severance agreements has been devised for corporate employees. Some of these severance agreements have drawn intense criticism from both the popular and business press. One broad category of these often criticized severance arrangements is the so-called parachute agreement which grants severance pay to individuals upon a change in control of a firm.

Today we see a wide range of parachute agreements. The first is the golden parachute which is designed to cover the top-level executives of a firm. The next is the silver parachute which usually covers managers the next level down. The last two are bronze parachutes which are constructed for mid- to lower-level management and tin parachutes which are aimed at covering all remaining employees.

In addition to the extent of coverage, another difference between the types of parachute agreements is the level of compensation. Golden parachutes are normally the most lucrative in terms of the compensation offered, while tin parachutes are the least. In recent years, however, the distinctions between these various parachute agreements have become somewhat blurred. Many parachute agreements now include middle and lower-level management as well as all non-managerial employees. This has served to diminish the distinctions between the non-golden (i.e., silver, bronze, and tin) parachutes.

Over the years there have been a number of high profile parachute payments. For example, in November 1985, just months prior to Beatrice's acquisition by Kohlberg, Kravis, Roberts and Company, the Board of Directors of the Beatrice Corporation awarded $24 million in parachute payments to six of the firm's managers. This award granted William W. Granger $7 million for his four-month tenure as CEO of Beatrice.[1] Another parachute payment receiving some notoriety was the package granted to Michael J. Bergerac of Revlon. After Pantry Pride acquired Revlon, Mr. Bergerac left Revlon with a total severance package of $35 million, $15 million of which represented his parachute.[2] And recently, in the pending takeover of Continental Bank Corp. by BankAmerica, Continental has agreed to pay seven of its departing executives over $15 million in parachute payments, almost $4 million of which will go to chairman Thomas Theobald.[3] Such severance packages represent substantial returns even for well-paid senior executives.

The magnitude of the above payments is an indicator of why, when first introduced, GPs drew substantial censure from both the business and general press. However, over the past two decades GPs have gone from being an oddity to being commonplace and, at the same time, the level of criticism has dropped dramatically. Given this shift in attention, the question arises as to what changes have occurred to GPs in particular and to parachute agreements in general which account for this alteration in public perception.

In the remainder of this article, we will address this question by exploring the range of parachute provisions in use today. However, due to the blurring in distinctions between the different types, we will focus on two broad categories of parachute agreements: golden parachutes, which cover top management, and tin parachutes, which cover all remaining employees.

GOLDEN PARACHUTES

In order for an agreement to be considered a golden parachute (GP) as defined by U.S. law, it must possess two characteristics. First, as defined by Section 280G of the Internal Revenue Code, a golden parachute is a contract in which a corporation agrees to make payment to certain *key officers* in the event of a change in control of the corporation. The term "key officers" refers to "any officer, shareholder, or highly compensated individual . . . who is one of the highest paid 1% of the employees of the corporation or, if less, one of the highest paid 150 employees of the corporation."[4] Thus, to qualify as a GP, the individuals involved must be members of top level management (this normally includes the CEO and various executive vice presidents).

Second, the payments must be contingent upon a change in control of the corporation. Though neither Congress nor the IRS have explicitly defined what constitutes a change in control, there has been general agreement that it can occur in a variety of ways. The most common is through a takeover. An examination of proxy statements shows that the acquisition of a substantial number of shares (normally 20%) or a turnover of more than half of the board of directors within a specified period of time (usually 6–12 months) is the general definition of a change in control used by most firms with GPs. Any agreement made between a corporation and members of its top management which calls for compensation to be given to

key officers in the event of a change in control is considered to be a GP by the IRS.

Until the mid 1980s, most GP agreements required only a change in control in order to be activated. This was known as a single trigger provision. The result was that executives with GPs could, in the event of a takeover, unilaterally choose to quit their firm and thus qualify to receive their severance benefits; that is, they could voluntarily pull their own ripcord. However, starting in the mid 1980s these agreements began to change. Though payments made upon a change in control were enough to qualify as a GP according to the IRS, many businesses began including a second provision which stated that GPs could only be activated if the covered individual was also terminated as a result of the change in control.[5] Termination must usually occur within two years of the change in control, and is normally defined as being either involuntary or constructive.[6] Involuntary termination occurs when the executive is dismissed from the company, while constructive termination arises from a change in job title, responsibilities, job location, or salary. This stipulation, that both termination and change in control are necessary to activate the parachute payment, is known as a **double trigger** parachute agreement.[7] Thus, in the vast majority of modern GP arrangements, both a change in control and termination (either involuntary or constructive) must occur before the executive can activate the agreement.

This switch from single to double trigger activation may have been, in part, a reaction to the intense public concern over the single trigger GP. Examination of earlier research indicates that the most significant criticisms of GPs revolved around the ability of executives to pull their own ripcord.[8] This shift to a double trigger is consistent with the issues life cycle model which suggests that once public concern reaches a certain level, organizations will change their behavior or face legislative action.[9] Though some legislative action was taken against GPs, it is interesting to note that, facing public criticism over single trigger parachute agreements, businesses acted to institute double trigger activation clauses in the vast majority of GPs.

Besides compensation based on salary, many GPs also include provisions for accelerating stock options and long-term incentive compensation. Bonuses also are estimated and paid, and fringe benefits (most often, insurance and pension) are included as well. The total compensation received by an individual is therefore a function of several variables and is difficult to determine before the execution of the GP.

In looking at the type of compensation offered, GPs tend to resemble the typical severance agreement. However, there is one major difference between these two arrangements. The average severance agreement is not dependent upon a change in control. Though a GP may be viewed as a type of severance agreement, it differs in this fundamental aspect.

Even though it is impossible to predict the exact contents of a GP, it is still possible to describe the general provisions of a typical GP. A typical agreement contains the following:

1. Coverage for the top 1% of a firm's employees;
2. Double trigger activation based upon both a change in control (normally defined as a majority turnover of the board of directors or the acquisition of over 20 percent of the outstanding stock by some distinguishable party) and termination of the individual (either involuntary or constructive);
3. Compensation consisting on average of two to three years salary plus accelerated stock options and retirement provisions, bonuses, and insurance benefits; and
4. A two-year time frame after a change of control in which termination will activate the GP.[10]

GOLDEN PARACHUTE LEGISLATION

In the late 1970s and early 1980s, the United States was experiencing an increased number of corporate takeovers. This led top executives to perceive a decrease in job security. This perception of job insecurity encouraged many executives to demand special severance packages that would go into effect in the event of a hostile takeover. Golden parachutes were thus invented. As GPs became increasingly larger and more lucrative, the level of public concern and criticism mounted. There were a number of well publicized cases of senior executives receiving millions and even tens of millions of dollars because they chose to quit their new firms after a successful takeover.

As part of the Deficit Reduction Act of 1984, Congress changed the tax treatment of GPs in order to address some of the public concerns. The changes were aimed at curbing "excessive" parachute payments. The new law, as amended in 1986, defined an excessive parachute payment as one where the executive would receive three or more times his or her annual base salary upon a change in control. Section 280G of the Internal Revenue Code (IRC) states that companies paying excessive parachute payments will not be able to deduct the expenses, while IRC 4999 states that recipients of these payments will be subject to a 20% excise tax on the total amount of compensation received in excess of their base salary.

Though the tax laws governing GPs affect most payments made which are based upon a change in control, there are a number of exemptions. First, any payments made before or after the change in control which can be proven to represent reasonable compensation for services rendered are exempt from IRC 280G. Second, payments made from qualified plans (e.g., pensions) are not considered part of a GP agreement. Third, any payments made from the change in control of a small company (as defined by IRC 1361B) are exempt from 280G. And fourth, any payments made in which 75% of the shareholders approve of the GP agreement, none of the stock of which is publicly traded immediately before the change in control, are also excluded from consideration.[11]

Establishing a golden parachute agreement requires a firm to undertake two actions. First, since the agreement constitutes a potential expense, the company must account for it by establishing a fund for the payment of possible claims.[12] Second, in accordance with SEC regulations, the firm must notify its shareholders as to the terms and conditions of the GP agreement by reporting it on the proxy statement.[13]

TIN PARACHUTES

At the other extreme are tin parachutes. Unlike a GP, which is designed to cover only top executives, the tin parachute is structured to cover all those employees of the corporation not already covered by GPs. Though these types of agreements have been around for nearly 20 years, the vast majority have only been in existence since 1986.[14]

Similar to most GPs, tin parachutes require double trigger activation; an employee must be either involuntarily or constructively terminated within a specified period (usually two years) following a change in control in order for payments to commence. These payments are typically based upon some calculation involving current wages and years of service (e.g., one month's pay per year of service). Most tin parachute agreements also provide for the continuation of health and life insurance benefits after termination as well as the acceleration of stock options. Furthermore, most tin parachutes are designed so that these benefits continue to accrue to the covered employee even if the terminated worker finds subsequent employment.[15]

Though tin parachute agreements appear similar to GPs, their treatment by government differs substantially. First, unlike GPs, companies are not required to report the creation of a tin parachute arrangement.[16] As mentioned previously, the SEC requires companies to disclose GP agreements in the proxy statement. However, tin parachutes do not require such disclosure. This fact makes it difficult to assess the extent of tin parachutes by researchers and shareholders alike, for companies tend to be rather secretive about the existence of such arrangements. Second, the IRS currently has no provisions regulating the exercise of tin parachutes. Thus, re-

cipients of these payments are not subject to a possible 20% excise tax, while businesses are able to fully deduct all payments related to tin parachute agreements. And lastly, unlike GPs, the creation of a tin parachute does not require a company to set aside funds to pay potential claims.[17]

Below is a summary of the provisions found in a typical arrangement:

1. Coverage includes all employees not previously covered by GPs;
2. Double trigger activation (requires involuntary or constructive termination within two years of a change in control);
3. Compensation is in the form of both a severance payment (typically one month's pay per year of service) and extended health and life insurance; and
4. Benefits are maintained even if an employee finds subsequent employment.[18]

ARGUMENTS FOR THE USE OF PARACHUTES

Align Managerial and Stockholder Interests. This argument which applies primarily to GPs suggests that when a company experiences a change in control the future status of the top management becomes uncertain. Acquiring firms do on occasion replace much of the top level management of acquired firms. In the absence of some type of change in control arrangement, top executives may try to thwart takeover attempts by other firms in order to protect their own jobs, even though a takeover may be in the best interests of their shareholders. One argument supporting the use of GPs is that they address this issue by promoting management objectivity. GP agreements may have the effect of reducing job uncertainty for top executives thereby allowing them to concentrate solely on the interests of company and its shareholders.[19]

Promote Dedication to the Firm. This argument implies that GPs and tin parachutes are justified on the basis of promoting loyalty by rewarding past service. Managers and employees may have spent many years developing knowledge and expertise relevant to a specific firm. This investment of their human capital may result in returns to the firm in future years. These individuals may see their later years of service as a reward for that investment. A successful takeover resulting in their dismissal would thus rob them of the fruits of this investment. Parachute agreements would protect their investment in the firm and would thereby enhance the level of top management and employee dedication to the corporation.[20] With this increased sense of dedication should come higher levels of employee morale. At the lower levels of the organization, greater employee morale would yield reductions in turnover and absenteeism, which ultimately would lead to increases in productivity. Thus from a human resource perspective, parachutes are "good for business."[21]

Retain and Hire Important Personnel. This argument is most commonly made in support of GPs. Here it is implied that GPs are necessary to attract and keep important personnel. The suggestion is that they encourage executives to stay with their firms, both during a takeover attempt and after the takeover is complete. This argument suggests that without GPs, the uncertainties surrounding a takeover might be sufficient to cause some key executives to leave at a time of severe organizational trial. GPs therefore buy the continued leadership of senior management, and as such are merely another form of executive compensation similar to bonuses, stock options, and so forth. Furthermore, firms offering change in control agreements may attract a more talented executive workforce than those not offering such arrangements.[22]

Secure Previously Arranged Benefits. Another argument which favors the use of GPs is that they protect the value of benefits from being lost. As Charles Feldman states, "Arrangements may be designed to protect the value of various employee benefits granted

in the ordinary course, such as supplemental executive retirement plans (SERPs) or stock options, from being lost or jeopardized by a change in control."[23] An example of this would be an arrangement where an executive would become fully vested in a retirement plan upon termination caused by a change in control.

Provides Incentives. This argument suggests that GPs can be used to motivate executives in order to achieve the goals of management. For example, management may want to develop a company into an attractive takeover candidate. To do so, management may establish arrangements whereby top executives would receive bonuses if the company is acquired at a price above a certain market value.[24] Some of these arrangements would include GP agreements with its executives which tie the acquisition price of the company to the parachute payment to be received. Such agreements would act as incentives for executives to keep the firm's stock price high, as well as to seek out potential suitors who would pay top dollar for the firm.

Provide Equity. This argument states that tin parachutes should be used in order to provide equity to employees not covered by GPs.[25] A fairness issue emerges when companies protect the highest paid employees from joy loss due to a change in control but offer no protection to those who need it most: the lower level employees. Thus it is argued that tin parachutes address this inequity by offering protection to all employees not covered by previous agreements (i.e., GPs). For example, when Herman Miller Inc., a large office-furniture manufacturer, instituted their tin parachute agreement, the argument used for implementing the agreement was fairness. As chairman Max DePree stated, "Severance contracts for the few do not meet our need for justice in corporate America."[26]

Takeover Defense. The last argument suggests that GPs and tin parachutes can be used as anti-takeover devices in order to ward off hostile takeover attempts. In the case of a takeover, the acquiring firm must pay the parachute agreements which become activated by the change in control. This has the effect of making the target firm more expensive to acquire. Takeover defenses may be of benefit to managers and other employees. As a result, fewer firms would be willing or able to attempt a takeover of a company which has entered into GP and tin parachute agreements with its workforce.

ARGUMENTS AGAINST THE USE OF PARACHUTES

In general, the concern about parachutes centers around five criticisms: the managerial performance criticism, the "arms length" criticism, the fiduciary responsibility criticism, the efficiency criticism, and the employee relations criticism. The first two of these criticisms are directed solely at GPs. They arise from the concern that GPs are implemented primarily in order to benefit existing management. These criticisms of GPs, therefore, fall within the general concerns of corporate governance; that is, the relationship which exists between management and shareholders. The next two criticisms, fiduciary responsibility and efficiency, apply to both golden and tin parachute agreements. The employee relations criticism addresses the use of GPs in the absence of tin parachute agreements.

Managerial Performance Criticism. This criticism has two dimensions. The first dimension suggests that GPs provide special compensation for managers to perform duties that they are already responsible to perform. This criticism is based on agency theory which states that the role of management is to serve as an agent for shareholders. Therefore, management is already charged with the responsibility of maximizing shareholder wealth. Providing additional compensation to get managers to objectively represent shareholder interests in a takeover

constitutes "double dipping"; that is, being paid twice for the same task.[27]

A second element of the managerial performance criticism relates to the relationship between managerial performance and takeovers. Takeovers generally occur only when some external group believes that they can manage the firm's assets more efficiently than can current management. This argument suggests that GPs are nothing more than multimillion dollar rewards to executives who have mismanaged a company, so that the company's stock price is depressed to the extent that an outside group is willing to pay a considerable sum to gain control of the target's assets.[28]

Arms Length Criticism. This criticism focuses on the relationship between executives and their boards of directors. The central premise of this criticism is that executives, through control of their boards, give themselves the golden parachutes. If so, then GPs would be yet another manifestation of the effects on a firm when control shifts from stockholders to managers—a phenomenon first discussed by Berle and Means in 1929 and thoroughly documented in the past two decades.[29]

Fiduciary Responsibility Criticism. This view is that management has an obligation to serve only the interests of the shareholders. The argument equates parachute agreements with theft if the agreements decrease the stock or takeover price of the firm. For example, if a purchasing firm is willing to pay only so much to acquire the target, and if the target successfully pumps up the costs of the acquisition by instituting these agreements, then the target is worth correspondingly less. For every additional million dollars that the purchasing firm must pay in parachutes, a million dollars is subsequently taken from the target's shareholders. Thus, by instituting parachute agreements, management violates its obligation to shareholders, for money which should go to the shareholders of the target firm is instead channeled into parachute payments.[30]

Efficiency criticism. This argument suggests that parachutes reduce the likelihood of a firm being acquired by another. Companies which have numerous, large sum parachute agreements may be less attractive to potential suitors. Because of this, inefficiently run firms with parachute agreements are less likely to be taken over and reorganized.

Employee Relations Criticism. This argument suggests that without tin parachute agreements, GPs have a detrimental effect on the morale of a company's workers. In a time of economic hardship and union givebacks, news of GPs can create a great deal of employee hostility. This anger could manifest itself as increased absenteeism, increased turnover, lower productivity, and the like. Thus, even if GPs can be justified economically, one must ask whether the existence of GPs compensates for the various costs associated with a hostile and/or demotivated workforce.

THE PRESENT STATE OF PARACHUTES

During the 1980s, GPs provoked major controversy in both the popular and business press over abuses of managerial perquisites. Although there have been a few notable instances of golden parachutes being refused by stockholders,[31] the trend appears to be toward an even greater use of this change in control arrangement. For example, in 1981, Hewitt Associates reported that 15% of the companies surveyed had GP agreements; by 1990, this figure had risen to 56%. Financial organizations are the most prevalent users of GPs (67%), though large industrial/service firms and small firms were not far behind (55% and 46%, respectively).[32]

Two factors have had a hand in the continued growth of GPs. First, though companies are required to report the adoption of golden parachute agreements in the proxy statement, very little shareholder resistance

has beep encountered. Second, the tax law legislation of 1984 and the change to double trigger GPs have seemed to quiet public concerns surrounding this issue. To assess the current status of GPs we need to examine the actual effects of the tax change on these arrangements.

With the presence of GP agreements now more the rule than the exception at most U.S. corporations, the question of how much compensation companies are offering in their GPs becomes of interest. The tax law changes of 1984 were intended to reduce the proliferation of excessive golden parachute payments. In responding to this change in the tax code, corporations offering GPs have pursued one of three strategies. The first of these is the cutback strategy. Here, firms reduce the parachute payment to 2.99 times the executive's base salary. This brings the executive's compensation below the "3 time base salary" limit, and therefore does not qualify as an excessive parachute payment according to the IRS. In turn, the executive escapes the 20% excise tax while the company is able to deduct the payment.[33]

The cut-back method of dealing with the tax law change was popular for the first couple of years after the creation of I.R.C. 280G and 4999; however, its popularity soon faded. The reason was because most executives would receive at least 3 times their base salary in stock options alone due to automatic vesting provisions arising from a change in control.[34] In order to qualify for the deduction and spare the executive the 20% excise tax, many companies would have to do away with GP payments altogether. Rather than risk upsetting their executives either by reducing their parachutes or subjecting them to a 20% excise tax, a number of companies pursued a different strategy known as "gross-up." Here, companies increased their executives' GP payments in order to offset any loss experienced by the excise tax.[35]

The last strategy for dealing with the tax treatment of GPs is the "do nothing" approach. As the name implies, corporations which follow this strategy neither raise nor lower their executives' parachutes. Instead, they let the "tax chips fall where they may."[36]

Though the do nothing approach eventually became the most common in addressing the tax law changes, the effect of these changes on GP compensation can certainly be seen. For as of 1989, approximately half of the companies with GP agreements limited their payments to below the three-times base salary ceiling.[37]

The use of tin parachutes is also becoming more widespread in corporate America. As of 1990, approximately 19% of companies reported having such agreements. This figure represents a threefold increase in the use of tin parachutes since 1988.[38] Though the exact causes leading to this phenomenal growth would be impossible to determine, there are three factors which have no doubt influenced the proliferation of these agreements. First, there are no tax regulations involving tin parachutes. This makes them inexpensive to implement for, unlike GPs, no funds need to be set aside to pay potential claims. Second, disclosure of tin parachute agreements is not required by the SEC. This fact reduces the likelihood of shareholder resistance to such arrangements and allows management to initiate these plans at will. Third, the presence of a tin parachute agreement tends to lessen the psychological impact of GPs on shareholders. In other words, having an agreement to protect all employees in case of a change in control can somewhat justify the existence of parachute payments for top executives, and hence reduce shareholder resistance to GPs.

One recent development concerning tin parachutes has occurred in the political arena. As of 1992, three states, Massachusetts, Pennsylvania, and Rhode Island, have enacted tin parachute laws which provide employees severance pay in the event of termination due to a change in control. Thus it appears that this type of agreement is becoming more popular for both business leaders and law makers alike.

PARACHUTE AGREEMENTS AND THE INTERESTS OF SHAREHOLDERS

Most of the arguments against the use of parachute agreements are based on the notion that parachutes negatively affect the interests of shareholders. Of the six criticisms mentioned above, the first five are directly concerned with shareholder welfare, while the last (employee relations criticism) argues that GPs indirectly affect shareholder interests by lowering employee morale and hence productivity. Given the importance shareholder welfare plays in the arguments against parachutes, an investigation of the relationship between these agreements and shareholder interests would shed much light on the validity of the criticisms. Thus, in this section we will begin by discussing the empirical findings of researchers who have examined the relationship. From there we will explore the rationale behind some criticisms of these agreements.

In a 1993 study by Born, Trahan, and Faria, the authors found that the adoption of a GP by a firm preceded an increase in its stock price.[39] Furthermore, another 1993 study by Machlin, Choe, and Miles found a positive relationship between multiple takeover offers and the existence of a GP. That is, firms with GPs would on average receive more than one takeover offer when they were in play while firms without GPs would normally receive only one offer.[40] Machlin et al. also found a positive relationship between the size of a GP and the magnitude of the takeover premium.

Though these two empirical investigations do not establish a causal connection between GPs and shareholder wealth, the correlations which were found are nonetheless of interest. If the arguments against the use of GPs were true, then one would expect to find a negative relationship between GP agreements and share price. However, this was not the case. The two studies mentioned above discovered the opposite relationship to exist. These findings therefore cast doubt on the criticisms against the use of GPs.

Very little has been said about the effects of tin parachutes The reason for this omission is simple: no empirical data are available which could help address this issue. Thus, the question as to whether tin parachutes negatively affect shareholder value remains unanswered.

In investigating the reasoning behind the criticisms of parachute agreements, some problems emerge. First, if parachutes are detrimental to the interests of shareholders, then shareholders should react very strongly against the adoption of a parachute agreement by the firm. This however has rarely happened. Though not required for tin parachutes, GP agreements must be reported in a firm's proxy statement. Thus, the shareholders—particularly the large and increasingly active institutional investors—of a firm can rescind any GP made between the firm and its executives. Though some GPs have been challenged and a few rescinded,[41] the overwhelming majority of GP agreements go unchallenged. This fact therefore suggests that most shareholders do not believe modern GPs constitute a significant raid on the assets of the firm.

A second problem concerns the argument that parachutes are detrimental to the interests of shareholders because they create inefficiencies by serving as anti-takeover devices. That is, firms adopt these agreements to ward-off unwanted suitors. In doing so, firms are able to operate less efficiently while the executives responsible for the inefficiencies maintain control. Thus, poor management is protected at the expense of shareholders. Though logically this argument is

valid, in reality it does not hold for several reasons. First, frequently the relative cost of an acquired firm's GPs is negligible.[42] Second, though tin parachute agreements cover many more employees and therefore are potentially more expensive, it is extremely unlikely that an acquiring firm will fire all the employees of the target upon acquisition. In reality, only a small percentage of a target firm's lower level employees lost their jobs due to a change in control. Thus the costs to the acquiring firm are again negligible, for the vast majority of tin parachute agreements are never activated.[43]

CONCLUSION

Parachute agreements are now a well-established fixture in the economic landscape. The overwhelming majority of firms have one or more such plans in place. Though historically many have been skeptical about their use, the change in their tax treatment and perhaps more importantly the movement (in response to the criticism) from single to double trigger activation has served to eliminate much of the public concern.

In addition, it appears that modern parachute agreements can yield many positive consequences. Properly designed GPs can operate to align the interests of managers and shareholders. Tin parachutes can promote equity within a firm and extend some protection to lower level employees in case of change in control. Although there still exists some potential for abuse in these agreements, safeguards such as restricted deductions for excessive payments and shareholder notification have sharply reduced the ability of managers to use GPs in an entirely self-serving manner.

NOTES

1. Steven Greenhouse, "Golden Chutes Under Attack," *New York Times*, Dec. 10, 1985, p. D2.
2. Amy Dunkin, and Laurie Baum, "Bergerac's Golden Parachute: The Biggest Ever," *Business Week*, May 5, 1986, p. 56.
3. "Continental Bank Bonuses," *New York Times*, May 29, 1994, p. 36.
4. I.R.C. § 280(c)(2) 1994.
5. "Golden Parachute Growth Noted," *National Underwriter*, February 27, 1989, p. 15.
6. Ibid.
7. Ibid.
8. Philip L. Cochran, and Steven L. Wartick, "Golden Parachutes: A Closer Look," *California Management Review*, Summer, 1984, pp. 111–125.
9. S. Prakash Sethi, "A Conceptual Framework for Environmental Analysis of Social Issues and Evaluation of Business Response Patterns," *Academy of Management Review*, 4 (January, 1979), pp. 63–74.
10. Ibid.
11. I.R.C. 280G
12. Joani Nelson-Horchler, "A Catchall Parachute," *Industry Week*, February 9, 1987, pp. 16–17.
13. Ibid.
14. Diana C. Robertson, and E. Webb Bassick IV, "Beyond Golden Bailouts: The Tin Parachute Is Landing," *Sloan Management Review*, Fall 1989, pp. 43–52.
15. Ibid.
16. Ibid.
17. Thomas J. Murray, "Here Comes the 'Tin' Parachute," *Dun's Business Month*, January 1987, pp. 62–64.
18. Robertson and Bassick IV, "Beyond Golden Bailouts," p. 44.
19. Charles F. Feldman, "Golden Parachutes Remain Popular Despite Strict Rules," *Taxation for Accounts*, October 1992, pp. 204–211.
20. Ibid.
21. Robertson and Bassick IV, "Beyond Golden Bailouts," p. 46.
22. Ibid.
23. Feldman, "A Bird's-Eye View," p. 70.
24. Feldman, "Golden Parachutes Remain Popular," p. 204.
25. Gary C. Hourhan, and J. Gregory Kunkel, "Should the Board Approve Tin Parachutes?" *Directors & Boards*, Winter 1988, pp. 26–27.
26. Nelson-Horchler, "A Catchall Parachute," p. 16.
27. Philip L. Cochran, and Steven L. Wartick, "Golden Parachutes: Good for Management and Society?" in *Business and Society* (eds. Sethi, S.P., and Falbe, C.), pp. 321–331.
28. Ibid.
29. Ibid.
30. Ibid.
31. Marcia Parker, "4 Companies Fight Votes on Parachutes," *Pensions & Investments*, January 8, 1990, p. 1, 31.
32. "More Firms Providing Takeover Protection," *Employee Benefit Plan Review*, October 1990, pp. 35, 38.
33. Arthur H. Kroll, "Stock Compensation: Parachutes to Ensure a Safe Landing," *The Tax Advisor*, May 1990, pp. 302–307.
34. Ibid.
35. Ibid.
36. Arthur H. Kroll, and Karen G. Krueger, "Current Parachute Arrangements Need Revising Due to Proposed Regs.," *Journal of Compensation and Benefits*, March/April 1990, pp. 261–268.
37. "Golden Parachute Growth Noted," *National Underwriter*.
38. "More Firms Providing Takeover Protection," *Employee Benefit Plan Review*.
39. Jeffery A. Born, Emery A. Trahan, and Hugo J. Faria, "Golden Parachutes: Incentive Aligners, Management Entrenchers, or Takeover Bid Signals?" *The Journal of Financial Research*, Winter 1993, pp. 299–308.
40. Judith C. Machlin, Hyuk Choe, and James A. Miles, "The Effects of Golden Parachutes on Takeover Activity," *Journal of Law and Economics*, October 1993, pp. 861–876.
41. Parker, "4 Companies Fight Votes," p. 31.
42. Robertson and Bassick IV, "Beyond Golden Bailouts," p. 49.
43. Ibid.

THE NOTION OF THE "GOOD CORPORATION" IN A COMPETITIVE GLOBAL ECONOMY

Moving from a socially responsible to a socially accountable corporation

S. Prakash Sethi

The American political debate and social psyche never seem to tire of their preoccupation with the role of the private sector—and especially the large corporation—and how it impacts all aspects of our lives. In a nation where the concept of "competitive markets" is elevated to a high moral principle from a mere system of ordering economic arrangements, we seem extremely reluctant to let private enterprise do what it ought to do in a market economy, and what is its wont, if we would only let it go about its business. Instead, we constantly seek and expect the private corporation to be a good citizen where definitions of good corporate citizenship cover the entire waterfront. These definitions are constrained only by the proclivities of various shareholders who seek a larger share of corporate resources than they could gain through market exchange. They are also imbued by the imagination and persuasiveness of social reformers who would like the corporation to help alleviate society's many other problems because "it is the right thing to do."

The schizophrenic nature of our expectations of a socially responsible corporation is all too apparent and manifests itself in countless confrontations between the corporation and other constituent groups. Thus, it is the same corporation that receives public accolades for exemplary behavior in one aspect of its business and is simultaneously hauled into the court of public opinion and judicial arena for acts of moral reprobation and illegal behavior in other aspects of its business.[1] While the eighties were condemned as the decade of corporate greed, the nineties are emerging as the decade of the heartless corporation. At the same time, we all have had our respective lists of the most admired, the most respected, the excellent and the most desired corporations to work for.[2]

Nowhere is this ambiguity more apparent than in the recent *Newsweek* article by Robert Samuelson (1993) where, using the trials and travails of IBM as a metaphor, he poignantly describes the demise of the "good corporation" and the terrible loss and hurt that is being inflicted on hundreds of thousands of our people and scores of our institutions. It would seem that our hitherto socially responsible corporations are no longer able to provide the wherewithal of a good life to their various constituencies as they go through the wrenching experience of downsizing to meet the new realities of international markets. The radical paradigm shift in our competitive environment, brought about by global competition, changing technologies, and a communication revolution, compels corporations to drastically

Research assistance in the preparation of this paper was provided by Ms. Linda M. Sama, a doctoral student, and is gratefully acknowledged.

205

alter their behavior in order to adapt, or risk obliteration.

This soliloquy is not intended to disparage the notion that we should demand and expect more of our corporate denizens beyond what market forces would impel them to deliver. Instead, we argue that "good" business conduct cannot be examined and evaluated outside the context of prevailing competitive economic structures and inter- and intra-institutional frameworks. To ensure "good" conduct on the part of corporations, one cannot rely, either solely or even primarily, on the principles and motivations of their socially conscious managers. Although, at the micro level, it is the individual conduct acting in a business context that gets reflected in the adverse social impact of the business institution, this conduct is seriously circumscribed by its macro-structural context. As economic activity increases in complexity and technological orientation, it requires collective action where each individual and institution contributes but a tiny fraction to the whole (Sethi, 1994a). The corporation can be either good or bad depending on who is making the trade-offs, at whose expense these trade-offs are being made, and the extent of discretionary resources available to the corporation and its managers: (a) to ameliorate some of the second-order effects, i.e., externalities, of their normal business activities; and, (b) to voluntarily meet non-market societal needs.

The paramount question for us to examine involves the circumstances, individual and contextual, that would induce business institutions and their managers to act in ways considered more socially desirable. We must ask whether there are market conditions that would define and limit the character of the "good corporation" regardless of the desires of certain segments of our society for it to be otherwise. And finally, we argue that for the "good corporation" to persist and prevail, we must meet three conditions:

1. The criterion for defining the "good corporation" would *not* be confined to what the corporation does, but would include the rationale that it employs for its specific actions.
2. It is not the magnitude of effort on the part of the "good corporation" that would be the determining factor; but its capacity to undertake such actions and the extent to which the corporations uses that capacity voluntarily.
3. The "good corporation" would be judged by the extent to which it forgoes its market power for the benefit of those stakeholders who are unfairly situated because of unequal bargaining power and leverage compared to the corporation.

It is these propositions that are the subject of our enquiry and to which we now turn our attention.

WHAT IS A "GOOD CORPORATION"?

The archetype of Samuelson's good corporation is a financially successful and economically efficient company that would marry profit-making with social responsibility; provide stable, well-paid jobs with generous benefits; support culture and the arts; encourage employees to become involved in their communities; and, be a good corporate citizen. Others have offered parallel although somewhat different visions of this idyllic corporate welfare state where managers combine market-competitive efficiency with enlightened stakeholder management to achieve the best of all possible worlds. For example, a recent issue of *Business and Society Review* (Fall, 1993) solicited the views of a selected group of scholars, activists and government leaders on the future of Samuelson's good corporation, that ranged all over the map.[3] However, most of the authors characterized the good corporation as doing more for its workers, consumers, etc., without offering much of a rationale for defining and evaluating the good corporation. Professor Rosabeth Moss Kanter of Harvard Business School, in response to how one might describe Samuelson's good corporation, conjures up a corporation committed to its workers, investing in human resources via a continuous process of training and development, and developing a pool of skilled workers to support envisioned future activities of the firm. These activities are the keys to what she terms "employability security." Moving from employees to customers, Tom Chappell, president of Tom's of Maine and author of *The Soul of a Business: Managing for Profit and the Common Good*, suggests that respect for customers generates needed feedback on company products and services, and that competition should be balanced by "goodness"—defined as a demonstration of care and concern for people, nature and the community. A contrasting perspective is offered by Doug Bandow of the Cato Institute who points to the costs of corporate welfare which, he contends, must be acknowledged and assessed against the potential benefits such welfare provides. Another contributor, U.S. Secretary of Labor, Robert B. Reich, emphasizes the long-term benefits of good corporate citizenship, particularly vis-á-vis employees, over the shorter-term payoffs of downsizing strategies. *Business and Society Review* Senior Editor, Milton Moskowitz, reminds us, appropriately, that capitalist markets by definition militate against doing well simply by doing good, bringing us to our next argument.

DOING WELL BY DOING GOOD

Good ethics is good business, we are told.[4] We would not be discussing this topic if this were indeed the case. Business people, being rational, would not need much prompting from outsiders to strive for ever higher standards of socially responsible behavior. All empirical evidence and economic logic indicate otherwise, however. Under conditions of rising competitive intensity and an uncontrollable free rider problem, companies cannot and will not do well. The relevant question to ask is not whether IBM is now more or less good but whether IBM has the luxury to be anything else. Those who put their naive faith in the idea that corporations can do well by doing good, i.e., good ethics is always

good business, are either assuming away the market advantages that these companies hold, or refusing to accept history as it exists and substituting instead their perception of reality as what it ought to be.

The reality of the "good corporation" is quite different as Samuelson himself readily admits. He concedes this point by bemoaning the pressure of increased global competition that compelled American companies to cut back the size and scope of the corporate welfare state. Lost in this argument is the fact of management complacence and incompetence that made them fritter away the opportunities for improving efficiency and productivity during periods of prosperity. Even under the best of circumstances, the good corporation can be viewed as "not all good" and "not good for everybody." It is easy to say, as the old cliche goes, make love not war, unless one asks the inevitable question, to wit, make love to whom and war against whom?

Consider the circumstances that made it possible for IBM to assume the mantle of the good corporation. By way of illustration, let me paint a somewhat cynical, although no less plausible rationale for IBM's actions. I might also say that this rationale is equally generalizable to other good corporations. IBM's ability to pay higher wages and offer lifetime employment was made possible through the superior profits that it could generate because of its dominant market position. Thus while IBM took care of its employees, managers, and shareholders, it showed no such concern for the customers of its products. It is only by charging its customers relatively high prices that IBM could generate above-normal profits, i.e., non-market rent, which would then enable the company to reward its other stakeholders with above-market benefits. It was not the highly competitive markets that made possible IBM's gains, but inefficient and imperfect markets which IBM helped create through its technological dominance and market power and then exploited to its own advantage. Is it, therefore, any wonder that unlike IBM's loyal workers and grateful shareholders, its abused and exploited customers would abandon ship at the first opportunity?

Clearly, it was in the best interest of IBM to maintain its non-normal profits. It accomplished this objective by:

(a) outbidding its competition for the best talent and resources; and,
(b) sharing some of its above-normal profits with other segments of the community and thereby garnering public goodwill and political support for its market dominance.

The afore-mentioned discussion should not detract us from the fact that IBM was a benevolent employer and a good corporate citizen. It could just as easily have been an arrogant corporation that would use its market power to maximize its gain to the detriment of its various stakeholders. However, the fact remains that it is the imperfect markets and their exploitation by corporations that create opportunities for "good" corporate behavior which, in turn, is largely dissipated when markets turn sour, a situation that is presently all too apparent.

DOING GOOD BY DOING WELL

Our objective, as a society, therefore, should be to create those structural conditions—economic and socio-political—that would induce all businesses to do good by doing well. An ancillary objective would be to create and support inter- and intra-institutional frameworks that would encourage good corporations to become better corporations.

This premise is based on the following assertions:

1. Highly competitive markets are inimical to the creation and sustenance of the "good corporation." Although competition makes business efficient, it does not make it virtuous. One could even argue that highly competitive markets provide greater opportunities for illegal and unethical behavior (Baumol, 1991; Sethi, 1994a). In other words, it is not possible

to sustain the axiom that a company can "do well by doing good."
2. Most markets become imperfect as they become large and complex, i.e., consumers and other factors of production, e.g., labor, lose their ability to bargain and compete with corporations on an equal footing.
3. Large corporations can survive only in imperfect markets. Therefore, they would take all necessary action to maintain these market imperfections so as to sustain their above-normal profits. The most logical behavior to expect from the corporation, under the circumstances, would be to do good generally when it is doing well, i.e., it would be first the economic imperative, and only secondarily the societal concerns, that would largely define both the nature and extent of "good" corporate conduct.

CREATING A CLIMATE FOR GENERALIZED SOCIALLY RESPONSIBLE BEHAVIOR

In the absence of economic rationale—both at the macro and micro levels—a corporation's socially responsible behavior is in the nature of public goods available to all members of society who stand to benefit from an enhancement of these values, regardless of their individual contribution to such enhancement. Unfortunately, this state of affairs creates real problems for those firms that wish to act in a socially responsible manner and thereby enhance the quality of life for the society as a whole. The economic concept is that of a "free rider." Since socially responsible firms have no control over the behavior of other firms who choose not to extend themselves, but nevertheless benefit from the social values and public goodwill created by the good firms, the latter group puts inexorable pressure on the former to create more and more good deeds and receive less and less social rewards—a situation that is simply not viable. While exemplary and extraordinary altruistic individual behavior might give us our heroes, they would certainly not be the heroes that ordinary mortals could emulate in the routines of their everyday lives. Nor do these heroes, and villains, provide us with an adequate basis for structural analysis of social institutions. The emphasis in our effort, therefore, must be on those social-structural underpinnings and institutional frameworks that are necessary for improving the ethical norms of corporate behavior (Sethi, 1994a).

One approach to limiting the free rider problem would be to raise the level of overall "good" corporate behavior, i.e., public or free goods in the form of ethically proactive behavior, that must be met by all business firms. This would be accomplished by raising public expectations and creating societal conditions to enforce them. In a sense this is nothing new. A great many business activities are already proscribed by legal statutes where they are perceived to be anti-competitive or contrary to public interest. Similarly, social customs and traditions may inhibit other forms of corporate behavior. The new approach, however is prescriptive and proactive. It would then make it possible—if you assume that most businesses do behave legally—that higher societal expectations would be met and that the problem of free rider would be minimized.

A great deal more is possible to improve the overall moral climate for the business community as a whole to behave at a higher level of socially responsible and ethically proactive behavior and thereby vastly improve the total stock of social good produced by the economic system. This would also raise the level of societal expectations and corporate social performance on the part of those companies that have enjoyed above-normal profits emanating from their exploitation of market imperfections. Religious leaders and moral philosophers have advocated some such approaches. There are also some socio-political movements in other parts of the world that are leaning in the same direction. For example, in his Encyclical *Centesimus Annus*, Pope John Paul II has outlined his vision of a just economic order with specific prescriptions for the role of property, just wages, fair profits, the value of work, distribution of wealth to help the poor and unfortunate amongst us, and the need for protecting the moral core of humanity, to name a few.[5] Although the Encyclical has been criticized in certain quarters for its selective use of history, ethno-centric bias, and fuzzy economic logic,[6] it nevertheless offers an approach to creating a more morally-based playing field for conducting economic activity.

A number of philosophers and ethicists have also argued in favor of certain universal standards of corporate behavior, ones that take into account the concept of human dignity, fairness and equity. Although these standards may be somewhat modified to accommodate certain local, culturally-based considerations, the latter cannot be used as an excuse to undermine the basic universalistic moral values and standards of human behavior.[7] Similarly, in the political arena, the International Labor Office of the United Nations as well as the European Community have advocated the creation of benchmark standards of worker's rights and a Social Charter involving corporations and their workers.[8]

These efforts, however, are more often flouted than adhered to by most players, including companies and countries involved. At best, they represent an ideal to be desired rather than a standard to be observed. No consensus currently exists as to the nature of more inclusive standards for the performance of market-based economic systems. There is considerable resistance to the injection of moral and ethical values in the capitalistic system which depends on individual choices and is supposedly value-neutral. Nevertheless, an improved an more comprehensive societal standard of corporate behavior—one that includes not only economic but ethical and moral values—would go a long way in making our system of market economy and private enterprise more humane and just while contributing to greater economic welfare.

FROM SOCIAL RESPONSIBILITY TO SOCIAL ACCOUNTABILITY

The final step in our analysis has to do with the criteria that one might use in evaluating the reasonableness and adequacy of "good" in the good corporation. The approach outlined below seeks to evaluate the "good corporation" in terms of the extent to which it voluntarily shares its market power and resultant pecuniary gains—and thereby yields accountability for its actions and performance—with those groups who have been adversely affected by that power. Broadly speaking, imperfect markets facilitate a corporation's above-normal returns from three sources covering three stages of interaction between the corporation and its stakeholders. These can be defined as: *information imbalance, bargaining and negotiating power imbalance,* and, *adjudication, or remedy and relief power* imbalance. They consist of, respectively:

- the amount and quality of information available to the two parties prior to entering into a transaction or exchange;
- the relative bargaining leverage of the opposing groups during negotiation; and,
- the ability of each group to seek proper adjudication of disputes and gain restitution for harm done when a transaction fails to yield desired and mutually satisfactory results.

We believe that these three general principles should be pertinent to all classes of stakeholders. However, their actual application would vary because of the differing magnitude of the "stakes" involved and the comparative strength of particular stakeholders.

RESTORING BARGAINING POWER AND SOCIAL ACCOUNTABILITY: THE CASE OF THE "GOOD CORPORATION" AND THE CONSUMER

An attempt is made here to demonstrate the operability of these principles using the illus-

tration of market exchange between corporations and consumers as a stakeholder group. Recall that under conditions of imperfect markets, a corporation stands to make above-normal profits through exploitation of imperfections in the marketplace. It follows, therefore, that under market conditions where a customer is reasonably fully-informed; has alternative sources of supply; can exercise independent choices; and, can enforce compliance; a corporation has no obligation to protect the customer from his/her stupidity, poor judgment, or failure to forecast the future correctly. Market rewards for good judgment must also carry penalties for poor judgment and consequent loss when potentially unacceptable levels of risk are assumed carelessly. A similar logic should apply to business dealings with other groups, e.g., employees, stockholders, suppliers and even the communities involved.[9]

1. Information Imbalance. Business gains from information imbalance because the lack of accurate information induces its customers to pay higher prices, accept products of lower quality, or choose different products/brands altogether. Thus the criteria for evaluating the "good" corporation in this case would be:

(a) the extent to which a firm provides its customers with information along the dimensions that he/she would need to make informed choices; and,

(b) the degree to which the firm renders the customer able to evaluate post-purchase effects in terms of his/her expectations and the producer's claims.

In one sense, there does not seem to be any dearth of information on products and services available to the consumer. Business firms alone spent over $131 billion in 1992 on total U.S. measured media of which the top 100 national advertisers accounted for 27.6% ($36.2 billion).[10] To this should be added accurate information on product labels, articles in the news media, government brochures and bulletins, and accounts of activities of consumer-based organizations.

In the logic of competitive markets, individual firms would provide customers only with the information that would encourage them to buy those companies' products. The customer is expected to learn about competitive products from other companies' advertising. However, in the real world things do not quite work out this way. In imperfect markets, firms put their major emphasis on differentiating their products and services—on the basis of both facts and perceived-illusory differences—so as to make it extremely difficult, if not impossible, for the consumer to make direct price-value comparisons amongst competing products and brands.

The information imbalance can be corrected at two levels:

The Industry—Efforts should be made to create uniform standards of product usage, labelling, and performance claims that could be compared by the customer in making buying decisions. This should be done through a cooperative effort among industry members, government agencies, and, responsible consumer organizations. There are a number of problems that must be overcome if this approach is to work. These include: the sheer enormity of the tasks in terms of products and brands, the cost of carrying out such a program, and the difficulty in persuading all significant stakeholders to participate in the process. Nevertheless, given a commitment on the part of industry and its important members, and pressure from public and private agencies, significant progress is possible in this direction. *In any case, the degree of progress measured against the potential for progress would be one measure of the industry's social responsiveness and accountability.*

The Firms—Companies should regularly survey consumers to objectively assess their information needs and devise means to communicate such information to the consumer. The objective would be to provide the consumer with the information that he/she would want, in addition to the information that the firm would like the customer to have so as to make a pro-firm purchase decision.

Secondly, where relevant, companies should maintain and regularly publish data on the volume and type of customer complaints and the nature of the companies response to such complaints. They should also disseminate information on current research and findings that might have an adverse effect on the quality or customer's use of those products. This approach is similar to the one used by firms in providing investors with information concerning current and projected losses in a firm's financial statements. If current and potential investors of publicly-held companies can demand such information to assess a firm's "quality of earnings," why should it be unreasonable for the current and potential customers to demand information on the "quality of product value" for the firm's offerings? *The measure of the good corporation would be the extent to which this information is provided voluntarily and the gap between the availability of such information and its importance to the customer.*

2. Bargaining Power Imbalance.

Under conditions of imperfect markets, a handful of companies control significant market shares, avoid price competition, and have a great deal of influence on the nature of goods to be produced and the manner in which they are to be sold. This market dominance is further reinforced by mass advertising and the creation of customer-brand loyalty based on real or spurious product attributes. Consumers, on the other hand, are largely unorganized, insufficiently informed and lack bargaining power to deal with companies on an equitable basis.

The "good corporation" will, therefore, seek ways to enable consumers to gain at least part of those benefits in terms of product quality, service and price that they would have achieved under conditions of a more level playing field in terms of information, resources, and organization. An example of such an approach would be for the companies to offer assurances as to the "effective and useful life" of a product backed by independent insurance or other means to ensure that customers are in effect getting what they believe they are paying for.

3. *Adjudication, and Remedy and Relief Imbalance.* The third area of restoring balance between producers and consumers has to do with adjudication of disputes and the receipt of prompt and fair settlement of claims. Most consumers suffer from a number of serious disadvantages in achieving this objective. Their individual claims are often small while their total impact on the company is quite large. Therefore, while the company has every incentive to fight such claims, the consumers have neither the time nor the resources to fight for equitable remedies. The two current approaches, i.e., small claims court and class action suits, are flawed from a macro perspective. In the former case, each claimant has to fight his/her dispute individually with no knowledge of the widespread nature of the problem and its resolution. The class action suits are at best haphazard and end up paying more to the lawyers than the plaintiffs.

The "good corporation" would institute procedures whereby affected customers can automatically receive adjudication of their disputes as well as fair settlement even when they did not have the knowledge of the harm done to them or had not initiated action against the offending company. The process suggested here could be termed "the internalization of class action suits" wherein remedy and restitution would become an integral part of doing business and would be automatically triggered upon the occurrence of certain events.

The following example will illustrate this point:

> Suppose a telephone company serves a particular area. Because of the nature of technology and usage patterns, a failure or malfunction rate of 2% is considered normal and has been factored into both the price of service and customers' quality expectations. Let us say that in a given period this rate has risen to

5%. Under normal procedures, the phone company might be expected to make refunds, but only to those customers whose service was actually disrupted. However, we would assume that while there may not have been actual disruption of service in other cases, there was a deterioration in the overall quality of service in the area. The telephone company should refund a proportion of the service fee that it charged to all of its customers in the impacted area. Similar measures can be developed for application to other types of products and services.

SUMMARY AND CONCLUSIONS

The private sector in general, and the corporate community in particular, have ample scope and opportunity to become more socially involved while incorporating a higher set of ethical values in their operating norms. We have previously argued that for corporations to be "good" beyond the minimal legal and market-based standards, they must have above-normal profits; must stand to benefit in some way from voluntarily sharing those profits with other groups; and, that the problem of free rider must be manageable. Notwithstanding, under conditions of imperfect markets, they certainly have the opportunity, and at least some inducement, to do so. However, ethical and social norms of corporate behavior cannot be left entirely to the personal preferences and predispositions of individual corporate managers, industry practices, fads of the moment, and the degree of successful pressure applied by community activists and other stakeholders.[11] None of these approaches are quite satisfactory and leave a large residue of distrust and bitterness. Corporate managers seek to act in ways that would enhance their self-image and peer group approval while protecting their vital business interests. Thus, their socially responsible behavior may deprive other businesses of critically needed resources in the economic arena because the latter could not compete with the superior resources of the former on an equal basis. In the social arena, it might also divert resources away from chronic social needs that lack glamour and are hard to tackle and, therefore, do not attract corporate interest.

Instead, an alternative approach is offered; one that is more objective and can be systematically applied in defining the nature and extent of corporate social performance in terms of corporate activities that are voluntarily undertaken, either to ameliorate the harm done to, or share gains with, its various constituencies who have suffered from the

exercise of market power by the corporation. This approach obviates the necessity of using subjective, disparate and non-comparable measures of corporate social performance given differences in financial and operating circumstances and external environments of different companies. At the same time, it is flexible enough to incorporate normative value-based standards and explicitly recognize the role of non-economic considerations and constituencies in shaping societal expectations of corporate behavior in eliciting appropriate corporate responses.

NOTES

1. Some of these ideas have been explored previously in an article by this author to appear in the April edition of the *Journal of Business Ethics* (Sethi, 1994a).
2. See, for example, Milton Moskowitz, Michael Katz and Robert Levering *The 100 Best Companies to Work for in America*.
3. For a fuller exposition of these views than that presented here, see the *Business and Society Review* Symposium on "Is the Good Corporation Dead?" Fall 1993, Number 87, specifically, Bandow, Chappell, Kanter, Moskowitz and Reich as listed in the references section of this paper.
4. Dennis P. Quinn and Thomas M. Jones, "An Agent Morality View of Business Policy." *Academy of Management Review*—Special Issue (January 1995). See also Blanchard & Peale (1988); Kotter & Heskett (1992).
5. See John Paul II: 1991, Encyclical Letter *Centesimus Annus* of the Supreme Pontiff, *On the Hundredth Anniversary of Rerum Novarum* (St. Paul Books and Media, Boston, MA). See also, Naughton and Laczniak (1993), Novak (1993), and Williams (1993).
6. See, for example, James Armstrong (1993), Green (1993), Hall and Ames (1993), Piker (1993), and Sethi and Steidlmeier (1993).
7. For a discussion of the application of universal ethics to market behavior, see, for example, Daly and Cobb (1989), DeGeorge (1993), Donaldson (1989), Etzioni (1988), Walton (1988) and Wogaman (1986). This list is by no means intended to be a comprehensive re-

view of the related literature, but rather, serves as illustrative of parallel points of view.
8. Research on the European Community's Social Charter is vast and the reader is directed to Bercusson (1990), Curwen (1992) and Hepple (1990) for a useful introduction.
9. For example, workers should have no claim on corporate largesse or escape penalties of future lay-offs when they or their representatives voluntarily entered into agreements with full knowledge of circumstances and potential for risks and rewards that might accrue in the future.
10. Media expenditures cited here do not include unmeasured advertising spending, which comprises direct mail, promotion, co-op, couponing, catalogs, business and farm publications and special events. The top 100 U.S. advertisers alone spent an additional $15.3 billion in 1992 on such unmeasured non-media advertising, according to estimates of Advertising Age. All numbers are obtained from *Advertising Age's Special Edition on the 100 Leading National Advertisers (LNA)* (September 29, 1993).
11. There is a rich body of literature that treats this subject under the rubric of Social Issues in Management and Business and Society. The variety of definitions, and scope of activities covered, to describe what is and what is not socially responsible behavior on the part of the business community are far too numerous and contentious to be described here.

There also remains the ultimate issue from the perspective of both the scholar and the practitioners; to wit, how should one link corporate social responsibility-responsiveness to corporate social performance. For an illustrative, and by no means exhaustive, set of writings, please refer to: Aram (1989); Aupperle, Carroll & Hatfield (1985); Cadbury

(1987); Carroll (1979, 1989); Epstein (1987); Frederick (1986); Freeman (1984); Gatewood & Carroll (1991); Gilbert (1989); Jones (1983); Keim (1978); Miles (1987); Sethi (1979, 1994b); Sethi & Falbe (1987); Sethi & Steidlmeier (1994); Votaw (1973); Votaw & Sethi (1973); Wartick & Cochran (1985); and Wood (1991).

REFERENCES

Advertising Age, Special Edition: "100 Leading National Advertisers," September 29, 1993.

Aram, J.D. 1989. The paradox of interdependent relations in the field of social issues in management. *Academy of Management Review*, 14: 266–283.

Armstrong, J. 1993. One protestant looks at *Centesimus Annus*. *Journal of Business Ethics*, 12(12): 933–944.

Aupperle, K.E., Carroll, A.B., & Hatfield, J.D. 1985. An empirical examination of the relationship between corporate social responsibility and profitability. *Academy of Management Journal*, 28: 446–463.

Bandow, D. 1993. Should we even bother to mourn? *Business and Society Review*, 87(Fall): 16.

Baumol, W.J. 1991. *Perfect markets and easy virtue: Business ethics and the invisible hand*. Cambridge, MA: Blackwell.

Bercusson, B. 1990. The European community's charter of fundamental social rights of workers. *Modern Law Review*. (September): 624–642.

Blanchard, K.H., & Peale, N.V. 1988. *The power of ethical management*. New York: William Morrow.

Cadbury, A. 1987. Ethical managers make their own rules. *Harvard Business Review*, 65(5): 69–73.

Carroll, A.B. 1979. A three-dimensional conceptual model of corporate social performance. *Academy of Management Review*, 4: 497–505.

Carroll, A.B. 1989. Business and society: *Ethics and stakeholder management*. Cincinnati, OH: South-Western.

Chappell, T. 1993. The pursuit of goodness. *Business and Society Review*, 87(Fall): 17.

Curwen, P. 1992. Social policy in the European Community. Working Paper.

Daly, H.E., & Cobb, J.B., Jr. 1989. *For the common good: Redirecting the economy toward community, the environment, and a sustainable future.* Boston, MA: Beacon Press.

DeGeorge, R.T. 1993. *Competing with integrity in international business*. New York: Oxford University Press.

Donaldson, T. 1989. *The ethics of international business*. New York: Oxford University Press.

Epstein, E.M. 1987. The corporate social policy process: Beyond business ethics, corporate social responsibility, and corporate social responsiveness. *California Management Review*, 29(3): 99–114.

Etzioni, A. 1988. *The moral dimension: Toward a new economics*. New York: The Free Press.

Frederick, W.C. 1986. *Theories of corporate social performance: Much done, more to do*. Working paper, University of Pittsburgh, Graduate School of Business.

Freeman, R.E. 1984. *Strategic management: A stakeholder approach*. Boston: Pitman.

Gatewood, R.D., & Carroll, A.B. 1991. Assessment of ethical performance of organization members: A conceptual framework. *Academy of Management Review*, 16: 667–690.

Gilbert, D.R., Jr. 1989. *Business ethics and three genres of stakeholder research*. Paper presented at the 3rd Conference on Quality of Life, Virginia Polytechnic Institute, Blacksburg, VA.

Green, R. 1993. *Centesimus Annus*: A critical Jewish perspective. *Journal of Business Ethics*, 12(12): 945–954.

Hall, D.L., & Ames, R.T. 1993. Culture and the limits of Catholicism: A Chinese response to *Centesimus Annus*. *Journal of Business Ethics*. 12(12): 955–963.

Hepple, B. 1990. The implementation of the community charter of fundamental social rights. *Modern Law Review*. (September): 643–654.

Jones, T.M. 1983. An integrating framework for research in business and society: A step toward the elusive paradigm? *Academy of Management Review*, 8: 559–564.

Kanter, R.M. 1993. Employability security. *Business and Society Review*, 87(Fall): 11–14.

Keim, G.D. 1978. Corporate social responsibility: An assessment of the enlightened self-interest model. *Academy of Management Review*, 3: 32–29.

Kotter, J.P., & Heskett, J.L. 1992. *Corporate culture and performance*. New York: Free Press.

LNA/Media Watch Multi-Media Service. 1993. *Ad$ Summary: January—September 1993*. New York: Competitive Media Reporting.

Miles, R.A. 1987. *Managing the corporate social environment*. Englewood Cliffs, NJ: Prentice Hall.

Moskowitz, M. 1993. In search of the good corporation. *Business and Society Review*, 87(Fall): 11.

Moskowitz, M., Katz, M., & Levering, R. 1985. *The 100 best companies to work for in America*. New York: New American Library.

Naughton, M., & Lacziniak, G.R. 1993. A theology of work in the Catholic social tradition. *Journal of Business Ethics*, 12(12): 981–994.

Novak, M. 1993. The creative person. *Journal of Business Ethics*, 12(12): 975–979.

Paul, Pope John II. 1991. Encyclical Letter *Centesimus Annus* of the Supreme Pontiff, *On the Hundredth Anniversary of Rerum Novarum*. St. Paul Books and Media, Boston, MA.

Piker, S. 1993. Theravada Buddhism and Catholicism: A social historical perspective on religious change, with special reference to *Centesimus Annus*. *Journal of Business Ethics*, 12(12): 965–973.

Quinn, D.P., & Jones, T.M. (forthcoming, 1995). An Agent Morality View of Business Policy. *Academy of Management Review—Special Issue* (January, 1995).

Reich, R.B. 1993. Stewardship of the future. *Business and Society Review*, 87(Fall): 10.

Samuelson, R.J. 1993. R.I.P.: The good corporation. *Newsweek*, July 5: 41.

Sethi, S.P. 1979. A conceptual framework for environmental analysis of social issues and evaluation of business response patterns. *Academy of Management Review*, 4: 63-74.

Sethi, S.P. 1994a. Imperfect markets: Business ethics as an easy virtue. *Journal of Business Ethics*, 13(4).

Sethi, S.P. 1994b. *Multinational corporations and the impact of public advocacy on corporate strategy: Nestle and the infant formula controversy*. Boston, MA: Kluwer Academic Publishers.

Sethi, S.P., & Falbe, C.M. 1987. *Business and society: Dimensions of conflict and cooperation*. Lexington, MA: Lexington Books.

Sethi, S.P., & Steidlmeier, P. 1993. Religion's moral compass and a just economic order: Reflections on Pope John Paul II's Encyclical *Centesimus Annus*. *Journal of Business Ethics*, 12(12): 901–917.

Sethi, S.P., & Steidlmeier, P. 1997. *Up against the corporate wall: Cases in business and society*, 6th ed. Upper Saddle River, NJ: Prentice Hall.

Votaw, D. 1973. Genius becomes rate. In D. Votaw & S.P. Sethi (Eds.), *The corporate dilemma: 11–45*. Englewood Cliffs, NJ: Prentice Hall.

Votaw, D., & Sethi, S.P. 1973. *The corporate dilemma*. Englewood Cliffs, NJ: Prentice Hall.

Walton, C.C. 1988. *The moral manager*. Cambridge, MA: Ballinger.

Wartick, S.L., & Cochran, P.L. 1985. The evolution of the corporate social performance model. *Academy of Management Review*. 10: 758–769.

Williams, O. 1993. Catholic social teaching: A communitarian democratic capitalism for the new world order. *Journal of Business Ethics*, 12(12): 919–932.

Wogaman, P. 1986. *Economics and ethics: A christian inquiry*. Philadelphia, PA: Fortress Press.

Wood, D.J. 1991. Corporate social performance revisited. *Academy of Management Review*, 16: 691–718.

ADDRESSING A THEORETICAL PROBLEM BY REORIENTING THE CORPORATE SOCIAL PERFORMANCE MODEL

Diane L. Swanson

This article identifies two major theoretical orientations in the business and society field. The corporate social performance (CSP) model illustrates their lack of integration and the problems posed for theory development. The model is reoriented so that it can be used to explore a synthesis of the two perspectives based on reframed principles of corporate social responsibility, processes of corporate social responsiveness, and outcomes of corporate behavior.

Conceptual developments in corporate social performance (CSP) literature have been organized into a research framework by Wood (1991a). This CSP model provides a coherent structure for assessing the relevance of research topics to central questions in the business and society field. It also highlights a central theoretical problem in the field: Its economic and duty-aligned perspectives are not integrated. The purpose of this article is to offer a research framework that can be used to explore their integration. To that end, this framework reorients Wood's CSP model.

The author gratefully acknowledges the helpful comments of Bill Frederick, Jim Weber, and Jim Wilson on related work. The author also acknowledges the insightful and constructive comments of the anonymous reviewers. An early version of this article was presented at an International Association for Business Conference. Financial support for the presentation was provided by the David Berg Family Fund.

First, the economic and duty-aligned perspectives are introduced as the dominant orientations to corporate social performance research. Although they overlap in a topic of mutual interest, they are not integrated. An examination of the CSP model illustrates this lack of integration and the problems it poses for theory development. Next, the perspectives are examined in more detail to underscore the obstacles to their integration and the inadequacies of both for theory development. To address these problems, a research strategy is proposed, and the two perspectives are reformulated. Then they are expressed in a reoriented CSP model in which they are linked across principles of corporate social responsibility, processes of corporate social responsiveness, and outcomes of corporate behavior. Finally, the importance of this new model for CSP research and theory development is discussed.

A CENTRAL THEORETICAL PROBLEM IN BUSINESS AND SOCIETY RESEARCH

An overview of the business and society field indicates that it contains two dominant orientations, referred to here as *economic* and *duty-aligned perspectives*. The *economic perspective*, largely expressed through management research, encompasses many social and ethical issues. It never, however, loses sight of the

216

firm's inviolable corporate economic responsibility to efficiently and profitably produce goods and services for society. This perspective accepts some tenets of the utilitarian ethic in neoclassical economics, including a teleological approach to ethics that judges economic activity by its consequences.[1]

Overall, neoclassical economics maintains that the greatest social satisfaction or good occurs when individuals are free to pursue their own self-interest in economic activity. It prizes not only efficient and profitable outcomes, but also autonomy and economic freedom. Further, because it factors power behavior and ill-will toward others out of economic activity and into the political realm, it takes self- and other interest to be mutually beneficial (Hirshman, 1981; March, 1992; Vogel, 1991). Consequently, it sees no compelling reason to account for benevolence or duty-based morality (Etzioni, 1988; Hausman, 1992; Sen, 1987). Neoclassical theory does, however, accept restraints from the public to the direction self-interest takes in business activity. In this spirit, Friedman (1962, 1970), a contemporary spokesperson, argued that managers need not be moral agents because their actions are already restrained by standards of public policy, the law, and ethical custom.

Lindblom (1977) referred to such restraints as forms of social control called "authority and persuasion." Authority, or legitimized power, is expressed in law and public policy (Harris & Carman, 1987). Persuasion can be based on morality and generally accepted norms and expectations embedded in social custom or tradition and reinforced by habit (Scott, 1987; Selznick, 1992). Like neoclassical theory, the economic perspective in the business and society field accepts these forms of restraints to business activity. It takes them to be means by which society directs business activity to be compatible with useful ends, i.e., those consequences consistent with sociocultural values (Buchholz, 1982, 1985; Chamberlain, 1973, 1977; Frederick, 1986; Jones, 1983; Steidlmeier, 1987).

The *duty-aligned perspective*, largely expressed through business ethics research, includes many managerial and economic issues. It never, however, loses sight of its primary interest in formulating rules for corporate moral behavior and expressing these rules as obligations or duties. Typically, it uses two closely related ethical approaches to do so: rights and justice. The first approach, a rights-based ethic, seeks protections or extensions of individual entitlements. More specifically, protections of entitlements are negative rights to be free from harm; extensions of entitlements are positive rights to have or pursue a benefit (Velasquez, 1982; Werhane, 1985). These rights invoke weak and strong forms of correlative duties. In weak form, negative duty protects negative rights by restraining action that can harm others. In strong form, positive duty supports positive rights by advocating a willing, active commitment to help others obtain their good. Both forms of duty reject the utilitarian assessment of action by consequences. Instead, they emphasize motivation, maintaining that ethical action requires the respect for the moral personhood of others described in Kant's duty-centered (or deontological) moral philosophy (Boatright, 1993; Brady, 1985; DeGeorge, 1990; Donaldson, 1989; Freeman & Gilbert, 1988; Velasquez, 1982).

The second approach, a justice-based ethic, prizes liberty, equality, and fairness of opportunity. It insists that an unfair distribution of harms and benefits be explained and defended on logical grounds (Frederick, 1987; Rawls, 1971). Standards of justice are closely related to those of rights because justice argues for the conditions that justify negative rights (the right to be free from harm) and positive rights (the right to have or pursue a benefit) (Beauchamp & Bowie, 1993). Concurrently, these conditions justify the negative and positive duties required by rights.

To summarize, business ethics research typically aligns rights and justice standards with rules about duties. This alignment occurs because the provision of closely-related rights and justice standards for individuals usually requires duties from others (Collins, 1989; Donaldson, 1989; Freeman & Gilbert 1988; Selznick, 1992; Velasquez, 1982). Their ethical motivation for doing so is the respect for others required by a duty-centered ethic (Rawls, 1971).

In principle, the economic and duty-aligned perspectives overlap significantly concerning the social control of business. Simply put, this topic is *the* central concept in the business and society field (Jones, 1983). Its centrality is due to the interest in negative duty or restraint to self-interest that the perspectives share. This mutual interest is not surprising because all ethical theories, including utilitarianism, agree on the importance of restraining self-interest (Selznick, 1992).

The following section examines the CSP model to show how this overlap is expressed in the field at large. This examination demonstrates that, even in their shared interest in social control the perspectives are antagonistic. Or, as Brady (1985) put it, they represent "Janus-headed" ethical views of business and society issues.

Frederick (1987) described this antagonism in terms of "trade-off and moral justification problems." The first problem occurs when the field's theorists argue for compliance with social controls because it is required by the law or public policy and because business may lose its much prized autonomy and economic freedom if it does not respond assuredly to social pressure. When such compliance seems costly, it invokes a trade-off between corporate economic goals and negative duty. For corporations to go beyond complying with social pressure and accept positive duty to society can appear even more costly. Put simply, a trade-off problem exists when profits and duty seem to collide.

The moral justification problem occurs when social control, and perhaps even positive duty, seems to serve corporate economic goals. Then the defense for corporate social

responsibility can be that it *pays* or is strategically wise (see Ackerman & Bauer, 1976; Mitnick, 1981; Preston & Post, 1975; Wood & Jones, 1994). However, ethicists never justify morality solely by economic criteria, even when the two happen to coincide (Beauchamp & Bowie, 1993; Donaldson 1989; Frederick, 1987). Consequently, even when the economic and duty-aligned perspectives do not pose a trade-off problem, they can fail to reveal the reasons *why* corporations should be socially responsible. This absence of clear moral directive is the moral justification problem.

Given the trade-off and moral justification problems, the field's dominant research orientations are not theoretically integrated, in spite of their strong shared interest in social control. The next section examines this lack of integration as it is expressed in the field at large.

THE CORPORATE SOCIAL PERFORMANCE MODEL REVISITED

A consolidated classification of research can be an important step toward theory development, especially for a field as eclectic as business and society. Such a framework can show interrelationships among diverse topics and provide a unifying theme and an agenda for future research (Jones, 1983). Wood's CSP model (see Table 1) is the most detailed classification to date, and it demonstrates interrelationships among three topics:

1. Principles of corporate social responsibility (CSR) expressed on the institutional, organizational, and individual levels.
2. Corporate processes of responsiveness as environmental assessment, stakeholder management, and issues management.
3. Outcomes of corporate behavior as social impacts, social programs, and social policies.

Wood's CSP model extends and revises Wartick and Cochran's (1985) model, which is, in turn, based on Carroll's (1979) work. These works are shaped by the field's man-

TABLE 1. The Corporate Social Performance (CSP) Model

Principles of Corporate Social Responsibility (CSR)

Institutional principle: legitimacy (Origin: Davis, 1973)
Organizational principal: public responsibility (Origin: Preston & Post, (1975)
Individual principle: managerial discretion (Origin: Carroll, 1979; Wood, 1990)
Processes of Corporate Social Responsiveness
    Environmental assessment
    Stakeholder management
    Issues management
Outcomes of Corporate Behavior
    Social impacts
    Social programs
    Social policies

FROM: "Corporate Social Performance Revisited, by D.J. Wood, 1991. *Academy of Management Review*, 16:694. Copyright 1991 by the Academy of Management. Adapted with permission of the author.

agement perspective. As a result, Wood's model does not give similar weight to the field's more recent business ethics research. This imbalance needs to be redressed because responsibility is a well-developed concept in business ethics (see Steidlmeier, 1987). Consequently, this ethics research has the potential to develop critically the normative dimensions of corporate social responsibility.

The following sections argue that because Wood's CSR principles lack this kind of normative development, they restrain corporate economic activity with social control that is normatively undefined. Further, they formulate corporate positive duty as optional altruism or philanthropy. These undeveloped interpretations of duty pose two major difficulties for comprehensive theory development. First, these interpretations invoke trade-off and moral justification problems in the CSR principles that render incompatible the economic and duty-aligned perspectives. Second, these interpretations render the CSR principles normatively inadequate for assessing processes of corporate social responsiveness and outcomes of corporate behavior. Essentially, the development of a general theory for the field awaits the integration of its

dominant perspectives into one that is normatively adequate for assessing corporate social performance.

The Institutional Principle of Legitimacy in Wood's CSP Model

The institutional principle originated with Davis's (1973) Iron Law of Responsibility. It states that business is a social institution that must use its power responsibly. Otherwise, society may revoke it. On this, Davis wrote

> Society grants legitimacy and power to business. In the long run, those who do not use power in a manner which society considers responsible will tend to lose it. (Davis, 1973: 314)

Sethi (1979) also held that if corporations ignore social expectations, they are likely to lose control over their internal decision making and external dealings.

As Wood (1991a) observed, the institutional principle expresses a prohibition rather than a positive duty. It implies that business should act on the threat of social control instead of on a positive commitment to society that disregards self-interest and consequences. Indeed, even if society expects positive duty from business, this expectation is contradicted if it is gained by threat of social coercion. Reinforcing such threat, Freeman's (1984) widely used stakeholder concept emphasizes that groups in society can *block* corporate goals (i.e., those groups that can affect or are affected by an organization). Related research describes how stakeholders can retaliate against questionable corporate practices (e.g., Collins, 1989).

By emphasizing negative duty, the institutional principle fails to legitimate the positive duty found in ethics research. Furthermore, it demonstrates the field's moral justification problem. Shaped by the economic perspective, it justifies social control by the loss of autonomy and economic freedom so valued by the business sector (see Cavanagh, 1990). By contrast, the duty-aligned perspective would instead justify social control by advocating that corporations be motivated to restrain certain business activity out of respect for their stakeholders. In sum, the institutional principle neither promotes positive duty nor advocates the moral motivation of respect. Thus, it is not infused with the sense of moral responsibility found in business ethics.

The Organizational Principle of Public Responsibility in Wood's CSP Model

Originating with Preston and Post's (1975) model that takes business and society to be interpenetrating systems, the organizational principle limits corporate duty to those social problems that can be traced to a firm's economic operations. Wood defined this principle:

> Businesses are responsible for outcomes related to their primary and secondary areas of involvement (i.e., economic impact) with society. (Wood, 1991a: 697)

Based on the neoclassical economic concept of an "externality," the organizational principle says that corporations are responsible only for solving the direct and indirect problems they cause. Solving these problems is their public responsibility. Despite its premise that business and society are symbiotic and mutually adaptive systems, this principle draws an economic boundary to corporate responsibility. Further, because it defines and enforces this responsibility with public policy, it emphasizes social control.

The concept of public responsibility is not entirely negative. Because it speaks of a mutually adaptive relationship between business and society, it has a constructive tone. Even so, it holds positive corporate duty to society at bay in three ways. First, it treats responsibilities beyond the problem-defined boundary as optional. Second, by linking corporate conduct to public policy, it emphasizes social control while it de-emphasizes a positive commitment to community that

might be expressed in a business-government partnership. Third, it does not address how corporate duty to society can be incorporated into managerial decision making so that social problems are minimized.

The Individual Principle of Managerial Discretion in Wood's CSP Model

Although the individual principle in Wood's CSP model does not resolve the latter concern, it does acknowledge that individual managers have moral discretion in decision making. Wood explained that

> [m]anagers are moral actors. Within every domain of corporate social responsibility, they are obliged to exercise such discretion as is available to them, toward socially responsible outcomes. (Wood, 1991a: 698)

This principle originated with Carroll's (1979) hierarchy of corporate responsibilities, which describes voluntary managerial duties that are not specifically prohibited or demanded of companies because of their other economic, legal, and ethical responsibilities (Wood, 1991a). This hierarchy means that managerial positive duty is discretionary because it is ranked last in importance, after the firm's known economic, legal, and ethical responsibilities.

The individual principle emphasizes social control in two ways. First, its legal category represents explicit social control of economic activity. Second, ethical responsibility invokes the threat of social control based on ethical custom. It does so by appealing to social expectations that corporations avoid "questionable" practices (see Carroll, 1979). So far, it is consistent with the contemporary articulation of neoclassical economics because it accepts restraints to economic activity from the law, public policy, and ethical custom. Even so, the individual principle goes beyond these forms of social control by addressing managers' discretion to choose positive duty. Yet, this discretionary range is narrow and per se voluntary compared to the more pervasive restraint to their behavior from social control.

The Normative Difficulties Posed by Wood's CSR Principles

Trade-Off and Moral Justification Problems. The economic and duty-aligned perspectives are not compatible in these three CSR principles, Rather, they are subject to trade-off and moral justification problems. The first problem occurs when negative duty appears costly in one of two ways. First, social control suggests implicit costs: Corporations forego profits when public policy, the law, and ethical custom restrain their pursuit of all economic opportunities. Second, social control suggests explicit costs: Corporations bear out-of-pocket costs when public policy, the law, and ethical custom require that they rectify the direct and indirect problems they cause. Because positive duty is formulated as discretionary and optional to social control, largely as altruism or philanthropy, it can appear even more costly. Also, because it is optional, it can be harder to justify, especially in difficult economic times.

Some CSP scholars take the trade-off problem seriously and counter it by asserting that, under certain conditions, corporate social responsibility can *pay*. Social control and positive duty may coincide with or even serve economic goals. This kind of argument implicitly accepts the primacy of economic standards in the CSR principles and judges negative and positive duty against such standards. This kind of justification is not acceptable from the duty-aligned perspective because it fails to advocate the importance of moral motivation. More specifically, it fails to advocate an attitude of respect toward others that would properly motivate corporate social responsibility.

Inadequate Normative Criteria for Responsiveness. The CSR principles lack adequate normative criteria for evaluating processes of responsiveness. These processes are corporate tools for assessing the environment and managing stakeholder issues. They are the action counterparts to responsibility (Wood, 1991a). The social control standard in the principles cannot effectively be used to assess these actions because it is normatively unclear in two ways. First, the principles do not identify what sociocultural values are at stake in social control issues. Instead, like Friedman's (1970) contemporary neoclassical view, the principles take these values to be embedded in public policy, the law, and ethical expectations, especially those of stakeholders who affect or are affected by business organizations. Thus, the CSR principles cannot answer what Jones (1983) asserted are two fundamental social control questions: How congruent are existing social control mechanisms with social values? How can they be made more congruent?

Corporations can provide answers to these questions when they use their tools of responsiveness to *change* social controls, to which they then adjust. Then they can be deemed responsible, according to the CSR principles. Clearly, corporations influence public policy, the law, and ethical expectations, and this influence is increasing (Wood, 1987). Quite simply, corporate economic power can become political power (Etzioni, 1988). Corporations can seek this power by lobbying Congress, building coalitions, using mass media, providing Congressional testimony, establishing political action committees, and using their public affairs function to manage social issues (Chomsky, 1987; Epstein, 1969; Sethi, 1982; Wartick & Cochran, 1985; Wartick & Rude, 1986).

The second way the CSR principles lack normative clarity is related to the moral justification problem. Eschewing a theoretical ethics base, the principles do not address the moral motivation of respect that supports duty. They instead rely on control and coercion. Although corporate social responsibility may be motivated by several factors, including respect for stakeholders it may also be strategically defensive and diversionary (see Sethi, 1982; Weidenbaum, 1977). Further, what appears to be corporate responsibility can be a paternalistic expression of corporate power instead of a responsible interaction with society (Frederick, 1987). Because the CSR principles do not deal with ethical motivation, they lack adequate criteria for making such distinctions.

Inadequate Normative Criteria for Outcomes. Outcomes of corporate behavior are subject to similar problems. For social impacts (e.g., pollution, payment of taxes, provision of jobs), it is a question of whether firms adhere to public policy, the law, and ethical expectations. Again, because corporations can influence these forms of social control, their adherence to them cannot be the primary standard for corporate social performance. The same holds for social programs and policies. They institutionalize motives and decision-making processes for managing social impacts (Wood, 1991a). In them, corporations house the means to influence their standards of social control. Again, the principles do not clarify the moral motivation for doing so.

To recapitulate, the economic and duty-aligned perspectives are not compatible in CSR principles because they encounter trade-off and moral justification problems that prevent their theoretical integration. Additionally, the principles restrain corporate economic responsibilities through normatively unclear social controls that can be influenced by a corporation's own responsiveness, programs, and policies. Moreover, the principles do not clarify the moral motivation for this influence and other corporate social behavior.

The Need for Broader CSR Principles

The emphasis on corporate economic responsibility in CSR principles is not misplaced. The vital social function of business is economic (Committee for Economic Development, 1971; Donaldson, 1989; Frederick, 1992; Preston & Post, 1975). Even so, business decisions consist of continuous interrelated economic and moral components (Etzioni, 1988; Frederick, 1986). The CSR organizational and

individual principles divide this interrelatedness, functionally, then hierarchically, with the standard of social control. This standard emphasizes negative duty or restraint to economic responsibility based on control. In turn, this control standard deemphasizes positive duty. On the institutional level, positive duty is not addressed; on the organizational level, it is not functionally linked to economic responsibilities; on the individual level, it is optional. Further, the principles do not address the moral motivation that would motivate a voluntary corporate commitment to both negative and positive social duties.

All of this renders these principles too narrow for comprehensive theory development. They do not articulate the field's primary interest in what constitutes a complete sense of corporate responsibility to society. The field's theorists recognize that the modern corporation operates on an expanded scale that requires a new business and societal relationship (Epstein, 1987; Frederick, 1986; Sethi, 1982; Wartick & Cochran, 1985; Wood, 1991b; Zeitlin, 1978). From the beginning, many researchers have been interested in defining corporate responsibility for social progress that matches an expanded agenda of human issues and needs (Bowen, 1953, 1978; Chamberlain, 1977; Davis, 1964; Eells, 1960; Frederick, 1986; Lodge, 1975; Preston, 1986; Steiner, 1983; Votaw & Sethi, 1969). This larger agenda requires broad standards for corporate social involvement, commitment, and responsibility to community (Buchholz, 1989; Frederick, 1986; Preston, 1986). To accommodate these broad standards, the CSP field needs to develop a larger theoretical perspective (Wood & Jones, 1994).

Presently, the CSR principles are not answering what Wood (1991c) argued is the field's most pressing question: How can and do corporations contribute to constructing "the good society"? To do so, their normative dimensions need to be developed in the following ways. First, the principles need to hold social control to normative standards. Second, they need to incorporate positive duty across their institutional, organizational, and individual levels. Finally, they need to address the moral motivation that supports both negative and positive expressions of duty. In other words, the CSR principles need to integrate the field's economic and duty-aligned perspectives into broader standards that can adequately assess corporation social performance by normative criteria.

THEORY BUILDING PROBLEMS IN CORPORATE SOCIAL PERFORMANCE

It has been argued that the economic and duty-aligned perspectives resist integration, despite their shared interest in social control. Indeed, recent attempts to integrate these two perspectives indicate that they are largely incompatible. For example, Donaldson (1989), a philosopher, restrained some corporate moral duties with economic cost standards, and Etzioni (1988), a sociologist, restrained economic activity within a duty-bound community. Certainly, it is unusual for a philosopher to yield to economic precepts and a sociologist to philosophic ones. This unusual situation occurs because the two perspectives, as presently formulated, resist blending for three interrelated reasons.

The Obstacles to Integrating the Perspectives

Incompatible Value Outcomes. The first reason the two perspectives resist blending is that they prize incompatible value outcomes. The utilitarian reasoning in the convention neoclassical economic perspective focuses on *gain for self*. It uses cost-benefit calculus to measure efficiency and to determine whether a net gain accrues to individuals in markets or to stockholders vis-á-vis corporate profits. Focused on this self centered end, it deemphasizes questions of rights and justice for others (see Wood, 1991a). In contrast, the duty-aligned perspective focuses on *duty to others* and, despite its emphasis on motivation, it weighs morality by the *extent* to which

others are treated dutifully by standards of rights and justice.

Because the economic and duty-aligned perspectives prize different value outcomes, they encounter the trade-off or moral justification problem. As noted in the CSR principles, the trade-off problem occurs when duty appears costly. This problem is also demonstrated by a proposed algorithm for ethical decision making, whereby economic, rights, and justice standards are trade-offs, except for those instances where they seem to coincide (Cavanagh, Moberg, & Velasquez, 1981). Even then, the economic and duty-aligned perspectives do not agree on the moral rationale for choice, the first judging by consequences and the second by moral motivation. Hence, they still encounter the moral justification problem.

Focus on Individual Choice. The second reason the perspectives resist blending stems from the first. In their emphasis on gain or duty, both perspectives focus mainly on the logic of individual choice (Steidlmeier, 1987). This focus on individual dynamics is misplaced because it deemphasizes how self- and other interests are played out in large, complex organizations and how group-influenced behavior affects the business and societal relationship. In these organizations, people function interdependently on an unprecedented scale (Lindblom, 1977). The logic of individual action does not necessarily explain their behavior, especially as it is expressed in groups (Cohen, March, & Olsen, 1972). Essentially, corporate social responsibility, responsiveness, and outcomes occur in tandem with organizational dynamics, not logical rules for individual choice. The disproportionate importance that both perspectives grant to the individual is not appropriate for a field interested in explaining social phenomena.

Narrow Value Orientations. Finally, because both perspectives focus on individual gain or duty, neither gives a broad accounting of social values. These values are well recognized and include communitarian standards like social justice (Jones, 1983; Steidlmeier, 1987). As some scholars observe, business research continues to formulate these standards individualistically (see Aram, 1993; Preston, 1986). This narrow value orientation is consistent with a reported lack of research in the business and society field on the social dimensions in the business environment (see Reed, et al., 1990).

Although self-interested gain and other-interested duty are important and deserve study, they co-exist with other value variations that operate dynamically across the individual, organizational, and societal levels (Rokeach, 1973; Williams, 1979). Neither the economic nor duty-aligned perspectives account for all the sociocultural values that can be expressed in business and societal interaction and the social control of it. Notably, neither develops the role of power as a sociocultural value that affects this interaction. This situation suggests that the field has not completely replaced the neoclassical separation of economic activity from politics, despite its organizational principle that takes them to interpenetrating systems. The point is that the field lacks a broad account of sociocultural values and how they can be expressed in the business and society relationship. Instead, its economic and duty-aligned perspectives narrowly focus on the value of individual gain or duty to others, reinforcing the field's trade-off and moral justification problems.

The Inadequacies of Both Perspectives for Theory Development

The two perspectives are not easily integrated because of their (a) incompatible value outcomes, (b) emphasis on individual choice, and (c) narrow value orientations. For these reasons, neither is an adequate foundation for a more comprehensive business and society theory development. Because of their relative simplicity, they cannot adequately account for the ongoing interaction between large, complex, and powerful business organizations and their complex, dynamic, and turbulent social environments. This interaction can be interwoven and adaptive. It involves complex value relationships across the individual, organizational, and societal levels. It involves power. The field needs a research perspective that can accommodate these dimensions of the business and societal relationship.

A RESEARCH STRATEGY

Despite shortcomings, the economic and duty-aligned perspectives bring important understandings to the field. Neither should be discarded. The first emphasizes vital corporate economic responsibility and the social expectation that it be carried out. Through managerial research and corporate experience, it has been sharpened into an organizational pragmatism that provides effective tools for corporate social responsiveness. Although these tools can influence social control, they can also enhance corporate economic survival in complex, dynamic, and turbulent environments. On the other hand, the duty-aligned perspective emphasizes the importance of the humanizing standards of rights and justice and the social expectation that business adhere to them. It also advocates a moral motivation for this adherence. Further, it provides reflective moral reasoning for examining these aspects of corporate duty.

Although the CSR principles demonstrate the field's central theoretical problem, they also demonstrate that the field may be poised to integrate its two dominant perspectives by reformulating and broadening its theoretical base. For instance, the principles diverge from neoclassical economics by recognizing the importance of three research topics. First, the institutional principle recognizes that business has power that affects its relationship with society. Second, the organizational principle recognizes that this power relationship is not partitioned but is interpenetrating and can be interwoven and adaptive. Third, the individual principle recognizes that managers are moral agents who can exercise positive duty. All in all, these topics acknowledge a relationship between business and society that involves more than economic restraint. It also involves power, collaboration, and positive duty. This acknowledgement hints that the field may be ready to broaden its CSR principles into more adequate standards for assessing corporate social performance. To do so, it needs to bring together the economic and duty-aligned perspectives in theoretically sound ways.

The proposed research strategy reformulates the perspectives so that they are normatively compatible and adequate for theory development. This strategy involves three overlapping approaches: (a) bridge the perspectives with the topic of decision making, (b) formulate decision making in terms of social processes, and (c) formulate social processes as ethical and value processes.

Bridge the Perspectives with Decision Making

What is considered "ethical" in business must be assessed within the context of reasoning that invokes actions (Weber, 1993). As a research topic, decision making can address reasoning that invokes action by addressing the motivation that prompts decisions. It can also address the consequences of these decisions. Thus, the topic of decision making has the potential to accommodate both moral motivation and economic consequences. Put differently, this topic may be a bridge between the duty-aligned and economic perspectives because it can accommodate the emphasis on moral motivation of the former and the economic consequentialism of the latter.

Formulate Decision Making in Terms of Social Processes

Decision makers in organizations can occupy different roles and hierarchical positions. Their decisions create ongoing organizational and environmental consequences that influence further decisions. Epstein (1987) described this interaction as a social policy process, and its features suggest that decision making be formulated as processes that can be linked across the individual, organizational, and societal levels. Consistent with general systems theory, this formulation is a powerful way to account for dimensions in business and societal interaction (Preston & Post, 1975). Consequently, it renders the two basic perspectives better candidates for theory development. Further, it rectifies two obstacles to their integration. One, it removes their undue emphasis on the individual (while keeping it as an important level of analysis). Two, it removes their fixed-ended reasoning.

Based on historical evidence, Boulding (1978) proposed three major social organizers or processes that have evolved to link individuals to productive organizations. These processes have been cross-validated by other research, including Lenski's (1966) large cross-cultural study of societies ranging from hunting and gathering to advanced industrial states (see also Capra, 1982; Harris, 1979). Briefly, these social processes are

> *Exchange process*: Involves an invitation to trade based on reciprocity. It is undergirded by production that is based on specialization and division of labor
>
> *Threat process*: Involves the use of force or dominance
>
> *Integrative process*: Involves cooperation that is based on shared identities among people in communities.

Formulate Social Processes as Ethical and Value Processes

Boulding asserted that ethics and values are bound up in the social processes. Ethics in the foregoing discussion has already been accounted for as negative and positive duty. Because values help explain action and its motivation (Freeman & Gilbert, 1988; Rokeach, 1973) it is particularly important to account for their role in the social processes. That done, values and ethics can be formulated as interactive processes in decision making that span the individual, organizational, and societal levels.

Frederick (in press) accounts for those values in the social processes relevant to business organizations. For the purpose at hand, this accounting broadens the concept of value beyond narrow gain or duty standards. Briefly, these value processes are

> *Economizing*: Refers to the ability of organizations efficiently to convert inputs to outputs through competitive behavior. This process provides the goods and services for exchange in markets.
>
> *Power-aggrandizing or seeking*: Refers to status-enforced, self-centered behavior in organizations that seeks to acquire and use coercive power through hierarchical arrangements.
>
> *Ecologizing*: Refers to symbiotic, integrative linkages between organizations and their environments that function adaptively to sustain life. These linkages are based on cooperative, collaborative behavior.

In terms of how these values are bound up in the social processes, economizing is necessary for exchange; power-seeking is part of threat systems; and ecologizing is part of the integrative process. Frederick also proposes a separate value set consisting of the personal values held by individuals in business organizations. Research on these values indicate that they are far too numerous to list here (e.g., England, 1967; Frederick & Weber, 1987; Posner & Schmidt, 1984). Even so, it is important to note that they include the extent to which individuals prize economic rights and justice standards.

THE REORIENTED CSP MODEL

According to the research strategy, the reoriented CSP model formulates decision making in terms of ethical and value processes that are linked across the (a) individual (e.g., executive, managerial, and employee), (b) or-

ganizational, and (c) societal levels. As such, it discards the assumption that the CSR principles are hierarchical. This reorientation suggests a theoretical picture that is interactive across principles, processes, and outcomes (Wood, 1991a). The model organizes this interaction in terms of four broad research topics: (a) CSR macroprinciples, (b) CSR microprinciple, (c) corporate culture, and (d) social impacts. In Figure 1, the research topics are in boxes; their interrelationships or linkages are denoted by arrows.

Macroprinciples of Corporate Social Responsibility

Institutional Level.   Organizations are special-purpose tools. When they adapt to social values beyond technical requirements, they become institutions (Selznick, 1957, 1993). As such, the institutional principle in Figure 1 states that corporations are economizing and ecologizing tools, a description that is congruent with the social contract conclusion that corporations are legitimate because they enhance the social good. They do so by producing goods and services on a scale that would otherwise be unattainable (Donaldson, 1989). That is, corporations can economize. Further, corporate legitimacy rests on their ability to adapt production to life-sustaining social needs and be integrated into society (Sethi, 1979). This integration requires that they forge cooperative, collaborative linkages with it (Etzioni, 1988). In this way, corporations can ecologize.

As a research topic, the institutional principle invites an examination of the interrelationships among (a) economizing, (b) ecologizing, and (c) negative and positive duty. Both the economic and duty-aligned perspectives agree that negative duty is a restraint to corporate action that harms society. The institutional principle implies that these harms are economic (e.g., industrial relocation that brings unemployment) and ecological (e.g., pollution), and the duty-aligned perspective insists that they are also violations of rights

FIGURE 14–1. The Reoriented CSP Model

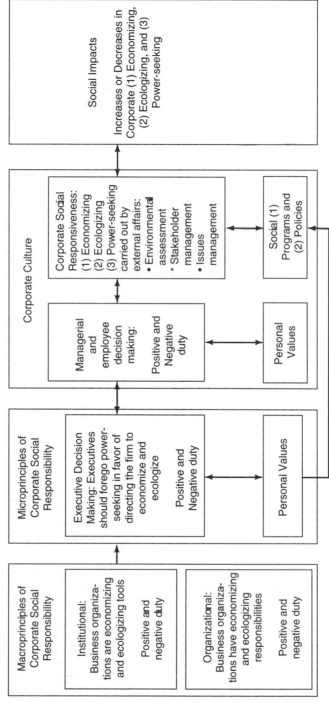

(e.g., the right to subsistence) and justice (e.g., fair and equitable on-the-job treatment). Additionally, the duty-aligned perspective views positive duty as a willing, constructive corporate commitment to provide rights and justice benefits to stakeholders. The institutional principle implies that these benefits can take economic and ecological forms. Supporting the importance of the latter, Selznick (1992) asserted that the integration of institutions into society is a major social benefit.

Organizational Level. Given the restated institutional principle, it follows that corporations have responsibilities to economize and ecologize and provide negative and positive duties to society. A more specific description of these organizational responsibilities awaits future research. In particular, this research would address how the interrelationships among economizing, ecologizing, and negative and positive duties can be manifest in *specific* industrial and social environments.

Microprinciples of Corporate Social Responsibility

Executive Decision Making, Ethics, and Personal Values. The microprinciple in Figure 1 states that executives should forego or limit power seeking as a personal or an organizational goal. Instead they should make decisions that direct the firm to economize and ecologize. This principle is consistent with Davis's iron law of responsibility; however, it is more concrete. It places the responsibility for legitimate use of power with the decision makers at the top of the corporate hierarchy.

Organizations have been described by some as tools of power for leaders whose interests are bound up with the expansion of corporate capital (Perrow, 1986; Zeitlin 1978). The microprinciple distinguishes between illegitimate and legitimate use of executive power. Illegitimate use, or "power seeking," relies on coercion and rank-order status. Its

motivation is self-interested empire building. In contrast, legitimate power involves the motivation and ability to direct organizational resources toward economizing and ecologizing. Negative and positive duty are important components of responsible executive decision making. Broadly, they provide a distinction between directing the firm to (a) restrain action that harms stakeholders and (b) provide action that promotes their good or benefit. Making these distinctions is related to executives' motives and personal values. Again, the latter includes economic, rights, and justice standards.

Corporate Culture and Normative Processes

Executives manage the belief systems or corporate cultures out of which organizations respond to their environments (Schein, 1985). Thus, the reoriented model links executive decision making to corporate culture. Figure 1 indicates that when corporate culture is understood in terms of normative processes, it allows interrelationships among several research topics, including

1. Linkages among normative executive decision making, corporate social programs and policies, and value-defined responsiveness carried out by an external affairs strategy. These linkages are consistent with Miles' (1987) finding that executive philosophy drives a firm's external affairs strategy.
2. Linkages between normative managerial and employee decision making and value-defined corporate social responsiveness.

Overall, the new model is capable of addressing two questions that Epstein (1987: 100) proposed are basic to understanding corporate management as a normative social policy process. They are

1. How can the leadership of a large, complex business organization best incorporate into their firm's decision-making processes the

difficult but essential task of defining (and redefining), evaluating, and institutionalizing the values that underlie its policies and practices as well as determine its unique culture?

2. What conceptual contributions can management thought make to business practitioners seeking to institutionalize value considerations into ongoing decision-making processes?

Social Impacts

Finally, the reoriented model allows linkages between normative processes occurring in corporate cultures and the social impacts of a company. Social impacts are depicted as increases or decreases in corporate economizing, ecologizing, and power seeking. Two-way arrows between research topics indicate that executive decision making, as well as social programs and policies, can be influenced by a firm's external affairs assessment of its social impacts.

CONCLUSION

In this article I propose a reoriented CSP model's construction that is consistent with Wood's (1991a) assertion that the CSR principles are analytical forms to be filled with value content that is operationalized. These operational processes—(a) economizing, ecologizing, and power-seeking values; (b) ethics as negative and positive duty; and (c) personal values—are interrelated. However, regarding the proposed model I do not propose functional relationships among them. Such relationships are research topics. The new model can be used to develop these topics and to assess whether the field's economic and duty-aligned perspectives can be integrated into an adequate normative theory for corporate social performance. By providing a conceptual framework for such research, the re-oriented model can make an important contribution to the field of corporate social performance.

NOTES

1. Economic theory represents a vast body of knowledge, including much research that explicitly addresses the ethical dimensions of economic activity (e.g., Arrow, 1951; Hirsch, 1976; Hirschman, 1985; Myrdal, 1970; Polanyi, 1944; Robinson, 1962; Sen, 1977, 1987). This article does not, however, address the many various strands of economic thought. Rather, it is interested in the extent to which the normative stance taken in contemporary expressions of neoclassical economic theory, has an impact on the corporate social performance field.

REFERENCES

Ackerman, R.W., & Bauer, R.A. 1976. *Corporate social responsiveness: The modern dilemma.* Cambridge, MA: Harvard University Press.

Aram, J.D. 1993. *Presumed superior.* Englewood Cliffs, NJ: Prentice Hall.

Arrow, K. 1951. *Social choice and individual values.* New York: Wiley.

Beauchamp, T.L., & Bowie, N.E. 1993. *Ethical theory and business.* Englewood Cliffs, NJ: Prentice Hall.

Boulding, K. 1978. *Ecodynamics.* Beverly Hills, CA: Sage Publications.

Bowen, H.R. 1953. *Social responsibilities of the businessman.* New York: Harper.

Bowen, H.R. 1978. Social responsibilities of the businessman—Twenty years later. In E.M. Epstein & D. Votaw (Eds.), *Rationality, legitimacy, responsibility: Search for new directions in business and society*: 116–130. Santa Monica, CA: Goodyear.

Brady, F.N. 1985. A Janus-headed model of ethical theory: Looking two ways at business/society issues. *Academy of Management Review*, 10: 568–576.

Buchholz, R.A. 1982. *Business environment and public policy*. Englewood Cliffs, NJ: Prentice Hall.

Buchholz, R.A. 1985. *Essential of public policy for management*. Englewood Cliffs, NJ: Prentice Hall.

Buchholz, R.A. 1989. *Business Ethics*. Englewood Cliffs, NJ: Prentice Hall.

Capra, F. 1982. *The turning point*. New York: Simon and Schuster.

Carroll, A.B. 1979. A three-dimensional model of corporate social performance. *Academy of Management Review*, 4: 497–505.

Cavanagh, G.F. 1990. *American business values*. Englewood Cliffs, NJ: Prentice Hall.

Cavanagh, G., Moberg, D., & Velasquez, M. 1981. The ethics of 36 organizational politics. *Academy of Management Review*, 6: 363–368.

Chamberlain, N. 1973. *The place of business in America's future: A study in social values*. New York: Basic Books.

Chamberlain, N. 1977. *Remaking American values*. New York: Basic Books.

Chomsky, N.C. 1986. *The Chomsky reader*. J. Peck (Ed.). New York: Pantheon Books.

Cohen, M., March, J., & Olsen, J. 1972. A garbage can model of organizational choice. *Administrative Science Quarterly*, 17: 1–25.

Collins, D. 1989. Organizational harm, legal condemnation and stakeholder retaliation: A typology, research agenda and application. *Journal of Business Ethics*, 8: 1–13.

Committee for Economic Development. 1971. *Social Responsibilities of business corporations*. New York: Author. Development.

Davis, K. 1964. The public role of management. *Proceedings of the Annual Meeting of the Academy of Management*: 3–9.

Davis, K. 1973. The case for and against business assumption of social responsibilities. *Academy of Management Journal*, 16: 312–322.

DeGeorge, R.T. 1990. *Business ethics*. New York: Macmillan.

Donaldson, T. 1989. *The ethics of international business*. New York: Oxford University Press.

Eells, R. 1960. *The meaning of modern business*. New York: Columbia University Press.

England, G.W. 1967. Personal value systems of American managers. *Academy of Management Journal*, 10: 107–117.

Epstein, E.M. 1969. *The corporation in American politics*. Englewood Cliffs, NJ: Prentice Hall.

Epstein, E.M. 1987. The corporate social policy process: Beyond business ethics, corporate social responsibility, and corporate social responsiveness. *California Management Review*, 29: 99–114.

Etzioni, A. 1988. *The moral dimension: Toward a new economics*. New York: Free Press.

Frederick, W.C. 1986. Toward CSR3: Why ethical analysis is indispensable and unavoidable in corporate affairs. *California Management Review*, 28: 126–141.

Frederick, W.C. 1987. Theories of corporate social performance. In S.P. Sethi & C. Falbe (Eds.), *Business and society: Dimensions of conflict and cooperation*: 142–161. New York: Lexington Books.

Frederick, W.C. 1992. Anchoring values in nature: Toward a theory of business values. *Business Ethics Quarterly*, 2: 283–303.

Frederick, W.C. In press. *Values, nature, and culture in the American Corporation*. New York: Oxford University Press.

Frederick, W.C., & Weber, J. 1987. The values of corporate managers and their critics. In W.C. Frederick & L.E. Preston (Eds.), *Research in corporate social performance and policy*, vol. 9: 131–152. Greenwich, CT: JAI Press.

Freeman, R.E. 1984. *Strategic management: A stakeholder approach*. Boston: Pittman/Ballinger.

Freeman, R.E., & Gilbert, D.R. 1988. *Corporate strategy and search for ethics*. Englewood Cliffs, NJ: Prentice Hall.

Friedman, M. 1962. *Capitalism and freedom*. Chicago: University of Chicago Press.

Friedman, M. 1970. The social responsibility of business is to increase its profits. *New York Times Magazine*. September 13: 33, 122–126.

Harris, M. 1979. *Cultural materialism*. New York: Random House.

Harris, R.G., & Carman, J.M. 1987. Business-government relations. In S.P. Sethi & C. Falbe (Eds.), *Business and society: Dimensions of conflict and cooperation*: 177–190. New York: Lexington Books.

Hausman, D.M. 1992. *The inexact and separate science of economics*. New York: Cambridge University, University Press.

Hirsch, F. 1976. *Social limits to growth*. Cambridge, MA: Harvard University Press.

Hirschman, A.O. 1981. *Essays in trespassing: Economics to politics and beyond*. New York: Cambridge Press.

Hirschman, A.O. 1985. Against parsimony: Three easy ways of complicating some categories of economic discourse. *Economic Philosophy*, 1: 7–21.

Jones, T.M. 1983. An integrating framework for research in business and society: A step toward the elusive paradigm? *Academy of Management Review*, 8: 559–564.

Lenski, G. 1966. *Power and privilege.* New York: McGraw-Hill.

Lindblom, C.E. 1977. *Politics and markets.* New York: Basis Books.

Lodge, G. 1975. *The new American ideology.* New York: Alfred Knopf.

March, J. 1992. The war is over and the victors have lost. *The Journal of Socio-Economics*, 21: 261–267.

Miles, R.A. 1987. *Managing the corporate social environment.* Englewood Cliffs, NJ: Prentice Hall.

Mitnick, B.M. 1981. The strategic uses of regulation—and deregulation. *Business Horizons*, 24(2): 71–83.

Myrdal, G. 1970. *The challenge of world poverty.* New York: Pantheon Books.

Perrow, C. 1986. *Complex organizations: A critical essay.* New York: McGraw-Hill.

Polanyi, K. 1944. *The great transformation.* New York: Farrar & Rinehart.

Posner, B.Z., & Schmidt, W.H. 1984. Values and the American manager: An update. *California Management Review*, 3: 202–215.

Preston, L.E. 1986. Social issues management: An evolutionary perspective. In D.A. Wren & J.A. Pearce II (Eds.), *Papers dedicated to the development of modern management: Celebrating 100 years of modern management: 50th anniversary of the Academy of Management:* 52–57.

Preston, L.E., & Post, J.E. 1975. *Private management and public policy: The principle of public responsibility,* Englewood Cliffs, NJ: Prentice Hall.

Rawls, J. 1971. *A theory of justice.* Cambridge, MA: Harvard University Press.

Reed, L., Getz, K., Collins, D., Oberman, W., & Toy, R. 1990. Theoretical models and empirical results: A review and synthesis of JAI volumes 1–10. In L.E. Preston (Ed.), *Corporation and society research: studies in theory and measurement:* 27–62. Greenwich, CT: JAI Press.

Robinson, J. 1962. *Economic philosophy.* Chicago: Aldine.

Rokeach, M. 1973. *The nature of human values.* New York: Free Press.

Schein, E.H. 1985. *Organizational culture and leadership.* San Francisco: Jossey-Bass.

Scott, R.W. 1987. *Organizations: Rational, natural, and open systems.* Englewood Cliffs, NJ: Prentice Hall.

Selznick, P. 1957. *Leadership in administration.* New York: Harper & Row.

Selznick, P. 1992. *The moral commonwealth.* Berkeley: University of California Press.

Sen, A. 1977. Social choice theory: A re-examination. *Econometrica*, 45: 53–89.

Sen, A. 1987. *On ethics and economics.* Oxford, England: Blackwell.

Sethi, S.P. 1979. A conceptual framework for environmental analysis of social issues and evaluation of business response patterns. *Academy of Management Review*, 4: 63–74.

Sethi, S.P. 1982. Corporate political involvement. *California Management Review*, 24: 32–42.

Steidlmeier, P. 1987. Corporate social responsibility and business ethics. In S.P. Sethi & C. Falbe (Eds.), *Business and society: Dimensions of conflict and cooperation:* 101–121. New York: Lexington Books.

Steiner, G.A. 1983. *Business and society.* New York: Macmillan.

Velasquez, M.G. 1982. *Business ethics: Concepts and cases.* Englewood Cliffs, NJ: Prentice Hall.

Vogel, D. 1991. The ethical roots of business ethics. *Business Ethics Quarterly*, 1: 101–120.

Votaw, D., & Sethi, S.P. 1969. Do we need a new corporate response to a changing social environment? *California Management Review*, 12(1): 3–31.

Wartick, S.L., & Cochran, P.L. 1985. The evolution of the corporate social performance model. *Academy of Management Review*, 10: 758–769.

Wartick, S.L., & Rude, R.E. 1986. Issues management: Corporate fad or corporate function? *California Management Review*, 29(1): 124–140.

Weber, J. 1993. Institutionalizing ethics into business organizations. *Business Ethics Quarterly*, 3: 419–436.

Weidenbaum, M. 1977. *Business, government, and the public.* Englewood Cliffs, NJ: Prentice Hall.

Werhane, P.H. 1985. *Persons, rights, and corporations.* Englewood Cliffs, NJ: Prentice Hall.

Williams, R. 1979. Change and stability in values and value systems: A sociological perspective. In M. Rokeach (Ed.), *Understanding human values:* 15–46. New York: Free Press.

Wood, D.J. 1990. *Business and society.* Glenview IL: Scott, Foresman (Harper Collins).

Wood, D.J. 1987. Strategic uses of public policy. In S.P. Sethi & C. Falbe (Eds.), *Business and society: Dimensions of conflict and cooperation:* 75–100. New York: Lexington Books.

Wood, D.J. 1991a. Corporate social performance revisited. *Academy of Management Review*, 16: 691–718.

Wood, D.J. 1991b. Social issues in management: Theory and research in corporate social performance. *Journal of Management*, 17: 383–406.

Wood, D.J. 1991c. Toward improving corporate social performance. *Business Horizons*, 66–73.

Wood, D.J., & Jones, R.E. 1994. *Research in corporate social performance: What have we learned?* Paper presented at the Conference on Corporate Philanthropy, sponsored by the Center for Corporate Philanthropy, University of Indi-

ana and the Mandel Center of Case Western Reserve, Cleveland.

Zeitlin, M. 1978. Managerial theory vs. class theory of corporate capitalism. In L.E. Preston (Ed.), *Research in corporate social performance and policy:* vol. 1: 255–263. Greenwich, CT: JAI Press.

THE STAKEHOLDER THEORY OF THE CORPORATION

Concepts, evidence, and implications

Thomas Donaldson
Lee E. Preston

The stakeholder theory has been advanced and justified in the management literature on the basis of its descriptive accuracy, instrumental power, and normative validity. These three aspects of the theory, although interrelated, are quite distinct; they involve different types of evidence and argument and have different implications. In this article, we examine these three aspects of the theory and critique and integrate important contributions to the literature related to each. We conclude that the three aspects of stakeholder theory are mutually supportive and that the normative base of the theory—which includes the modern theory of property rights—is fundamental.

If the unity of the corporate body is real, then there is reality and not simply legal fiction in the proposition that the managers of the unit are fiduciaries for it and not merely for its individual members, that they are . . . trustees for an institution [with multiple constituents] rather than attorneys for the stockholders.

E. Merrick Dodd, Jr.
Harvard Law Review, 1932

The idea that corporations have *stakeholders* has now become commonplace in the manage-

The development of this article benefited greatly from discussions held at the Conference of Stakeholder Theory at the University of Toronto, May 1993, and from the specific comments of many people, including Professors Aupperle, Carroll, Clarkson, Halal, Freeman, Jones, and Sethi.

ment literature, both academic and professional. Since the publication of Freeman's landmark book, *Strategic Management: A Stakeholder Approach* (1984), about a dozen books and more than 100 articles with primary emphasis on the stakeholder concept have appeared. (Significant recent examples include books by Alkhafaji, 1989; Anderson, 1989; and Brummer, 1991; and articles by Brenner & Cochran, 1991; Clarkson, 1991; Goodpaster, 1991; Hill & Jones, 1992; and Wood, 1991a,b; plus numerous papers by Freeman and various collaborators, individually cited). *Stakeholder management* is the central theme of at least one important recent business and society text (Carroll, 1989), and a diagram purporting to represent the *stakeholder model* has become a standard element of "Introduction to Management" lectures and writings.

Unfortunately, anyone looking into this large and evolving literature with a critical eye will observe that the concepts *stakeholder*, *stakeholder model*, *stakeholder management* and *stakeholder theory* are explained and used by various authors in very different ways and supported (or critiqued) with diverse and often contradictory evidence and arguments. Moreover, this diversity and its implications are rarely discussed—and possibly not even recognized. (The blurred character of the stakeholder concept is also emphasized by Brummer, 1991.) The purpose of this article is

233

to point out some of the more important distinctions, problems, and implications associated with the stakeholder concept, as well as to clarify and justify its essential content and significance.

In the following section we contrast the stakeholder model of the corporation with the conventional input-output model of the firm and summarize our central thesis. We next present the three aspects of stakeholder theory—descriptive/empirical, instrumental, and normative—found in the literature and clarify the critical differences among them. We then raise the issue of justification: Why would anyone accept the stakeholder theory over alternative conceptions of the corporation? In subsequent sections, we present and evaluate the underlying evidence and arguments justifying the theory from the perspective of descriptive, instrumental, and normative justifications. We conclude that the three approaches to stakeholder theory, although quite different, are mutually supportive and that the *normative* base serves as the critical underpinning for the theory in all its forms.

THE CENTRAL THESIS

We summarize our central theses here:

> **Thesis 1:** The stakeholder theory is unarguably descriptive. It presents a model describing what the corporation is. It describes the corporation as a constellation of cooperative and competitive interests possessing intrinsic value. Aspects of this model may be tested for descriptive accuracy: Is this model more descriptively accurate than rival models? Moreover, do observers and participants, in fact, see the corporation this way? The model can also serve as a framework for testing any empirical claims, including instrumental predictions, relevant to the stakeholder concept (but not for testing the concept's normative base).

> **Thesis 2:** The stakeholder theory is also instrumental. It establishes a framework for examining the connections, if any, between the practice of stakeholder management and

the achievement of various corporate performance goals. The principal focus of interest here has been the proposition that corporations practicing stakeholder management will, other things being equal, be relatively successful in conventional performance terms (profitability, stability, growth, etc.).

> **Thesis 3:** Although Theses 1 and 2 are significant aspects of the stakeholder theory, its fundamental basis is normative and involves acceptance of the following ideas: (a) Stakeholders are persons or groups with legitimate interests in procedural and/or substantive aspects of corporate activity. Stakeholders are identified by their interests in the corporation, whether the corporation has any corresponding functional interest in them. (b) The interests of all stakeholders are of intrinsic value. That is, each group of stakeholders merits consideration for its own sake and not merely because of its ability to further the interests of some other group, such as the shareowners.

> **Thesis 4:** The stakeholder theory is managerial in the broad sense of that term. It does not simply describe existing situations or predict cause-effect relationships; it also recommends attitudes, structures, and practices that, taken together, constitute stakeholder management. Stakeholder management requires, as its key attribute, simultaneous attention to the legitimate interests of all appropriate stakeholders, both in the establishment of organizational structures and general policies and in case-by-case decision making. This requirement holds for anyone managing or affecting corporate policies, including not only professional managers, but shareowners, the government, and others. Stakeholder theory does not necessarily presume that managers are the only rightful locus of corporate control and governance. Nor does the requirement of simultaneous attention to stakeholder interests resolve the longstanding problem of identifying stakeholders and evaluating their legitimate "stakes" in the corporation. The theory does not imply that all stakeholders (however they may be identified) should be equally involved in all processes and decisions.

The distinction between a stakeholder conception of the corporation and a conventional input-output perspective is highlighted by the contrasting models displayed in Figures 1 and 2. In Figure 1, investors, employees, and suppliers are depicted as contributing inputs, which the "black box" of the firm transforms into outputs for the benefit of customers. To be sure, each contributor of inputs expects to receive appropriate compensation, but the liberal economics, or "Adam Smith" interpretation, of this model in long-run equilibrium is that input contributors, at the margin, receive only "normal" or "market competitive" benefits (i.e., the benefits that they would obtain from some alternative use of their resources and time). Individual contributors who are particularly advantaged, such as possessors of scarce locations or skills, will, of course, receive "rents," but the rewards of the marginal contributors will only be "normal." As a result of competition throughout the system, the bulk of the benefits will go to the customers. (There is, of course, a Marxist-capitalist version of this model in which both the customer and the investor arrows are reversed, and the object of the game is merely to produce benefits for the investors. This interpretation now seems to be confined almost exclusively to the field of finance.)

The stakeholder model (Figure 2) contrasts explicitly with the input-output model in all its variations. Stakeholder analysts argue that *all* persons or groups with legitimate interests participating in an enterprise do so to obtain benefits and that there is no prima facie priority of one set of interests and benefits over another. Hence, the arrows between the firm and its stakeholder constituents run in both directions. All stakeholder relationships are depicted in the same size and shape and are equidistant from the "black box" of the firm in the center. The distinctive features of this conception, as contrasted with conventional input-output conceptions, will become apparent as our analysis proceeds.

This summary of the stakeholder theory and our discussion throughout this article refer specifically to the theory's application to the investor-owned corporation. Although stakeholder concepts have been applied in other settings (e.g., government agencies and social programs), these situations are fundamentally different, and simultaneous discussion of a variety of possible stakeholder relationships leads, in our view, to confusion rather than clarification. The critical corporate stakeholder issues, both in theory and in practice, involve evidentiary considerations an conceptual issues (e.g., the meaning of property rights) unique to the corporate setting.

It is also worth noting at the outset that the extent to which the stakeholder theory is understood to represent a controversial or

FIGURE 1. Contrasting Models of the Corporation: Input-Output Model

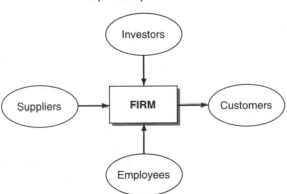

FIGURE 2.   Contrasting Models of the Corporation: The Stockholder Model

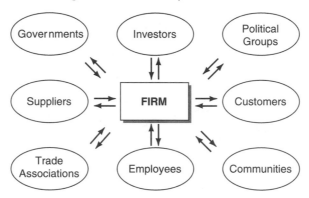

challenging approach to conventional views varies greatly among market capitalist economies. These differences are highlighted in a recent issue of *The Economist* (1993: 52):

> In America, for instance, shareholders have a comparatively big say in the running of the enterprises they own; workers . . . have much less influence. In many European countries, shareholders have less say and workers more . . . [I]n Japan . . . managers have been left alone to run their companies as they see fit— namely for the benefit of employees and of allied companies, as much as for shareholders.

ALTERNATIVE ASPECTS OF STAKEHOLDER THEORY: DESCRIPTIVE/EMPIRICAL, INSTRUMENTAL, AND NORMATIVE

One of the central problems in the evolution of stakeholder theory has been confusion about its nature and purpose. For example, stakeholder theory has been used, either explicitly or implicitly, for descriptive purposes. Brenner and Cochran (1991: 452) offered a "stakeholder theory of the firm" for "two purposes: to describe how organizations operate and to help predict organizational behavior." They contrasted this "theory," which they developed only in outline form, with other "theories of the firm," but they did not ask whether the various theories cited have comparable purposes.

In fact, different theories have different purposes and therefore different validity criteria and different implications. For example, according to Cyert and March (1963), the neoclassical theory of the firm attempts to explain the economic principles governing production, investment, and pricing decisions of established firms operating in competitive markets. In contrast, their behavioral theory of the firm attempts to explain the process of decisionmaking in the modern firm in terms of goals, expectations, and choice-making procedures. Aoki's (1984) cooperative game theory of the firm attempts to explain internal governance, particularly the balance between owners' and workers' interests. In contrast to all of these contributions, transactions cost theory attempts to explain why firms exist (i.e., why economic activities are coordinated through formal organizations rather than simply through market contacts) (Coase, 1937; Williamson & Winter, 1991). (Although all these theories are put forward as "positive" or "scientific" conceptions, there is a tendency for them to be used for normative purposes a well.)

The stakeholder theory differs from these and other "theories of the firm" in fundamental ways. The stakeholder theory is intended both to explain and to guide the structure and operation of the established corporation (the "going concern" in John R. Commons' famous phrase). Toward that end it views the corporation as an organizational entity through which numerous and diverse participants accomplish multiple, and not always entirely congruent, purposes. The stakeholder theory is general and comprehensive, but it is not empty; it goes well beyond the descriptive observation that "organizations have stakeholders." Unfortunately, much of what passes for stakeholder theory in the literature is implicit rather than explicit, which is one reason why diverse and sometimes confusing uses of the stakeholder concept have not attracted more attention.

The stakeholder theory can be, and has been, presented and used in a number of ways that are quite distinct and involve very different methodologies, types of evidence, and criteria of appraisal. Three types of uses are critical to our analysis.

Descriptive/Empirical

The theory is used to describe, and sometimes to explain, specific corporate characteristics and behaviors. For example, stakeholder theory has been used to describe (a) the nature of the firm (Brenner & Cochran, 1991), (b) the way managers think about managing (Brenner & Molander, 1977), (c) how board members think about the interests of corporate constituencies (Wang & Dewhirst, 1992), and (d) how some corporations are actually managed (Clarkson, 1991; Halal, 1990; Kreiner & Bhambri, 1991).

Instrumental

The theory, in conjunction with descriptive/empirical data where available, is used to identify the connections, or lack of connections, between stakeholder management and the achievement of traditional corporate objectives (e.g., profitability, growth). Many recent instrumental studies of corporate social responsibility, all of which make explicit or implicit reference to stakeholder perspectives, use conventional statistical methodologies (Aupperle, Carroll, & Hatfield, 1985; Barton, Hill, & Sundaram, 1989; Cochran & Wood, 1984; Cornell & Shapiro, 1987; McGuire,

Sundgren, & Schneeweis, 1988; Preston & Sapienza, 1990; Preston, Sapienza, & Miller, 1991). Other studies are based on direct observation and interviews (Kotter & Heskett, 1992; O'Toole, 1985; see also, O'Toole, 1991). Whatever their methodologies, these studies have tended to generate "implications" suggesting that adherence to stakeholder principles and practices achieves conventional corporate performance objectives as well or better than rival approaches. Kotter and Heskett (1992) specifically observed that such highly successful companies as Hewlett-Packard, Wal-Mart, and Dayton Hudson—although very diverse in other ways—share a stakeholder perspective. Kotter and Heskett (1992: 59) wrote that "[a]lmost all [their] managers care strongly about people who have a stake in the business—customers, employees, stockholders, suppliers, etc."

Normative

The theory is used to interpret the function of the corporation, including the identification of moral or philosophical guidelines for the operation and management of corporations. Normative concerns dominated the classic stakeholder theory statements from the beginning (Dodd, 1932), and this tradition has been continued in the most recent versions (Carroll, 1989; Kuhn & Shriver, 1991; Marcus, 1993). Even Friedman's (1970) famous attack on the concept of corporate social responsibility was cast in normative terms.

Contrasting/Combining Approaches

Each of these uses of stakeholder theory is of some value, but the values differ in each use. The *descriptive* aspect of stakeholder theory reflects and explains past, present, and future states of affairs of corporations and their stakeholders. Simple description is common and desirable in the exploration of new areas and usually expands to the generate explanatory and predictive propositions. (All such activities shall be called *descriptive* for our purposes.) *Instrumental* uses of stakeholder theory make a connection between stakeholder approaches and commonly desired objectives such as profitability. Instrumental uses usually stop short of exploring specific links between cause (i.e., stakeholder management) and effect (i.e., corporate performance) in detail, but such linkage is certainly implicit. The much-quoted Stanford Research Institute's (SRI) definition of stakeholders as "those groups without whose support the organization would cease to exist" (SRI, 1963; quoted in Freeman, 1984: 31) clearly implies that corporate managers must induce constructive contributions from their stakeholders to accomplish their own desired results (e.g., perpetuation of the organization, profitability, stability, growth).

In *normative* uses, the correspondence between the theory and the observed facts of corporate life is not a significant issue, nor is the association between stakeholder management and conventional performance measures a critical test. Instead, a normative theory attempts to interpret the function of, and offer guidance about, the investor-owned corporation on the basis of some underlying moral or philosophical principles. Although both normative and instrumental analyses may be "prescriptive" (i.e., they may express or imply more or less appropriate choices on the part of decision makers), they rest on entirely different bases. An instrumental approach is essentially hypothetical; it says, in effect, "If you want to achieve (avoid) results X, Y, or Z, then adopt (don't adopt) principles and practices A, B, or C." The normative approach, in contrast, is not hypothetical but categorical; it says, in effect, "Do (Don't do) this because it is the right (wrong) thing to do." Much of the stakeholder literature, including the contributions of both proponents and critics, is clearly normative, although the fundamental normative principles involved are often unexamined.

A striking characteristic of the stakeholder literature is that diverse theoretical approaches are often combined without acknowledgement. Indeed, the temptation to seek a three-in-one-theory—or at least to

slide easily from one theoretical base to another—is strong. Clarkson, (1991: 349) for example, asserted an explicit connection among all three when he concluded that his stakeholder management model represents a new framework for describing, evaluating, and managing corporate social performance.

All three types of theory are also to be found in the work of Freeman, whom many regard as the leading contributor to the stakeholder literature. In his original treatise, he asserted that changing events create a descriptive fit for the theory:

> Just as the separation of the owner-manager-employee required a rethinking of the concept of control and private property as analyzed by Berle and Means (1932), so does the emergence of numerous stakeholder groups and new strategic issues require a rethinking of our traditional picture of the firm . . . We must redraw the picture in a way that accounts for the changes. (1984: 24)

At the same time, he also endorsed the theory's *instrumental basis*. We should, he noted, "explore the logic of this concept in practical terms, i.e., in terms of how organizations can succeed in the current and future business environment" (1984: 25). Instrumental concerns are also reflected in Freeman's extensive discussion of stakeholder management implementation techniques, both in his 1984 treatise and in other papers (Freeman & Reed, 1983; Freeman & Gilbert, 1987). In a later work, however, Evan and Freeman (1988: 97) justified stakeholder theory on normative grounds, specifically its power to satisfy the moral rights of individuals. They asserted that the theory of the firm must be reconceptualized "along essentially Kantian lines." This means each stakeholder group has a right to be treated as an end in itself, and not as means to some other end, "and therefore must participate in determining the future direction of the firm in which they have a stake."

The muddling of theoretical bases and objectives, although often understandable, has led to less rigorous thinking and analysis than the stakeholder concept requires. To see the significance of the distinctions among descriptive, instrumental, and normative uses of the stakeholder concept, consider the current controversy over the special privileges of top managers in large corporations, particularly in connection with mergers and acquisitions. There is considerable evidence that in the burst of large corporate takeovers during the 1980s, share values typically rose for acquired firms and fell for acquiring firms. Many observers have speculated that self-serving managerial activity accounts for both results (Weidenbaum & Vogt, 1987; Jensen, 1989). The acquired firms gain in value because, prior to the takeover, they were burdened by inefficient, self-serving managers, and the acquiring firms lose in value because the impetus for the acquisition was not return on investment for owners but ego gratification and career advancement for their top managers. If this analysis is accurate, and if managers' nests are often feathered in other ways (e.g., salaries, bonuses) at the expense of shareowners, then it is descriptively true that managers' interests have priority over those of other stakeholders, including shareowners. But we cannot move directly from an *is* claim—the de facto priority of manager's interests—to an *ought* claim in either instrumental or normative contexts. Moreover, even if it were true that higher paid managers did, in fact, achieve higher levels of profitability (thus meeting instrumental criteria), it would still not follow that higher pay/profit results were normatively justifiable. (Witness the near-universal condemnation of the income/profit achievements of the 19th century robber barons.)

THE PROBLEM OF JUSTIFICATION

The underlying epistemological issue in the stakeholder literature is the problem of justification: Why should the stakeholder theory be accepted or preferred over alternative conceptions? Until this question is addressed, the distinctions among empirical, instrumental, and normative approaches can be papered over. Moreover, the answer to this question must be related to the distinct purpose that the theory is intended to serve. That is, reasons to accept the stakeholder theory as a descriptive account of how managers behave, or of how the business world in constituted, are different from reasons to accept the stakeholder theory as a guide for managerial behavior, and so on.

The stakeholder theory is justified in the literature, explicitly or implicitly, in ways that correspond directly to the three approaches to the theory set out in the previous section: descriptive, instrumental, and normative. Descriptive justifications attempt to show that the concepts embedded in the theory correspond to observed reality. Instrumental justifications point to evidence of the connection between stakeholder management and corporate performance. Normative justifications appeal to underlying concepts such as individual or group "rights," "social contract," or utilitarianism. (Brummer's recent survey of this literature ignores descriptive issues but emphasizes "power and performance," i.e., instrumental and "deontological," i.e., normative, arguments; cf. Brummer, 1991.)

In our view, the three aspects of the stakeholder theory are nested within each other, as suggested by Figure 3. The external shell of the theory is its descriptive aspect; the theory presents and explains relationships that are observed in the external world. The theory's descriptive accuracy is supported, at the second level, by its instrumental and predictive value; *if* certain practices are carried out, *then* certain results will be obtained. The central core of the theory presumes the truth of the core normative conception, insofar as it presumes that managers and other agents acts *as if* all stakeholders' interests have intrinsic value. In turn, recognition of these ultimate moral values and obligations gives stakeholder management its fundamental normative base. In the following sections, we sur-

FIGURE 3.   Three Aspects of
Stakeholder Theory

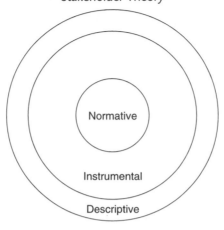

vey the evidence and argument involved in each of these approaches to the justification of the stakeholder theory.

DESCRIPTIVE JUSTIFICATIONS

There is ample descriptive evidence, some of which has already been cited, that many managers believe themselves, or are believed by others, to be practicing stakeholder management. Indeed, as early as the mid-1960s, Raymond Baumhart's (1968) survey of upper-level managers revealed that about 80 percent regarded it as unethical management behavior to focus solely in the interest of shareowners and not in the interest of employees and customers. Since then, other surveys asking similar questions about the stakeholder sensitivity of managers have returned similar results (Brenner & Molander, 1977; Posner & Schmidt, 1984). Ongoing empirical studies by both Clarkson (1991) and Halal (1990) attempt to distinguish firms that practice stakeholder management form those that do not, and both investigators found significant numbers of firms in the first category. Managers may not make explicit reference to "stakeholder theory," but the vast majority of them apparently adhere in practice to one of the central tenets of the stakeholder theory,

namely, that their role is to satisfy a wider set of stakeholders, not simply the shareowners (Note, however, that the 171 managers surveyed by Alkhafaji (1989) did not believe that the corporate governance roles of any stakeholders, including shareowners, should be increased. Perhaps not surprisingly, they strongly favored increased dominance of corporate governance by management).

Another kind of descriptive justification for the stakeholder theory stems from the role it plays as the implicit basis for existing practices and institutions, including legal opinion and statutory law. Recent court decisions and new legislation have weakened the so-called "Business Judgment Rule," which vests management with exclusive authority over the conduct of a company's affairs only on the condition that the financial welfare of stockholders is single-mindedly pursued (Chirelstein, 1974: 60). At last count, at least 29 states have adopted statutes that extend the range of permissible concern by boards of directors to a host of non-shareowner constituencies, including employees, creditors, suppliers, customers, and local communities (Orts, 1992). Furthermore, courts have tended to support these statutes. For example, the well-known Delaware Supreme Court decision in Unocal, although requiring corporate directors to show that a "reasonable," threat exists before fighting hostile takeover offers, nonetheless allowed a number of concerns to affect the determination of such "reasonableness," including "the impact [of the takeover] on 'constituencies' other than shareholders (i.e., creditors, customers, employees, and perhaps even the community generally)" (*Unocal Corp. v. Mesa Petroleum Co.*, 1985). In a more recent Delaware case, *Paramount Communications, Inc. v. Time, Inc.*, (1990) the Unocal rationale was expanded to allow directors to include factors such as long-range business plans and a corporation's "culture." In one of the most dramatic challenges to the ownership rights of hostile acquirers, the Supreme Court of the United States upheld an Indiana statute that in the Court's own words "condition[s] acquisition of control of a corporation on approval of a majority of the *pre-existing* disinterested shareholders" (emphasis added) (*CTCS Corp. v. Dynamics Corp. of America* 1987.)

As Orts noted, this trend toward stakeholder law is not solely a U.S. phenomenon and is reflected in the existing and emerging laws of many developed countries. The so-called codetermination laws of Germany require employee representation on second-tier boards of directors. The Companies Act of Great Britain mandates that company directors shall include the interests of employees in their decision making (*Companies Act*, 1980). The new "harmonization" laws of the European Community (EC) will, when approved, include provisions permitting corporations to take into account the interests of creditors, customers, potential investors, and employees. (Orts, 1992). Finally, the well-known corporate governance model in Japan—through both law and custom—presumes that Japanese corporations exist within a tightly connected and interrelated set of stakeholders, including suppliers, customers, lending institutions, and friendly corporations.

Another series of legal developments in the U.S. asserts the interests of third-party stakeholders—specifically, unsuccessful job applicants—in business operations. Title VII of the Civil Rights Act of 1964 explicitly makes it a violation of law for an employer "to fail or refuse to hire . . . any individual" on the basis of discriminatory criteria (42 U.S.C. §§2000e-2a(1) & (2), 1982). This legislation has become the focus of numerous legal complaints and some substantial settlements. In a class action suit involving Potomac Electric Power Co., Washington, DC, complainants charged that the company had hired far fewer Blacks from its applicant pool than would have been expected on statistical grounds. The judge certified a "class" of more than 7,000 unsuccessful Black applicants, most of whom will be eligible for compensation out of a $38.4 million settlement pool (which is also available to employees experiencing discrimination) (*The Washington Post*, 21 February 1993).

Both of these sets of legal developments reinforce our initial statement that stakeholders are defined by *their* legitimate interest in the corporation, rather than simply by the corporation's interest in *them*. But neither the legal developments nor the management survey results provide definitive epistemological justification for the stakeholder theory. Managers adopting the stakeholder approach may be relieved to learn that they are not alone, and indeed that they are conforming to the latest management or legal trends, but both the survey results and legal developments are, at bottom, simply facts. They do not constitute the basis for the stakeholder (or any other) theory of management. Indeed, even if the stakeholder concept is implicit in current legal trends (a proposition that is not universally accepted), one cannot derive a stakeholder theory of management from a stakeholder theory of law any more than one can derive a "tort" theory of management from the tort theory of law.

The hazards of using purely descriptive data, whether jurisprudential or otherwise, as justification for a broad theory are well known. There is the problem of the so-called "naturalistic fallacy," moving from *is* to *ought* or from *describe* to *evaluate*, without the necessary intervening analysis and explanation (Moore, 1959: 15–16). Then, again, there is the simple problem of hasty generalization. By the logic of descriptive justification, if new surveys showed that managers were abandoning stakeholder orientations, or if the legal support for broad stakeholder interests were to weaken, the theory would be invalidated. But this observation offers a significant clue about the nature of the theory itself, because few if any of its adherents would be likely to abandon it, even if current legal or managerial trends were to shift. This suggests that the descriptive support for the stakeholder theory, as well as the critiques of this support to be found in the literature, are of limited significance and that the most important issues for stakeholder theory lie elsewhere.

INSTRUMENTAL JUSTIFICATIONS

Because the descriptive approach to grounding a stakeholder theory is inadequate, justifications based on a connection between stakeholder strategies and organizational performance should be examined. Consider, for example, the simple hypothesis that corporations whose managers adopt stakeholder principles and practices will perform better financially than those who do not. This hypothesis has never been tested directly, and its testing involves some formidable challenges. (Clarkson's ongoing work is the only significant effort of this type known to us; cf. Clarkson, Deck, & Shiner, 1992.) The view that stakeholder management and favorable performance go hand in hand has, however, become commonplace in the management literature, both professional and academic. The earliest direct statement is probably that of General Robert E. Wood, then-CEO of Sears, in 1950: "All I can say is that if the other three parties named above [customers, employees, community] are properly taken care of, the stockholder will benefit in the long pull" (quoted in Worthy, 1984: 64). A recent effort to

introduce practicing managers to the stakeholder concept and to improve their ability to implement stakeholder management practices is the work of Savage, Nix, Whitehead, and Blair (1991). Brummer (1991) cited not only Freeman (1989) but also Ackoff; Manning; Maslow; Peters, and Waterman; Starling; Sturdivant; and others in support of stakeholder theory's instrumental base.

Unfortunately, the large literature dealing with the connections, if any, between various aspects of corporate social performance or ethics, on one hand, and conventional financial and market performance indicators, on the other, does not translate easily into a stakeholder theory context. Whatever value the social/financial performance studies may have on their own merits, most of them do not include reliable indicators of the stakeholder management (i.e., the independent variable) side of the relationship. There is some evidence, based on analysis of the *Fortune* corporate reputation surveys, that the satisfaction of multiple stakeholders need not be a zero sum game (i.e., that benefits to one stakeholder group need not come entirely at the expense of another) (Preston & Sapienza, 1990). As previously noted, Kotter and Heskett's (1992) case studies of a small number of high-performance companies indicated that the managers of those companies tend to emphasize the interests of all major stakeholder groups in their decisionmaking. However, there is as yet no compelling empirical evidence that the optimal strategy for maximizing a firm's conventional financial and market performance is stakeholder management.

Analytical Arguments

Even without empirical verification, however, stakeholder management can be linked to conventional concepts of organizational success through analytical argument. The main focus of this effort in the recent literature builds on established concepts of principal-agent relations (Jensen & Mechling, 1976) and the firm as a nexus of contracts (Williamson & Winter, 1991). Agency theory and firm-as-contract theory, although arising from different sources, are closely related and share a common emphasis: efficiency. (They also share the terminology and methodology of the new transactions costs literature, cf. Williamson, 1985.) Agency theorists argue that corporations are structured to minimize the costs of getting some participants (the agents) to do what other participants (the principals) desire. Firm-as-contract theorists argue that participants agree to cooperate with each other within organizations (i.e., through contracts), rather than simply deal with each other through the market, to minimize the costs of search, coordination, insecurity, etc.

Hill and Jones (1992: 132, 134) are responsible for the most ambitious attempt to integrate the stakeholder concept with agency theory (see also Sharplin & Phelps, 1989). These authors enlarged the standard principal agent paradigm of financial economics, which emphasizes the relationship between shareowners and managers, to create "stakeholder-agency theory," which constitutes, in their view, "a generalized theory of agency." According to this conception, managers "can be seen as the agents of [all] other stakeholders." They noted that stakeholders differ among themselves with respect to (a) the *importance* (to them) of their stake in the firm and (b) their *power* vis-à-vis the managers. They also noted that there is considerable friction within the stakeholder-agent negotiation process—some of it because of some participants' ability to retard equilibrating adjustments that are unfavorable to themselves. They therefore argued that there is no reason to assume that stakeholder-agent relationships are in equilibrium at any particular time. (This contrasts sharply with the "perfect markets" hypothesis favored in the finance literature.) In their view, the process, direction, and speed of adaptation in stakeholder-agent relationships, rather than the equilibrium set of contributions and rewards, should be the primary focus of analysis. This brief summary cannot

do justice to their rich conception, but the key point for current purposes is that the stakeholders are drawn into relationships with the managers to accomplish organizational tasks as efficiently as possible; hence, the stakeholder model is linked instrumentally to organizational performance.

A similar theme emerges from the firm-as-contract analysis of Freeman and Evan (1990; see also Evan & Freeman, 1988). They recommended integrating the stakeholder concept with the Coasian view of the firm-as-contract and a Williamson-style analysis of transaction costs to "conceptualize the firm as set of multilateral contracts over time." According to Freeman and Evan,

> Managers administer contracts among employees, owners, suppliers, customers, and the community. Since each of these groups can invest in asset specific transactions which affect the other groups, methods of conflict resolution, or safeguards must be found. (1990: 352)

They emphasized that all parties have an equal right to bargain, and therefore that a minimal condition for the acceptance of such multi-partite arrangements by each contracting party is a notion of "fair contract," i.e., governance rules that "ensure that the interests of all parties are at least taken into consideration" (1990: 352). Once again, the stakeholder model (and its implementation through a set of acceptable implicit contracts) is seen as essential to successful organizational performance.

The stakeholder interpretations of both agency theory and firm-as-contract theory give special attention to the differential position and special role of managers vis-à-vis all other stakeholders. Hill and Jones (1992: 140) emphasized "information asymmetry" between managers and other stakeholders and contrasted the concentration of resource control by managers with the diffusion of control within stakeholder groups in which there may be no mechanism to gain command over a significant portion of the group's total resourcep. Evan and Freeman (1993: 102–103) asserted that "management has a duty of safeguarding the welfare of the abstract entity that is the corporation" and of balancing the conflicting claims of multiple stakeholders to achieve this goal. They further declared

> A stakeholder theory of the firm must redefine the purpose of the firm. . . . The very purpose of the firm is, in our view, to serve as a vehicle for coordinating stakeholder interests. (102–103)

According to this perspective, success in satisfying multiple stakeholder interests—rather than in meeting conventional economic and financial criteria—would constitute the ultimate test of corporate performance.

But how will multiple and diverse stakeholders be assured that their interests are being coordinated in ways that lead to the most favorable possible results for themselves (i.e., the most favorable results consistent with the requirements of other stakeholders)? Hill and Jones (1992: 140–143) stressed the importance of (a) monitoring devices that have the effect of reducing information asymmetry (e.g., public reporting requirements) and (b) enforcement mechanisms, including law, "exit" (the possibility, or credible threat, of withdrawal from the relationship), and "voice." Freeman and Evan (1993) emphasized the notion of fairness. Going beyond the notion of "fair contracting," they recommended that the criterion of "fairness" in stakeholder bargains be a Rawlsian "veil of ignorance." Under a "veil of ignorance," parties to a bargain agree upon a set of possible outcomes prior to determining which outcome will be received by which party (e.g., one person cuts the cake, another takes the first slice) (Rawls, 1971, cited in Freeman & Evan, 1990: 352–353).

Both pairs of analysts, Hill and Jones and Freeman and Evan, placed greater emphasis on the process of multiple-stakeholder coordination than on the specific agreements/bargains. Both groups stressed that mutual and voluntary acceptability of bargains by all contracting stakeholders is the necessary criterion for efficient contracts. Both neglected the roles of potential stakeholders not conspicuously involved in explicit or implicit contracts with the firm. The two pairs of authors differed slightly in one respect: Hill and Jones saw the network of relationships as consisting of separate implicit contracts between each stakeholder group and "management" (as a central node), whereas Freeman and Evan ultimately viewed the firm "as a series of multilateral contracts among [all] stakeholders" (1990: 354).

Weaknesses of Instrumental Justifications

Perhaps the most important similarity between these two independent attempts to justify the stakeholder model lies in the fact that although they draw initially on the conceptual apparatus of instrumental or efficiency-based theories (i.e., principal-agent relations and "firm-as-contract" theory), they ultimately rely upon noninstrumental or normative arguments. This shift is less conspicuous in the case of Hill and Jones, who implied that monitoring and enforcement mechanisms will be sufficient to curb opportunistic behavior by managers at the expense of other stakeholders. The authors would no doubt agree, however, that the ultimate success of stakeholder-agency theory would require a fundamental shift in managerial objectives away from shareowners and toward the interests of all stakeholders; such a shift would necessarily involve normative, rather than purely instrumental, considerations. Freeman and Evan's recourse to a Rawlsian concept of "fairness" as the ultimate criterion for stakeholder bargains is an overt elevation of normative criteria over instrumental ones. No theorist, including Rawls, has ever maintained that bargains reached on the basis of a "veil of ignorance" would maximize efficiency. By elevating the fairness principle to a central role, Freeman and Evan shifted their attention from ordinary economic contracts of the sort envisaged by Coase, Williamson, and the mainstream agency theorists, which are governed by individual efficiency considerations. Instead, they emphasized what have been called "heuristic" or "social" contracts that rest upon broad normative principles governing human conduct (Donaldson & Dunfee, 1994a,b).

It should come as no surprise that stakeholder theory cannot be fully justified by instrumental considerations. The empirical evidence is inadequate, and the analytical arguments, although of considerable substance, ultimately rest on more than purely instrumental grounds. This conclusion carries an important implication: Although those who use the stakeholder concept often cite its consistency with the pursuit of conventional corporate performance objectives (and there is no notable evidence of its *in*consistency), few of them would abandon the concept if it turned out to be only *equally* efficacious as other conceptions. O'Toole (1991: 18–19) for example, examined a case in which the economic consequences of stakeholder vs. conventional management "ended up neutral"; he stressed that "it is the *moral consequences* that are at issue" and described stakeholder analysis as "the sine quo non of business virtue" (emphasis in the original).

NORMATIVE JUSTIFICATIONS

The normative basis for stakeholder theory involves its connection with more fundamental and better-accepted philosophical concepts. The normative assumptions of traditional economic theory are too feeble to support stakeholder theory, and the concept of a free market populated with free and rational preference seekers, however correct and important, is compatible with both stakeholder and nonstakeholder perspectives. Of course, the two normative propositions stated at the beginning of this article—that stakeholders are identified by *their* interest in the affairs of the corporation and that the inter-ests of all stakeholders have intrinsic value—can be viewed as axiomatic principles that require no further justification. Unfortunately, this approach provides no basis for responding to critics who reject these propositions out of hand.

One way to construct a normative foundation for the stakeholder model is to examine its principal competitor, the model of *management* control in the interests of shareowners, as represented by the business judgment rule. As noted in previous sections, there is considerable criticism of this model on descriptive grounds. Pejovich (1990: 58) noted that in the modern corporation (as opposed to the owner-managed firm) the rights of shareowners are "attenuated" by the dispersion of ownership and by high agency costs; he stressed that "the *economic system*," not "the *legal system*," is responsible for this "attenuation of the right of ownership" (emphasis in original). Many direct observers (e.g., Geneen & Moscow, 1984; Pickens, 1987) have questioned managers' devotion to shareowner welfare, and survey results such as those of Alkhafaji (1989) and Posner and Schmidt (1992) provide statistical support for these perceptions.

But the management serving the shareowners model (i.e., the principal-agent model in its standard financial economics form) is not only descriptively inaccurate; careful analysis reveals that it is normatively unacceptable as well. Changes in state incorporation laws to reflect a "constituency" perspective have been mentioned. The normative basis for these changes in current mainstream legal thinking is articulated in the recent American Law Institute report, *Principles of Corporate Governance* (1992). The relevant portion of this document begins by affirming the central corporate objective of "enhancing corporate profit and shareholder gain," but it immediately introduces qualifications: "Even if corporate profit and shareholder gain are not thereby enhanced," the corporation *must* abide by law and *may* "take into account ethical considerations" and engage in philanthropy (Sec. 2.01(a)(b); 1992: 69). The accompanying commentary explicitly affirmed the stakeholder concept:

> The modern corporation by its nature creates interdependencies with a variety of groups with whom the corporation has a legitimate concern, such as employees, customers, suppliers, and members of the communities in which the corporation operates. (1992: 72)

The commentary further noted that response to social and ethical considerations is often consistent with long-run (if not short-run) increases in profit and value, but it continues

> Nevertheless, observation suggests that corporate decisions are not infrequently made on the basis of ethical consideration even when doing so would not enhance corporate profit or shareholder gain. *Such behavior is not only appropriate, but desirable. Corporate officials are not less morally obliged than any other citizens to take ethical considerations into account, and it would be unwise social policy to preclude them from doing so.* . . . [The text] does not impose a legal obligation to take ethical considerations into account. However, the absence of a legal obligation to follow ethical principles does not mean that corporate decisionmakers are not subject to the same ethical considerations as other members of society. (American Law Institute, 1992: 80-82, emphasis added)

FORMAL ANALYSIS: THEORY OF PROPERTY

To go beyond this practical rejection of the "management serving the shareowners" model, more formal normative justifications of stakeholder theory might be based either on broad theories of philosophical ethics, such as utilitarianism, or on narrower "middle-level" theories derived from the notion a "social contract" exists between corporations and society. A comprehensive survey of this terrain would go far beyond the scope of this article, and much of it has been recently traversed by others (Brummer, 1991; Freeman, 1991; see also, Donaldson, 1982). Here, we offer a brief sketch of a normative basis for

the stakeholder theory that combines several different philosophical approaches and that is, we believe, original in the literature. We argue that the stakeholder theory can be normatively based on the evolving theory of property.

There is a subtle irony in proposing that the stakeholder model can be justified on the basis of the theory of property, because the traditional view has been that a focus on property rights justifies the dominance of shareowners interests. Indeed, the fact that property rights are the critical base for conventional shareowner-dominance views makes it all the more significant that the current trend of thinking with respect to the philosophy of property runs in the opposite direction. In fact, this trend—as presented in the now-classic contributions of Coase (1960) and Honore (1961) and in more recent works by Becker (1978, 1992a,b,c) and Munzer (1992) —runs strongly counter to the conception that private property exclusively enshrines the interests of owners.

Considerable agreement now exists as to the theoretical definition of property as a "bundle" of many rights, some of which may be limited. More than 30 years ago, Coase (1960: 44) chided economists for adhering to a simplistic concept of ownership:

> We may speak of a person owning land . . . but what the land-owner in fact possesses is the right to carry out a circumscribed list of actions. The rights of a land-owner are not unlimited . . . [This] would be true under any system of law. A system in which the rights of individuals were unlimited would be one in which there were no rights to acquire.

Honore (1961) specifically included the notion of restrictions against harmful uses within the definition of property itself. Pejovich (1990: 27–28) probably the most conservative economic theorist working in this area, emphasized that "property rights are relations between individuals" and thus "it is wrong to separate human rights from property rights"; he further noted that "the right of ownership is not an unrestricted right."

The notion that property rights are embedded in human rights and that restrictions against harmful uses are intrinsic to the property rights concept clearly brings the interests of others (i.e., of non-owner stakeholders) into the picture. Of course, which uses of property should be restricted and *which* persons should count as stakeholders remain unspecified. Simply bringing non-owner stakeholders into the conception of property does not provide by itself justification for stakeholder arguments assigning managerial responsibilities toward specific groups, such as employees and customers. The important point, however, is that the contemporary theoretical concept of private property clearly does not ascribe unlimited rights to owners and hence does not support the popular claim that the responsibility of managers is to act solely as agents for the shareowners. (The necessary compromise between individual property rights and other considerations is highlighted in the "takings" issue—i.e., modified to protect the interest of others or society in general. For a survey of current views on this complex matter, see Mercuro, 1992.)

These comments examine the *scope* of property rights, but it is also relevant to examine their *source* (i.e., What basic principles determine *who* should get (and be allowed to keep) *what* in society?) Unless property rights are regarded as simple, self-evident moral conceptions, they must be based on more fundamental ideas of distributive justice. The main contending theories of distributive justice include Utilitarianism, Libertarianism, and social contract theory (Becker, 1992). The battle among competing theories of distributive justice is most often a battle over which characteristics highlighted by the theories— such as need, ability, effort, and mutual agreement—are most relevant for determining fair distributions of wealth, income, etc. (The role of theories of justice within organizations is attracting considerable current attention, cf. Greenberg, 1987.)

For example, when the characteristic of *need* (a feature highlighted by Utilitarianism) is the criterion, the resulting theory of prop-

erty places formidable demands upon property owners to mitigate their self-interest in favor of enhancing the interests (i.e., meeting the needs) of others. When *ability* or *effort* (features highlighted by Libertarianism) are the criteria, the resulting theory leaves property owners freer to use their resources (acquired, it is assumed, as a result of ability and effort) as they see fit. Social contract theory places primary emphasis on expressed or implied understandings among individuals and groups as to appropriate distributions and uses of property.

Many of the most respected contemporary analysts of property rights reject the notion that any *single* theory of distributive justice is universally applicable. Indeed, it seems counterintuitive that any one principle could account for all aspects of the complex bundle of rights and responsibilities that constitutes "property." Beginning with Becker's (1978) analysis, the trend is toward theories that are pluralistic, allowing more than one fundamental principle to play a role (Becker, 1992a; see also, Munzer, 1992). But if a pluralistic theory of property rights is accepted, then the connection between the theory of property and the stakeholder theory becomes explicit. All critical characteristics underlying the classic theories of distributive justice are present among the stakeholders of a corporation, as they are conventionally conceived and presented in contemporary stakeholder theory. For example, the "stake" of long-term employees who have worked to build and maintain a successful business operation is essentially based on effort. The stake of people living in the surrounding community may be based on their need, say, for clean air or the maintenance of their civic infrastructure. Customer stakes are based on the satisfactions and protections implicitly promised in the market offer, and so on. One need not make the more radical assertion that such stakes constitute formal or legal property rights, although some forceful critics of current corporate governance arrangements appear to hold this view (Nader & Green, 1973). All that is necessary is to show that such characteristics, which are the same as those giving rise to fundamental concepts of property rights, give various groups a moral interest, commonly referred to as a "stake," in the affairs of the corporation. Thus, the normative principles that underlie the contemporary pluralistic theory of property rights also provide the foundation for the stakeholder theory as well.

MANAGERIAL IMPLICATIONS

A full discussion of the managerial implications of this analysis would require much more discussion. As a summary, the two points we emphasize are (a) the recognition of specific stakeholders and their stakes by managers and other stakeholders and (b) the role of managers and the *management function*, as distinct from the *persons* involved, within the stakeholder model. These two issues are intimately intertwined.

It is the responsibility of managers, and the management function, to select activities and direct resources to obtain benefits for legitimate stakeholders. The question is Who are the legitimate stakeholders? Some answers in the literature are, in our view, too narrow; others are too broad. The firm-as-contract view holds that legitimate stakeholders are identified by the existence of a contract, expressed or implied, between them and the firm. Direct input contributors are included, but environmental interests such as communities are also believed to have at least loose quasi-contracts (and, of course, sometimes very specific ones) with their business constituents.

We believe that the firm-as-contract perspective, although correct, is incomplete as a description of the corporation. For example, many business relationships with "communities" are so vague as to pass beyond even the broadest conception of "contract." The plant-closing controversy of the last couple of decades clearly shows that some communities had come to expect—and sometimes were able to enforce—stakeholder claims that

some firms clearly did not recognize. As another example, potential job applicants, unknown to the firm, nevertheless have a stake in being considered for a job (but not necessarily to get a job). Lacking any connection to the firm, these potential employees are difficult to view as participating in the firm by reason of a *contract*, either implied or explicit. (We do not mean, however to rule out possible relevance of so-called social contracts to such situations, cf. Donaldson & dunfee, 1994b). Stakeholders are identified through the actual or potential harms and benefits that they experience or anticipate experiencing as a result of the firm's actions or inactions. In practice, and in addition to legal requirements, appraisal of the legitimacy of such expectations is an important function of management, often in concert with other already recognized stakeholders.

Excessive breadth in the identification of stakeholders has arisen from a tendency to adopt definitions such as "anything influencing or influenced by" the firm (Freeman, 1984, quoting with approval Thompson, 1967). This definition opens the stakeholder set to actors that form part of the firm's environment—and that, indeed, may have some impact on its activities—but that have no specific stake in the firm itself. That is, they stand to gain no particular benefit from the firms's successful operation. The two types of interests that have cropped up most frequently in this connection are (a) competitors and (b) the media. Competitors were introduced as factors that have "an influence on managerial autonomy" in Dill's 1958 article, which is appropriately cited in the literature as a precursor of stakeholder analysis. However, neither the term *stakeholder* nor the notion of a *stake* (i.e., potential benefit) were explicitly introduced in Dill's analysis. In any event, in the normal course of events, competitors do not seek benefits from the focal firm's success; on the contrary, they may stand to lose whatever the focal firm gains. Competitive firms may, of course, join in common collaborative activities (e.g., through trade associations), but here the shared (noncompetitive) interests account for the stakeholder relationship. The notion that the media should be routinely recognized as stakeholders was originally introduced by Freeman (1984), but it seems to have been eliminated (without explicit explanation) from his later writings. It is essential to draw a clear distinction between influencers and stakeholders: some actors in the enterprise (e.g., large investors) may be both, but some recognizable stakeholders (e.g., the job applicants) have no influence, and some influencers (e.g., the media) have no stakes.

The role of managers within the stakeholder framework described in the literature is also contradictory. Aoki (1984), for example, recognized only investors and employees as significant stakeholders and saw managers as essentially "referees" between these two stakeholder groups. He acknowledged neither (a) the essential role of management in the identification of stakeholders nor (b) the fact that managers are, themselves, stakeholders—and, indeed, a very privileged class of stakeholders—in the enterprise. Williamson (1985) is almost alone among academic analysts in emphasizing the fact that the managers of a firm are one of its most important and powerful constituencies and that—wittingly or unwittingly—they are extremely likely to practice opportunistic and self-aggrandizing behavior.

This last point is absolutely critical for our argument, and recognition of it confirms our most important proposition: that the stakeholder theory is fundamentally normative. We observed at the close of our discussion of instrumental justifications that the instrumental case for stakeholder management cannot be satisfactorily proved. Here we restate that observation and add that the ultimate managerial implication of the stakeholder theory is that managers *should* acknowledge the validity of diverse stakeholder interests and *should* attempt to respond to them within a mutually supportive framework, because that is a moral requirement for the legitimacy of the management function.

It is feared by some that a shift from the traditional shareowner orientation to a stakeholder orientation will make it more difficult to detect and discipline self-serving behavior by managers, who may always claim to be serving some broad set of stakeholder interests while they increase their powers and emoluments. Indeed, Orts (1992: 123) saw this as the "greatest danger" of the new "constituency statutes" for corporate governance, although he nevertheless supported the constituency approach.

Our response to this fear is twofold: First, the conventional model of the corporation, in both legal and managerial forms, has failed to discipline self-serving managerial behavior. In this era of multi-million dollar CEO compensation packages that continue to increase even when profits and wages decline (Bok, 1993), it is difficult to conceive of managers having greater scope for self-serving behavior than they have already. Second, the stakeholder model we have advanced here entails comprehensive restrictions on such behavior. Indeed, its very foundation prohibits any undue attention to the interests of any single constituency. To be sure, it remains to implement in law the sanctions, rules, and precedents that support the stakeholder conception of the corporation; in short, it remains to develop the legal version of the stakeholder model. [See, for example, Eisenberg's (1976) attempt to restructure the legal model of the corporation.] Yet over time, statutory and common law are almost certainly capable of achieving arrangements that encourage a broader, stakeholder conception of management—one which eschews singleminded subservience to shareowners' interests—while at the same time restraining the moral hazard of self-serving managers.

CONCLUSION

We have argued that the stakeholder theory is "managerial" and recommends the attitudes, structures, and practices that, taken together, constitute a *stakeholder* management philosophy. The theory goes beyond the purely descriptive observation that "organizations have stakeholders," which, although true, carries no direct managerial implications. Furthermore, the notion that stakeholder management contributes to successful economic performance, although widely believed (and not patently inaccurate), is insufficient to stand alone as a basis for the stakeholder theory. Indeed, the most thoughtful analyses of why stakeholder management might be casually related to corporate perfor-

mance ultimately resort to normative arguments in support of their views. For these reasons, we believe that the ultimate justification for the stakeholder theory is to be found in its normative base. The plain truth is that the most prominent alternative to the stakeholder theory (i.e., the "management serving the shareowners" theory) is morally untenable. The theory of property rights, which is commonly supposed to support the conventional view, in fact—in its modern and pluralistic form—supports the stakeholder theory instead.

REFERENCES

Alkhafaji, A.F. 1989. *A stakeholder approach to corporate governance: Managing in a dynamic environment*. New York: Quorum Books.

American Law Institute. 1992. *Principles of corporate governance: Analysis and recommendations*. Proposed Final Draft (March 31, 1992). Philadelphia.

Anderson, J.W., Jr. 1989. *Corporate social responsibility*. New York: Quorum Books.

Aoki, M. 1984. *The co-operative game theory of the firm*. Oxford: Clarendon Press.

Aupperle, K.E., Carroll, A.B., & Hatfield, J.D. 1985. An empirical examination of the relationship between corporate social responsibility and profitability. *Academy of Management Journal*, 28(2): 446–463.

Barton, S.L., Hill, N.C., & Sundaram, S. 1989. An empirical test of stakeholder theory predictions of capital structure. *Financial Management*, 18(1): 36–44.

Baumhart, R. 1968. *An honest profit: What businessmen say about ethics in business*. New York: Holt, Rinehart and Winston.

Becker, L.C. 1978. *Property rights*. London: Routledge & Kegan Paul.

Becker, L.C. 1992a. Property. In L.D. Becker & C.B. Becker (Eds.), *Encyclopedia of ethics*, vol. 2: 1023–1027. New York: Garland.

Becker, L.C. 1992b. Places for pluralism. *Ethics*, 102: 707–719.

Becker, L.C. 1992c. Too much property. *Philosophy and Public Affairs*, 21: 196-206.

Berle, A., & Means, G. 1932. *Private property and the modern corporation*. New York: Macmillan.

Bok, D. 1993. *The cost of talent: How executives and professionals are paid and how it affects America*. New York: Free Press.

Brenner, S.N., & Cochran, P. 1991. *The stakeholder theory of the firm: Implications for business and society theory and research*. Paper presented at the annual meeting of the International Association for Business and Society, Sundance, UT.

Brenner, S.N., & Molander, E.A. 1977. Is the ethics of business changing? *Harvard Business Review*, 58(1): 54–65.

Brummer, J.J. 1991. *Corporate responsibility and legitimacy: An interdisciplinary analysis*. New York: Greenwood Press.

Carroll, A.B. 1989. *Business and society: Ethics and stakeholder management*. Cincinnati, OH: South-Western.

Chirelstein, M.A. 1974. Corporate law reform. In J.W. McKie (Ed.), *Social responsibility and the business predicament*: 41–78. Washington, DC: The Brookings Institution.

Civil Rights Act. Title VII: 42 USC §§ 2000e-2a(1) & (2). 1982.

Clarkson, M.B.E. 1991. Defining, evaluating, and managing corporate social performance: A stakeholder management model. In J.E. Post (Ed.). *Research in corporate social performance and policy*: 331–358. Greenwich, CT: JAI Press.

Clarkson, M.B.E., Deck, M.C., & Shiner, J.J. 1992. *The stakeholder management model in practice*. Paper presented at the annual meeting of the Academy of Management, Las Vegas, NV.

Coase, R.H. 1937. The nature of the firm. In O.E. Williamson & S.G. Winter (Eds.), *The nature of the firm: Origins, evolution, and development:* 18–33. New York: Oxford University Press.

Coase, R.H. 1960. The problem of social cost. *Journal of Law and Economics*, 3: 1–44.

Cochran, P.L., & Wood, R.A. 1984. Corporate social responsibility and financial performance. *Academy of Management Journal*, 27(1): 42–56.

Companies Act, 1980. Great Britain.

Cornell, B., & Shapiro, A.C. 1987. Corporate stakeholders and corporate finance. *Financial Management*, 16: 5–14.

The Economist. 1992. [Corporate governance special section] September 11: 52-62. *CTS Corp. v. Dynamics Corp. of America.* 1987. U.S. Supr., 481, 69, 87.

Cyert, R.M., & March, J.G. 1963. *A behavioral theory of the firm.* Englewood Cliffs, NJ: Prentice Hall.

Dill, W.R. 1958. Environment as an influence on managerial autonomy. *Administrative Science Quarterly*, 2: 409–443.

Dodd, E.M., Jr. 1932. For whom are corporate managers trustees? *Harvard Law Review*, 45: 1145– 1163.

Donaldson, T. 1982. *Corporations and morality.* Englewood Cliffs, NJ: Prentice Hall.

Donaldson, T., & Dunfee, T.W. In press. Integrative social contracts theory: A communitarian conception of economic ethics. *Economics and Philosophy.*

Donaldson, T., & Dunfee, T.W. 1994b. Towards a unified conception of business ethics: Integrative social contracts theory. *Academy of Management Review.* 252–284.

Eisenberg, M.A. 1976. *The structure of the corporation: A legal analysis.* Toronto: Little, Brown.

Evan, W.M., & Freeman, R.E. 1988. A stakeholder theory of the modern corporation: Kantian capitalism. In T. Beauchamp & N. Bowie (Eds.), *Ethical theory and business:* 75–93. Englewood Cliffs, NJ: Prentice Hall.

Freeman, R.E. 1984. *Strategic management: A stakeholder approach.* Boston: Pitman.

Freeman, R.E. (Ed.) 1991. *Business ethics: The state of the art.* New York: Oxford University Press.

Freeman, R.E., & Evan, W.M. 1990. Corporate governance: A stakeholder interpretation. *The Journal of Behavioral Economics*, 19(4): 337–359.

Freeman, R.E., & Gilbert, D.R., Jr. 1987. Managing stakeholder relationships. In S.P. Sethi & C.M. Falbe (Eds.), *Business and society:* 397–423. Lexington, MA: Lexington Books.

Freeman, R.E., & Reed, D.L. 1983. Stockholders and stakeholders: A new perspective on corporate governance. *California Management Review*, 25(3): 88-106.

Friedman, M. 1970. The social responsibility of business is to increase its profits. *New York Times Magazine*, September: 32–33: 122, 126.

Geneen, H., & Moscow, A. 1984. *Managing.* Garden City, NY: Doubleday.

Goodpaster, K.E. 1991. Business ethics and stakeholder analysis. *Business Ethics Quarterly*, 1(1): 53–73.

Greenberg, J. 1987. A taxonomy of organizational justice theories. *Academy of Management Review*, 12(1): 9–22.

Halal, W.E. 1990. The new management: Business and social institutions in the information age. *Business in the Contemporary World.* Winter: 41–54.

Hill, C.W.L., & Jones, T.M. 1992. Stakeholder-agency theory. *Journal of Management Studies*, 29: 131–154.

Honore, A.M. 1961. Ownership. In A.G. Guest (Ed.), *Oxford essays in jurisprudence:* 107–47. Oxford: Clarendon Press.

Jensen, M.C. 1989. Eclipse of the public corporation. *Harvard Business Review*, 67(5): 61–74.

Jensen, M., & Mechling, W. 1976. Theory of the firm: Managerial behavior, agency costs, and capital structure. *Journal of Financial Economics*, 3 (October): 305–360.

Kotter, J., & Heskett, J. 1992. *Corporate culture and performance.* New York: Free Press.

Kreiner, P., & Bambri, A. 1991. Influence and information in organization-stakeholder relationships. In J.E. Post (Ed.), *Research in corporate social performance and policy*, vol. 12: 3–36. Greenwich, CT: JAI Press.

Kuhn, J.W., & Shriver, D.W., Jr. 1991. *Beyond success: Corporations and their critics in the 1990s.* New York: Oxford University Press.

Marcus, A.A. 1993. *Business and society: Ethics, government and the world economy.* Homewood, IL: Irwin.

McGuire, J.B., Sundgren, A., & Schneeweis, T. 1988. Corporate social responsibility and firm financial performance. *Academy of Management Journal*, 31: 354–372.

Mercuro, N. (Ed.). 1992. *Taking property and just compensation.* Boston: Kluwer.

Moore, G.E. 1959. *Principia ethica* (1903) Cambridge, England: Cambridge University Press.

Munzer, S.R. 1992. *A theory of property.* New York: Cambridge University Press.

Nader, R., & Green, M.J. (Eds.). 1973. *Corporate power in America.* New York: Grossman.

Orts, E.W. 1992. Beyond shareholders: Inter-preting corporate constituency statutes. *The George Washington Law Review*, 61(1): 14–135.

O'Toole, J. 1985. *Vanguard management*. Garden City, NY: Doubleday.

O'Toole, J. 1991. Do good, do well: The business enterprise trust awards. *California Management Review*, 33(3): 9–24.

Paramount Communications, Inc. v. Time, Inc. 1990. Del.Supr., 571A. 2d 1140.

Pejovich, S. 1990. *The economics of property rights: Towards a theory of comparative systems*. Dordrecht, The Netherlands: Kluwer Academic Publishers.

Pickens, T.B. 1987. *Boone*. Boston: Houghton Mifflin.

Posner, B.Z., & Schmidt, W.H. 1984. Values and the American manager. *California Management Review*, 26(3): 202–216.

Preston, L.E., & Sapienza, H.J. 1990. Stakeholder management and corporate performance. *Journal of Behavioral Economics*, 19: 361–375.

Preston, L.E., Sapienza, H.J., & Miller, R.D. 1991. Stakeholders, shareholders, managers: Who gains what from corporate performance? In A. Etzioni & P.R. Lawrence (Eds.), *Socio-economics: Toward a new synthesis*: 149–65. Armonk, NY: M.E. Sharpe.

Rawls, J. 1971. *A theory of justice*. Cambridge, MA: Harvard University Press.

Savage, G.T., Nix, T.W., Whitehead, C.J., & Blair, J.D. 1991. Strategy for assessing and managing organizational stakeholders. *Academy of Management Executive*, 5(2): 61–75.

Sharplin, A. & Phelps, L.D. 1989. A stakeholder apologetic for management. *Business and Professional Ethics Journal*, 8(2): 41–53.

Thompson, J. 1967. *Organizations in action*. New York: McGraw-Hill.

Unocal Corp. v. Mesa Petroleum Co. 1985. Del. Supr., 493 A.2d 946.

Wang, J., & Dewhirst, H.D. 1992. Boards of directors and stakeholder orientation. *Journal of Business Ethics*, 11: 115–123.

Washington Post. 1993. Pepco bias suit heads for 38 million settlement. February 21: A1.

Weidenbaum, M., & Vogt, S. 1987. Takeovers and stockholders: Winners and losers. *California Management Review*, 29(4): 157–168.

Williamson, O.E. 1985. *The economic institutions of capitalism*. New York: Free Press.

Williamson, O.E., & Winter, S.G. (Eds.). 1991. *The nature of the firm: Origins, evolution, and development*. New York: Oxford University Press.

Wood, D.J. 1991a. Corporate social performance revisited. *Academy of Management Review*, 16: 691–718.

Wood, D.J. 1991b. Social issues in management: Theory and research in corporate social performance. *Journal of Management*, 17: 383–405.

Worthy, J.C. 1984. *Shaping an American institution: Robert E. Wood and Sears, Roebuck*. Urbana: University of Illinois.

SOCIETAL PRESSURES ON BUSINESS

In whose interest?

Oliver Williams

Social responsibility resolutions, almost non-existent less than twenty years ago, are now an important force in the corporate world. In 1989, 170 resolutions came to a vote, while in 1988 only 156 were presented to the shareholders. In the 1990s, a typical year might have some 200 resolutions, presented, for the most part, by religious organizations. These resolutions concern a wide array of social responsibility issues including the environment, affordable housing, family farms, smoking and health, food irradiation, transfer of technology, South Africa, Northern Ireland, infant formula, military issues, animal issues, the world debt crisis, energy issues, political action committees, and equal employment.[1]

The social responsibility resolution is only one of the tools used by citizen groups to directly affect the corporation; other direct measures include demonstrations and boycotts as well as lawsuits brought against companies. Indirectly, interest groups have an enormous influence on corporate America by actively participating in all phases of the public policy process; much of the social regulation in place today can trace its origin to the initiative, lobbying and research of one or a coalition of interest groups. The number of interest groups and lobbies in Washington, D.C. is staggering; for example, over 30 groups are lobbying for women's issues, 15 for the elderly, 50 for minorities and 30 groups focus on environmental issues. The names of many of these groups have become household words: Common Cause, the Sierra Club, the National Wildlife Federation, Ralph Nader's Congress Watch, Friends of the Earth, The Council on Economic Priorities, the National Organization for Women, and TransAfrica, to name but a few.[2]

The focus of this article will be to outline some of the reasons for the dramatic increase in citizen activism, particularly from church institutions. It will also analyze several recent cases where activists have directly confronted corporate policy in order to glean some insight that may be helpful for the future.

LIVING BETWEEN THE TIMES

Church coalitions and other activist groups that are critical of business ultimately attribute their opposition to their interest in advancing a more humane society; their protests are a tangible way of moving toward this vision. Yet it was not so long ago that there was a strong social consensus that the best way for business to advance a humane society was to compete efficiently in the mar-

Part of this article appeared in an earlier version in Oliver F. Williams, "Business and Church Activism in America" in *Business and Society*, eds., S. Prakash Sethi and Cecilia M. Falbe (Lexington, MA: Lexington Books, 1987), pp. 378–390.

ket. Providing quality goods and services at the best price was taken to be business's contribution to the common good. Executives today are living between the times; that is, they are caught between the time when there was a strong social consensus that the market mechanism was the best way to control business activity, and some possible future time when society has a clear consensus about how business institutions ought to advance human welfare.

We are living in a time when this new consensus is in the making. What is clear is that economic language—the language that traditionally often provided the sole rationale for corporate decisions—is not in itself acceptable to religious activists and many other socially concerned persons. Listening to many discussions between management and corporate critics, one is struck by the fact that they are often speaking different languages: management defends decisions in the economic language of profit and loss, and critics question the same decisions in the ethical language of justice and rights. The parties of such discussions usually pass like ships in the night; in the end, these conversations generate much heat and little light.

The implications of living between the times are far-reaching and affect how managers come to think of themselves. Most people want to be decent and moral, and they would like their efforts in business to reflect these characteristics. Under the former consensus on values in the social environment, managers could have some confidence that they were meeting their obligation to human welfare by participating in the market. Today, business executives are often caught in the middle. While most would acknowledge that they must consider the social costs of economic decisions, it is seldom clear where the moral person should draw the line in assessing the social and economic values at issue. We know business corporations are not the Red Cross, but what should they be? It is here that constructive dialogue with church and other activists may be helpful.

Until relatively recently, market and legal signals were the only major social forces that caught the attention of top management. Consumer sovereignty reigned in that astute management carefully tracked consumer needs and expectations and responded with the appropriate product and price to capture the market in question. Now top management must also respond to a whole array of non-market forces in the form of the activities of the various interest groups referenced above. What is at stake is the very legitimacy of the business corporation, for what is going on today is a rewriting of the implicit social contract between business and society. Society has more comprehensive expectations for business and, to some extent, business had better respond. However, while it is clear that a business has a responsibility to monitor and correct the problems it has caused in society, its so-called externalities such as pollution, it is unclear how much business can tackle other social ills in a community which are unrelated to the industry. Business must develop its own vision of its role in society and some sense of what it can and cannot do for society.

Implicit in the shareholder resolutions and various political strategies of the interest groups is a new vision of the role of business in society. Business is taken to be a major actor in a dynamic social system and the activists are attempting to forge the shape of business's new role. The challenge for top management is to be interactive in this process and have a hand in shaping its future destiny before public policy limits prerogatives.

WHY SO MUCH ACTIVISM?

What has given rise to this rather sudden increase in nonmarket forces or interest group activism? One of the most formative experiences that may have set the tone for activism in the United States was the civil rights movement of the 1960s. The many who participated in this event, both actively and passively, came to feel a new power to transform society. Evil did not have to be tolerated; unjust social structures could be changed with strategy and persistence. In my view, the experience of the civil rights movement, its use of the media and its creation of heroes provided the model and the power that brought the current activist movements to birth.

At the same time, several other important developments provided fertile soil for the growth of the activist movements. Traditionally the two major political parties were the vehicles that carried the concerns of the people through the public policy process, but they no longer function effectively in the eyes of many people. Interest groups today carry out many of the roles that were abdicated by the political parties. Also, during the last thirty years the media has achieved significant power to shape public opinion on social issues. Informed public opinion has led to financial and other support for a wide variety of groups championing social issues.

CHRISTIAN BELIEFS AND THE BUSINESS WORLD

While many can understand the proliferation of interest groups and the rise of shareholder activism with social responsibility resolutions as a development from an environment as described above, what is not clear is why the churches have become so prominent in some of these movements. For example, in any given year the majority of social responsibility resolutions have been initiated by church groups. It may be helpful to examine the historical evolution of church involvement in the economic life of the nation.

Religion has always been considered an important force in the shaping of American life. The Frenchman Alexis de Tocqueville, writing some one hundred fifty years ago, observed that religion played an essential role in America by shaping citizens who valued just and wholesome communities; he saw religion as crucial to the fabric of the nation.[3] Max Weber, in his famous *The Protes-*

tant Ethic and the Spirit of Capitalism, argues that capitalism would have never developed without the religious influence; some of the core virtues of religion—honesty, industry, frugality, and thrift—formed communities of men and women who were the most productive and creative in their work.

Today many mainline Protestant and Catholic churches, rather than foster "the spirit of capitalism," often appear to be its harshest critics. Through proxy resolutions, boycotts, removal of funds from banks with objectionable policies, and other strategies, church groups are increasingly applying direct pressure to business corporations. What sorts of religious convictions motivate church groups in their dealing with business? Are the churches intent on creating a culture adverse to business, or can corporate managers forge a more cooperative relationship with these powerful institutions?

Many business leaders are puzzled as to why mainline Protestant and Catholic churches are often critical of business corporations. Understanding the religious convictions of these church leaders is essential. A core conviction of Christians is that the ministry of Jesus was to proclaim the coming Kingdom of God. While this conviction has been unchanging, the way in which the term *Kingdom of God* has been understood in the Christian community has changed radically at various periods. A new meaning of *Kingdom of God* today has resulted in a self-understanding that often prompts Christians to oppose business corporations vigorously.

The first generation of Christians understood themselves as a special community chosen by God to prepare for the sudden arrival of his kingdom. They thought the world as they knew it was about to end, and that they would be part of a transcendent Kingdom of God, a new world somehow discontinuous with the present one. Later generations came to believe that the church was to be that community that strives for and points toward the Kingdom of God, a kingdom that would finally arrive in God's good time. The notion of a coming kingdom finds resonance in the human heart, for people have always been restless for a land of peace and happiness, of "milk and honey." In the Hebrew Scriptures the prophets speak of a time of the kingdom when the lion will lie peaceably with the lamb. Christian Scriptures record the teaching of Jesus and portray a vision of the qualities of the kingdom—peace, justice, harmony, and brotherhood. Throughout the history of Christian communities there have been a variety of ways of relating the kingdom of the times. While the notion of the kingdom provides a vision of the sort of life we ought to have, the question is whether one should try to realize the kingdom here and now, approximate it, or anticipate it?

For most of Christian history the Kingdom of God was thought to be present in the institutional church in a small way, only to be fully realized by God at the end of time. In the church communities, men and women, in the spirit of Christ, could grow in charity, compassion, generosity, and so on. They could live virtuous lives and anticipate the final coming of God's kingdom where his rule of love would finally reign. The intellectual giant who fashioned the theological synthesis that shaped the Catholic Church for over seven hundred years is Thomas Aquinas (1225–1274).[4] Aquinas, as a person of the time, was not primarily concerned with changing social structures or making the world a better place to live. For him, the whole purpose of life in this world was to become virtuous and thereby to prepare for eternal happiness in the next world. Focusing on the virtues highlighted in the Bible—faith, hope, and charity—and Aristotle's four cardinal virtues—wisdom, justice, fortitude, and temperance—Aquinas encouraged Christians to lead lives and to form societies that would accent growth in virtue.

Life as Aquinas knew it, in the thirteenth century, was based on an agricultural economy and, by contemporary standards, almost everyone was poor. Society was understood to be static, on a model ordained by God, where the ideal was for all to have sufficient goods for their particular state in life. Lords, peasants, craftsmen, and merchants were taken to be in their role according to the divine plan. Upward mobility was foreign to this world, and for one to strive to accrue wealth beyond one's level was thought to be sinful—the sin of avarice. Aquinas and other theologians of the time supplied much practical guidance on just prices, usury, and trade in order to promote and protect the virtuous character of Christians, but they would never go so far as to encourage the creation of wealth. Trade and all forms of wealth creation were suspect, for making money cultivates greed in the merchant's heart and greed corrupts the life of the community. In the Thomist perspective, honor ought to be given to virtuous persons, yet if some citizens are particularly ingenious at making money, honor will likely be bestowed on them for their riches; this will slowly erode the high moral quality of the community.

Until recent times the vision of life's purpose espoused by Aquinas was the dominant one of the churches. Today, however, there is the realization that God's plan entails that all should enjoy the good things of creation; the proclamation of the kingdom is understood to entail working for sociopolitical changes that are likely to alleviate the plight of the poor. While Christians have always been taught to be concerned for the poor, the traditional response was personal charity. Although the sixteenth-century reformers, following Martin Luther, championed structural changes in society to eliminate the causes of poverty, this emphasis was short-lived. Only in our own time do we hear the loud call from the churches for systemic changes in institutions so that wealth might be more equitably distributed.

The efforts toward systemic change and reform of business corporations are understood to be mandated by that belief that the church is the "budding and beginning of the Kingdom," and that this future kingdom, the one that God will finally bring about, lights up the visions of Christians and spurs them on to work for political forms of justice and peace here and now. The new role of the churches is to labor for the values of the Kingdom of God—justice, love, peace, brotherhood, and so on—in the sociopolitical order. To be sure, the churches never intend to deemphasize in any way their spiritual mission, but rather seek to draw out and make explicit the implications in the social order of living the Gospel. This new perspective is fully incorporated into the teachings of the churches.

THE SOURCES OF CONFLICT

In its basic thrust, the new church's emphasis on making the world a better place is quite congruent with the ideals of many business persons and organizations. To be sure, there will always be some tension, for the church perspective highlights God's intentions to have a world of peace and justice, and speaks in terms of ultimates that are only to be realized in eternity. The business perspective focuses on more proximate objectives and must always calculate the tradeoffs involved in employing resources efficiently; freedom is a key value for corporate managers, for the wider the scope of management prerogatives, the more likely the goal in question will be achieved.

The trick is to keep the inherent tension between business and the churches on a creative track rather than a destructive one. For example, where liberation theology dominates the church discussion, there has seldom been fruitful dialogue with the business community. Some discussion of the origin and aims of liberation theology may be helpful, since this theology is often influential in the churches of developing countries.

LIBERATION VERSUS GRADUALISM: A CONTEMPORARY DEBATE

In 1970, the World Council of Churches founded the Commission for the Churches Partici-pation in Development (CCPD); this commission has championed structural changes in society and advocated a liberation style of change in preference to the traditional gradualist approach. The World Council is presently dominated by Third World countries and its statements are sometimes militant and decidedly anticapitalist. John C. Bennett, noted Protestant social ethicist and leader in ecumenical affairs, comments that the "World Council . . . no longer reflects the older and more disciplined ethical thinking of the First World."[5] While critical, he is sympathetic to the Third World intellectuals; he goes on to say that "the First World theologians can be criticized for provincialism and complacency."

The liberation style of doing theology has its roots in the Catholic Church of Latin America, and is intended to be a direct challenge to Christians who seem all too comfortable with suffering and deprivation in this present world. The writings of these Latin American theologians are characterized by a concern to see the world from the viewpoint of poor persons, and by an all-pervasive call to realize justice and liberation from poverty, and to realize this vision soon. The dominant motif is the people's participation in overcoming their oppression. It is an emphasis on a rapid change in social structures that is characteristic of the liberation approach. Not surprisingly, liberation theology is often marked by strong anticapitalist and anti-American rhetoric; from a liberationist perspective, the United States and its economic system hold little promise for Third World development. Some church leaders, although they may not fully espouse liberation theology, often speak from its militant posture. For example, in an interview in *Forbes* magazine, Paulo Evaristo Carinal Arns Catholic archbishop of Sao Paulo, Brazil, when asked about the problems of inflation and unemployment in Brazil, responded, "These problems (are) consequences of the installation of the multinational corporations and of a savage capitalism that can produce these ills in order to reap greater profits later."[6] Many detailed studies by economists and scholars most sympathetic to the terrible plight of the poor in Brazil offer a much different analysis. In fact, many argue that multinationals and capitalism, with appropriate government regulation, are the only hope for the poor in Brazil.

Although there is agreement within the churches that the plight of the poor must be alleviated, there is debate over the appropriateness of liberation theology. Many are concerned with its affinity with leftist political movements. Some accuse it of too easily advocating violence as a means of social change. There are others, however, who consider it as one of the valid means of transforming society. Persons espousing this theology are sensitive people who have been deeply touched by the condition of the poor and want transformations now. There is little appetite to wait a century and a half—the time it took to fashion such wealth-producing capabilities in the West. There is scant mention of the cultivation of habits of industry and other virtues. From a liberation perspective, the key issues are not these. Rather, the focus in proclaiming the Kingdom of God is on a positive strategy to overcome "oppression of the poor by the rich" and a great optimism that together humankind can fashion a different sort of world. Gustavo Gutierrez, a pioneer in this theology, makes the point well in his *A Theology of Liberation.*[7]

From the point of view of today's corporate leaders, a key feature of this theology is that it has little patience in its crusade to make the world a better place. The champions of this theology are strident in their condemnation of multinationals and corporate capitalism. However, an important point here is that church leaders who espouse the more extreme forms of liberation theology are not typical, and that it would be a mistake to characterize mainline Protestant and Catholic leaders in this militant mold. For example, the March 1995 United Nations World Summit for Social Development held in Copenhagen reflected a marked interest by church leaders in market-based solutions to economic development as did the 1991 Roman Catholic encyclical Centesimus Annus (1991).

STRATEGIES OF CHURCH ACTIVISTS IN THE UNITED STATES

As two of the world's largest multinational institutions, the church and the business corporation have a pervasive influence throughout the world. While churches have always highlighted the essential connection between personal and social ethics, it is only in the last fifteen years that they have formulated strategies designed to influence the social impact of business corporations. The initial concern of churches was that their own considerable economic resources be invested with an eye toward social responsibility. Stemming from the doctrine of private property, church teaching stressed that ownership entails responsibility, and the churches tried to be models of what good economic stewardship might be.

To assist church bodies in their judgments on investment, the National Council of Churches established the Corporate Information Center (CIC) in 1971. In 1974, the CIC merged with an ad hoc group of Catholic religious orders and Protestant denominations that had formed to protest a proposed corporate mining venture in Puerto Rico. This new coalition, housed in the New York City headquarters of the National Council of Churches, is known as the Interfaith Center on Corporate Responsibility (ICCR). The staff of the center provides research on corporate social performance, and coordinates and formulates church activist strategies.

A good argument can be made that church critics are capitalism's best friend. The professional staffs of churches link the local congregations with national structures through a vast network. Activists form the church staffs and ICCR provide one channel for business leaders to keep informed of the fresh ideas of public concern. Social concern shareholder proposals, even if only representative of a minority, serve as an important safety valve. Many of the reforms enacted in business and government first surfaced in the writings and activities of church critics. Business's ability to respond to public concern is one reason it is still accepted as a vital part of our society. The continued legitimacy of the business corporation depends upon its ability to meet public expectations.

In a typical year, church proponents file over one hundred and fifty shareholder proposals but withdraw about 20 percent of these after dialogue and negotiation with the companies in question. The point here is that the church activists can be thought of as providing a service by surfacing issues of public concern such as equal employment opportunity, environmental issues, and plant closings, and that many of the apparent conflicts are settled in a spirit of mutual respect by communication and discussion.

For the most part, religious social teaching has always accepted the American economic vision of growth with equity. On balance, however, there have been many more words said about justice than growth. Often religious documents do not exhibit a clear understanding of the inevitable trade-offs necessary in any economic system. The point of most mainline religious criticism of Western capitalism has been that the virtues of entrepreneurship, productivity, creativity, and individual achievement have been stressed at the expense of concern for the fairness of the results. Most of the activities of church critics can be seen as a counter-balance, trying to ensure that the benefits and burdens of corporate activity are equitably distributed, and that the rights of the least advantaged are not neglected. From experience with a number of business leaders, it is my impression that many see a genuine value in church activist groups. Sensitive leaders understand that the legitimacy of their institutions depends on public approval and support. Insofar as activists mirror the convictions of thoughtful members of the

society, their work ensures that business, with social approval, will continue to perform its vital function of providing goods and services.

Church groups have come to assume that dialogue with business groups without pressure or the threat of pressure will not be effective in resolving injustices under discussion. While there is clearly some experience on which to justify this premise, many observers, both within and outside of the churches, have cautioned activists about the unintended consequences of such a strategy. For example, consider the widely reported infant formula controversy.

THE INFANT FORMULA CONTROVERSY

The substantive issue underlying the controversy was the extremely high infant mortality rates in developing countries; corporation leaders and their critics agree on this. While no one is claiming that infant formula is the sole cause of these deaths, the critics have argued that the aggressive marketing practices have persuaded many women to shift from breastfeeding to bottlefeeding. The use of infant formula and bottlefeeding has two adverse consequences:

1. the loss of protective antibodies from breast milk; and
2. the potential to misuse the formula either by using impure water or by diluting the formula to make it last longer

There is also the problem of illiteracy in many areas so that often the product's instructions cannot be properly understood. In addition, refrigeration was not available for most users. With this sort of analysis, in 1970, Dr. Derrick B. Jelliffe, then head of the Caribbean Food and Nutrition Institute in Jamaica, recommended that all commercial formulas be withdrawn from the market in developing countries. Needless to say, his recommendation was not without controversy. In 1975, the ICCR, along with some of its member groups, presented shareholder resolutions requesting information on marketing practices in the Third World to two of the major formula companies, Bristol-Myers and American Home Products. Abbott Laboratories, through its Ross Laboratories division, also was challenged in a shareholder resolution by church groups to examine its overseas marketing practices.

In 1977, the University of Minnesota Catholic Newman Center founded the Infant Formula Action Coalition (INFACT). This organization, along with the ICCR, organized a national boycott against the Swiss-based Nestle S.A., the largest supplier of commercial formula in the Third World. This consumer boycott continued for 6 1/2 years and was the subject of much media attention and conflict before it was suspended in late January 1984. More than seventy American organizations representing churches, doctors, nurses, teachers, and other professionals had joined the boycott.

Drawing support largely from church organizations, the Nestle boycott leaders mounted a major campaign on the premise that a serious problem could be remedied by changing objectionable marketing practices in the Third World. In 1981, the coalition's efforts to have an international code on the marketing of infant formula adopted by the World Health Organization (WHO) were successful. The voluntary code suggests that free samples, mass advertising to consumers, and a number of other sales lures should be suspended. The focus of the boycotting groups was now to pressure the industry to implement the International Code. All Nestle products and services, from Nestle Crunch candy bars to Stouffer hotels and restaurants, were under the boycott.

Throughout the conflict, charges were traded by both sides. For example, before a U.S. Senate hearing on the issue in 1978, a Nestle's spokesman argued that the protest was directed by "a worldwide church organization, with the stated purpose of undermining the free enterprise system." A June 1983 newsletter of INFACT reported a typical

statement of boycott leaders: "Malnutrition, the pain of diarrhea and disease, and the constant threat of death are not the natural birthright of a child, but the result of a social system informed and directed by powerful corporations working for their own selfish interests."

Although Nestle agreed in 1982 to abide by the WHO code, it was not until 1984, after much hostility, that the church groups finally suspended the boycott. Because some multinational corporations (MNCs) have changed the way they market infant formula in the less-developed countries (LDCs), church groups may have a claim to some success. But the length of the Nestle boycott and the seeming intractability of its leaders, even in the face of Nestle's acquiescence, caused some damage both to the company and to the cohesiveness of the church groups.[8]

A senior official of Nestle said the boycott's principal cost was employee morale. When religious groups engage in protracted conflict with business, in this case to "save starving babies," it is difficult to gauge the damage to both esprit de corps and the public perception of the legitimacy of business and the economic system. Experience from this conflict between industry and religious activists would seem to indicate two sorts of serious errors. On the one hand, industry should not assume all critics are Marxist and are seeking a revolutionary socialistic system. Critics should be listened to and their remarks carefully assessed. On the other hand, critics should be straightforward with the goals they are seeking. No matter how good the end, a less than forthright means is beneath the dignity of church representatives. The church as a moral leader ought to ensure that its representatives are beyond reproach. In this light, consider the strategy on infant formula summarized by James Post in a recent article.

Societies often have difficulties in shaping "sensible" policy solutions to complex policy issues. The reason that children die in developing nations is not because infant formula is a bad product. Rather, there is an environment of poverty, illiteracy, inadequate sanitation, unhealthy water, and limited health services that create dangerous conditions for the use of formula. Marketing did not create these conditions, but marketing was a more *actionable* aspect of the problem than poverty, water, or education . . . Because business corporations are responsive to external pressure, action targeted at them has a better chance of producing change than actions aimed at such underlying conditions as poverty and illiteracy. A marketing code will not alleviate the problems of poverty, illiteracy, and poor sanitation, but it can help to ensure that companies do not exploit such conditions to their own advantage.[9]

While this may be acceptable strategy of some consumer groups, is it the most appropriate one for the church—the model of what human community ought to be like? The church indeed must be concerned to better the lost of the poor, but are not straightforward attempts to influence public policy much more fruitful? Should not the churches' major effort be directed at securing public policy aimed at improving the underlying conditions of poverty, illiteracy, and so on? Is settling for a marketing code, settling for too little? To be sure, the churches must be involved on both levels, criticizing injustices in business as well as initiating discussion of just public policy. Too much energy spent on the former, however, may leave little for the latter. The prospect of collaborative efforts with corporations to solve poverty problems will be unlikely if churches are alienated from business. To view this point from another angle, it may be helpful to consider another recent controversy, the dispute over investments in South Africa.

THE CASE OF THE ETHICS OF INVESTMENTS IN SOUTH AFRICA

As business corporations begin to assume the task of integrating ethical concerns into their economic decisions, it is becoming increasingly clear that this task is fraught with diffi-

culties. "Business leaders must be accountable for their exercise of power, not only to stockholders but to stakeholders—all those major constituencies affected by a business: employees, suppliers, local communities, area hospitals, schools, and so on."[10] Once this dictum from the scholars in ethics and management has been accepted and actually employed in the policy process by managers, often new and unintended consequences loom on the horizon. In the pages that follow, a brief summary of the attempt by business to follow an ethical course with investments in South Africa will be discussed. The case illustrates the difficulty of trying to please the major constituencies of a business corporation and may yield much insight for managers as they struggle to integrate ethics into policy decisions in the decades ahead.

APARTHEID: AN EVIL

During the summer of 1985, I was in South Africa researching the ethics of U.S. investments there. After nearly four weeks of traveling throughout the country and interviewing almost one hundred persons—religious leaders, labor leaders, business executives, members of Parliament, black workers, and so on—I had little hope that South Africa would soon be a peaceful land. About that time I had an interview with Bishop Desmond Tutu. As I walked into his office in Johannesburg, I was greeted by an exuberant Bishop Tutu. My first question was to ask him how he kept so hopeful in the midst of such oppression and violence. He said, "Let's pray before we talk." We prayed together for several minutes. His prayer called to mind that Jesus Christ came face to face with evil, suffered death at its hands, and finally rose again, overcoming evil once and for all, and that as followers of Christ we believe that same pattern can be repeated in each of our lives. Bishop Tutu's challenge is not unlike the challenge that we all face: each of us, in our own way, and in our own circumstances, is challenged to overcome evil with good.

All of us know evil from personal experience, but seldom do we encounter evil structured in society so firmly and resolutely as it was in the apartheid laws of South Africa. While there are more oppressive systems in the world, apartheid was the only one based on skin color. Over 300 racial laws in South Africa denied blacks many of the rights we take for granted—the right to vote, to move about freely in their own country, to attend the better white schools and to have the opportunity for decent housing.

I met any number of blacks who had important executive positions in business firms in South Africa and yet they still had to live in a ghetto—not because they could not afford better but because, according to the Group Areas Act, land was zoned by race. South Africa's white towns and cities are generally surrounded by black townships, often bleak, dusty and despair-ridden places. Estimates are that 25 percent of the 12 million urban blacks are unemployed. The situation of over 12 million blacks living in the so-called "homelands" is much worse. South Africa appears, for the most part, to be a beautiful and wealthy country. But not for the great majority of its inhabitants. It is dominated by the 5 million whites who control 80 percent of the land.

Learnings for the Future

In April 1994, in a move almost as dramatic as the fall of the Berlin Wall, South Africa had its first national election where all—blacks and whites—could vote. This vote was the culmination of several years of intense negotiations among all the major groups in the country. In order to learn from this experience of advancing political rights, it may be helpful to examine the strategies employed by activists and the business community. A key factor to keep in mind is that many analysts, while not denying the great achievement of attaining political rights, continued to look forward during the struggle to the day when overcoming *economic* apartheid would be the challenge. That challenge, which is the current one, requires a well-developed infrastructure

and a critical mass of multinationals to attract new investment and job creation as well as a renewed emphasis on affirmative action.

Was it reasonable in 1985 to expect a quick and peaceful solution to the racial injustices of South Africa? Almost everyone said "No." The problem was in the numbers: whites were outnumbered by blacks almost by a factor of six. The whites had tried all kinds of schemes to maintain all the power—the homelands, white job reservation, restrictions of black business, and so on—and for a while these policies had worked. The strategy of the white ruling class seems to have been to do anything that would hinder the emergence of a unified black political group. The name of the game was survival, and the Afri-kaaners (the white ruling class) played it well. In the early 1990s, however, the nation was at a crossroads. The blacks were, with good cause, increasingly agitating for political and economic rights, to the point of disrupting the white economy. Could the whites broaden the democratic processes to include blacks without losing all they had ever worked for? Although the government under State President F. W. de Klerk had spoken of a number of changes, as of 1990 none had been enacted which touched the core of apartheid and opened the way toward a full scale multiracial society. Many were hopeful that this transition would take place in the not too distant future, and that a bloodbath could be avoided. Others argued that only violence would achieve the desired result, a society that guarantees political and civil rights for all.

On February 2, 1990, South African President Frederik W. de Klerk announced some major steps that signaled an opening to a negotiated settlement. President de Klerk legalized the African National Congress and many other opposition groups, promised to free political prisoners, declared a moratorium on executions, released press restrictions, and most significantly, he called upon all parties in contention to meet at the negotiating table to form a new constitution for South Africa. While hopeful, most South Africans realized that there would be no easy path to a new political order. Only time would tell whether the white minority would freely redistribute power in the political and economic realms.

Apartheid and U.S. Businesses in South Africa

It was in this context that even in 1990 many powerful groups continued to argue that the only moral course was for all foreign firms to withdraw from South Africa. This would weaken the economy and hasten the end of apartheid as the white leaders would compromise in the face of economic disaster. The operative image here seems to have been that of a glass half empty, implying that apartheid was still the vision of the white leadership and that only an economy in ruins would force the leadership to negotiate a new dispensation. However, others argued that apartheid had long been in its death throes and that the white leadership, even under P.W. Botha, knew the old era was short lived (the glass was half full). Thus, for this group a moral course was for the companies to remain in South Africa and take measures to assist the blacks in their struggle and also to prepare the way for job creation through new investment in the post-apartheid South Africa. Fortunately, both groups found adherents.

Today there is a recognition that business is part of a dynamic social system. Because business in perceived as being powerful and effective, people have come to expect that business will help solve social and political problems of a society. This expectation can be a heavy burden for business. In the South African context, the problem was even more complex, for many argued that capitalism thrived from the cheap labor afforded by apartheid and hence business interests had been apartheid's ally. For a small group of black intellectuals in South Africa, capitalism was the enemy. For the millions who earned their livelihood in the businesses of South Africa, the record was more ambiguous. There is no question that almost all blacks in South Africa were "very unhappy" with apartheid; on the other hand, one of the most reliable surveys indicated that only 24% of urban blacks supported total disinvestment. If companies will use their influence and dramatically oppose apartheid, 75% of the blacks would support their presence, according to this research study.[11] In principle, most blacks did not equate capitalism with apartheid.[12]

Multinational businesses from the U.S. have had operations in South Africa for over fifty years. It is a country that has vast potential for new markets, and major companies from all over the globe sought to get a position there. At its height, the U.S. corporate presence included over 280 companies with direct investments totaling some $2 billion. What is often overlooked, however, is that South Africa is a relatively wealthy country, and that only about 4 percent of all direct investment was from foreign multinational companies; only one-fifth or .8 percent of all direct investments in South Africa were from U.S. firms in 1976, although some strategic areas, such as the major share of the computer and petroleum industries, were serviced by U.S. multinationals.

Overcoming Apartheid: A Brief Overview of Initiatives in the U.S.

Concern about racist policies in South Africa on the part of U.S. groups dates back to 1912 when the NAACP provided assistance to what later became the Africa National Congress of South Africa. It was not until the mid-sixties, however, that college students, civil rights leaders, and church groups began to devise strategies in response to the evil of apartheid. In 1973 a major offensive was launched by church groups against bank loans to the Republic of South Africa (R.S.A.). Forty-seven banks, including some of the major U.S. banking institutions, were threatened with a mass withdrawal of deposits unless loans to R.S.A. ceased. Although the campaign did not have a significant effect on the loan policy of the banks, it did give much visibility to the apartheid problem. In 1971 the first shareholder resolution on South Africa calling for the termination of General Motors operations in R.S.A. was presented by the Episcopal Church. At the time, church officials candidly stated that their goal was *not* to have GM leave South Africa, but rather to pressure the company to use its power to help change R.S.A. government policy on the races and to better the lot of blacks at home and the workplace.[13] Until the late 1980s, this was the strategy of most U.S. church groups, even though their official positions advocated total withdrawal of U.S. firms. Since 1971 there have been over five hundred shareholder resolutions on South Africa targeted at dozens of U.S. corporations.

Initially the majority of U.S. businesses with operations in South Africa responded to the churches' call to help solve the racial problem in South Africa by adopting the code of conduct developed by the Reverend Leon H. Sullivan. Sullivan, for many years a leading black pastor in Philadelphia and a member of the Board of Directors of the General Motors Corporation, called 12 major U.S. companies together in 1977 and drew up a code of conduct that has come to be known as the Statement of Principles. If U.S. companies were in South Africa, they must pursue the following policies:

1. Non-segregation of the races in all eating, comfort and work facilities;
2. Equal and fair employment practices for all employees;
3. Equal pay for all employees doing equal or comparable work for the same period of time;
4. Initiation and development of training programs that will prepare blacks, coloreds, and Asians in substantial numbers for supervisory, administrative, clerical, and technical jobs;
5. Increasing the number of blacks, coloreds, and Asians in management and supervisory positions;
6. Improving the quality of employees' lives outside the work environment in such areas as housing, transportation, schooling, recreation and health facilities, and
7. Working to eliminate laws and customs that impede social and political justice.

(Point 7 was added in 1985 and was not in the original code.) Even though U.S. corpora-

tions employed only about 90 thousand of the 9 million workers in South africa, the case was made that the efforts to dismantle apartheid by American firms served as a beacon and a catalyst in generating reform throughout business and industry. If the non-U.S. companies who also adopted a code similar to the Statement of Principles are counted, almost one million blacks in South Africa enjoyed the protection of the code.

By 1985, within the workplace, the code and similar measures by non-U.S. firms became standard policy, and many blacks reported that their lives were much more humane because of them. Outside the workplace,land was still zoned by skin color and there were over 300 laws designed to enforce apartheid, the Afrikaans word for separate development (literally "Separatehood"). In 1985, in a bold new development, the Rev. Sullivan and the signature companies added a new requirement to the code: All U.S. companies operating in South Africa would "support the ending of all apartheid laws."[18] This now became point number seven in the Statement of Principles listed above.

U.S. companies following the Statement of Principles were now actively lobbying the South African government to end apartheid laws. The lobbying, for the most part, was done through the Signatory Association, an industry association of all the U.S. firms in South Africa which have subscribed to the Principles. The American Chamber of Commerce in South Africa (AMCHAM) wrote a hard-hitting document that placed industry squarely in opposition to the apartheid laws. Their position paper covered urbanization and influx control, housing removals, migrant labor, black business rights, and citizenship. It also argued for channels for democratic participation at all levels of government, the means of which were to be arrived at by negotiation and consultation with all leaders of the various constituencies. The final document was officially presented to a special R.S.A. Cabinet Committee and it was widely publicized. In a dramatic move, the major business groups of South Africa gave the then President, P.W. Botha, an ultimatum: He must begin to negotiate with key black leaders to abolish apartheid. To stress the urgency, some of the most prominent leaders of industry flew to Zambia and met with the leaders of the outlawed African National Congress. All this was in 1985; still, there was no significant reform, although by 1989, there was some hope that the new President, F.W. de Klerk, would meet the challenge of dismantling apartheid.

Would the South African government respond to the growing demands for change, demands both from within the country and from the international community? In all fairness, most analysts candidly admitted agnosticism on this point. The Reverend Leon Sullivan, in June 1987, carrying out a promise he made two years earlier, called for all U.S. companies to withdraw from South Africa by March 1988. He also asked that the U.S. initiate a total economic embargo "until statutory apartheid is ended and blacks have a clear commitment for equal political rights." While he acknowledged that the principles had been "a tremendous force for change," he stated that much remains to be done and that more pressure was needed to force the R.S.A. government to negotiate with blacks.

U.S. companies with operations in South Africa found themselves in the midst of a major domestic controversy: determining the "right" thing to do was exceedingly difficult. In 1986, 50 U.S. corporations left South Africa. Between 1986 and 1989, over 90 more companies withdrew. These companies included some of the giants, such as IBM, GM, Kodak, and Xerox. The reasons for the departures were well summarized in a *Wall Street Journal* story on the Xerox disinvestment in 1987. Quoting Xerox chairman, David T. Kearns, the *Journal* wrote:

> Mr. Kearns said he still feels staying put is best for South Africa's 23 million blacks. But he now says leaving is what is best for Xerox. "It was clear things were continuing to deteri-

orate on all fronts," he said. The nation's economy and social climate were worsening; pro-disinvestment groups' criticism was rising; and Xerox was beginning to lose sales in the U.S. to local governments that were banning contracts with companies doing business there.[15]

What was the goal of the pro-disinvestment groups? My research on the South Africa question focused on the types of arguments being made by the various leaders and groups in the struggle for black rights in the R.S.A. It may be helpful to outline this work.

The Logic of the Arguments Concerning Disinvestment

After surveying the many ethical arguments made for and against investments in South Africa, three main approaches emerged:

1. the "clean hands" approach;
2. the "solidarity with victims" or prophetic approach; and
3. the "stewardship" approach

Each style has a unique dominant concern. Advocates of the clean hands approach were mainly concerned to avoid complicity in the evil of apartheid. Followers of the prophetic style emphasized the crucial need to identify with the oppressed of South Africa in a clear and dramatic manner, while followers of the stewardship approach sought to determine the best way to use corporate and government power to advance the welfare of black South Africans. Most often those arguing in the "clean hands" and prophetic modes were strong advocates of disinvestment, while the followers of the stewardship ethic often argued the case for continuing investment. Those in the debate from religious groups will find that there is not one position which is *the* Christian or Jewish answer; all three approaches can be appropriate expressions of Christian faith, for example. One's unique vocation as a Christian often determines one's ethical stance, whether it be a prophet, a steward, or pacifist. Secular humanists, analogously, may well gravitate to one of the three logics in analyzing moral issues.

The "Clean Hands" Approach. Apartheid, as a statutory system that bestows rights on the basis of color and race, is a denial of the fundamental value of human dignity, a value which for Christians and Jews follows from the conviction that all people are created in the image of God, and which for all humankind is enshrined in the United Nations Declaration of Human Rights. Apartheid was, without a doubt, an evil system, and many argued that as such it should not enjoy the cooperation of people of good will in any shape or form. In this view, then, the claim on conscience to avoid evil may take precedence over the claim to fashion political and economic strategies to promote justice where these strategies entail cooperation with institutions involved with evil. Until apartheid is dismantled, economic and political cooperation is censored, according to some. Disinvestment is *the* answer. The problems many have noted with this solution however, is that it fails to help those most in need, those suffering under apartheid.

To be sure, there were very thoughtful responses to apartheid employing the "clean hands" sort of logic. Consider the position of Clifton R. Wharton, Jr., formerly the top officer of TIAA-CREF and an advocate of removing all U.S. investments from South Africa:

> Finally there comes a point so incompatible with one's respect for humanity itself that compromises with conscience can no longer be tolerated or rationalized. When a human situation so fundamentally affronts every tenet of human values, a public expression of personal opposition is a moral obligation.[17]

Wharton was not claiming that his stand would make things turn out right in South Africa; rather, he refused to be an accomplice in the evil of apartheid. To participate in the apartheid system is to be morally culpable and the proper response, in this view, is to disassociate oneself.

The Prophetic Approach. People who espouse the second model primarily want to make a prophetic statement so that men and women of compassion will join ranks and show solidarity with the oppressed of South Africa. This ethic generally calls for disinvestment and strong economic and trade sanctions. It draws on the biblical witness that we are all one people and are called to express our solidarity with those in special need.

Walter Fauntroy, the then representative of the District of Columbia in the U.S. House of Representatives and pastor of New Bethel Church in Washington, D.C., followed the prophetic logic. Fauntroy, as one of the original founders of the Free South Africa Movement, advocated a total withdrawal of U.S. investment. For Fauntroy, joining the movement and pressing for disinvestment was a moral requirement. However, he was not primarily concerned for "clean hands," as in the model just discussed. Rather, he was making a prophetic statement, hoping that his stance would evoke similar sentiments from others who would join the resistance. The strength of this position is that it unambiguously challenges evil and wrongdoing. The weakness of this approach is that it assumes that this is the unique moment of crisis in South Africa, when an overwhelming show of solidarity will mobilize widespread support. Yet should the broad coalition of resistance not materialize, the oppressed blacks may be more demoralized.

The Stewardship Approach. In the quest for justice in personal and communal life, the stewardship ethic acknowledges that often one is faced with choices, all of which have a regrettable aspect. Although U.S. corporate presence in South Africa may indirectly support an apartheid regime by paying taxes, that presence may at the same time be a constructive force to dismantle apartheid, and the lack of that presence may have dire consequences for many who depend on it for their livelihood. In this account, the U.S. corporate presence was moral, even though it may have involved cooperation with evil, for that presence is actually creating the conditions to end apartheid. In technical language, the "directly voluntary" consequence, achieving the good, occurs while reluctantly allowing an "indirectly voluntary" consequence, an evil. The judgment is made that there is a proportionately grave reason for permitting the evil effect to occur.[18]

A stewardship ethic was exemplified in the writings of Gatsha Buthelezi, Chief Minister of Kwazulu, President of Inkatha and a cabinet officer in the Mandela administration as of May 1994. Buthelezi has little use for arguments from moral purity or prophetic witness but rather focuses on how corporate power could most effectively advance the welfare of blacks:

> To stand on American indignant principles by withdrawing diplomatically and economically from South Africa is a luxury that the vastness of American wealth could afford. But indulgence in that luxury for the sake of purity of conscience, whatever genuine motives produce that conscience, would do no more than demonstrate the moral ineptitude of a great nation in the face of challenges from a remote area of the globe.[19]

To be sure, Buthelezi was not uncritical of U.S. corporations in South Africa; he was always prodding them to be "good stewards" and use their influence more aggressively to dismantle apartheid. Yet he was fighting to keep U.S. corporations and investments in South Africa because he needed their leverage in his struggle to overcome apartheid and he needed jobs for his people. He never lost sight of the needs of the post-apartheid South Africa in the struggle.

It has become fashionable in some quarters to consider Buthelezi as having sold out since during the apartheid years he was the Chief Minister of Kwazulu. Such a position is a serious mistake. A *New York Times* editorial put it well:

> Chief Buthelezi is unfairly caricatured by black militants as an Uncle Tom. The truth is more interesting. He has repeatedly called for the unconditional release of Nelson Mandela, jailed leader of the African National Congress. Though the chief preaches moderation, he has scorned attempts to draw him away from Mr. Mandela into talks with Pretoria on a "new dispensation" meant to prolong minority rule.[20]

Many institutional shareholders who continued to hold stock in U.S. corporations with operations in South Africa, during the apartheid years, and a number of others argued for the morality of investments in R.S.A. with the stewardship ethic. The reasoning here was that since the business community has lent its active support to the black cause, the dismantling of apartheid had begun, however slowly. In five years, from 1985–90, more changes had been consummated than in the fifty before: the repeal of the Immorality and Mixed Marriages Act, the recognition of black trade unions to the point that over one million blacks were union members, the ending of "whites only" job reservations, the repeal of the law forbidding nonracial political parties, the establishment of a franchise for mixed-race and Indians (unsatisfactory as it is), and the granting to blacks the right to hold the deed to their land in black townships. The repeal of the pass laws and the toleration of the erosion of the Group Areas Act soon followed. More important, U.S. business had been on the forefront of initiatives to abolish existing legislation that continued apartheid. Such matters as urbanization and influx control, housing, removals, migrant labor, black business rights, and citizenship were major items aggressively lobbied for and promoted by the business community in South Africa. The centerpiece of this business initiative was that all these matters ought to be negotiated with the acknowledged black leaders of R.S.A. While advocates of continuing U.S. investment in South Africa understood that the internal pressure of blacks themselves was crucial for dismantling apartheid, they also considered the pressure from the business community as an important aid in the struggle.

The stewardship ethic also argued that an important consequence of U.S. investments in South Africa was the attention that R.S.A. received by the U.S. media and other institutions of U.S. society. For example, higher education in the United States has been involved in a number of programs to contribute to black advancement in South Africa. The New England Board of Higher Education was involved in a program to raise funds to support scholarships for blacks in universities in R.S.A. The Carnegie Corporation, with the presidents of major U.S. universities, funded an planned a number of cooperative ventures with higher education in South Africa. The U.S. South Africa Education Program (SAEP) has brought over 300 black South African students to the United States from 1979 to 1990 for graduate and undergraduate study. Many of these same blacks are now part of the government of the new South Africa. A crucial need now is to provide numbers of blacks the education and training that the new South Africa requires. The U.S. corporate presence is presently a major source and catalyst for that education.

It is interesting to note that Clifton R. Wharton, Jr. originally argued from a stewardship ethic that the consequences of the U.S. corporate presence in South Africa—"practicing nondiscrimination" and "providing a progressive example"—morally justified the investments. As stated earlier, however, six years later in 1985, Wharton was an advocate of complete disinvestment. Acknowledging that the new initiatives from the business community might offer a glimmer of hope, Wharton felt compelled to champion economic withdrawal.

> For the small minority of blacks employed by progressive U.S. corporations, there have been some changes for the better. But these gains are overwhelmed by the clear evidence that for the vast majority, things have gotten steadily worse, not better, during the last decade.[21]

To be sure, by 1985 a serious recession had depressed South Africa, there had been an increased loss of freedom under the state of emergency, and press coverage was censored. Yet many, on the basis of gains in the previous five years, were still hopeful that U.S. investments could help. For example, the former Episcopal Bishop of Washington, D.C., the late John T. Walker, an important black clergyman until his death in 1989, argued for the continued presence of U.S. companies in South Africa so long as they aggressively opposed apartheid and empowered blacks with jobs and skills. "I don't see why liberals think there's only one way of going about accomplishing what you want to accomplish. . . . My views are not far removed form Desmond Tutu's in a practical sense."[22]

In order to understand why people like Wharton and the Rev. Leon Sullivan finally called for disinvestment, it is well to recall that most people seem to have a point beyond which they will not go in the use of the stewardship ethic; deciding when the pace of change is too slow is a very personal judgment. Some continue to ask, "Slow, compared to what?" Others reach the breaking point and say, "Here I stand; I can do no other."[23]

Sanctions and Disinvestment: The Appropriate Response?

The American public increasingly had become aware of apartheid for the evil that it was, and new public policy reflected this concern. In October 1986, overriding President Reagan's veto, Congress passed the Comprehensive Anti-apartheid Act of 1986. The bill involved a ban on new U.S. loans and investments in South Africa, and a prohibition on certain imports from R.S.A. including coal, steel, uranium, agricultural products, iron and textiles. While no one was under the illusion that the economic sanctions of the bill would cripple or even moderately harm the South African economy, for the items prohibited were not the major imports, the bill did send a strong signal that the U.S. supported the black cause.

To be sure, sending a signal indicating which side the U.S. is on is an important move, but could U.S. economic sanctions ever be reasonably expected to yield enough pressure to move the R.S.A. government to dismantle apartheid? That is, could the departure of U.S. corporations and the cessation of U.S. bank loans and trade bring the South African economy to its knees and, therefore, its leaders to the negotiating table? In terms of the conceptual framework presented above, can economic sanctions be the primary tool of a stewardship ethic, or are they more properly the means of a prophetic or clean hands ethic. We know U.S. economic pressures can symbolically demonstrate where our loyalties are; it is a point of dispute whether such sanctions actually did hasten the dismantling of apartheid. We do know that every company that disinvested in South Africa made job creation in the post-apartheid nation all the more difficult.

In an insightful study for the Institute for International Economics of 78 cases of economic sanctions, Clyde Hufbauer and Jeffrey Schott concluded that the success of sanctions depends on a number of factors. Successful uses of sanctions were generally cases marked by the following characteristics:

1. a narrowly defined objective;
2. an economically large sender country imposing the sanction on small target;
3. sanctions had an immediate effect with little chance for the target country to adjust;
4. minimal economic costs to sender;
5. economic sanctions could be imposed unilaterally without need of cooperation from other countries to be effective.[24]

Unfortunately, items 3 and 5 were almost impossible to implement in the South Africa case. To be sure, because of disinvestment a number of workers did lose their jobs—mostly black workers—but this small increase in the already large unemployment ranks held little promise for marshalling significant pressure. More importantly, the U.S. has had little success in convincing other major trading partners to join the sanctions campaign. A March 12, 1987, UPI story discussed a report from the Secretary-General of the United Nations, Javier Perez de Cuellar, where he noted that as U.S. firms were pulling out of South Africa, West Germany's Daimler-Benz and Bayerische Motorenwerke (BMW) were expanding and Italy's Olivetti Co. was building a plant. Assuming that the U.S. could persuade the major trading partners—Japan, U.K. and the Federal Republic of Germany—to withdraw from South Africa, this only accounts for about 50% of South Africa's trade.

While there is merit to strategic sanctions, that is, carefully crafted sanctions designed to achieve a limited objective (for example, the cultural and sport sanctions or the denial of landing rights for South African Airways or the refusal to roll over loans from international banks), it was never clear that the call for total disinvestment could achieve any proportional good. Since total disinvestment never happened, one can only speculate, but this speculation may be most helpful in guiding policy in other situations such as China and the human rights struggle.

The basic premises of the sanctions advocates need much more scrutiny, that is, the premise that all trading partners will join the cause and the premise that the power wielders of a government will respond positively and restore human rights under the pressure of the withdrawal of foreign trade and capital. While in South Africa external pressure played some role, changes in the apartheid laws were all enacted in situations of *internal* pressure when the State President had the right flank in check. In 1985, the pillars of apartheid were slowly crumbling and the black experience in the business community often prepared the way. Through the participation in trade unions, the blacks got a taste of solidarity which united them in the face of the evil of apartheid. The experience of solidarity increasingly united blacks in consumer boycotts and other activities designed to win their civil and political rights; this, of course, assumed the blacks continued to have jobs and consumer power.

Often the call of disinvestment from South Africa was meant to be a form of economic pressure but not actually a call for all foreign investment to depart. In this scenario, disinvestment threats play a role somewhat analogous to the concept of deterrence in nuclear ethics. According to this doctrine, a threat to use nuclear weapons against an adversary deters that adversary from using military force. Of course, if the policy is effective, the nuclear weapons will never be used. Similarly, if the policy of threatening disinvestment is effective, that is, if the South African government dismantles apartheid and starts a negotiating process with acknowledged black leaders, actual disinvestment need never occur. The May 2, 1986, "Statement of the Southern African Catholic Bishops' Conference" employs this logic.

> We, ourselves, believe that economic pressure has been justifiably imposed to end apartheid. Moreover, we believe that such pressure should continue and, if necessary, be intensified should the developments just referred to show little hope of fundamental change. However, we do not need to point out that, in our view, intensified pressure can only be justified if applied in such a way as not to destroy the country's economy and to reduce, as far as possible, any additional suffering to the oppressed through job loss. (Paragraph 10)

In the late 1980s, however, the "hassle factor" caused many major U.S. multinationals to depart from South Africa. It may be that this total disinvestment strategy could not yield the desired objective. The call for increasing economic sanctions was often assumed to be coming from the great majority of South African blacks. Although black leaders of the African National Congress (ANC) and the United Democratic Front (UDF) consistently called for sanctions, leaders of Inkatha, the large, predominantly Zulu group, regularly opposed all sanctions and encouraged foreign investment. As indicated above,

reliable surveys do not confirm any widespread support for disinvestment of South African blacks. To be sure, the findings of these surveys are disputed by some analysts who point to the fact that it was against the law to advocate sanctions in R.S.A. Yet the fact remains that all reputable surveys indicated that if disinvestment means loss of jobs, then blacks were not in favor of it. In any event, in 1994 President Nelson Mandela called upon all those firms who never disinvested from R.S.A. to help develop new investment and create jobs in South Africa.

The Need "To Do Something": Shareholder Democracy

For the most part, the business managers believed that their operations in South Africa were helping to dismantle apartheid. As blacks become more prosperous, they become better customers; as they become free of travel restrictions, transport and recruitment costs go down. Thus, for moral as well as for self interest reasons, business was interested in ending apartheid. The dilemma for firms with operations in South Africa was that in the U.S. the idea had caught on that sanctions and disinvestment would bring about the downfall of apartheid. Stakeholder democracy insures that the firms, given a strong message, will finally take action. The companies will depart even though the managers who know the South African scene had serious reservations that disinvestment would be a tool to dismantle apartheid. Many antiapartheid activists in South Africa feared that even if sanctions yielded lower living standards for whites they would adjust to the slower economy rather than yield black political rights with their backs to the wall. The managers must listen to their many constituencies in South Africa as well as in the United States, but finally they must listen to their shareholders and other stakeholders. Thus many firms departed South africa although, fortunately for the new, nonracial government trying to attract new investment and create jobs, many multinational firms did remain in RSA maintaining the essential infrastructure required for a dynamic growth economy.

Most often, the stakeholders do not speak forcefully on social responsibility issues; most do not vote the proxies or initiate boycott legislation, however, the South Africa issue was an exception and it may set the pattern for other forthcoming issues. With the South African apartheid question, there was a growing impatience and a feeling that we must do something now. Calls for sanctions and disinvestment are a very appealing response to the need "to do something." Such moves may be a dramatic statement of where we stand ("Clean Hands" or "Prophetic" stance), but they have yet to demonstrate that they can achieve the objective ("Stewardship" ethic). One thing is certain: the departure of American business from South Africa because of pressures exerted in the U.S. has usually resulted in new non-U.S. owners who were much less interested in solving social problems. In considering the proper response to the deprivation of human rights, in China or Burma, for example, disinvestment must be carefully scrutinized. The Investor Responsibility Research Center, a Washington, D.C. research group respected for its objectivity, concluded a 1988 study with the following observation: "The most notable changes in corporate conduct following disinvestment have been the cutbacks in funding for community development programs and organizations that challenge apartheid policies, as well as some rechanneling of funds from the more progressive organizations to those deemed politically acceptable in South African terms."[25] Those arguing for withdrawal of all foreign businesses have rendered an important service in the fight against apartheid in that they have raised the general level of awareness in the U.S. of the evil of that system. The media attention given to a university endowment selling the stock of firms with operations in South Africa or to a city, county or state passing an ordinance forbidding purchases from such companies have enabled many Americans to have a fairly good idea of the injustice that permeated the daily life of the non-whites—80% of the population of South Africa. That these moves aided in the removal of apartheid laws—the ultimate goal—remains to be studied and analyzed.

Like most difficult problems, it may be that a plurality of strategies offers the best hope for restoring human rights. The disinvestment lobby placed all of its chips on the hope that the continued withdrawal of foreign investment would so weaken the eco-nomy that the South African white leadership would come to see the wisdom of negotiating a new constitution for multiracial society. Yet many sympathetic South Afri-cans, both black and white, counseled against such a "scorched earth" policy and fortunately that advice was heeded by some. This critical mass of firms that remained in South Africa are now the building blocks for the future.

There is no doubt, in my view, that external pressure was required to eliminate statutory racism in South Africa. One weapon providing pressure to eliminate apartheid that I believe gets far too little credit is the whole effort of the U.S. companies that remained in South Africa that falls under the Statement of Principles Program, the endeavor that was founded and guided by the Reverend Leon Sullivan and continued until 1994 under a National Advisory Council. As a member of the National Advisory Council, I was not naive about the clout of the U.S. companies that remained in South Africa—only 58 of the companies were in R.S.A. in 1994 with over 180 having sold their holdings. The U.S. companies' role in the fight against apartheid was to be a model, a catalyst, spurring on the vastly more numerous domestic and non-U.S. foreign companies to some significant involvement in activities to overcome apartheid. Some would say the U.S. companies were lighting a candle rather than cursing the darkness, but I and many others were more hopeful.

A typical annual report on the activities of the U.S. companies in South Africa, compiled by Arthur D. Little, Inc., as a part of the requirements of the Statement of Principles for South Africa Program, notes that some 60 U.S. companies provided more than 30 million dollars a year to programs designed to eliminate apartheid.[26] Some of these dollars went to assist in black educational endeav-ors but many went to activities that most South Africans considered too risky because they directly challenged the status quo and advanced social change. For example, the Colgate Palmolive Company provided the funds and personnel to organize a black consumer boycott of the stores in Boksburg after the local city council tried to restore segregation in the downtown city park. Other companies directly challenged white merchants in Johannesburg by assisting blacks in exercising their newly legislated freedom to do business in the downtown areas; this assistance was not only start-up funding, but also training in business skills and entrepreneurship.

Several companies, such as the Kellogg Company, used their influence and resources to secure the freedom of union leaders who were being detained by the police. Companies, such as Johnson & Johnson, also spent money to encourage non-racial education and medical care, a direct confrontation to the then current structures based on a racial hierarchy. Many companies, such as John Deere, bought homes in white areas, making it possible for blacks to assume ownership, thus challenging and eroding the Group Areas Act that zones land by race.

The obvious objection to all these examples of incremental change is that it took so long to dismantle apartheid. Yet it just might be that there was no quick fix for this evil. At least we ought to allow for this possibility and encourage a plurality of strategies in similar situations in the future. Companies that are willing to take up the challenge and oppose an evil system deserve the support of the public—or at least its toleration.

A MANAGERIAL PERSPECTIVE

History may well show that the terms of the discussion about South Africa needed a fresh review. What is the objective in calling for disinvestment and sanctions? It is clear that in the early stages of the campaign church activists, while calling for disinvestment, were primarily seeking to enlist the support of business in anti-apartheid projects. Their efforts were largely successful; through the Statement of Principles founded by Leon Sullivan and other similar codes, business identified with the black cause. To be sure, for some this identification came late, but better late than never. Because of a growing impatience that the evil system of apartheid had continued to perdure, in 1985 a broad coalition of black activists, church groups and political leaders in the U.S. rallied around the call for disinvestment and sanctions. Fortunately many multinationals remained in South Africa and continued programs to empower blacks and oppose apartheid structures. In 1994 enlightened R.S.A. leadership forged a new multi-racial alliance which gave birth to the first national election and a new State President, Nelson Mandela. It is noteworthy that President Mandela has not only not taken reprisals against the companies that did not follow the call to disinvest but rather he has praised them for their leadership and creating jobs and encouraging new investment.

Reviewing the role of business in society in the last fifty years, it is surprising how the responsibilities of business have dramatically increased. Clearly, capitalism is not static but is what some have called a moving target. Business is part of a dynamic social system, and as new social and political problems have been identified, society has repeatedly turned to business for solution. Business is perceived as being powerful and effective. However, business is also mistrusted. Bigness has always been suspect in America. Corporations often have appeared insensitive to human values; some clearly have been. Many still think that profit maximization is the sole motive of business, even though a careful analysis of many corporations would yield a much more complex pattern.

The Nestle case as well as the South Africa case are instances where multinationals assumed additional responsibilities for the complex sociocultural and environmental systems within which it was operating. However, the assumption of this responsibility was initiated and accompanied by protests, largely from religious organizations that applied pressure directly to the corporations. More prompt action may have avoided such coalitions. In the case of Nestle, there was still a protest organization operating long after many of the original supporters judged the founding problem to have been solved. The most effective business response may be to have managers who are adept at responding promptly to those societal expectations that are feasible and judged appropriate.

Church leaders too must scrutinize their "prophets." Moral language, especially when used by church personnel, is powerful. It has a remarkable ability to arouse passions and motivate persons of religious conviction. However, moral language can be abused when it is used without careful analysis. The churches could dilute an essential part of their heritage, should they fail to exercise diligence in the use of moral language. Business leaders who are church members could perform a great service for the religious community by offering their perspective to the church. As a matter of course, top management of the future would do well to know moral language and ethical analysis, not only to protect themselves but, more importantly, to consciously expand the horizon for decision making.

NOTES

1. See "Preliminary Preview of 1990 Social Responsibility Resolutions" published by the Investor Responsibility Research Center, Inc., Suite 600, 1755 Massachusetts Avenue, N.W., Washington, DC 20036.
2. For a survey of the various interest groups, see John M. Holcomb, "Citizen Activism and Corporate Political Strategies: Evolution from 1970–1985" in *Business and Society*, eds., S. Prakash Sethi and Cecilia M. Falbe (Lexington, MA: Lexington Books, 1987), pp. 353–378.
3. Alexis de Tocqueville, *Democracy in America*, ed., Phillips Bradley (New York: Vintage Books, 1945), vol. I, p. 316. Part of this section appeared in earlier articles: "Religion: The Spirit or the Enemy of Capitalism," *Business Horizons* 26(6):6–13 (1983); and "Catholic Bishops Take on Economics," *Business and Society Review* S4(3):21-26 (1985).
4. For further elaboration of this discussion on Aquinas, see *The Judeo-Christian Vision and the Modern Corporation*, eds. Oliver F. Williams and John W. Houck (Notre Dame, IN: University of Notre Dame Press, 1982).
5. John C. Bennett, "Protestantism and Corporations," in *The Judeo-Christian Vision and the Modern Corporation*, p. 88.
6. Norman Gall, "When Capitalism and Christianity Clash," *Forbes*, September 1, 1980, pp. 100–101.
7. Gustavo Gutierrez, *A Theology of Liberation*, trans. Sister Caridad Inda and John Eagleston (Maryknoll, NY: Orbis Books, 1973).
8. The Nestle case is discussed in more detail in my article, "Who Cast the First Stone," *Harvard Business Review* 62(5):151–160 (1984).
9. James E. Post, "Assessing the Nestle Boycott: Corporate Accountability and Human Rights," *California Management Review* 27(2): 127 (1985).
10. For a discussion of "stakeholders" by a top manager, see Catherine B. Cleary, "Women in the Corporation: A Case Study about Justice," in *The Judeo-Christian Vision and the Modern Corporation*, eds. Oliver F. Williams

and John W. Houck (Notre Dame, IN: University of Notre Dame Press, 1982) pp. 292–305. Also see R. Edward Freeman, *Strategic Management: A Stakeholder Approach* (Boston: Pitman, 1984).

11. M. Orkin, *Divestment: The Struggle and the Future* (Johannesburg, South Africa: Raven Press, 1986).

12. For an insightful analysis of capitalism and apartheid, see Mere Lipton, *Capitalism and Apartheid* (Totowa, NJ: Littlefield, Adams & Company, 1985).

13. See David Vogel, *Lobbying the Corporation: Citizen Challenges to Business Authority* (New York: Basic Books, 1978), pp. 169–200.

14. For a full discussion of the Statement of Principles, see my *The Apartheid Crisis* (San Francisco: Harper & Row, 1986).

15. Dennis Kneale, "Xerox, Finally Succumbs to Pressure, Says It Will Sell South African Unit," *The Wall Street Journal*, 20 March 1987, p. 42.

16. This section has been previously published in Chapter Four of my *The Apartheid Crisis*.

17. Clifton R. Wharton, Jr., "Economic Sanctions and Their Potential Impact on U.S. Corporate Involvement in South Africa," House of Representatives Committee on Foreign Affairs, Subcommittee on Africa; 99th Congress, 1st Session, January 31, 1985, p. 105.

18. For an elaboration of my position on proportionality, see Oliver F. Williams, "Business Ethics: A Trojan Horse?" *California Management Review* 24, 1982, 14–24.

19. Mangosuthu Gatsha Buthelezi, "Disinvestment Is Anti-Black," *The Wall Street Journal*, 20 February, 1985, p. 32.

20. "The Gods Are Crazy in Pretoria," *The New York Times*, 2 December, 1986, p. 34.

21. Wharton, p. 50.

22. Michael Isikoff, "Cleric Questions Firms' Pullout From S. Africa," *The Washington Post*, 20 October, 1986, pp. 19–20.

23. For an insightful discussion of these two ethics, see Max Weber, "Politics as a Vocation," *From Max Weber: Essays in Sociology*, ed. and trans., H.H. Gerth and C. Wright Mills (New York: Oxford University Press, 1946), pp. 77–128.

24. See Clyde Hufbauer and Jeffrey Schotte, *Economic Sanctions in Support of Foreign Policy Goals* (Washington, D.C.: Institute for International Economics, 1983). The summary of the characteristics is quoted from William H. Cooper, "South African-U.S. Economic Ties: Emerging Issues," Congressional Research Service Issue Brief, 23 October, 1986, pp. 9–10.

25. Jennifer Kibbe and David Hauck, *Leaving South Africa: The Impact of U.S. Corporate Disinvestment* (Washington, D.C.: Investor Responsibility Research Center, 1988), p. 34.

26. See the *Thirteenth Report on the Signatory Companies to the Statement of Principles for South Africa* available from the Industry Support Unit, Inc., Room 7E #1601, 150 East 42nd Street, New York, New York 10017-5666.

ECOCENTRIC MANAGEMENT
FOR A RISK SOCIETY

Paul Shrivastava

ABSTRACT: A central feature of postindustrial modernization is the proliferation of technological and environmental risks and crises. These risks and crises in modern society emanate from corporate industrial activities. The traditional management paradigm is limited in several ways for responding to demands of the risk society and should be abandoned. I propose an alternative "ecocentric" paradigm for management in the risk society context, which advocates an ecologically centered conception of interorganizational relations and internal management activities. Thus, organizations are reviewed as situated within bioregionally sustainable industrial ecosystems, relating to each other through a logic of ecological interdependence. Within this context, ecocentric management seeks to minimize the environmental impact of organizational vision, inputs, throughputs, and outputs. Implications of this paradigm for management practice and research are examined.

The last quarter of this century has been a period of transition from an industrial to a postindustrial era. Previously, industrial societies were focused primarily on the creation of wealth through technological expansion and,

Many ideas and arguments in this article were stimulated by and discussed on the ONE-L network of the Organizations and the Natural Environment Interest Group of the Academy of Management. I would like to thank the ONE-L members for their contribution and support.

secondarily, on distribution of the wealth (societal welfare). In contrast, postindustrial societies are centered on the risks that accompany the creation of and distribution of wealth. Consequently, the management paradigm that should be used for postindustrial societies is different from the management paradigm developed in the literature during the past three decades.

In this article, I examine the nature of postindustrial modernization. Important characteristics of postindustrial "risk societies," and the worldwide proliferation of risks are described. Next, four key limitations of the traditional management paradigm are examined. Finally, I propose both an alternative ecocentric management paradigm and the implications it can have for organizational research and practice.

BARE OUTLINES
OF THE RISK SOCIETY

To set the stage for my argument, I must first distinguish between industrial and *postindustrial modernization*. Industrial modernization covered the period from the industrial revolution to the mid-20th century. This tremendous period of industrial progress was characterized by scientific and technological advancements in agriculture, medicine, communications, transportation, energy, chemicals, electronics, and other sectors.

Such dazzling progress blinded people to the risks that were simultaneously imposed by industrialization.

Theories of industrial modernization proposed by Marx, Habermas, Parsons and others share a utopian evolutionism. Proponents of these theories associate industrial modernization with steady progress, and they downplay discontinuities and crises, especially in the ecological arena. They use the concepts of development of means of production, communicative rationality, and structural differentiation and functional integration, as the mechanisms behind the exceptional evolutionary economic and social transformation (Habermas, 1989; Parsons, 1982).

Postindustrial modernization represents the past 30 years in industrialized Western societies. Postindustrial societies are characterized by the following economic, social, and political attributes: (a) much of the economic production occurs in service and hightechnology sectors; (b) there is increasing globalization of finance, production, labor, and product markets; (c) economic growth is confronted with ecological limits; and (d) there is a movement toward democratization of markets and politics (Bell, 1975; Giddens, 1990).

A number of social theorists have examined the transition that industrial societies make when they become postindustrial societies. These theories of reflexive modernity place *risk* at the center of the modernization process (Beck, 1992a; Douglas & Wildavsky, 1982; Giddens, 1990, 1991; Lash, 1993). These theories have viewed postindustrial modernization as processes of critically assessing and dealing with the risks created by industrialization, and their central concern has been with *technological and environmental risks*. The most compelling analysis in this genre is the work of Ulrich Beck (1992a,b), from which I draw generously in this section.

Risk is a complex concept that has been studied in numerous social science disciplines. *Webster's Ninth New Collegiate Dictionary* defines risk as "exposure to possible loss,

injury, or danger." This basic idea of risk as possible loss has been interpreted differently in different disciplines. Psychologists define risk in terms of perceptions of people exposed to potential loss. They use psychometric measures of risk perceptions to measure risk (Slovic, 1987). Economists define risk as uncertainty about economic gains and losses. They use statistical probability models to measure this uncertainty. Financial analysts extend this economic concept of risk to include risks based on different sources of uncertainty (e.g., market risks, inflation risk, liquidity risk, credit risk, interest rate risk, currency risk, structural risk, reinvestment risk and prepayment risk) (Bernstein, 1992). In risk management, authors use the probability of event times the impact of the event as a measure of risk (Kliendorfer & Kunreuther, 1987; Lave, 1987). Sociologists define risks as social processes and systems for dealing with hazards (Perrow, 1984; Krimsky & Golding, 1992; Short & Clarke, 1992).

Sociological definitions of risk best fit my needs for discussing the risks of postindustrial modernization. *Risk* is defined here as "a systematic way of dealing with hazards and insecurities induced and introduced by modernization itself" (Beck, 1992a: 21). Modernization risks are produced concomitantly with the production of wealth. Modernization processes seek to fulfill human needs through the development of technological productivity and the creation of wealth. Exponential growth in productive forces unleashes hazards, potential threats, and risks. Thus, excessive production of hazards and ecologically unsustainable consumption of natural resources are the root sources of modern risks.

In the classical industrial society, the logic of wealth production dominated the logic of risk production; thus, risks were minor, and they could be treated as latent side effects or "externalities" of production. In the postindustrial society, this relationship is reversed: The logic of risk production and distribution dominates processes of social change. Just as production and distribution of wealth (social welfare) were central organizing concepts in the classical industrial society, *risk* is the central organizing concept in the postindustrial society. Beck called postindustrial society, "the risk society"—a society in which "the productive forces have lost their innocence in the reflexivity of modernization processes" (Beck, 1992a: 12–13). Increasing production and accumulation of wealth also increases the potential for loss, in other words risks.

Risks induce systematic and often irreversible harm in humans and the natural environment. They represent continued impoverishment of nature, and often are invisible, at least when they begin because knowledge about them is riddled with the uncertainty.

Definitions of risk are based on causal interpretations; that is, risks exist only in terms of the *knowledge* about them. They can be changed, modified, magnified, channeled, and dramatized by knowledge. Risks are highly susceptible to social definition and social construction; consequently, perceptions of risk are reality for many practical purposes (Clarke, 1989).

In this perceptually and socially mediated relationship between risk and knowledge, science's monopoly on the rationality of risk decisions is broken. Multiple competing and conflicting "scientific" claims about risk from different stakeholders are merged in the process of defining the causes and the effects of risk. Science does not provide a single unambiguous consensual answer to questions about risks. Scientific rationality is no longer an adequate arbiter of risk disputes. In resolving risk disputes, multiple (corporate vs. government vs. people's) scientific interpretations are moderated by their respective political interests.

Thus, knowledge of risks has great political significance. Knowledge or expertise is a source of political power. Risks politicize knowledge (scientific and otherwise) in unique ways; they cast doubts on scientific and social rationalities (Nelkin, 1979).

Risks are *ascribed* by epoch and civilization. A person is afflicted by risks by both being part of a civilization and by being aware of these risks. In this sense, risks have been part of every era; however, in earlier times the main sources of risks were acts of God or nature (earthquakes, plagues, pestilence, diseases, etc.). Blame for these risks lay outside of society. In contrast, modern risks are characterized by a *lack*: the impossibility of an *external* attribution of hazard. Instead, risks in modern times are acts of society or reflections of human actions and omissions. They depend on decisions—political, economic, social, and organizational ones. Risks are not caused by people's ignorance of solutions; they are caused by unintended and unforeseen effects of the solutions themselves. Thus, the source of danger is not ignorance but knowledge (scientific and technological) (Beck, 1992a).

Unlike the risks of earlier civilizations, modernization risks are rooted in ecologically destructive industrialization and are global, pervasive, long term, imperceptible, incalculable, and often unknown. Radioactivity and chemical contamination are examples of such risks. Risks emanating from the Chernobyl nuclear accident were geographically pervasive, temporarily transgenerational, crossed national boundaries, and remain incalculable.

Ecological degradation contradicts the interests that advance industrialization, and it has differential impacts on people. Differential distribution of risks puts people in different *social risk positions*. Risks cross economic class, gender, ethnic, generational, and national boundaries. Risk positions exacerbate inequalities based on these variables, but wealth or power do not provide complete protection from modernization risks. These risks can have a boomerang effect on their producers; thus, producers are not immune to the risks they produce. Therefore, risks can transcend traditional boundaries of class, race, and nation (Clarke, 1989; Luhmann, 1990).

The logic of risk production, risk diffusion and risk commercialization is only loosely coupled to the logic of capitalism or social-ism (Communism), and it is *self-referential*, (i.e., independent of the surrounding satisfaction of human needs). Modernization, in seeking economic growth, inadvertently but systematically unleashes risks and hazards. Once created, such risks can expand and evolve independently of economic gains.

Risk Proliferation.   Modernization risks have proliferated through population explosion, industrial pollution, environmental degradation, and the lack of institutional capacity for risk management. People in communities all over the world have been experiencing these risks in the form of visible negative influences on their quality of life.

World population has doubled during the past 40 years; it is presently about 5.5 billion. It will double again during the next 40 years to approximately 11 billion. The tremendous ecological burden such a population explosion places on the earth's ecosystems is apparent from the depletion of natural resources (Ehrlich & Ehrlich, 1991). Widespread damage to world fishery (50% depletion during the last 50 years), wild life, rain forests (42,000 square miles lost each year), soil degradation by industrial agriculture, desertification (26,000 square miles lost each year), has now been documented (Brown et al. 1991). To simply provide basic amenities to 11 billion people will require increasing all world economic products by five to thirty times the current levels. At the most probable rates of consumption growth, world reserves of oil, natural gas, coal and all minerals will be depleted within the next century (Clark, 1989; Daly, 1977; McNeil, 1989; World Commission on Environment and Development, 1987).

Additionally, because of industrial pollution risks to health and environment also have expanded, and urban air pollution, smog, global warming, ozone depletion, acid rain, toxic waste sites, nuclear hazards, obsolete weapons arsenals, industrial accidents, and hazardous products are manifestations

of these risks. An idea of their scale may be gleaned from the data for one type of pollution—toxic wastes.

In the United States alone, there are over 30,000 documented uncontrolled toxic waste sites, and these are increasing at the rate of 2,000 to 3,000 per year. Of these sites, over 2,500 are on the National Priority List because they represent active danger to human health. Estimates for cleaning up these sites range from \$25 billion to \$150 billion. Payment devoted for cleanup during the past ten years has averaged approximately \$0.5 billion per year. The net result of this incommensurate remedy is the cumulative increase of toxic wastes and risks each year (Carson, 1962; Commoner, 1990; Likens, 1987).

This pattern of *accumulating risks and inadequate remedies* is true for most of the other pollution problems I have listed. Such is the situation today in the United States, despite this country's immense financial and technological resources for cleanup, great public awareness of ecological problems, and stringent environmental regulations. The situation in the rest of the world is worse.

Environmental and technological risk have been created by institutions (corporations and government agencies) that also are in charge of controlling and managing these risks. This self-policing of risks is partly responsible for risk proliferation. Because of complexities and error proneness of technological systems, traditional risk managers' approaches have failed to prevent both accidents and the escalation of these risks (Perrow, 1984; Short & Clarke, 1992).

People who have been affected by "technoenvironmental" risks are experiencing an increased dependency on obscure and inaccessible social institutions and actors. They have developed a skeptical attitude (private reflexivity) toward risk-related institutions, such as corporations and government regulatory agencies. Communities also progressively have taken risk decisions into their own hands. This action has been evidenced in the United States through the rise of the

NIMBY (Not in My Back Yard) movement. NIMBY is a grass-roots resistance movement that opposes hazardous industrial and urban development projects within communities (Couch & Kroll-Smith, 1991; Douglas & Wildavsky, 1982; Goldstein & Shorr, 1991; Krimsky & Golding, 1992; Piller, 1991).

Public perceptions of technoenvironmental risks have been heightened by frequent high-profile industrial accidents. Chernobyl, the *Exxon Valdez*, and the incident in Bhopal have raised world consciousness about these technoenvironmental risks. Heightened perceptions of risks have fostered political pressures for regulating environmental hazards. During the past two decades, increasing regulations worldwide have changed the competitive dynamics of many industries (Mitroff & Pauchant, 1990; Shrivastava, 1994; Smith, 1992).

This bare outline of the postindustrial risk society serves as the context for management problems of the coming century. Environmental degradation and risks, as central consequences of modernization, pose new challenges for corporate managers and public policy officials. Technological and environmental risks are the core management problems of the risk society.

In this context, it is not sufficient to manage corporations to optimize production variables, such as profits, productivity, jobs, and growth. Corporations must manage risk variables, such as product harm, pollution, waste, resources, technological hazards, and worker and public safety. This type of management does not mean simply an expansion of the management agenda to include new risks: It implies a fundamental reversal in the focus of managers' attention; that is, substituting the production orientation of existing paradigms with the risk orientation of a new paradigm proposed later in this paper.

The traditional management paradigm was developed for the industrial society; thus, it is inherently limited in many ways for meeting the challenges of the "risk" society. I examine four key limitations of this tradi-tional paradigm compatible with needs of this risk society.

LIMITATIONS OF THE TRADITIONAL MANAGEMENT PARADIGM

At the beginning, let me acknowledge that authors of the management literature do not agree on a single coherent management paradigm (Burrell & Morgan, 1978). There are many management theories and approaches that loosely fit into a dominant managerial worldview. In the traditional worldview, organizations have been described as economic and legal entities created by groups of people who have common or, at least, compatible goals. Organizational promoters invest their own and borrowed resources to accomplish their goals. Organizations are systems of production, serving the goals of stakeholders and operating in a dynamic economic, social, and political environment. Economic organizations or corporations have received much attention by researchers in organizational/management theory. Hence, this article also focuses on management in the context of modern corporations.

Within this general view of organizations, different management theorists have sought to optimize different types of productivity and returns from organizations. Organizational theorists examine the contingent match among organizational structure, size, environment, technology, resources, and decision processes (Aldrich, 1979; Hall & Quinn, 1983; Pfeffer 1982; Scott, 1981). Strategic management theorists have sought to align organizational resources with environmental demands to achieve objectives and optimize returns to investors (Porter, 1980; Schendel & Hofer, 1979). In addition, organizational behavior and human resource management theorists have sought to optimize the use of organizational personnel (Miner, 1984).

Also, researchers of cultural theories of organization have examined organizational values, beliefs, assumptions, norms, and mores, seeking to understand these ideas as cultural entities (Frost, et al., 1985; Deal & Kennedy, 1982). The literature corporate social responsibility (CSR) literature has examined the changing role of corporations in society, seeking to make corporations more responsive to societal needs (Sethi & Steidlmeier, 1991; Freeman, 1984; Wood, 1991).

All of these organizational theories (except for the CSR literature) do not address ecological issues seriously. CSR authors have periodically focused on ecological problems as a social issue of concern to management (Buchholz, Marcus, & Post, 1992; Hoffman, Frederick, & Petry, 1990; Post, 1991). However, ecology is not central even to the CSR literature. It is *one of many* social problems confronting corporations. Other problems include race and gender discrimination, business ethics and fraud, corporate philanthropy, minority concerns, community welfare, and stakeholder demands (Carroll, 1979; Preston, 1985).

Other theorists that have argued for ethical and moral conduct of organizations (Etzioni, 1988; Goodpastor, 1989). Complex moral, social, and administrative motives are discernible in the creation and running of organizations. Not all organizations are driven by a single-minded objective to maximize profits; some instead, pursue multiple objectives (March & Simon, 1958/1993).

Collectively, these organizational theories constitute a formidable body of literature. They cannot be described in the limited space of this paper. Useful critical assessments have been conducted by other researchers (Alvesson, 1992; Burrell & Morgan, 1978; Fischer & Sirianni, 1993; Shrivastava, 1986; Whitley, 1984).

In this article, I simply want to identify four key assumptions (common to these organizational approaches) that act as limitations in dealing with the organizational challenges of a risk society: (a) a denatured view of organizational environment, (b) production/consumption bias, (c) financial risk bias, and (d) anthropocentrism. These assump-

tions are not equally and uniformly common to all theories in the traditional management paradigm. However, most traditional management theorists subscribe to some version of these assumptions.

Denatured View of the Environment.   In the traditional management paradigm a narrow concept of "organizational environment" is used, which emphasizes the economic, political, social, and technological aspects of organizational environments. Economic aspects of environments, especially variables characterizing markets, industries, competitors, and regulations, receive primary emphasis. This approach virtually ignores the natural environment (Emery & Trist, 1965; Fahey & Narayanan, 1984).

Organizational environments are portrayed as abstract, disembodied, and ahistorical external influences on organizations. The environment has been described as a bundle of resources to be used by organizations. The emphasis is on understanding both how environments influence organizations and how organizations can procure, exploit, or compete for environmental resources. The reverse relationship—how organizations have an impact on their natural environment—has received little attention (Shrivastava, In press; Throop, Starik & Rands, 1993).

It is worth noting that although management theorists have adopted a narrow view of environments, management practitioners have begun to incorporate a broader and more holistic view of the environment into their practices. The rise of environmentalism and environmental regulations have led corporations to acknowledge the physical environmental base of organizational activities.

To fully appreciate the ecological consequences of organizational activities, the relevant organizational environment must be reviewed as an *economic biosphere*, which includes not only economic, social, technological, and political elements, but also biological, geological, and atmospheric ones. The environment of business consists of (a) the ecology of the planet earth; (b) the world economic, social, and political order; and (c) the immediate market, technological, and sociopolitical context of organizations (Davis, 1991; Smith, 1992; Stead & Stead, 1992).

Production/Consumption Bias. There are two linked assumptions of the traditional management paradigm that exacerbate environmental degradation. First, is the assumption that business organizations are neutral, rational, technological "systems of production" that serve the interests of many stakeholders. Business activities, education, and research are geared toward improving organizational *productivity* and *efficiency*, and they should benefit stakeholders. This focus on production, ignores destructive aspects of organizations. Environmental destruction and harm caused by organizations, such as environmental pollution, toxic products and wastes and technological and occupational hazards and risks are ignored and treated as external forces.

Second, is the assumption that unconstrained consumption is not a problem and should be promoted. Traditional management theorists accept the *consumerist society* ideal of Western industrialism. In the United States, over $100 billion is spent each year in advertising aimed at increasing the consumption of goods. The basic logic of continually producing new products for limitless consumption has remained unquestioned by proponents of the traditional management paradigm (Commoner, 1990; Smith, 1992). These assumptions are now challenged by the mounting evidence of widespread environmental destruction and public health risks caused by organized industrial production and unsustainable consumption patterns.

Financial Risk Bias. Another limiting assumption of the traditional management paradigm involves the *concept of risk*. Financial risk dominates the idea of risk in business studies. Company employees assume that the primary risks they face are related to financial and product markets. They assess and manage financial risks in relation to eco-

nomic returns. They also manage product-market risks that involve uncertainty about product demand caused by changing economic conditions, consumer preferences, market demographics, competitive pressures, and regulatory changes.

They ignore the risks posed by technology, its location, its waste products, and its impact on the natural environment. This mindset ignores the numerous ecological, technological, and health risks emanating from industrial hazards that described previously. Industrial hazards also impose risks due to the disruption of larger economic, social, political, and cultural systems.

This narrow-minded discussion of risks in organizations (i.e., how to face risks and how to manage them (March & Shapira 1989) predominates studies of organizations. Little attention has been paid to risks that have been imposed by organizations onto diverse stakeholders or the distribution of these risks among different sectors of society.

Anthropocentrism. Another fundamental limitation of traditional management paradigm is *anthropocentrism*, an ideology that asserts the separateness, uniqueness, primacy, and superiority of the *human* species. This concept legitimizes human welfare as the central purpose of societal institutions. Accordingly, nature is reviewed as an expendable resource for furthering the interests of humans. Humans, thus, have a right to exploit nature without any real concern for maintaining its integrity. Preservation of nature is meaningful only as a condition of human self-interest. Therefore, nature may be protected and conserved so that humans may use it to the "max," both at the present time and in the future. According to anthropocentric assumptions, human beings have no moral obligation to minimize their impact on nature (Devall & Sessions, 1985; Nash, 1989).

Anthropocentrism is part of the traditional management paradigm at a very deep level. It is part of the basic assumptions borrowed from neo-classical economics, which is in itself anthropocentric. Thus, ideas such as, "property rights" over the natural resources, "free market" exchange with linked ecological externalities, "economic rationality" in organizational decision making, denaturalized theories of the firm, and insatiable consumption need of *homo economicus*, are taken for granted in organizational studies (Daly & Cobb, 1989).

Under anthropocentric assumptions, organizational exploitation of natural resources is legitimate, even desirable. Concerns about natural resource extinction rarely surface as strategic organizational issues. When they do, they are prompted not by a preservationist sentiment, but rather by fears of price inflation and future shortages. This anthropocentric attitude has fostered the unchecked exploitation of resources by organizations (Pauchant & Fortier, 1960).

SHIFTING PARADIGMS: ECOCENTRIC MANAGEMENT IN INDUSTRIAL ECOSYSTEMS

If organizations can effectively address the ecological degradation inherent in risk societies, they must use a new management orientation. They need an orientation that focuses centrally on technological and environmental risks; that is, one that does not treat risks as externalities but treats them as the *core problems* of management.

Moving risk to center stage of organizational theory and practice can be accomplished in many ways. My approach here is to adopt the perspective of the stakeholder that bears the most risks from industrial activities: *Nature!* Why? Because nature is fundamental to all life, and certainly human welfare depends on it. Placing nature (and derivatively human health, not wealth) at the center of management/organizational concerns is the hallmark of the alternative ecocentric management paradigm that I proposed.

In this section I provide a preliminary description of the ecocentric management paradigm. My purpose is to help create a vision of ecologically sustainable organization-environment relations. This paradigm is simply a place for management researchers to start from, and consequently, it is tentative, provisional, and incomplete. In the next paragraphs I suggest two basic concepts—*industrial ecosystems* and *ecocentric management* that re-envision interorganizational relations and internal organizational elements. Industrial ecosystems provide a vision of organizational populations and interorganizational relations that are compatible with bioregional natural systems. Ecocentric management in contrast, seeks ecologically sustainable organizational designs and practices.

Industrial Ecosystems

The ecocentric conception of organizational populations and interorganizational relations is based on both the ecological interdependence and ecological performance of organizational communities. Therefore, an industrial ecosystem concept parallels the natural ecosystem concept, a network of connected interdependent organisms and their environment that give and take resources from each other to survive. For example, in a marine ecosystem, big fish eat little fish; little fish eat insects; and insects eat weeds and plankton. Products of natural photosynthesis and waste of fishes and insects serve as nourishment of weeds, plankton, and fish habitats. This arrangement constitutes a self-sufficient, dynamically balances ecosystem.

The industrial ecosystem seeks to emulate this idea of natural ecosystems. Conceptually, it consists of a network of organizations that jointly seek to minimize environmental degradation by using each others waste and by-products, and by sharing and minimizing the use of natural resources (Allenby, 1993; Ayres & Simonis, 1992).

Implicit in such an arrangement is the belief that it is possible to reduce the ecological impact of industrial activities and to use ecological resources more effectively, through cooperative strategies. This cooperation can occur at several levels: (a) the simplest industrial ecosystem network could involve a few proximally located organizations and (b) more extensive industrial ecosystems establish cooperative relations at the local, regional, and even national levels. Ideally, bioregionally bounded ecosystems are desirable because they make the most of natural bioregional capacities for resources, energy, markets, and waste sinks (Frosch & Gallapoulos, 1992; Tibbs, 1991).

A network of companies in Kalundborg, Denmark exemplifies a simple industrial ecosystem. It consists of a power plant, an enzyme plant, a refinery, a chemical plant, a cement plant, a wall-board plant, and some farms. These plants use one another's wastes and by-products as raw materials. They coordinate their use of raw materials, energy, and water, and their waste management practices. Figure 1 shows the flow of resources between them.

The coal-fired Asnaes power plant sells its used steam to the Novo Nordisk enzyme plant and Statoil refinery, instead of condensing it and dumping it into the fjord. The power plant also sells its fly ash to a cement company and its surplus heat to the city for heating. Statoil, in turn, supplies Asnaes with treated waste water for cooling. It also sells the power plant desulphurized gas to burn, saving 30,000 tons of coal a year.

The power plant ships high-sulphur gas emissions to a sulphuric acid plant. Asnaes removes pollutants from its smokestacks and sells the limestone gunk to Gyproc, the wall-board plant. The wall-board plant also receives low-grade (below construction-grade specifications) cement from the cement plant, which cuts the import of mined gypsum. Asnaes warms a fishery that produces 200 tons of trout and turbot each year, and local farms use waste from the fishery and from Novo's enzyme plant as fertilizer.

The conservational impact of this industrial ecosystem on the natural environment is impressive. It saves water, which is pumped from Lake Tisso (seven miles away). The

FIGURE 1. An Industrial Ecosystem

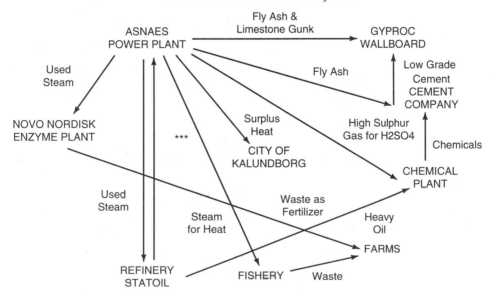

*** Treated Waste Water for Cooling and Desulphurized Gas for Fuel
Result:
Minimization of water use
Maximization of energy use
Resource reuse/Recycling

Ecology cooperation
Image/Public relations

amount of waste sent to landfills is minimized. It reduces pollution that would otherwise be emitted into the atmosphere, and it conserves energy resources in the community. Thus, companies cooperate on ecological problems and are provided a forum for ongoing improvement of environmental performance. In addition, participating companies receive good publicity and enjoy a healthy image.

Viewing organizations as components of industrial ecosystems suggests fundamental changes in their operational scope, strategies, cost structures, location, and management practices. Creating organizations as parts of bioregionally desirable ecosystems requires very different criteria for new product development, venture financing, entrepreneurial forms, and infrastructural services.

Large-scale adoption of the industrial ecosystem model for restructuring interorganizational relations will require new economic and industrial regulations, new industrial infrastructure services, new roles for markets, and new markets for ecologically sound products. Many reasonable proposals for these larger societal changes at the regional, the national, and the international levels have been made in numerous studies. Due to space limitations and the organizational focus of this paper, I will not discuss these, but instead I refer the reader to the following authors: Allenby, (1993), Costanza, (1992), Daly and Cobb, (1989), Naess, 1987; and World Commission on Environment and Development, (1987).

Ecocentric Management

The second part of the ecocentric paradigm focuses on the management of organizational elements that have an impact on nature. The outcome would be to align organizations with their natural environments. This alignment involves a different view of organizational goals, values, products, production systems, organization, environment, and business functions. Table 1 summarizes the

key differences between traditional and ecocentric paradigms. The dichotomies and opposing ideal types represented by the 2 columns of Table 1 are an analytical artifact In reality, the researcher is unlikely to find paradigm in its "pure" type.

The ecocentric paradigm aims at creating sustainable economic development and improving the quality of life worldwide for all organizational stakeholders. It is based on ecocentric and postpatriarchial values that seek freedom from domination of all types. These values reject human domination over nature. They appreciate the importance of intuition and understanding over scientific rationality.

The action consequences of ecocentric management proliferate all aspects of organizations—their mission, inputs, throughputs, and outputs. Ecocentric management seeks ecofriendly products through ecological designs, packaging, and material use. It encourages the use of low energy, smaller amounts of resources, and environmentally efficient and appropriate technologies of production.

Organizations in the ecocentric paradigm are appropriately scaled, provide meaningful work, have decentralized participative decision making, have low earning differentials among employees, and have nonhierarchical structures. They establish harmonious relationships between their natural resources and to minimize waste and pollution.

All business functions assume more ecologically centered roles. Marketing seeks to educate consumers about responsible consumption, instead of promoting unrestricted consumption. Finance aims for long-term sustainable growth, instead of short-term profits. Accounting seeks to incorporate social and environmental costs of production, instead of externalizing them. Management seeks to provide meaningful work and safe working conditions, instead of single-mindedly pursuing labor productivity.

The concept of total quality environmental management (TQEM) provides a framework for managing the environmental im-

TABLE 1.   Traditional Versus Ecocentric Management

Traditional Management	Ecocentric Management
Goals:	
Economic growth & profits	Sustainability and quality of life
Shareholder wealth	Stakeholder welfare
Values:	
Antropocentric	Biocentric or Ecocentric
Rationality and packaged knowledge	Intuition and understanding
Patriarchal values	Postpatriarchal feminist values
Products:	
Designed for function, style, and price	Designs for the environment
Wasteful packaging	Environment friendly
Production System:	
Energy and resource intensive	Low energy and resource use
Technical efficiency	Environmental efficiency
Organization:	
Hierarchical structure	Nonhierarchical structure
Top-down decision making	Participative decision making
Centralized authority	Decentralized authority
High-inome differentlals	Low incom differentials
Environment:	
Domination over nature	Harmony with nature
Environment managed as a resource	Resources regarded as strictly finite
Pollution and waste are externalities	Pollution/waste elimination and management
Business Functions:	
Marketing aims at increasing consumption	Marketing for consumer education
Finance aims at short-term profit maximization	Finance aims at long-term sustainable growth
Accounting focuses on conventional costs	Accounting for social and environmental costs
Human resource management aims at increasing labor productivity	Human resources management aims to make work meaningful the workplace safe/healthy

pacts. TQEM involves systematic greening of organizational missions, inputs, through-puts, and outputs (Shrivastava & Hart, 1992; Council on Environmental Quality, 1993).

Mission.   Traditionally, corporate missions have had a national and financial orientation. They have aimed at satisfying the demands of a narrow set of stakeholders, primarily investors and customers and, secondarily, government and communities (David, 1989). Ecocentric management espouses corporate missions oriented toward long-term, global, and environmental issues. In addition to seeking financial gains, ecocentric companies

actively seek harmony with the natural environment. Nature is a primary stakeholder, both in the regions where a company operates and globally. Ecocentric companies have their commitments to nature clearly articulated in mission statements (Campbell & Young, 1991).

Corporate missions and visions provide the "glue" which holds together other elements of organizations. In fact, alignment of the organization's strategies, structure, systems, and processes is greatly facilitated by a widely shared vision. In ecocentric companies, such a mission and vision includes corporate commitment to:

1. Minimizing the use of virgin materials and nonrenewable forms of energy.
2. Eliminating emissions, effluents, and accidents.
3. Minimizing the life cycle cost of products and services.

Inputs.   Ecocentric managers reject uncontrolled organizational use of inputs in the form of natural resources and energy. They subscribe to the principle of *sustainable* use of natural resources. *Sustainable use* means pacing the exploitation of renewable resources in such a way that they can regenerate themselves through natural processes. It also involves minimizing the use of nonrenewable resources. The basis for this principle is recognition that the earth's resources are finite.

Ecocentric management seeks to *minimize the use of virgin materials and nonrenewable forms of energy.* This goal can be achieved by (a) reducing energy and material use through conservation measures; (b) making greater use of recycled or renewable materials and energy; or (c) offsetting consumption with replenishment.

The practical possibilities in resource and energy conservation are immense. Many companies are already developing innovative conservation programs. For example, the National Audubon Society's new headquarters building cuts its use of energy by 40 percent through solar architectural design, use of energy efficient lighting fixtures, and conservation-oriented maintenance and energy use programs. Herman Miller abandoned the use of virgin timber in their top lines of furniture, turning instead to wood grown on a sustained yield basis. The Body Shop is replenishing the fossil fuel-based energy it buys from utilities. It has established a wind energy plant in Scotland, which supplies energy back to the electric grid.

Throughputs.   The throughput system or production process is often associated with environmental risks, occupational and public health risks, and inefficient use of material and human resources. Ecocentric management seeks to *eliminate emissions, effluents, workplace hazards, and risks of accident.* The production process aims at achieving a "zero discharge" goal, and a "zero risk" goal. It focuses efforts toward the virtual elimination of waste. It espouses a preventative approach rather than controlling approach after pollution and hazards are created.

The potential for ecocentric production systems is exemplified by Dow Chemical's new ethylene plant in Fort Saskatchewan, Canada. This facility was designed to minimize discharges of waste water. It will release only 10 gallons of waste water per minute, compared to 360 gallons per minute for a traditional plant. Corporations are realizing that throughput process improvement have a cost-saving effect and can even generate revenue. Evidence of these benefits is provided by 3M Company's Pollution Prevention Pays (3P) Program, Dow Chemical's Waste Reduction Always Pays (WRAP) Program, and Chevron's Save Money and Reduce Toxics (SMART) Program (Hunt & Auster, 1990; Kleiner, 1991).

3M saved nearly $500 million and prevented 500,000 tons of pollution between 1975 and 1989 through its 3P Program. This program has been based on pollution reduction at the source through product reformulation, process modification, equipment redesign, and recycling and reuse of materials. Each project undertaken by the 3P program must meet four criteria; (a) eliminate or reduce pollution, (b) save energy or materials and resources, (c) demonstrate technological innovation, and (d) save money.

Outputs.   Products and waste are the two primary outputs of organizations. Product choice and design have important implications for the natural environment. Products that lack durability or are difficult to repair place greater demand on the resource base of new materials and energy. Products that are difficult or expensive to reuse or recycle result in unnecessary costs for waste and disposal. Ecocentric management seeks to *mini-*

mize the life-cycle cost of its products and services. Life-cycle costs attaches a monetary figure to every impact of a product, that is, disposal costs, legal fees, liability for product harm, loss of environmental quality, and so on. Product-development decisions have been based not only on projected cash flow, but also on the projected future costs associated with each product design (Buzzelli, 1991).

Ecocentric managers view organizational waste both as an environmental problem and as a business opportunity. They seek to minimize and treat waste in a manner least harmful to the environment. Waste-management strategies include waste reduction, reuse, and recycling. Then, remaining waste is incinerated or placed in a landfill. The opportunities in waste management include both in cost reduction and the safe dealing with the enormous inventory of hazardous waste. In fact, the business opportunity in hazardous waste management is estimated to be over $200 billion (EPA, 1990).

Systems Approach. A systems approach to managing environmental impacts of organizational activities is central to ecocentric management. If managers consider jointly all of the aspects of the organizational system, this awareness helps to prevent the shifting of environmental harm from one subsystem to another. This approach can be facilitated by organizations adopting life-cycle assessment methodology for minimizing the ecological impacts of products from "cradle to grave." Ultimately, the corporation should close the loop of output and input processes.

CHALLENGES OF ECOCENTRIC MANAGEMENT

The ecocentric management paradigm has serious implications for management practice and theory. Corporate managers face many strategic and operational questions. For example, how should they redesign and navigate their business portfolios to meet ecological limitations and bottlenecks? What are the human resource needs of ecocentric organizations? How do ecological costs change the financial structure of investment projects and firm competitiveness? What are the market potentials for ecofriendly technologies and "green markets?"

The ecocentric management paradigm also poses important challenges to the traditional management paradigm and theories. It calls for revising them significantly: that is, adopting a management theory that is not anthropocentric. A theory that researchers can use to acknowledge ecological risk and degradation as central variables in organizational analysis. This theory would not be biased towards ecologically unsustainable production and consumption. This theory would help researchers and practitioners alike to understand technological and environmental factors as key corporate risks.

Ecocentrism calls for questioning the very concept of organizations. If the organizational environment is viewed as an ecobiosphere, it forces those in the field of management to question the simplistic assumption that organizations are innocent *systems of production* that produce products desired by consumers. Accordingly, this theory suggests that organizations also must be seen as *systems of destruction* because they systematically destroy environmental value. This destruction cannot be dismissed as an "externality" of production that the firm must not account for. It must be treated as a central and systematic feature of organized economic activity.

This view of firms suggests revising management's basic concepts of *organizational objectives and strategy*. Objectives of the firm that maximize (or satisfice) variables like profits, revenues, and productivity, are incomplete and inadequate. Such objectives also must include minimizing the negative and destructive effects of organizational activities.

This new concept of strategy deals with the co-alignment of organization with its environment. A firm's strategy cannot be limited to defining both its domain of operation and scope at the corporate level and its competitive approaches at the business-unit level. This strategy must include some conception of the firm's relationship with the natural environment. It must address issues of impact of the firm's activities on the natural and social environments, and it must provide avenues for renewal of environmental resources that the organization uses.

Today, the challenge facing organizational researchers is momentous: for each management theory, proponents must reflexively identify implications of ecocentrism. Reconceptualizing fundamental concepts like *orga-*

nizations, objectives, and *strategies,* forces researchers and practitioners to rethink much of what they know about organizations. Part of this rethinking involves making the functional areas of business (operations, accounting, marketing, finance, administration, and human resource management) more ecocentric. Fortunately, "green marketing" and "green accounting" have already been put to use in making progress toward ecocentrism in both theory development and practice (Gray, Bebbington, & Walters, 1993). My hope is that in the coming years we (in management) will see the flowering of green organizational/management theories and practices.

REFERENCES

Aldrich, H.E. 1979. *Organizations and environments.* Englewood Cliffs, NJ: Prentice Hall.

Allenby, B.R. 1993. *Industrial ecology.* New York: Prentice Hall.

Alvesson, M. 1992. *Critical organizational theory.* Newbury, CA: Sage.

Ayres, R.U., & Simonis, U. (Eds.) 1992. *Industrial metabolism.* Tokyo: UN University Press.

Beck. U. 1992a *Risk society: Towards a new modernity.* Newbury Park, CA: Sage.

Beck, U. 1992b. From industrial society to risk society. *Theory, Culture, and Society,* 9(1): 97–123.

Bell, D. 1975. *The coming of post-industrial society.* New York: Basic Books.

Bernstein, P.L. 1992. *Capital ideas: The improbable origins of modern Wall Street.* New York: Free Press.

Brown, L., Chandler, W.U., Flavin, C., Jacobson, J., Polock, C., Postel, D., Starke, L., & Wolf, E.C. 1991. *State of the World.* Washington, DC: Worldwatch Institute.

Buchholz, R., Marcus, A., & Post, J. 1992. *Managing environmental issues: A case book.* Englewood Cliffs, NJ: Prentice Hall.

Burrell, G., & Morgan, G. 1978. *Sociological paradigms and organizational analysis.* London: Hienemann.

Buzzelli, D. 1991. Time to structure an environmental policy strategy. *Journal of Business Strategy* 12(2): 17–20.

Campbell, A. & Young, S. 1991. Creating a sense of mission. *Long Range Planning,* 24: 10–20.

Carson, R. 1962. *Silent Spring.* Greenwich, CT: Fawcett.

Carroll, A.B. 1979. A three-dimensional conceptual model of corporate social performance. *Academy of Management Review,* 4, 497–505.

Clark, M. 1989. *Ariadne's thread.* New York: St. Martin's Press.

Clarke, L. 1989. *Acceptable risk: Making decisions in a toxic environment.* Berkeley: University of California Press.

Commoner, B. 1990. *Making peace with the planet.* New York: Pantheon Books.

Costanza, R. 1992. *Ecological economics.* New York: Columbia University Press.

Couch, S., & Kroll-Smith, S. 1991. *Communities at risk.* New York: Peter Lang.

Council on Environmental Quality. 1993. *Total Environmental Quality Management.* Washington, DC: CEQ.

Daly, H.E. 1977. *Steady state economics.* San Francisco: Freeman.

Daly, H., & Cobb, J. 1989. *For the common good.* New York: Beacon Press.

David, F. 1989. How companies define their mission. *Long Range Planning,* 22: 15–24.

Davis, J. 1991. *Greening business.* Oxford, England: Blackwell.

Deal, T.E., & Kennedy, A.A. 1982. *Corporate cultures.* Reading, MA: Adisson Wesley.

Devall, B., & Sessions, G. 1985. *Deep ecology: Living as if nature mattered.* Salt Lake City, UT: Peregrine Smith Books.

Douglas, M., & Wildavsky, A. 1982. *Risk and culture.* Berkeley: University of California Press.

Ehrlich, P., & Ehrlich, A. 1991. *The population explosion.* New York: Touchstone.

Emery, F.E., & Trist, E.L. 1965. The casual texture of organizational environments. *Human Relations*, 18: 21–32.

EPA. 1990. Environmental investments: The cost of a clean environment. Washington, DC: U.S. Government Printing Office.

Etzioni, A. 1988. *The moral dimension.* New York: Free Press.

Fahey, L., & Narayanan, V.K. 1984. *Environmental analysis.* St. Paul, MN: West.

Fischer, F., & Sirianni, C. 1993. *Critical perspectives on bureaucracy.* (2nd Rev. ed.). Philadelphia: Temple University Press.

Freeman, R.E. 1984. *Strategic management: A stakeholder approach.* Boston: Pitman.

Frosch, R.A., & Gallapoulos, N.E. 1992. Towards an industrial ecology. In A.D. Bradshaw (Ed.), *The treatment and handling of wastes.* London: Chapman Hall.

Frost, P., Moore, L.F., Louis, M.R., Lundberg, C.C., & Martin, J. 1985. *Organizational culture.* Beverly Hills, CA: Sage.

Giddens, A. 1990. *The consequences of modernity.* Stanford, CA: Stanford University Press.

Giddens, A. 1991. *Modernity and self identity in the late modern age.* Cambridge, England: Cambridge University Press.

Goldstein, R.L., Shorr, J.K. 1991. *Demanding democracy after Three Mile Island.* Gainesville: University of Florida Press.

Goodpaster, K. 1989. *Business ethics: The state of the art.* New York: Oxford University Press.

Gray, R., with Beggington, J., & Walters, D. 1993. *Accounting for the environment.* London: Chapman.

Habermas, J. 1989. *A theory of communicative action.* Boston: Beacon Press.

Hall, R.H., & Quinn, R.E. (Eds.). 1983. *Organization theory and public policy.* Beverly Hills, CA: Sage.

Hannan, M. and Freeman, J. 1989. *Organizational Ecology.* Cambridge, MA: Harvard University Press.

Hoffman, W.M., Frederick, R., & Petry, E.S. 1990. *The corporation, ethics, and the environment.* New York: Quorum Books.

Hunt, C., & Auster, E. 1990. Proactive environmental management: Avoiding the toxic trap. *Sloan Management Review*, 31(2): 7–18.

Kleindorfer, P., & Kunreuther, H. 1987. *Insuring and managing hazardous risks: From Seveso to Bhopal and beyond.* New York: Springer-Verlag.

Kleiner, A. 1991. What does it mean to be green? *Harvard Business Review*, 69(4): 38–47.

Krimsky, S., & Golding, D. 1992. *Social theories of risk.* Westport, CT: Praeger.

Lash, S. 1993. Reflexive modernization: the aesthetic dimension *Theory, Culture, and Society*, 10(1): 1–23.

Lave, L. (Ed.). 1987. *Risk assessment and management.* New York: Plenum Press.

Likens, G. 1987. Chemical wastes in our atmosphere—An ecological crisis. *Industrial Crisis Quarterly*, 1(4): 13–33.

Luhmann, N. 1990. Technology, environment, and social risk: A systems perspective. *Industrial Crisis Quarterly*, 4(3): 223–232.

March, J.G., & Simon, H. 1958/1993. *Organizations.* New York: Wiley.

March, J.G., & Shapira, Z. 1989. Managerial perspectives on risk and risk taking. *Management Science*, 33, 11, 1404–1421.

McNeill, J. 1989. Strategies for sustainable economic development. *Scientific American*, September 155–165.

Miner, J.B. 1984. Theories of organizational behavior. New York: McGraw-Hill.

Mitnick, B. 1980. *The political economy of regulation: Creating, designing, and removing regulations.* New York: Columbia University Press.

Mitroff, I., & Pauchant, T. 1990. *We are so big and powerful nothing bad can happen to us.* New York: Carol.

Naess, A. 1987. *Ecology, community and lifestyle: Ecosophy.* 1987. Cambridge, England: Cambridge University Press.

Nash, R.F. 1989. *The rights of nature.* Madison: University of Wisconsin Press.

Nelkin, D. 1979. *Controversy: Politics of technical decisions.* Newbury Park, CA: Sage.

Parsons, T. 1982. *On institutions and social evolution.* Chicago, IL: University of Chicago Press.

Pauchant, T., & Fortier, J. 1990. Anthropocentric ethics in organizations, strategic management, and the environment. In P. Shrivastava & R. Lamb (Eds.), *Advances in strategic management*, vol. 6: 99–114. Greenwich, CT: JAI Press.

Perrow, C. 1984. *Normal accidents: Living with high-risk technologies.* New York: Basic Books.

Pfeffer, J. 1982. *Organizations and organization theory.* Boston: Pitman.

Piller, C. 1991. *The fail-safe society: Community defiance and the end of American technological optimism.* New York: Basic Books.

Porter M.E. 1980. *Competitive strategy.* New York: Free Press.

Post, J.E. 1991. Management as if the earth mattered. *Business Horizons*, 34(4): 32–38.

Preston, L. (Ed.) 1985. *Research in corporate social performance.* Greenwich, CT: JAI Press.

Scott, R.W. 1981. *Organizations: Rational, natural and open systems.* Englewood Cliffs, NJ: Prentice Hall.

Schendel, D., & Hofer, C.W. 1979. *Strategic management: A new view of business policy and planning.* Boston: Little, Brown.

Sethi, S.P., & Steidelmeier, P. 1971. *Up against the corporate wall.* Englewood Cliffs, NJ: Prentice Hall.

Short, J.F., & Clarke, L. 1992. *Organizations, uncertainties, and risk.* Boulder, CO: Westview.

Shrivastava, P. 1986. Is strategic management ideological? *Journal of Management*, 12(3): 79–92.

Shrivastava, P. 1994. *Greening business: Towards sustainable corporations.* Cincinnati, OH: Thompson Executive Press.

Shrivastava, P. In press. Castrated environment: Greening organizational studies. *Organization Studies.*

Shrivastava, P., & Hart, S. 1992. Greening organizations—2000. *International Journal of Public Administration*, 1763–4: 607–635.

Siomkos, G. 1989. Managing product harm crises. *Industrial Crisis Quarterly*, 30(1): 41–60.

Slovic, P. 1987. Perception of risk. *Science*, 236(4799): 280–285.

Smith, Dennis, 1992. *Business and the environment.* London: Chapman.

Stead, W., & Stead, J. 1992. *Management for a small planet.* Newbury Park, CA: Sage.

Throop, G., Starik, M., & Rands, G. 1993. Sustainable strategy in a greening world. In P. Shrivastava, A. Huff, & J. Dutton (Eds.), *Integrating the natural environment into strategic management*, Vol. 9: 63–92. Greenwich, CT: JAI Press.

Tibbs, H. *Industrial ecology: An environmental agenda for industry.* Boston: Technology and Product Development Directorate, Arthur D. Little, Inc.

Tinker, A. 1989. *Paper prophets: A critique of the social role of accounting.* (photocopy).

Whitley, 1984. Management studies as a fragmented adhocracy. *Journal of Management Studies*, 2: 109–119.

Williamson, O.E. 1985. *The economic institutions of capitalism: Firms, markets, and relational contracts.* New York: Free Press.

Wood, D. 1991. Corporate social performance revisited. *Academy of Management Review*, 16: 691–718.

World Commission on Environment and Development. 1987. *Our common future.* New York: Oxford University Press.

TOO CLOSE FOR COMFORT

*How the business press protects
the corporate status quo*

Charles A. Riley, II

The key to understanding the coverage of corporate policy and behavior in the business press lies not in an examination of the reporters and editors, but their audience and sources. There is a sacred loop connecting the upper-level managers who read the magazine and those who are quoted in it. Like a computer program that loops around and repeats itself in a pattern—neither creative nor original—the echoes created by this closed circuit of opinion and dogma have made business magazines and television programs into staunch defenders of the status quo. The fault of the writers and editors, and their corporate bosses in the major news organizations, lies in snuggling up too close to these sources and entering the conversation as yet another echo of their cliches.

Ideally, good journalists have the ability to set aside their own interests and opinions to allow sources and readers to communicate directly. The journalist as medium is most effective when, like a transparent window, he or she intervenes least in the passage of information and opinions from expert sources to readers uncolored by the journalist's views and opinions. In the case of business, this can be a difficult task, particularly given the average reader's relatively low level of interest in serious business issues, particularly technical or ethical problems, and the reader's specialized and often narrowly defined knowledge as compared with the broader,

though much less specialized, stance of a young, well-educated magazine staff working and living in Manhattan.

Some of this can be illustrated through a comparison of the three groups involved: readers, sources, and journalists. Although no definitive study of the sources has been done, pinpointing factors like age, educational level and other characteristics, by design there is a match between sources and readers. They are nearly a mirror image of one another. If anything, the sources are somewhat richer and more powerful, certainly by virtue of appearing in the magazine more celebrated, and that plays up to one of the fundamental psychological factors in the business press: The love of a fantasy or dream to which many readers aspire which takes particular shape in the photographs and details offered by the magazine. There is a whole "lifestyle of the rich and famous" element to the profiles and other stories in *Fortune*, *Forbes*, *Business Week* and other business publications. When a low-level manager picks up the magazine and sees a rich and powerful person on the cover, he or she imaginatively replaces the face with his own in a kind of fantasy that extends through all the photos of the huge office, the smiling family with a beautiful, usually younger and blonde "trophy" wife (the subject of a whole cover feature in one notorious issue of *Fortune*), the fast cars and the huge set of golf clubs or polo ponies or yacht that are the basic props for these photo shoots. Much of the writing in these magazines, like the trappings in the photographs, is meant to tease the reader into fantasies of having an immense staff of secretaries and a limo waiting outside the Beechcraft corporate jet, meeting with heads of state in Eastern Europe and China to close on gargantuan deals, and heading off to Singapore to pick up the 100-foot yacht for a sail around Bali to relax. My own experience as a reporter led me to find precious space in an article for details about the bowling alley and private tennis and basketball courts of one corporate raider, and I was continually on the alert to note the personal art collections and paintings by Monet, Miro, Picasso or Roy Lichtenstein hanging in the offices or homes of the subjects I interviewed. Where trade-offs are made in choosing the kind of "color" and detail that can go into a story after all the editing is done and the huge reporting files were culled for the essentials on a story, all too often tidbits about the lifestyle or perks would make it into the final version while hours of significant interviews or piles of financial figures would end up on the cutting room floor.

The demographics of the journalists do not match that of the readers or sources, particularly in terms of age or income, and the disparity means that reporters have to accommodate the perspective of an older, richer, far more conservative audience that reflects the "voice of management" in the magazine's pages. The revealing demographic studies done by magazines in order to produce beautifully printed and presented "subscriber portraits" are mainly tools for advertising sales representatives, but they also serve as a guide to editors and writers who abide by the principle that the reader, like the customer, is always right. The writers at *Fortune*, to take one example, have a constant visual reminder of whom they were writing for in the form of the magazine's cover images of heavy-set, greying American business leaders in French-cut tailored shirts, Hermes ties and loud Brooks Brothers suspenders looking earnest-ly out at us from the newsstands: Fallen angels like Ross Johnson formerly of RJR Nabisco, the late lamented John Akers of IBM, or Lee Iaccocca of Chrysler, as well as those who have managed to hang on like Jack Welch of General Electric, leveraged buy-out sharks like Carl Icahn and Henry Kravis, clothing tycoons such as Leslie Wexner and Donald Fisher, the cagey Warren Buffett of Berkshire Hathaway, Ford's Harold "Red" Poling and others of their ilk. One of the most welcome changes in this rogue's gallery in the past two decades was the chance to put the bespectacled whiz-kid of Microsoft, Bill Gates, on the cover in his tieless Lacoste shirt.

WRITING CORPORATE HAGIOGRAPHY

The driving force behind the use of these famous faces and personal stories involves, naturally, revenues from both advertising and circulation. While advertising accounts for more than 75 percent of most magazines' annual sales, followed by subscriptions and, a long way behind, newsstand sales figures, there is a direct correlation between the newsstand battles and the ability of the advertising sales representatives to land big contracts. Less importantly, but psychologically more revealing, is the battle of egos among the business magazines that peg their sense of success upon the measured factor of which one outsells the other at the newsstand.

Without question, a "hot face" sells magazines. During the 1970s, Iaccocca's portrait on a business magazine would clinch the newsstand prize every time, on a par with the latter-day magnetism in another magazine field that was wielded by pictures of Princess Diana. While John Sculley and Bill Gates come close, their appeal was more constricted, and Donald Trump is still too big a joke to command the attention of real business readers. This is obviously "people journalism" at work, of the kind that spurred Time Inc. to take a column out of the back pages of their flagship magazine and make it into one of their topselling weeklies: *People*. By focusing on the personalities and idiosyncrasies of individuals, it arguably diverts attention from the business, economic and political issues that some might assume should have priority in a magazine that calls itself, for example, *Business Week*. This is one of the reasons that so many journalists revere the work of *The Economist*.

The cult of the business personality, and in particular the romanticization of certain business figures, has a strange effect on journalism. It seduces writers into becoming hagiographers, in the tradition of the Medieval scholiasts who in earnest devotion labored over the lives of the saints. The formula for these articles is a basic one. A public relations officer from a major company, often one whose chairman is on the board of McGraw-Hill or Time Inc. or is a close personal friend of one of the top executives at the media giant owning the magazine, pitches the idea of an in-depth profile of the CEO. An associate editor is dispatched to the company's headquarters, at the magazine's expense (most magazines forbid writers to accept travel money from the subjects they are covering) and is wined and dined for at least a day by the public relations team, which fill the writer in on background and prepare him or her for the interviews. Then a day is set aside for the writer to follow the CEO around, often from breakfast at his home through the arrival at the office and a few meetings, followed by luncheon with beaming employees and perhaps a speech or conference in the afternoon and an evening at the ballet or the art museum where the CEO is a patron or board member. Carefully choreographed, this "unlimited access" is the big attraction for journalists, who are supposed to get "inside the mind of management," as *Fortune*'s old advertising slogan puts it. The next two days are spent interviewing the number two and number three executives and a few division heads, with an obligatory trip to the shop floor or a bit of wandering in the hallways. You can imagine the degree of

candor and critical distance these secondary interviews offer. Who is going to criticize the boss, in print in a major magazine and for the record?

Upon returning to New York, the writer is given a reporter associate who is in charge of going through a Lexus/Nexus search for financials on the company as well as doing a bit more phone interviewing. Perhaps the sister or cousin or an old business school professor can provide the obligatory story about how the CEO was a math prodigy or a killer player at Monopoly that fleshes out the biographical element in the story. On top of that, either the writer or reporter calls a few Wall Street analysts, either picked from Nelson's Directory according to the industries they cover or out of the Rolodex full of reliable analysts that a beat reporter should have if he or she has been covering telecommunications or automotives or any other field for a period of time. Finally, the story is put together, along the lines of a particular formula (just like the hagiographies of old) with the quotes and information in all the right places.

A key moment in the editing process comes when the managing editor's office calls the writer, reporter, art director and photo researcher into a little projection room and about 50 different slides are flashed on the screen from the photo shoot that occurred, generally after the writer has left town (most photo shoots do not involve an interviewer who is present, but are done by professional freelancers). Of these, probably four or five will be chosen. The process can take anywhere from 15 minutes to an hour, and is thought through and argued with tremendous care. Although the attempt to be creative is obvious—the technique was perfected by the staged *Sports Illustrated* photo shoots—the body language is fairly standard from one CEO profile to the next. The head shot is fundamental. For the "candids," the body language is everything. Virtually all the top-ranking women pictured in the magazines will have their arms folded sternly across their chests. It is also a favorite pose for men, along with the foot up on the chair or desk, or the hand thrust out imploringly from the podium at the annual meeting. An image of the CEO with his jacket off, his French cuffs rolled up and one button undone with his tie judiciously loosened while he talks to subordinates earnestly is also useful. Hard hat shots used to be fashionable but are out now, replaced by the CEO at the computer keyboard, plugging away in an effort to show that he is as high-tech as he is supposed to be (surveys show that many of them lack computer skills).

One of the most recent examples of this kind of hagiography is a cover story that appeared in *Fortune* in May 1994, with the cover tag line, "Is Herb Kelleher America's BEST CEO?" followed by the little teaser, "He's wild, he's crazy, he's in a tough business—and he has built the most successful airline in the U.S." Kelleher, the 63-year-old chairman of Southwest Airlines, is shown on the cover with an idiotic grin on his face evidently jumping—a metaphor for flying—with his arms outspread in an old leather aviator's hat and goggles, his red tie flapping in the breeze against a bright blue sky. On the table of contents, in the same getup, he is staring in a visionary trance up into that blue sky, apparently looking for his squadron. The corny caption reads: "Southwest Airlines Chairman Herb Kelleher has lofty ambitions for his operation—and a decided flair for keeping things hopping at work."

Right away you know where the story is headed. By using an offbeat, clownish personal style, and a "work should be fun" attitude, Kelleher earns the loyalty of his employees and helps sales enough to make a success in the patently disastrous airline industry. The cover piece was written by Kenneth Labich, who is in his own right one of the fun-loving, and funny, members of the magazine's staff, a big Falstaffian bear of a man who has been covering the airlines for about two decades and knows the executives and the companies so thoroughly that he is perfectly capable of revealing both their deepest problems and the highlights. The

glowing prose he lavishes on Kelleher has more to do with the magazine's bullish agenda on American business than it does with Labich's personal sense of what is right and wrong in the airline industry. His comments about many of the subjects he writes about are acerbic and deadly in their accuracy, but his writing has to serve a function.

Whenever you read a business magazine's cover story, take a moment to peruse the "Editor's Desk" or publisher's memo at the front of the issue, in which a few inside tips on how the story was done are offered to readers in an almost club-like gesture of letting the subscriber backstage at a performance. The "Editor's Desk" is based on quick interviews with the writers at the conclusion of the editing process and just before the issue goes to bed. For the May issue that featured Kelleher, Labich shares the limelight with Bill Saporito, another member of the *Fortune* board of editors, who provides a profile of Wal-Mart CEO David Glass in the same issue. In all likelihood, Labich and Saporito were in a benign competition to get the cover, and Labich's story won because Wal-Mart is overexposed in the press. The photos on the "Editor's Desk" show Saporito, in sunglasses and a Yankees cap (he is a huge baseball fan) sitting at a preseason Kansas City Royals game with CEO Glass, who is also chairman of the Royals franchise, and his family. Saporito, beer in hand, is enjoying a joke with Glass and his son Dan under a bright blue sky with palm trees in the background. In the center of the page, Labich is pictured in a head shot, in his tie and jacket, looking like a modern-day version of one of Holbein's portraits of Henry VIII.

The text of the "Editor's Desk" weaves the two pictures together. The theme of the two stories is "people really matter," according to managing editor Marshall Loeb, who signs the "Editor's Desk." There is a joke about Saporito, the Yankees fan, and Glass, the Royals's chairman, debating the merits of their beloved ball clubs. Then the text cuts to Labich, who "loves the Chicago Cubs but gets his real lift from airlines." Labich has picked Kelleher "who just may be America's best CEO," because of his attention to people. Then Labich is quoted offering his own opinion, as a way of allowing him to express what he thinks in an editorial fashion as opposed to the reporting that is supposed to be objective in the story. "In a service business, how you treat people *counts*. They're going to pass that along to the customer." The "Editor's Desk" wraps up by saying that Saporito coincidentally ran into Kelleher, Labich's prey, at Sam Walton's funeral in 1992, and found that Kelleher was an admirer of the late Walton, "a man who could laugh at himself." The other similarity that Saporito notices was that both Kelleher and Walton ran companies that are "incredibly cheap" since Kelleher personally approves any expenditure over $1,000, a disciplinary tidbit that does not appear in the main story. The kicker to the "Editor's Desk" is Saporito's observation that "The Wal-Mart folks stay at Motel 3, where they don't even leave the lights on for you." Even before we turn inside to the articles themselves, we have a perfect picture of the tight circles along which business journalism traces its path. The writers enjoying a ballgame with the CEO, going to Sam Walton's funeral, bumping into the same tightly knit group of American corporate leaders seemingly wherever they go. This is not criticism of either Labich or Saporito, as they are doing their job—getting "inside the mind of management"—and working their connections. But critical distance is missing.

The Kelleher feature is vintage *Fortune* hagiography, down to the story about the CEO who will stay out with a mechanic in a bar until four a.m. to help figure out what is wrong with a plane. The business magazines run both corporate profiles and individual profiles, and it is significant that both follow the same format. Incidentally, the libel laws covering both are virtually the same, so that a corporation can sue a writer or magazine for libel just as an individual can. The logical connection is the focus on "style" and personality, as though a whole corporation takes its cue from the personal style of one individ-ual or a company can be written about in the same way that a person can be, as a character that behaves according to psychological patterns of behavior. This identification of a corporate style with an individual style is also part of the rationale behind "people" journalism in business. Traditionally, an *ad hominem* approach to political or financial phenomena was frowned on, particularly in the case of an attack. In our time, *ad hominem* is the path that writing about business most frequently takes.

The article, which follows a scene-by-scene construction in the same way that a movie's shooting script is put together, opens in the ballroom of a midtown Manhattan hotel where Kelleher, the successful joker, has a crowd of 300 airline industry officials in stitches with a speech. "Kelleher—Herb to even his most fleeting acquaintances—is not just the current darling of U.S. aviation. He is also the airline industry's jokemeister, the High Priest of Ha-Ha, a man who has appeared in public dressed as Elvis and the Easter Bunny, who has carved an anti public persona out of his affection for cigarettes, bourbon, and bawdy stories. A fair percentage of the crowd have been up late swapping lies with Herb a time or two, and now they are waiting for him to say something . . . *outrageous*," writes Labich. Masterfully, one might add, because with his touches of Tom Wolfe and Hunter S. Thompson and his sly hints of juicy jokes and stories to come, Labich has concocted the perfect opener. Who would not want to read on?

The point is that "Kelleher owns this crowd," and his charisma allows him to own his employees as well. The next section of the article quotes Wall Street analysts and the U.S. Department of Transportation surveys along the lines of proving that Southwest really is a success story, and the sentences are generously laced with numbers that show rising revenues, 25% annual earnings increases, and relatively low debt to total capitalization rates compared with the miserable numbers posted by United, American, Delta and other U.S. carriers. Then Labich returns to Kelleher, "the Metternich of the Metroplex" with his "wolfish grin," as he offers a thumbnail sketch of his origins, his father's position as general manager of Campbell Soup where Kelleher worked on the factory floor, his days as a star athlete in high school, college and law school, and the whole drama of starting up Southwest. The narrative is compressed, straightforward, and peppered with little quips from Kelleher to keep the humor flowing, as well as little references to the $86 million in exercisable stock options Kelleher currently owns just to remind readers of the serious money involved.

After the bio, the brief look at Kelleher on the job and his thoughts on management follow, as well as a fairly dry section on how an airline has to be run in order to make a profit with particular attention to the thorny problem of labor disputes. Labich is careful to relate how well Kelleher's people take care of customers and how highly they think of him and his "hoo-ha brio." It makes the whole idea of working for Kelleher a kind of "cause" or movement, that you either buy into or cannot handle, and the bond uniting his 12,000 workers is likened to "some sort of religious cult," a comparison that Kelleher says he finds flattering.

The next scene takes us back to Kelleher the man, his fondness for parties, Wild Turkey bourbon, cigarettes and a huge stuffed turkey an admirer sent to him that holds a half gallon jug of bourbon—when you pull up on the tail feathers the liquor comes out the beak. Labich relates that Kelleher is about to celebrate his 40th wedding anniversary, and has put four kids through college, that he loved a recent biography of Winston Churchill, hunts and fishes in Wyoming and has plenty of stamina left for the kind of "hell-raising that he has always enjoyed."

PRECEDENT: THE SECOND LOOP

In addition to the circuit formed by nearly identical readers and sources, there is another closed loop that determines how business is covered. Once a magazine has taken a position on an issue, all further coverage of the issue is expected to adhere to that position. The significance of previously published articles, like the weight of precedence in the law, can shape the presentation of a rolling story for a decade or more. It is fairly clear, from the perspective of 1993, that most business writers missed the AIDS story and often mishandled the facts, but it is not the purpose of this study to simply harp on these mistakes. As Martin Mayer observes, "Second-guessing the coverage of an event is an easy sport and —given the self-righteousness of the executives of news organizations (not the grunts in the trenches, who are often self-critical)—it is an all but irresistible sport. But news is necessarily unreflective."[1] In the case of AIDS, this has been particularly evident at *Fortune, Business Week* and most dramatically *Barron's* where editors have consistently hammered the Federal government for spending too much on AIDS research. The relative silence at *Forbes* on the issue was attributed by many in the field to the possibility that Malcolm Forbes Sr., whose bisexuality was well known in the world of business journalism, may have died of AIDS.[2] Given the conservative bent of the readership, it should come as no surprise that the general editorial slant of the major business books is also conservative despite the left-leaning privately held views of many of the reporters and the general effort made to make features as objective as possible. The editorials only reflect the bias, and then future staff writers are obliged to adhere to the line year after year.

The business press coverage of AIDS offers a focal point for a number of problems afflicting not only the media but also business itself. Because the loop of sources and audiences is so tight, and the precedents are so strong, the *status quo* is inevitably preserved. Any attempt to break through to an Archimedean point of reference to study the key problems facing American business is stifled. It is typical of business thinking to return again and again to old policies, and it is typical of the media to recycle old stories with new numbers. One longtime observer of this phenomenon is Andre Alkiewicz, a former British intelligence officer who runs a think tank in Connecticut called Perception International. Alkiewicz spends his day culling the world press for signs of change that will be of interest to his corporate clients, including AT&T, Ford, Conrail and a number of investment firms. He is continually frustrated by the difficulty he faces in getting executives as well as business reporters to face the changes and observe the links between signs of a trend that is first taking shape as a series of connected anomalies. "With TK, as with a number of other crises that have affected American business in the last decade, the trouble is that nobody noticed the early warning signs, and asked what caused the anomaly. Behind the big picture is a still bigger picture, involving social and political as well as economic factors."[3] It is precisely this bigger picture that has eluded both business journalists and the business leaders they cover.

THE PREVAILING ATTITUDE

Understanding the attitude of business leaders is surprisingly easy for a writer or editor. In addition to being in contact with the major players at every *Fortune 500* company, we had privileged information on our readers. The research departments at *Fortune, Business Week* and *Forbes* maintain sophisticated profiles of the typical reader, tracking income and wealth, education and corporate responsibilities. At *Fortune*, the reader profile also included information on what he drinks (Vodka for 54 percent, Scotch for 46 percent), drives (75 percent drive American cars, and 10 percent drive a BMW), does on the weekend (48 percent play golf, 38 percent go to art galleries, 77 percent watch American movies) and wears (100 percent buy suits worth $400 or more). The use of "he" in that sentence is neither accidental nor sexist. In 1988, when I

was working on my story about AIDS for *Fortune*, 85 percent of the readers were men, 76 percent were married, half were between the ages of 35 and 54 and 12 percent were over 65. Their average income was $147,000, and their average net worth was $1,218,000.[4] By 1992, the percentage of married readers was up to 79, and the average income had grown to $165,300. The magazine prides itself on reaching the top management (48 percent) of business, industry or professions (91 percent) at large corporations (37 percent run companies with more than 10,000 employees and 25 percent are in charge of organizations with annual sales in excess of $5 billion). The questionnaire does not include race or sexual preference, but reliable sources indicate that 2 percent of *Fortune* readers are gay, and less than 10 percent are African-American and Hispanic.[5]

As far as advertisers are concerned (subscriber's portraits are prepared and packaged in lavish booklets in order to lure buyers of ad space) these are dream demographics. For writers trying to sell an AIDS story, they are a nightmare. The demographic portrait of the business reader is, in short, an exact match for the Center for Disease Control's demographic portrait of the lowest risk group for AIDS, not only in terms of the high proportion of married white males but with respect to educational and income levels as well. Only the high concentration of readers in the Northeast and West, including San Francisco and New York, is at odds with the overwhelmingly heavy statistical indications that *Fortune* readers are unlikely to have any personal stake in the story. Using the criterion of personal vulnerability or connections to the disease it is clear that AIDS is likely to have a very low interest rating, compounded by squeamishness about AIDS even among a group that is university-educated (more than 76 percent).

For this reason alone, AIDS ideas are a tough sell at editorial meetings, where one-page story memos are reviewed by the managing editor along with the editorial board of the magazine. In addition to the obvious stigma of popular distaste and discomfort regarding the disease itself, the subject lacks appeal to editors because all science stories receive traditionally low reader scores on the meticulously graded subscriber surveys that are prepared for the marketing department and shared with the editorial staff. At *Fortune*, executive editor Walter Kiechel regularly began meetings of the Wall Street beat reporters and writers with a quick look at the reader scores, and the staff groaned at the low scores constantly registered by international stories (only 41% of readers are interested, and few finish the pieces) as well as science and technology. Personal investing traditionally ranks first, followed by profiles of companies, economic forecasts, politics and profiles of entrepreneurs and business leaders and manufacturing always did far better. While 58 percent of readers favor stories about new technologies, less than 4 percent are willing to read straight science stories, even about health which, in other magazine sectors, has grown in popularity since 1980. Business readers need an investment hook to pull them into a story about AIDS.

Beyond the general subscriber portrait, when I worked on my AIDS story at *Fortune* in 1988 I also had the benefit of a groundbreaking, invaluable survey of American executives—as yet unpublished—sponsored by the same in-house research group together with Lieberman Research, another marketing research firm, and Allstate Insurance that indicated the attitude of my readers toward AIDS. The questionnaire was prepared with the help of a 20-person advisory panel that included representatives from the American Cancer Society, the American Council of Life Insurance, the Centers for Disease Control, the National Center for Health Statistics, the National Leadership Coalition on AIDS as well as insurers like Allstate and Metropolitan Life, major corporations with large AIDS-education programs like Wells Fargo Bank and IBM, drug manufacturers like Bristol-Myers and activists from the Gay Men's

Health Crisis. Conducted in 1988, "The Business Response to AIDS" marked one of the earliest attempts on the part of business to gauge its own membership's response to the issue, and the figures it produced are revealing. To start with, it was unusually difficult to get the 2,500 companies targeted to respond. Only 623 completed questionnaires came back, a disappointing 26 percent completion rate. Nearly double that percentage completed similar surveys conducted in 1989 about marketing luxury cars and the unification of Europe in 1993. As the preface on "method" for the AIDS survey indicates, the response rate was "quite acceptable considering the sensitivity of the subject matter and the depth of attitudinal and behavioral information requested."[6]

One of the most valuable aspects of the study was the way it broke down the response by the size of the company, indicating an important split in attitudes between the chairmen of large corporations (1,000 employees or more) and small businesses with fewer than 100 employees. It also suggested there was a stronger awareness of AIDS and degree of involvement in the service sector than in manufacturing. The executives with larger, service-oriented firms were more likely to have had some kind of experience with AIDS in the workplace, particularly those in the Northeastern and Western regions. Not surprisingly, they outscored the Southern and Midwestern industrial executives in their knowledge of AIDS as well. For the whole group, 16 percent indicated that some of their employees had been infected with HIV, 17 percent said some employees had full-fledged AIDS, and 13 percent reported that some employees had died of AIDS. Just to indicate how those figures have changed, a survey published by the Centers for Disease Control in May 1993 shows that now half the nation's workers are in the at-risk 25-to-44-year-old group, and more than two-thirds of companies with 2,500 to 5,000 employees have experienced an employee infected with HIV, while nearly one in 12 small businesses have had an employee infected with AIDS. By 1992, the average cost for medical treatment, including lost tax revenue and productivity along with medical costs to employers and insurers, was up to $102,000 for the average 20 months between diagnosis of AIDS and death. These figures are among the controversial statistics that are continually massaged and inflated to suit one agenda or another.

The study touched on a number of vital concerns in business. Because it was a management survey, it provided solid data on decisions regarding policy decisions on AIDS education, testing, hiring and firing, public image and benefits. In 1988, AIDS ranked third among the most important issues facing the United States. The Federal deficit is the nation's biggest problem, according to 81 percent of the executives, followed by drug abuse (56 percent), AIDS (45 percent) and the negative balance of payments (40 percent). Back in 1988, the threat of recession was on the minds of only 20 percent of the executives, and the environment was only slightly more worrisome (21 percent), while homelessness (7 percent) and unemployment (4 percent) ranked near the bottom of the list. While 64 percent indicated that their companies were concerned about AIDS in 1988, a stronger 84 percent predicted that they would be concerned in five years, including 42 percent who said their companies would be "very concerned." That level of concern is not shared by small companies, however, except that while large companies are most concerned about the AIDS epidemic, small companies are more concerned about how the public would react if some of their employees had AIDS, just as Midwestern and Southern companies both large and small are more concerned about public reaction. While 79 percent of large companies were concerned about AIDS, only 53 percent of small companies shared that concern.

The degree of experience with AIDS is an important factor. While nearly half of the large companies' executives reported that employees in their work force have experienced AIDS, only 2 percent of small companies reported having employees who have tested positive or died of the disease.

One of the most interesting statistics in the 1988 and 1992 subscriber portraits is the extent to which readers took part in public or civic activities. Nearly half of *Fortune*'s readers do volunteer work and are active in civic, church or charitable groups, and 35 percent report that they take an active role in a civic or social issue. Well over half the subscribers' households have done charity or political work.[7] You might think that this would soften their stance on AIDS, and it is surprising to compare this level of political and social activism with some of the responses to questions regarding AIDS organizations in the survey of executives about AIDS. Only 14 percent said their company had made a contribution to an AIDS organization, and 37 percent indicated that they would be likely to do so. Among the factors that would get a company more involved in the AIDS problem, outside appeals from AIDS organizations ranked next to last (appeals from celebrities in sports, the arts or entertainment were at the bottom of the list), with only 10 percent saying it would help increase involvement. This is a far cry from the 92 percent who indicated that AIDS experience (such as the infection of employees, friends, or family members) would make a company become more involved, followed by the company impact on morale or costs (86 percent) and employee advocacy (75 percent, but only 15 percent if the labor unions pushed for it). In general, outside voices from other companies, community leaders, the President of the United States or government officials, were presumed to be ineffective in making companies more involved. While *Fortune* readers are inclined to be part of these groups, it is clear that their word is not heeded when it comes to issues of this kind.

It is easy for the outsider to overlook one of the most important aspects of the business press, particularly vis-a-vis a subject like

AIDS. The Big Five in the United States, *Fortune* (circulation: 672,000), *Business Week* (circulation: 900,000), *Forbes* (circulation: 740,000) *The Wall Street Journal* (circulation: 1,860,000) and *The Economist* (circulation: 166,000 in the United States) dominate the popular image of the business press. Among the more specialized publications that share the limelight are the *Harvard Business Review* (circulation: 204,000), *Financial World* (circulation: 442,000), *Personal Investor* (circulation: 110,000), *CFO* (circulation: 303,000) and *Black Enterprise* (circulation: 250,000) among others. Articles about AIDS in these publications were often much better than those in the bigger books like *Fortune* and *Business Week*. For example, *Harvard Business Review* back in November-December 1991 ran a three-part case study of how an employee with HIV should be managed over time, the May-June of 1989 ran an in-depth study of Pacific Bell's response to AIDS, and before that a strong article on "The Fear of AIDS" appeared in the July-August 1986 issue. These pieces predated by several years the trend toward management-oriented articles on dealing with AIDS in the workplace that would appear in *Business Week* and *The Wall Street Journal*.

At *Black Enterprise*, a fine story on the cost to business of AIDS, "AIDS: We All Pay in Different Ways," was written by editor Frank McCoy for the February 1993 issue, but since then it has been hard to get AIDS stories through the editorial board. A short piece in the same issue asked "Do Black Reps Fight AIDS," and examined the responsibility of the Congressional Black Caucus and black lawmakers in the funding battle on Capitol Hill. Unlike most business magazines, the point of view of *Black Enterprise* is that the existing funding is insufficient, and even the $2 billion budget for research for 1994 will not be adequate. But for the most part, the magazine is wary about doing AIDS stories. As Rhonda Reynolds, a *Black Enterprises* reporter who has covered AIDS in short pieces, observes, "They don't want to hear about it now. For one thing, it reflects badly on black

folks that they are in a high-risk category, and besides it is becoming an old story."[8]

THE LEVEL PLAYING FIELD: TRADE MAGAZINES

Beyond this tight circle of what can be roughly categorized as "consumer" publications is vast realm of largely unknown trade publications—including magazines, tabloids and newsletters—that in revenues and circulation actually dwarf the mainstream business press. Over 4,000 trade and specialized business magazines, employing more than 100,000 journalists, reach audiences in 150 distinct industry classifications. They are descended from the banking news sheets that were America's first journalism. These compilations of shipping and commercial news, like the contents of arriving and departing ships as well as port conditions and pirate action, were distributed in the coffeehouses of New York, Boston, Providence and Philadelphia during the early 1700s. Ultimately, the earliest of them is the *Neue Zeitunger*, a newspaper produced by the late 15th-century banking empire known as the House of Fugger. The publication reported information sent in by Fugger's agents throughout the world. In the United States, the specialized press has grown from 1,100 business publications in 1920 to the current round figure of 4,000, and electronic media services are sprouting up all over to add to that number. The revenues have grown from $45 million in 1942 to about $4 billion today, and circulation in that time has gone from 1.3 million readers to more than 123 million readers, about three times the combined circulation of *Fortune*, *Forbes*, *Business Week* and *The Wall Street Journal*.

There are magazines for taxidermists, hog producers, chemists, art dealers, car mechanics and contractors as well as any number of other arcane trades. More importantly for the purposes of this study, there are several magazines and newsletters covering industries like insurance, personnel and benefits, health services and management, biotechnology and medical disposal. For the most part, the coverage of AIDS in these periodicals was more advanced and accurate than the coverage in the big business books, and it came years earlier. According to a recent NEXUS search, there are at least 100 stories in the specialized press to every one in the big four magazines including the *Journal*. The best of them are in insurance publications like *Best's Review, National Underwriter* and *Business Insurance*, all of which have carried superb coverage of AIDS since 1983. Remarkably accurate and detailed articles on AIDS have also appeared, perhaps surprisingly, in *Advertising Age*. More specialized journals involving employee relations provided excellent coverage long before the major publications, including articles in *Occupational Hazards, Across the Board, Regulation, Employee Benefit Plan Review, Personnel Journal, Employment Relations Today, Employee Relations Law Journal, Review of Public Personnel Administration, Personnel Administrator* and the *Journal of Compensation and Benefits*. Similarly, there were fine stories on AIDS in more investment-oriented publications such as *Industry Week, Pensions & Investments*, and *Institutional Investor*, which had a piece on "AIDS in the Workplace" in its February 3, 1986 issue. Finally, trade magazines like *Communication World* and *American Demographics* as well as the health care books like *Risk Management, Business and Health, Modern Health Care* and the *Journal of Health Care Marketing* were on top of the story sooner than the mainstream media. In 1984, according to Kinsella's account of the development of the AIDS story, there were scarcely a thousand items in the mainstream press on AIDS. By 1985, in the third quarter, the total jumped to 1,744 and 2,086 for the fourth quarter. It rose again to over 3,000 articles per quarter in 1987 and 1988.[9] The main business magazines offered scarcely a tenth of these totals even after 1986, and in 1987 just 100 articles on AIDS appeared in *Business Week, Fortune, Forbes* and *The Wall Street Journal* including minor news briefs. However, the totals for the specialized press are far higher than both the mainstream media and the major business periodicals. The specialized press had well over 1,000 articles on AIDS in 1983, and doubled that figure each year through 1985, when it soared to nearly 14,000 articles in 1987 and 1988. And, unlike in the major business media, the pace has not slackened.

The reason for this more extensive and better coverage is simply the fact that AIDS is a matter of business survival for the audience served by the specialized press, particularly the insurance and health books. They cannot afford to ignore the crisis, and they cannot afford to understate the figures. *Best's Review* and *National Underwriter*, which have published outstanding articles on AIDS since 1984, have writers on the topic full-time, despite their limited staff resources. In many ways, their heightened awareness is not unlike that of the gay publications studied by James Kinsella, who pointed out in his book *Covering the Plague* how much more effective *The Native* and *The Advocate* were than *The New York Times* when the story was first reported.[10] Since writers at *Fortune* and the other major magazines subscribe to these trade publications and steal from them regularly, it was inevitable that as the coverage of AIDS in the trade press crested in 1987 the mainstream business press would have to take notice.

IN THE TRENCHES

It was nearly six on a Friday evening, the first week of November in 1987, and the grey-carpeted corridors of *Fortune*'s offices on the fifteenth floor of the Time/Life Building were silent. While the editors up on the sixteenth floor were still beavering away on the December 7th issue, the reporters and writers one flight below them were stealthily packing up for the weekend and preparing to play a little game of roulette, sneaking out five minutes early in the hope that the phone did not ring with a query or abrupt summons to a late editorial conference over a story. I was nearly out the door when, from around the corner, I heard a loud groan and an uncharacteristic string of expletives coming from the office of Stuart Gannes, one of this country's premier science journalists and, ordinarily, a soft-spoken thorough gentleman. Stu was 37, the father of two and a veteran science reporter who had been with Time Inc.'s ill-fated *Omni* magazine before joining *Fortune* as an associate editor in 1985. Since I had been assigned to be Stu's reporter associate on a story about the race for an AIDS vaccine, I felt it was my business to investigate.

Stu was looking pretty disconsolate, his chin on his hands and his chair pushed way back from his desk where, on top of an immense pile of notes, library files and science magazines, I spotted the first draft of his story. He had just been up to the office of Keith Johnson, our section editor, who had given the story a first reading before the weekend. "Look at this bullshit," Stu growled as he handed me the editor's copy. Scrawled across the top in pencil was a quick note, the only mark on the fourteen pages of neatly doublespaced Atex printout. It took me a while to decipher it, but then I realized that Stu was not just having one of those ego fits that writers often have after days of work on a story that an editor chooses to criticize.

The editor's note read, "Rework and bring in line with our earlier articles on this." Having helped gather the clips and government information for Stu, I thought our article was the magazine's first shot at covering the search for an AIDS vaccine. I did not realize—and Stu had forgotten"that just two and a half months before our Washington editor, Lee Smith, had written a story for the politics and policy section of the August 31 issue about AIDS research titled "Throwing Money at AIDS." The editor wanted our piece to adhere to the line that Smith had established, specifically with regard to the overzealousness of Washington in its funding of research and educational programs. The piece had generated a ton of negative mail charging insensitivity and narrow-mindedness although

nobody had written to correct the facts (which is the most serious kind of letter, in the eyes of the reporter). With the kind of second-party, rigorous fact checking process used by *Fortune*, it is unlikely that gross distortions—such as those that regularly cloud the credibility of *The Village Voice* when it covers AIDS—are unlikely. The accuracy of the magazine's coverage of AIDS has never been in question, but this is one example of how accuracy and fairness can part ways.

Lee Smith is a smooth veteran who in the summer of 1987 had just arrived in *Fortune*'s small but important Washington bureau after a triumphant three years as bureau chief in Tokyo. Renowned at the magazine for his outrageously bright silk ties and acidic satirical gifts, the 51-year-old, married member of the magazine's board of editors has a great knack for finding the story that combines social and political issues that affect business. His AIDS piece picks apart the Reagan administration's $800 million budget for AIDS education, testing and research, and declares that the projected $3.8 billion, including Medicaid costs, that is likely to be spent in 1991 is ridiculous. In fact, the figure for 1991 was even higher, and by 1993 the proposed budget for spending on AIDS calls for authorized spending of $4.9 billion through September 30, a rise of 118 percent since George Bush took office in 1989, making it the top government expenditure on research into any disease except cancer.

The tone of Smith's AIDS piece is powerful. After noting that the Federal government planned to spend $1 billion a year on research and another $1 billion on education and testing, Smith cracks, "Nice round numbers."[11] Then he proceeds to dissect the government's approach to AIDS while asserting that the risk to heterosexuals is too slim for more drastic steps to be taken. One of the most interesting aspects of Smith's opening paragraph is the way in which he refocuses attention on the class distinction between those at risk and those that are most emotionally involved in the disease:

The wrong people are frightened. Some of those who are at greatest risk seem oblivious, while those who seem to be at almost no risk are panicky. AIDS has become an obsession, especially among the upper classes, and this gets translated into a demand that the federal government attack it with a lot of money. AIDS is without question a horrible disease that deserves a high ranking on the list of national concerns. But as things are going, the country will spend far more money on AIDS than can be put to good use.[12]

The key issue in Smith's eyes is the relation of the cost of AIDS programs to benefits, particularly as weighed against the need for money to be spent on other problems such as the reduction of the budget deficit and other health problems, including alcohol abuse and schizophrenia.

Remember, only 45 percent of managers viewed AIDS as an urgent problem, while the federal deficit was ranked number one at 81 percent and the balance of payments had a strong 41 percent. Smith is particularly opposed to spending more on AIDS education, knocking the $248 million proposed for that and counseling as well as voluntary testing in 1989 as "too much." He scoffs at the Madison Avenue approach to AIDS as a product that scarcely needs a boost in name recognition. While he cites a few programs as deserving, including a Manhattan-based, $200,000-a-year educational program for addicts run by a reformed heroin user, Smith generally urges caution with regard to programs that promote AIDS testing and counseling, largely on the grounds that the AIDS tests would not be cost-effective as the Red Cross has also found. Smith's greatest sympathy is for the infants born with the disease:

> For their sake and the sake of other victims, present and potential, the government should spend a lot of money on AIDS. But as with all public spending, the architects of programs and the appropriators of funds should not disregard ratios of costs to benefits. Nor should they fail to compare amounts spent on

> AIDS with spending on programs to combat or alleviate other ills . . . At the very least, the federal government should keep its money out of programs that are patently misguided, such as broad plans to teach everyone about AIDS.[13]

For the purposes of our article on the search for the vaccine, Smith's brief interview with Dr. Anthony Fauci of the National Institutes of Health was the most important part of the piece. He criticizes the $179 million that the NIH planned to spend on finding a cheaper and more effective treatment than AZT—"a palliative, not a cure," in Smith's words—and also knocks the $52 million spent by the NIH on vaccine research:

> NIH should probably not try to expand its AIDS budget to that $1 billion-a-year goal set by the National Academy of Sciences panel. It is far from clear that the agency can put that much money to good use. NIH might have to resort to its practice of 1983 and 1984, when to get some AIDS projects rolling, it discarded the usual pattern of financing one request out of three and tossed money at every respectable application for AIDS research funds. Such unselective largess can make for poor science. Moreover, putting too much money into AIDS could begin to cut funding for research on other ills.[14]

With those brief sentences—quintessential Smith and *Fortune* work, picking at big budgets and hewing close to the numbers—the entire spin of Stuart Gannes's article on vaccine research was reversed. Gannes wanted to call for an increase in funding for vaccine research, at the urging of Fauci, Dr. Mathilde Krim of the American Foundation for AIDS Research, Michael Haseltine and every other scientist and AIDS expert he interviewed. Because of Smith's strong precedent—and to a lesser degree because of his higher rank on the masthead—significant changes would have to be made in Gannes's piece to bring it into line. The process gave me the best lesson in journalism as it is really practiced that I have ever received.

The re-write started at the top. It is unusual for headlines and "decks"—the subheading that often explains, at greater length, the headline—to remain the same through the editing process, and editors at publications like *Fortune* are prone to making radical changes to suit their own take on the subject. Stu's working headline was "Can Science Outsmart the AIDS Virus?" and his deck read, "Research is spending ahead to develop an AIDS vaccine. But the obstacles are formidable. It will take a major breakthrough to stop the killer microbe." The optimistic note reflects Stu's confidence in the ability of science to solve problems. He frequently lamented the difficulty he had in persuading top editors to let him write in-depth pieces on basic science and its importance to American industry, and nurtured a deep conviction that given the proper support the major labs could work wonders, including the discovery of a vaccine for AIDS. The only part of Stu's head and deck that made it to the final version of the story is the metaphor of the race with obstacles—"The Race for an AIDS Vaccine"—but by the time the piece was published the sprint had become a marathon and the hurdles had priority.

The lead paragraph of the first version, which actually remained intact through the editing process, puts forward the race metaphor: "Three years after scientists identified a virus as the cause of AIDS, somebody has finally crossed the starting line in the race to prevent the incurable disease." The news peg for the piece was the first clinical trials at the NIH to determine the safety of an experimental vaccine developed by biotech start-up MicroGeneSys, which was the first prototype to get FDA approval for preliminary testing. When we put the piece together, two dozen companies including Merck and Bristol-Myers were in the running for a vaccine, and our job mainly was to handicap the race, providing investors with a tip sheet on who would win, place and show.

The trouble began with a pair of quotes from scientists who claimed they were more interested in solving the puzzle of AIDS than in making profits. Bernard N. Fields, a virologist at Harvard Medical School, and David W. Martin, chief of research at Genentech in South San Francisco, suggested that the chance to work at the cutting edge of science was all they wanted. "The risk is what drives us. We don't necessarily think an AIDS vaccine is a wonderful business opportunity. We just think it's something biotech has to tackle," claimed Martin. This was too pure for *Fortune*, and it was cut before the second version came out of the Atex printer five days later. Stu's scientific agenda was beginning to clash with the financial needs of the editors. At one point, the editor combined "intellectual adventure" with "the sweet smell of a possible Nobel prize" as the motivational factors that vie with "mundane business considerations." Stu lobbied to remove the Nobel Prize crack, and won.

The clash of cultures between science and commerce is nothing new for journalists like Stu Gannes. It has been played out many times before, particularly during the dramatic rise of the computer start-ups in Silicone Valley, one of the plum assignments for business journalists, who found the computer pioneers disarmingly naive about money and even reluctant to talk about it. Similarly, many sources for AIDS stories who work in the labs—even those who are sponsored by Merck and Genentech and Ciba Geigy—are disgusted by the way in which stock prices move up and down on the slightest news. By 1993, the backlash against media hype would be significant, particularly in the scientific community as well as among gay activists. In March, a 31-year-old Harvard medical student named Yung-Kang Chow thought he had discovered the "Achilles Heel" of HIV and proposed a three-drug "cocktail" of AZT to kill the virus. He took pains to avoid the media and downplay the significance of the discovery, noting that it worked only *in vitro* and might be ineffective in humans. But the *New York Times* and other publications put him on the front page. Dr Martin S. Hirsch, a well-known AIDS researcher at Massachusetts General Hospital who supervised Chow's work, called the effect of the publicity on the project "devastating." Chow himself said, "It has been blown out of all proportion." As *Business Week* noted in an article cruelly titled "Red Faces in White Coats," the Chow strategy may not have been so original after all and is yet to be proven. "But stories of new treatments for AIDS have a way of taking on a life of their own," Geoffrey Smith wrote.[15] This is just the latest episode in the escalating tension between the press pool and the laboratory team.

Stu Gannes is not an idealist in the way that some AIDS activists are, but he is at home with the can-do spirit of researchers at Cambridge BioScience or Repligen, both in Massachusetts, Oncogen, MicroGeneSys in West Haven, Connecticut, Wyeth Labs or Chiron in Emeryville, California, where small teams of virologists work away daily on the vaccine as an intellectual problem rather than as a goldmine. This can be a problem when your readers are more interested in the one sure bet they can place with their brokers. The difference in agendas is articulated by David Webber, the editor of *Biotech Investor*, a monthly investment newsletter headquartered in Manhattan that tracks the latest developments in biotechnology for Wall Street analysts and a few subscribers who ante up $45 a year for an early peek at products before the FDA gives final approval. According to Webber, "Most of these companies are still research-driven. For them to work on a commercial AIDS vaccine is comparable to Compac or Apple Computer trying to develop a superconducting personal computer." In other words, the high-risk research on the vaccine, as Gannes pointed out, is hardly justifiable when so much basic science is yet to be done. This is almost as true in 1995 as it was in 1987.

Readers of *Fortune* are far more interested in the prospects of Merck, which sponsored Repligen's research to the tune of $7.5 million for the first year with guarantees of further funding, royalties and the rights to manufacture the vaccine, or Ciba-Geigy which supported six similar projects at Chiron involv-

ing not only AIDS but herpes and malaria as well. When Stu pitched the feature to the editors, he dropped the names of Merck, Bristol-Myers and Ciba-Geigy and the Institut Merieux, which funded Cambridge BioScience, while playing up the "blockbuster product" angle on a vaccine that would have a virtually universal market. The large drug companies are identified as the angels that make it possible for small bio-tech start-ups, "scientist-entrepreneurs," to try their hand at major research projects like the AIDS vaccine:

> In fact, AIDS vaccine research is a godsend for many young biotech companies. Since the advent of gene splicing in the late 1970s, scientist-entrepreneurs have been looking for projects that put their specialized know-how to work. Most of these start-ups have focused on health care, which offers vast markets for useful new drugs. But few biotech companies can conduct specialized research without outside financial help. As the epidemic worsens, money is flowing into biotech houses in ever-increasing amounts.[16]

Stu's trouble with the editor had nothing to do with corporate funding for research. The problems arose when it came time to discuss the role of the NIH and federal funding in general, as well as the severity of the epidemic and who it affects. As it is, these figures are always massaged by different sources with different agendas, each hoping to amplify or downplay the severity of the disease in order to attract attention and money. As Stu completed his first draft on November 4, without referring to the earlier *Fortune* article about the waste of federal resources on the vaccine, he was convinced that more money was needed not merely from the major drug companies but from the NIH as well to complete the job of finding a working vaccine. In his first version, he left blank the dollar figure coming from the NIH. We should have lifted the number—$52 million to be spent by the NIH on AIDS in 1988 for vaccine research from Lee Smith's article in the August issue. Previous issues of *Fortune* within the same year are considered a "red check" source for numbers or names, so the fact checker—I was Stu's fact checker on the piece—would not have to double check the figures with an outside source. However, from the NIH I learned that $134.7 million was earmarked for AIDS research in general for 1986, and we put $135 million into the first edited version on November 9th just after ten in the evening, when we were hoping Johnson wasn't looking. It made it through.

Unfortunately, while we were not looking Johnson cut a key paragraph from near the end of the story that did contradict the thesis of Smith's article. Gannes had written:

> Not all smaller biotech companies have been able to enlist bigger partners from the private sector, so the government has decided to help them out. Early next year the NIH plans to spend about $5 million to fund six new National Cooperative Vaccine Development Groups. "We want to encourage the linkage between academic and commercial investigators," says John E. Nutter, the NIH official who will direct the program. "Most of the early vaccine efforts are focused on the external covering of the virus. We want to ensure that we're creating a good, firm base of information about AIDS in case these earlier approaches don't pan out."

Johnson cut the whole paragraph. Various arguments can be made for cutting a paragraph. The 14 lines of text needed to be saved, or the amount of money and projects seemed too minor. In the past, *Fortune* was always very enthusiastic about reporting collaborations between scientific and commercial enterprises. Unfortunately, on top of the previous information about NIH support, this paragraph suggests the federal government can do more and provide a safety net for further research, and that contradicted the party line at *Fortune* as established by Smith's article, so it went.

We were also unlucky with the figures for the number of victims or those at risk. In his first version, Stu went with the statistics provided by Mathilde Krim of AmFar and Dr. Paul Volberding, head of the AIDS clinic at San Francisco General Hospital, who both reported that there were an estimated two million Americans harboring the HIV virus, and the number of heterosexuals infected had jumped 69 percent in the past year. The edited version inserted the fact that the number of AIDS cases resulting from heterosexual activity was "only 1,644 cases . . . a mere 4 percent of the U.S. total," a phrase that Stu felt was minimizing the sense of risk for most readers but which corroborated Smith's assertion that the disease had not dramatically affected any but the high-risk groups. Stu was under pressure to lower the figures and downplay the risk to heterosexuals. A little after 10:30 on the morning of November 16, Stu received a message over the Atex system from Johnson, who relayed a caution from executive editor Allan Demaree concerning the totals for how many people are affected. Demaree was the top editor on the piece, meaning that he would work it over after Johnson. Demaree's first topedit version came out on November 11th, a week after Stu filed. On November 16th, topedits two and three came out in the afternoon, preceded by Johnson's memo to Stu, which read:

> Allan, who saw Randy Shilts on *60 Minutes* over the weekend, wants to make sure we're clear in the story that so far as is known everyone who is infected with the virus eventually gets AIDS. He also wonders whether there are any other viruses that lie dormant for a time before they become active; I thought of herpes, which at least has active and dormant phases. Finally, there were radio reports over the weekend that the presidential commission on AIDS is about to produce numbers for AIDS infectees and victims that are only about half the U.S. totals we and everyone else have been using. Would you please explore that and figure out what we should be saying?

It was my job to call Washington and try to find the figures. I had a good source on the commission, Dr. James L. Baker, who helped me on November 16th with an estimate of between one and 1.7 million, which was half the total we used in the first draft. He also indicated that thus far they had found 30 to 50 percent go on to be "symptomatic," but that the consensus among scientists was that it will be as high as 100 percent as time goes on. Stu inserted a sentence on this, which made it to the final version: "Taking the long view is especially difficult with AIDS, which kills everyone who gets it." By the time the piece came out, the figure for the total number of people with HIV was changed to read: "With estimates of the number of Americans now harboring the virus ranging from 800,000 to more than 2 million." The change came about because Smith had used the figure 1.5 million, attributing it to "public health officials," and 40,000 for people who have developed AIDS. Actually, the Centers for Disease Control had reported 44,757 cases of Americans with AIDS, 25,644 of whom had died, and we had those figures from an Associated Press bulletin received on November 5th. But in the sidebar on "The Continuing Search for a Cure," the figures were halved and we reported that 20,000 cases of AIDS had occurred in the United States per the report that Johnson had spotted. Similarly the number of cases from transfusions was reduced from 12,000 (per the Centers for Disease Control in Atlanta) to 1,100, per Smith's article, and Johnson himself offered the calculations that suggested that 170 new AIDS cases annually could result from transfusions, given that the incidence of the virus in blood supplies is less than one unit in 50,000 and there are more than 8.5 million transfusions a year. In fact, the danger to hemophiliacs was far higher and the number of cases annually was nearly triple what we reported.

In addition to headlines and openers, the spin on a piece is mainly determined by the way it closes. From his first draft, Stu wanted to place the virologists at work on AIDS in the heroic tradition of Edward Jenner and other great scientists whose achievements were due in part to "lucky accidents" as well as diligence. The first ending he wrote actually ended up being the ending that appeared. It diverges from the metaphor of the race, except insofar as marathoners often stumble across the finish line: "With so many scientists focused on AIDS, there is always the chance that one of them will stumble across an idea which makes everything fall into place." While not completely cynical in the Lee Smith vein, the ending did manage to convey the exasperated sense of hope that Stu and I felt as we finished the piece.

It is unfair to be too critical of Johnson and *Fortune* and the way they turned the article on the vaccine on its ear. Johnson is one of the best editors in the magazine business, a man of humor and sharp instincts who recognizes a good story and knows how to deliver it to his audience. He and Demaree were just giving the readers what they expected, and it would be more than their jobs were worth to do anything else. In 1993, it is easy to mock the wrong numbers and lack of foresight that troubled editors and writers who did not understand the disease and its severity back in 1987. As far as the business press went, it was still early in the game for AIDS coverage. Ours was only the third feature among the major magazines devoted to any kind of AIDS research, although *The Wall Street Journal* had provided some coverage of AIDS research and particularly Jonas Salk and the Manhattan-based venture capitalists led by dealmaker Morton Davis of D.H. Blair who put up $1 million of his own money and raised $5 million more to back Salk's firm, Immune Response.[17] By the second quarter of 1987, the number of AIDS stories in the mainstream media had crested to 3,221, and in the third quarter the figure was 3,210 stories. It was the high point for media coverage, reflecting increased awareness of the threat to ordinary Americans rather than simply the high-risk groups.[18] The high-impact *Newsweek* cover story, "The Search for a Cure" by Vincent Coppola whose brother was dying of the disease, had appeared back in April 18,

1993, and our own colleagues at *Time* had already run a score of major features about AIDS before *Fortune* got around to it. Business books were behind, but as new AIDS-related companies popped up in 1987, and fancy investors including Robert Maxwell, Lord Rothschild, Allen F. Campbell, Japan's Nissin Food Products, SmithKline Beckman, the Rockefellers' Venrock, Euclid Partners and other venture capital firms became interested the need for business coverage became apparent. By the fall of 1987, the list of new companies working on AIDS included Amnion, Applied Biotechnology, Athena Neurosciences, Biopure, British Biotechnology, Candace Pert, DSW Laboratories, Gensia, IDEC, Immune Response, Mikromed Screening, Quidel, Tanox, United Biomedical, Viro Research International and the start-ups we covered in the article.

It's not easy walking right in and doing a story on AIDS, even for a veteran science reporter like Stu Gannes. No general business magazine has a regular AIDS beat, so the writer and reporter are basically tuning in to an ongoing debate in progress, hoping to maintain a degree of impartiality and to be able to sift through mountains of data and interpretive versions that are in conflict. Naturally, the big money talks, particularly in the case of stories with a Washington element where lobbying organizations are drawn to reporters from the major magazines almost as soon as they check into their hotels. I used to have at least four messages from lobbyists waiting for me at the desk of the Ritz-Carlton when I checked in, and it might be four days before I could get anyone at the FDA or any other government agency to return my calls on the same issue. In 1987 the debate was far less shrill than it is today—there was no ACT-UP, and AmFar was very polite. The major drug firms had their lobbyists, chiefly the American Pharmaceutical Manufacturers Association in Washington, and the social activists in San Francisco and New York were concentrating on waking up the mainstream media to gain more televi-sion and newsweekly coverage. Much of the extensive research Stu and I did came in the form of analysts' reports from Morgan Stanley as well as Kidder Peabody, annual reports and press kits from the growing public relations offices of Abbott, Ciba-Geigy, Amgen, Merck and other firms, and interviews with leaders in the health field. Access to Fauci, Krim, Haseltine, Gallo and Salk was no problem for *Fortune* reporters, because the scientist-stars saw greater exposure and funding opportunities in the million readers, including political and business leaders, who receive the magazine.

Among the many sources of frustration and regret I felt as the piece came out, beyond the skewed figures and revised language of the piece, was the lack of interviews with those who had been personally affected by the disease. None of the features in any of the business magazines or *The Wall Street Journal* used interviews with AIDS victims until well after the beginning of 1988, with the exception of a brilliant pair of articles in *Money* magazine, *Fortune*'s downmarket sister publication on which most editors and writers frowned, by freelancer Andrea Rock. The first was a story about the "Billion-Dollar Business of Blood" published in March 1986. Her piece pulled no punches about the danger of AIDS, and used more dramatic figures than *Fortune* had. It won the 1987 Page One Award for Crusading Journalism from the Newspaper Guild. The article took aim at the Red Cross—which fired off a hot letter of rebuttal that *Money* published in its next issue—as well as the for-profit blood companies that in the interest of cost-effectiveness were skimping on the basic screening precautions. The second was an even harder-hitting piece, "What You Don't Know About AIDS But Should," that appeared in November 1987 issue just as Stu and I were submitting our first draft. Rock's anecdotal lead relates the story of Tema Luft, a single, 34-year-old telephone company technician from Baltimore, whose picture appears and who said she caught the disease from one of only three lovers she had in the past 14 years. It proceeds to lambast politicians and public health authorities for their poor job in combating the disease:

> Yet there is troubling evidence that these figures, and the projections based on them, understate the severity of the existing disease and its potential for spreading to the broader population. Even more disturbingly, the record shows that many of the politicians and public health authorities entrusted with combating AIDS have failed us. They have consistently underestimated the scope of the epidemic, downplayed the risk that it could be transmitted heterosexually, and in some cases, deliberately minimized bad news in a misguided effort to avoid panicking an already frightened public. The result? Needless delay in implementing the policies that could have slowed the epidemic, and, at a deeper level, a false sense of security that helped lull us into thinking there would be a quick fix for AIDS. There will not be, and until we and our leaders acknowledge that, we cannot hope to bring AIDS under control.[19]

Rock's feature, which appeared in a special section on "The Cost of AIDS," is the first business magazine story on AIDS that used interviews with real people who have AIDS, with attribution, and its slant is entirely different from that of *Fortune*, which might prove that despite having the same corporate parent it is possible for contrasting editorial perspectives to develop in two magazines within one large communications firm. It is worth noting that Rock is not a staffer, but a freelance writer and a woman. More pragmatically, a glance at the demographics of *Money* magazine subscribers will indicate why the article could be so different. Poorer, younger, less educated and more likely to be in contact with AIDS than the *Fortune* readers, the *Money* audience is also likely to be far more liberal in its political and social attitudes.

Business press coverage of AIDS, even after Rock's more humane and emotional articles, continued along the lines of what we had done at *Fortune*. Its emphasis was on investment opportunities and the competitive nature of the race to the marketplace for new drugs.

BREAKING NEW GROUND

As the *Fortune* stories show, AIDS coverage in the business press was becoming predictable. From a problem that was virtually ignored by business leaders and editors as late as 1985 to a science and technology sidebar in 1986 and then a financially focused "goldmine" piece in 1987, the AIDS story had progressed further to the "middle of the book" core of business journalism. Finally, it was time for a human-interest feature on the ways management deals with employees with AIDS. But that story did not appear for another five years, and I was still surprised to see it on the cover of *Business Week* in February 1993. The cover, "Managing AIDS" by Ron Stodghill, a New York staff reporter, marked an important first for a mainstream business periodical. It ran at about the same time as a series in *The Wall Street Journal* on AIDS in the workplace by Judith Valente, like Rock a freelancer and a woman. But Stodghill's story was something different, and arguably more powerful. Its full effect on the business press is still difficult to measure.

At *Business Week* the attitude toward AIDS stories was virtually identical to the in-house feeling at *Fortune*. This is not surprising, since the demographics of the readership are almost identical, and there is a marked similarity between the staff makeup of both magazines. According to John Carey, *Business Week*'s editor for health policy stories in Washington, AIDS stories are a very tough sell with the top editors in New York. "We do AIDS stories mainly as science and technology pieces, but it is very hard to get a story through on AIDS policy and the social effort to prevent the disease. There's no interest at all in that."[20] Carey wrote a whole story on what he calls the "horrible job" being done in the United States on prevention particularly among intravenous drug users. It was supposed to run as part of a big health care package in April of 1993, but when the editors in New York received it they killed it right away. "They felt that they had read it all before and they had read enough on AIDS," Carey explains.

This is what makes the cover story by Stodghill all the more shocking. "That piece was seen as quite important from the beginning, and they felt that it presented the problem in a new light," Carey explains. Stodghill's editor in New York, Mike O'Neal, had the green light from the beginning. "We knew we wanted it on the cover and we wanted it to be different," says O'Neal.[21] Stodghill lived in Blue Bell, Pennsylvania for two weeks where he put together the research on the small sales and service office of Digital Equipment Corporation that is the sole focus of the article. There, he taped multiple interviews with employees and in particular with Jean Langone Smith, the 39-year-old office manager, and Frank Daloisio, a 40-year-old sales rep who has AIDS. Their story, in intimate detail, is the whole basis of the six-page feature with an appended shorter piece by Stodghill, Russell Mitchell in San Francisco, Karen Thurston in Atlanta and Christina Del Valle in Washington on "Why AIDS Policy Must be a Special Policy."

The first clue that Stodghill's story is something different lies in the photographs and captions. On the cover, Daloisio and Jean Langone Smith are shown standing close together against a black backdrop, but the right side of Daloisio's face is in shadow. Their lips pressed together, their eyes bloodshot and full of fear and concern, it is a striking picture, with Smith, the manager, appearing just over Daloisio's left shoulder. In white type with a red initial cap, the teaser starts on a note that is unfamiliar to *Business Week* readers, who are unaccustomed to emotion in their hard news reporting: "This is the story of how one mid-level executive at Digital Equipment struggled with managing an employee suffering from AIDS. It is a tale of fear

and compassion, denial and hope, anger and humanity. It is a story that is being played out, in one way or another, in virtually every major American corporation."

The theme of the piece is encapsulated in the first pull-quote: "As Jean discovered, the disease is too complex for policy manuals."[22] The opening is given to Smith, who in 1993 is still unable to calmly answer interview questions about the day that Daloisio told her he had AIDS. She criticizes herself for not being more sympathetic when, on a Monday morning in December, Daloisio tried to explain:

> Frank's first attempt to break the news to Jean ended with the revelation that he was terminally ill. But that was all he said. Then, on an icy Monday morning a few weeks later, he sat down in Jean's office and rambled on about a friend who had died of AIDS. Both of them knew what he was trying to say, but neither knew how to express it. Finally, Frank stopped and asked: "You know what it is, don't you?" "Yes, I do," she said. "It's a terrible thing in our society." Jean still stings from the shame she felt. "What a dumb, impersonal thing to say," she chided herself. "The man is dying, for God's sake!"[23]

Beyond the degree of intimacy and the openness with which AIDS is discussed in the piece, the other factor that distinguishes the article from most business journalism is the critical approach it takes to management and its treatment of labor. Since these magazines are overwhelmingly pro-management, it is a daring perspective. In a story that is terribly complicated from the first, Stodghill also adds the problem of depicting the female manager as initially too tough, and finally softer. The business press has made a concerted effort to write more about women bosses and how tough they have to be, and this article goes against the grain in that regard as well. Finally, the article calls on executives at major corporations to beef up their educational effort to help managers like Smith to cope with the situation.

The article is a detailed, blow-by-blow account of the way Smith juggled the responsibility she felt for DEC's declining sales in her region with the obligation to Daloisio she also felt. It adds candid remarks from co-workers on the situation, many of them showing the resentment and homophobia felt by people who felt Daloisio was getting a break because of his disease. The piece is superbly balanced between the points of view of Daloisio and Smith, and exceptional in its respect for Daloisio's need for privacy. Stodghill provides thumbnail sketches of the two figures and their rise from working class backgrounds to white-collar jobs, Smith from the secretarial pool and Daloisio from the repair department. It confronts the technical questions about Daloisio's rights and benefits, but it steers clear of the questions of money and costs. The strength of the article lies in its description of delicate emotional scenes. At one point, Smith blows up in anger at Daloisio, who refuses to answer her at a meeting, prompting her to storm out of the room. Daloisio sends her a message on the voice mail requesting a meeting with the human resources representative. Smith's anger turns to fear and paranoia. She passes a sleepless night and takes it out on her husband, then asks Daloisio why he does not trust her enough to just talk to her. Her ignorance of DEC's policies is candidly admitted, and her resentment when Daloisio takes several days off after a lot of sick leave just to attend a friend in the final stages of AIDS is related. The article concludes on a cautionary note, after Smith insists that she had to handle the trauma of managing AIDS on her own, without the head office coming in to run her business. Stodghill does a fine job of opening up a small office and showing the concentric effects of the crisis it contained that could ripple through the entire business community:

> It's not exactly Jean's style to psychoanalyze herself. "As a manager ,it raised the bar for what I need to be," she says flatly. Others

think she's changed a lot. "In the past, people didn't feel comfortable going in and saying what was on their mind, or just shooting the breeze," says Betty Ann. "But after Frank's ordeal, Jean seemed to become more agreeable to hearing your thoughts and just letting you talk to her." Jean opened up, and that was crucial. DEC's policy on AIDS, and others like it, represent an enlightened effort to institutionalize compassion. Rules, though, are merely rules. For Jean and her co-workers, managing AIDS came down to discovering a greater humanity within themselves. For Frank, it meant marshaling the courage to confront his problem openly. Offices aren't typically the crucible for a mixture so personal and emotional. But there's nothing typical about AIDS.[24]

There is an ironic footnote to this remarkably gutsy cover story in *Business Week*. The last page of every issue of the magazine is devoted to three unsigned editorials by senior staffers, and one of them usually addresses an issue raised by the cover story. The lead editorial is another example of the typical business magazine approach to the AIDS policy questions. It takes the government to task for not making progress, and suggests that too much money is spent on the wrong projects. It might have appeared in any issue of any business magazine from 1985 to the present. It reads in part:

> There is plenty of room for improvement in managing AIDS research. A top priority of the new appointee should be a reshuffling of the National Institutes of Health AIDS-research bureaucracy. After spending $15 billion over the past decade, researchers have staked reputations and careers on scientific approaches that have led to few treatments and no cure for the deadly disease. Despite vast expenditure, the nucleus of researchers specializing in AIDS still does not know precisely what causes the disease . . . Throwing money at the old AIDS-research bureaucracy will not solve the problem.[25]

Since Stodghill's cover story appeared, a few other articles on the sociological aspect of the disease, often written from the management perspective, have dealt with the issue without constant recourse to the question of profits and costs. This has been accompanied by a marked increase in politics and policy stories on President Clinton's new health care reforms and the high cost of AIDS cases to the federal government as well as employee assistance programs at major corporations. Most business journalists agree that there is only one big AIDS story left to write: reporting the discovery of a cure or vaccine. Until then, editors remain skeptical until new angles on the old story are brought to them.

NOTES

1. Martin Mayer, *Making News* (Boston: Harvard Business School Press, 1993), p. 35.
2. My main source for this is Reed Abelson, a reporter at *Fortune* who had worked closely with Malcolm Forbes at *Forbes* just before joining the *Fortune* staff, as well as numerous comments by writers and editors at *Fortune*, *Business Week* and *The Wall Street Journal*.
3. Personal interview, July 1993.
4. The source for all the figures in this paragraph are *Fortune* subscriber portraits prepared in 1988 and 1992. In the summer of 1988 the survey of paying subscribers was prepared by Erdos and Morgan, a Manhattan-based marketing research organization. After successive mailings of the eight-page questionnaire to 4,000 individual subscribers —accompanied by letters from Jim Hayes, Fortune's publisher, and dollar bills as incentives—the total usable response was 2,125. In the winter of 1992, the research was also done by Erdos and Morgan, and 1,906 usable returns came back. *Fortune* continues to use the 1992 survey as its advertising sales vehicle.
5. According to a former director of market research at *Fortune*, Merle Sprinzen, along with information provided by the Media Industry Newsletter and interviews with Lane Cooper, editor of the Newsletter.
6. *Business Response to AIDS: A National Survey of U.S. Companies*, p. 3.
7. *Fortune*, National Subscriber Portrait, p. 53.
8. Personal interview, July 1993.
9. James Kinsella, *Covering the Plague* (New Brunswick: Rutgers University Press, 1989), p. 156.
10. Kinsella, *Covering the Plague*, pp. 25–47.
11. Lee Smith, "Throwing Money at AIDS," *Fortune* magazine, August 31, 1987, p. 64.
12. Ibid.
13. Ibid., pp. 65-67.
14. Ibid., p. 68.
15. Geoffrey Smith, "Red Faces in White Coats: Did Mass General Oversell an AIDS 'Breakthrough,'" *Business Week*, March 8, 1993, p. 37.
16. Gannes, "The Race for the AIDS Vaccine," p. 116.
17. Marilyn Chase, "Chic Disease: Venture Capitalists See Ways to Make Money in Combating AIDS," *The Wall Street Journal*, September 28, 1987.
18. Source: Center for Disease Control, "News Media Coverage of AIDS: Based on Computer Search of NEXUS Library, January 1982–March 1988," 1988.
19. Andrea Rock, "What You Don't Know about AIDS but Should," *Money*, November 1987, pp. 90–91.
20. Personal interview, July 1993.
21. Personal interview, July 1993.
22. Ron Stodghill, "Managing AIDS," *Business Week*, February 1, 1993, p. 48.
23. Ibid., p. 48.
24. Ibid., p. 52.
25. "Overhaul AIDS Research, " *Business Week*, February 1, 1993, p. 82.

FALLEN HEROES

Social drama on Wall Street

Mitchel Y. Abolafia

He emerged as the foremost villain of the age not merely by piling up a fortune; that was acceptable, even desirable, so long as one did it in the proper way with appropriate gestures toward convention. His rise to success followed the classic pattern of the rags-to-riches myth except in the crucial area of *method*. . . . In business he was ruthless and devious, clever and unpredictable, secretive and evasive. Above all, he was imaginative, not only brilliant but thoroughly original.

> from Klein,
> *The Life and Legend of Jay Gould*, 1986: 492

This study focuses on a small but notorious subculture of bond traders: those who pushed and redefined the limits of self-interested behavior on the trading floor in the 1980s. We are interested both in the process of redefinition and in the restraint this elicited. These actors, the best known of whom is Michael Milken, shared the self-interested goals of their peers in the market, but developed innovative means for their achievement. As Robert Merton explains, such "innovators" are not uncommon in our economic history.

This study is drawn from chapter 7 of the author's manuscript *Making Markets: Self-Interest and Restraint on Wall Street* (Harvard University Press, forthcoming).

On the top economic levels, the pressure toward innovation not infrequently erases the distinction between business-like strivings this side of the mores and sharp practices beyond the mores. As Veblen observed, "It is not easy in any given case—indeed it is at times impossible until the courts have spoken—to say whether it is an instance of praiseworthy salesmanship or a penitentiary offense." The history of the great American fortunes is threaded with strains toward institutionally dubious innovation as is attested by many tributes to the Robber Barons. The reluctant admiration often expressed privately, and not seldom publicly, of these "shrewd, smart, and successful" men is a product of a cultural structure in which the sacrosanct goal virtually consecrates the means. This is no new phenomenon.[1]

Such innovators are deviant in the sense that their *methods* (*means, strategies*) are outside the currently accepted practices, rather than implying any psychologically aberrant or irrational behavior. In fact, their methods may eventually come to define the new norm. Merton goes on to explain that those most predisposed to be deviant innovators are those for whom access to approved means is blocked. This suggests that in financial markets the deviant innovators will come not from the top tier firms, those that are already dominant, but rather from those firms with less access to the best customers and their pools of capital.

Merton also notes that these innovations are the product of a "cultural structure" in which the goal of extraordinary wealth "consecrates" normative violation. An extreme version of this culture existed in the overheated bond market in the 1980s. This culture is to be differentiated from the more radical and innovative behavior to be described here. Opportunism and innovation are not the same thing, although both share positive connotations in this culture and both thrive in conditions of high incentive and low restraint. The general culture of opportunism in the bond market at this time was probably a necessary and conducive condition for the success of the more radical innovative action.

What Merton fails to note is that much of this "institutionally dubious innovation" is accompanied by considerable conflict in the business community. Existing elites, defenders of the status quo, often fight the "innovators" tooth and nail. At times they win. At times they lose. Frequently, they adjust to the new methods of profit. This study assumes that deviant innovation often elicits such conflict. The social drama model, derived from diverse work by Victor Turner,[2] Northrup Frye,[3] and Martin Kilduff,[4] will be used to illuminate a conflict that confronted deviant innovators on Wall Street in the 1980s. This model describes the process by which an innovator's breach of norms captures the attention of community elites who feel compelled to respond. The resulting crisis undermines the legitimacy of one group or the other. Protagonists compete to define the newly emerging business reality. Outcomes are dependent on the interpretive skills of the conflicting parties, as well as their ability to mobilize resources. This study focuses on the social drama involving Michael Milken and the junk bond "revolution." It uses government documents and investigative reports to construct a re-interpretation of these events.

The deviant innovators in social dramas are often portrayed, and often portray themselves, as heroes.[5] They are the renegades who propose to shake up an industry or the corporate raider who has arrived to save a firm. On the trading floor they are the "entrepreneurs" who take the greatest risks, develop new instruments, and add most significantly to the firm's bottom line. But like all heroes, they run the risk of a tragic fall into defeat and humiliation. The onetime hero may be redefined by his powerful opponents as a fraud and a public villain. In such a case, the hero's romantic image is exploded and the conventional social order is reaffirmed.

MICHAEL MILKEN AND JUNK BONDS

We will begin with the paradigmatic social drama of the financial markets in the 1980s. Its protagonist is Michael Milken, a Wall Street hero who took what many in the community believe to be a tragic fall from his once lofty pedestal. I am less concerned with the criminal fraud for which Milken was indicted and found guilty than I am with the grand innovations he brought to bond trading, most of which were once resisted and are now accepted practice.[6] Michael Milken nurtured and controlled the junk bond market of the 1980s. His firm accounted for more than 50 percent of all junk bond trading during most of those years. Eventually, it was the use of junk bonds to finance leveraged buy-outs and hostile takeovers that shook the financial community and brought the conflict to public attention. The rise and fall of Michael Milken was a social drama in American finance. It is a conflict in which the protagonists continue to offer competing and alternative interpretations of what happened.

We will focus our attention on these competing interpretations and how their creators strategically succeeded or failed in defining the situation and the outcome of the conflict. Michael Milken cast himself as the underdog hero in a drama of societal change. As early as 1970, in an op-ed piece that was rejected by *The New York Times*, Milken compared himself to other Berkeley graduates of that turbulent time. "Unlike other crusaders from Berkeley, I have chosen Wall Street as my battleground for improving society. It is here that the government's institutions and industries are financed."[7] Later, at the height of his success, Milken became messianic. He told a group of money managers in Boston in 1986, "We're faced with change. And all of us have resisted this change. Our regulators have resisted change, our politicians have resisted change, portfolio managers have resisted change, traders have resisted change, salesmen have resisted change. . . . The common perception is that capital is scarce, but in fact capital is abundant. It is vision that is scarce."[8] Milken had the vision. He led an increasingly large following into new forms of financing. He used the model of crusading hero to guide his actions and to influence others' interpretations and behavior.

Modeling the rise and fall of Michael Milken as a social drama is not to belittle its significance. The rise and fall of Milken changed corporations and markets. In the course of the drama a huge new debt market was created in which mid-sized firms like Turner Broadcasting and MCI financed their explosive growth. Major corporate restructurings were accomplished, among them RJR Nabisco, the largest ever. Companies from Gulf Oil and TWA to Beatrice Foods changed hands. In fact the rise and fall of Milken involved the self-conscious production of financial history. The protagonists pursued such goals as changing the way corporations are financed, ending the dominance of old guard investment banks, and stopping the speculative mania of the raiders and their bankers on Wall Street.

Who are the protagonists in this social drama? First, there is Michael Milken, head of the junk bond operation at Drexel Burnham Lambert, an investment bank. It was he, and his colleagues at Drexel, who made the junk bond revolution possible. He was opposed by a series of increasingly important participants in the drama. In the early stages of the drama, he was opposed by other bond traders and salespeople at investment banks, inside and outside his own firm. Later he was opposed by actors in the wider corporate and political communities representing order, convention, and the status quo in corporate financing and ownership. Among these adversaries were chief executive officers of leading corporations as well as prominent members of the banking community. These leaders were joined by important actors from government including Paul Volcker, the director of the Federal Reserve Board, and several important Congressional leaders.

A final and extremely important set of actors in the drama was the media. In the early 1980s *Business Week* ran Milken on their cover. He was hailed as a hero. The media promoted his heroic self-image, dubbing him the "king" of junk bonds and his customers as leaders of a revolution in corporate finance. By 1988 Connie Bruck, in her bestselling book, was calling his customers predators, and by 1991 James Stewart, who won a Pulitzer prize for his reporting on Milken, made him out as the worst of a "den of thieves." The media made this drama public and highly visible.

All of these protagonists employed strategies and rhetorics designed to capture the attention and sympathy of various publics. They grounded their performance in the myths and metaphors of the society. By playing the conflict to various audiences, the actors produced a text or script which we may analyze in an effort to understand the conflict and what it reveals.

DRAMATIC PHASES

The Breach. A breach occurs between actors in the same social system as the result of the violation of "some crucial norm regulating the intercourse of the parties."[9] This violation is more than a faux pas, it is a deliberate effort to challenge the establishment. The breacher sees himself as acting altruistically, as a representative of others, whether these others are aware of it or not. That characterization seems to fit Milken's self-image. At least since the time of his op-ed piece, he has cast himself as a crusader for change engaged in "the improvement of society."

Milken's first significant violation of the norms came very early in his career. During his years at Berkeley, he became interested in "fallen angels," bonds that had been downgraded by the rating agencies to "below investment grade." He came across a study by Braddock Hickman of every corporate bond issued between 1900 and 1943 showing that a portfolio of widely diversified low-grade fallen angels could be more profitable than a portfolio of high-grade bonds, especially if you got in while they were undervalued. The barrier to selling fallen angels was the rating agencies, Standard and Poor's and Moody's. They controlled the definition of acceptable risk that investment firms used when recommending bonds to their customers. As a result most bond traders and salesmen considered it unacceptable to trade in or offer such instruments.[10]

Milken took his first full time job at Drexel Firestone in 1970. He soon asked to be moved from research to bond sales and trading. He began to focus on the low-grade (high yield) bonds, doing meticulous research into the companies in order to promote what Stewart called "the gospel of high yield bonds."[11] Milken's colleagues on the trading floor disliked the securities he traded and saw his behavior as a breach of tradition. As Connie Bruck explains, "Most of his colleagues looked askance at Milken and his low rated bonds." She quotes a former Drexel executive who said, "The high-grade bond guys considered him a leper. They said, 'Drexel can't be presenting itself as banker to these high grade, Fortune 500 companies and have Mike out peddling this crap.'" Milken was segregated off in a corner of the trading floor but survived. By 1973 he was making a 100 percent profit on his trading position. The firm increased his capital and gave him increasing autonomy. They allowed him to keep one dollar for every three he made. He made $5 million for the year by 1976.

During these years Milken built a clientele for low-grade bonds. He did this not only by convincing customers of the bond's high yield and underlying value, but by promising to bid on the bonds personally if the customer wanted to get out, i.e., he promised liquidity. Among Milken's early clients were small and medium sized insurance companies that bought for their portfolios, executives at the recently deregulated savings and loan associations, and aggressive fund managers looking for high returns. Among Milken's customers was an inner circle who knew each other and traded in each other's debt and equity through Milken. As Stewart point out, among Milken's biggest clients were a small group of entrepreneurs—Saul Steinberg, Meshulam Riklis, and Carl Lindner —who had been rebuffed on Wall Street for their aggressive tactics or had been under investigation by the SEC.[13]

By 1977 Milken had established Drexel as the only firm willing to act as a market-maker in below investment grade bonds. Milken stood ready to buy and sell throughout the day, albeit at a large mark-up of 3 or 4 points compared to the eighths and quarters in investment grade bonds. That same year, 1977, Lehman Brothers and Goldman Sachs underwrote the first important original issues of low grade bonds for LTV, Fuqua, and Pan Am.[14] But it was Milken, who already had a ready group of buyers for such issues, who made it into a significant new form of financing. Fred Joseph, a partner in corporate finance at Drexel, brought Milken a client, Texas International, that wanted to issue low grade bonds.[15] Milken helped Texas International issue $30 million in new debt. Drexel did seven more issues in 1977. By 1978 Drexel dominated the market for issuing what soon came to be known as "junk bonds." It completed fourteen issues that year. Its next closest rival, Lehman Brothers, did six. At its peak, Drexel held almost 70 percent of the market share in this business.[16] When the traditional "white shoe" investment banks became interested in this profitable market, Milken antagonized them by refusing to share initial offerings with a syndicate of firms.

The clients for this business were mostly mid-sized firms without previous access to such a market. The alternative for these companies had been the further dilution of their equity or taking on restrictive loan covenants. Milken felt strongly that these companies, and their entrepreneurial leaders, were being denied capital by the financial establishment. In an interview, Milken framed the issue, "To me it was a form of discrimination—to discriminate against the management and employees of a company which offered value-added products and services, all because (they) didn't get a certain rating. It seemed grossly unfair. so I would not have been true to myself if I didn't use the tools I had, to try and raise capital for these people."[17] Milken cast himself as the champion of the mid-sized firm. He used a charged word—"discrimination"—to attack the establishment banks for denying access to relatively cheap capital. Milken had clearly found his cause.[18]

THE CRISIS

Breaches of crucial norms in a community threaten the status quo and often elicit acts of repression. If such a breach is not "sealed off" it is likely to escalate into a mounting crisis.[19] The breach and its escalation usually reveal some existing cleavage, a state of affairs that had been previously covered over. The escalating nature of the breach seems to dare the establishment to deal with the menace. In the current instance, the breach was not repressed. The extension of junk bond financing to actors outside the traditional corporate elite escalated dramatically in the 1980s. Observers began to talk of a junk bond "revolution" as if it might be a turning point in corporate finance. In retrospect, it appears as a moment of suspense in which assumptions about corporate ownership and control were called into question.

The escalation of the breach is best represented by a single key innovation, one that threatened the corporate establishment and made Milken dangerous, i.e., using junk bonds to finance hostile take-overs. Although the breach was initiated in the corporate finance department at Drexel, it was made possible by Milken's ability to sell debt. Milken is said to have feared that the extra risk involved might hurt the junk bond market he had created, but he clearly overcame any reluctance. He was widely perceived as the engine that made the rapid growth of the junk bond financed hostile take-over possible.

The merger wave of the 1980s had begun with a series of friendly leveraged buy-outs in which large conglomerate firms were taken private and restructured. In some of the largest of these, such as Beatrice Companies, the deal would not have been possible without billions in junk bonds, sold by Milken. But it was the hostile take-overs that drew the greatest public attention and resistance. The hostile take-over itself was not a new innovation. Such take-overs have a long history. But they were always accomplished by a larger firm acquiring the stock of a smaller, attractive target. Milken's ability to sell large amounts of junk bonds made it possible for his customers to go after targets in corporate America that had previously been immune from the threat of take-over. Many of the most notorious raiders had strong alliances with Milken: Henry Kravis, Ron Perelman, Saul Steinberg, Victor Posner, T. Boone Pickens, and Carl Icahn. These men shared Milken's taste for innovative methods and his anti-establishment view of the existing corporate leadership. But, increasingly, it was Milken who was perceived as the man who made their dreams possible.[20]

It was the hostile offers for major oil companies, like Gulf Oil and Unocal, that extended the junk bond breach into a crisis. These actions revealed the extent to which entrenched senior managers would go to maintain their control and prerogatives.[21] More importantly, it revealed a vulnerability to disruption of their control for which these managers were unprepared. It was raiders like

T. Boone Pickens who fearlessly taunted the corporate elite using the junk bond breach as their weapon. He argued that size should not protect stagnant management and that underachievers should not be safe just because of their size. In the Gulf deal, in 1984, Milken informed Pickens that he would be able to raise $1.7 billion for the campaign. This would enable Pickens' Mesa Petroleum to acquire a firm more than twenty times its size. Historian Robert Sobel believes that this deal was a turning point that established a sense of crisis and revealed the outlines of the ensuing conflict.

> Later, those within the industry would recognize this interaction as a critical juncture in the history of the junk era—the moment Milken emerged as a superstar. Armed with such backing as Drexel could provide, raiders could go after just about any large, fat corporation. In his ability to raise enormous sums of money quickly, Milken had no peer—and major corporate targets had no greater adversary.[22]

REDRESS

Once the disturbance of the social order has become manifest, powerful members of the community may act to limit its spread. The means of redress include informal persuasion or mediation as well as recourse to formal legal restraints. The redressive actions may themselves escalate depending on the status of the parties and their degree of resistance. There may also be a regression to the crisis phase or the two phases may go on simultaneously. Although the leaders of establishment may attempt to restore the status quo, this may not be possible. What starts as redress often continues as prolonged conflict. In the case of Milken and junk bonds, the corporate elite applied a broad cross-section of remedies in an effort to halt the escalating crisis. The initial remedy was simply for corporate targets to resist the raiders. This included both defensive and offensive strategies. As the crisis escalated, the redressive action came to include action in the political arena.

Redressive action consists of both pragmatic techniques and symbolic action.[23] In the early part of the redressive phase the pragmatic techniques consisted mainly of defensive efforts by the target firms to either make themselves unattractive (changes in charter, taking on debt) or find a "white knight" to protect them from the raider by acquiring them on more friendly terms. Offensive strategies included threatening to acquire the raider (the pac man strategy), bringing injunctions against the raider, suing the raider, or paying off the raider (greenmail). Pragmatic action also included efforts in the political arena. The Business Roundtable, made up of the 200 largest U.S. corporations, began lobbying Congress in 1984 to pass legislation against take-overs. Several committees held hearings. A ban on mergers among the top 50 oil companies was proposed by Senator Johnson from Louisiana.[24] In response to T. Boone Pickens' raid on Unocal, its Chairman, Fred Hartley wrote to Paul Volcker, Chairman of the Federal Reserve Board, asking for an investigation of "abuses by some banks and financiers that are feeding a take-over frenzy that strikes at the economic well being of this country."[25] On December 6, 1985 the Fed curbed the use of junk bonds in acquisitions. By the end of that year more than thirty-one bills had been proposed in Congress to limit take-over activity. Individual firms lobbied in their home states. By 1987, thirty-seven states had passed laws restricting take-over activity.

In social dramas, symbolic action frequently plays a significant role in the ultimate achievement of redress. Protagonists are involved in an interpretive conflict over the definition of heroes and villains. The corporate establishment launched a rhetorical attack on Milken and junk bonds. Corporate leaders created opportunities in government and the media to impose their frame on events. Lobbyists and political action committees encouraged congressmen to defend the largest corporate investments in their home districts. Congressional hearings became the stage for demonization of Milken and the "junk bond bust-up hostile take-over." Nicholas Brady, investment banker for Unocal, and later Secretary of the Treasury, wrote an op-ed piece for *The New York Times* titled "Equity Is Lost in Junk Bondage." He also told a reporter, "These are the people you want to keep off the streets. . . . The best you can say is they are gamblers and hustlers."[26] Felix Rohatyn, another investment banker wrote an op-ed piece in the *Wall Street Journal* called "Junk Bonds and Other Securities Swill." The tone of this rhetoric is colorfully represented by Fred Mercer, CEO of Goodyear.

> Let me tell you what's wrong with Mike Milken and company. You have to start by asking, what does he provide to society? What does he create? What actually happens in the way of building products that help our standard of living to be either maintained or improved? And the answer is nothing . . . and incidentally, it pays quite well. It pays a lot better than what I've been paid.[27]

From such rhetoric, the lines of cleavage were unmistakable. Leaders of the corporate establishment were attempting to limit the spread of the crisis. They employed the powerful cultural frame of the outsider, speculator (gambler, hustler) who does not work for his wages, and does not deserve to be in the "game."[28] Drexel responded with a series of advertisements showing the mid-sized companies that Milken had funded, but the establishments' evocative anti-speculator imagery seemed to hold more salience for a broader public.

REINTEGRATION

The final phase of social drama involves either a reintegration of the violators or an irreparable schism. Neither is a return to the status quo ante. Even reintegration suggests an altered community. Positions in the status system may have changed and new norms may have emerged during the crisis. This reordering of the social order allows the ana-

lyst to assess the role of power relations in shaping the outcome.

There has been no schism on Wall Street or in corporate America. Rather, most of the radical innovators and most of their normative breaches have been reintegrated into the community. Junk bonds have become an accepted part of the financial world. After a short decline, starting with the demise of Drexel and continuing during the recession in 1990 and 1991, new issues of junk bonds returned to the market. In 1993, 341 new issues came to market, exceeding the 226 issues in the peak year of 1986. The amount borrowed has grown from $33 billion in 1986 to $57 billion in 1993. Several of the junk bond raiders joined the corporate establishment, actually running the firms they acquired, e.g., Icahn (TWA) and Perelman (Revlon). But the critical breach, the one that elicited the redress, has been curbed. Whereas 67.5% of junk bonds issued in 1987 were used in take-overs, only 11.2% were so used in 1993.[29] The largest corporations are once again safe from raiders and free to focus on the competition.[30]

Where do Milken's felony convictions fit in this drama? Like many dramatic heroes, Milken had a fatal flaw. Some saw it as greed. I think it was hubris. Milken had developed an exaggerated sense of himself in relation to the rules and norms of his community. We have seen that his success was built on an escalating series of normative violations. Each deviant innovation brought greater success. There were no restraints for Michael Milken. The crimes for which he was imprisoned all occurred during the take-over mania of the mid-eighties. They reflect the recklessness of an overheated deal-maker: evasion of net capital rules, filing false statements with the SEC, concealing ownership of stock.

The crimes for which Milken was punished are of relatively small consequence when compared with the consequences of the breach he made possible: the junk bond hostile take-over. This tool was the basis for widespread asset redistribution, large-scale corporate restructuring, and tremendous personal dislocation. Yet, it is hard not to see

Milken's trial and imprisonment as the symbolic resolution of this social drama. By the time he was sentenced, Milken's breaches had become symbolic not only of speculative frenzy, but of corporate indifference and the disruption caused by a decade of corporate restructuring. Had Milken held himself to higher standards, thereby avoiding prison, the social drama would have had a slightly different denouement. Action by the Federal Reserve Board and the state legislatures had stopped the hostile take-overs anyway. What was missing was a ritualized rite of censure and cleansing in the wake of a disruptive decade. Milken's personal fall and removal from the market became a symbolic redress and the basis for reintegration of the community. In place of the crusading hero of Wall Street, Milken became its foremost modern villain.

DISCUSSION

It is worth noting that most innovative breaches never become full blown social dramas. Rather, most breaches, innovative and otherwise, are repressed. Their appearance, rapid repression, and demise signal the reaffirmation of the boundaries of acceptable behavior. The culture of Wall Street, like culture in general, is fundamentally conservative, seeking to reproduce itself rather than change. But occasionally, a challenger of the status quo will gather sufficient support, despite the resistance of the elite, to change some aspect of the normative structure. If the breach is widely adopted, new logics of action will be generated to legitimate the once deviant behaviors.

It seems that the kind of deviant innovation described here is both addictive and blinding. It is addictive because once one has succeeded in challenging the establishment it is terribly tempting to try again and to see how far the establishment can be pushed. When the innovation is generously rewarded, it becomes a game to see how much more rewarding the next step might be. But this escalating success at outsmarting the estab-

lishment can also be blinding. The innovator develops a distorted sense of his own power and position. In cases like Milken's and perhaps the Salomon Brothers scandal, the one-time innovator begins to violate rules of transaction that get in the way (squeezing markets, exceeding limits, disguising ownership, etc.). At the same time, the establishment elite has not evaporated and there are still lines to be crossed that may threaten establishment interests. Either through over-confidence or political naivete, the innovator threatens the interests of those who are most invested in the status quo. At this point, the heroic innovator has, through his own excess, given his opponents the tools to demonize him. In the end, the redressive powers of the community are used to send a message to others about what happens to those who threaten the status quo.

History will always be ambivalent about such characters. It will paint them as both robber barons and industrial giants. Milken nurtured a new market in debt for mid-sized firms that is thriving today but squandered his reputation on securities violations. Salomon built itself into a powerhouse of Wall Street, but its top leaders left in disgrace. If the expansion of capital is a good thing, then these people are heroes. Their downfall was in failing to heed their community's restraints. Capitalism will always produce such characters. As long as incentives exist, people will step over the line. Innovators will develop new and deviant methods to achieve wealth. When incentives are at their highest and restraints at a minimum, as they were on Wall Street in the 1980s, a new generation will emerge to rise and fall in this recurring social drama.

CONCLUSION

The story of Milken and junk bonds is a story of deviant innovation and the resulting social conflict within a community. But most of the scandals on Wall Street in the 1980s were not social conflicts. They were about greed and fraud, individuals engaged in deceit for the purpose of lining their pockets. Although Milken engaged in blatant fraud, it is a small part of his drama. On the other hand, Dennis Levine and Ivan Boesky were not innovators. They offered no vision of change on Wall Street and did not threaten the power of any establishment. Rather, they used their guile to garner "inside information" and then used this information to take advantage of others in the market. They were extreme opportunists.

But, as the Milken story suggests, there does seem to be an association between deviant innovation and deviant opportunism. Although most opportunists are not innovators, it may be that deviant innovators are more likely in opportunistic cultures and that, in turn, successful deviant innovation creates an environment conducive to even greater excesses of opportunism. The innovations themselves may balance out as either positive or negative from the perspective of society's greater welfare. They will be tested by time. But the opportunism associated with such activity is clearly negative. Nevertheless, both deviant innovation and opportunism seem to be inherent in the system. Their recurrence on Wall Street throughout its history suggests that both culture and incentives are conducive to their generation. The dilemma for society is to identify a degree of restraint that will inhibit the opportunism without forestalling the innovation.

NOTES

1. Robert K. Merton, *Social Theory and Social Structure*, N.Y.: Free Press. pp. 195–196.
2. Victor Turner, *Dramas, Fields, and Metaphors*, Ithaca, N.Y.: Cornell University Press, 1974.
3. Northrup Frye, *Anatomy of Criticism*, Princeton, N.J.: Princeton University Press, 1957.
4. Martin Kilduff and Mitchel Abolafia, "The Social Destruction of Reality: Organizational Conflict as Social Drams," Paper Presented at the American Sociological Association Meeting, Chicago, Illinois, August 1987.
5. The robber barons, and more recently, Michael Milken, are the subject of continuous revisionist battles. For some, the railroad industrialists were heroes. For other, robbers. Recently, Alfred Chandler (*The Visible Hand*, Cambridge, Belknap Press, 1977) has made the case that Jay Gould was the leading "system builder" of the railroad age. He writes, "no man had a greater impact on the strategy of American railroads than Jay Gould, the most formidable and best known of the late nineteenth century speculators (p. 148)." There is a mini-industry thriving on the competing interpretations of Michael Milken. See Bruck, C., *Predators Ball*, (N.Y.: Simon and Schuster, 1988), Stewart, J., *Den of Thieves*, (N.Y.: Simon and Schuster, 1991), Bailey, F., *Fall from Grace*, (N.Y.: Birch Lane Press, 1992) and Kornbluth, J., *Highly Confident: The Crime and Punishment of Michael Milken*, (N.Y.: 1992).
6. For an analysis of the fraud see Mary Zev, *Banking on Fraud*, Hawthorne, N.Y.: Aldine de Gruyter, 1993.
7. Quoted in "The Golden Age of Junk" by Roger Alcaly, *New York Review of Books*, May 26, 1994, p. 28.
8. Quoted in Connie Bruck, *Predators Ball*, N.Y.: Simon & Schuster, 1988, p. 271.
9. Victor Turner, *Dramas, Fields, and Metaphors*, Ithaca: Cornell University Press, 1974.
10. This story is told in Bruck, C., *Predator's Ball* (1988), Bailey, F., *Fall from Grace* (1992), and Steward, J., *Den of Thieves* (1991).
11. Stewart, J., Ibid. p. 45.
12. Bruck, G., *Predator's Ball*, p. 29.
13. Stewart, J., *Den of Thieves*, p. 46.
14. Sobel, R., *Dangerous Dreamers*, (N.Y.: John Wiley, p. 78).
15. Stewart, J. *Den of Thieves*, p. 48.
16. Bruck, C., *Predator's Ball*, p. 48.
17. Ibid., p. 57.
18. It was during this period, in 1978, that Milken moved the junk bond department of Drexel to Beverly Hills. Some observers have suggested that this was an attempt to get out from under Drexel's control. This may be so, but it seems equally likely that as Milken claimed, he simply wanted to go home to southern California. (He bought a house a few blocks from his parent's home in Encino.) He merely had no compunction about challenging the norm which said that all sig-

nificant investment banking is done in New York. It was part of his challenge to the establishment.

19. Turner, V., *Dramas, Fields, and Metaphors*, p. 38.
20. Sobel, R., *Dangerous Dreamers*, p. 128.
21. There are a number of books which make this argument. See T. Boone Pickens, *Boone* (Boston: Houghton Mifflin, 1987), Bailey, F., *Fall from Grace*, Sobel, R., *Dangerous Dreamers*, 1993.
22. Sobel, R., *Dangerous Dreamers*, p. 143.
23. Turner, V., *Dramas, Fields, and Metaphors*, p. 41.
24. Sobel, R., *Dangerous Dreamers*, p. 148.
25. Bailey, F., *Fall from Grace*, p. 116.
26. Ibid., p. 117.
27. Quoted in Bailey, *Fall from Grace*, p. 125.
28. Paul Hirsch ("From Ambushes to Golden Parachutes: Corporate Takeover as an Instance of Cultural Framing," *American Journal of Sociology*, vol. 91, January 1986: 821) notes that the normative framing of the junk bond raiders (Steinberg, Icahn, and Pickens) by their targets was more extreme than in contests among large corporate status equals.
29. All figures in this paragraph are from Alcaly, R., "The Golden Age of Junk," p. 29.
30. It is impossible to know with certainty what ended the wave of hostile take-overs because merger waves seem to always have a limited life span, but it is clear that the threat of legislation, inspired by the corporate elite, was a critical factor in the timing.

LOSING GROUND

*In the latest recession, only Blacks suffered net
employment loss. Firms added Whites, Asians,
and Hispanics overall, but they deny any
bias effects of seniority, location.*

Rochelle Sharpe

The last recession seriously eroded equal opportunity for America's black workers.

Blacks were the only racial group to suffer a net job loss during the 1990–91 economic downturn, at the companies reporting to the Equal Employment Opportunity Commission. Whites, Hispanics and Asians, meanwhile, gained thousands of jobs, according to *Wall Street Journal* analysis of EEOC records.

The computer aided study shows that some of the nation's largest corporations shed black employees at the most disproportionate rate. At Dial Corp., for instance, blacks lost 43.6% of the jobs cut, even though they represented 26.3% of Dial's work force going into the recession. At W.R. Grace & Co., they held 32.2% out, while they accounted for 13.1% of the company's pre-recession payroll. At BankAmerica Corp. and ITT Corp., blacks lost jobs at more than twice the rate of their companies' overall work-force reductions.

Companies say the sudden demographic shift is a statistical fluke, the unintentional fallout of corporate cutbacks and reorganizations. But some civil rights advocates argue that something more insidious is going on.

"This is subconscious, deep-seated racism," says George Fraser, who publishes directories of black professionals. "People don't even know these patterns and behaviors are being initiated until you begin to see the pieces of the puzzle together and look at the numbers."

In an analysis of the 35,242 companies that filed EEOC reports for more than 40 million workers in both 1990 and 1991, the *Journal* found:

- Blacks lost a net 59,479 jobs at these businesses during the recession, which officially began in July 1990 and ended in March 1991. Overall, blacks' share of jobs at the companies dropped for the first time in nine years, wiping out three years of gains. Black employment at the companies fell in 36 states and in six of nine major industry groups.
- By contrast, Asians and Hispanics, who in recent years have become more vocal about getting their share of jobs, both made gains. Asians gained a net 55,104 jobs during the recession and Hispanics a net 60,040 jobs. Whites, who outnumber blacks nearly eight to one at these companies, gained 71,144 jobs.
- Blacks workers were especially hard hit in blue-collar jobs, losing nearly one-third of the net 180,210 such slots lost. They were the only group to lose service-worker positions, dropping 16,630 such jobs while businesses added 53,548 new ones. They were the only group to lose sales jobs.
- Blacks did show some progress in several highly prized white-collar job categories. They gained a disproportionately high number of managerial, professional and technical jobs. But they held such a small percentage of these jobs before the recession began that their actual gains were meager. Companies added a net 2,719 black managers during the recession,

bringing the 1991 number to 248,915, which is just 5.2% of the total for all races.

Even with the job losses, black workers represent a higher share of the staffs of EEOC companies than of the U.S. population (11.8%) or of the overall U.S. work-force (10.4%). Considering the size and locations of the EEOC companies, they could be expected to have more than the nationwide proportion of black workers.

Yet blacks, who accounted for 12.5% of the work force of companies filing with the EEOC, not only lost a disproportionately high share of jobs in companies that cut staff, but also gained a disproportionately low share of positions added during the recession. They lost 15% of the jobs at the roughly half of EEOC firms that had net employment cuts, and gained just 11.4% of new jobs at firms that added staff.

"The recession in America means depression in the black community," says Carol Massey, president of the Los Angeles chapter of the National Black MBA Association.

The losses can be partially explained by blacks' relatively low seniority in companies and their heavy concentration in the types of jobs eliminated. Corporations' continuing decisions to abandon inner-city offices, factories or franchise outlets didn't help blacks, either.

But the demographic change suggests something more fundamental has occurred, a pronounced shift in the way affirmative action operates. Several companies with poor records of retaining blacks say they were mostly concerned with their aggregate minority employment rates and never calculated whether blacks bore a disproportionate share of cutbacks. Thus, they could claim to the government continued progress by minorities as a whole even as blacks were suffering reversals—in some cases dramatic ones.

Black workers had their biggest setbacks at retailers. About half of their losses were in retailing, where blacks lost jobs at a 50% higher rate than the overall work force.

At Sears, Roebuck & Co., for example, blacks lost 54.3% of jobs cut, according to the company's original filing with the EEOC. After extensive interviews with the *Journal*, the company said it had discovered a gargantuan addition error in the numbers it gave the government and printed in its annual reports for three years—a mistake that exaggerated blacks' proportion of job losses. The revised records, which the EEOC is now investigating for accuracy, still show blacks losing a disproportionate 20% of the jobs cut by Sears. The company's work force was 15.8% black in 1990.

SEARS says its black work force wasn't hurt because of inattention to diversity but by the need to eliminate expensive distribution centers in the inner cities. The giant retailer closed two major urban distribution centers in 1991, relocating part of the operations to suburbs largely inaccessible to blacks without cars.

"It's not like we set out to eliminate black jobs," says a Sears spokesman. "We set out to streamline our catalog and distribution centers to make them more competitive." The centers, built in the early 1990s, had been designed to house relatively small merchandise and be accessible to railroads, the spokesman says. The new ones, he says, are built in the suburbs to be more convenient to trucks.

But several former black managers at Sears believe that corporate indifference toward affirmative action caused them problems during the recession and that this attitude grew throughout the 1980s as federal enforcement declined. "It appeared the company discontinued its emphasis on having a diversified work force," says Bob Johnson, Sear's first black vice president, who retired in 1991.

Like Sears, most companies say blacks' job losses were completely unrelated to affirmative action. At W.R. Grace, for instance, where blacks lost jobs at more than twice the rate of overall work-force cuts, officials say the drop was due entirely to Grace's extensive restructuring.

"This issue has nothing to do with diversity," says Fred Bona, a company spokesman. "The restructuring has to do with a worldwide business strategy, involving which businesses we should be in." The company sold several businesses unrelated to its basic chemical manufacturing work, such as restaurants, he says. He argues that blacks' share of Grace's work force rose if one excludes a Mexican fast-food business that was partially divested.

But some black employees complain of persistent racial bias. "They are very, very prejudiced," Frank Bellow, a machinist, says of Grace's management at its Lake Charles, LA, catalyst manufacturing plant. When the company makes personnel decisions, he asserts, they revert "to the old Jim Crow ways."

Mr. Bona says Grace as addressed the black employees' complaints.

Critics consider many companies' explanations about black job losses hollow excuses, designed to hide unspoken bias. Charges Wesley Poriotis, who heads Wesley, Brown & Bartle, one of the nations's oldest minority search firms: "There's a deep sourness in corporate America that they had to hire minority professionals. Downsizing has been their first opportunity to strike back."

For many firms that cut a high percentage of blacks in the recession, the reasons are the same: They closed or sold operations in inner cities. But whether the cutbacks reflect bias isn't easily clear.

McDonald's Corp., for instance, says the statistic that blacks accounted for 36.5% of its job losses in the 1990–91 period merely reflects the sale of 270 company owned restaurants to franchisees. While most of these blacks probably now have jobs with the new franchisees, the corporate switch could indicate McDonald's was unloading many of its inner-city restaurants to blacks; the fast-food chain declines to say where the stores are located, but contends the changes reflect nothing about its inner-city policies.

Yet what looks like abandoning the inner city may really be giving economic opportunity to an underprivileged group. Even attorneys who sued McDonald's on behalf of black franchisees credit the company with giving blacks liberal franchising terms, making it possible for some to own a business for the first time in their lives.

Geography plays a major role in black-employment patterns. At BankAmerica, blacks did poorly during the recession because of attrition combined with the fact that the company expanded in states that have low black populations, such as Arizona and New Mexico, says spokesman Russ Yarrow. Blacks accounted for 28.1% of the lost jobs, even though they made up just 7.9% of the company's work force before the recession.

Companies say they didn't deliberately reduce their black work forces. A high percentage of blacks got laid off, though, because they held more of the jobs companies decided to eliminate. ITT says its black work force was hurt when it stopped managing the Sheraton hotels in Dallas, St. Louis and West Palm Beach, Fla. Blacks accounted for 27.4% of the jobs lost at ITT during the economic slump, despite constituting 11.8% of the company's pre-recession work force, primarily because of these hotel losses, says Jim Gallagher, an ITT spokesman. Blacks held 402 of the 1,109 jobs at these hotels, mainly as waitresses and room attendants, he says.

In most companies, blacks were concentrated in the most expendable jobs. More than half of all black workers held positions in the four job categories where companies made net employment cuts: office and clerical, skilled, semi-skilled and laborers, according to EEOC records.

Many companies may not even realize how their black employment shifted during the recession. Personnel executives often focus primarily on minorities' overall progress, in part because that is what the federal government focuses on when it evaluates affirmative-action efforts.

Even at companies with aggressive diversity programs, such as Dial, black workers can lose ground. Dial says its attorneys carefully reviewed layoff plans for adverse impact before any downsizing took place. But company officials say they assessed the effect on overall minority and female employment rather than on blacks, Hispanics or Asians separately.

Blacks at Dial lost jobs at a rate two-thirds higher than did its work force as a whole. Dial's overall record for minorities, however, looks exemplary, especially if white females are included, because Dial added Asians and American Indians and laid off a disproportionately small percentage of white women.

"I feel confident that the process we established ensures equitable treatment," says Joan Ingalls, Dial's vice president of human resources. "It's not appropriate to offer preferential treatment."

Like Dial, Sears boasts of inroads made by its minority staff, which occurred because Asians and Hispanics fared better during the recession than Sear's overall work force. Comparing blacks' achievements to other minorities is "a skewed point of view," says William Griffin, Sear's director of human resources. What matters, he says, is Sear's overall minority employment record. "What we hold our managers accountable for is work-force diversity."

Civil-rights attorneys are skeptical of such explanations. "The first thing that makes me suspicious is if companies are aggregating all the minorities together," says Barry Goldstein, a prominent civil-rights lawyer.

But the office of Federal Contract Compliance Programs, which investigates discrimination at businesses that receive government money, decides which companies to audit by analyzing their records on overall minority employment. Only after companies are selected for an audit will investigators consider examining records on individual ethnic or racial groups, says Annie Blackwell, the program's policy director. And they will do the individual ethnic analysis, she says, only "if there's a reason to do it."

Civil-rights advocates argue that under the guise of fairness for all, employers can hide differential treatment of blacks. "Affirmative action has gotten so diluted that companies can trade one minority against the other," says Aileen Hernandez, who was an EEOC commissioner under President Johnson.

For years, advocates such as Ms. Hernandez have considered the federal government inept as a watchdog. They complain that agencies such as the EEOC began being trimmed during the Reagan administration, and officials started promoting the notion of lumping all minorities together to treat them as one bid disadvantaged group. The EEOC also shifted its enforcement efforts away from class-action suits against companies, focusing instead on individual cases of discrimination.

Affirmative action was weakened even more during the recession because of a series of Supreme Court decisions that made it harder for individuals to sue companies for discrimination. By the late 1980s, companies were much more fearful of private litigators than the government, says Jonathan Leonard, a professor at the University of California at Berkeley, who studies workplace discrimination. With the court's Wards Cove decision in 1989, which made it tougher for minorities to use statistics to prove racial bias, companies suddenly became nearly immune to job discrimination challenges until the Civil Rights Act was passed in 1991, he argues.

At Sears, Mr. Johnson, the former vice president, and other black employees say they felt the impact of Reagan and Bush administration policies almost immediately. They saw the government's broad-based race and gender discrimination investigation into Sears during the late 1970s transformed into a weak sex-discrimination case in the 1980s that the company ultimately won. And in the middle of the EEOC's lawsuit against Sears, they watched then-Sears Chairman Edward Telling stop doing business with the federal government to protest what he perceived as the Labor Department's "campaign of harassment."

What resulted, says Mr. Johnson, was a gradual, steady erosion of black workers that occurred quietly and with little discussion. The number of blacks who held the key buyers' jobs dwindled from 25 in 1981 to 14 in 1985 to seven or eight in 1990, he says. Sears won't release the numbers, but says the drop of blacks was proportional.

The reduction wasn't due to any deliberate campaign to eliminate blacks, Mr. Johnson and others say. It was a combination of the old-boy network playing a stronger role during layoff decisions, they say, plus black workers getting so discouraged by the atmosphere that they became eager to take early retirement buyouts.

Barbara Samuels, who joined Sears in 1963, says she took early retirement at age 54 in 1991 because "I felt the place was being detrimental to my mental and physical health." One month after she was named the company's buyer of the year in 1987, she says, her boss gave her a performance evaluation of only "meets expectations." Another supervisor delighted in telling ethnic and sexist jokes around her, she says.

Sears declines to comment on Ms. Samuel's experience, but a spokesman says it has strived to create a work environment that "is sensitive to employees." Although blacks bore a disproportionate share of job losses at Sears in the recession, their share of the Sears work force—15.85%—was notably higher than blacks' representation in the overall U.S. work force.

Certainly, many whites lost their jobs during corporate downsizing, too. But blacks say they began to notice that at least some of their white counterparts would eventually be hired back to take jobs in the newly restructured divisions, something that rarely happened to them. "It's the old FBI syndrome: friends, brothers, and in-laws," says Bill Hawkins, who runs a search firm in Los Angeles. "If you don't have an FBI, you're in a good position to lose your position."

Blacks who held jobs involving public contact had an especially rough time during the recession, EEOC records show.

They lost 5,823 sales jobs overall in 1991, for instance, even though companies added a net total of more than 63,000 white, Asian and Hispanic sales workers. "There's a continuing problem that white companies will not buy from a black salesman," says John Work, a career consultant and author of "Race, Economics and Corporate America."

At least one recent study suggests that racism still plays a role in some personnel decisions. In 1990, the Urban Institute sent out teams of black and white job applicants with equal credentials. The men applied for the same entry-level jobs in Chicago and Washington, D.C., within hours of each other. They were the same age and physical size, had identical education and work experience, and shared similar personalities. Yet in almost 20% of the 476 audits, whites advanced farther in the hiring process, researchers found.

"The simple answer is prejudice," says Margery Turner, a senior researcher at the Urban Institute involved in the study. "Clearly, blacks still suffer from unfavorable treatment."

Of course, not all job applicants have similar credentials. Most blacks can't even be considered for highly skilled jobs because they don't have enough education. Only 13.1% of blacks in the work force have college degrees, compared with 24.6% of whites and 38.6% of Asians, according to the 1990 Census.

The better-educated Asians managed to gain jobs even in states that cut tens of thousands of workers. Overall, Asians gained jobs in midsize and big business in 39 states, while blacks lost ground in 36 states.

Blacks were hit particularly hard in Florida, losing jobs at EEOC corporations at a rate more than five times that of the overall workforce reductions. They were the only racial group to lose jobs there as well as in Illinois, where 43.4% of jobs lost were held by blacks; in 1990 they represented 13.4% of all workers in the state. Their work force was devastated in New York, where they lost more than 21,000 of the 91,746 jobs cut in businesses. And they also got slammed in California, losing more than 11,000 of the 72,230 jobs eliminated while Asians were gaining more than 9,000 positions.

Only in three Southern states—Alabama, Arkansas, and Louisiana—did blacks add a substantial number of jobs.

With comparably little education, blacks often get stuck in lower skilled, blue-collar jobs. And only seniority saves many blue-collar workers from the unemployment line these days.

Since blacks were often among the last hired for these jobs, they were frequently the first to go. At USX Corp., which lost nearly a tenth of its already decimated work force in 1991, employees at some plants had to have almost 20 years' experience to keep their jobs. Blacks lost nearly 20% of those jobs lost at the company, even though they made up just 12.6% of the work force going into the recession.

Discrimination problems in the steel industry were supposed to have been solved in the 1970s, when the EEOC required companies to change their rules on promotions and transfers. Until then, openings weren't posted throughout plants, and people who wanted to change departments lost their seniority.

Initially, the changes helped blacks get better jobs. Even if they had been hired into a dirty, dangerous unit, they had the chance to learn about and accept better positions, knowing their seniority was secure.

But at USX, the new rules that allowed blacks' advancement in the 1970s ended up accelerating their job losses in the 1980s, when the company had massive layoffs. That's because of USX's plantwide labor pool, which allowed blue-collar workers who were laid off to bump people out of jobs in other departments, if they met qualifications and had seniority.

Blacks who could overcome the seniority hurdles often stumble when faced with the company's new testing requirements, says Billy Hawkins, chairman of a union grievance committee at USX's plant in Gary, Ind. Suddenly, blacks with 25 years' seniority were being rejected for jobs because they couldn't read rulers—even though rulers weren't even used on the job. USX says the stiffer tests are all job related and needed since the steel industry is more technology-driven than before.

Blacks could no longer get training to qualify for skilled jobs either, as USX eliminated its Craft-training programs in the mid 1980s because of the availability of unemployed craftsmen. As a result, parts of the plant that were traditionally black have started turning white, Mr. Hawkins says.

"It's really ironic," adds Frank Webster, another union representative. "Blacks were caught by the very thing that was supposed to protect them. We're seeing the end results of discrimination. We're right back to square one."

How Black Workers Fared at Leading Companies

	Total Employees 1991	Decline from 1990	Black Employees 1991	Black Decline from 1990	Blacks' % of 1990 Workforce	Blacks' % of Total Decline	Black Job-loss Index
Allied Signal	70,803	4,777	8,232	416	11.44%	8.71%	0.76
Alcoa	35,322	2,092	3,338	276	9.66	13.19	1.37
American Cyanimid	18,159	1,334	1,841	336	11.17	25.19	2.26
American General	17,948	2,106	1,734	175	9.52	8.31	0.87
American Home Products	24,291	960	2,047	96	8.49	10.00	1.18
AT&T	149,080	18,525	24,497	2,953	16.38	15.94	0.97
Anheuser Busch	47,587	1,736	5,975	10	12.13	0.58	0.05
BankAmerica	57,311	932	4,342	262	7.90	28.11	3.56

How Black Workers Fared at Leading Companies *(cont'd.)*

	Total Employees 1991	Decline from 1990	Black Employees 1991	Black Decline from 1990	Blacks' % of 1990 Workforce	Blacks' % of Total Decline	Black Job-loss Index
Bank of Boston	12,439	1,152	1,247	137	10.18	11.89	1.17
Bank of New York	14,296	1,435	3,141	417	22.62	29.06	1.28
Black & Decker	21,783	3,029	2,602	334	11.83	11.03	0.93
Boeing	152,861	3,500	7,983	143	5.20	4.09	0.79
Borden	26,684	2,459	2,904	366	11.22	14.88	1.33
Burlington Northern	31,782	1,807	1,315	48	4.06	2.66	0.65
Campbell Soup	26,548	2,265	4,053	671	16.40	29.62	1.81
Caterpillar	39,893	2,596	2,652	147	6.59	5.66	0.86
Centel Corp.	10,526	1,744	1,144	76	9.94	4.36	0.44
Central & South West	7,905	532	442	17	5.44	3.20	0.59
Chase Manhattan	28,202	2,223	6,109	298	21.06	13.41	0.64
Chemical Banking	26,247	952	5,536	46	20.52	4.83	0.24
Chrysler	92,607	7,577	20,051	652	20.66	8.60	0.42
Citicorp	49,852	3,752	7,532	157a	13.76	a	—
Coca-Cola Enterprises	19,072	894	3,195	376	17.89	42.06	2.35
Conrail	27,001	2,083	1,339	95	4.93	4.56	0.92
Contel Cellular	13,672	7,139	750	504	6.03	7.06	1.17
Cooper Industries	41,896	2,382	5,709	171	13.28	7.18	0.54
Corning	13,785	2,864	910	44	5.73	1.54	0.27
Deere & Co.	26,540	1,160	1,092	80	4.23	6.90	1.63
Dial Corp.	28,161	3,317	6,829	1,445	26.29	43.56	1.66
Digital Equipment	62,530	5,409	4,052	597	6.84	11.04	1.61
Walt Disney	50,070	1,007	3,666	0	7.18	0.00	0.00
Dow Chemical	28,420	2,195	2,019	224	7.33	7.33	1.39
Dupont	78,254	18,259	9,197	1,436	11.02	7.86	0.71
Eastman Kodak	74,783	835	5,565	5	7.37	0.60	0.08
Eaton Corp.	25,976	2,627	1,692	171	6.51	6.51	1.00
Emerson Electric	41,772	1,912	2,805	201	6.88	10.51	1.53
Entergy	13,059	920	2,088	206	16.41	22.39	1.36
First Union	19,594	1,448	2,769	164	13.94	11.33	0.81
Fluor	26,316	16,864	1,894	3,143	11.67	18.64	1.60
FMC Corp	18,499	846	1,222	19a	6.22	a	—
Fruit of the Loom	24,463	670	6,853	153	27.88	22.84	0.82
General Dynamics	86,107	14,903	5,699	715	6.35	4.80	0.76
General Electric	194,872	15,932	14,574	2,000	7.86	12.55	1.60
General Motors	405,452	6,055	68,011	1,252	16.83	20.68	1.23

How Black Workers Fared at Leading Companies *(cont'd.)*

	Total Employees 1991	Decline from 1990	Black Employees 1991	Black Decline from 1990	Blacks' % of 1990 Workforce	Blacks' % of Total Decline	Black Job-loss Index
Georgia Pacific	53,550	5,183	10,716	913	19.80	17.62	0.89
Gerber Products	11,407	3,186	1,065	411	10.11	12.90	1.28
W.R. Grace	34,219	939	4,299	302	13.09	32.16	2.46
Hercules	18,113	3,591	1,787	34	8.39	0.95	0.11
Hewlett-Packard	54,651	3,634	2,084	134	3.81	3.69	0.97
Honeywell	39,632	14,362	2,113	968	5.71	6.74	1.18
Ingersoll-Rand	22,977	1,798	1,894	110	8.09	6.12	0.76
IBM	203,981	18,174	18,677	1,545	9.10	8.50	0.93
ITT	79,141	1,186	9,159	325	11.81	27.40	2.32
James River	28,160	3,599	2,302	71	7.47	1.97	0.26
Johnson Controls	22,924	1,925	1,900	145	8.23	7.53	0.92
Kerr-McGee	6,616	1,154	782	27	10.41	2.34	0.22
Lockheed	70,912	9,494	4,697	960	7.04	10.11	1.44
Louisiana-Pacific	12,490	814	2,046	146a	14.28	a	—
Marriott	193,742	22,818	41,671	6,972	22.46	30.55	1.36
Martin Marietta	60,955	3,293	5,338	289	8.76	8.78	1.00
Maytag	16,575	1,402	1,161	93	6.98	6.63	0.95
McDonald's	98,663	8,009	21,816	2,925	23.19	36.52	1.57
McDonnell Douglas	102,525	14,937	11,114	1,708	10.92	11.43	1.05
J.P. Morgan	8,081	658	1,268	182	16.59	27.66	1.67
Norfolk Southern	32,401	1,876	4,698	205	14.30	10.93	0.76
Occidental Petroleum	45,182	2,805	2,822	188	6.27	6.70	1.07
Paccar	8,437	1,176	491	105	6.20	8.93	1.44
Parker Hannifin	19,624	1,402	1,299	15	6.25	1.07	0.17
Pet	7,197	614	859	212	13.71	34.53	2.52
PPG Industries	20,976	1,678	2,152	222	10.48	13.23	1.26
Quaker Oats	14,336	1,734	1,460	41	9.34	2.36	0.25
Raytheon	68,221	1,703	3,589	59a	5.05	a	—
RJR Nabisco	39,727	2,672	7,049	436	17.65	16.32	0.92
Rockwell International	78,517	7,028	4,788	514	6.20	7.31	1.18
Safeway	78,685	664	6,736	104	8.62	15.66	1.82
Schering-Plough	10,618	1,639	1,714	468	17.80	28.55	1.60
Scott Paper	18,235	676	2,219	41	11.95	6.07	0.51
Sears Roebuck	414,736	10,259	61,783	5,573	15.85	54.32	3.43
Shawmut National	7,351	4,152	972	367	11.64	8.84	0.76
Sherwin-Williams	17,620	645	1,569	22	8.71	3.41	0.39
Snap-on Tools	6,048	644	193	29a	2.45	a	—

How Black Workers Fared at Leading Companies *(cont'd.)*

	Total Employees 1991	Decline from 1990	Black Employees 1991	Black Decline from 1990	Blacks' % of 1990 Workforce	Blacks' % of Total Decline	Black Job-loss Index
Society Corp.	8,939	1,009	1,294	5	13.06	0.50%	0.04
Tandem Computers	7,013	1,330	196	34	2.76	2.56	0.93
Tenneco	11,124	1,494	537	41	4.58	2.74	0.60
Texas Instruments	44,735	3,731	4,325	381	9.71	10.21	1.05
Textron	46,066	3,641	3,896	400	8.64	10.99	1.27
Times Mirror	28,582	1,860	3,520	322	12.62	17.31	1.37
Travelers	32,746	3,212	3,739	404	11.52	12.58	1.09
TRW	45,496	1,340	3,999	186	8.94	13.88	1.55
Union Texas Petroleum	664	789	80	37	8.05	4.69	0.58
Unisys	51,950	4,697	3,102	87	5.63	1.85	0.33
United Technologies	97,651	5,315	8,882	383	9.00	7.21	0.80
Upjohn	11,196	1,587	705	147	6.67	9.26	1.39
USX Corp.	46,439	4,580	5,500	903	12.55	19.72	1.57
VF Corp.	38,259	1,601	6,907	223a	16.77	a	—
Weyerhaeuser	37,971	4,699	3,807	430	9.93	9.15	0.92

SOURCE: EEOC, Data Tapes of Company Reports, 1990, 1991.

BLACKS DID BETTER AT SOME COMPANIES

Not all companies lost a disproportionate share of their black employees in the last recession.

American Telephone & Telegraph Co. managed to retain its percentage of black workers, despite job cuts. "We monitored what was happening, and we worked awful hard," says Anne Fritz, an AT&T human resources manager. "We tried to be fair to everybody."

But most companies that lost only a small percentage of black workers, or even gained blacks, did so mainly because of a geographical fluke, such as selling business or trimming staff in largely white neighborhoods. Like corporations that lost a disproportionate share of blacks, these companies say they had no idea their restructuring would have such a disparate impact on its employees.

Black employees also benefitted from early-retirement programs at a few companies. Blacks lost only five of 835 jobs in Eastman Kodak Co.'s early-retirement buyout because most of the workers who qualified for the program were white males hired in the 1950s and '60s. The departures of these employees created some vacancies that were filled by a greater share of minorities, Kodak says.

AT&T had similar early-retirement offers in the 1980s, which allowed it to maintain its level of staff diversity despite massive downsizings. But when the company began layoffs in the 1990s, it decided to look for other ways to ensure that minorities wouldn't be hit harder than the overall staff. AT&T says it wanted to avoid any undoing of an intensive affirmative action effort dating back to 1973, following the filing of sex and race discrimination charges against it by the EEOC.

So, during the recession, AT&T began reducing its payroll by offering employees two-year unpaid leaves of absence. It also laid off workers, but offered them several ways to try to stay with the company. AT&T launched an in-house employment service to help these employees find other jobs at the company, and created a temporary work pool enabling them to receive reduced pay while awaiting temporary assignments inside AT&T.

These efforts seem to have worked. The company's payroll was 16.4% black in 1990.

And of 18,525 employees who lost their jobs in the recession, about 16% were black.

For most companies, however, black job gains came by chance. "There isn't any specific consideration given to minority status," says Barry Lacter, a spokesman for Louisiana-Pacific Corp., where the black work force grew by 7.7% in 1991, even as the company cut its overall staff by 6.1%.

The reason for the gain? Location, location, location. The Company eliminated jobs in its rural Northern California plants that had few minorities, while adding workers in Southern states with large black populations.

HOW THE DATA WERE ANALYZED

To examine how black workers fared in the recession, *The Wall Street Journal* analyzed employment changes at 35,242 companies that filed reports with the Equal Employment Opportunity Commission in 1990 and 1991. More than 40 million employees, or about a third of the labor force, work for these concerns. The *Journal* also analyzed changes in black employment at each of about 400 of the nation's largest federal contractors in terms of market capitalization.

The reports provide a comparison of employment at the nation's larger businesses before and after the latest economic downturn, which officially began in July 1990 and ended in March 1991. (In 1990, the companies had to report personnel information for one payroll period between January and March; but because of a regulation change, they didn't have to file their 1991 reports until the third quarter, after the recession ended.)

Businesses with 100 or more employees must tell EEOC yearly the number of women and minorities they employ, with breakdowns, for specific job categories. Companies with 50 or more employees and a U.S. government contract of at least $50,000 must file reports too.

The *Journal* obtained computer tapes of all 1990 and 1991 EEOC reports, but with the company names deleted. To compare individual companies, the *Journal* used the Freedom of Information Act to obtain summary employment filings for the largest federal contractors from the Labor Department's Office of Federal Contract Compliance Program.

To analyze blacks' treatment at federal contractors where total employment fell by 500 or more between 1990 and 1991, the *Journal* calculated what percentage of each company's work force was black in 1990 and then determined what percentage of the employment decline between 1990 and 1991 represented black workers. The black job-loss index was computed by dividing the first calculation into the second. If a company had a staff that was 16% black in 1990 but blacks accounted for 24% of its decline in employment, the company's black job-loss index would be 1.50.

Thus, the larger the black job-loss index, the more disproportionate the staff reduction was for blacks. A number of less than one indicates the jobs of blacks were eliminated at a lower rate than their 1990 representation at the company.

The reports submitted by the federal contractors aren't adjusted for corporate actions such as the sale or acquisition of a business. Thus, the year-to-year comparisons show the changing racial makeup of a company's work force, not necessarily actual layoffs.

HOW AND WHY ORGANIZATIONS
ARE CULTURES

Harrison Trice
Janice Beyer

Humans build their cultures, nervously loquacious, on the edge of an abyss.

Kenneth Burke[1]

Human cultures emerge from people's struggles to manage uncertainties and create some degree of order in social life. People in organizations face many uncertainties. Their environments change due to economic conditions, technological developments, or the actions of competitors. To compete in a fast-developing global economy, people in organizations must deal with different types of customers and a large array of possible new competitors. Concerned citizen groups and legislatures ask them to deal with problems of environmental pollution, environmental preservation, deterrence of drug and substance abuse, and even elder and child care. Meanwhile, the explosion of information and knowledge means they must try to coordinate the activities of specialists with many different kinds of expertise when each does not fully understand the other and when their diverse views often conflict. They must do all this even as the social order within their organizations and their boundaries are changing due to mergers, reorganizations, and downsizing. From all of these uncertainties, many ambiguities arise. It is often far from clear

what is the best course of action for managers and others to take to ensure their organizations' survival and continued prosperity. If they fail, they face other threats and uncertainties, including loss of job, social status, and self-esteem. Thus, it is not surprising that, like people in other settings, people in organizations develop cultures.

Their cultures provide organizational members with more or less articulated sets of ideas that help them individually and collectively to cope with all of these uncertainties and ambiguities. People in organizations, as in social life generally, generate ideologies that tell them what is, how it got that way, and what ought to be. Such ideologies form the *substance* of cultures. They are not rationally based belief systems. Rather they are relatively implicit sets of taken-for-granted beliefs, values, and norms. Also, ideologies are more emotionally charged and resistant to change than rational beliefs because they give people some sense of confidence in facing the threats posed by uncertainties, and because they arise in the very circumstances that cannot be fully understood or predicted by rational means. In addition, by endorsing some actions and forbidding others, ideologies channel people's actions so that most of the time they repeat apparently successful patterns of behavior, mesh together in predictable ways, and avoid certain dangers and

333

conflicts. Table 1 gives some examples of ideologies that have grown up at Southwest Airlines, an organization that has faced and surmounted many uncertainties.

Cultures also help people to cope with uncertainties by providing them with accepted ways of expressing and affirming their beliefs, values, and norms. Cultures have repertories of cultural *forms* that members use to express the substance of their cultures. Table 1–1 also gives examples of some of the cultural forms used at Southwest Airlines. Cultural forms imbue actions and other entities with meanings; they enable people to communicate and celebrate their ideologies in

many different ways. This is possible because most human actions have dual consequences—they both accomplish certain technical and practical ends and express some subset of cultural meanings (Leach 1968).

To summarize, cultures are collective phenomena that embody people's responses to the uncertainties and chaos that are inevitable in human experience. These responses fall into two major categories. The first is the *substance* of a culture—shared, emotionally charged belief systems that we call ideologies. The second is *cultural forms*—observable entities, including actions, through which members of a culture express, affirm, and communicate the substance of their culture to one another. Clearly, people in organizations develop both cultural substance and cultural forms. Out of these processes, cultures grow. Cultures are a natural outgrowth of the social interactions that make up what we call organizations.

CULTURE'S ROLE IN MANAGING CHAOS

Human beings lack the genetic programming other animals have to ensure that they will behave in predictable ways that promote collective survival. Instead, humans have a relatively open nervous system that permits individuals to behave in many different ways (Geertz 1970). By comparison, many animal species, especially the lower forms, have quite closed and fixed central nervous systems. Amazing performances are made possible by inborn genetic programs that pattern actions within narrow predetermined ranges of behavior. There is an amazing precision, an almost breathtaking exactness, about the web building of the black widow spider and the nest building of the oriole.

Because human behavior is less specifically regulated by genetic programs, it exhibits greater variability and pliability. Throughout human history, cultures have provided much of the additional guidance needed for human beings to collectively survive, adapt,

---

TABLE 1. Examples of Ideologies and Cultural Forms at Southwest Airlines

---

Distinctive Ideologies[a]

As expressed by Herbert Kelleher, CEO of Southwest Airlines:
Failure is a natural result of the competitive process.
One organization's problem can become another organization's opportunities.
Competition and conflict are inevitable and can be turned to an organization's advantage.
One way to compete is to make work fun.
The crucible of competition made our employees very dedicated, very mission oriented, close knit, and high-spirited.
We give the best service in the business.

Examples of Cultural Forms

Once each quarter, officers of the company work as baggage handlers, ticket agents, and flight attendants.[b]
Employees traditionally wear costumes on Halloween, Valentine' Day, and other special occasions and don "fun uniforms" every Friday.[c]
One Christmas Day, at a time of intense competition with America West, SW flight attendants on a flight out of Phoenix donned red spandex pants, sweatshirts with a candy cane design, necklaces of jingle bells and tree bulbs, and headbands with sprigs of mistletoe.[d]
The entrance hall to corporate headquarters at Love Field in Dallas is covered with plaques earned by employees for outstanding contributions to the company.[e]
Every Friday at noon, employees in Dallas gather in the parking lot for a cookout.p[f]

---

[a] Adapted from Freiberg 1987, pp. 152–55.
[b] From Farnham 1989, p. 78.
[c] From Carey 1988, p. 6F.
[d] From Lucas 1988, p. 28
[e] From Freiberg 1987, p. 309.
[f] From Jarboe 1989, p. 104.

and achieve. For what the genetic code does not provide, human beings have developed cultural codes. "We are, in sum, incomplete or unfinished animals who complete ourselves through culture—and not through culture in general, but through highly particular forms of it." (Geertz 1970, p. 61) To be human

> is not just to talk; it is to utter the appropriate words and phrases in the appropriate social situations in the appropriate tone of voice. . . . It is not just to eat; it is to prefer certain foods cooked in certain ways and to follow a rigid table etiquette in consuming them; it is not even just to feel, but to feel certain quite distinctive emotions—patience, detachment, resignation, respect. (Geertz 1970, p. 64)

The potential diversity of human behavior can lead to chaos. It usually doesn't because human beings interactively create and perpetuate social order and some measure of control over events by means of their cultures. Without cultures, human life would be harsh and the qualities that we associate with being human would not exist. By producing some degree of orderliness and regularity from baffling, precarious, and disorderly circumstances (Leach 1976b), cultures smooth human life and allow people to get on with the necessities of living. This ongoingness, in turn, permits the accumulation of human learning over time. Each generation does not need to discover anew the solutions to recurrent uncertainties and problems. But chaos always threatens because new uncertainties arise. Thus some analysts suggest that cultures only cover up the ultimate disorder of existence (Moore and Myerhoff 1977, p. 17) and construct a precarious social reality that keeps chaos at bay (Berger and Luckmann 1966, p. 103). Indeed, scientists of all kinds now realize that "chaos seems to be everywhere" (Gleick 1987, p. 5).[2]

Organizations, like other social collectivities, tend to produce and preserve shared responses and shared experiences of uncertainty and chaos. People who belong to a given organizational culture share to some degree its basic properties: its substance and its forms. Collectively, they hold certain ideologies about how to deal with recurrent problems and uncertainties. They arrive at their shared ideologies through collective experience and repeated social interactions over time. They use cultural forms to communicate and reinforce these shared ideologies. Organizational cultures, like other cultures, develop as groups of people struggle together to make sense of and cope with their worlds.

WHAT'S DIFFERENT ABOUT CULTURES

While cultural anthropologists who studied tribal societies tended to include all aspects of social life as part of cultures, their all-encompassing approach does not seem suited to the analysis of modern, complex organizations. Research in management fields like organizational behavior, human resources, and strategy, and in the social sciences disciplines of sociology, psychology, and political science has already developed many useful ways of looking at people in work organizations. Each of these approaches, however, greatly simplifies reality by treating only selected aspects of human behavior in organizations. Thus, each offers only a partial explanation—and one that can sometimes be misleading to the degree it ignores valuable insights provided by other approaches or misses important aspects of behavior. Cultural approaches to the study of organizations tend to be more encompassing, but because life in modern work organizations is so multifaceted and complex, cultural approaches do not try to encompass everything. We believe a cultural approach is most useful for organizational analysis when (1) it calls attention to and helps explain various aspects of organizations that are neglected or overlooked by other approaches; and (2) it pulls in and helps to integrate various concepts developed by these other approaches with cultural approaches.

The purpose of this introductory section is to set the stage for the more detailed examinations in later chapters by briefly discussing some of the general features of cultures. Some of these features are unique to cultures; others have a distinctive twist when looked at from a cultural perspective. Together they delineate what makes this perspective different from others. We will begin by outlining some characteristics and consequences of cultures on which most analysts agree. We will then discuss briefly other characteristics over which there is considerable controversy. We will end this section with a discussion of some features that organizational cultures do *not* have but that are sometimes ascribed to them.

Characteristics of Cultures

Table 2 lists six major characteristics of cultures on which most analysts agree. Some of these were already mentioned in our general description of cultures. The words in Table 1–2 are seldom used in traditional analyses of organizations and management. They describe phenomena that are largely ignored in other approaches to analyzing organization. Together they capture the essence of what makes cultures different. All will be described briefly here and revisited many times throughout this book.

Collective.   Cultures cannot be produced by individuals acting alone. They originate as individuals interact with one another. Individuals may originate specific ways of managing the fundamental insecurities of life, but until these specific ways come to be collectively accepted and put into practice they are not part of a culture. Cultures are the repositories of what their members agree about. Persons who do not endorse and practice prevailing beliefs, values, and norms become

marginal and may be punished or expelled. Belonging to a culture involves believing what others believe and doing as they do—at least part of the time.

Emotionally Charged.   Because cultures help to manage anxieties, their substance and forms are infused with emotion as well as meaning. To some extent, all culture is a "gigantic effort to mask" life's fundamental insecurities (Kluckhohn 1942, p. 66). People cherish and cling to established ideologies and practices because they seem to make the future predictable by making it conform to the past. People's allegiances to their ideologies and cultural forms thus spring more from their emotional needs than from rational consideration. When ideologies and cultural practices are questioned, their adherents react emotionally. They may be able to advance elaborate rationales for them, but the depth of the feelings they bring to their arguments indicates that more than rationality is at work. Members of a culture rarely dare to question core beliefs and values.

> . . . man [sic] dreads both spontaneity and change. . . . Conventions and institutions . . . originate as group expedients which have some social value at some time, but they remain the objects of passionate adoration long after they have outlived their usefulness. Men fight and die for them. (Ferguson, 1936, p. 29)

Cultural ideologies and forms also help to channel emotions into socially accepted channels. As one analysis of myths pointed out, "Emotion is assisted by the repetition of words that have acquired a strong emotional coloring, and this coloring again is intensified by repetition" (Hocart 1939, p. 208). The performance of rites and rituals heightens awareness of shared sentiments. Rites and rituals may also provide ways for individuals to sublimate antisocial impulses (Kluckhohn 1942, p. 74).

Historically Based.   Cultures cannot be divorced from their histories and they do not

TABLE 2.   Some Characteristics of Cultures

Collective	Inherently symbolic
Emotionally charged	Dynamic
Historically based	Inherently fuzzy

arise overnight. To develop a culture, people need to spend time together to interact and share with one another common uncertainties and some ways of coping with them. Thus, a particular culture will be based in the unique history of a particular group of people coping with a unique set of physical, social, political, and economic circumstances. Once individuals in a cultural group come to share some set of ideas and cultural practices, these ideas and practices begin to have a kind of life of their own. They often persist within that group after the uncertainties that gave rise to them are no longer present, and their originators and early proponents have left. Thus, a thorough examination of a culture will usually uncover residues of cultural ideas and practices that originated at earlier points in its history to deal with uncertainties that may no longer be present. Even though these historical residues are buried under current preoccupations and relatively hidden from awareness, they can still have powerful effects in guiding current behavior.

Inherently Symbolic. To say that cultures are symbolic is to emphasize the expressive, rather than the technical and practical side of human behavior. While, as pointed out earlier, human actions both do and say things, it is their expressive side that cultural analysis explores. Symbolism plays a very important role in cultural communication and expression. Things often stand for other things. Symbols so infuse cultural communication that they are considered the most basic unit of cultural expression (Turner 1967). They occur frequently as part of other cultural forms. Thus, while in one sense symbols are a specific type of cultural form, they are, in another sense, the most general and pervasive of cultural forms. Some organizational theorists therefore focus on symbolism in organizations rather than on the broader concept of culture (Pondy et al. 1983; Pfeffer 1981a; Turner 1990a).

Dynamic. While cultures create continuity and persist across generations of members, they are not static, but dynamic. Cultures continually change. Some of the reasons follow.

First, no communication is ever perfect. Thus, all members do not learn exactly the same things about what a culture endorses and expects. Even if they intend to conform perfectly to what others expect, their understandings of a culture may be too imperfect to make that possible. Second, individuals have considerable discretion, even in very traditional cultures, to create their own variants of expected behavior. The degree of individualism varies across societies and over time but is probably always sufficient to produce some degree of innovativeness and creativity in responding to life's problems and challenges. Third, so much of culture is taken for granted that its transmission and reception occurs at a nonconscious level. Members are often unaware of what their cultures really say about a specific issue or event. As one common expression notes, "It would hardly be fish who discovered the existence of water." Fourth, the fact that so much of cultural communication is symbolic makes it inherently imprecise. Symbols often have more than one meaning (Turner 1990b). What members receive from their cultures is often more like a series of clues than direct messages; they must often translate and extrapolate from these clues to get at core meanings. Fifth, organizations, in particular, must often assimilate new groups and practices to deal with new demands and opportunities in their changing environments. New importations, whether they involve techniques, equipment, or people, are likely to carry with them some cultural baggage that will affect existing cultures.

While not exhaustive, this list of reasons helps to show how and why cultural persistence is imperfect and why there is considerable change in how any culture manifests itself over time.

Inherently Fuzzy. Not only are cultures inherently symbolic, they are inherently fuzzy (Leach 1976b; Gluckman 1963a; Pierce 1977; Moore 1975) in a variety of other ways. A leading anthropologist provides an instructive metaphor:

> . . . The appropriate image . . . of cultural organization is neither the spider web nor the pile of sand; it is rather more the octopus, whose tentacles are in large part separately integrated, neurally quite poorly connected with one another and with what in the octopus passes for a brain, and yet who nonetheless manages to get around and to preserve himself, for a while anyway, as a viable, if somewhat ungainly entity. (Geertz 1966, p. 66)

Cultures are not monolithic single sets of ideas, but rather incorporate contradictions, ambiguities, paradoxes, and just plain confusion. Anthropologists characterize modern cultures as "deeply ambiguous" (Keesing 1987, p. 162) and characterized by "enormous multiplicity" (Geertz 1983, p. 161). The more complex and fragmented the circumstances a human group confronts, the more likely it will mirror these elements in its culture with fuzziness.

Since modern organizations often operate in uncertain and confusing environments, observers have noted how the cultural elements they encounter in team are rather miscellaneous (Riley 1983), full of double binds (Cameron and Quinn 1988, p. 2), multiple meanings (Young 1990; Chatov 1973), ambiguous ceremonials (Mechling and Wilson, 1988), and stories and metaphors (Feldman 1991). Some contradictions undoubtedly arise from residues of the past and from imperfect cultural transmission; others arise because of the many subcultural influences in organizations that emanate from occupational groups with different work-related uncertainties and experiences. Still others arise from the emergent, interactive nature of cultures and organizations; organizations and their cultures are perpetually in the process of becoming organized (Weick 1985). As actions go forward, people often discover some lack of shared and coincident meanings that needs to be worked out.

One analyst divided cultures into their core or central elements and those that are more peripheral. Fuzziness marks the peripheries, while the central elements and core values generate sufficient consensus to produce some cooperation and coordination and to permit members to "recognize their common identity through time and across lines of conflict" (Shils 1975, p. xii).

Consequences of Cultures

Table 3 lists the most prominent and distinctive consequences of cultures about which most experts agree. The words on this list do sometimes appear in traditional treatments of management and organizations. But, with the exception of *uncertainties* and *commitment*, the words are infrequently used. While the other consequences listed are central to understanding what cultures are about, they play a very minor role in most noncultural analyses. Considering each in some detail should therefore contribute to our understanding of what makes cultures different.

Management of Collective Uncertainties. Through ideologies and cultural forms, cultures supply "fixed points in a world of bewildering change and disappointment" (Kluckhohn 1942, p. 68). Even in contemporary U.S. society, where change itself is highly valued and pursued, conformity to core cultural expectations is considered a virtue. People do not want everything in their worlds to change at the same time. They want to be able to take some things for granted. Ideologies and cultural forms grow up particularly around "those sectors of experience which do not seem amenable to rational control and hence where human beings can least tolerate insecurity" (Kluckhohn 1942, p. 68). They persist because they "reduce the

TABLE 3.   Some Consequences of Cultures

Management of collective uncertainties	Generation of dual consequences
Creation of social order	Technical and expressive
Creation of continuity	Latent and manifest
Creation of collective identity and commitment	Functional and dysfunctional
Encouragement of ethnocentrism	

anticipation of disaster" (Kluckhohn 1942, p. 68). Even in contemporary U.S. society, where change itself is highly valued and pursued, conformity to core cultural expectations is considered a virtue. People do not want everything in their worlds to change at the same time. They want to be able to take some things for granted. Ideologies and cultural forms grow up particularly around "those sectors of experience which do not seem amenable to rational control and hence where human beings can least tolerate insecurity" (Kluckhohn 1942, p. 68). They persist because they "reduce the anticipation of disaster" (Kluckhohn 1942, p. 69). It is not hard to see how the ideologies and forms listed in Table 1 help managers and employees of Southwest Airlines to face the uncertainties engendered by the fierce competition and fluctuating environmental demands in the airline industry.

The ideologies and associated forms that cultures develop vary in the degree to which they are grounded in some sort of practical experience and confrontation with reality or based in purely imagined events and superstitions. Obviously, ideologies that match realities imposed by the physical world and other circumstances will serve to help members of a culture adapt to and perhaps surmount those realities better than ones that do not. Also, of course, it can be dangerous to misunderstand genuine threats or to rely on magic to dispel them. Cultures that persist in unrealistic beliefs jeopardize their very survival.

Creation of Social Order. Cultures create social order from the potential chaos that emanates from the open-ended nature of the human nervous system. Recurrent patterns of behavior form; people begin to see them as right and proper ways to behave and become emotionally attached to them. The result is norms—quite specific and taken-for-granted expectations for how people should behave in a myriad of circumstances. Norms control behavior because members of a culture will sanction violations of their norms with disapproval and more concrete punishments.

The degree of social control that cultures produce, however, varies across societies and time periods. Cultures never completely control individuals; some refuse to conform and become deviants. Also, some cultures are pluralistic, with each subculture having only partial control over members. While the social control that cultures produce can be used for sinister ends and all cultures can be seen as constraining individual freedoms to some degree, people do not reach their full potential as human beings nor live happily and contentedly without cultures. Examples of people living outside their cultures are provided by individuals who reject or lose contact with the norms of any social groups in their societies. This social condition, known as anomie, greatly increases the probability of suicide (Durkheim 1964). Also, frequently occurring accounts of feral children (Shattuck 1980)—children growing up outside human society, usually raised by animals—attest to the anxieties people have and the negative consequences they ascribe to being without culture.

Creation of Continuity. Human cultures so uniformly generate continuity of their beliefs and practices that a special term is used to refer to this process. The ways in which cultural substance and forms are passed from member to member over time is called socialization. To socialize someone is to impart to that person how to think and behave to conform to a social group's needs and to attach emotional significance to those thoughts and behaviors. Thus, individuals are shaped to fit within and continue the prevailing social order. Failures to socialize are costly to cultural continuity and social order. Social life is disrupted when individuals do not know how or refuse to conform to important expectations. If disruptions are serious and widespread, the prevailing culture may be pressured into change.

Many agencies and institutions in modern society—most notably religions, the family, the schools, and peer groups—socialize members for their general social roles. Schools and higher education play an especially important role in socializing members for work roles. To the degree that these agents instill values and behaviors consistent with the past, some degree of cultural continuity is assured. To the degree that they fail, cultural continuity is imperiled and the general level of uncertainty will rise because people cannot count on one another as they used to do.

Creation of Collective Identity and Commitment. Members of cultures come to be bonded together not only by shared views of the world, but by many social ties and commitments. People come to know themselves as well as others in terms of their place within a culture. They assume a certain social identity within the cognitive, emotional, and social frameworks provided by the culture. To a great degree this identity is acquired reflexively as people interact with others and interpret others' reactions to them (Mead 1934). People develop an image of themselves as part of a particular social group with particular cultural beliefs and practices. If they move to a new social group and become part of its culture, their self-image will change.

Within social groups that persist long enough to form cultures, members also develop a sense of a common identity. They are aware, at some level, of the similarities that they and other members share and how this makes them different from others. They, in effect, develop some degree of consciousness and pride in what makes their group unique (Martin et al. 1983). Cultural groups also become reference groups for their members. People look to other members of their cultures for emotional support and confirmation of the meanings they ascribe to events. They also look to them for approval and disapproval of their and others' behaviors. From these reactions and from the models other members' behaviors provide, people construct their understandings of their worlds.

People's dependence on each other for emotional support and for making sense of their worlds also builds commitment to their cultural groups. They come to depend on other members of their culture to help them get through life's uncertainties and difficulties. They do not want to disrupt the ties that provide them with these assurances and so become committed to their continuity. Members' experiences in the culture pile up positive rewards and hurts avoided that increase their positive attachments to their cultures.

Encouragement of Ethnocentrism. The next characteristic of cultures listed in Table 3—that they encourage ethnocentrism—calls attention to some unpleasant possibilities associated with cultures. People who endorse one set of ideas often come to distrust, fear, and dislike people with other ideas. The stronger and more emotionally charged the ideas, the more likely that their adherents will come to have intolerant and emotionally charged reactions to people who hold other ideas. The very term ideology; which we use in this book to represent the substance of cultures, has an unpleasant connotation because of its association with groups who use their ideas to justify their domination of other groups of people. While it seems clear that ideologies are not used exclusively to advance selfish interests (Beyer, Dunbar, and Meyer 1988), it also seems clear that they carry the danger of enhancing feelings of group superiority. For example, the residues of the caste system of India and racist ideologies everywhere provide rationales for some ethnic groups to mistreat others. But many other cultural and subcultural differences that occur in organizations—especially occupational, departmental, and status boundaries—can also produce ethnocentrism. In organizations, as elsewhere in society, such feelings are likely to interfere with cooperation and coordination among groups and lead to such phenomena as passing the buck or blaming the victim.

Generation of Dual Consequences. The consequences of cultures include at least three dualities that have rather different implications for organizations. The first of these— *technical and expressive* consequences—has already been mentioned. While some cultural analysts, especially cultural anthropologists, might consider all of the technical activities and ideas of organizations as part of their cultures, the approach followed in this analysis is to focus on the expressive side of activities in organizations as the essence of their cultures. Other approaches to analyzing organizations focus on their technical and practical side. We do not intend, by focusing on the expressive, to deny that organizational activities have technical or practical outcomes. Nor do we feel that most activities have exclusively one or the other set of consequences. Rather, these dimensions represent dual consequences in the sense that both are present in most situations.

The second set of consequences of cultural activities is their *latent and manifest* consequences. Latent consequences are those that are hidden from view; manifest consequences are those that are evident. This duality means that cultures operate simultaneously at various levels of awareness. While some components of culture may be deeply buried and unconscious, others are relatively close to the surface and more accessible to examination (Schein 1985). Although there is some controversy on this point, it seems unlikely that core cultural elements are so unconscious that they never come to the surface of people's awareness. If this were so, people would not know when their or others' actions violated basic cultural assumptions. It does seem likely, however, that much of culture is taken for granted and unexamined most of the time. It takes something out of the ordinary, something that makes a specific element in the culture salient, to make people become aware of what is ordinarily latent (Louis 1980, 1985a).

The third duality along which cultural consequences can be arrayed is their *functional and dysfunctional* aspects. In social science terms, functional consequences are those that are beneficial, useful, and help to maintain current social arrangements; dysfunctional consequences are harmful, not useful, and tend to upset current social arrangements. Because many early cultural anthropologists tended to analyze features of tribal societies in terms of how they helped to maintain those

societies, their work was criticized as one-sided and as providing rationales for the continuance of current societies with whatever imperfections and injustices they included. Similarly, some early treatments of organizational cultures treated them relatively uncritically as functional (Peters and Waterman 1982). Whole areas of organizational and management research have tended to focus on discovering and explaining what is functional in organizations and thus ignored their dysfunctional aspects (Pondy and Mitroff 1979). There has been a strong tendency in analyses of organizational cultures to "overemphasize the integrative and cohesion-producing side of culture" (Van Maanen and Kunda 1989, p. 49).

Other analyses of organizational cultures have suggested that considering only the positive aspects of culture is misleading. Cultures can be "equally dysfunctional" (Trice 1985, p. 248). They have many downside risks and costs, even in companies that are admired for both their performance and cultures. Some of the general drawbacks of corporate cultures identified in a recent study of firms in the electronics industry include:

- making employees vulnerable to burnout from working too hard
- making people unwilling to change what they do
- coloring the interpretation of information and events
- encouraging behaviors that few people do well
- encouraging ego involvements that heighten the emotionality of events

Many other drawbacks were identified for specific types of corporate cultures in this industry (Jelinek and Schoonhoven 1990, pp. 370–402).

In general, most activities in organizations can be seen to have both functional and dysfunctional consequences. This is illustrated by such popular expressions as "the trade-off is. . . . ," "the other side of the coin," and "the folly of good intentions." Sometimes activities have functional consequences for one set of people and dysfunctional ones for another set. Sometimes activities have both sets of consequences for the same people. An awareness of this duality raises the important question of how functional and dysfunctional consequences are distributed. History is replete with cultures that espoused ideologies that oppressed members of certain groups to the advantage of others. This third duality warns us that the same possibilities exist for organizational cultures. Also, organizational cultures that were functional for one period of time can become dysfunctional as the environment or other circumstances change (Starbuck, Greve, and Hedberg 1978; Miller 1990).

Some Controversial Characteristics of Cultures

All scientific fields give rise to controversies. So it is not surprising that anthropologists and other researchers of cultures disagree on some basic issues. In addition, the study of organizational cultures is relatively new. Those working in the area were trained in a variety of social science disciplines and thus bring different perspectives to their research. They, in effect, come from a variety of scientific subcultures. Table 4 lists several major issues on which the experts on organizational cultures do not agree. Each is important as well as controversial.

Single Culture vs. Multiple Cultures. The revival of cultural analysis of organizations in the 1980s was sparked by a few popular books written largely for a managerial audience (Peters and Waterman 1982; Deal and Kennedy 1982; Ouchi 1981). These books gave the general impression that whole organizations can have distinctive cultures and that top management has a great deal of say

TABLE 4.   Controversial Aspects of Organizational Cultures

Single culture	vs.	Multiple cultures
Consensus	vs.	Dissensus
Distinctive	vs.	Universal elements
Rigid	vs.	Malleable cultures

in shaping those cultures. Some managers, many consultants, and perhaps a few scholars still hold to such views. Several organizational scholars reacted to these popular treatments by emphasizing how pervasive and important subcultures were in organizations (Gregory 1983; Riley 1983; Barley and Louis 1983). This multicultural perspective is dominant today (Trice and Morand 1991). Few scholars doubt the presence of subcultures in organizations, but some doubt that organizations have organization wide umbrella cultures.

The perspective to be taken in this book is that many organizations have both. While subcultures undoubtedly grow up more readily than organizationwide cultures, the testimony of various careful scholars indicates that some organizations have distinctive organizationwide cultures (Clark 1970; Pettigrew 1979; Whipp, Rosenfeld, and Pettigrew 1989; Child and Smith 1987; Hackman 1984). The disputes over this point may stem from different conceptions of culture.

Consensus vs. Dissensus. Many scholars agree that some consensus about cultural substance and forms is a distinguishing feature of cultures, but disagree about whether to include within the term *culture* rather fragmented, shifting collections of people with different, even conflicting, views. A recent analysis suggests that there are three perspectives on organizational cultures: integrated, differentiated, and fragmented (Meyerson and Martin 1987; Martin and Meyerson 1988; Meyerson 1991; Martin 1991). The integrated view emphasized organizationwide consensus, internal consistency, and clarity; the differentiated view emphasizes consensus within subcultures, inconsistencies between them, and clarity only within subcultures; the fragmented view emphasizes a lack of consensus both organizationwide and in subcultures, a lack of either clear consistency or inconsistency, and the pervasiveness of ambiguity.

It is important to note that the first perspective is the same as the organizationwide approach already mentioned. The second is close to the multicultural approach already mentioned. The two really differ only in the level at which cultures occur; in both, cultures are characterized by substantial consensus.

The third perspective departs from traditional definitions of culture by its emphasis on ambiguity and dissensus. While this view has some basis in the literature on culture (Turner 1969; Moore 1975), it so emphasizes ambiguity and confusion that it is hard to see how such a set of relationships could form the basis of a culture. If ambiguity and fragmentation are the essence of relationships, and if the feeble and transitory consensus that does form fluctuates constantly with various forces, there is no culture as most scholars (e.g. Moore 1975; Jones, Moore, and Snyder 1988; Schein 1990) define one. Such a culture, if it can be said to exist, would do little to help people grapple with ongoing uncertainties. Also, from a dynamic perspective, such a set of relationships seems likely to either degenerate over time into a collection of individuals, each doing his or her own thing, or develop mechanisms for resolving conflict and ambiguity (Trice 1991) and thus produce some consensus. What enables cultures to arise in such situations is not the pervasive confusion and ambiguity, but the presence of a minimal degree of consensus and clarity about some issues.

For example, an observer of social workers in hospitals described their cultures as fragmented ones, yet they were observed to use special, unstructured meetings in which "anything goes" to express their anxieties and reduce tensions and conflict (Meyerson 1991b, p. 264). Furthermore, attendance was especially good at these meetings, strongly suggesting that they had some shared value to the participants. These meetings undoubtedly functioned as rites of conflict reduction that helped members cope with the ambiguities that seemed to permeate their occupational roles. If nothing else, the social workers shared an understanding that they could share their perceptions of ambiguity on these occa-

sions. Thus, there was some consensus about how to handle ambiguity even in this fragmented occupational subculture. They also shared some basic orientations and knowledge about their occupation, faced similar problems, and had comparable experiences (Meyerson 1991a, p. 131; Feldman 1991).

Perhaps the best resolution that can be made for this issue is to acknowledge that all of these perspectives have some truth, but that none is the whole story. As already discussed, organizational cultures have various characteristics that produce ambiguities, conflicts, and dissensus: they reflect history and carry forward residues of the past; they are inherently symbolic and fuzzy; they are dynamic and not static; they include multiple, often contradictory, sets of ideas; and they have dual sets of consequences. It is therefore unlikely that any single culture will fit completely into any of the three perspectives identified. All cultures have areas of dissensus, and all cultures have at least a core of consensus. Also, cultures have centers and peripheries; some members and some ideas are more marginal than others. Some degree of dissensus and ambiguity among marginal members must be expected (Shils 1975).

> Consistency, consensus, harmony, and integration do occur even though in the midst of inconsistencies, ambiguities, conflicts, disruptions, and dissolution. These two sets of forces appear to be reciprocal to one another. It is even conceivable that they somehow are essential to each other. Such a condition is the ultimate paradox in the puzzle of organizational behavior. (Trice 1991, p. 304)

To avoid endless confusion, it seems sensible to reserve the term *culture* for situations in which there is some core of consensus. Because people try to reduce uncertainties, organizations will have pockets of consensus somewhere within them if any members are around long enough to share some of the same uncertainties and their ways of coping with them.

Distinctive vs. Universal Elements. Anthropologists developed two very different schools of thought about the relative uniqueness of the substance and forms of cultures. To simplify a bit, one school argued that certain universals occur in all cultures (Levi-Strauss 1963; Leach 1970). Applying this idea to organizations would argue that some commonalities can be found across various organizational cultures. The other anthropological school argued that to generalize beyond a single culture would be inaccurate because this would rip the cultural elements out of the social context that gave them their meaning (Geertz 1973). To apply this idea to organizations would argue that we cannot generalize from research conducted in one organization to anything in another. This controversy presents especially thorny issues for the analysis of organizational cultures because users of such analyses often want to be able to apply results from one organization to another. Managers and management researchers, in particular, seek results from which generalizations for theory and practice can be drawn.

The methods that cultural researchers use reflect this controversy. Researchers who believe that there are generalizable properties in organizational cultures often use *etic* methods, in which they apply a typology or explore some prior set of concepts in one or more organizations. Some of them use methods like questionnaires or structured interviews that yield quantified measures. Researchers who believe that cultures are unique and specific to a particular group will use *emic* methods—unstructured interviewing, observation, and other qualitative techniques—designed to elicit the "native point of view."[3] Emic researchers try hard to avoid imposing their own category systems or other ideas on a culture, seeking rather to bring to the surface category systems and ideas that members of the culture themselves use to think about their worlds (Naroll and Naroll 1973). Emic researchers are likely to study one organization or one group in an organization at a time.

Clearly, both of these approaches have value. The middle ground is to realize that without etics, comparisons lack a frame; without emics, comparisons lack meat. Emic and etic data do not constitute a rigid dichotomy, but instead often present the same data from two points of view (Harris 1976). Thus, the most sensible resolution of this controversy appears to be to avoid carrying either approach to an extreme, except when the research or practical question at hand clearly demands that approach. Rather, some combination of these approaches seems advisable, with the particular mix depending on how much is known about the group under study in advance and what sorts of issues the researchers are interested in exploring. There seems to be room for both explorations of general properties of cultures and for explorations of specific cultures yielding relatively unique insights.

We will not try to categorize all past research on organizational cultures in terms of this controversy. Table 5, however, presents a partial listing of various types of organizational cultures that management researchers have advanced and discussed. Such typologies imply an etic orientation in that they seek to generalize some cultural properties across more than one organization. Their diversity suggests, however, that they were devised using emic methods. Obviously, the theories of researchers are not always consistent with their methods in terms of the issue of universality. Also, this controversy is clearly far from resolved in the management field. The contents of Table 5 illustrate that little consensus has emerged about how to categorize cultures, even though there is some overlap on the kinds of issues on which they might be categorized. If organizational cultures have universal properties, they have not yet been convincingly demonstrated.

Rigid vs. Malleable Cultures. A few observers fear cultures are so unchanging as to confront managers with "unbridled rigidity" (Bennis and Nanus 1985, p. 183). For reasons

TABLE 5.   Some Examples of Typologies of Organizational Cultures[a]

Types of Organizational Cultures	Dominant Ideologies	Authors
Type A	Hierarchical control, high specialization, short-term employment, individual responsibility, individual decision making	
Type J	Clan control, low specialization, lifetime employment, collective responsibility, collective decision making	
Type Z	Clan control, moderate specialization, long-term employment, individual responsibility, consensual decision making	Ouchi and Jaeger, 1978; Ouchi, 1981
Process	Low risk, "cover your ass" mentality, tight hierarchy	Deal and Kennedy, 1982
Tough-guy–Macho	High risk, quick feedback, fluctuating structure	
Work-hard–Play-hard	Moderately low risk, race to the quick, flexible structure	
Bet-your-company	Very high risk, slow feedback, clear-cut hierarchy	
Sensation-thinking	Impersonal, abstract, certainty, specificity, authoritarian	Mitroff and Kilmann, 1975
Intuition-thinking	Flexible, adaptive, global notions, goal-driven	
Intuition-feeling	Caring, decentralized, flexible, no explicit rules or regulations	
Sensation-feeling	Personal, homelike, relationship-driven, nonbureaucratic	
Apathetic	Demoralizing and cynical orientation	Sethia and Von Glinow, 1985
Caring	High concern for employees, no high performance expectations	
Exacting	Performance and success really count	
Integrative	High concern for employees with high concern for performance	
Paranoid	Fear, distrust, suspicion	Kets de Vries and Miller, 1984
Avoidant	Lack of self-confidence, powerlessness, inaction	
Charismatic	Drama, power, success, abject followership	
Bureaucratic	Compulsive, detailed, depersonalized, rigid	
Schizoid	Politicized, social isolation	

[a] To save space, the table summarizes only some of the points used by these authors to describe their types.

already explained, however, most analysts agree that various characteristics of cultures internally generate some amount of spontaneous change on a pretty continuous basis. This change may be gradual, it may be sporadic, but over time it nonetheless produces significant amounts of change.

There is less agreement on whether cultures can be deliberately changed, especially in a relatively short time. Some cultural researchers argue that, because cultures emerge spontaneously from informal interactions, any changes must also emerge spontaneously (Dorson 1971). Such a stance implies that cultures cannot be deliberately managed or planned. Other analysts argue that cultures can be deliberately changed, but only a little, or only with great difficulty. Some suggest, for example, that managers may be able to "slightly modify the trajectory of a culture"

(Martin and Siehl 1983, p. 53). Another view is that changing cultures cannot be accomplished without replacing existing social learning processes (Schein 1985, 1990)—no simple or quick undertaking.

Still other reasons that have been identified as making deliberate cultural change difficult include: that cultures are too elusive and hidden to be accurately diagnosed, managed, or changed (Uttal 1983); that the techniques and skills involved are rare and take too long to make deliberate change practical (Uttal 1983; Schwartz and Davis 1981); and that the many subcultures existing in most organizations act against coordinated change (Barley and Louis 1983). Undoubtedly the most basic reason that analysts expect deliberate cultural change to be difficult is that cultures help to sustain people through life's difficulties (Beyer 1981; Boje, Fedor, and

Rowland 1982), and people therefore hold onto their cultures with some tenacity.

Other analysts treat cultures as if they can be readily manipulated, suggesting that direct, intentional actions not unlike those used in other management tasks can be used to change corporate cultures (Peters and Waterman, 1982; Deal and Kennedy 1982; Kilmann 1982). For example:

> Can every company have a strong culture? We think it can. But to do that, top management first has to recognize what kind of culture the company already has, even if it is weak. The ultimate success of a chief executive officer depends to a large degree on an accurate reading of the corporate culture and the ability to hone it and shape it to fit the shifting needs of the marketplace. (Deal and Kennedy 1982, p. 18)

Again, both positions have some validity. Cultures are undoubtedly resistant to change —especially changes that do not emerge from within the cultural group. If they were too malleable, cultures would not provide the continuity and certainty that people come to depend on to give their lives order and meaning. On the other hand, cultures do change, and sometimes that change occurs as the result of deliberate interventions. The large-scale changes produced by charismatic leaders like Martin Luther King, Jr., and Mahatma Gandhi illustrate that people's deliberate efforts can change cultures dramatically. If such changes can be accomplished in whole societies, it is certainly conceivable that organizational cultures can be deliberately changed.

Recent thinking suggest some of the variables that need to be considered in assessing how difficult it would be to change a given culture. Three factors identified as likely to affect cultural persistence are: the fluidity of current ideologies, members' commitment to them, and the availability of alternative ideologies (Wilkins and Dyer 1988). The greater the fluidity and availability of alternatives, and the lower the members' commitment, the easier it will be to effect cultural change.

Obviously, to say that change is possible is not the same as saying it is easy or frequent. Because organizations are complex and their managers tend to think more in terms of ostensibly rational rather than expressive processes, planned cultural change is not a simple matter. It requires a thorough understanding of how cultures work, what factors about them are likely to produce what sorts of resistance to change in a given situation, and what levers cultures offer for producing change.

What Cultures Are Not

As already stated, one danger in using a cultural perspective is that everything in human behavior will be viewed as culture. For the purposes of management research and practice, we favor using the term relatively narrowly. Thus, it may help to eliminate some confusion by pointing out what organizational cultures are not. While some may view the issues we raise in this section as still controversial, we feel there are sufficient reasons to decide them in the directions indicated. As before, our motive is to reserve the culture concept for phenomena that are distinctive and not encompassed in other, more traditional approaches.

Not Climate.   In the management literature the concepts of culture and climate are sometimes confused. The two concepts, however, have distinctly different origins that give them rather different meanings. As originally conceptualized, organizational climate referred to psychological environments in which the behaviors of individuals occurred. Studies focused on individually perceived, rather immediate experiences of organizational members (Campbell et al. 1970; Hellriegel and Slocum 1974). Attitudinal reactions or perceptions of these experiences were measured by items in questionnaires. The appeal of the climate construct was that it seemed to give researchers a way to combine a broad array of variables already studied into a single omnibus concept that would simplify the process of characterizing and comparing the psychological environments of individuals. Thus it focused on measuring the perceptions of individuals about their organizations, rather than beliefs, values, or norms shared by groups of people. While others have since argued for and applied the concept at a collective level (Joyce and Slocum 1984), the measures used continue to be anchored in individual perceptions and thus reflect individual rather than shared experiences (Jackofsky and Slocum 1988). Although statistical techniques can then uncover clusters of people holding similar perceptions, alone they cannot tell us how individuals who perceive their climates similarly arrived at their shared perceptions.

Another basic difference between climate and culture is that the primary techniques used to measure climate were developed to measure attitudes. They are etic techniques that hold the danger of imposing researchers' views of the world on those being studied. In addition, it is far from clear that what they ask about is cultural, either in the sense of emerging from shared experiences, or in the sense of reflecting people's core understandings of their organizations. If attitudes reflect culture at all, they do so at only the most superficial level. For good reason, the traditions of cultural research call for intensive data collection using primarily emic methods over a substantial period of time. Otherwise, the subtleties that characterize cultures, as listed in Tables 2 and 3, cannot be uncovered or understood.

Another basic difference between climate and culture is that the primary techniques used to measure climate were developed to measure attitudes. They are etic techniques that hold the danger of imposing researchers' views of the world on those being studied. In addition, it is far from clear that what they ask about is cultural, either in the sense of emerging from shared experiences, or in the sense of reflecting people's core understandings of their organizations. If attitudes reflect culture at all, they do so at only the most

superficial level. For good reason, the traditions of cultural research call for intensive data collection using primarily emic methods over a substantial period of time. Otherwise, the subtleties that characterize cultures, as listed in Tables 2 and 3, cannot be uncovered or understood.

Still another difference between the concepts of climate and culture is that climate lacks unique indicators. So many different variables have been subsumed under the climate concept by various researchers that it overlaps with most constructs in organizational behavior (Glick 1985, p. 606), as well as with structure, technology, formalization (James and Jones 1974), and effectiveness (Lawler, Hall, and Oldham 1974). By contrast, culture has many unique indicators like myths, symbols, rites, and stories. Recent attempts to link climate to culture assume that employees' reports of what they perceive to be prevalent organizational procedures and practices are somehow equivalent to these rich cultural manifestations (Schneider 1990). This seems highly unlikely.

Although some researchers use methods and concepts similar to those used in research on climate to study culture (Hofstede 1980b; Cooke and Rousseau 1988; Hofstede et al. 1990; Rousseau 1990; O'Reilly, Chatman, and Caldwell 1991), other experts on culture feel such attempts are bound to miss the essence of what culture is all about.

Not Groupthink. A misplaced emphasis on the notion that shared meanings by themselves, are the essence of culture can create some confusion between the concepts of groupthink and culture. Groupthink describes situations where people behave in certain ways that tend to not only make them think similarly but also hide any differences in how they feel and think (Hellriegel, Slocum and Woodman 1986, pp. 249-52). It consists of "a collective pattern of defensive avoidance, lack of vigilance, unwarranted optimism, sloganistic thinking, suppression of worrisome defects, and reliance on shared rationalizations . . . " (Janis 1972, p. 399). While the phenomenon of groupthink resembles culture in some respects, it is usually used in reference to relatively small, face-to-face groups. Thus, the concept has some overlap with subcultures, but seems inappropriate to apply at the more encompassing level of a large subunit or organization. Most important, the phenomenon of groupthink lacks such cultural characteristics a historical base, symbolism, dynamism, fuzziness, cultural forms, and the duality of technical and expressive consequences. Nor do the descriptions of groupthink portray the kinds of on-goingness and inclusiveness that characterize cultures.

Not Social Structure.   Another controversy concerns the relationship between culture and social structure. While cultures pattern behaviors, and social structure is often defined as recurrent patterns of behavior, cultures are *not* the same as social structures. Social structures in societies, organizations, or other collectivities consist of the tangible and specific ways that human beings order their observable relations with each other. Cultures, on the other hand, consist of systems of abstract, unseen, emotionally charged meaning that organize and maintain beliefs about how to manage physical and social needs. A clear illustration of the difference between social structure and culture and their relative independence of each other is " . . . the existence of highly organized insect societies with at best a minimal rudimentary component of culture . . . " (Kroeber and Parsons 1970, p. 87). Human societies, however, do not yield examples where the two are so clearly independent.

The structure-culture controversy revolves around how closely the two are related to each other in human society. If they are inextricably intertwined and highly interdependent, then it would be hard to argue that they are separate entities (Radcliffe-Brown 1952; Singer 1968). Most analysts conclude that culture and social structure are "distinct,

though interrelated: neither is a mirror reflection of the other—each must be considered in its own right" (Keesing 1974, p. 83). One important reason that culture and structure cannot be too interdependent is that such a relationship would leave little possibility for change; the two would be interlocked in a static state, in which neither could change because it was constrained by the other. In reality, much social change arises from the relatively loose interplay of culture and structure (Geertz 1957).

Not Metaphor.   Finally culture is not merely a metaphor for describing organizations or other cultural groups. Cultures exist; they are naturally occurring, real systems of thought, feeling, and behavior that inevitably result from sustained human interactions. They occur in nations, corporations, occupations, unions, gangs, and scientific research laboratories.

One advantage of the cultural approach to organizational analysis is that it can displace two old metaphoric notions that have prevailed in organizational analysis—that organizations are like machines or like organisms (Lundberg 1985a, p. 197). But to adopt a metaphoric view that organizations are *like* cultures implies that culture is something an organization *has* (Smircich 1983). To reject the metaphoric view is to assert that "organizations don't *have* cultures; they *are* cultures . . . " (Weick 1983, p. 27). This seems to us the more valuable perspective.

Not Necessarily the Key to Success.   A recent analysis of the literature on organizational cultures from 1980 to 1985 indicates that over time academic researchers became more concerned with the relationship of organizational cultures to organizational success (Barley, Meyer, and Gash 1988). The practitioner literature, which paid little attention to culture until the 1980s, was understandably always concerned with how cultures might improve organizational performance. At least four different positions can be identified in the writings on this issue by academics and practitioners.

The first of these identifies *certain cultural configurations* that characterized excellent companies (Peters and Waterman 1982) and thus presumably provide formulas for success. This line of reasoning and the evidence for it, while attracting practitioners, did not persuade many academics (Pfeiffer 1984; Carroll 1983; Johnson, Natarajan, and Rappaport 1985). Data showed the exemplary companies identified were not superior to other Fortune 1000 companies in terms of performance or in terms of following the so-called principles of excellence (Hitt and Ireland 1987). Also, examination of the performance of Peters' and Waterman's "excellent" firms just a few years later showed that several were experiencing many difficulties (*Business Week* 1984). Apparently, cultural configurations associated with success at one point in time are not necessarily successful at other times when environmental conditions have changed.[4]

In a more amorphous way, early comparisons of U.S. and Japanese organizational cultures also implied that certain cultural components were associated with high levels of organizational performance (Ouchi 1981; Pascale and Athos 1981). Managers and consultants were quick to embrace some Japanese ideas and practices, and such devices as quality circles proliferated in U.S. firms. Their success has been mixed at best (Lawler and Mohrman 1987).

The second position is that *strong cultures* lead to success; it is exemplified in the earlier quote from Deal and Kennedy's book (see p. 18), which begins with a chapter entitled "Strong Cultures: The New 'Old Rule' for Business Success." Unfortunately, these authors failed to clarify what they believe constitutes a strong or a weak culture. This gap was filled by another analyst, who suggested that the strength of a culture is determined by its thickness, extent of sharing, and clarity of ordering (Sathe 1985, p. 15). He suggested strong cultures have many ideologies that are widely shared and clearly ordered in terms of their relative importance. Also, according to this analysis, strong cultures produce more intense behaviors. Since studies show that influential cultures can be dysfunctional and thereby detrimental to overall organizational success (Starbuck, Greve, and Hedberg 1978; Miller 1990), it seems dangerous to assume that having a strong culture always insures success. The very strength of a culture could serve to discourage needed change.

The third position is the other side of the coin; it argues that some cultures are sick—*neurotic* is the term used. The central idea of this analysis is that cultures may derive unhealthy modes of functioning from the psychopathological problems of their chief executives (Kets de Vries and Miller 1984). The implication is that strong cultures, in the sense of influential or powerful ones, are not necessarily healthy. While the authors do not directly address the issue of success, it is hard to imagine that the neurotic firms they describe are financially successful for very long.

The fourth position on the relationship between culture and organizational success tries to set forth certain conditions under which cultures are more important for and conducive to success. One analysis assesses whether cultures are efficient means of control in terms of how well they govern needed transactions. It concludes that cultures are more efficient when (1) transactions occur under conditions of ambiguity, complexity, and interdependence; (2) enough people share the same set of ideas that set forth appropriate orientations; (3) the costs of maintaining the culture are not too high; and (4) subunits do not develop cultures that operate to the detriment of a larger organization lacking in culture. From this perspective: "Some organizational culture will presumably be irrelevant to performance; some forms of culture will promote and some will inhibit efficient operation, depending on the conditions listed above" (Wilkins and Ouchi 1983, p. 478).

Another analysis specifies three conditions that must be met before a culture will contribute to sustained superior financial performance: (1) the culture must be valuable in the sense that it leads the firm to behave in ways that lead to high sales, low costs, high margins, and other factors adding financial value to the firm; (2) it must be rare in the sense that other firms do not have the same or very similar cultures; and (3) it must not be easy to imitate so that competitors cannot readily change their cultures to include the same advantageous characteristics (Barney 1986, p. 658). This analysis clearly envisions culture as a possible source of competitive advantage.

The works cited are only examples of these four perspectives. Each implies that organizational cultures tend to contribute "in some way to the systematic balance and effectiveness of an organization" (Smircich and Calas 1987, p. 237). Although the last perspective makes the relationship between culture and success contingent on certain conditions, it still tends to oversimplify. Cultures can vary on many different characteristics (Table 1–2) that these analyses gloss over. Also, financial or other kinds of practical success are not the only criterion by which organizational cultures can be assessed, nor is it necessarily the most useful and insightful perspective from which to examine them. A thorough and exhaustive review of the relevant studies concluded that " . . . these studies have not definitely established an empirical link to financial performance . . . if we continue, either explicitly or implicitly to use culture as yet another determinant of performance related outcomes, we will fail to realize the full potential of studying culture" (Siehl and Martin 1990, pp. 30, 34). We would rather see the cultural perspective on organizations liberate researchers and managers from past assumptions and ways of thinking about organizations and suggest new paradigms for their study and management (Beyer, 1984; Barley, Meyer, and Gash 1988; Smircich and Calas 1987).

A BRIEF HISTORY OF CULTURAL RESEARCH ON ORGANIZATIONS

Cultural research on organizations is not a recent development. While it became more prominent in the 1980s following the publication of popular books like *In Search of Excellence* and *Theory Z*, there had been a fairly steady stream of research on cultural phenomena in organizations dating back to the 1930s. Especially influential were the activities of a group of scholars at the University of Chicago who interacted extensively with the business community. Other efforts were scattered. All of this research did not come from a consistent theoretical perspective, but much of it has yielded valuable insights that have been important for the study of organizations. Thus, it may be useful to describe some of this research and summarize its findings to underline in still another way how the cultural approach is distinctive. This review will also provide a background for the more detailed discussions to follow in later chapters.

The Pioneers

The first systematic attempt to understand modern work organizations in cultural terms occurred in the early 1930s during the last phase of the well-known Hawthorne studies at the Western Electric Company in Chicago, Illinois. In this, as in so many other ways, these studies proved to be seminal for the study and understanding of human behavior in work organizations.

The Hawthorne studies began with experiments on the relationships between productivity and the physical work environment. This phase of the studies grew naturally out of the concerns of industrial engineers employed by the company. When the results of these experiments proved puzzling and not explicable in purely technical terms, the company decided to turn to behavioral scientists and incorporate them into the program of ongoing research.

Elton Mayo, a faculty member in the Harvard Business School, was hired as a consultant by Western Electric. He, in turn, had to persuade the business school dean to allow him to employ an experienced, but still young assistant professor from the anthropology department to assist him in the Hawthorne studies. The young anthropologist was W. Lloyd Warner. Mayo argued that Warner would adapt the anthropological methods he had employed to uncover social structure and belief systems in tribal societies to the current work community within the Western Electric plant. This had never been done before—no wonder the dean needed persuading. The result of Mayo and Warner's discussions was the famous bank wiring room observation study, which began in November 1931 and lasted until May 1932. Careful analysis indicates that "this study was primarily designed by W. Lloyd Warner" (Moore 1989, p. 3).

Warner did not come to this new challenge totally unprepared. He had not only done classical anthropological fieldwork among the Murngin of Northeast Australia, he had also recently begun an extensive ethnographic study of the community of Newburyport, Massachusetts. One of the purposes of the community study was "to shed light on the way in which behavior, values, and attitudes that had shaped the community influenced the behavior, values, and attitudes of employees in the workplace" (Moore 1982, p. 117). This classic and very influential research, begun in 1929 and not completed until 1937, was eventually published in six volumes, known as the Yankee City Series. In one of these volumes Warner focused on how a community's culture shaped the cultures of workplaces within it (Warner and Low 1947). At Western Electric he focused on how work group cultures affected worker behavior and productivity in a specific work setting.

Undoubtedly because of Warner's influence, a new phase in the Hawthorne studies began. The bank wiring room study introduced anthropological field methods of observation and interviewing into the Hawthorne studies; the kinds of data collected were very similar to those usually collected by cultural anthropologists. Observations and interviews were aimed at describing three kinds of social relations occurring in the room: the technical, the social, and the ideological (Roethlisberger and Dickson 1946; Moore 1982). Technical relations arranged the flow of materials to machines, tools, and their output. The social structure organized the work, both formally in terms of specific designated relations, and informally in terms of those friendships and cliques that naturally formed outside the formal, prescribed relationships. The third kind of relations, the ideological, concerned the workers' culture—their shared beliefs and understandings regarding the work setting.

An observer, seated at the back of the room, made records of what he heard and saw. An interviewer talked to each employee on a regular basis. Their data showed that the social structure in the room informally broke into two cliques, and that this division came about largely because of differences in tasks. In addition, the investigators detected a well-defined status structure in which, for example, selector-wiremen were decidedly superior to soldermen, connector-wiremen were decidedly superior to soldermen, and connector-wiremen were superior to selector-wiremen. The ideologies these workers shared were extracted from the interviews; they consisted of beliefs about fairness, a living wage, and the right to work. Workers used these ideologies to justify and explain why they restricted output, pressured fellow employees to withhold production, and frequently violated company rules. This phase of the Hawthorne studies marked the first well-publicized cultural explanations for workers' behaviors in the management literature (Roethlisberger and Dickson 1946).[5]

Warner went on to complete his research for the Yankee City Series (Warner and Lunt 1941) and joined the faculty of the University of Chicago in 1935. From there he and his students began another community study—this time of the Deep South (Davis et al. 1941). Unfortunately, Warner himself did not continue to do anthropological studies within work organizations. However, he stayed at Chicago, where he and one of his students, Burleigh B. Gardner began a consulting firm to help employers deal with personnel problems. An influential businessman in Chicago, who was a trustee of the University of Chicago, learned of their consulting firm and convinced Warner and Gardner that their efforts should be under the aegis of the university. Gardner was offered a full-time position in the School of Business after completing his Ph.D degree. He taught the first course in applied industrial anthropology at the University of Chicago business school in 1942 and continued to do so until the end of World War II. Gardner also wrote the first textbook that took a cultural perspective on work organizations (Gardner 1945).

Meanwhile, in late 1942, the Committee on Human Relations on Industry was established at the University of Chicago with Warner as chairperson and Gardner as executive secretary. Faculty from various departments became members of the Committee. A young sociologist, David G. Moore, introduced Gardner to James C. Worthy, a senior personnel executive of Sears Roebuck, who was trying to figure out how to study the personnel side of that organization (Muhs 1989). Almost immediately, Gardner began to collaborate with Worthy on a study of the effects of a simple, flat store organization. After four years Gardner left the university to do full-time consulting. The position of executive secretary of the Committee was filled by another student of Warner's—William Foote Whyte.

Whyte carried the cultural approach forward until after World War II. After finishing a famous community study of north Boston called *Street Corner Society* (Whyte 1943) that became his Ph.D. dissertation, Whyte returned to the University of Chicago in 1944 and carried out an ethnographic study of the restaurant industry at Warner and Gardner's invitation. In it Whyte focused primarily on the informal social structure, as he had done in *Street Corner Society*, but also analyzed organizational symbols (Whyte 1948).

All of this research occurred more than three decades before popular books made organizational culture a management fad in the early 1980s. It was made possible by an unusual degree of close cooperation between the progressive managers of two major corporations—Western Electric and Sears Roebuck—and a group of capable and respected academic researchers. Without the long-term access to workplaces, provided by these corporations' managers, such research is not possible. Writing in 1978, Whyte commented, "This strong beginning justified hopes that organizational studies would become a major field for applied anthropologists, yet in succeeding years, very few anthropologists joined these pioneers" (Whyte 1978, p. 130). Unfortunately, Warner and Whyte moved on to other interests and pursuits—Warner to further community studies, Whyte to the study of social values and economic development in Peru. We can only speculate that managers and the dominant forces in academia were not sufficiently receptive to their pioneering work on organizational culture to make its continuance attractive to them. As a consultant, Gardner continued to research the social organization of work for Sears Roebuck (Worthy 1991). Much of this work, however, consisted of quantitative surveys—a technique which was then being developed to measure employee morale. Moore worked with Gardner and completed his dissertation during this period (Moore 1954), but Gardner's research for Sears was not published.

Other than Warner, cultural anthropologists had shown little interest in the workplace. Under the influence of Claude Levi-Strauss, the trends in anthropology moved toward examination of exotic and distant cultures rather than those close to home. Even Warner himself had done little actual fieldwork in work organizations. While Whyte did extensive fieldwork, his work focused mostly on group phenomena and only peripherally on cultural matters—specifically on symbolism. In organizational sociology there was a steady decline of interest in small groups and a concomitant turn toward formal structure. The promise inherent in a cultural approach to the study of organizations had only been partially implemented; descriptions and interpretations of cultural forms in the workplace, such as myths, stories, or rites, were rare.

At the same time, the qualitative field methods that characterize the cultural approach were being supplanted by the heady attractions of the computer. High-speed computing permitted the collection of large bodies of quantitative data and the flowering of the techniques of the social survey. The trend had begun with research carried out on the military during World War II; the statistical approaches developed for that research (Stouffer et al. 1950) could now be diffused and practiced by anyone with appropriate training and access to a high-speed computer. Soon a torrent of quantitative studies appeared; they encouraged research into other questions. The structural and psychological variables and theories that lent themselves to quantification became the dominant trends in organizational research from the 1960s to the late 1970s.

But there had been a beginning for the cultural approach. "In five short years there was an unusual flourishing of anthropological and sociological research . . . a unique combination of circumstances involving academia, business, a great industrial city, and the times" (Moore 1982, p.121). It did not revolutionize all of the research on organizations or all of management thought—as quantitative methods and the computer did later. But it did provide the foundation for a modest stream of insightful research and writing on work and organizations done primarily by industrial ethnographers (Gamst 1977).

Scattered Effects

During the 1950s and 1960s, a few American researchers continued the anthropological tradition begun by Warner and his students. Perhaps the most sustained efforts were made by Donald Roy (1952, 1953, 1954, 1960), who used participant observation to study culture within small work groups and produced results resembling those from the bank wiring room in the Hawthorne studies. Undoubtedly the best-known work from this period was Melville Dalton's *Men Who Manage* (1959). Dalton, who worked in the two companies he studied, focused his research on the extent to which subcultures naturally emerged from workers' needs and documented how these informal groups actually governed much of what happened in these companies. In his accounts, the formal system of rules, titles, and the like served as a backdrop for the real dynamics of social life in industry.

Somewhat related and far more influential in mainstream organizational research was the work of scholars like Philip Selznick, who described the interactions of affected communities and the fledgling Tennessee Valley Authority[6] in terms of how institutions respond to changing circumstances (Selznick 1949). Selznick used the term institution to indicate that organizations were more than rational instruments—they were infused with value beyond the technical requirements of tasks (Scott 1987; Selznick 1957). Although a sociologist, Selznick conducted his research much like a cultural anthropologist, gaining his insights on cooptation and institutional leadership from long-term observations and extensive interviewing in the organizations and communities studied.

Meanwhile, in England, a group of social scientists known as the Tavistock Institute began to do research on organizations as cultural systems (Jacques 1951). They experimented in introducing various innovations into organizational cultures, especially beliefs about the positive value of worker participation in organizational decision making. A U.S. researcher in this tradition was F.L.W. Richardson (1955, 1961), who showed how the stress and conflicts generated by the structuring of work relations affected social interactions, employees' feelings, and productivity in a large electrical design and manufacturing concern.

A few cultural studies of atypical workplaces also appeared during this period. For example, Hortense Powdermaker (1950) did extensive observation in the motion picture industry on the relations of film making crews with those behind the scenes—writers, producers, and studio executives. William Caudill (1958) studied the day-to-day personal relations of doctors, ward personnel, and patients in a psychiatric hospital. Jules Henry's (1963) study of public schools documented how the schools acted as the cultural transmitters of the values of thrift, industry, competitiveness, and cleanliness.

But it was not until the late 1960s that the efforts of several researchers broke through the relative obscurity to which cultural research had been relegated in organizational and management studies. In the United States, a team of researchers led by Harrison Trice interpreted their observations of personnel practices as cultural rites and ceremonials (Trice, Belasco, and Alutto 1969). In England, Barry Turner (1971) wrote a book explicitly exploring both the substance and forms of organizational cultures. His analysis relied heavily on the concepts of British cultural anthropologists. Somewhat later, Andrew Pettigrew, an English sociologist, studied a large retail firm on a long-term basis. His detailed study of the introduction of computers into a retail firm (1973) not only continued the anthropological tradition of participant observation, but also capitalized on multiple methods and sources of data collection to achieve added confidence in the results of his qualitative observations. A few years later, in a highly influential article, he went on to delineate the concept of organizational culture for management research:

In the pursuit of everyday tasks and objectives, it is all too easy to forget the less rational and less instrumental, the more expressive social tissue around us that gives those tasks meanings. Yet, in order for people to function within any given setting, they must have a continuing sense of what that reality is all about in order to be acted upon. Culture is the system of such collectively accepted meanings operating for a given group at a given time . . . and the offsprings of the concept of culture I have in mind are symbol, language, ideology, belief, ritual, and myth. (Pettigrew 1979, p. 574).

A second important study done in the United States at about the same time was Burton Clark's *The Distinctive College* (1970), which documented the importance of what he called organizational sagas in the long-term survival and relative prosperity of three of these institutions. His concept of saga is very similar to that of organizational culture; he may have chosen the term *saga* to emphasize the important role that founders and historical tradition played in these colleges (1972). In an earlier study, he had focused on how organizational values shifted as school organizations adapted to their environments (Clark 1956). Both of these studies used qualitative methods.

The work of another researcher focused attention on the value of qualitative methods *per se*. Quantitative methods had become so dominant in mainstream management research that it was almost revolutionary when Henry Mintzberg systematically observed managers at work. His reports of this research on *The Nature of Managerial Work* (1973) received considerable scholarly attention and were rewritten for several popular publications, including the *Harvard Business Review* (Mintzberg 1975). Although Mintzberg did not focus on organizational culture, his detailed observations of the daily activities of five managers uncovered some cultural aspects of the managerial role. Perhaps because of the topic, or perhaps because of the business-oriented academic circles in which he moved, Mintzberg's work made systematic qualitative methods—the primary tools for studying culture—once again respectable in many circles that had largely ignored qualitative work by sociologists and anthropologists.

The rediscovery of the benefits of qualitative methods, in turn, led to an influential special issue of the *Administrative Science Quarterly* (1979). While this issue did not focus on culture *per se*, the guest editor was John Van Maanen, a professor at the Massachusetts Institute of Technology, who specialized in studying occupational cultures.

The research findings of Pettigrew, Clark, and Mintzberg caught the attention of prominent organizational and management scholars. Their work was published in leading journals and their books were widely cited. Such was not the case for the industrial ethnographers who were active over the same period. They were based in anthropology or folklore departments, where their work was hardly the vogue, and where they had little contact with organizational researchers, who were in sociology departments or management schools. Five researchers of this type deserve mention. Frederick C. Gamst (1980a, 1980b) and Robert S. McCarl (1974, 1976) studied the cultures of colorful occupations. C.S. Holzberg and M.J. Giovannini (1981) integrated a broad range of prior research on work cultures from many different societies in an annotated bibliography. Marietta Baba (1986) summarized the practical implications of these and other studies for workplace cultures. An exception is Michael O. Jones, Director of the Folklore and Mythology Center at the University of California at Los Angeles, who not only encouraged cultural research in organizations, but reached out to address the issues of application that concern researchers in organizations and management (Jones 1988).

Recent Revitalization

Although the study of organizational cultures was not new, it certainly received a big impetus in the 1980s. Two best-selling books were widely interpreted as saying that organizational cultures were important for organizational productivity and adaptability. Peters and Waterman's *In Search of Excellence* (1982) and Ouchi's *Theory Z* (1981). At about the same time, two other books on organizational cultures garnered widespread attention from managers and the press (Pascale and Athos 1981; Deal and Kennedy, 1982). Many business and trade magazines featured articles on the topic. Between March 1983 and October 1984, five major conferences on corporate culture and organizational folklore and symbolism were held (Jones 1984, p. 8), many of them bringing managers and scholars together. The proceedings of three of these were published as books (Pondy et al. 1983; Frost et al. 1985; Kilmann et al. 1985). Three academic journals—*The Journal of Management Studies* (1982), *Administrative Science Quarterly* (1988), and *Journal of Management* (1985), and one journal oriented to managers, *Organizational Dynamics* (1983)—published special issues on the topic. Two academically oriented textbooks on organizational cultures appeared in 1985 (Schein 1985; Sathe 1985). More recently, four books of readings (Jones, Moore, and Snyder 1988; Turner 1990c; Gagliardi 1990; Frost et al. 1991), another textbook (Ott 1989), a book-length research report (Denison 1990), and a book-length ethnography (Kunda 1991) have appeared.

During the early 1980s, meetings of professional associations like the Academy of Management and the Institute for Decision Sciences began to include special symposia on culture. Since 1980, an international group of scholars calling themselves The Standing Committee on Organizational Symbolism has held annual conferences in Canada and Europe and published a newsletter, *SCOS Note-Work*. Inevitably, new courses sprang up in degree programs at numerous colleges and universities. A listing of Ph.D. theses by the library of the Industrial and Labor Relations School at Cornell University revealed that between 1980 and 1985 nineteen doctoral dissertations dealing with some aspect of organizational culture were written. Researchers reported that in 1979 they found about fifty studies with the word *myth* in the title or abstract; by late 1981, they found more than five hundred such articles (Broms and Gahmberg 1982, p. 30)—an increase of more than 1,000 percent in just two years!

What made the concept of organizational culture suddenly so attractive to managers, the press, and scholars? Two sets of parallel developments led in this direction. One was the turbulence and difficulties that U.S. firms were experiencing in competing with organizations from countries with very different cultures. The second was a growing realization by some organizational scholars that structural-rational approaches to understanding organizations missed crucial aspects of how organizations functioned and how they affected the lives of their members (Pondy and Mitroff 1979).

Following World War II, the supremacy of U.S. management went practically unchallenged. Many other societies looked to the United States to solve major productivity problems of the world with technical and managerial knowhow. But in the 1970s, the superiority of U.S. managerial skills and ideas came into question as Japan, a country with a drastically different culture, became the United States' chief competitor for economic leadership of the world. The question on everyone's mind was whether it was cultural differences that accounted for the unparalleled productivity of Japanese organizations. The cultures of U.S. work organizations became candidates for blame. Environmental forces were demanding change and many U.S. managers began to see that past practices may have discouraged innovation, quality, and cooperation; they apparently even failed to achieve the high productivity to which they were oriented. Managers and analysts also began to realize that changing organizations would not be easy without an understanding of the cultures that had grown up within these organizations; they began to see culture as both an impediment to change and a possible vehicle for achieving it.

The downturn in the U.S. economy in the 1970s had generated much anxiety and conflict between workers and management. Many U.S. workers and managers were unemployed for the first time in their lives. Learning of the apparent harmony in Japanese workplaces, U.S. managers began to see culture as a way to integrate managers' and workers' concerns to create some consensus and cooperation in their organizations. Managers and workers needed reassurance; increasing the coherence of the internal cultures in their organizations seemed a good way to achieve it. And if harmony could be achieved, it was bound to contribute to managerial control, increase performance and profits, and generally help to make U.S. industry competitive again. Culture became in some managers' eyes just another seductive "quick fix" for their problems (Kilmann 1984).

Even before the 1970s, some organizational scholars were growing disillusioned with the assumptions inherent in largely rational, bureaucratic models of organizations. The rational model had been modified and stretched to its limits (Thompson 1967), and still something essential to the realities of organizational life was missing. Perhaps the most influential work to set forth an alternative, much more subjective, view of organizations was Karl Weick's *The Social Psychology of Organizing*, published in 1969. Weick emphasized how people's cognitive processes and social interactions shaped organizations in nonrational ways. Like its title, his analysis also emphasized the fluidity and emergent nature of organizational life. Other researchers had become frustrated trying to apply the bureaucratic model to universities (Cohen, March, and Olsen 1972) and to Japanese organizations. One set of researchers, who studied Japanese-managed organizations in the United States, reported " . . . we cannot describe adequately how different the atmosphere is in an organization where 50 to 80 percent of the personnel have Japanese origins . . . " (Lincoln, Olson, and Hanada 1978, p. 834). By the late 1970s, several researchers had advanced theories that severely questioned the rational bureaucratic view; they suggested organizations were loosely coupled systems (Weick 1976) and were permeated with myth and ceremony (Trice, Belasco, and Alutto 1969; Meyer and Rowan 1977).

Closely aligned with models of organizations are the methods used to study them. Some researchers were also becoming disillusioned with quantitative methods and quasi-experimental designs (Ouchi and Wilkins 1985) because of the relatively trivial amounts of variance they explained, the lack of comparability of results across studies, their failure to achieve much predictive validity, and the incomprehensibility their sophisticated methods contributed to reports of research. Furthermore, causality was often indeterminate or so complex that managers could not gain much insight from such research into how to change organizations in beneficial ways (Van Maanen 1982). In addition, critics point out, quantitative methods encouraged researchers to separate themselves from the phenomena that made up organizational life and spend limited time—if any—in organizations to collect their data (Beyer 1984). The resulting reports seemed sterile; they missed the drama, excitement, and high emotion that characterized much of what happens daily in organizations.

In an effort to be scientific, organizational researchers had reduced their phenomena to such simplistic models that it had lost its richness and human character. Managers were understandably suspicious of the relevance of such abstracted research because it ignored many of the specificities their experience told them were important; so they did not use its results. Research on utilization found that managers were more likely to use the results of more detailed, qualitative studies (Beyer and Trice 1982).

These dissatisfactions led to a revival of interest in qualitative methods as well as in culture. Each revival reinforced the other, for qualitative methods almost invariably surface something of cultural significance and

the accepted ways of doing cultural research involve qualitative methods. While there has been a drop-off of managerial attention to culture since the early 1980s, organizational research seems to have been permanently transformed. More researchers have been doing more qualitative studies than in the past, and more of these focus specifically on cultural phenomena. The accumulated literature is already large and of sufficient quality to merit study by students aspiring to become managers and those aspiring to become researchers of organizations and management.

SUMMARY

People in organizations develop cultures as they interact and share ways of managing and coping with uncertainties. Cultures have two components: (1) substance, which consists of shared systems of beliefs, values, and norms; and (2) forms, which are observable ways that members of a culture express cultural ideas. By reducing the potential variability of human behavior, cultures provide some degree of order and continuity in social life. Cultures have many distinctive characteristics that highlight aspects of organizations missed by other approaches and that make the analysis and study of organizational cultures both fruitful and challenging. Analysts do not agree on all aspects of culture. There is some danger that the concept will be used so broadly that it will lose its value. Also, some confusion has arisen between related concepts and culture.

Cultural research in organizations is not a recent development. The Hawthorne studies at Western Electric in the early 1930s involved an anthropologist and included observations of workgroup cultures. This work stimulated a brief flowering of cultural research in work organizations and provided the foundation for scattered efforts by sociologists and anthropologists until the 1970s. The books of the early 1980s that made culture a popular fad among managers followed a series of influential studies and publications by English and U.S. organizational scholars that revived qualitative methods and illustrated their value with new insights. The revival of interest in organizational cultures has continued in academic circles throughout the 1980s and has produced a substantial body of research.

But many gaps remain in our knowledge of organizational cultures. Also, the cultural approach focuses primarily on the expressive side of organizations.

NOTES

1. Quote attributed to Kenneth Burke by Clyde Kluckhohn. "Myths and Rituals: A General Theory" *The Harvard Theological Review* 35 (1942: 45–79).

2. A new interdisciplinary branch of science developing to study chaos has underlying assumptions that are radically different from those of traditional science. Seeing the world as a chaotic place focuses scientists' attention on process rather than state, or becoming rather than being. The cultural approach to studying and analyzing organizations has similar potential to question traditional scientific assumptions and focus attention on the process of people becoming organized.

3. The two types of research spring from different research traditions and have different aims. Quantitative research typically employs statistics to test hypotheses or to determine the probability of events. This procedure requires deciding in advance what is important and how it will be measured. Qualitative research is more exploratory and open ended. Qualitative researchers typically observe and interact with groups of people in their social settings over a substantial period of time in order to discover the participants perspectives and understand their so-

cial worlds as they do. Some qualitative researchers are content to produce rich descriptions of social life while others use their observations to develop new theory.

4. Perhaps the most telling criticism of the Peters and Waterman approach, from a cultural perspective, is that it ignores the differing environmental contingencies and other contextual circumstances of organizations, apparently assuming that similar cultural features are equally plausible and likely to be successful in all circumstances.

5. Although Professors Elton Mayo and W. Lloyd Warner played major roles in the initiation and collection of data in these studies, it was another Harvard Professor, Fritz Roethlisberger, and William J. Dickson, at the time Chief of Employee Relations Research Department at Western Electric, who analyzed the data and undertook to write a full account of the research studies (Trahair 1984). For a retrospective view of the research effort see Roethlisberger (1977).

6. The Tennessee Valley Authority was created by the U.S. federal government in 1933 to develop the Tennessee River and its tributaries in order to promote inexpensive electrical power, irrigation, and flood control.

REFERENCES

Administrative Science Quarterly, Special Issue 1979, 24(4), Guest editor: John Van Maanen.

Baba, Marietta L. 1986, *Business and Industrial Anthropology: An Overview*, Washington D.C.: American Anthropological Association.

Barley, Stephen R. and Meryl Louis. 1983, Many in one: Organizations as multicultural entities. Paper presented at the annual meeting of the Academy of Management, August 14–17, Dallas, Tex.

Barley, Stephen R., Gordon W. Meyer, and Deborah C. Gash. 1988, Cultures of cultures: Academics, practitioners and the pragmatics of nor-

mative control. *Administrative Science Quarterly*, 33: 24–60.

Barney, Jay B. 1986, Organizational culture: Can it be a source of sustained competitive advantage? *Academy of Management Review*, 11: 656–65.

Bennis, Warren, and Burt Nanus. 1985, *Leaders*. New York: Harper & Row, Pub.

Berger, Peter L., and Thomas Luckmann. 1967, *The Social Construction of Reality*. 3rd ed. Garden City, N.Y.: Anchor Books.

Beyer, Janice M. 1981, Ideologies, values and decision-making in organizations. Pp. 166–97 in

Nystrom, Paul, and William H. Starbuck (eds.) *Handbook of Organizational Design*, vol. 2. London: Oxford University Press.

Beyer, Janice M. 1984, Cultures within cultures: Whose are we talking about? Paper presented at the Annual meeting of the American Institute of Decision Sciences, Toronto, Canada.

Beyer, Janice M., Roger L. Dunbar, and Alan D. Meyer. 1988, Comment: The concept of ideology in organizational analysis. *Academy of Management Review*, 13(3): 483–89.

Beyer, Janice M., and Harrison M. Trice. 1982, The utilization process: A conceptual framework and synthesis of empirical findings. *Administrative Science Quarterly*, 27: 591–622.

Boje, David M., Donald B. Fedor, and Kendrith M. Rowland. 1982, Mythmaking: A qualitative step in OD interventions. *Journal of Applied Behavioral Science*, 18: 17–28.

Broms, Henri, and Henrick Gahmberg. 1982, *Mythology in Management Culture*. Helsinki, Finland: School of Economics.

Business Week. 1984, Who's excellent now? November 5, pp. 76–88.

Cameron, Kim S., and Robert E. Quinn. 1988, Organizational paradox and transformation. Pp. 1–18 in Cameron, Kim S., and Robert Quinn (eds.) *Paradox and Transformation*. Cambridge, Mass.: Ballinger Publishing.

Campbell, J.P., M.D. Dunette, Edward E. Lawler III, and Karl E. Weick, Jr. 1970, *Managerial Behavior, Performance, and Effectiveness*. New York: McGraw-Hill.

Carey, Christopher. 1988, Southwest Airlines sets its own rules. *St. Louis Post Dispatch*, December 25, 1988, pp. 1, 6F.

Carroll, Daniel T. 1983, Review of Thomas J. Peters and Robert W. Waterman, Corporate Cultures: The Rites and Rituals of Corporate Life. *Harvard Business Review*, 6(November–December): 78–88.

Caudill, William. 1958, *The Psychiatric Hospital as a Small Society*. Cambridge, Mass.: Harvard University Press.

Chatov, Robert. 1973, The role of ideology in the American corporation. Pp. 50-75 in Votaw, Dow and S. Prakash Sethi (eds.) *The Corporate Dilemma: Traditional Values Versus Contemporary Problems*. Englewood Cliffs, N.J.: Prentice Hall.

Child, John, and Chris Smith. 1987, The context and process of organizational transformation—Cadbury Limited in its sector. *Journal of Management Studies*, 24(November): 565–93.

Clark, Burton R. 1956, Organizational adaptation and precarious values: A case study. *American Sociological Review*, 21: 327–36.

Clark, Burton R. 1970, *The Distinctive College: Antioch, Reed, and Swathmore*. Chicago: Aldine.

Clark, Burton R. 1972, The organizational saga in higher education. *Administrative Science Quarterly*, 17: 178–83.

Cohen, Michael D., James G. March, and Johan P. Olsen. 1972, A garbage can model of organizational choice. *Administrative Science Quarterly*, 17: 1–25.

Cooke, Robert A., and Denise M. Rousseau. 1988, Behavioral norms and expectations: A quantitative approach to the assessment of organizational culture. *Group and Organization Studies*, 13: 245–73.

Dalton, Melville. 1959, *Men Who Manage*. New York: John Wiley.

Davis, Allison, Burleigh B. Gardner, Mary R. Gardner, and W. Lloyd Warner. 1941, *Deep South: A Social Anthropological Study of Caste and Class*. Chicago: University of Chicago Press.

Deal, Terrence E., and Allan A. Kennedy. 1982, *Corporate Cultures: The Rites and Rituals of Corporate Life*. Reading, Mass.: Addison-Wesley.

Denison, Daniel R. 1990, *Corporate Culture and Organizational Effectiveness*. New York: John Wiley.

Dorson, Richard M. 1971, Applied folklore. Pp. 40–42 in Sweterlitsch, Dick (ed.) *Papers on Applied Folklore*. Bloomington, Ind.: Folklore Forum Bibliographic and Special Series #8.

Durkheim, Emile. 1964, *Suicide*. New York: Free Press.

Farnham, Alan. 1989, The trust gap. *Fortune*, December 4, pp. 56–74, 78.

Feldman, Martha S. 1991, The meanings of ambiguity: Learning from stories and metaphors. Pp. 145–56 in Frost, Peter, Larry F. Moore, Meryl R. Louis, Craig C. Lundberg, and Joanne Martin (eds.), *Reframing Organizational Culture*. Newbury Park, Calif.: Sage Publications, Inc.

Ferguson, Harvey. 1936, *Modern Man: His Beliefs and Behavior*. New York and London: Knopf.

Freiberg, Kevin L. 1987, The heart and spirit of transformation leadership: A qualitative case study of Herb Kelleher's passion for Southwest Airlines. A dissertation in partial fulfillment of requirements for degree of Doctor of Philosophy, University of San Diego.

Frost, Peter J., Larry F. Moore, Meryl R. Louis, Craig C. Lundberg, and Joanne Martin (eds.).

1985, *Organizational Culture*. Beverly Hills, Calif.: Sage Publications, Inc.

Gagliardi, Pasquale (ed.). 1990, *Symbols and Artifacts: Views of the Corporate Landscape*. New York: Walter de Gruyter.

Gamst, Frederick C. 1977, An integrating view of the underlying premises of an industrial ethnology in the U.S. and Canada. *Anthropological Quarterly*, 50(1): 1–9.

Gamst, Frederick C. 1980a, Toward a method of industrial ethnography. *Rice University Studies*, 66(1): 15–42.

Gamst, Frederick C. 1980b, *The Hoghead: An Industrial Ethnology of the Locomotive Engineer*. New York: Holt, Rinehart & Winston.

Gardner, Burleigh B. 1945, *Human Relations in Industry*. Chicago: Richard D. Irwin.

Geertz, Clifford. 1957, Ritual and social change: A Javanese example. *American Anthropologist*, 59: 991–1012.

Geertz, Clifford. 1966, *Person, Time, and Conduct in Bali: An Essay in Cultural Analysis*. Yale Southeast Asia Program, Culture Series #14.

Geertz, Clifford. 1970, The impact of the concept of culture on the concept of man. Pp. 47–65 in Hammel, Eugene A., and William S. Simmons (eds.) *Man Makes Sense*. Boston: Little, Brown.

Geertz, Clifford. 1973, *The Interpretation of Cultures*. New York: Basic Books.

Geertz, Clifford. 1983, *Local Knowledge: Further Essays in Interpretive Anthropology*. New York: Basic Books.

Gleick, James. 1987, *Chaos: Making a New Science*. New York: Penguin.

Glick, William H. 1985, Conceptualizing and measuring organizational and psychological climate: Pitfalls in multilevel research. *Academy of Management Review*, 10(3): 601–16.

Gluckman, Max. 1963a, *Order and Rebellion in African Tribal Society*. London: Cohen and West.

Gregory, Kathleen L. 1983, Native view paradigms: Multiple cultures and culture conflict in organizations. *Administrative Science Quarterly*, 28: 359–76.

Hackman, J. Richard. 1984, The transition that hasn't happened. Pp. 29–59 in Kimberly, John R., and Robert E. Quinn (eds.) *New futures: The challenge of managing corporate transitions*. Homewood, Ill.: Dow Jones-Irwin.

Harris, Marvin. 1976, History and significance of the emic/etic distinction. *Annual Review of Anthropology*, 5: 329-50.

Hellriegel, Don, and John W. Slocum, Jr. 1974, Organizational climate: measures, research and contingencies. *Academy of Management Journal*, 17: 255–80.

Hellriegel, Don, John W. Slocum, Jr., and Richard W. Woodman. 1986, *Organizational Behavior*, 4th ed. New York: West Publishing Co.

Henry, Jules. 1963, *Culture against Man*. New York: Random House.

Hitt, Michael A., and R. Duane Ireland. 1987, Peters and Waterman revisited. *The Academy of Management Executive*, 1(2): 91–98.

Hocart, Arthur M. 1939, Ritual and emotion. *Character and Personality*, 7: 201–11.

Hofstede, Geert. 1980b, *Culture's Consequences: International Differences in Work-Related Values*. Beverly Hills, Calif.: Sage Publications, Inc.

Hofstede, Geert, Bram Neuijeu, Denise Daval Ohayv, and Geert Sanders. 1990, Measuring organizational cultures: A qualitative and quantitative study across twenty cases. *Administrative Science Quarterly*, 35: 286–316.

Holzberg, C.S., and M.J. Giovannini. 1981, Anthropology and industry: Reappraisal and new directions. *Annual Review of Anthropology*, 10: 317–60.

Jackofsky, Ellen F., and John W. Slocum, Jr. 1988a, A longitudinal study of climates. *Journal of Organizational Behavior*, 9: 319–34.

Jacques, Elliott. 1951, *The Changing Culture of a Factory*. London: Tavistock Publications.

James, Lawrence R., and A.P. Jones. 1974, Organizational climate: A review of theory and research. *Psychological Bulletin*, 81: 1096–1112.

Janis, Irving. 1972, *Victims of Group Think: A Study of Foreign Policy Decisions and Fiascoes*. Boston: Houghton Mifflin Company.

Jarboe, Jan. 1989, A boy and his airline. *Texas Monthly*, 17(4): 98–104.

Jelinek, Mariann and Claudia B. Schoonhoven. 1990, *Innovation Marathon: Lessons from High Technology Firms*. Cambridge, Mass.: Basil Blackwell, Ltd.

Johnson, W. Bruce, Ashok Natarajan, and Alfred Rappaport. 1985, Shareholder returns and corporate excellence. *Journal of Business Strategy*, 6(2): 52–62.

Jones, Michael O. 1984, Corporate natives confer on culture. *The American Folklore Society Newsletter*, 13(October): 6, 8.

Jones, Michael O. 1988, In search of meaning: using qualitative methods in research and application. Pp. 31–49 in Jones, Michael O., Michael D. Moore and Richard C. Snyder (eds.) *Inside Organizations: Understanding the Human Dimension.* Beverly Hills, Calif.: Sage Publications, Inc.

Jones, Michael O., Michael D. Moore, and Richard C. Snyder (eds.). 1988, *Inside Organizations: Understanding the Human Dimension.* Beverly Hills, Calif.: Sage Publications, Inc.

Journal of Management Studies, Special Issue. 1982, *Organizations as Ideological Systems.* Guest Editor: William H. Starbuck.

Journal of Management, Special Issue. 1985, *Organizational Symbolism*, 11(2): Guest Editor: Peter J. Frost.

Joyce, William F., and John W. Slocum, Jr. 1984, Collective climate: Agreement as a basis for defining aggregate climates in organizations. *Academy of Management Journal*, 27: 721–42.

Keesing, Roger M. 1974, Theories of culture. *Annual Review of Anthropology*, 3: 73–97.

Kets De Vries, Manifred F.R., and Danny Miller. 1984, *The Neurotic Organization.* San Francisco: Jossey-Bass.

Kilmann, Ralph H. 1982, Getting control of the corporate culture. *Managing*, 3: 11–17.

Kilmann, Ralph H. 1984, *Beyond the Quick Fix: Managing Five Tracks to Organizational Success.* San Francisco: Jossey-Bass.

Kilmann, Ralph H., Mary J. Saxton, and Roy Serpa and Assoc. (eds.). 1985, *Gaining Control of the Corporate Culture.* San Francisco: Jossey-Bass.

Kluckhohn, Clyde. 1942, Myths and rituals: A general theory. *The Harvard Theological Review*, 35(January): 45–79.

Kroeber, Alfred L., and Talcott Parsons. 1970, The concepts of culture and of social system. Pp. 85–87 in Hammel, Eugene A., and William S. Simons (eds.) *Man Makes Sense.* Boston: Little, Brown.

Kunda, Gideon. 1991, *Engineering Culture: Control and Commitment in a High Technology Corporation.* Philadelphia: Temple University Press.

Lawler, Edward E., III, Douglas T. Hall, and Gregory R. Oldham. 1974, Organizational climate: Relationships to organizational structure, process and performance. *Organizational Behavior and Performance*, 11: 139–55.

Lawler, Edward E., and Susan A. Mohrman. 1987, Quality circles: After the honeymoon. *Organizational Dynamics*, 15(Spring): 42–54.

Leach, Edmund. 1968, Ritual. *International Encyclopedia of the Social Sciences*, 13: 520–26.

Leach, Edmund. 1970, *Claude Levi-Strauss.* New York: Viking Press.

Leach, Edmund. 1976b, Social anthropology: A natural science of society? *British Academy of Science Proceedings.* 62: 157-80. London: Oxford University Press.

Levi-Strauss, Claude. 1963, *Structural Anthropology.* New York: Basic Books.

Lincoln, James R., Jon Olson, and Mitsuyo Hanada. 1978, Cultural effects on organizational structure: The case of Japanese firms in the United States. *American Sociological Review*, 43(6): 829–47.

Louis, Meryl R. 1980, Surprise and sense making: What newcomers experience in entering unfamiliar organizational settings. *Administrative Science Quarterly*, 25: 226–51.

Louis, Meryl R. 1985a, A investigator's guide to workplace culture. Pp. 73–93 in Frost, Peter J., et al. (eds.) *Organizational Cultures.* Beverly Hills, Calif.: Sage Publications, Inc.

Lucas, Charlotte-Anne. 1988, The plane facts: Southwest Airlines and America West try to clip each other's wings. *New Times*, 19(7): 26–28, 30, 32.

Lundberg, Craig C. 1985a, On the feasibility of cultural intervention in organizations. Pp. 169–85 in Frost, Peter J., et al. (eds.) *Organizational Culture.* Beverly Hills, Calif.: Sage Publications, Inc.

Martin, Joanne. 1991, A personal journey: From integration to differentiation to fragmentation to feminism. Pp. 352–66 in Frost, Peter J., Larry F. Moore, Meryl R. Louis, Craig Lundberg, and Joanne Martin (eds.) *Reframing Organizational Culture.* Newbury Park, Calif.: Sage Publications, Inc.

Martin, Joanne, Martha S. Feldman, Mary Jo Hatch, and Sim B. Sitkin. 1983, The uniqueness paradox in organizational stories. *Administrative Science Quarterly*, 28(September): 438–52.

Martin, Joanne, and Debra Meyerson. 1988, Organizational cultures and the denial, channeling, and acknowledgement of ambiguity. Pp. 93–125 in Pondy, Louis R., Richard Boland, Jr., and Howard Thomas (eds.) *Managing Ambiguity and Change.* New York: John Wiley.

Martin, Joanne, and Caren Siehl. 1983, Organizational culture and counterculture: An uneasy symbiosis. *Organizational Dynamics*, 12(2): 52–65.

McCarl, Robert S. 1974, The production welder: Product, process, and the industrial craftsman. *New York Folklore Quarterly*, 30: 244–53.

McCarl, Robert S. 1976, Smokejumper initiation: Ritualized communication in a modern occupation. *Journal of American Folklore*, 81: 49–67.

Mead, George H. 1934, *Mind, Self, and Society.* Chicago: University of Chicago Press.

Mechling, Jay and David S. Wilson. 1988, Organizational festivals and the uses of ambiguity: The case of picnic day at Davis. Pp. 303–17 in Jones, Michael O., Michael D. Moore, and Richard C. Snyder (eds.) *Inside Organizations: Understanding the Human Dimension.* Beverly Hills, Calif.: Sage Publications, Inc.

Meyer, John W., and Brian Rowan. 1977, Institutionalized organizations: Formal structure, myth, and ceremony. *American Journal of Sociology*, 83: 340–61.

Meyerson, Debra E. 1991a, Normal ambiguity? A glimpse of an occupational culture. Pp. 131-44 in Frost, Peter, Larry F. Moore, Meryl R. Louis, Craig C. Lundberg, and Joanne Martin (eds.) *Reframing Organizational Culture.* Newbury Park, Calif.: Sage Publications, Inc.

Meyerson, Debra E. 1991b, Acknowledging and uncovering ambiguities in cultures. Pp. 254–70 in Frost, Peter, Larry F. Moore, Meryl R. Louis, Craig C. Lundberg, and Joanne Martin (eds.) *Reframing Organizational Culture.* Newbury Park, Calif.: Sage Publications, Inc.

Meyersin, Debra, and Joanne Martin. 1987, Cultural change: An integration of three different views. *Journal of Management Studies*, 24: 623-48.

Miller, Danny. 1990, *The Icarus Paradox.* New York: Harper Business.

Mintzberg, Henry. 1973, *The Nature of Managerial Work.* New York: Harper & Row, Pub.

Mintzberg, Henry. 1975, The manager's job: Folklore and fact. *Harvard Business Review*, 53(4): 49–61.

Mintzberg, Henry. 1979a, An emerging strategy of "direct" research. *Administrative Science Quarterly*, 24(December): 582–88.

Mitroff, Ian, and Ralph H. Kilmann. 1975, Stories managers tell: A new tool for organizational problem solving. *Management Review*, (July): 18–28.

Moore, David G. 1954, *Managerial Strategies in Organizational Dynamics in Sears Retailing.* Unpublished Ph.D. thesis, Department of Sociology, University of Chicago.

Moore, David G. 1982, The committee on human relations in industry at the University of Chicago. Pp. 117–21 in *Academy of Management Proceedings.* Kae H. Chung (ed.) 42nd Annual Meeting, New York.

Moore, David G. 1989, Comments during a symposium on the Committee on Human Relations in Industry at the University of Chicago. Working paper of the Management History Division, William Muhs (ed.).

Moore, Sally F. 1975, Epilogue: Uncertainties in situations, indeterminacies in culture. Pp. 210–39 in Moore, Sally F., and Barbara G. Myerhoff (eds.) *Symbols and Politics in Communal Ideology.* Ithaca, N.Y.: Cornell University Press.

Moore, Sally F., and Barbara G. Myerhoff. 1977, Secular ritual: Forms and Meaning. Pp. 3–25 in Moore, Sally F., and Barbara G. Myerhoff (eds.) *Secular Ritual.* Assen, Amsterdam, The Netherlands: Van Gorcum.

Muhs, William (ed.). 1989, *Symposium on Committee on Human Relations in Industry at University of Chicago*, Academy of Management, August 1982, New York.

Naroll, Raoul, and Frada Naroll (eds.). 1973, Introduction. Pp 1–23 in *Main Currents in Anthropology.* Englewood Cliffs, N.J.: Prentice Hall.

O'Reilly, Charles A., Jennifer Chatman, and David F. Caldwell. 1991, People and organizational culture: A profile comparison approach to assessing person-organization fit. *Academy of Management Journal*, 34: 487–516.

Organizational Dynamics. 1983, 12(2): Autumn.

Ott, J. Steven. 1989, *The Organizational Culture Perspective.* Pacific Grove, Calif.: Brooks/Cole Publishing.

Ouchi, William. 1981, *Theory Z: How American Business Can Meet the Japanese Challenge.* Reading, Mass.: Addison-Wesley.

Ouchi, William G. and Alfred M. Jaeger. 1978, Type Z organization: Stability in the midst of mobility. *Academy of Management Review*, 3: 305–13.

Ouchi, William G., and Alan L. Wilkens. 1985, Organizational culture. *Annual Review of Sociology*, 11: 457–83.

Pascale, Richard T., and Anthony G. Athos. 1981, *The Art of Japanese Management.* New York: Simon & Schuster.

Peters, Thomas J., and Robert H. Waterman. 1982, *In Search of Excellence: Lessons from America's Best Run Companies.* New York: Harper & Row, Pub.

Pettigrew, Andrew W. 1973, *The Politics of Organizational Decision-Making.* London: Tavistock Publication.

Pettigrew, Andrew W. 1979, On studying organizational cultures. *Administrative Science Quarterly*, 24: 570–81.

Pfeffer, Jeffrey. 1981a, Management as symbolic

action: The creation and maintenance of organizational paradigms. *Research in Organizational Behavior*, 3: 1–52.

Pfeiffer, John. 1984, Schlock for sale: A review of *In Search of Excellence*. Science '84, 5(3): 90–94.

Pierce, Joe E. 1977, Culture: A collection of fuzzy sets. *Human Organization*, 36(2): 197–200.

Pondy, Louis R., Peter J. Frost, Gareth Morgan, and Thomas C. Dandridge (eds.). 1983, *Organizational Symbolism*. Greenwich, Conn.: JAI Press.

Pondy, Louis R., and Ian I. Mitroff. 1979, Beyond open system models of organization. *Research in Organizational Behavior*, 1: 3–39.

Powdermaker, Hortense. 1950, Hollywood, the dream factory. An anthropologist looks at the movie-makers. Boston: Little, Brown.

Radcliffe-Brown, Alfred. 1952, *Structure and Function in Primitive Society*. New York: Free Press.

Richardson, F.L.W. 1955, Anthropology and human relations in business and industry. Thomas W.L. (ed.) *Yearbook of Anthropology*. Special publication of the American Anthropological Association.

Richardson, F.L.W. 1961, Talk, work and action: Human reactions to organizational change. Monograph No. 3. Society for Applied Anthropology. Ithaca, N.Y.: School of Industrial and Labor Relations, Cornell University.

Riley, Patricia. 1983, A structurationist account of political culture. *Administrative Science Quarterly*, 28(3): 414–37.

Roethlisberger, Fritz J. 1977, *The Elusive Phenomenon*. Cambridge, Mass.: Graduate School of Business Administration and Harvard University Press.

Roethlisberger, F.J., and William J. Dickson. 1946, *Management and the Worker*. Cambridge, Mass.: Harvard University Press.

Rousseau, Denise M. 1990, Assessing organizational culture: The case for multiple methods. Pp. 153–92 in Schneider, Benjamin (ed.) *Organizational Climate and Culture*. San Francisco: Jossey-Bass.

Roy, Donald. 1952, Quota restriction and gold bricking in a machine shop. *American Journal of Sociology*, 57: 427–42.

Roy, Donald. 1953, Work satisfaction and social reward in quota achievement. *American Sociological Review*, 18: 507–14.

Roy, Donald. 1954, Efficiency and the fix: informal intergroup relations in a piece-work machine shop. *American Journal of Sociology*, 60:255–66.

Roy, Donald. 1960, Banana Time: Job satisfaction and informal interaction. *Human Organization*, 18: 158–61.

Sathe, Vijay. 1985, *Culture and Related Corporate Realities*. Homewood, Ill.: Richard D. Irwin.

Schein, Edgar H. 1985, *Organizational Culture and Leadership*. San Francisco: Jossey-Bass.

Schein, Edgar H. 1990, Organizational culture. *American Psychologist* 45(2): 109–19.

Schneider, Benjamin (ed.). 1990, *Organizational Climate and Culture*. San Francisco: Jossey-Bass.

Schwartz, Howard M., and Stanley M. Davis. 1981, Matching corporate culture and business strategy. *Organizational Dynamics*, Summer: 30–48.

Scott, W. Richard 1987, *Organizations: Rational, National, and Open Systems*, 2nd ed. Englewood Cliffs, N.J.: Prentice Hall.

Selznick, Philip. 1949, *T.V.A. and the Grass Roots*. Berkeley, Calif.: University of California Press.

Selznick, Philip. 1957, *Leadership in Administration*. New York: Harper & Row, Pub.

Sethia, Nirmal K., and Mary Ann Von Glinow. 1985, Arriving at four cultures by managing the reward system. Pp. 400–20 in Kilmann, Ralph H. et al. (eds.) *Gaining Control of the Corporate Culture*. San Francisco: Jossey-Bass.

Shattuck, Roger. 1980, *The Forbidden Experiment: The Story of the Wild Boy of Aveyron*. New York: Farrar, Straus & Giroux.

Shils, Edward. 1975, *Center and Periphery: Essays in Macrosociology*. Chicago: University of Chicago Press.

Siehl, Caren, and Joanne Martin. 1990, Organizational culture: A key to financial performance. Pp. 241–82 in Schneider, Benjamin (ed.). *Organizational Climate and Culture*. San Francisco: Jossey-Bass.

Singer, Milton. 1968, Culture. *International Encyclopedia of the Social Sciences*, 3: 527–43.

Smircich, Linda. 1983, Concepts of culture and organizational analysis. *Administrative Science Quarterly*, 28(3): 339–58.

Smircich, Linda, and Maria B. Calas. 1987, Organizational culture: A critical assessment. Pp. 228–63 in Jablin, F.M., L.L. Putnam, K.H. Roberts, and L.W. Porter (eds.) *Handbook of Organizational Communication*. Beverly Hills, Calif.: Sage Publications, Inc.

Starbuck, William H., Arant Greve, and B.L.T. Hedberg. 1978, Responding to Crisis. *Journal of Business Administration*, 9: 121–37.

Stouffer, Samuel A., Louis Guttman, Edward A. Suchman, Paul F. Lazarsfeld, Shirley A. Star, and John A. Clausen. 1950, *Measurement and Prediction*. New York: John Wiley.

Thompson, James D. 1967, Organizations in Action. New York: McGraw-Hill.

Trahair, Richard C.S. 1984, *The Humanist Temper:*

The Life and Work of Elton Mayo. New Brunswick, N.J.: Transaction Books.

Trice, Harrison M. 1985, Rites and ceremonials in organizational cultures. *Research in the Sociology of Organizations*, 4: 221–70.

Trice, Harrison M. 1991, Comments and discussion. Pp. 298–309 in Frost, Peter J., Larry F. Moore, Meryl Louis, Craig Lundberg, and Joanne Martin (eds.) *Reframing Organizational Culture*, Newbury Park, Calif.: Sage Publications, Inc.

Trice, Harrison M., James Belasco, and Joseph A. Alutto. 1969, The role of ceremonials in organizational behavior. *Industrial and Labor Relations Review*, 23(October): 40–51.

Trice, Harrison M., and David Morand. 1991, Cultural diversity: Organizational subcultures and countercultures. Pp. 69–105 in Miller, Gale, *Studies in Organizational Sociology—Essays in Honor of Charles K. Warriner.* 10: 69–105, Greenwich, Conn.: JAI Press.

Turner, Barry A. 1971, *Exploring the Industrial Subculture.* London: The Macmillan Press.

Turner, Barry A. 1990a, The rise of organizational symbolism, Pp. 83–96 in Hassard, John, and Denis Pym (eds.) *The Theory and Philosophy of Organizations: Critical Issues and New Perspectives.* London: Routledge & Kegan Paul.

Turner, Barry A. 1990b, Introduction. Pp. 1–11 in Turner, Barry (ed.). *Organizational Symbolism.* New York: Walter de Gruyter.

Turner, Barry A. 1990c, (ed.) *Organizational Symbolism.* New York: Walter de Gruyter.

Turner, Ralph H. 1969, The theme of contemporary social movements. *British Journal of Sociology* 20(4): 390–405.

Turner, Victor W. 1967, *The Forest of Symbols: Aspects of Ndembu Ritual.* Ithaca, N.Y.: Cornell University Press.

Uttal, Bro. 1983, The corporate culture vultures. *Fortune*, October 17, Pp. 66–72.

Van Maanen, John. 1982, Introduction. Pp. 7–10 in Van Maanen, John, J.M. Dobbs, Jr., and R.R. Faulkner (eds.) *Varieties of Qualitative Research.* Beverly Hills, Calif.: Sage Publications, Inc.

Van Maanen, John, and Gideon Kunda. 1989, "Real feelings": Emotional expression and organizational culture. *Research in Organizational Behavior*, 11: 43–103.

Warner, W. Lloyd, and O.J. Low. 1947, *The Social System of the Modern Factory* New Haven, Conn.: Yale University Press.

Warner, W. Lloyd, and Paul S. Lunt. 1941, *The Social Life of a Modern Community.* New Haven, Conn.: Yale University Press.

Weick, Karl E. 1969, *The Social Psychology of Organizing.* Reading, Mass.: Addison-Wesley.

Weick, Karl E. 1976, Educational organizations as loosely-coupled systems. *Administrative Science Quarterly*, 21(March): 1–19.

Weick, Karl E. 1983, Letter to the editor. *Fortune*, October 17, p. 27.

Weick, Karl E. 1985, Sources of order in underorganized systems: Themes in recent organization theory. Pp. 106–36 in Lincoln, Yvonne S. (ed.) *Organizational Theory and Inquiry.* Beverly Hills, Calif.: Sage Publications, Inc.

Whipp, Richard, Robert Rosenfeld, and Andrew Pettigrew. 1989, Culture and Competitiveness: Evidence from two mature U.K. Industries. *Journal of Management Studies*, 26(November): 561–85.

Whyte, William F. 1943, *Street Corner Society: The Social Structure of an Italian Slum.* Chicago: University of Chicago Press.

Whyte, William F. 1948, *Human Relations in the Restaurant Industry.* New York: McGraw-Hill.

Whyte, William F. 1978, Organizational Behavior Research. Pp. 129–46 in Eddy, Elizabeth M., and William L. Partridge (eds.) *Applied Anthropology in America.* New York: Columbia University Press.

Wilkins, Alan, and W. Gibb Dyer, Jr. 1988, Toward culturally sensitive theories of culture change. *Academy of Management Review*, 13(4): 522–33.

Wilkins, Alan L. and William G. Ouchi. 1983, Efficient cultures: Exploring the relationship between culture and organizational performance. *Administrative Science Quarterly*, 28: 468–81.

Worthy, James C. 1991, Personal correspondence, August 5.

Young, Ed. 1989, On the naming of the rose: Interests and multiple meanings as elements of organizational culture. *Organizational Studies*, 10(2): 187–206.

MANAGING CULTURE
AS A COMPETITIVE RESOURCE

*An identity-based view of sustainable
competitive advantage*

C. Marlene Fiol

ABSTRACT: How can organizations manage the cognitive processes by which a firm invests in resources for competitive advantage? Studies of organizational culture, as currently framed, have not provided adequate answers to this question. By focusing either on culture as underlying beliefs or on culture as behavioral manifestations, these studies have overlooked the critical links between beliefs and behaviors that are at the very core of managing cognitive processes for sustained advantage.

This article reframes the culture concept to highlight the role of contextual identities in linking behaviors and their social meaning in organizations. Drawing on theories from cultural linguistics and structural anthropology, it argues that cognitive processes in organization do not directly reflect either behaviors or underlying beliefs. Rather they represent the interface between the two. To manage cognitive processes for competitive advantage requires that we attend to the identities by which people make sense of what they do in relation to a larger set of organizational norms.

Sustainable competitive advantage is the unique position of a firm in relation to its competitors that allows it to outperform them consistently (Hofer & Schendel, 1978; Porter 1985). Though firms may gain competitive ad-

I wish to thank Jay Barney, Roger Dunbar, Praveen Nayyar, I.G. Thomas, and the anonymous referees for helpful comments on earlier drafts of this article.

vantages in numerous ways (e.g., size, location, access to superior resources (Ghemawat, 1986), or just plain luck (Barney, 1986a), much of the research on competitive advantage has focused on organizational competencies as a major source of advantage (Nelson & Winter, 1982; Reed & DeFillippi, 1990; Selznick, 1957).

A firm's competency includes the particular set of skills and resources it possesses as well as the way that those assets are used to produce action outcomes (Reed & DeFillippi, 1990). Competency thus encompasses more than a firm's stock of tangible assets. It encompasses the cognitive processes by which the stock is understood and translated into action.

If follows, then, that the management of competencies for competitive advantage involves not only acquiring the right number, type, and mix of *tangible* assets, but also managing the *cognitive* decision rules that determine how people transform those assets into action outcome (Nelson & Winter, 1982; Prahalad & Bettis, 1986). Theories pertaining to the management of tangible assets for competitive advantage rest on a consistent body of research coming out of economics, finance, marketing, and accounting. Theories pertaining to the management of cognitive processes for competitive advantage, in contrast, appear sporadically (e.g., Barney, 1986b; Nelson & Winter, 1982; Prahalad & Bettis, 1986), and without consistent grounding in a particular discipline.

Though there is a general recognition that the tool kits of economics and finance contain little that affords a useful analytical grip on issues pertaining to cognitive processing in organizations (Nelson & Winter, 1982), there is less agreement about where to look for more useful tools. Culture theories, based in anthropology and sociology, though explicitly addressing the question of how cognitive rules emerge and function in organizations, have in the past not added much to traditional economic tool kits. This is partly because culture studies suffer from schizophrenia. On the one hand, students of "high" culture in organizations (Krefting & Frost, 1985), argue that cognitive processes reside in and are ruled by deeply ingrained repertoires that are beyond conscious manipulation. This first view of culture potentially undermines the whole undertaking of normative strategic analysis by suggesting that organizational cognition is a function of deep-level assumptions and beliefs that cannot be managed. On the other hand, culture theorists focusing on observable manifestations of culture (Peters & Waterman, 1982; Schwartz & Davis, 1981), have equated an organization's culture with the trappings and behaviors it engenders. The second view of culture adds very little to the traditional tool kits of competitive analysis because, like economic approaches, it shifts the focus away from cognitive processes themselves to the behavioral inputs and outputs of the processes.

This article reframes the culture concept to highlight the linkages between behaviors and their social meanings in organizations. It argues that the management of cognitive processes for competitive advantage depends on an understanding of those linkages. Following previous research, it defines high culture as a set of unobservable and usually unspoken rules that govern an organization's definition of what it is. Artifacts and behaviors are observable expressions of the system of rules. Deviating from previous work, however, this article argues that cognitive processes in organizations do not directly reflect

either behaviors or underlying rules. Rather, they represent the interface between the two. That interface is problematic because there is not always a one-to-one correspondence between multiple observable expressions in a firm and an underlying set of rules. To understand the linkages between behaviors and rules, researchers must focus on how organizational members and subunits differentially make sense of their actions and how those sense-making processes relate to an underlying system of rules.

Organizational members make sense of their actions on the basis of an intermediate set of beliefs referred to as *identities* (Albert & Whetten, 1985; Dunbar & Fiol, 1990; Dutton & Dukerich, 1989). Identities reflect how individuals or subunit parts of an organization define what they do in relation to their understanding of what the organization is. Identities thus represent aspects of culture translated into a specific context. To manage the cognitive dimension of competency is to manage the linkages between abstract cultural values and behavioral expressions of those values. This requires attention to the intermediate identity beliefs that define the linkages.

The article begins by reviewing and highlighting the role of culture in the management of organizational competency. After a brief review of existing research on organizational culture, a model of cultural evolution is presented. The model high-lights the importance of the contextual articulation of rules as the source of all meaning. These contextual rules function as the missing link in existing culture research applied to organizations. The article borrows generously from the work of anthropologists and cultural linguists who have used natural language systems as a model for understanding how other social systems of meaning develop and change.

COMPETENCY AS A COMPETITIVE RESOURCE

A considerable body of research has developed around the idea that the superior performance of some firms results from their imperfectly imitable competencies (Hofer & Schendel, 1978; Lippman & Rumelt, 1982; Nelson & Winter, 1982; Selznick, 1957). Integrating previous definitions of competency, Reed and DeFillippi (1990:90), recently defined it as the "particular skills and resources a firm possesses, and the superior way in which they are used." The definition highlights the dual aspects of the concept. Organizational competency refers not only to a particular asset stock, but also to the processes that define that stock in use.

The first aspect of competency, relating to characteristics of the asset stock, is well developed in the literature. Researchers agree that to provide a firm with a sustainable advantage, competencies must be superior and they must be imperfectly imitable by rival firms (Reed & DeFillippi, 1990). Firms have achieved barriers to imitation when their rivals cannot understand the competencies on which the advantage is based because of "basic ambiguity concerning the nature of the causal connections between actions and results" (Lippman & Rumelt, 1982:420. According to Reed and DeFillippi (1990), the existing literature suggests three characteristics of competencies that can be sources of ambiguity: tacitness, complexity, and specificity. *Tacitness* arises from learning by doing, which results in a lack of codification of the competency. *Complexity* arises from large numbers of technologies, such that their combination makes imitation difficult. *Specificity* arises from a close symbiosis in the exchange relationships of a firm's transactions, so that the competencies are too transaction-specific for a firm's rivals to copy. Integrating the three characteristics drawn from previous research, the authors state that the "interaction effects of tacitness, complexity, and specificity serve to heighten ambiguity effects and barriers to imitation" (Reed & DeFillippi, 1990:94). Finally, the authors tell us that in order to sustain the ambiguity that is a source of advantage, firms must constantly reinvest in the causally ambiguous characteristics (i.e., support people with tacit knowledge, protect the security of complex processes, and increase levels of asset specificity).

Reed and DeFillippi's (1990) conceptualization contributes to our understanding of how competency can be managed as a source of sustained competitive advantage by specifying the relationships among three attributes treated separately in previous research. Their work does not, however, take us beyond the traditional bounds of competency research. Though they begin with a definition of competency as both a stock and a process, their analysis focuses on characteristics of the asset stock, with minimal attention to how managers of a firm make sense of their stock of assets to manage the processes by which it is used and renewed.

Prahalad and Bettis (1986) warned against the dangers of concentrating solely on the tangible characteristics of a firm's resources. In the context of firm diversification, for example, they argued that diversity results not from the characteristics of the assets themselves. Rather, it results from the variety of management logics for processing and understanding those assets. They described managers as carrying around "beliefs, theories, and propositions" (489) about the relationship between assets and action outcomes. Over time, those beliefs get into an organization-wide "dominant logic" that governs the decision rules people use to translate resources into action. One of the most challenging jobs of managing resource configurations, then, is managing the multiple and often contradictory logics that they embody.

How can organizations manage their repertoire of decision rules if they are to invest simultaneously in resources that are specific, complex, and tacit? To address this question, we must better understand how people's implicit "beliefs, theories, and propositions" emerge in the form of organizational logics and how these govern the processes by which resources are transformed into action outcomes. This article turns next to how theories of organizational culture have contributed to this understanding.

ORGANIZATIONAL CULTURE AND COMPETENCY

Organizational culture is a metaphor drawn from anthropology and sociology and refers to the webs of meaning that bind individuals into collectivities (Smircich, 1983). Studies of organizational culture focus explicitly on the beliefs, theories, and propositions that govern the processes by which resources are transformed into action outcomes. Theories of organizational culture would thus appear to provide a useful framework for studying the poorly understood cognitive component of organizational competency.

Though potentially comparable partners in the study of organizational competency, theories of organizational culture and strategy theories of competitive advantage have long been uneasy bed partners. This is because the two streams of research differ in their theoretical assumptions about what is meaningful as a subject of study and about the basic objectives of study. Strategy theorists have traditionally been concerned with observable organizational phenomena. Their studies tend to be prescriptive, suggesting ways to improve observable aspects of organizations. Culture theorists, in contrast, have traditionally been concerned with unobservable organizational phenomena. Their studies tend to be descriptive, suggesting ways to better understand those forces in organizations that cannot be seen or touched. Each plays a potentially important role in understanding organizational competency. Given the disparate assumptions and objectives, however, researchers have found it difficult to bridge the two streams of work.

Rather than finding a way to bridge the differences between culture and strategy research, recent studies of organizational culture have increasingly side-stepped or ignored the differences, leading some researchers to argue that "culture" and "strategy" are substitutable concepts (Weick, 1985). The result has been the emergence of two camps of culture research. Although some researchers have clung to original notions of culture as deep-level assumptions, others have taken a different route. Largely side-stepping issues of problematic meanings and a lack of one-to-one correspondence between behaviors and their meanings, they have collapsed the two approaches to suggest that cultures can be managed and changed through behavioral manipulations (e.g., Peters & Waterman, 1982; Schwartz & Davis, 1981).

The first camp of culture research, interested in how organizations can be understood as cultures, holds a culture purist's view (Smircich, 1983). It assumes that culture is an emergent process that has as its source a set of deep, underlying values. Studies following this stream of research have focused on what it means to be organized. The objective has been to describe the organizing processes, rather than to explain or predict an outcome. The relevant features of culture are the largely unconscious and deeply rooted sources of values and beliefs (Krefting & Frost, 1985).

In contrast, the second camp of culture research, interested in culture as something an organization has, holds a culture pragmatist's view (Smircich, 1983). It assumes that culture is a key to unlocking organizational commitment, productivity, and profitability. Studies following this stream of research have focused on culture as a tool for achieving a desired organizational outcome. Given these premises and research objectives, it is not surprising that the relevant features of culture in these studies have been surface-level manifestations of culture that are observable and thus can be managed: espoused values, reward structures, dress codes, and so on (e.g., Peters & Waterman, 1982; Schwartz & Davis, 1981; Siehl, 1985; Tichy, 1982).

Pulling culture research squarely into the strategic management paradigm, Barney (1986b) argued that in order for a firm's culture to provide sustained competitive advantages, three conditions must be met: (a) the culture must be valuable, enabling the firm to do things that lead to economic value, (b) the culture must be rare or unique, and (c) the culture must be imperfectly imitable so that competing firms cannot easily change their cultures to include the desired characteristics.

Barney's first two conditions mirror the approach of culture pragmatists. The value and uniqueness of an organization's culture are attributes that may lead to a desired outcome. His third condition, however, puts an interesting twist on the normative implications of managing cultures. He argued that if firms can adopt or generate a valuable and rare culture, then it is not imperfectly imitable. Competing firms can do the same. The rather pessimistic implication is that the management of culture is useful only for those firms that already have a rare and valuable culture. Organizations can manage to *sustain* what they already possess. Culture research, however, according to Barney's argument, cannot help firms attain valuable and rare cultures because any efforts toward this end are, in principle, imitable.

In discussing the first two conditions, Barney argued that the approach of culture pragmatists has added little to traditional strategy tool kits for studying competitive advantage. A view of organizational culture as a manipulatable tool, like economics-based views, focuses on attributes of a stock of competencies that rivals can imitate. It contributes little to understanding the cognitive processes that drive those competencies.

Barney's third condition for culture as a competitive resource, imperfect imitability, espouses the research premises of culture purists. It pushes aside observable manifestations of culture as imitable features that may be a reflection, but are not a source of sustainable advantage. The source of valuable and rare cultures is embedded in a firm's history and heritage. The only prescription that emerges from this view is to attempt to understand the meaning of valuable threads of the past, a concern that is central to the objectives of culture purists. Taking a stand, ultimately, as a culture purist, Barney leaves little room for studies of culture, as currently framed, to contribute to our understanding of how organizations gain or re-establish cultural features as a basis for sustained competitive advantage. Drawing on the two predominant streams of culture research, culture as deep meanings and culture as observable manifestations, he discards the latter as imitable and the former as unmanageable.

Given the two predominant approaches to the study of organizational culture, it is difficult to argue with Barney's conclusions. This article, however, provides a reframing of the culture concept that may lead to different conclusions. In developing this reframing, the first step is to note that the problems with current applied culture research lie not in its conclusions, but in its basic premises. The predominant focus on either deep-level assumptions or surface-level behavioral manifestations masks the critical meaning-making processes that mediate between the two. Those processes lie at the very heart of the poorly understood cognitive component of organizational competency. Though the study of meaning-making processes has a long history in anthropology and cultural linguistics, management research to date has incorporated little of it.

THE MISSING LINK IN CULTURE AND COMPETENCY RESEARCH

The cognitive component of organizational competency centers around how people make sense of particular skills and assets and how they use them to transform them into action outcomes. Cognitive processes are thus not equivalent to the behaviors themselves. Nor are they equivalent to an abstract set of beliefs. Though they are shaped by both, they reside in the linkages between behaviors and their social meanings. They represent beliefs in use that determine how particular behaviors come to "mean" what they do.

To establish the premises of such an argument and to illustrate its applicability, the following section of the paper presents linguistic and anthropological views of how something comes to mean and how those meanings are conveyed (Barthes, 1967; Levi-Strauss, 1976; Saussure, 1916). In particular, it draws on semiotic theories of meaning to describe the processes by which underlying cultural rules are translated into observable expressions and how patterned expressions, in turn, generate underlying rules.

Semiotics is the study of how signs combine to convey meaning. The approach uses natural language as a model to show how meaning is generated and conveyed in other systems of signification (i.e., mannerisms, behaviors, and the like) (Eco, 1979). Natural language systems are made up of words, speech acts, and a set of underlying rules that determine the way meaning is generated in a language. Words are the only observable components of this system. Speech acts are communicated ideas. Underlying rules are embodied in the grammatical system that distinctly defines different languages. Grammar systems provide the rules by which words convey meanings. Yet to understand how words combine to convey meaning, linguists rely on speech acts that reflect a contextual understanding of the relations between words and the grammar rules of a language. Understanding the evolution of language and the emergence of new words that are incorporated into a language requires attention, not exclusively to individual words nor to their underlying rule system, but to the speech acts that link the two.

A critical assumption of a semiotic approach to the study of meaning in organizations is that natural language systems and the speech acts that link them to words can be taken as models to describe and explain the links between expressions and rule systems of any social system of meaning. Language rests on a set of underlying rules, just as organizational culture does. How different members of an organization use those rules to make sense of what they do is analogous to how people use language, through speech acts, to make sense of discrete words.

Understanding how linguistic theories explain the evolution of natural language systems can guide us toward a different understanding of how to manage cultural evolution and change for competitive advantage. A linguistic approach, in its emphasis on *contextual articulation* as the source of all meaning, provides a way to explain and manage cultural meanings by focusing neither on high culture nor on surface-level manifestations, but rather on the bridge between them. The following describes how a semiotic perspective identifies the bridge between surface expressions and underlying meanings. The bridge is described within a linguistic model of meaning and a parallel cultural model of meaning.

LANGUAGE, SPEECH ACTS, AND WORDS

Words are the signs that combine to convey meaning in natural language systems. Grammatical rules govern their meaningful combinations. Each word-sign has two components: a signifier or expression component, and a signified or content component. Expression components are observable, for example, when people say a particular word. The content attributed to an expression, however, depends on unobserved linkages that a semiotic analysis seeks to make explicit and explain.

Language users generally make the connections between expression and content without conscious awareness of applying any rules. We learn to speak without explicitly learning grammatical rules. Yet rules underlie and govern the meanings of our words. The fact that they are not made explicit, or that they may not even be known as such, does not negate the existence of rules.

Though a general language system governs the meaning of words, there is not a direct one-to-one correspondence between words and a grammatical system. A given word can mean different things in the same language. *Dog*, for example, means one thing when my son refers to his pet, another when I use it in a business policy session on portfolio analysis, and yet another when a man pejoratively characterizes a woman. The meanings we attach to the expression *dog* are not arbitrary, however. A particular speech act implies a context within which words are linked to a set of rules that give them meaning.

The three components of language, then, include an underlying and unobservable set of rules, observable expressions in the form of words, and speech acts that contextualize words and thus serve as a link to the system of rules. None of the components can be understood without the others. Grammatical rules are the result of patterned speech acts over time that, in turn, are the result of patterned word use over time. Patterned word use in a particular context, however, also results from an understanding of existing grammatical rules. Natural language evolves through an iterative process involving all three components simultaneously.

There are forces for both maintenance and change embedded in language systems. A focus on grammatical rules highlights those forces that serve to maintain the language as a stable system that cuts across multiple speech contexts. A focus on patterned word use in a particular context highlights those forces that may over time change the contours of the system through processes of addition and substitution.

Language evolves through addition when words and grammatical forms not previously part of the lexicon are incorporated into the language. Examples include the addition of words such as *ointment*, and *beauty* from French, and *genius* and *immune* from Latin in the 13th century. Recent examples include the additional meanings of words such as *debug* and *interface* in the context of the computer world.

Language evolves through substitution when the meaning of words and grammatical forms is replaced by new meaning. In his outline history of the English language, Whitehall (1983) reported that about 85% of the Old English vocabulary has been lost to modern English partly because of replacements from French and Latin and partly because of the development of idiomatic phrases. He noted, however, that much of this lost vocabulary consists of synthetic compounds of which the simplex elements still survive (e.g., *law-book* and *earth-craft* are gone, but the component elements remain).

The preceding examples of changes through the addition and substitution of words illustrate a critical aspect of language evolution. Simultaneous and interacting forces for the maintenance and change of meaning have undergirded the evolution of the English language. Had changes occurred strictly through addition, with no deletion or substitution, the language system would have become unmanageably complex and fragmented. Had changes occurred only though pure substitution, with no maintenance of original expressions, the result would have been a new language.

The evolution of a language system is thus managed by balancing additions and substitutions with meanings that carry over from the original. It reflects a process of "renewal" (a re-writing of the old) as opposed to "transformation" (a discarding of the old).[1] Evolution through renewal requires that changes in the meanings of words are simultaneously *incorporated* into and *differentiated* from an existing language system. To understand and manage such an evolution, linguists do not focus on particular word changes within the system. They focus instead on the speech acts of a particular speech community that define what is common and different about the word patterns. The focus on speech communities as the links that bind different word usages to a common language is illustrated in the common practice in dictionaries of listing multiple meanings of a word, each within an explicitly defined speech community.

Finally, there is another interesting parallel between the study of language and culture. Linguists, like culture researchers, are divided between purists and pragmatists (Chomsky, 1957). The former are concerned primarily with the written language and its principles; the latter are concerned primarily with the spoken word. Like their culture counterparts, these two camps have developed rather independently. However, those linguists concerned with describing and explaining language evolution are inevitably drawn to the intermediate level of speech acts in context.

CULTURE, IDENTITIES, AND BEHAVIORS

Drawing on the linguistic model of meaning generation presented above, the following paragraphs present a parallel model of culture. Surface-level behaviors and the results of those behaviors are the signs that combine to convey meaning in organizations as cultural systems. Underlying beliefs and assumptions are thought to govern their meaningful combinations. Each behavior-sign, like word-signs, has two components: a signifier or expression component, and a signified or meaning component. Expression components are observable, for example, when a research faculty member writes a paper or a manager invests in a new technology. The meaning attributed to an expression, however, depends on unobserved linkages that a semiotic analysis seeks to explain.

Organizational actors generally make the connections between behavioral expressions and their meaning without conscious awareness of applying a set of rules. Corporate ladder-climbers, for example, regularly work late without always consciously linking that behavior to a rule system that determines the meaning of the behavior. Yet rules underlie and govern the meaning of what we do. The fact that they are often not explicit and are often not known as such does not negate their existence.

Though a general system of rules is thought to determine the meanings of behaviors in organizations, there is no direct one-to-one correspondence between behaviors and their meaning. A given behavior can mean different things to different people within the same organization. An investment in a new technology may mean "innovation" to people in R&D and manufacturing depart-

ments; it may mean "consumer orientation" to people in a marketing department; and it may mean "waste" to people in the comptroller's office. The meanings people attach to the behavior are not arbitrary, however. People's organizational *identity* provides the context within which behaviors are linked to the rules that give them meaning.

Identity is a concept rooted in psychology and sociology where it is used to characterize an individual in relation to a larger cultural system (Goffman, 1967). It is essential to note that the concept refers not to the larger system *per se*, but to people's understanding of themselves in relation to the system/s. It thus serves as a critical link between people's particular behavioral contexts and the underlying values that give them meaning.

Within the context of organizations, identity describes what people define as central, distinctive, and enduring about their organization (Albert & Whetten, 1985). Those definitions will vary depending on "where [people] sit" in the organization (Dutton & Jackson, 1989). An organization's structure is thus one important source of subunit identities. Formal organizational structures dictate fairly unique and patterned behaviors for subgroups within most large organizations. There is increasing evidence that subgroups with structurally differentiated roles within a firm also differ in the way they make sense of organizational events and situations (Dearborn & Simon, 1958; Dougherty, 1989; Douglas, 1986; Jackson & Dutton, 1989; Nystrom, 1986; Walsh, 1988). Organizational members working in different parts of an organization exhibit different perceptions, make different attributions, and use different cognitive orientations.

Different subunit identities, however, may not always mirror an organization's departmental structure. Multiple subunit identities may arise due to hierarchical differentiation, geographic dispersion, product diversity, functional orientation, or any other factor that would tend to differentiate behaviors over time. Walsh (1988), for example, conducted a study in which managers who belonged to one of four different areas of management (accounting/finance, human relations, marketing, and general management) read a case and then wrote a description of what they considered to be the most important problem facing the company. He found that the marketing group saw more external management problems than did the human relations group or the generalist group. The managers were given identical data. Yet their interpretations of it reflected systematic differences relating to their functional orientation.

Albert and Whetten (1985) illustrated the identity concept in terms of the modern research university. They described universities as having a dual identity. The institution began with a normative identity—like a church—oriented toward ideology and "governed by cultural, educational, and expressive values" (282). Over time, identity "drifts" caused it to add a utilitarian identity—like a business—oriented toward economic productivity and "governed by values of economic rationality" (281). The authors suggested that over an organization's life cycle, it is normal for it to evolve from having a single identity toward acquiring multiple identities. It is how people cope with and make sense of their behaviors in light of changing conditions. Paralleling linguists' descriptions of the evolution of language, they described identity drifts as occurring through processes of *addition* and *subtraction* of behaviors (275).

Table 1 depicts the parallels drawn in this article between natural languages and cultures as systems of meaning. The three components of the systems include an underlying and unobservable set of rules defining a language system/culture, observable expressions in the form of words/behaviors, and speech acts/organizational identities that contextualize the expressions and thus serve as the link to a broader system of rules. As in the case of the components of a language-meaning system, the components of organizational culture can only be understood in relation to each other. The evolution of the culture of today's research university, for example, can only be understood if we examine discrete behavioral changes (e.g., shifting to quantitative tenure criteria) in relation to the utilitarian logic that gives them meaning. To understand how such a logic emerged and has been sustained as part of our university systems, however, one must understand its relation to the earlier religious logic that once defined and continues to partially define the institution. An organization's culture, like a natural language, evolves through an iterative process involving all three components of meaning.

TABLE 1. Language, Speech Acts, and Words
Culture, Identities and Behaviors

	Language/Culture	Speech Acts/Identities	Words/Behaviors
Definition	General system of rules that governs meanings.	Contextual understanding of rules.	Observable expressions/behaviors that combine to form speech acts/identities.
Boundaries	Describes a whole system.	Describes a contextual frame that links parts of a system to a whole.	Describes observable parts of a system.
Source	Result of multiple converging speech acts/identities over time.	Result of patterned word use/behaviors over time.	Result of existing system and new contexts.
Function	**Maintenance:** General standard against which the meanings of discrete speech acts/identities are understood.	**Renewal:** Incorporation and differentiation of new contextual understanding.	**Change:** Additions/substitutions to fit changing contexts.

There are forces for both maintenance and change in meaning systems, whether linguistic or cultural. A focus on the beliefs and assumptions defining high culture emphasizes those forces that serve to maintain the stable norms that cut across multiple identities. A focus on behavioral expressions in a particular context highlights those forces that may over time change the contours of the entire system. To understand and manage the evolution, however, requires a focus on the identities that link people's understanding of their behaviors to a broader system of meaning.

MANAGING CULTURE FOR SUSTAINABLE COMPETITIVE ADVANTAGE

As stated earlier, previous research on organizational culture as a competitive resource has focused either on culture as an abstract system of rules or on discrete manifestations of those rules, largely ignoring identities as a critical intermediate level of meaning generation. Identities result from patterned ways of behaving over time. Such patterns color how subunits understand themselves in relation to the organization. Following the prescriptions of the linguistic model presented earlier, managing changes in a firm's culture requires incorporating new *identities*, rather than *behaviors*, into an existing cultural system. In the evolution of natural language systems, new word-forms are not linked directly to a general system of rules. They are linked to a speech context, and that speech context is integrated as part of the linguistic system. So too, by focusing on the integration of contextual meanings, rather than on the integration of behaviors, managers are able to introduce shared understanding of changed behaviors without neutralizing the differences that the behaviors bring to the firm.

Managing the cognitive component of organizational competencies, then, requires a dual focus on (a) the linkages between behaviors and the identities that grow up around those behaviors, and (b) the linkages between identities and a larger system of values. Albert and Whetten (1985) discussed at length the first set of links—between identities and observable behaviors within an organization. They referred to the two identities of modern universities as two logics of management reflected in different technical functions and in different types of responses to external stimuli. They described the function of identities as providing a way for individuals or organizational subunits to make sense of changing events by locating them as an instance of a more general law or framework.

But how did the new forms of behavior become central, distinctive, and enduring features of universities? The linguistic-based model developed in this article suggests that new forms of behavior result in organizational identity drifts when overseers of a firm (top management) explicitly decouple the new behaviors from an existing set of cultural rules and gradually integrate the contextual meanings of those behaviors into a set of central organizational values.

Albert and Whetten were not explicit about the links between identities and a larger cultural system. Though they mentioned in a footnote that identities are part of a larger value system (293), they stopped short of examining the links between organizational subunit identities and a broader set of norms. As a result, they were not able to discuss the mechanism by which the single dominant religious identity of early universities made way for the drift toward dual identities. Nor were they able to examine how the dual identities continue to be maintained in an uneasy balance that preserves the institution's external legitimacy and internal integrity.

Fiol and Dunbar (1990) recently argued that a common set of core values underlies and governs the meanings of even the most behaviorally diverse firms. As an example, they described the diverse behaviors of beer firms. Their central argument was that despite apparent diversity and contradiction between those aspects of beer firms that promote consumption and those that promote moderation, there is a deeper system of meaning at the level of the organization that allows each aspect to be a competitive resource for the firm without pulling it apart over time. To relate their point to the case of Albert and Whetten's universities, the emerging utilitarian identity had to have been recognized as both unique and valuable within some broader concept of universities than simply as religious institutions.

A focus on the linkages between identities and the cultural systems to which they relate highlights an important difference between language systems and other social systems of meaning. Language systems, as compared with organizational cultures, represent relatively separate and non-overlapping systems of meaning. For example, though English has evolved through exposure to speech (e.g., the influence of Latinos on American English), it is not as a language embedded in a higher-order grammatical system. Organizational cultures, in contrast, are embedded in a hierarchy of meaning systems whose boundaries are not as clearly defined. The culture of an organization is embedded in the culture of an industry, for example, which in turn is embedded in the cultural norms of a society.

A semiotic model of contextual articulation as a source of meaning emphasizes an intermediary perspective, regardless of the level of analysis, that one must adopt in order to explain how organizational meanings evolve. Within such a framework, identity does not refer to a particular level of analysis. It refers to a perspective. It describes the way that parts of a cultural system, at any level of analysis, define themselves in relation to the system. One may thus view a group of individuals sharing the same function and role within an organization as an organizational subculture or occupational culture (Van Maanen & Barley, 1984) if one is interested in understanding the norms that define the group as a system. If, on the other hand, the aim is to understand the relationship of the group to a larger system of meaning, a

shift to a focus on identities provides a more relevant and useful framework. To focus on the group's identity is to focus on its contextual understanding of a broader set of cultural norms.

Identities, rather than behaviors or general cultural systems, must be the focus of our efforts to understand the management of culture for sustainable competitive advantage. The close correspondence of identities and the behavioral contexts from which they emerge leads to the possibility of consciously managing their evolution. The presence of a larger rule system, which serves as a central referent for multiple identities, leads to imperfectly imitable links between discrete behaviors and the beliefs that guide them.

The following section describes and illustrates several ways of managing culture as a competitive resource. First, it describes the limited conditions under which culture can be managed through behavioral manipulations. Second, it illustrates the more generally relevant opportunity for firms to manage their culture through a focus on identities.

MANAGING CULTURAL CHANGE THROUGH BEHAVIORAL SUBSTITUTION OR ADDITION

Albert and Whetten (1985) noted that different identities may be incorporated in organizations through either substitutions or additions of patterned forms of new behavior. Neither process, by itself, however, ensures that the differences will be incorporated into an existing culture. To assume that behavioral additions or substitutions alone lead to cultural change is to follow the path of culture pragmatists that assume a one-to-one correspondence between multiple different sets of behaviors and a single set of rules that determines how those behaviors are understood.

To manage cultural change through addition or substitution is to focus on behaviors in relation to an overall system of meaning of an organization. Just as pure substitution of words may lead to a new language, so too may pure substitutions of behavior patterns lead to a new culture. And just as pure additions of words may result in new dialects that develop their own rule system, so too may pure additions of behavior patterns result in multiple subcultures with their own separate cultural norms. In both cases, culture changes directly mirror behavioral changes. There are two scenarios in which cultural change is possible through the manipulation of behaviors. The following describes each of them.

Behavioral Substitution

In some instances, the behaviors of members of a firm are all interpreted through a common lens. This leads to the possibility of managing the firm's culture by substituting one set of behaviors for another. Such a direct link between behaviors and culture, however, is likely only in situations where a few powerful people have personal control over all of a firm's activities.

Proposition 1a: Substitution of Behavior Patterns Will Lead to Cultural Change Only if the Behavior-Culture Interface Is Controlled by a Powerful Few. The possibility of managing cultural change through the substitution of behaviors is illustrated by the experience of a small privately owned shirt shop on the east side of lower Manhattan. In the 1970s, the proprietor sold low-priced shirts that appealed to young men who were interested in the latest fashions. As the young clientele aged into Yuppies and Wall Street boomed, it became evident that growth opportunities lay not in low-priced fashionable shirts, but in top-of-the-line, custom-tailored dress shirts. Within months, the proprietor changed the physical image of the store, the design of her advertisements, and the nature of her merchandise to pursue the high-end market. Anyone observing the changes saw more than a product change. It was a change of identity, which in the case of this shirt business resulted in the substitution of the entire organizational culture for another.

Such changes, not only in a firm's *pattern of behaviors*, but in its entire *cultural definition*, are difficult if not impossible for businesses that are not personally controlled by a single proprietor. The case above illustrates a successful culture shift through behavioral substitution when the identity and culture of the firm are one. When an organizational culture encompasses multiple identities, however, as is most often the case, contextual differences are likely to prohibit such a one-to-one correspondence between behaviors and the firm's cultural values. Moreover, a complete substitution of the patterns of behaviors of only one subunit would leave the firm with no common set of values.

Proposition 1b: The Management of Cultural Change through the Substitution of Behavioral Patterns Will Not Ensure a Sustainable Competitive Advantage because the Changes Are Not Imperfectly Imitable. Even in situations where a powerful few have the personal control needed to effect cultural changes through behavioral substitutions, their efforts may not lead to sustained superior performance. This is because, as Barney (1986b) noted, changes in the behavioral manifestations of a culture are easily imitated. The one-to-one correspondence between behaviors and the rule system that governs them allows the redefinition of culture through behavioral interventions. That one-to-one correspondence, however, also means that rivals may adopt what is valuable about the culture simply by replicating the behaviors. The tight coupling between strategic behaviors and cultural norms that makes it possible for insiders to manage beliefs through behavioral changes, also makes it possible for outsiders to replicate the changes.

Behavioral Addition

In some instances, the culture of a firm, as a whole, changes through the addition of subunits, each with its own cultural norms. This often occurs through the acquisition of a unit with differing behaviors and norms into an existing value system. Each subunit retains its own set of beliefs and values, which may be quite distinct from those of its sibling units.

Proposition 2a: Additions of New Behavior Patterns Will Lead to Cultural Change only if the Additions Are Clustered into Autonomous Units Whose Own Distinct Culture Is Allowed to Emerge as Separate from That of the Original Culture. Such is the well known case of GE's diversification from its core appliance businesses. New identities were acquired along with the new sets of behaviors. The firm did not, at the time of the acquisitions, incorporate those identities into a common set of organizational values. The old identity (self-definition as an appliance manufacturer) remained intact, but the new contexts were so disconnected from the old that it became difficult to speak of a cohesive meaning system binding the pieces of the organization together.

As the firm added multiple disparate behaviors to an organization that once prided itself for its strong cultural system, the leadership became more and more concerned with learning to speak a common language. GE today runs corporate seminars on a full-time basis with the explicit purpose of coming together on "who we are." It faces a formidable challenge, given that each business unit is contextually decoupled from the others. This decoupling has resulted in undesirable fragmentation, both in behaviors and the values that give meaning to those behaviors.

Proposition 2b: The Management of Cultural Change through Additions of New Behavioral Patterns Will Not Ensure a Sustainable Competitive Advantage because the Changes Are Not Imperfectly Imitable. As in the earlier example of the Manhattan shirt producer, cultural change at GE reflected a one-to-one correspondence between newly acquired sets of behaviors and the cultural norms that mirrored those behaviors. The firm acquired new cultures as it acquired new behavioral competencies. There was little attempt, early on,

to integrate the multiple contexts into a common corporate language. Again, in this case, GE's organizational culture shifts afford it no particular advantage over its rivals. Once again, if distinct cultural norms are a direct reflection of distinct patterns of behaving, the former can be replicated by simply replicating the behavior.

The two cases provide examples of cultural change made possible through behavioral manipulation. In both cases, the changes were managed, not through a renewal of an existing set of organizational values, but through either substituting it with another or neutralizing it through fragmentation. In both cases, underlying beliefs, theories, and propositions were maintained in an unchanged relation to a patterned set of behaviors. Separate new behaviors led to separate new beliefs.

MANAGING CULTURAL CHANGE THROUGH RENEWAL

The majority of firms we study, however, are unable or unwilling to undergo massive cultural revolutions or cultural fragmentation. Rather, they are challenged to change what they do to keep up with changing environmental conditions while trying to hang onto a stable sense of who they are. Therein lies the real challenge of managing culture as a competitive resource. In such cases, an existing culture, as a historically derived set of beliefs and values, is recognized as a competitive resource.

According to the framework developed in this article, the challenge of managing such a resource in a changing environment involves two things. First, management must decouple new behavior patterns and their related identities sufficiently from traditional organizational values so that identities are able to drift with the changing tides. Second, management must sustain a common underlying core of what the organization is that gradually incorporates the newly emerging identities. That is, the meaning of the new behaviors must be allowed to emerge in context, independent of an existing set of organizational norms. Once established, those contextual meanings can be incorporated into the larger system. By initially decoupling new behaviors from an existing set of norms, an organization allows new meanings to emerge. Then, by explicitly defining new contexts as part of the original system, rather than new behaviors or a new system, an organization can adjust its culture through renewal, rather than addition or substitution, to continual changes in a firm's patterns of behavior.

Proposition 3a: Cultural Renewal Results from (a) Tight Coupling of New Behaviors and Their Contextual Meaning, (b) Uncoupling of New Behaviors and a Traditional System of Meaning, and (c) Loose Coupling of Multiple Contextual Meanings and a General System of Cultural Norms. Managing for cultural renewal rather than cultural transformation requires that managers pay attention to the way new behavior patterns in subunits of the firm lead those subgroups to define themselves differently in relation to the firm. The way to manage such emergent differences as competitive resources, according to the framework developed in this article, is explicitly to *decouple* the new behavior patterns from an existing set of cultural norms, and to manage *coupling* at the level of identities or contextual meanings.

The experiences of six US forest products firms during the environmentally turbulent early 1980s illustrates the challenge of managing emerging identities without subsuming them into an existing culture. Most of the 1970s represented a stable period for the forest products industry. The six largest firms were vertically integrated and for decades had held dominant positions in upstream lumber operations. Behaviors historically associated with successful vertical integration included efficient production techniques, large contract negotiation skills, and heavy capital outlay. These ingrained behaviors

over several decades had molded a single and dominant identity for these firms that regularly referred to themselves as the "forest giants" of the industry (Arthur Andersen, 1979, 1980, 1981). Heavy spending patterns, in particular, became so much a part of their cultural belief system that the behaviors became an assumed rather than a conscious part of strategy evaluations.

Huff (1990) and others have referred to strategies as maps that provide firms with a sense of direction and a point of reference. Internal annual planning documents continued to serve as maps that guided these firms' planning behaviors. However, the behaviors that these maps signified had been memorized to the point where they were not explicitly addressed in the planning review process. The map automatically signified a set of ingrained routes.

In the early 1980s, firms in the industry were faced with drastic changes as a result of the rising cost of capital, the rise of lumber imports, and the rapidly shifting demand patterns from upstream lumber to downstream specialty paper products. Industry analysts and internal strategic planners in all six firms recognized the need for a shift in both strategic positioning (toward end-user markets) and resource allocation (from production to packaging and selling skills) for the integrated firms.

What the new strategy map signified was clear to all six firms. Their internal planning documents as well as statements to the public as early as 1980 reflected a general awareness of the need to change their pattern of behaviors. However, the integrated giants were challenged to manage not only their behaviors or strategic maps, but also the deeper-level organizational values or culture maps that had become tightly coupled with an outdated set of behaviors—heavy capital spending on upstream lumber operations.

The reorientation process of two of the firms is a particularly interesting study of contrasts. One of the firms responded to the changed environment by specifying a new set of objectives in its planning documents—a move to downstream markets. Other than that, the firm changed none of its planning document formats or planning procedures. The planning group continued to use the format of earlier years, simply inserting a new set of objectives. The planning procedures followed the same timetable and involved similar personnel. The necessary changes in this firm's resource allocations were never implemented. Insiders reported that people paid lip service to the new destination on their strategy map, but everyone continued with business as usual. There appears to have been no way to separate the new strategy map from the culturally ingrained routes, even though a new destination had been specified. The new strategy map clearly signified a change in behaviors, but the culture map, tightly coupled with an ingrained and outdated set of behaviors, did not signify a change.

Another of the six integrated firms also responded to the changed environment by specifying a new strategy destination toward downstream markets. In addition, top management put the entire formal planning system on hold. Project teams were set up to plan resource allocation programs for the changed destination. The organization forcefully separated the new strategy map, whose signified behaviors heralded an emerging new identity, from the formal planning process that was steeped in a traditional definition of who the firm was. In this firm, resources were successfully repositioned to take advantage of the growth in downstream markets.

By separating the strategy map with a clear one-to-one correspondence to required new behaviors from the culture map whose meanings had to be redefined, the second organization managed a cultural renewal. New patterns of behavior were not managed directly in relation to an existing definition of the firm through processes of addition or substitution. Rather, new patterns of behavior were seen as valuable, but different, con-

textual realities. They were not added to a list of destinations on a map that had become too familiar. Nor were the listed on a map as substitutes of previous destinations. By managing the change process as a valued and separate part of ongoing operations, the second organization allowed those involved in the process to develop a view of their organization based on a different context. The emerging identity was incorporated into the regular planning process only after its differences were sufficiently developed and understood so as to not be neutralized by an ingrained organizational self-definition.

Proposition 3b: The Management of Cultural Renewal through a Decoupling of New Behaviors from a Firm's Traditional Values and a Coupling of New Contextual Meanings with a Firm's Traditional Values Will Ensure a Sustainable Competitive Advantage because the Renewal Is Imperfectly Imitable. The managers of the second firm in the illustration above did not attempt to manage the culture of their firm through behavioral manipulation. Though one might argue that the removal of the new planning process from ingrained routines represented an imitable behavioral manipulation, this behavior per se did not lead to cultural renewal. The management of the firm's formal structures allowed a process to emerge that might otherwise have been stymied. Structural management did not, however, lead to the new forms of cultural self-definition that emerged. By managing the interface between the ingrained cultural system and a new contextual awareness, the managers paved the way for an imperfectly imitable process to occur.

DISCUSSION AND CONCLUSION

Organizational competency is a critical competitive resource. In particular, the ambiguity of decision rules that link skills/assets and action outcomes is an essential ingredient for achieving a sustainable competitive advantage. This factor raises a host of largely unanswered questions about the possibility of managing the cognitive processes by which a firm reinvests in such ambiguity, both to sustain and to renew its competitive edge.

Previous research has drawn on culture theories to attempt to address these questions. The results have been largely untenable because of the persistent separation of the pragmatic study of behaviors and the purist study of the beliefs that determine the meaning of behaviors. By reframing the organizational culture concept to highlight the linkages between behaviors and beliefs, this article offers an integrative framework that can potentially add to the tool kits of both purists and pragmatists. The reframing recognizes cultural belief systems as the glue that binds the diverse aspects of a firm (Nord, 1985). However, this article also suggests that in most cases it may be both difficult and ineffective to manage the gluing process at the level of behaviors in relation to an organization-wide system of beliefs. The two are most often not direct reflections of each other. Behavior patterns reflect unique identities or contextual beliefs. This is where the glue metaphor may be most appropriate. Those identities, rather than the discrete behaviors that drive them, are the keys to understanding and managing behaviors in relation to an over-all belief system.

The approach suggests to researchers, consultants, and managers alike, that we not limit our concern to *either* behaviors or underlying values. They are interactive components of systems of meaning. They are neither substitutable as Weick (1985) suggested, nor are they independent of each other, as much of previous research implies. The management of day-to-day behaviors always has an impact (encouraging either maintenance or change) on people's organizational identities. That is, the management of behaviors leads to confirming or disconfirming the contextual meanings of those behaviors. Those identities, in turn, are always defined in terms of a more general

set of beliefs. We need to be concerned about how our management of behaviors affects the identities of individuals and organizational subunits and how those identities reflect and are reflected by an organization's broader set of beliefs.

The further development of such an approach will contribute to the tool kits now available for understanding the management of organizational competency. In addition to prescribing that managers invest in people with tacit knowledge (Reed & DeFillippi, 1990), for example, it prescribes that managers listen to how those people make sense of their role in relation to the organization. That is, the approach suggests a broadened emphasis that includes not only the behaviors of people with tacit knowledge, but also the contextual beliefs that reflect how those people define themselves in relation to the organization as a whole.

Finally, an identity-based approach to managing organizational competencies encourages a dialectical view of coupling or relatedness in organizations. Orton and Weick (1990) argued that organizational coupling is not a unidimensional construct ranging from loose to tight. A singular focus on tangible structures/behaviors on the one hand or beliefs on the other, however, by definition leads to a view of coupling as either loose or tight along a single dimension. A focus on identities as a bridge between behaviors and beliefs leads to a multi-dimensional view of organizational coupling. Couplings may be tight between identities and culture, as was the case of the proprietorship in the example above. Or couplings may be tight between behaviors and identities but loose between behaviors and an existing set of cultural norms, as was the case of the successful forest product firm.

By arguing that culture can be managed by attending to the interface between high culture and multiple emerging identities, this article begins to show how the dialectics of loose coupling may arise. The approach calls for tight coupling of different patterns of behavior and the identities they spawn. Yet it simultaneously calls for explicit decoupling of behaviors from a single overarching system of meaning.

An appreciation of this dialectic may bring us closer to explaining and managing what Prahalad and Bettis (1986) called *meta-learning* in organizations. Rather than transforming organizations through additions or substitutions of knowledge, meta-learning involves learning to simultaneously conceptualize different and contradictory forms of knowledge. Understanding what meta-learning means in the organizations we study may require that we, as researchers, engage in the process ourselves. The challenge is to recognize the differential value of our different tool kits and to employ them for the renewal of our joint research efforts.

NOTES

1. Taken from Karl Weick's address at the meeting of the Academy of Management. San Francisco, August, 1990.

REFERENCES

Albert, S., & Whetten, D.A. 1985. Organizational identity. *Research in Organizational Behavior*, 7:263–295.

Arthur Anderson, 1979, 1980, 1981. *Forest products*. Arthur Andersen.

Barney, J.B. 1986a. Strategic factor markets. *Management Science*. 32:1231–1241.

Barney, J.B. 1986b. Organizational culture: Can it be a source of sustained competitive advantage? *Academy of Management Review*. 11:656–665.

Barthes, R. 1967. *Elements of semiology*. Boston: Beacon Press.

Chomsky, N. 1957. *Syntactic structures*. Paris: The Hague.

Dearborn, D.C., & Simon, H.A. 1958. Selective perception: A note on the departmental identification of executives. *Sociometry*. 21:140–144.

Dougherty, D. 1989. *Why don't departments work well together on innovation? Thought worlds and collective action in large firms*. Working paper, Wharton Business School.

Douglas, M. 1986. *How institutions think*. Syracuse, NY: Syracuse University Press.

Dunbar, R.L.M., & Fiol, C.M. 1990. *Organizational identity and organizational images: A distinctive theme with variations*. Working paper, New York University.

Dutton, J.E., & Dukerich, J.M. 1989. *Keeping an eye on the mirror: The role of image and identity in organizational adaptation*. Paper presented at the Workshop on Managerial Thought and Cognition, Washington, DC.

Dutton, J.E., & Jackson, S. 1989. *Does what you see depend on where you sit?: Linking context and strategic issue categories*. Paper presented at the Academy of Management meetings, Washington, DC.

Eco, U. 1979. *A theory of semiotics*. Bloomington: University of Indiana Press.

Fiol, C.M., & Dunbar, R.I.M. 1990. *Identifying the basis for organizational cohesion: The tight side of loose coupling*. Working paper. New York University.

Ghemawat, P. 1986. Sustainable advantage. *Harvard Business Review*, 64(5):53–58.

Goffman, I. 1967. *Interaction ritual*. New York: Anchor Books.

Hofer, C.W., & Schendel, D. 1978. *Strategy formulation: Analytical concepts*. St. Paul, MN: West.

Huff, A.S. 1990. *Mapping strategic thought*. London: Wiley.

Jackson, S.E., & Dutton, J.E. 1989. Discerning threats and opportunities. *Administrative Science Quarterly*, 33:370–387.

Krefting, L.A., & Frost, P.J. 1985. Untangling webs, surface waves, and wildcatting. In P.J. Frost & Associates (Eds.), *Organizational culture*. Beverly Hills: Sage, 155–168.

Levi-Strauss, C. 1976. *Structural anthropology*. New York: Basic Books.

Lippman, S.A. & Rumelt, R.P. 1982. Uncertain imitability: An analysis of interfirm differences in efficiency under competition. *The Bell Journal of Economics*, 13:418–438.

Nelson, R.R., & Winter, S.G. 1982. *An evolutionary theory of economic change*. Cambridge, MA: Harvard University Press.

Nord, W.R. 1985. Can organizational culture be managed? A synthesis. In P.J. Frost & Associates (Eds.), *Organizational Culture*. Beverly Hills: Sage, 187–196.

Nystrom, P.C. 1986. Comparing beliefs of line and technostructure managers. *Academy of Management Journal*, 29:812–819.

Orton, J.D., & Weick, K.E. 1990. Loosely coupled systems: A reconceptualization. *Academy of Management Review*, 15:203–223.

Peters, T.J., & Waterman, R.H. 1982. *In search of excellence*. New York: Harper and Row.

Porter, M.E. 1985. *Competitive advantage: Creating and sustaining superior performance*. New York: Free Press.

Prahalad, C.K., & Bettis, R.A. 1986. The dominant logic: A new linkage between diversity and performance. *Strategic Management Journal*, 7: 485–501.

Reed, R., & DeFillippi, R.J. 1990. Causal ambiguity, barriers to imitation, and sustainable competitive advantage. *Academy of Management Review*. 15:88–102.

Saussure, F. de 1916. *Cours de linguistique generale*. Paris: Payot.

Schwartz, H., & Davis, S. 1981. Matching corporate culture and business strategy. *Organizational Dynamics*, 10:30–48.

Selznick, P. 1957. *Leadership in administration*. New York, Harper and Row.

Siehl, C. 1985. After the founder: An opportunity to manage culture. In P.J. Frost & Associates (Eds.), *Organizational Culture*. Beverly Hills: Sage, 125–140.

Smircich, L. 1983. Concepts of culture in organizational analysis. *Administrative Science Quarterly*, 28:339–358.

Tichy, N. 1982. Managing change strategically: The technological, political, and cultural keys. *Organizational Dynamics*, 11:59–80.

Van Maanen, J., & Barley, S.R. 1984. Occupational communities: Culture and control in organizations. *Research in Organizational Behavior*, 6:287–365.

Walsh, J.P. 1988. Selectivity and selective perception: An investigation of managers' belief structures and information processing. *Academy of Management Journal*, 31:873–896.

Weick, K.E. 1985. The significance of corporate culture. In P.J. Frost & Associates (Eds.), *Organizational Culture*. Beverly Hills: Sage, 381–390.

Whitehall, H. 1983. Outline history of the English language. In *Webster's New Universal Unabridged Dictionary*. New York: Simon & Schuster, vii–xi.

WORKING THROUGH DIVERSITY
AS A STRATEGIC IMPERATIVE

Susan E. Jackson
Eden B. Alvarez

Organizations that attack the diversity issue with full force do so because they believe that taking action is a strategic imperative. For most organizations, simply knowing the facts about workforce diversity—which are now parading as headlines in our daily newspapers—does not stimulate major changes in management practices. The facts about the nature of the workforce are important, but their significance s most obvious when they are considered in the context of the changing business environment.

One hundred years ago, as the 19th century drew to a close, Americans in every major urban center were experiencing the industrial revolution, which dramatically altered the nature of their work. Small, home-based businesses closed their doors, and fathers and sons headed out to work in the factories. Independent artisans who offered customized goods and services to their local communities traded in their life-style to work on assembly lines, where work was divided into simple tasks performed by man-and-machine teams. With the industrial revolution, the social intimacy and personalized business relationships that characterized work were replaced by isolation, mass production, and impersonal bureaucracy.

Now, as we approach the beginning of a new millennium, another revolution is transforming our work lives. The economic forces shaping this new revolution are many and varied, but two are particularly relevant to the topic of workforce diversity: the shift from a manufacturing-based economy to a service economy and the globalization of the marketplace. These changes are bringing more and more people from diverse backgrounds into contact with one another, and, at the same time, mean that businesses are becoming more reliant on person-to-person contact as a way to get things done. Add to these trends the changing demographics of both consumers and the workforce, and the stage is set for diversity to emerge as a strategic business issue.

THE SERVICE ECONOMY

As of May 1991, 78% of all U.S. employees (74% of employees in the private sector) worked in service-based industries (Bureau of Labor Statistics, 1991), and projections for the future show a continuing upward trend. However, these figures underestimate the true importance of services in our economy. Manufacturers also know that service is important, and they woo customers by providing it for their products. Services hidden within the manufacturing sector of our economy include activities such as maintenance and repair of automobiles, household appliances, computers, and industrial equipment;

customer training; customized design work; and deliveries. Also hidden from these figures are the myriad internal service exchanges that occur within companies.

Defining services is difficult, but capturing the essence of them is easy. As one person put it, "Services is something which can be bought and sold but which you cannot drop on your foot" (Gummesson, 1987, p. 22). That is, services are intangible. More importantly for the topic of diversity, a service is produced and consumed on the spot, during an exchange that involves both the provider of the service and the customer. During a service encounter, production, marketing, and quality control all occur simultaneously.

Bell (1973) described service work as a "game between persons." For companies to win at this game, they need employees who can read their customers and interact with them in a nearly flawless manner. Employees must be able to understand the customer's perspective, anticipate and monitor the customer's needs and expectations, and respond sensitively and appropriately to fulfill those needs and expectations. In the service game, "customer literacy" is an essential skill. But achieving customer literacy is an illusive goal. As some companies are beginning to realize, employing a workforce that mirrors the customers is one step in the right direction. Maryland National Bank in Baltimore discovered this when it studied the customer retention records for its branches. The best branches recruited locally to hire tellers who could swap neighborhood gossip. Of the 20 branch managers, one of their best—located in a distant suburb—was described as dressing "very blue-collar . . . she doesn't look like a typical manager of people. But this woman is totally committed to her customers" (Sellers, 1990, p. 60).

As service activities gain in importance, so do issues of diversity. In a service economy, interactions between people are pervasive, and effective communications are essential to business success. Similarities between people help smooth these basic processes, whereas differences between people can interfere. Ironically, having discovered they can communicate more effectively with their customers by hiring employees who are similar to those customers, employers soon realize they have increased their internal diversity and must find ways to counter the resulting internal communication difficulties among employees plus the challenge of effectively managing and retaining their new, diverse workforce.

GLOBALIZATION SPURS ORGANIZATIONAL RESTRUCTURING

The globalization of business activities is another environmental force that pushes issues of diversity into the foreground as firms envision their strategic objectives. A recent *Harvard Business Review* survey of 12,000 managers from 25 different countries documented how common international expansion has become. Worldwide, 45% of larger companies (10,000 or more employees) had experienced some international expansion in the past 2 years. In the United States, about 26% of all respondents indicated that their company had recently expanded internationally (Kanter, 1991).

As trade barriers fall, foreign sourcing becomes more attractive and new growth opportunities are created. For example, for U.S. pharmaceutical companies, the portion of annual sales coming from foreign markets was recently estimated to be 40% (Business International Corporation, 1991). To capture large shares of foreign markets, licensing agreements and joint ventures with non-U.S. firms are often desirable and sometimes necessary. For large companies, these alliances may require coordinating activities in 100 or more countries. Smaller companies may have alliances involving only one or two foreign locations, but these are critical if corporate survival hangs on their ability to manage them successfully.

For managers, experiences with new international partners can be like a slap in the face that forces them to realize the value of employees with cross-cultural sensitivities, as well as the need for organizational systems that knit multiple cultures together to form a seamless whole. When perfected, such systems will enable organizations to fully utilize the talents of employees from all parts of the world with no interference due to the static created when cultures clash.

But globalization has more subtle consequences, as well. These affect companies that are not even reaching out for a share of the global market. For example, globalization means U.S. firms now compete with companies from around the world for customers who were once a safely isolated home market. With more options to choose from, all consumers of goods and services have more power to insist that their needs and preferences be satisfied. Successful U.S. firms have learned how to get close to their customers, regardless of whether those customers are individuals or businesses, internal or external customers, in the home market or in foreign markets.

As they struggle to get closer to customers abroad and at home and to win their loyalty, many firms are changing their organizational structures. Some of these changes, such as increased use of work teams, merely highlight the importance of working through domestic demographic diversity. Other changes, such as new strategic alliances, reveal new types of diversity that must be managed, including differences in the cultures that host a company's foreign operations.

New Business Strategies Require More Teamwork

In response to the increased pressure created by global competition, many U.S. businesses focused first on articulating a competitive strategy and then began adapting themselves to fit that strategy. For many, increasing the quality of products and services became a high-priority strategic objective. Indeed, quality enhancement strategies have become pervasive since the federal government legitimized and institutionalized such efforts by launching the Malcolm Baldrige National Quality Award. Other companies focused on innovation—a tactic U.S. firms had historically exploited successfully. To succeed at beating the competition through innovation, more creative products and services had to be developed and speedily made available to consumers.

What is clear now is that use of work teams can facilitate the pursuit of quality and the drive for innovation. For example, since Ford Motor Company adopted its "Quality Is Job One" philosophy, it has engaged in a massive program of organizational change. To produce quality products, Ford believes that employees must be involved in and committed to their jobs and that team-based work engenders this commitment, so teams have proliferated throughout the organization (see Banas, 1988). The same philosophy prevails at Corning Glass, where employees are organized into some 3,000 teams (Dumaine, 1990) and is gaining favor with a growing number of service companies ("Work Teams," 1988).

Besides improving quality, teams facilitate innovation by bringing together experts with dissimilar knowledge bases and perspectives and providing an environment for creative thinking. Armed with more creative ideas, companies can also shorten the cycle time from product inception to production by using concurrent engineering, which is a design process that relies on multifunction teams of experts from design, manufacturing, and marketing.

To ensure that new ideas are successfully transferred from the research and development lab to the marketplace, both suppliers and the intended customer may become team members as well. A Nobel Prize winner at Bell Labs described this new order as follows: "Five years ago managers here didn't even use the word 'customer.' Now each of us has two jobs; working in corporate research and serving on a team connected to one of AT&T's product areas" (Bylinski, 1990, p. 72).

Together, multifunction tams plus liaisons with suppliers and customers should speed technology transfer, which is essential for high-technology U.S. firms trying to regain their competitive positions. There is nothing high-tech about the process of managing these technical teams, however. According to a senior vice president at Texas Instruments: "You delude yourself if you think that the emphasis in technology transfer is on technology. It's a humanistic task, not a technical one" (Bylinski, 1990, p. 73). Stripped to its core, the task is to make sure that the right people are in contact with one another and supporting one another's efforts. In addition to listening to their customers, the members of successful multifunction teams must break through the walls that have long separated their organizational departments and learn to cooperate.

Teams may not cure all of a company's ills, but many American business leaders apparently agree with Texas Instrument's chief executive officer (CEO) that "no matter what your business, these teams are the wave of the future." A survey by the American Productivity and Quality Center found that half of the 467 large firms in their study planned to be relying significantly more on self-managing teams (Dumaine, 1990). When teams are formed, diversity is inevitable— sometimes it is intentionally designed into teams to stimulate creativity, and sometimes it is simply a natural by-product of drawing team members from a diverse employee population. Either way, it is inescapable.

Mergers and Alliances Require Managing Diverse Corporate Cultures

Employees are not the only ones teaming up with one another. Companies are teaming up, too. Although the rate of corporate merger has eased since the mid-1980s, it remains high. And, in addition to the traditional merger, where two companies are joined into one, there are a host of minimergers occurring between organizations. As Kanter puts it, companies that were once adversaries are now becoming "PALs"—pooling, allying, and linking together in order to improve their competitive capacity (Kanter, 1989). These are the alliances formed by firms as they tighten their relationships with suppli-

ers and customers. Such alliances often require that two units from two different organizations meld together to act as a linking pin between the firms involved. As in full-fledged mergers, participants in minimergers must learn to cope with diverse corporate cultures.

Working through corporate culture diversity is a major challenge: Respondents to the *Harvard Business Review* survey mentioned earlier were asked to report on the problems their companies had with customer and client alliances. The *most* frequently cited source of problems was differences in corporate cultures. "Different corporate cultures" created problems in 59% of the companies with such alliances, making it considerably more troublesome than "coordinating plans," which was the next most common problem (experienced by 43% of the companies).

Anyone who has experienced a merger, or has simply left a company to take another job, probably knows that organizational cultures can differ in terms of which ideals are most valued, customs and rituals, the shared expectation employees have for how they should behave, and the way members of the organization interpret events. Like national cultures, corporate cultures serve as unobtrusive backdrops, often going unnoticed except between changing scenes. But when scenes change, as during a merger, the textures of the corporate cultures that must be knit together become apparent. For example, in the aftermath of the merger between Delta Airlines and Western Airlines, the informal, intimate, "Californian" culture at Western Airlines could be appreciated more fully by some employees when they saw how it contrasted to the "Southern" culture at Delta (Kanter, 1989). Similarly, the corporate cultures that dominated U.S. auto companies a decade ago became more salient after Japanese transplants and joint ventures exposed auto workers to radically different corporate environments.

As this discussion of the new business environment shows, in the 21st century communications and the people they connect will be the lifeblood of business. Regardless of who is doing the communicating, and regardless of whether people are connecting with one another face-to-face, fax-to-fax, or phone-to-phone, high-fidelity transmissions will be essential. Through effective communications, business will assess customers' needs and desires, create new products and services, market their products and services to a global audience, and manage the production and delivery of products and services across borders of all types, including geographic, economic, cultural, and organizational.

THE CHANGING LABOR MARKET

The shift to a service-based economy and increasing global competitiveness should make the importance of excellent workforce management practices obvious. These should be reason enough for business leaders to list continuous improvement of human resource management (HRM) as a top priority in their strategic agenda. And, given the current environment, it seems inevitable that any organization looking for ways to improve human resources management will see the management of diversity as one issue with broad implications. But for those who have let other priorities distract them from continuous HRM improvement, a third change in the environment should help focus their attention—a tightening of the supply of qualified employees. As one CEO put it, "We're used to competing for customers, but now we'll be faced with a growing need to compete for our workforce" (Sellers, 1990, p. 59).

In the recent past, the labor market could be characterized as a buyer's market. Labor was in abundant supply and therefore it was relatively cheap and easy to acquire. When "traditional" employees were abundant, employers did not need to recruit from the pool of "nontraditional" workers whose differences may have required organizations to make adaptive changes. However, in the near future the labor market will become more and more of a seller's market. The shortage of appropriately skilled labor will force employ-

ees to compete to attract, retain, and effectively manage all available employees.

Many companies are already feeling the pinch. According to one survey (Towers Perrin & Hudson Institute, 1990), shortages of technical, secretarial/clerical, professional, and supervisory/management skills make recruiting difficult now for at least half of U.S. employers, and the problem is expected to worsen in the near future. Particular types of labor shortages are slightly worse in some geographic regions and in some industries, but regional and industry variations are relatively minor—the problem is pervasive.

To cope with the scarcity of potential employees, employers are responding with a number of initiatives: They are developing new recruiting strategies designed to find new sources of labor, such as students, immigrants, and retirees; they're devising new benefits packages that better fit the needs of the new workforce, hoping to make their organizations more attractive to job applicants; and they're becoming more flexible regarding employment conditions, for example, by allowing employees more input in the determination of the length and scheduling of their work weeks, offering opportunities for extended leaves of absence, and arranging for job sharing. Such initiatives help companies attract talent from a broader and larger labor pool, buffering the company from the tightening labor market.

Increased employee diversity is a natural consequence of such initiatives. Colleagues working together in the future will be less alike with respect to gender, cultural background, and age. These differences are important because they are associated with differences in perspectives, life-styles, attitudes, values, behaviors, and thought patterns.

Gender Diversity

In the late 1950s, when many of today's CEOs were entering the labor force as young professionals, they were being joined almost exclusively by other men. Back then, men were receiving 95% of the MBA degrees awarded and 90% of the bachelor's degrees in business. As these men are finishing their careers, 30 years later, the picture is dramatically different. In 1990, women received approximately 31% of the MBA degrees awarded, as well as 39% of the law degrees, 13% of engineering degrees (Butruille, 1990), and half of all undergraduate degrees.

Today, females are better educated than ever before *and* more are choosing to be in the active labor force. By the year 2000, the workforce is expected to be almost completely balanced with respect to gender. Furthermore, gender-based segregation within organizations is gradually decreasing. By 1987 women represented 35% of the population of the executive, management, and administrative workforces (Selbert, 1987), although in 1990 women held less than one-half of 1% of top jobs in major corporations (Fierman, 1990).

Working through gender diversity offers two major challenges to organizations. Ensuring that women's talents and abilities are fully utilized on the job is one challenge. Because women represent such a large portion of the workforce, maximizing their level of productivity is essential to achieving competitiveness. This often requires attacking the artificial barrier of a male-dominated corporate culture. As the CEO of Avon Products has noted, "Cultural discrepancies can come out in little ways. We used to have a lot of white male traditions at Avon. We bought season tickets to sporting events, and we called the annual management outing President's Golf Day. Our first two women officers complained . . . We realized these activities were no longer appropriate. They were too male-oriented and unwittingly made others feel like outsiders" (Edwards, 1991, p. 60). According to one recent survey, 60 % of women executives in larger firms feel that their firm's male-dominated corporate culture is an obstacle to the success (i.e., productivity) of women ("Welcome to the Woman-Friendly Company," 1990). These women may be underestimating the problem, however. A poll of 241 Fortune 1000 CEOs found that nearly 80% of these CEOs said there were barriers

that kept women from reaching the top. And of those who admitted that barriers exist, 81% identified stereotypes and preconceptions as problems women face (Fierman, 1990).

Many of the obstacles in corporations can be traced to society's stereotypes about men and women, which can create a catch-22 situation for women seeking advancement. A recent *New York Times* article describing the treatment of male and female politicians vividly depicted the situation:

> In 1987, she [Pat Schroeder, the Colorado Democrat] was denounced for reinforcing the stereotype that women are unable to coolly make tough decisions because she cried as she announced she would not run for President. When President Bush misted up as he addressed the Southern Baptist Convention in Atlanta a couple weeks ago, and confessed to crying when he made the decision to send Americans to war, *Time* magazine gushed over "his new expansiveness," his "more confiding" tone and his "new human dimension." (Dowd, 1991).

Adjusting to the fact that women in our society shoulder a disproportionate share of the responsibility for family care is a second challenge employers face. Failure to adjust to the differing needs of women (vs. men) with family responsibilities interferes with the ability of a company to fully utilize the talents of many of its female employees. When the family responsibilities of these women combine with outdated organizational norms that assume families put few restrictive demands on talented employees, artificial constraints block their promotion into jobs that could make full use of their skills and abilities. By adjusting to the differing family needs of various employees, employers will be better positioned to utilize more fully the talents of all employees. In addition, because the children in the families of today's workforce are the workforce of tomorrow, helping parents be both good family members and productive employees represents an investment in the future. As Peter Lynch, former head of the Magellan Mutual Fund, put it upon retiring at the age of 46 to spend time with his family, "Children are a great investment. They beat the hell out of stocks" ("Managing Generational Diversity," 1991).

Cultural Diversity

After gender diversity, cultural diversity is the second most frequently noted change in the workforce. *Workforce 2000* projections indicate that during this decade, only 58% of new entrants into the labor force will come from the "majority" population of white native Americans, with 22% of new entrants expected to be immigrants and the remainder being mostly African-Americans and Hispanic-Americans. The figures for new entrants contrast sharply with the status quo. Of the 1985 workforce, 83% were white native Americans. By the end of this decade, it is likely that less than 75% of the workforce will be white native Americans (Kutscher, 1989).

However, national figures do not tell the whole story. Regional differences are substantial. For example, our Hispanic population is concentrated in four regions: Mexican-Americans reside mostly in California and Texas, Puerto Ricans favor New York, and a majority of Cuban-Americans live in Florida. Our Asian population, which doubled in size during the 1980s, tends to be located in California, New York, and Hawaii. Our African-American population is more dispersed throughout the country, yet residential statistics for the cities they populate reveal greater segregation of African-Americans than that experienced by the more recently established Asian-American and Hispanic populations (Jaynes & Williams, 1989).

Use of broad labels such as *immigrant, native white, African-American, Hispanic-American,* and *Asian-American* conceals part of the story also, for within each of these broad categories hide many distinct ethnic cultures and subcultures. For example, the 1980 U.S. Census included 10 different categories for

Asian-American respondents to use to describe their ancestry, 4 categories for native respondents of Spanish origin, and 16 categories for white native respondents. And several more categories were added to assess the country of origin of foreign-born respondents.

Cultures have consequences that are easily experienced but more difficult to describe. For many people, the concept of culture conjures up images of the exotic customs, religions, foods, clothing, and life-styles that make foreign travel—as well as trips into the ethnic enclaves in our local cities—both stimulating and enjoyable. These aspects of a foreign culture can be experienced without ever engaging in conversation with someone from that culture. It is also easy for businesses to accommodate these aspects of cultural diversity—the cafeteria can offer a variety of ethnic foods and flexible policies can allow employees to observe whichever holidays they choose.

However, the deeper consequences of culture—such as values and ways of interpreting the world—cannot be handled merely by changing menus and policies. And it is these deeper consequences that organizations are struggling with today. When people with different habits and world views come together in the workplace, misunderstandings and conflicts inevitably occur as a result of dissimilar expectations and norms. Employees who behave according to the cultural adage that "the squeaky wheel gets the grease" may be viewed as offensive and undesirable teammates by employees who were taught that "the nail that sticks out gets hammered down." Employees behaving according to the latter adage may be viewed as ineffective by the former group of employees. Such misunderstandings can mean that valuable feedback about problems and successes is poorly transmitted or never becomes available for the organization's use and improvement.

Some readers might question whether cultural diversity is anything new. Skeptics might point out that the proportion of our population who are African-Americans has been relatively stable and the number of immigrants entering our country in recent years is only slightly higher than it was at the beginning of the century, when Europeans were the predominant newcomers (Richman, 1990).

Several factors seem to account for employers' current recognition that cultural diversity requires active management. First, although the proportion of African-Americans in this country has remained stable, their employment patterns have changed considerably during the recent affirmative action era, during which substantial integration occurred for clerical, technical, and skilled crafts (see "Race in the Workplace," 1991). Although often overlooked, education levels of African-Americans have risen during this time, also, providing another stimulant for workplace integration. Second, although the number of immigrants entering this country each year is relatively small, over the years the number of employees with strong ties to another national culture grows due to the continuing impact of nationality on second- and even third-generation citizens (e.g., see Fugita & O'Brien, 1991; Mydans, 1991). Third, the variety of the immigrant population has itself increased, as Asians and Latins from dozens of countries join the European immigrants. Fourth is the changing nature of the work, which requires that employees interact continuously with one another, with customers, and with suppliers. Fifth, and finally, global competition means that cultural diversity among working Americans is only part of the challenge. Insightful business leaders recognize that the common cultural experiences Americans share with one another make it easier to develop multicultural competence at home than abroad. Thus, they can use their multicultural domestic workforce as an educational resource and training ground for learning some of the tough lessons associated with conducting business internationally.

Age Diversity

Age diversity has received relatively little attention to date. Instead, attention has been directed to the implications of a graying workforce. In developed countries such as the United States, the median population age has been increasing. Along with this comes the bulging ranks of "older" employees trying to climb the corporate ladder, which creates havoc for traditional, hierarchical organizations. Such organizations are structured to accommodate large cohorts of entry-level employees and smaller cohorts of employees at more advanced career stages. These organizations tend to segregate employees by age. Organizational elders supervise the cohort that will soon replace them, who in turn supervise their own replacements. In such organizations, higher-ranked managers seldom rub elbows with the incoming generation of employees. As Mark Pastin put it, "You find CEOs who think the best thing about being CEO is that they don't have to mix it up with the riffraff" (Farnham, 1989). For managers who consider isolation from the lower ranks a perk, the ideal form of "contact" with lower-level employees may be sending them a memo or preparing a video for them to view.

But these old hierarchies are a dying breed. Competitive pressures have forced organizational restructuring and modern organizations to sport a new profile. At the same time that walls between organizational subunits are being torn down, the structure is being flattened. As layers of hierarchy are removed, previously segregated generations of employees find themselves working together and even rotating jobs amongst themselves.

Other factors contributing to greater intergenerational contact in the workplace include the entry (and reentry) into the workforce of middle-aged women, who often work in positions dominated by younger employees at the early stages of their careers; employment among former "retirees," who discover that their savings, Social Security checks, and other retirement benefits are inadequate to sustain their life-styles; and programs designed to capture more younger workers, such as internships and apprenticeships that permit high school students to work while earning academic credits.

In addition, in many organizations, the higher education levels of younger employees are considered more valuable than the experience accrued by older employees. Often, the result of all of these forces is an unfamiliar reversal of roles. As one restaurant manager put it, giving orders to older workers "is sort of like telling your grandma to clean the table." If younger generations find this uncomfortable, it is easy to imagine that their grandparents' generation does as well. As one retiree explained: "For 30 years I was a supervisor, and then one night I step out of one role and into another. . . . When you're being supervised by someone younger, you see a lot of things that aren't going to work, but you have to bite your tongue" (Hirsch, 1990, p. B1).

The combination of changes in the age distribution of employees and new flatter organization structures mean that four generations of workers can find themselves working side by side: the swing generation (1910-1929), who survived the Great Depression and World War II and are now over 60 years old; the silent generation (1930-45), which is a relatively small cohort that includes most of our current business and political leaders; the baby boomers (1946-64), whose large size gives them substantial social and economic clout; and the baby bust generation (1965-76), which has been characterized as distinguished by the wide schism that separates the haves and the have-nots ("Managing Generational Diversity," 1991). Even if employees from these four generations were all native Americans, they would differ fundamentally in their values and attitudes about work (see Elder, 1975; "Work Attitudes," 1986), their physical and mental functioning (Rhodes, 1983), and the everyday concerns that reflect their stages in the life cycle. Of course, within each generation, gender and cultural variety also abound, yielding a workforce that reflects the complete palette of human potential.

THE CHALLENGES OF WORKING THROUGH DIVERSITY

By now it should be clear that diversity is important to everyone in today's business organizations. In the longer term, effectively working through diversity is a strategic imperative for success in a highly competitive, global environment. More immediately, diversity is simply a fact of life that influences the recruitment, retention, motivation, and performance of employees. Short-term and long-term responses to diversity must address three challenges: availability, fairness, and synergy.

The Availability Challenge

In the past, employers often dealt with diversity by minimizing it where they could and by trying to ignore it when they couldn't get rid of it. This approach fits the efficiency mind set that has dominated the industrial era. When the supply of labor was abundant relative to demand, employers could control the diversity in their workforce by using selective hiring practices and by imposing standard operating procedures. From a position of relative power, companies could refuse to hire employees who were unable to work the standard workweek and punish those who were too often absent or tardy, or who just simply didn't fit in. Any negative side effects of such practices, such as lower morale or higher turnover, were treated as justifiable costs paid to ensure a smooth-running organization.

But as qualified employees become more scarce, employers must become more flexible. They can no longer say, "This is when and where you must be available for work, and this is the way we will treat you while you are here." Now they must adapt to potential employees who say: "This is when and where the work must be available for me to do it, and this is the way I must be treated if you want me to stay."

The Fairness Challenge

Flexible policies and practices help employers solve the availability issue created by a tight supply of diverse labor and inevitably bring them face to face with a second challenge, namely, ensuring that all employees and potential employees are treated fairly and feel that they are treated fairly. Employers who fail to meet this challenge squander their hard-won human resources.

During the past quarter century, concerns about fair employment practices were often driven by fear of the repercussions associated with discrimination lawsuits. Whether a company treated employees (and job applicants) fairly was, ultimately, judged by the courts using technical criteria, which were negotiated by attorneys, psychologists, and psychometricians. In this context, fair treatment came to mean equal treatment. Supervisors and managers were admonished to act as if they were blind to differences among employees, especially if those differences might be linked to sex, race, ethnicity, age, or national origin.

Ironically, in this context employees stimulated battles over fairness, but once those battles began, employees' evaluations of fairness were not the stakes companies sought to win. The stakes were money, reputation in the community (perhaps), and freedom to continue conducting business as usual. Times are changing, however. Now, regardless of whether employers find themselves fighting legal battles over fair employment practices, they must take employees' perceptions of fair treatment seriously.

From the perspectives of employees, issues of fairness are not constrained to sex, cultural background, age, or other legally protected attributes. Many other aspects of personal orientation are deemed worthy of tolerance and respect as well, including polit-ical views, sexual orientations, family situations, and various personal idiosyncracies. Employers who appear to favor some personal orientations and stifle others risk paying the price of low productivity due to a restricted pool of applicants, employee dissatisfaction, lack of commitment, turnover, and perhaps even sabotage.

The Synergy Challenge

The third challenge in working through diversity is unleashing and taking full advantage of the latent potential of groups. Groups are powerful motivational tools. When running effectively, work teams can be both more productive and more creative than individuals working alone. But when they function poorly, groups can have disastrous consequences for organizations, because the same social forces that push people to reach their fullest potential can also push people into unproductive and even destructive behavior patterns.

It is the potential for positive synergy that attracts employers to group-based organizational structures. For this potential to be realized, relationships among team members must be relatively positive. A long history of psychological research shows that excessive group conflict interferes with productivity (see Jackson, 1991). Conflict can close down communication channels, waste group energy, and create excessive amounts of turnover. This is not to say that all conflict should be squelched. To the contrary, constructive conflict must be encouraged to stimulate creative problem solving. Too little conflict may be a sign of complacency or stale, routine approaches to addressing new problems. The challenge for employers is to ensure that destructive conflict, which often arises when group members are unable to get along on a personal level, is minimized while ensuring that people with diverse ideas and perspectives are challenged to find resolutions to problems that everyone can endorse.

THE ROLE OF HUMAN RESOURCES MANAGEMENT PROFESSIONALS

Tackling these three challenges of workforce diversity is a key responsibility of modern human resources management professionals. They are the ones who are best able to educate business leaders about the strategic importance of working through diversity and to mobilize them to take immediate actions. And they are the ones with the knowledge and skills needed to analyze what their organizations need to do to respond to simultaneous changes in the nature of competition and the labor market. Finally, human resources professionals have available to them a wide range of tools for changing the attitudes and behaviors of their organization's employees. These tools include recruiting and selection methods, performance evaluation and appraisal, compensation and reward systems, training and development techniques, and models for redesigning both jobs and the organization within which jobs are performed.

To organizations that succeed in meeting these challenges will go the rewards of greater workforce productivity and improved organizational health. At the same time, employees in successful organizations will reap the benefits of employment conditions that are congruent with their individual needs and aspirations.

REFERENCES

Banas, P.A. (1988). Employee involvement: A sustained labor/management initiative at the Ford Motor Company. In J.P. Campbell & R.J. Campbell (Eds.), *Productivity in organizations: New perspectives from industrial and organizational psychology* (pp. 388–416). San Francisco: Jossey-Bass.

Bell, D. (1973). *The coming of post-industrial society: A venture in social forecasting*. New York: Basic Books.

Bureau of Labor Statistics. (1991, June). *Employment and earnings*. Washington, DC: U.S. Department of Labor.

Business International Corporation. (1991). *Developing effective global managers for the 1990s*. New York: Author.

Butruille, S.G. (1990, April). Corporate caretaking. *Training & Development Journal*, 25, 49–55.

Bylinski, G. (1990, July 2). Turning R&D into real products. *Fortune*, pp. 72–77.

Dowd, M. (1991, June 30). When men get a case of the vapors. *New York Times*, sect. E, p. 2.

Dumaine, B. (1990, May 7). Who needs a boss? *Fortune*, pp. 52–60.

Edwards, A. (1991, January). Special Report: Cultural diversity in today's corporation. *Working Woman*, pp. 45–60.

Elder, G.H., Jr. (1975). Age differentiation and the life course. *Annual Review of Sociology*, 1, 165–190.

Farnham, A. (1989, December 4). The trust gap. *Fortune*, pp. 56–78.

Fierman, J. (1990, July 30). Why women still don't hit the top. *Fortune*, pp. 40–62.

Fugita, S.S., & O'Brien, D.J. (1991). *Japanese American ethnicity: The persistence of the community*, Seattle: University of Washington Press.

Gummesson, E. (1987). Lip services—a neglected area of services marketing. *Journal of Services Marketing*, 1, 1–29.

Hirsch, J.S. (1990, February 26). Older workers chafe under young managers. *Wall Street Journal*, pp. B1, B6.

Jackson, S.E. (1991). Team composition in organizational settings: Issues in managing an increasingly diverse work force. In S. Worchel, W. Wood, & J.A. Simpson, (Eds.), *Group process and productivity* (pp. 138–173). Newbury Park, CA: Sage.

Jaynes, G.D., & Williams, R.M., Jr. (1989). *A common destiny: Blacks and American society*. Washington, DC: National Academy Press.

Kanter, R.M. (1989). *When giants learn to dance*. New York: Simon & Schuster.

Kanter, R.M. (1991, May-June). Transcending business boundaries: 12,000 world managers view change. *Harvard Business Review*, pp. 151–164.

Kutscher, R. (1989). Projections, summary and emerging issues. *Monthly Labor Review*, 112 (11), 66-74.

Managing generational diversity. (1991, April). *HRMagazine*, pp. 91–92.

Mydans, S. (1991, June 30). For these Americans, ties to Mexico remain. *New York Times*, p. L12.

Race in the Workplace: Is Affirmative Action working? (1991, July 8). *Business Week*, pp. 50–63.

Rhodes, S.R. (1983). Age-related differences in work attitudes and behavior: A review and conceptual analysis. *Psychological Bulletin*, 93, 328–367.

Richman, L.S. (1990, January 29). Let's change the immigration law—now. *Fortune*, p. 12.

Selbert R. (1987, November 16). Women at work. *Future Scan*, 554, pp. 1–3.

Sellers, P. (1990, June 4). What customers really want. *Fortune*, 58–68.

Towers Perrin & Hudson Institute. (1990). *Workforce 2000: Competing in a seller's market*. Valhalla, NY: Towers Perrin.

Welcome to the woman-friendly company where talent is valued and rewarded. (1990, August 6). *Business Week*, pp. 48–55.

Work attitudes: Study reveals generation gap. (1986, October 2). *Bulletin to Management*, p. 326.

Work teams can rev up paper-pushers, too. (1988, November 28). *Business Week*, pp. 64–72.

CORPORATE AND EXECUTIVE CRIMINAL LIABILITY

Appropriate standards, remedies, and managerial responses

John M. Holcomb and S. Prakash Sethi

American society has long been concerned with constraining corporate behavior to ensure that it remains within the parameters of societal expectations. Large corporations, as private collections of capital and resources, are correctly seen as vehicles of economic growth and societal prosperity. At the same time, bigness is viewed with alarm because the resources of private corporations are seen as giving them relative immunity from prosecution.

Historical evidence justifies such a belief. Legal and social action against corporate and management misbehavior* comes in large doses, but only periodically, often in response to major scandals, e.g., the Credit Mobilier and Whiskey Ring scandals after the Civil War, the Teapot Dome Scandal of the 1920s, Watergate and the illegal political payments of the 1970s, and the insider trading scandals of the 1980s. Big business has been unpopular since its rise at the turn of the century, and, in the aftermath of the latest scandals, two-thirds of the public has concluded that business executives put profit ahead of morality.[1]

Until the 1960s, corporations were rarely prosecuted; and executives, rarely prosecuted, were much less put in jail. Most perpetra-

---

Throughout this paper, the terms "corporate misbehavior," "corporate law violations," and "corporate crime" are used to include both the corporation and its top managers whether acting individually or collectively.

tors of white-collar crimes were treated more lightly than other criminals. When white-collar criminals were indeed prosecuted and punished, most cases pertained to violations of securities law—law protecting investor-owners from the misdeeds of managers. Such protection was considered critical to the survival of the corporate form of organization and the working of securities markets, which must depend on the trust of individual investors for professional managers. Though the Securities Act of 1933 and the Securities Exchange Act of 1934 have created a most efficient U.S. securities market, the stock-market crash of 1987 and the insider-trading violations of the 1980s have led to tougher legislation. The SEC may seek a penalty of three times the victim's damages under the Insider Trading Sanctions Act of 1984, and 1988 legislation provides penalties of up to ten years imprisonment and a $1 million fine for individuals, and a $2.5 million fine for firms.[2]

Other corporate law violations have included: corporate misbehavior that distorted the functioning of competitive markets and thereby harmed consumers. The prohibited activities included price-fixing, market collusion, and deceptive advertising, to name a few. The Sherman, Clayton, and Federal Trade Commission Acts regulate such conduct. One of the single largest criminal prosecutions for price-fixing was brought against electrical equipment manufacturers, including General Electric and Westinghouse, in 1960. Forty-five corporate officers pleaded guilty, and seven spent brief periods in jail. Total fines of $1.9 million were paid, and almost two thousand civil suits were settled for over $400 million.[3] Since that time, criminal sanctions under the Sherman Act have increased to fines of $100,000 and prison sentences of up to three years for individual offenses, and fines up to $1 million for corporate offenses.

In the last decade the definition of corporate crimes and the extent of society's determination to curb those crimes have expanded. Collectively called social welfare crimes, they deal with such issues as environmental pollution, workplace hazards, and product safety. Society's concern to create a balance between corporate power and public safety in these areas is, in part, reflected in the creation of such agencies as the Consumer Product Safety Commission, Environmental Protection Agency (EPA), Occupational Health and Safety Administration (OSHA), and the enactment of laws dealing with production, transportation, and disposal of hazardous wastes in air, water, and on ground; workers' right to know about the hazards of their work environment and protection from employer pressure to work under unsafe working conditions; elimination of discriminatory employment practices; and, consumer protection through product testing and approval, establishment of safety standards, labelling, inspection, and product recall requirements.

Legislation and enforcement regarding social welfare crimes have expanded rapidly *and* contentiously. This development has the potential to dramatically affect corporate growth and profitability and the manner in which corporations are organized and managed. Not only are we now defining as crimes acts of omission, as well as commission, but also violations of legality *regardless* of their ultimate impact on corporate actions and their societal consequences. Furthermore, the gradual stripping of respectability from corporate executives is leading to their treatment as common criminals. Prosecutors are deploying new powers and using new strategies to bring corporations and executives to justice under laws such as The Racketeer Influenced and Corrupt Organizations Act (RICO).[4] Thus, the United States is now catching up with Western Europe where concern with social welfare crimes has long been an integral part of the legal and social fabric.

MAGNITUDE AND SCOPE OF CORPORATE CRIMES

There has been a surge in the reporting and prosecution of corporate crime. The National Institute of the Law Enforcement Assistance Administration (LEAA), seeking to determine the frequency of "initiation[s] of enforcement action" by twenty-four federal agencies during 1975 and 1976 against violators of the law, analyzed data for the 582 largest publicly owned corporations (477 manufacturing, 18 wholesale, 66 retail, and 21 service). LEAA found that at least one action had been initiated against 60 percent of those corporations. In the manufacturing sector, an average of 4.8 actions were taken against 300 parent corporations. Almost half of the parent manufacturing corporations had one or more serious or moderate violations. More than 40 percent of the manufacturing corporations engaged in repeated violations. Over three-fourths of all actions were in the manufacturing, environmental and labor area.[5] Though no current studies exist, a 1982 study by *U.S. News and World Report* found that more than 20 percent of Fortune 500 companies had been convicted of at least one major crime or had paid civil penalties for serious illegal behavior between 1970 and 1980.[6]

Since the Department of Justice organized its environmental-crimes unit in 1982, former Attorney General Richard Thornburg observes, 703 indictments and 517 convictions have been obtained; fines, restitution, and forfeitures totalling over $56 million have been assessed; and more than 316 years

TABLE 1.   Recent Punishments for Financial and Security Crimes by Corporations. Corporations and Executives Charged for Criminal and Civil Violations Under SEC Act.

Corporations	Crime	Punishment
1. Drexel Burnham Lambert Group (DBL)	Criminal charges of mail, wire and security fraud against DBL. Mr. Michael Milken, Head of Junk Bond Operations, charged with 98 counts of insider trading, mail fraud, racketeering, etc.	In 1988, DBL pleaded guilty to six felonies and paid $650 million in fines and restitution. DBL was also barred from paying a bonus of $200 million to Milken. DBL was barred by FSLIC from underwriting junk bond issues from which it drew 90 percent of its profits. Milken pleaded guilty to six felonies in 1990, agreed to pay $600 million in penalties, and was later sentenced to 10 years in prison, 3 years of probation and 5,400 hours of community service. In 1992, Milken has agreed to pay an additional $500 million to settle all civil litigation against him, and 200 other Drexel executives have agreed to pay $800 million toward the civil settlement.
2. Ivan F. Boesky Co.	Criminal charge of conspiring to file false statements.	Ivan Boesky pleaded guilty and was sentenced to 3 years in prison. He was also fined $100 million as a penalty.
3. Lincoln Savings and Loan Co., California	Fraud and mismanagement.	Lincoln Co. was seized by government management and its collapse will cost the taxpayers $200 million. Charles Keating was convicted of 17 California securities-fraud violations in 1992, and several law and accounting firms paid over $200 million to settle civil charges for failing to disclose Lincoln's fraud.
4. Warner Lambert Co.	Death of 6 employees due to explosion was tried as 6 counts of manslaughter and 6 counts of criminally negligent homicide.	Eventually the W. L. Co. was exonerated of criminal charges. However, a judgment approved by the court involved more than $16 million to be paid: Warner Lambert $11 million; $0.5 million each from Hamac Hansella, a west German machinery manufacturer; Petrochemicals, Texas; and Liquid Carbonics, New Jersey. Additional payments were made by 12 other defendants. The Warner factory was closed and the company spent another $7 million to help employees who lost their jobs.

SOURCE: S. Prakash Sethi and Praveen Chopra, "Corporate Crimes and Executive Liability: Analysis, Trends and Policy Guidelines," in S. Prakash Sethi, Paul Steidlmeier, and Cecilia M. Falbe, eds., *Scaling the Corporate Wall: Readings in Social Issues of the Nineties* (Englewood Cliffs, NJ: Prentice Hall, 1991), 203–30.p

of jail time have been imposed.[7] A great many of the environmental statutes have been amended to reclassify misdemeanor offenses to felonies.[8] Enforcement of these laws has been stiffened. For example, The Pollution Prosecution Act of 1990 provides for a quadrupling of the number of special agents by 1995 and increases technical support and training of state and federal law enforcement officials.[9] Meanwhile, state law enforcement offices have also strengthened their attack on environmental crimes.[10]

Currently, 20 to 30 percent of all prosecuted offenses involve antitrust violations;

government fraud cases, 20 to 25 percent; environmental prosecutions, 10 to 15 percent; private fraud cases 10 to 15 percent; and lesser percentages for currency-reporting violations, tax fraud, import and export violations, and food and drug violations.[11] While the penalties for corporate environmental violations are the most vivid, sanctions for other corporate violations have increased as well. Between 1987 and 1990, the average total sanction for corporate violators, based on a biased sample that likely overstates the increase somewhat, went from a little over $320,000 to nearly $2.4 million.[12] As a result of the more vigorous prosecution of corporate crime and increasing penalties, corporate lawyer Joseph H. Flom has stated, companies face "a greater threat to corporate control from inadequate management [resulting in] a failure to be vigilant in terms of what is potential criminal conduct" than from hostile takeovers.[13] Both corporations and their executives must contend with the rising tide of criminal enforcement: about 70 percent of indictments for federal environmental crimes are brought against individuals, while 30 percent are brought against corporations.[14]

The above data notwithstanding, the extent of corporate criminal activity and its rate of growth remain unknown. The institutional nature of corporate crimes and the technical nature of many law violations make detection and prosecution extremely difficult. This is especially so for more serious crimes where the complicity of the entire organization impedes identification of the individual wrongdoer and the person ultimately responsible. At the same time, there is a widespread and increasing public belief that most corporate crimes remain undetected, and, moreover, that laws concerning corporate and executive crimes, especially those in the social-welfare arena, are weakly enforced and lightly punished.[15] Corporate and executive law violations and their punishment have, therefore, emerged as one of the major concerns of public-policy debate in the United States and are likely to remain so for the foreseeable future.

SCOPE OF THE PAPER

In theory, corporations and managers make economically rational decisions, which by definition are premeditated. Therefore, a system of well designed punishment (fines and incarceration) ought to yield optimum general and specific deterrence, equitable and fair restitution, and compensation for the victims of such acts. However, corporate-law violations occur in an environment of internal and external factors that severely limit the scope of "rational" behavior. There is also a large gap between "law in books" and "law in action." Corporate executives do not always act rationally, either on behalf of their corporations or themselves. And a great many of our laws and enforcement procedures are developed without much regard to institutional character and ethos, organization structure and decision-making processes, competitive environment, and peer group pressures. Absent such regard, many laws fail to achieve their intended purposes, and also cause much unintended social injury in terms of productivity, innovation, risk-taking, economic growth, and societal welfare.

This paper presents a framework which examines market and institutional characteristics that lead to corporate and executive crimes and how these processes must be linked to any remedial procedures incorporated in various laws and enforcement actions. Next, it discusses various legal issues pertaining to corporate and executive liability for corporate crimes. Finally, it identifies some of the unresolved issues and suggests policy guidelines and future research.

A FRAMEWORK FOR ANALYZING CORPORATE ILLEGAL BEHAVIOR

Corporate illegal behavior may be best analyzed in terms of major areas of activity and market and institutional control mechanisms [Figure 1].[16] It follows, therefore, that opportunities and rewards for illegal behavior will increase in direct proportion to the failure of these mechanisms to operate efficiently. Ex-

FIGURE 1. Business-Society Interface: Modes of Societal Control

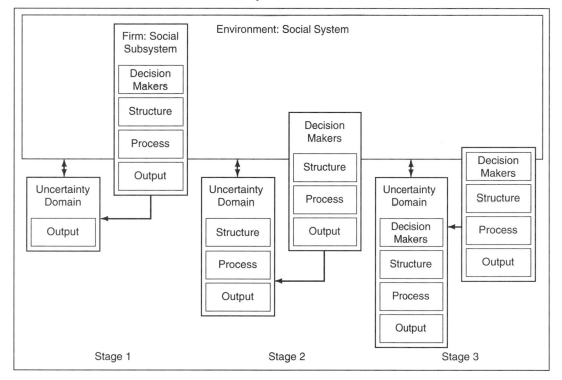

ploitation of opportunities for illegal behavior will also depend on competitive market pressures, corporate ethos, personal predilections, and ethical standards of individual managers, and group norms both within the organization and in the reference corporate community. Any legal measures designed to curb existing corporate practices deemed socially undesirable, or to channel future corporate activities in a more socially desirable direction, must, therefore, take into account the point of impact of such laws and enforcement actions within the corporate decision locus, market and competitive conditions, and social norms of behavior.

Corporate Illegality Arising Out of Failures of Market Institutions. In a competitive market, social control over economic organizations is exercised through the nature of a company's output. When a corporation's services or products do not meet society's needs,

they are not purchased; the corporation's ability to acquire and pay for physical and human resources is restricted and owners-entrepreneurs are not rewarded for the use of their capital and assumption of risk. Under this system, all needed changes are communicated to the corporation via the market's responses to its products and services. Companies must respond to these needs or eventually cease to exist. No other social-control mechanisms are considered necessary [Figure 1, Stage 1].

As companies become large and diversified, however, they become increasingly immune to market discipline. Through strategic planning, product innovation, and market domination, corporate managers constantly strive to insulate their companies from the tyranny of the marketplace. To the extent they succeed, market signals for change become weak and diffuse. Corporate managers become unwilling or unable to initiate orga-

TABLE 2. Punishments for Recent Corporate Crimes of Health and Safety. Corporations and Executives Charged for Criminal and Civil Violations Under OSHA.

Corporations	Crime	Punishment
1. Iowa Beef Processors	Worker injuries due to safety hazards.	The initial fine of $2.6 million was increased to $5.6 million for lack of cooperation on the part of management to create safe working conditions through modernization of plant as ordered by OSHA. This is OSHA's largest fine ever.
2. National Film Recovery Systems Inc., Illinois	Criminal charge of murder and involunatary manslaughter for the death of a worker due to use of cyanide about which worker was uninformed. In addition, management was charged on 20 counts of reckless conduct.	Owner as well as manager involved were each sentenced to 25 years in the custody of the Illinois Department of Corrections and also fined $10,000 each on murder convictions. In addition, each defendant was fined $10,000 for involuntary manslaughter and $14,000 each for reckless conduct conviction.
3. Sabine Consolidated Inc.	Death of 2 construction workers on the job was tried as criminally negligent homicide.	Three executives were indicted on criminal charges.
4. United American Bank	Illegal loans.	The Chief Loan Officer, Mr. Barr, was sentenced twice to federal penitentiaries and is currently serving 18 years. FDIC was required to pay $700 million for illegal loans.
5. Vernon Savings and Loan, Texas	Falsification of financial statements. Sham transactions to earn bogus profits and generating two sets of minutes for board meetings.	Vernon Savings declared insolvent. Don Dixon who pushed the bank into over $350 million of debt by sham transactions has been charged by FSLIC for racketeering. Almost all of its thrift loans were in default.

SOURCE: S. Prakash Sethi and Praveen Chopra, "Corporate Crimes and Executive Liability: Analysis, Trends and Policy Guidelines," in S. Prakash Sethi, Paul Steidlmeier and Cecilia M. Falbe, eds., *Scaling the Corporate Wall: Readings in Social Issues of the Nineties* (Englewood Cliffs, NJ: Prentice Hall, 1991), 203–30.

nizational changes that would enable them to respond to changing societal expectations because to do so would mean giving up part of the benefits generated through earlier efforts at market insulation.

When changes in corporate behavior become difficult to effect through market signals, social forces are directed to effect changes through control of a corporation's production processes and decision-making structures—that is, by controlling and modifying the corporation's internal environment. Thus, elements of the decision-making structure and process previously internal to the organization become subject to outside pressure, external scrutiny, and control. A regulatory framework is developed to achieve this end [Figure 1, Stage 2].

Process Controls.   Process controls direct corporations to undertake their production and sales activities in a pre-specified manner. Thus, such controls tend to create uniformity in operating behavior, thereby taking away any competitive advantage a firm may have in using different production and marketing techniques. In the traditional areas of government regulation of economic activities, process controls have included types of marketing practices considered unfair and, therefore, illegal. New social legislation in such diverse areas as pollution controls and environmental safeguards, in-plant worker safety, and protection of employees from job discrimination based on sex, color, age, or ethnic origin, has imposed a variety of process controls on corporations.

Controls on Persons.   A failure to change corporate behavior through regulation of output results in attempts to modify behavior of decision makers through punishment and deterrence [Figure 1, Stage 3]. The belief is that imposing penalties on managers will divert along more socially desirable paths ingenuity and resourcefulness previously employed to subvert legal requirements. By imposing performance criteria on managers, government obviates the need to demonstrate how a given objective might be accomplished and shifts the burden of explaining why it has not been achieved.

LEGAL APPROACHES TO CURBING CORPORATE AND EXECUTIVE ILLEGAL BEHAVIOR

Society has a right to use criminal penalties and imprisonment of executives to deter corporate misdeeds. There may indeed be circumstances where corporate executives are held to higher standards of accountability than those imposed on individuals acting in their own capacities. The highly complex and difficult to detect nature of many corporate crimes; the higher level of intellect and premeditation needed to commit and conceal those crimes; and the potential harm inflicted on society because of the enormous resources of the corporation justify such a criterion. Law violations by corporations and executives not only inflict enormous pain and injury on large segments of society, they also undermine the working of a market economy and private enterprise, thereby eroding the very foundations of society. The question, therefore, is not about the right, necessity and desirability of imposing such penalties, but about designing a system of punishment that is appropriate to the magnitude of the crime, is well crafted as an instrument of general and specific deterrence, and is equitable and fair both to the culprit and victim in specific terms and serves the larger purposes of society in general terms. A system of criminal penalties for corporations and executives should serve four basic objectives: deterrence, rehabilitation, incapacitation, and retribution.

Deterrence.   For deterrence to be effective, either in specific or general terms, the costs of committing the act to the corporation and the executives involved, either in terms of fines or other penalties, must exceed its current and potential benefits. It has been argued that civil, as opposed to criminal, penalties under such circumstances are equally effective and more efficient in terms of time and costs. This argument, however, suffers from faulty logic. Not all executives and corporations are always driven only by economic considerations nor are they deterred from illegal acts solely because of financial pain. Given a firm's competitive position and an executive's power in the organizational hierarchy, all or most of financial penalties may be transferred to other groups, e.g., consumers, investors, and so on. In theory, a fine that harms shareholders should motivate them to ensure that a diligent management team is in place, one that will create the internal controls necessary to prevent illegal behavior. In reality, absent mass tort litigation, it is uncertain what level of fine is necessary to activate the owners of the corporation to assert control.

The cost-benefit deterrence analysis also ignores noneconomic values to be served by criminal prosecution that also advance the goal of deterrence. Since the effect on the victims of corporate economic crimes is not so different from that of common burglaries—both deprive the victims of their money—a sense of social justice requires that corporate executives be subjected to the painful experience of incarceration. Moreover, the stigma attached to a criminal conviction may damage the reputation of a company, thereby affecting its earning potential and corporate power. Similarly, corporate criminals may have a greater fear from the stigma of incarceration and, therefore, may be deterred from committing such illegal acts.[17]

Rehabilitation.   The rehabilitative effect of criminal penalties occurs by prompting executives to reflect on the social harm they have caused, even though in many cases they may have acted solely for the benefit of their corporations. However, it would be gratuitous to absolve an intelligent executive from the consequences of his/her illegal acts just because they were performed in the corporations's interest. Criminal penalties for the corporation will force executives to avoid criminal acts in order to protect their reputation. Although, corporations cannot be incarcerated, their managers will, nevertheless, be mindful of the enormous economic costs and potential loss of authority and even of their jobs that might occur should the stigma of criminal conviction induce other companies and individuals to refrain from doing business with them.[18]

Incapacitation. Recidivism in the case of corporate crime occurs. Therefore, criminal penalties, such as restrictions from engaging in particular lines of business, frequent reporting to regulators, and in extreme cases, closing down the enterprise are legitimate uses of criminal penalties to protect society from repeated criminal behavior.[19]

Retribution. Just as criminal law is more effective than civil law at incapacitating both executives and corporations, so also it is more adroit at exacting retribution. The concept of fairness underlying retributive justice requires that corporations be punished for gaining an unfair advantage over other corporations or over their stakeholders through criminal activity.[20]

INDIVIDUAL EXECUTIVE LIABILITY

Prior to the current initiatives of the Department of Justice in prosecuting corporate executives for environmental crimes, court cases have validated criminal liability for individual executives, especially high corporate officials. In the first major Supreme Court precedent in this regard, *U.S. v. Park*,[21] the chief executive officer of Acme Markets, a national retail grocery chain, was held criminally liable for violating provisions of the Food, Drug and Cosmetic Act. Mr. Park failed to insure that Acme Markets eliminate rodent infestation from a Baltimore warehouse. He claimed he had delegated that responsibility, even though the company had been given a previous warning by the FDA. But the U.S. Supreme Court concluded that, due to Park's authority and "responsible relationship" to the violations, he was personally liable for failing to ensure compliance with the FDA order.

In the second case, *People* v. *Film Recovery Systems, Inc.*,[22] the Cook County State's Attorney in Illinois brought murder charges against three corporate officers, the president of the company, the plant manager, and the plant foreman. After exposure to a "mixing" tank in the plant that contained sodium cyanide, a worker died of acute cyanide toxicity. Before the incident all three corporate officials were aware of the dangers of cyanide poisoning at the plant. Nevertheless, no corrective actions had been taken. Each defendant was sentenced to twenty-five years in prison on the murder charge, and the company and its parent were each convicted of involuntary manslaughter and fourteen counts of reckless conduct for which they were fined a total of $34,000.

In a third case, *People* v. *Warner-Lambert Co.*[23] four managers were eventually acquitted of criminally negligent homicide and manslaughter on fairly narrow grounds in a much criticized decision. An explosion in a Freshen-Up chewing gum plant had injured fifty workers and six died from the incident. The company's insurer had previously warned the company of the hazardous condition at the plant and had recommended various methods to reduce the danger, all of which were rejected by the company in favor of a less expensive short-term solution. The New York Court of Appeals concluded that without precise evidence of the actual triggering cause of the explosion, it could not find that the defendants should have foreseen its cause. Despite its ruling on the foreseeability barrier, the court did not broadly rule that the four managers were otherwise exempt from liability.

CORPORATE CRIMINAL LIABILITY

Corporate criminal liability in the United States follows one of two standards, i.e., vicarious liability and the standard set forth in the Model Penal Code (MPC). Federal criminal liability is based on vicarious liability, while the states are divided over embracing vicarious liability or the MPC. In addition, both federal and state governments may write specific statutes to encompass certain crimes, e.g., the charges brought in the Exxon Valdez case.

Vicarious liability, or respondeat superior, is a tort law concept that has gradually been absorbed into the criminal law. Under this concept, the criminal intent of a corporate agent is automatically imputed to the corporation when the agent commits a crime within the scope of employment with the intent of benefitting the corporation. A string of court cases has made the last two qualifications almost meaningless, thereby creating corporate culpability by the mere fact of an agent's committing a crime. Thus vicarious liability is said to accrue even where such conduct was specifically forbidden by corporate policy and the corporation made good-faith efforts to prevent the crime. Similarly, courts deem criminal conduct by an agent to be "with the intent to benefit the corporation" even when the corporation had no knowledge of the criminal conduct and received no actual benefit from the offense.[24] Most legal commentators believe that such a broad construction of a corporation's vicarious liability goes too far, because the courts have rendered nugatory the distinction between criminal and civil law: when there is no evidence of actual corporate intent, a finding of vicarious criminal liability against corporations trivializes the criminal law; moreover, there must be evidence of moral culpability to merit application of the criminal law. Broad-ranging vicarious liability invites contempt for the law.

While federal law follows vicarious liability, several states follow the definition of liability created by the Model Penal Code. The essential components of MPC are: strict liability for certain regulatory offenses; liability for negligent supervision of employees; and liability if the offense was authorized, requested, commanded, performed or recklessly tolerated by the board of directors or by a high managerial official. Of the three, the third standard applies to most corporate criminal violations. Since a corporation can be liable only if there is involvement by a high corporate official, and since board members and officers may have little to do with the daily operations of the firm, the MPC standard seems to excessively restrict liability. A corporation is not held liable when it should be. Furthermore, since lack of awareness by senior executives may be a defense for the corporation in such a case, the MPC standard encourages top management to insulate itself from knowledge of corporate illegal behavior.[25]

The MPC standard offers one major advantage over the vicarious liability standard: it provides for a "due diligence defense," by allowing corporations to absolve themselves of liability by demonstrating that senior executives had taken steps to prevent the illegal conduct, which nonetheless occurred. Courts, however, have ruled that the mere existence of prohibitive policies is not sufficient for a due diligence defense. Corporations must take the next step and enforce those policies. For example, in cases involving worker safety, employers must demonstrate that they have preventive policies, have taken steps to discover violations, and have penalized such violations.[26] This is analogous to the defenses that corporations must mount to escape vicarious liability for sexual harassment offenses by managers.

The result of this examination is that neither the vicarious liability standard nor the

Model Penal Code standard may be adequate to confront the issue of corporate criminal liability. While the doctrine of respondeat superior is over-inclusive and may create excessive corporate liability, even when the firm attempts to control the illegal acts of its agents, the MPC standard seem under-inclusive and fails to establish corporate liability except when there is willful ignorance by top management.

U.S. SENTENCING COMMISSION GUIDELINES

In an effort to increase the deterrence effect of fines and create some uniformity in imposing sentences, the U.S. Sentencing Commission created sentencing standards, covering individuals and organizations convicted of antitrust offenses, that went into effect on November 1, 1987. Guidelines covering all other organizational offenses went into effect on November 1, 1991. According to the guidelines, fines can be levied for up to four times the pecuniary loss caused by, or four times the pecuniary gain resulting from, an offense.[27]

Sufficient experience has not yet been accumulated in working with the guidelines. However, legal scholars have pointed out some obvious drawbacks. They argue that if society derives a benefit from an activity, firms should be fined only on the basis of the harm caused, and not the economic gain accrued. For example, if fines for oil spills were based on economic gain derived from oil exploration, rather than the harm caused, oil exploration itself could be over-deterred.[28] Basing fines instead on the social harm created encourages prosecutors to target more egregious offenses against society.

A further problem with the sentencing guideline, even if it is restricted to penalizing a firm solely on the basis of harm caused, is its failure to consider economic sanctions other than federal criminal fines. Such fines might be based on twice the harm caused, and additional financial penalties might also be assessed against a firm, perhaps by other

governmental units,[29] thereby greatly increasing the magnitude of total fines to a level where, by discouraging companies from taking entrepreneurial risks, they might prove counterproductive. Conversely, it is not always possible to quantify the harm—for example, that caused by certain food and drug violations—inflicted by the corporate offender.[30]

For a fine to be effective in deterring a corporate offender and for the offender to rationally calculate the costs and benefits of violating the law, it is not sufficient for the potential violator to know that fines are increasing. The offender must also realize the probability of being detected and punished. Becker's analysis of "optimal penalties" suggests that the penalty should equal the net social cost of the crime divided by the probability of detection.[31] Cohen suggests, therefore, that criminal sanctions should be inversely related to the probability of detection. "Offenses that are always detected do not require large punitive multiples, while those that are difficult to detect may require fines that are multiples of losses in order to account for the possibility that some offenders will not be caught."[32] A major barrier to the effectiveness of even large fines, however, is the improbability of detecting many corporate crimes. Some authorities believe that most corporate violations can be easily concealed, and that many victims of corporate crime do not realize they have been injured. Moreover, "we lack even an approximate estimate of how much white-collar crime occurs or how often it results in conviction."[33] To increase fines when a corporation believes its violations are invulnerable to detection serves little deterrent purpose.

Another important aspect of the sentencing guidelines on monetary sanctions is the consideration of corporate size in the level of the fine. The reasoning is that: (a) compared to the total number of organizations, relatively few are large corporations; (b) the difficult issue of vicarious liability is typically more critical for larger organizations; and, (c) a larger fine is needed to sufficiently punish and deter a larger organization.[34] Large corporations have been convicted and fined less often than small companies, a trend that has been especially troubling to environmental advocates.[35] However, there is evidence from 1988-1990 data that the number of large corporations prosecuted and sentenced has been increasing.[36] Meanwhile, there is disagreement over the extent to which large corporations actually *commit* more crime than smaller firms. Etzioni, in testimony to the Sentencing Commission, stated that two-thirds of large corporations have been involved in significant illegal acts.[37] Based on earlier studies, other commentators believe that large corporations are more likely than small ones to commit criminal violations, and that those violations will be more serious.[38] Others, however, believe that managers in large corporations commit fewer crimes, because they are more risk averse and benefit less from the economic gains of illegal behavior than managers in smaller firms.[39]

The sentencing guidelines also presume that *aggravating factors* are present in any corporate conviction, and place the burden on the defendant to show any mitigating factors that might prevent imposition of the maximum sentence. Such mitigating factors include:

- noninvolvement in the offense of any policy-influencing personnel;
- appropriate steps to prevent the commission of crimes;
- appropriate steps to detect crimes that have been committed;
- self-reporting of offenses to authorities;
- cooperating fully with the government's investigation; accepting responsibility;
- swift, voluntary remedial action;
- disciplining individuals responsible for the offense; and
- responding to the occurrence of an offense by taking steps to prevent further offenses.[40]

Moreover, in 1991, the Department of Justice announced guidelines for the prosecution of environmental crimes that embody some of the same elements as the recently adopted sentencing guidelines. The DOJ decisional factors include: whether the disclosure was voluntary; degree of cooperation; extensiveness of compliance program and efforts to prevent violations; pervasiveness of noncompliance; internal disciplinary action; and, subsequent compliance efforts.[41]

The new Sentencing Guidelines also create a new standard of "probation or probationary period" that can be imposed as a type of sentence, not simply as an alternative to the imposition of a sentence. Probation may be ordered to: impose restitution, a remedial order, or community service; to safeguard the defendant's ability to make payments on a deferred fine; or "to ensure that changes are made within the organization to reduce the likelihood of future criminal conduct."[42]

DIFFICULTIES IN IMPOSING CRIMINAL PENALTIES FOR CORPORATE AND EXECUTIVE CRIMES—DRAWBACKS IN THE CURRENT SYSTEM

Assessing criminal liability for corporations and executives poses a number of problems related to finding the locus of a particular crime, determining culpability, establishing the appropriate level of penalties, persuading the judges and juries to impose them, and evaluating their deterrent effect. Analysis must keep in mind that neither the crimes nor their punishment can be evaluated outside their social context.

Corporate Executive as "the Criminal."   Most laws dealing with corporate crimes and their enforcement are aimed at people with a *high socioeconomic status* who share an affinity—through schools, clubs, professional backgrounds, religious affiliation and other social institutions—with the groups responsible for making laws and enforcing them, legislators, judges, and prosecutors. Differences between ordinary law offenders and the law-violating executives are that the latter group often has an elaborate and widely accepted ideological rationalization for the offenses and possesses great social significance and economic power.[43] The violator may identify himself as a law breaker but not as a criminal. Kadish, calling this the problem of moral neutrality, questions the criminalization of morally neutral conduct.[44] White-collar crimes often carry nominal penalties, even when the executive is sentenced to prison.

Connected to the issue of culpability is the concept of *mens rea*, i.e., there must be a guilty mind or wrongful purpose for a criminal offense to be punishable. In determining the presence or absence of *mens rea*, three elements must be considered:

- Did the individual make a choice to commit a wrongful act?
- Was this choice freely made? and
- Did the individual know or could he have recognized the wrongfulness of his act?

It is usually quite difficult to amass the evidence of such individual *mens rea*.

A third problem has to do with the *communal character of many corporate crimes* and the difficulty in *identifying particular individual(s) who should be held responsible* for a particular offense. The group orientation of corporate crimes depersonalizes business leadership. Thus, while the impact of corporate crime may be serious for the society and often more violent in its consequences than a multiplicity of individually committed street crimes, the corporate personality diffuses the individual burden of guilt. Through a battery of accountants, lawyers, scientists, and other experts, management can demonstrate the bureaucratic imperative of shared responsibility, thereby denying or seriously weakening the notion of personal obligation.[45] It is often impossible to pinpoint the locus of any decision.[46] Moreover, some decisions are genuinely collective.

Courts have acted on this reality by holding corporations liable on the basis of their collective knowledge. In *United States* v. *T.I.M.E.-D.C., Inc.*,[47] a regulatory case, the court held that the requisite knowledge for a violation need not be vested exclusively in one person and concluded that, "the corporation is considered to have acquired the collective knowledge of its employees."[48] Because corporate acts are often the products of collective knowledge and collective intent, it is futile to try to locate specific individuals responsible for such acts. On the basis of the concept of collective knowledge, it is a small step to recognize the concept of organizational *mens rea*. Some legal analysts and judges have already moved in that direction.

A fourth issue concerns the impact of individual punishment on the behavior of the corporate entity. If only the individual executive is liable, there may be overwhelming pressures by the corporation to engage in illegal activity, for the sake of servicing its bottom-line interests. The internal sanction for avoiding risk, either demotion or dismissal, may approach the severity of a criminal sanction for preferring risk and crossing over the line into criminal behavior. Even if criminal punishment is viewed as a more severe consequence, its probability of application may be viewed as much lower, considering slight chances of either detection or prosecution.[49]

If the strategy of criminal prosecutors would be to pursue individual executives, that would provide an incentive for corporations to take legal violations less seriously. As one writer has put it, "Corporate policies may encourage illegal behavior, often implicitly, then simply allow the individuals who are caught to be jettisoned."[50] Even the record of the accelerated environmental enforcement of recent years demonstrates that most of the defendants are lower level managers, or "custodians."[51] A legal approach that targeted individuals would encourage corporations to essentially designate "vice presidents responsible for going to jail."[52] "In such an environment, the agents are cogs in a wheel. Those convicted are simply replaced by others whose original propensity to obey the law is similarly overcome by a corporate ethos that encourages illegal acts."[53] Only through corporate liability is there a motivation for structural reform.[54]

Corporate Entity as "the Criminal." Treating corporations as criminals also creates a series of ticklish issues pertaining to identifying crimes, assessing their magnitude, and creating penalties that meet the criteria of general and specific deterrence in accord with social norms. These problems generally fall into two categories, involving the current standards of corporate liability and the common remedies applied in the form of cash fines.

Conflict with Social Mores. The impact of violations in social welfare crimes, e.g., pollution controls, is highly diffuse and indirect, while the cost of compliance can be shown to have immediate and direct effect on certain identifiable constituencies that exert constant pressure on management to minimize the impact of these costs. The manager's group norms do not consider a violation of these laws to be antisocial. The statutes are considered nuisances or regulations imposed by overzealous bureaucrats. Support from group norms for the manager's behavior tends to break down further his self-perception as a law violator. Fines are sometimes considered license fees or nuisance payments for doing business, and, therefore, of little value either as specific deterrents (discouragement of repeated violations by the same individual) or as general deterrents (discouragement of others from law violations). Evidence does exist, however, that higher fines can lead to a higher level of legal compliance.

Organizational Mens Rea. Some commentators take the position that intent is not simply an attribute of persons but that corporations can manifest it through their policies. Some philosophers even maintain that such policies, structures, and incentives manifest moral intent, not just legal intent.[55] Various legal tests might be applied by judges to determine the existence of a corporate intent.

One commentator suggests the following three-part test:

- Did a corporate practice or policy violate the law? or,
- Was it reasonably foreseeable that a corporate practice or policy would result in a corporate agent's violation of the law? or,
- Did the corporation adopt a corporate agent's violation of the law?[56]

Evidence of such a corporate intent might be ascertained through standard operating procedures, policy statements, or minutes of committee, task force, or board meetings.

Protection of Innocent Shareholders. Corporate fines are often opposed because they harm "innocent shareholders," but some economists would argue that is part of the risk shareholders assume by participating in the financial marketplace. As one commentator points out, "A fine that nullifies expected gain merely counterbalances the positive side of a shareholder's risk equation: the chance that his corporation will engage in criminal activity and will escape undetected."[57] Moreover, shareholders may neutralize their risk by diversifying their share holdings, and any risk might be reflected in a lower share price at the time of acquisition. If the market notifies shareholders that there is a risk in an investment, they can assume responsibility by advocating corporate internal-control policies to minimize the risk.

Post Hoc Character of Many Corporate Crimes. It would be inaccurate to assume than an increase in highly visible types of corporate law violations indicates widespread flouting of laws by corporations. An important segment of corporate crimes is highly technical in nature, and only after the courts have spoken can one say a law has been broken. It is often difficult to distinguish, without benefit of hindsight, between innovative business practices that will eventually be approved and those that will eventually be stigmatized and punished as crime.[58] Landmark cases may indicate a propensity to probe the law's farthest limits—quite a different practice from deliberate infractions of a known law.[59] The vagueness of many of the more recent statutory violations creates still additional compliance problems. Because of the difficulty of defining proscribed conduct, courts are reluctant to impose penalties on conduct whose specific illegality is doubtful. Finally, many laws, such as environmental statutes and campaign finance regulations, contain technical reporting requirements, violations of which may not manifest the requisite criminal intent that judges are prone to punish.

THE UNRESOLVED AGENDA AND GUIDELINES FOR FUTURE ACTION

The trend toward harsher penalties for corporate executives comes just when opinion polls indicate that business credibility in the public eye is extraordinarily low. Notwithstanding the expanding scope of statutory corporate crimes and stiffer penalties, there continues a widespread perception that corporations and their executives do not get their just deserts. Environmental activists and other business critics maintain that the enforcement record is still insufficient. On the basis of reports from the General Accounting Office and various environmental groups, the Natural Resources Defense Council has concluded, "It is clear from this widespread non-compliance . . . that stricter criminal penalties are needed to deter . . . irresponsible conduct."[60] According to one study, "Until 1984, no large corporation was criminally prosecuted under federal environmental legislation. Of the corporations prosecuted under federal environmental laws since 1984, only 6 percent were among the nation's 500 largest industrial corporations in 1989. In fact, only 1.6 percent of the Fortune 500 have ever been prosecuted for an environmental violation."[61]

The first step required is the development of a theoretical framework linking sociopolitical conditions that would support criminal penalties with those corporate activities susceptible to modification. The framework should also link the severity of penalties with corporate structures and executive span of control. Clearly, fines and imprisonment judiciously employed can create a measure of specific and general deterrence. However, it would be folly to depend exclusively, or even primarily, on these measures. In addition, we must consider alternative remedies that may provide, under certain circumstances, a more effective outcome. But the task is subtle. Deterrents to corporate crime must be effective *without* smothering the risk-taking and innovation critical to corporate success in an increasingly challenging global environment. There follows a discussion of some of the issues such a theoretical framework will have to take into account.

Concept of Liability. Despite weaknesses in its dominant standards, there are advantages to retaining some variant of corporate liability. First, a stigma does more readily attach to a criminal than to a civil sanction, very important in an era when the public views corporate crime as increasingly serious, more serious, according to some polls, than ordinary street crime. Moreover, criminal justice is more swift and certain than civil justice. Finally, an adverse criminal finding can invite a wave of private tort suits, as more courts follow the doctrine of collateral estoppel (the findings of fact in a criminal case are biding in future private litigation).[62] In this sense, corporations must take criminal liability very seriously, since the monetary fines assessed may merely be the opening wedge of heavier damages later.

Suggestions have been made to expand the criminal liability of corporations, including one comment that companies not be allowed, as they are under the Moral Penal Code, to exonerate themselves by demonstrating that top corporate officials were unaware of the illegal conduct. Instead, corporations should be required to establish a due diligence defense,[63] thereby providing them an incentive to establish internal controls. Another authority believes that due diligence should not be allowed as an affirmative defense, to demonstrate lack of intent, but should only be a consideration at sentencing.[64]

There are other ways by which criminal penalties can be made more effective. For example:

1. The frequency and incidence of prison sentences should be increased significantly so . . . they convey to the public a true picture of the widespread nature of crimes, if that is case. The sentences should bear a close relationship to the severity of the crime so that judges would not be reluctant to impose them.
2. Under extreme circumstances, firms convicted of violations could be prohibited from doing business with other firms whose executives had been convicted of criminal violations, as specified by law or condition of sentencing. Such restrictions are already imposed in Nevada's gambling industry where firms known to have been associated with mob-tied businesses are barred from operating in the state. Settlements in trials of major securities violators, including Michael Milken and Dennis Levine, have included provisions that the defendants not work in the securities industry in the future. The same concept could be extended to social welfare crimes such as environmental offenses, barring a guilty executive from working in a particular industry, e.g., the chemical industry, in the future.
3. Corporations whose operations have been in violation of criminal laws should be subjected to special reporting requirements. The company or its officers could, for example, be required to make regular periodic statements to the court stating that no violations existed. If violations were later proved, the firm or individual could be convicted of perjury as well as the violation, and the penalties naturally would be harsher.[65]

Limitations of Monetary Fines.   The use of monetary fines for deterring corporate misconduct has been criticized by many legal scholars and corporate executives. According to Coffee, fines face what he calls the "deterrence trap." Since the assets of even the richest corporations are finite, and, therefore

are to be expended judiciously, and assuming that corporations are rational economic actors, a fine beyond a certain point loses its deterrent value. Corporations will weigh the possible economic gain from illegal behavior against the possible economic loss of a fine, discounted by the chance for detection and apprehension. If the change of detection is slight, even a fine beyond a company's ability to pay would not deter if from acting illegally.[66]

Monetary fines have been criticized also because they assume that corporate managers, whose behavior they are intended to affect, share the same economic calculus as the ideal rational actor. However, as noted earlier, other personal motivations often intrude in a manager's decision. Organization theorists have found many such motivations, including the urge for power and expansion, the need to compete and move up the corporate ladder, the desire for prestige, the creative impulse, the need to identify with a group, the desire for security, the urge for adventure, and the desire to serve others.[67] Furthermore, even assuming that managers shared the economic calculus of the firm, they live in a world of imperfect knowledge and lack the information to make a cost-benefit analysis concerning each illegal act. Frequently, it is not possible for a firm or an executive to assess the risk of apprehension or conviction.[68] Moreover, social psychologists have shown that people are less risk averse when they behave in groups.[69] Finally, both management and legal scholars point to the greater loyalty that managers and employees often demonstrate to their subunit, department, or division within the corporation than to the corporate entity. Such loyalty may encourage illegal behavior, for what benefits the subunit, especially in the short term, may have adverse long-term legal consequences for the firm.[70]

Beyond the rational-actor model, the legal literature cites two other theories that help to explain corporate behavior. One is the organizational-process model just referred to; the other, the bureaucratic-politics model. The latter speaks of coalition behavior among subunits in the organization, and of decisions made according to bargaining and compromise, standard features of the political process.[71] If the firm is not purely an economic actor, solely economic sanctions may falter on two levels, the organizational and the managerial.

Another major weakness of the monetary-fine remedy is the spillover problem it creates by externalizing the cost to various corporate stakeholders. Beyond the impact the fine might have on the so-called innocent shareholders, a monetary fine might also have an adverse impact on employees, suppliers, and customers. To the extent that a fine can be passed on in the form of higher prices, customers might be hurt. While the ability to pass on the cost of a fine is more certain in oligopolistic industries and in companies where risky behavior is an industrywide phenomenon, those firms in competitive industries will be more constrained in their pricing behavior. If the solvency of a firm is threatened by a fine, an austerity and work-force-reduction program would adversely affect both employees and suppliers.[72] The spillover problem, in turn, leads to the problem of nullification. If judges and juries perceive that the primary effect of a penalty will fall on innocent parties, rather than be felt by culpable managers, they may resist imposing a harsh fine.[73] Under the sentencing guidelines, however, nullification and leniency are basically precluded, though judges can interpret an offense to be a "lower" guideline crime than it actually is.

Cohen suggests an approach to making monetary fines more effective as deterrents. He argues that criminal sanctions should be inversely related to the probability of detection. "Offenses that are always detected do not require large punitive multiples, while those that are difficult to detect may require fines that are multiples of losses in order to account for the possibility that some offenders will not be caught."[74] For a fine to be effective in deterring a corporate offender, and for the offender to rationally calculate the costs and benefits of violating the law, it is not sufficient for the potential violator to know that fines are increasing. The violator must also realize the probability of being detected and punished. Becker's analysis of "optimal penalties" suggests that the penalty should equal the net social cost of the probability of detection."[75]

Additional Remedies.   Scholars and critics have proposed a variety of additional remedies that might be used—either alone or in combination with criminal penalties—to curb illegal corporate behavior. These include: equity fines; organization restructuring; greater use of adverse publicity for corporate violators; probation and monitoring of corporate performance; a corporate-ethos standard for corporate intent; and, a reactive corporate-fault standard for *mens rea*.

Equity Fines.   Coffee[76] suggests equity fines as an alternative to monetary penalties for deterring corporate crimes. Under this system, a convicted corporation would be required to issue shares to a state victims'-compensation fund equivalent in market value to a cash fine designed to deter corporate misconduct. Such an authorization of new shares would dilute the value of outstanding shares, concentrating the impact of the remedy on the shareholders and those executives holding stock options. The major benefits claimed by Coffee from the proposal are:

- it would reduce the spillover impact on workers and consumers while concentrating it on shareholders;
- it would alleviate the nullification problem by reducing the threat to workers and customers, giving judges and juries less hesitation to punish the firm;
- it would facilitate much higher penalties without affecting the market valuation of the firm;
- it would align management's interests more closely with shareholders by focusing the adverse impact on the declining values of the firm's shares;
- it would instill in management the fear of a takeover due to the issuance of a new block of shares; and,

- since shareholders would be awakened from their slumber of indifference through a greater fear of risky shares, they would demand greater internal controls on corporate misbehavior.

There are some drawbacks to this proposal, however. It might magnify the harm on shareholders, yet not directly intervene to create structural reform. Managers might evade the incentive for self-policing produced by the proposal, at least partially, by forsaking stock options entirely in exchange for other benefits, thereby avoiding the adverse impact of these fines.[77]

Corporate Restructuring. One of the major problems with discovering corporate illegal behavior is the complexity of corporate decision making where any given decision involves many layers of personnel and no clear locus of authority. A corporate organization is designed to pinpoint areas of responsibility and authority so as to increase both cost efficiencies and profit performance. It is not designed to minimize corporate malfeasance, especially as it pertains to social welfare crimes, which often have the result of increasing a firm's cost efficiencies and profit performance. Two approaches might accomplish the goals of maximum prevention of harmful acts, easy determination of responsibility of executives committing these acts, and fairness in the imposition of penalties.

- Every law that proscribes certain activities in health, safety, and environmental areas should require that the corporation designate an executive who will be responsible for ensuring corporate compliance with the law. Since this would be tantamount to prewarning, the executive so designated could not offer a "lack of knowledge" defense. To avoid the problem of a "vice-president in-charge of going to jail," these designated executives must be shown to have the necessary competence and authority within the organizational hierarchy commensurate with their responsibility for the risk.
- Corporations might develop "social accountability centers" similar in purpose and goals

to "profit centers." Profit centers are organized on a rational basis since the performance of a business unit or a manager has to be isolated and measured. Top management rewards a manager on the basis of a profit center's performance. With a "social responsibility center," all harmful and dangerous acts would be charged to the manager of the center. This approach might cause responsibility for compliance with certain laws to be distributed among more than one person within a corporation. However, it has the distinct advantage of segmenting areas of corporate activities so that an executive's responsibility is clearly established.[78]

Organization restructuring may also be ordered by a court as a condition of probation. Allied Chemical, following the Kepone spill, implemented an SEC consent order requiring the company to launch an independent investigation of environmental risk and to take appropriate action. As a result, the company established a Toxic Risk Assessment committee, composed of legal, medical, and scientific experts, which has been hailed by the EPA as an industry model. Moreover, Allied revised its compensation system so that one-third of a plant manager's pay would be based on safety performance.[79] Though such a scheme is interventionist, it relies on a self-study and initiatives proposed by experts, not only by regulators or judges. It also has two major advantages over the incentives provided by fines. It serves not only deterrence but also the criminal-justice goal of rehabilitation.[80]

Adverse Publicity. A corporation's goodwill has a measurable market value, which would be likely to suffer from adverse publicity. The mandate for such court-ordered publicity would be to "get the word out" to investors and others in the corporate community. Such a course would also have the effect of creating "a societal consensus on the undesirability of corporate crimes; prison sentences could be accompanied by a public apology from the corporation and the executive, together with a description of their deeds. Such apologies are common in both Germany and Japan and seem to have been effective in bringing public attention—and public condemnation—to violators."[81] Such measures have also been endorsed by environmental groups as a way of bringing public opprobrium upon corporate polluters,[82] while others have questioned their potential effectiveness. Coffee offers six criticisms:

- the government is a relatively poor propagandist;
- government publicity may be drowned out because the communication channels of our society are already inundated with criticism of corporations;
- corporations can dilute this sanction through counter-publicity;
- the efficacy of publicity in cases involving consumer fraud or jeopardy to the public safety does not imply that publicity will be equally effective in dealing with "regulatory crimes";
- if publicity directed against the corporation is effective, it will produce the same externalities as cash fines;
- civil liberties issues surround the use of publicity as a sanction.[83]

This criticism, however, does not take into account the field evidence from counter advertising, e.g., in the case of cigarettes and tobacco, which seemed to have been quite effective and moved the tobacco companies to accept a ban on cigarette advertising in the broadcast media rather than allow counter advertising on the air waves.[84] Moreover, it is not necessary that the corporate offender be forced to engage in adverse publicity or that government should play such a role. Instead, part of the funds generated through fines can be used for launching a media campaign that could even include broader aspects of public education. A model for this approach has been presented in congressional testimony.[85] More recently, California state authorities have used funds levied on cigarettes to publicize dangers of smoking and have achieved measurable results among the targeted audiences of teenagers.[86]

Corporate Probation. Corporate probation may take many forms. At one extreme, prison sentences could be combined with a probationary period. An executive who is convicted of criminal wrongdoing should be barred from holding an executive-level position in a publicly held company for a prescribed number of years following release from prison.[87] At another extreme, a presentence report could be mandated as a condition of corporate probation. Coffee suggests a model such as the McCloy report on Gulf Oil, a meticulous study of the company's domestic and foreign political payments. The impact of the report was major, as it led to internal reforms within Gulf and hastened the resignation of senior corporate officials.[88] While in major corporate scandals, such as that involving Michael Milken and Drexel Burnham Lambert, an enterprising reporter or author might come on the scene with a precise and revealing study,[89] there is no guarantee that will happen except in dramatic instances of corporate illegality. Mandated studies do make sense.

Environmental advocates suggest that probation imposed as a sentence for environmental crimes might also contain some of the following types of conditions:

- cleanup of the damage caused by the violation;
- restoration or replacement of material resources damaged or destroyed by the illegal conduct;
- full restitution to individuals for any loss or damage to health or private property, or trust funds when immediate harm is impossible to determine or compensate;
- conducting or funding of studies necessary to ascertain the full extent of damage to health and environment;
- adequate notification to members of the public who may have been, or who may be, affected by the illegal conduct; and
- comprehensive environmental audits of the organization's facilities, conducted by outside experts, to ensure that similar violations do not occur in the future.[90]

To the extent that a corporation already has developed systems of internal social evaluations and corporate public disclosure, the firm will be that much better prepared for the imposition of probation or to even avoid any sentence.

Corporate Ethos Standard. The culture of a corporation—its traditions and ethos—exerts strong influence on the behavior of its managers and employees.[91] Corporate ethos thus should play an important role in determining the intent or *mens rea* of a firm in cases of corporate crime. As Bucy states, "The corporate ethos test does not require that the government prove which individual is at fault. It does, however, require the government to prove that the criminal conduct was committed by a corporate agent and that a corporate ethos existed that encouraged the criminal conduct."[92]

In this sense, a corporate-ethos standard would create both a broader and a more precise corporate liability than either the federal vicarious-liability standard or the Model Penal Code. Each of the latter two standards attach liability to the corporation only when either a specific identifiable manager or high-level official is implicated in the illegal act, a burden not imposed by the corporate-ethos standard. That standard, similar to the collective-intent standard, creates liability based on the goals and policies of the firm even when specific individual violators cannot be identified. However, corporate liability is simultaneously narrower and more precise under the corporate-ethos standard than under the vicarious-liability standard or the MPC, in that corporations are not automatically held vicariously liable for the illegal acts of managers. Only those firms whose policies encourage such actions are held liable. The ethos standard distinguishes between conscientious firms and those that deserve to be punished, rewarding "those corporations that make efforts to educate and motivate their employees to follow the letter and spirit of the law."[93]

There are eight components to the corporate ethos standard:[94]

- *hierarchy*—this standard would include an examination of the firm's organizational structure, including the effectiveness of its board of directors;[95]
- *corporate goals*—the ethos standard would weigh the extent to which bottom-line goals are pushed, at the expense of legal reporting requirements or fairness to customers;
- *educating corporate employees about legal requirements*—to the extent that government contractors organize seminars to prevent fraud or to discuss law and ethics, and to the extent that any human-resources department enlightens corporate employees on the nature of prohibited sexual harassment, the more protection the firm would enjoy under an ethos standard;
- *monitoring compliance with legal requirements*—companies that institute effective operational audits or inventories of corporate social performance,[96] an ombudsman or other procedures to protect corporate whistleblowers, and special compliance letters or other internal-reporting systems would be less apt to be found liable under a corporate-ethos standard;
- *involvement of high-level officials*—evidence of such high-level involvement would not constitute conclusive support for corporate liability, as it does under the Model Penal Code, but it is partial proof that a negative corporate ethos exists that encourages criminal behavior;
- *corporate reaction to past violations and violators;*
- *compensation incentives for legally appropriate behavior;*
- *indemnification*—if a corporation indemnifies a convicted executive for fines, penalties, and attorney fees, the executive has less motivation to obey the law, again reflecting a negative corporate ethos.

While corporate-probation proposals, such as those of Stone and Coffee, impose the same types of control mechanisms, their proposals are more intrusive than those of the corporate-ethos standard. Corporate-probation standards mandate that corporations adopt specific measures as a condition of probation.[97] The corporate-ethos standard operates more like a market mechanism. Corporations are given an incentive, in order to avoid a finding of criminal intent, to adopt such control mechanisms voluntarily and before the fact.[98] The U.S. Sentencing Commission also encourages the adoption of such internal controls, by lowering the amount of a fine when such controls are utilized by a firm.

Reactive Corporate Fault Standard. The corporate-ethos standard may be seen as a form of proactive corporative fault, i.e., culpability is based on the type of internal controls devised by the corporation *before* the violation is committed. Some authorities, however, believe that a reactive corporate-fault standard—how the firm acts to rectify the harm created by the offense and to protect the relevant stakeholders (e.g., consumers, workers, the community or the environment)—is a better standard than a proactive one for determining criminal liability.[99] This would especially be the case where the firm had received a compliance order from a judge or government agency, detailing its reactive obligation after the offense had been committed. Currently, a corporate offender's reactions may help mitigate a sentence, but a reactive corporate fault standard would be more powerful, in that it, like the corporate-ethos standard, would determine corporate intent prior to conviction. A reactive corporate-fault standard might be applied in instances of corporate crisis management and would yield differ-ent results in various cases. For example Firestone's failure to promptly institute a recall of its 500 radial tire, in response to complaints of product danger from consumers and a leading public interest group, might have constituted persuasive evidence of reactive liability.[100] Likewise, Exxon's delayed and decentralized response to the Exxon Valdez oil spill, along with its inadequate oil-spill response plan, would surely have created liability based on a reactive corporate-fault standard.[101] On the other hand, Johnson & Johnson's reaction to the Tylenol deaths of the early 1980s, including a prompt recall of all Tylenol capsules, cooperation in the investigation of the deaths, and the development of tamper-resistant packaging would likely have exonerated the company under a reactive corporate-fault standard.

Given the number and complexity of issues that must be addressed, the task of constructing a theoretical model for the development of effective deterrents to corporate crime—deterrents that do not simultaneously debilitate the corporation—is formidable. Considering the stakes, however, it must be undertaken.

NOTES

1. Seymour Martin Lipset and William Schneider, *The Confidence Gap* (New York: The Free Press, 1983).
2. F. William McCarty and John W. Bagby, *The Legal Environment of Business* (Homewood, IL: Richard D. Irwin, 1990).
3. William G. Shepherd, *Public Policies Toward Business* (Homewood, IL: Richard D. Irwin, 1985), 256–57.
4. Anthony J. Celebrezze, Jr. and Steven J. Twist, "The Racketeer Influenced and Corrupt Practices Act (RICO): Constraint on Corporate Crime or Unfair Business Weapon?" in S. Prakash Sethi and Cecilia M. Falbe, eds., *Business and Society: Dimensions of Conflict and Cooperation* (Lexington, MA: D.C. Heath 1987), 506–28.
5. Marshall B. Clinard, *Illegal Corporate Behavior*, National Institute of Law Enforcement and Criminal Justice, Law Enforcement Assistance Administration, U.S. Department of Justice, October 1979; U.S. Congress, "White Collar Crime: The Problem and the Federal Response," Subcommittee on Crime of the Committee on the Judiciary, 95th Cong., 2nd sess., 1978; and, S. Prakash Sethi and Praveen Chopra, "Corporate Crimes and Executive Liability: Analysis, Trends and Policy Guidelines," in S. Prakash Sethi, Paul Steidlmeier, and Cecilia M. Falbe, eds. *Scaling the Corporate Wall: Readings in Social Issues of the Nineties* (Englewood Cliffs, NJ: Prentice Hall, 1991), 202–30.

6. Dick Thornburg, "Criminal Enforcement of Environmental Laws: A National Priority," *George Washington Law Review* 59, no. 4 (April 1991): 778.

7. James W. Starr, "Turbulent Times at Justice and EPA: The Origins of Environmental Prosecutions and the Work that Remains," *George Washington Law Review* 59, no. 4 (April, 1991): 907, points out that felony offenses were created by amendments to the Resource Conservation and Recovery Act in 1988, to the Superfund Law in 1988, through the Emergency Planning and Community Right-to-Know Act of 1986, the Clean Water Act of 1988, the Safe Drinking Water Act of 1988, and the Clean Air Act of 1990.

8. James M. Strock, "Environmental Criminal Enforcement Priorities for the 1990s," *George Washington Law Review* 59, no. 4 (April 1991): 926.

9. Mark A. Cohen, "Environmental Crime and Punishment: Legal/Economic Theory and Empirical Evidence on Enforcement of Federal Environmental Statutes" (forthcoming) in *Journal of Criminal Law and Criminology* 82, no. 4 (1992): 29.

10. Mark A. Cohen, "Corporate Crime and Punishment: An Update on Sentencing Practice in the Federal Courts, 1988–1990" *Boston University Law Review* (forthcoming).

11. Ibid., 12. The $2.4 million average, however, includes a $115 million settlement paid by Sundstrand for defense procurement overcharges and the $660 million sanction paid by Drexel Burnham Lambert. The total sanction goes beyond fines paid to the government. Cohen defines it as including "all government imposed sanctions, such as federal criminal fines, restitution, administrative penalties, state criminal or civil fines, clean-up costs ordered to be paid by the offender, voluntary restitution made known to the judge prior to sentencing, *and* court-ordered payments to victims or other third parties." The total sanction, however, does not include private settlements made to victims.

12. Milo Geyelin and Ellen Joan Pollock, "Prison Terms in Fraud Cases Are Redefined," *Wall Street Journal*, 6 December 1991, B6.

13. Cohen, "Environmental Crime and Punishment," 31.

14. Robert W. Adler and Charles Lord, "Environmental Crimes: Raising the Stakes," *George Washington Law Review* 59, no. 4 (April 1991): 795–96.

15. The discussion of the framework is drawn, in large part, from S. Prakash Sethi, "Liability without Fault? The Corporate Executive as an Unwitting Criminal," *Employee Relations Law Journal* 4, no. 2 (Autumn 1978): 185-219. See, also, the two subsequent expansions and revisions of this article, i.e., S. Prakash Sethi, "Corporate Law Violations and White-Collar Crime," in Sethi and Falbe, ed., op. cit., 471–506; and S. Prakash Sethi and Praveen Chopra, op. cit., 202–30.

16. Comment, "Developments in the Law Corporate Crime: Regulating Corporate Behavior Through Criminal Sanctions," *Harvard Law Review* 92, no. 6 (April 1979): 1365–66; and, Brent Fisse and John Braithwaite, *The Impact of Publicity on Corporate Offenders* (Albany: State University of New York Press, 1983), a study of adverse publicity on seventeen corporations.

17. Brent Fisse, "Reconstructing Corporate Criminal Law: Deterrence, Retribution, Fault, and Sanctions," *Southern California Law Review* 56 (1983): 1154.

18. Michael B. Metzger, "Corporate Criminal Liability for Defective Products: Policies, Problems, and Prospects," *Georgetown Law Journal* 73 (October 1984): 10.

19. Fisse, 1180; Cohen, "Corporate Crime and Punishment," 7, explains ". . . all of these goals can just as easily be served through a combination of tort and administrative remedies. For example, treble damage awards and civil penalties might offer deterrence, while debarment and license revocation are forms of incapacitation. Although rehabilitation has fallen out of favor by many policy makers as a realistic goal, examples of sanctions that attempt to rehabilitate are certain forms of negotiated remedies such as environmental audits. Retribution may also be exacted through punitive damage awards in tort actions. The only exception is the case of incapacitating individuals—which can only be done through incarceration or some less restricting alternative such as home detention."

20. 421 U.S. 720 (1975). See also S. Prakash Sethi and Robert N. Katz, "The Expanding Scope of Personal Criminal Liability of Corporate Executives—Some Implications of United

States v. Park" 32, *Food, Drug, Cosmetic Law Journal* (1977): 544–70.

21. Steven C. Yohay and Garen E. Dodge, "Criminal Prosecutions for Occupational Injuries: An Issue of Growing Concern," *Employee Relations Law Journal* 13, no. 2 (Autumn 1987): 197-223, and Jay C. Magnuson and Gareth C. Leviton, "Policy Considerations in Corporate Criminal Prosecutions After People v. Film Recovery Systems, Inc.," *Notre Dame Law Review* 62, no. 5 (Autumn 1987): 913–39.
22. 51 N.Y. 2d 295, 414 N.E. 2d 660, 434 N.Y. S. 2d 159 (1980), cert. denied, 450 U.S. 1031 (1981). See also Stephen A. Radin, "Corporate Criminal Liability for Employee-Endangering Activities," *Columbia Journal of Law and Social Problems* 1 (1983): 39–75.
23. Pamela H. Bucy, "Corporate Ethos: A Standard for Imposing Corporate Criminal Liability," *Minnesota Law Review* 75, no. 4 (April 1991): 1102–03.
24. Bucy, 1103–05; Coffee, 445; and , Foerschler, 1294–95.
25. United States v. Beusch, 596 F.2d 871, 878 (9th Cir. 1979); Yohay and Dodge, 203; *Meritor Savings Bank v. Vinson* 477 U.S. 57 (1986).
26. U.S. Sentencing commission, *Supplementary Report on Sentencing Guidelines for Organizations*, August 30, 1991, 10–11.
27. Mark A. Cohen, "Environmental Crime and Punishment," 12–13, 74.
28. See note 11 for the definition of the total sanction.
29. Mark A. Cohen, "Corporate Crime and Punishment: A Study of Social Harm and Sentencing Practice in the Federal Courts, 1984–87," *American Criminal Law Review* 26, no. 3 (Winter 1989): 646–47, 652.
30. Gary S. Becker, "Crime and Punishment: An Economic Approach," *Journal of Political Economy* 76 (1968): 169–217.
31. Mark A. Cohen, "Environmental Crime and Punishment," 76–77.
32. John C. Coffee, Jr., 390, 394.
33. U.S. Sentencing Commission, 8–9, 24.
34. cohen, "Corporate Crime and Punishment: An Update on Sentencing Practice in the Federal Courts, 1988-1990," 6, and Frank Edward Allen, "Few Big Firms Get Jail Time for Polluting," *Wall Street Journal*, 9 December 1991, B2.
35. Adler and Lord state on 795-96: "Until 1984, no large corporation was criminally prosecuted under federal environmental legislation. Of the corporations prosecuted under federal environmental laws since 1984, only 6 percent were among the nations 500 largest industrial corporations in 1989. In fact, only 1.6 percent of the Fortune 500 have ever been prosecuted for an environmental violation."
36. Cited in Adler and Lord, 796, 809.
37. Steven L. Friedlander, "Using Prior Corporate Convictions to Impeach," *California Law Review* 28, no. 5 (October 1990): 1325–28.
38. Cohen, "Environmental Crime and Punishment," 17.
39. U.S. Sentencing Commission, 43.
40. Cohen, "Environmental Crime and Punishment," 25.
41. Adler and Lord, 829, 834.
42. S. Prakash Sethi, "The Expanding Scope of Executive Liability (Criminal and Civil) for Corporate Law Violations," 492-93.
43. Sanford H. Kadish, "Some Observations of the Use of Criminal Sanctions in the Enforcement of Economic Legislation," in *White Collar Crimes: Offenses in Business, Politics and Professions* (Geis and Meier, eds., 1977), 304–15.
44. S. Prakash Sethi, "Liability Without Fault? The Corporate Executive as an Unwitting Criminal," *Employee Relations Law Journal* 4, no. 2 (1978): 205–07.
45. Foerschler, 1298; Bucy, 1119; Radin, 57; and Metzger, 56.
46. 381 F. Supp. 730 (W.D. Va. 1974).
47. Foerschler, 1304-05. See, also, *United States v. Bank of New England*, 821 F.2d 844 (1st. Cir.), cert. denied, 484 U.S. 943 (1987).
48. John C. Coffee, Jr., "'No Soul to Damn: No Body to Kick': An Unscandalized Inquiry into the Problem of Corporate Punishment," *Michigan Law Review* 79 (January 1981): 409–10.
49. Ann Foerschler, "Corporate Criminal Intent: Toward a Better Understanding of Corporate Misconduct," *California Law Review* 78, no. 5 (October 1990): 1289.
50. Adler and Lord, 807.
51. John Braithwaite, *Corporate Crime in the Pharmaceutical Industry* (London: Routledge and Kegan Paul, 1984), 308.
52. Bucy, 1101.
53. Foerschler, 1291; Michael B. Metzger, "Cor-

porate Criminal Liability for Defective Products: Policies, Problems, and Prospects," *Georgetown Law Journal* 73 (October 1984): 61.

54. S. Prakash Sethi, "Liability Without Fault? The Corporate Executive as an Unwitting Criminal," *Employee Relations Law Journal* 4, no. 2 (1978): 205–07.

55. Fisse 1148–49; Kenneth Goodpaster and John Matthews, "Can a Corporation Have a Conscience?" *Harvard Business Review* (January-February, 1982): 132–33; Peter A. French, "Corporate Moral Agency," *Business Ethics: Readings and Cases in Corporate Morality*, W. Michael Hoffman and Jennifer Mills Moore (New York: McGraw-Hill, 1984).

56. Foerschler, 1306.

57. Christopher Kennedy, "Criminal Sentences for Corporations: Alternative Fining Mechanisms," *California Law Review* 73 (1985): 452.

58. Sethi, "The Expanding Scope of Executive Liability," note 42, 494.

59. Kadish, op. cit., 299–301.

60. Robert W. Adler and Charles Lord, "Environmental Crimes: Raising the Stakes," *George Washington Law Review* 59, no. 4 (April 1991): 709. Adler and Lord also point out (p. 802) that "Overall, average fines are up but have leveled off at one-fifth of the maximum allowed by the respective statutes. Average prison terms have also increased over the past few years, but the time actually served is as low as one-twentieth to one-hundredth of the statutory maximum. For all of the statutes, the percentage of convicted individuals who actually go to jail has dropped as the average sentence has increased."

61. Adler and Lord, 795-96.

62. Fisse, 1151; Metzger, 84; Coffee, 447.

63. Comment, "Developments in the Law Corporate Crime," *Harvard Law Review* 92 (1979): 1243–45.

64. Coffee, 446.

65. S. Prakash Sethi, "Corporate Law Violations and Executive Liability." Testimony on H.R. 4973 before the Subcommittee on Crime of the House Judiciary Committee, December 13, 1979. Cited in S. Prakash Sethi, "The Expanding Scope of Executive Liability," 471–506.

66. Coffee, 389–90.

67. Numerous authorities cited in Fisse, 1155; and Metzger, 19.

68. Coffee, 294.

69. Coffee, 395; Metzger, 17.

70. Coffee, 397; Metzger, 20-21; Christopher D. Stone, *Where the Law Ends* (New York: Harper & Row Publishers, 1975), 45.

71. Fisse, 1157-59; Foerschler, 1301-02.

72. Kennedy, 449, 455-56; Coffee, 400-05; Fisse 1219.

73. Coffee, 405-07; Kennedy, 456; Radin, 52.

74. Mark A. Cohen, "Environmental Crime and Punishment," 76-77.

75. Gary S. Becker, 169–217.

76. Coffee, 413-20. Regarding the final advantage of his proposal, Coffee further writes, "If the premise that stock market pressures induce at least some forms of corporate misconduct is correct, the equity fine is a punishment which truly fits the crime, for its primary effect is to dampen stock market pressure for the aggressive pursuit of illicit short-term gain. . . . punishment will, to a degree, precede the crime as companies perceived to be run in a manner that encourage illegal behavior will see their stock values decline. As noted earlier, corporate managers will have an incentive to institute preventive monitoring controls to forestall this decline—just as today they have an apparently more than adequate incentive to maximize short-term profits," 419–20.

77. Fisse, 1236; Metzger, 70; Kennedy, 460–68. Kennedy elaborates: "Nevertheless, the shareholders continue to bear the burden of the penalty to the same extent and in the same proportions as they would a cash fine. And for a stockholder whose holdings are substantial, the loss might be severe," 461. "The mere expedient of shifting the target of the fine from assets to equity surely will not improve shareholder awareness of fines. A typical stockholder, who would not take notice of a change occasioned by a fine in the assets portion of a financial statement, would hardly be jolted by an equivalent change to the 'shares issued and outstanding' line of the same statement. A change in share values would likewise be of no greater moment to stockholders if brought about by an equity fine than if caused by a cash fine. It is not the mechanism of the equity fine that might awaken the shareholders. Rather, it is the larger fines that could result from the lessened overspill of an equity fining system. While larger fines of any kind would help to counteract indifference, such fines are more

likely to materialize if courts are permitted to levy them on equity," 465–66.

78. S. Prakash Sethi, "Corporate Law Violations and Executive Liability." Testimony on H.R. 4973 before the Subcommittee on Crime of the House Judiciary Committee, December 13, 1979. Cited in S. Prakash Sethi, "The Expanding Scope of Executive Liability (Criminal and Civil) for Corporate Law Violations," 471–506.

79. Coffee, 451, 456.

80. Fisse, 1155; Metzger, 71–73.

81. S. Prakash Sethi, "Corporate Law Violations and Executive Liability." Cited in S. Prakash Sethi, "The Expanding Scope of Executive Liability," 471–506.

82. Adler and Lord, 841; Fisse, 1155–56, 1229–31; Metzger, 64.

83. Coffee, 425-28.

84. "The Tobacco Industry and the Smoking Controversy," in S. Prakash Sethi, *Up Against the Corporate Wall: Modern Corporations and Social Issues of the Eighties*, 4th ed. (Englewood Cliffs, NJ, 1982), 398–421.

85. S. Prakash Sethi, "IRS Administration of Tax Laws Relating to Lobbying." Testimony before the Subcommittee of the Committee on Government Operations, 95th Cong., 2nd sess., July 20–21, 1978; see, also, S. Prakash Sethi, *Advocacy Advertising and Large Corporations: Social Conflict, Big Business Image, News Media and Public Policy* (Lexington, MA: D.C. Heath, 1977); and, S. Prakash Sethi, "Beyond the Fairness Doctrine: A New War on Corporate 'Propaganda,'" *New York Times*, 10 August 1986, 3-F.

86. Sonia L. Nazario, "California Anti-Cigarette Ads Seem To Reduce Smoking," *Wall Street Journal*, 31 October 1990, B1, B9; Richard W. Stevenson, "Tough Anti-Smoking Effort Aims at Cigarette Marketers," *New York Times*, 26 April 1990, C1, C21.

87. S. Prakash Sethi, "Corporate Law Violations and Executive Liability," 471-506.

88. Coffee, 430–31.

89. See James Stewart, *Den of Thieves*, (New York: Simon and Schuster, 1991).

90. Adler and Lord, 831–832.

91. See Terrence E. Deal and Allan A. Kennedy, *Corporate Cultures: The Rites and Rituals of Corporate Life* (Reading, MA: Addison-Wesley Publishing Co., 1982); see, also, Thomas J. Peters and Robert H. Waterman, Jr., *In Search of Excellence: Lessons from America's Best-Run Companies* (New York: Harper & Row, 1982); see, Edgar H. Schein, *Organizational Culture and Leadership*, (San Francisco: Jossey Bass, 1985); see, also, Clarence C. Walton, *The Moral Manager* (New York: Harper & Row, 1988).

92. Bucy, 1128.

93. Bucy, 1100.

94. Bucy, 1129–44.

95. Bucy, 1129–33.

96. See Raymond A. Bauer and Dan H. Fenn, Jr., *The Corporate Social Audit* (New York: Russell Sage Foundation, 1972); Task Force on Corporate Social Performance, *Corporate Social Reporting in the United States and Western Europe* (Washington, DC: U.S. Department of Commerce, 1979).

97. John C. Coffee, Richard Gruner, and Christopher D. Stone, "Standards for Organizational Probation: A Proposal to the United States Sentencing Commission," *Whittier Law Review* 10, no. 1 (1988): 77–102.

98. Bucy, 1159, elaborates on this advantage. "The corporate ethos standard also allows corporations to choose and design procedures best suited to them. The more effective the chosen procedures are, the better chance the corporation has of avoiding liability if a corporate agent later violates the law . . . because the corporate ethos standard addresses criminal liability in the first instance rather than after the criminal conduct has occurred, the internal controls that this standard encourages are more likely to actually reduce corporate crime."

99. Fisse, 1195–1213.

100. Fisse, 1206.

101. Claudia H. Deutsch, "The Giant With a Black Eye," *New York Times*, 2 April 1989, F1, F8; Steven Fink, "Prepare for Crisis, It's Part of Business," *New York Times*, 30 April 1989, F3; John Holusha, "Exxon's Public Relations Problem," *New York Times*, 21 April 1989, D1, D4; Charles McCoy, "Alyeska Record Shows How Big Oil Neglected Alaskan Environment," *Wall Street Journal*, 6 July 1989, A1, A4; Gerry Sikorski, "Exxon Slips Away," *New York Times*, 7 September 1989, A23; Alanna Sullivan, "Exxon's Holders Assail Chairman Rawl Over Firm's Handling of Alaska Oil Spill," *Wall Street Journal*, 19 May 1989, A3.

CORPORATE CRIME AND CORPORATE SANCTIONS IN JAPAN

William S. Laufer and Alison J. Cohen

For years American sociologists have marveled at the low rates of conventional or "street crime" in Japan. In the United States, in contrast, the 1990 homicide rate was seven times higher and the rape rate over twenty times higher than in Japan.[1] In order to explain recently stable and declining Japanese crime rates, scholars and commentators have considered the contribution of a homogeneous culture, cohesive family unit, shared personal value system, and the strict crime-control philosophy that guides Japan's efficient criminal-justice system.[2] There is, however, a conspicuous absence of scholarship and commentary on the effectiveness of existing sanctions, as compared with informal social controls, in deterring or inhibiting corprate crime in Japan. This is surprising, given a series of stock scandals at major brokerage houses over the past decade, as well as recent criminal charges of price-fixing and other monopolistic acts by corporations.[3] The absence of such scholarship is also unfortunate. For the last three years debate has raged over the effort by the United States Sentencing Commission to fashion appropriate penalties for corporations convicted of crimes under federal law; had that scholarship existed, and assuming that the Commission would have consulted it, the Commission might have gained insight into the effectiveness of certain sanctions by considering Japan's experience.

In this article, we examine corporate crime and sanctions in Japan. We first contrast Japanese and American crime statistics and current explanations for conventional and white-collar crime. Next, we contrast corporate criminal liability and corporate crime in the United States and Japan. We then consider recent securities scandals and their effect on the creation of new regulatory bodies as well as the revision of apparently ineffective securities legislation. Finally, we consider corporate sanctions in Japan.

CRIME IN AMERICA AND JAPAN

Conventional Crime

Over the last forty years, criminological theory has focused on three main explanations for conventional crime: strain theory, cultural-deviance theory, and social-control theory.[4] Strain theorists maintain that all members of society subscribe to one set of cultural values—those found in the middle class. These middle-class values emphasize material acquisition and financial success. Frustration and strain sets in with lower-class persons who subscribe to these middle-class values, but do not have legitimate means to attain the goals these values reflect. Thus, one possible result of this disjunction between goals and means is the commission of a crime.[5]

419

Cultural-deviance theorists make a number of different arguments. Those who subscribe to social-disorganization theory argue hat rapid changes in industrialization or urbanization may result in a decline of formal and informal forces which ensure norm conformity in neighborhoods or communities. The result is an intergenerational transmission of deviant values within socially disorganized and disintegrating inner-city neighborhoods.[6]

Neither strain nor cultural-deviance theories adequately explain the low crime rate in Japan (Table 1). Given rapid changes in the rates of urbanization, industrialization, and modernization after World War II, strain and social-disorganization theorists would have predicted significant increases in Japanese crime rates. But those crime rates did not precipitously increase. Indeed, they remained stable or actually declined.

The failure of these theories to explain crime in Japan may be due to the fact that they are tightly tied to the nature of social structure, as opposed to social processes. Needed is a "process perspective" that considers human relationships and complex social relations which ensure norm allegiance and conformity. Such a perspective must consider a wide range of influences, ideologies, norms, customs, and laws which create and then foster social bonds among individuals, the family, organizations, and society. Social-control theory has been the obvious candidate of many commentators.

SOCIAL CONTROL THEORY

The construct of social control is elastic. As a theoretical perspective, it has been broadly defined as all characteristics of society as well as forces which influence norm conformity or obedience to customs, rules, or law. It also has been employed narrowly to explain society's formal response to deviance. A brief consideration of four prominent models of social control will assist in explaining norm conformity in Japan.

Inspired by the writings of Auguste Comte (1798–1857) and Emile Durkheim (1858–1913), a normative vision of social control emerged at the turn of the century; the early work of Ross[7] and Cooley[8] best represents this broad conceptualization of social control which served as a foundation for the sociological study of social and moral order.

According to Ross, social control is a natural extension of complex social relations. As society evolves, and personal or intimate relations are replaced by impersonal, contractual relations, there is a burgeoning of self-interest. Ross reasoned that the "natural bonds, . . . so many and firm . . . [in] the rural neighborhood or village community . . . , no longer bind men . . . in the huge and complex aggregates of the day."[9]

With such a development, Ross maintains, instinctive controls, such as empathy, sociability, a sense of equity, and solidarity, become insufficient to control and curb self-interest. Thus, as natural communities mature into "artificial societies," the regulation of conduct to quell temptation and resist the exploitation of unethical opportunities demands a means of control which is more formal and systematic. Quite simply, with societal institutions demanding impersonal relations and producing an amalgam of private interests, an artificial order is required.

Ross argues that the means of control to ensure social order in economically and socially developed communities include: public opinion, law, beliefs or values, social suggestion or the influence of tradition and convention, education, custom, religion, social roles or types, ceremony, art, personality, enlightenment, illusion, social valuations, ethics, and class control. These social mechanisms allow for an accommodation of natural and artificial order. In post-industrial societies with complex economic transactions, social order is maintained by accommodating the natural order, which derives from personal control, with sufficient artificial constraint. A second model specifically concerns law as a response to deviance.

TABLE 1. Number of Crimes Known to Police, Crime Rates, and Clearance Rates (1988) in Japan and United States

Category	Japan	United States
Population	122,783,000	245,807,000
Homicide		
Number of cases	1,441	20,675
Crime rate	1.2	8.4
Clearance rate (%)	97.1	70.0
Rape		
Number of cases	1,741	92,486
Crime rate	1.4	37.6
Clearance rate (%)	86.4	52.1
Robbery		
Number of cases	1,771	542,968
Crime rate	1.4	220.9
Clearance rate (%)	78.5	25.6
Larceny		
Number of cases	1,422,355	12,356,865
Crime rate	1,158.4	5,027.1
Clearance rate (%)	55.7	17.5

SOURCE: National Police Agency, *White Paper on Police.* Tokyo: Government of Japan, 1990, p. 132.

SOCIAL CONTROL OF DEVIANCE

In a ground-breaking work, Black[10] discussed law as a quantitative variable which has four styles: penal, compensatory, therapeutic, and conciliatory. Each style results in a qualitatively different brand of social control—punishment, payment, help, and resolution. Black's work paved the way for a powerful formulation of social control—one which identified the law as a primary locus of control. Studies which emerged from this perspective used this locus as means of understanding deviance, the response to deviance, and the control of deviance.[11]

Social Control of Power

A third control perspective attempts to explain group-level conformity by exploring: (a) conscious attempts by powerful segments in society to control stakeholders or constituents; (b) the socioeconomic planning under-

taken by governmental agencies and agents; and (c) the sociology of influence and power in society.[12] Thus, social control can have a positive meaning, i.e., one in which norm and rule conformity is enhanced by a type of social or administrative guidance; or the term can take on a negative meaning, i.e., one which fosters oppressive, restrictive, or corrupt control by those in power.

These three models of social control are easily distinguished by examining what they explain: the relation between natural and artificial order, deviance, and responses to power. They also may be distinguished by considering the level of their explanation. Each model explains group behavior. A fourth perspective, however, explains individual and group action.

Social Control of Social Bonds

Social control also may be conceptualized in terms of social bonds. The best predictor of law and norm conformity, accordingly, is the strength of one's attachments, conventional involvements and commitments, and beliefs in the moral and political order. Social bonds act as a powerful press toward conformity by placing an individual's attachments, for example, in jeopardy through the disclosure of a law violation. This view may be traced back to a series of studies on delinquency causation that suggested that crime results from: a failure to internalize socially accepted and prescribed norms of behavior, a dismantling of individual controls, and a breakdown in the effectiveness of external controls.[13]

The idea that internal or individual control can be established through a stake in conformity, while external controls are grounded in social organization added to a limited, but emerging tradition of integrating conceptions of psychosocial control. This tradition continued with studies that considered the notion that a number of different control factors may operate concomitantly in constraining human behavior.[14] For example, some researchers have argued that internalized control is a product of guilt brought about by the conscience. Indirect control, which might be considered quasi-external in form, comes from an individual's identification with appropriate non-criminal objects, e.g., parents and well socialized friends. Finally, direct control, a pure external control factor, is a function of extant rules, restrictions, and punishments.[15]

Social control theory reached its most modern form in the United States with the work of Travis Hirschi.[16] Hirschi proposed that the greater the perception of attachment to family and friends, commitment to and involvement in conventional activities, and devotion to commonly held beliefs, the more likely it is that one will engage in prosocial behavior. Since, the consequences of law violation would likely place significant relationships in jeopardy, the bond of affection between spouses, or a parent and child, becomes the primary deterrent to nonconformity.

The extent of this deterrent is conditioned upon the depth and quality of the attachment. The bond between the parent and child, for example, forms a path through which conventional paternal or maternal ideals and expectations can pass. This bond is strengthened by: the amount of time the child spends with the parent(s), the intimacy of communication between the parent and child, and the affectional identification between parent and child.

The next set of bonds concerns an individual's commitment to and involvement in conventional activities. Hirschi, in keeping with the psychosocial tradition described earlier, identified a number of stakes in conformity or commitments which include vocational aspirations, educational expectations, and educational aspirations. Once again, law-violative behavior is associated with decreased stakes in law abidance.

Finally, Hirschi discussed the importance of sharing a common or central societal value system. He concluded that law violations are in part determined by a person's belief in the moral validity of prosocial norms.

SOCIAL CONTROL IN JAPAN

The social control of deviance, power, social bonds, and natural-order perspectives provide an excellent framework for the explanation of norm conformity in Japan.[17]

One of the central theses of the social-control-of-deviance perspective is that law varies inversely with other forms of control. Thus, in societies with elaborate legal systems, detailed laws, and vast law-enforcement capabilities, other less formal mechanisms of ensuring social order are unnecessary. The converse is true for Japan. If law is conceptualized as a quantitative variable, then Japan has little law. As one scholar has noted: "Japan enjoys a freedom from legal restraints in a manner unparalleled by any other industrialized society."[18]

Weak Formal Controls

The conspicuous weakness of formal social-control mechanisms, as well as the unusual strength of informal social-control forces in Japan has been observed by scholars for many years. For example, a significant number of criminal prosecutions each year are suspended; i.e., the prosecution of a criminal charge is held in abeyance by a judge, pending the outcome of future behavior.[19] In fact, suspension of prosecution (kiso yuyo) is prevalent for almost all categories of crimes. Estimates range from 30 percent of all penal-code prosecutions to 36 percent of special-offenses prosecutions are suspended as a result of an accused's apology, payment of restitution, or expression of contrition.[20]

In relation to the prevalence of suspension, consider the role of apology in Japanese law. A written apology is often accepted as an alternative to filing of a criminal complaint.[21] An apologetic attitude of an accused can result in the police not referring the case to the prosecutor. Once charges are filed, the Penal Code of Japan allows a prosecutor the discretion to withdraw the prosecution (koso no torikeshi), thus dismissing the case, if an apology meets with approval. Evidence of an apology and remorse also may be considered a mitigating circumstance by sentencing judges; it may even result in a suspended sentence. Finally, once convicted or once considered blameworthy by the public, a ministry official or corporate executive often may tender a formal, written, ceremonial apology (shimatsusho). Shimatsusho have the effect of reinforcing an individual's submission to the hierarchical order, often for the sake of maintaining harmony. Confession, repentance, and absolution are considered underlying themes of the process of criminal justice in Japan.

The weakness of formal social control may be illustrated as well by considering the role of administrative guidance (AG) or *guosei shido*, AG is a form of persuasion by a governmental agency, practiced since the beginning of the Meiji era (1868-1912), which seeks to ensure that an organization conducts its business in a certain way.[23] Conforming to this persuasion is typically not required by law, and in most cases is entirely voluntary. The different types and functions of AG are found in Table 2.

AG has been extraordinarily effective in ensuring legal and normative compliance—without resort to law. At least four reasons may account for this. First, there is a conscious appreciation in Japan that the interests of the government override those of any individual organization. Though the subject of much debate, Chie Nakane's work on the social structure of society and groups in Japan provide some plausible suggestions for the vertical subordination of these interests.[23] Perhaps the best suggestion is found in the generalization of the relationship between parent and child, considered the smallest community of interest, to other social relationships, such as teacher and pupil, employer and employee, parent corporation and subsidiary, and governmental agencies and corporations.

Another reason for the acceptance of AG may be found in an important part of the fabric of human relations in Japan, captured by the term *Amae*, the desire to be loved. *Amae* reflects the core features of the mother-child relationship, e.g., trust, dependency, safety, and unconditional love. Accordingly, *amae* prompts compromise on the part of corporations, as well as a willingness to build consensus, or *ringi-sei*, in relations with government bodies.

The success of AG has been attributed, at least in part, to the reciprocal nature of favors, or *on*. Favors in Japan prompt reciprocation, or *giri*. A favor commands a like action. Given the connectedness of government and business and the history of the government's effort to build and rebuild corporate Japan, it is not surprising that there are ongoing reciprocal and dependent relations.

Finally, AG is far more flexible than more formal legal mechanisms. For instance, sanctions for organizational crime in Japan are generally limited to fines. Administrative agencies, on the other hand, have significant discretion in fashioning sanctions. Consider how the Health and Welfare Ministry (HWM) responded to Nippon Chemiphar, when it was revealed that employees had faked clinical data in order to obtain approval for seven new drugs.[24] MHW closed down the entire company for a period of eighty days. Nippon Chemiphar's warehouse and two factories were sealed. Mr. Akira Yamaguchi, Nippon Chemiphar's president, accepted full responsibility and promptly resigned.

The prominence of social control as an explanation of norm conformity may be seen

TABLE 2: Types and Functions
of Administrative Guidance

Types
- Guidance authorized by statute which allows for the issuance of recommendations or *kankoku*,
- Guidance issued under regulatory statutes which may provide more formal mechanisms such as orders or license requirements, and
- Guidance not authorized under a statute, but under the law establishing the relevant ministry.

Functions
- Regulatory guidance or *kisei shido*, e.g., restriction of production
- The provision of promotion or support or *sokushin josei*
- Harmonizing conflicting interests or *chosei*

SOURCE: Adapted from John O. Haley, "The Oil Cartel Cases: The End of an Era." *Law in Japan* 15: 1–11 (1982), and Wolfgang Pape, "Gyosei Shido and the Antimonopoly Law." *Law in Japan* 15: 12–24 (1982).

in a number of other aspects of culture and tradition. For instance, social control is seen in Japanese cultural and ethnic homogeneity, as well as cultural loyalty to a common tradition.

Homogeneity and Harmony

Japan has been called a nation-family, suggesting the obvious—that there exists significant cultural and ethnic homogeneity. Scholars discussing Japanese homogeneity have suggested that common values, norms, and customs are but a few of the important dimensions underlying a singular culture. In part, it is the submission of individuality in the name of homogeneity that distinguishes Japan from other countries.[25] It is, as well, the undifferentiated co-existence of an individual in relation to the group, the country, and the gods. Thus, homogeneity is as clearly reflected in population demographics as it is in Japan's conformist cultural ideology.

Part of this ideology is an unwavering belief in harmony, or *wa*. *Wa* has been touted as providing a basis for Japan's imperial system, is considered implicit in the notion of *amae*, and is said to have originated in shinto—an ancient native religion.[26] At the core of *wa* is the subordination of individuality in order to support group consensus. *Wa* is a social control which consistently exerts a powerful social influence. This social influence is literally "a web that binds," an intricate constellation of interacting obligations among individuals, groups, the country as a whole, and the world.[27]

But the web does more than subordinate, obligate, and bind an individual. *Wa* has the effect of individual dissolution through enlightenment. Expectations, standards, feelings of self-esteem and self-worth originate and then reside within the group. The group takes on a meaning which transcends the aggregate of individuals. Just like the social-control-of-social-bonds perspective, deviation from the group incurs risks of loss and shame. This is so because deviance places attachments in jeopardy.

Japan has been labeled a "communitarian" society with its emphasis on harmony, reciprocity, group allegiance, and individual subordination. Communitarianism is the antithesis of individualism.[28] The elements of communitarianism are a uniform interdependency, requiring reciprocal obligation, trust, and loyalty.[29]

CORPORATE CRIMINAL LIABILITY AND CORPORATE CRIME

In the United States, as elsewhere, liability is a threshold issue—"should the act which has been alleged be subjected to criminal punishment"? As Table 4 indicates, the United States and Japan differ with regard to the criminal liability of corporations. Corporate criminal liability in America exists in state and federal law in different forms. The codification of the Model Penal Code (MPC) by the American Law institute in 1962 ushered in a new era of uniform liability for most state corporate criminal-law violations.[30] A majority of states, following the MPC, vest power in prosecutors to proceed against corporations in one of three ways. First, corporations are liable for minor, regulatory offenses where a clear legislative purpose exists to make them so, and the agent who has acted has done so on behalf of the corporation, within the scope of his authority. The basis of liability here is vicarious, grounded in the doctrine of respondeat superior. Second, a corporation is liable where the offense is based upon a failure to discharge a specific duty of performance imposed by law. Finally, corporations are liable for all penal law violations, with few exceptions, where the "offense was authorized, requested, commanded or recklessly tolerated by the board of directors or by a high managerial agent acting in behalf of the corporation within the scope of his office or employment."[31] This final category, which has been the subject of much deliberation and debate, rejects the broad respondeat superior approach discussed above and confines liability to a narrow class of criminal acts—those which concern high managerial agents whose acts reflect the policy of the corporate body. States have been slow to adopt these liability rules in their entirety. Most state legislatures, it appears, have used them as a rough guide for drafting often less restrictive provisions.[32]

Federal statutory law, in comparison, fails to explicitly provide general principles of liability for corporations. Rather, case law has evolved under principles of vicarious responsibility where corporations are criminally liable for the conduct of employees acting within the scope of their employment or apparent authority. More elaborate rules for the federal courts have been proposed. Liability rules were first discussed at length by the National Commission on Reform of Federal Criminal Laws (Brown Commission) over twenty years ago. The Brown Commission suggested corporate liability for any offense committed by an agent and authorized, commanded, or requested by the board of directors, or those with managerial power.[33]

The failure of Congress to incorporate these rules into a comprehensive reform of the federal criminal law has resulted in some inconsistency, as well an uncertainty with regard to the extent of liability for acts committed by agents of corporations.[34]

In Japan, there is only partial corporate criminal liability (Table 3). The Japanese Penal

TABLE 3. Comparative Corporate Criminal Liability

Full Corporate Criminal Liability
- Canada
- England
- Netherlands
- United States

Partial Corporate Criminal Liability
- Belgium
- Denmark
- France
- Japan

No Corporate Criminal Liability
- Austria
- Germany
- Italy

SOURCE: Adapted from L.H. Leigh, "The Criminal Liability of Corporations and other Groups: A Comparative View," *Michigan Law Review*, 80: 1508–1528 (1979).

Code does not include explicit reference to corporate actors.[35] Thus, corporations rarely, if ever, are charged with offenses against a person, e.g., criminal homicide. Significant liability does exist outside the Penal Code. A host of regulatory and non-regulatory statutes include corporate actors as "legal persons" subject to liability. These statutes, like those found in the United States Code, do not share a common or explicit set of liability rules. To make matters more complex, legal commentators and courts appear to differ with respect to which statutes impose direct versus vicarious liability. Nonetheless, a host of statutes do in fact impose criminal liability (Table 4).

Table 5 reveals the extent to which corporations in Japan are regulated by statutory law. The category Dispositions reflects the number of criminal charges filed against corporate entities during the 1990 calendar year —over 3,800 charges against corporations. Notably, a sizeable percentage of these prosecutions were suspended. Corporations were most often charged with violations of the Industrial Safety and Health Law (831 instances), Law for the Safety of Vessels (367), Waste Disposal and Public Cleaning Law (322), Law on Control and Improvement of Amusement Business (311), Marine Pollution Prevention Law (249), and Labor Standards Law (208).

Of the 165 cases that went on to the District Court for trial, only two were acquitted (Table 5). All corporations found guilty were fined. Guilty verdicts, were returned, for example, in eighty-four corporate tax cases, twenty-one anti-prostitution cases, and eleven trademark cases.

Contrasting the number of corporate prosecutions in 1990 with the number of reported homicides, rapes, or robberies in Japan, it appears, at first glance, that corporations suffer unmercifully under Japanese law. The number of corporate prosecutions also looks impressive when compared with data on organizations prosecuted over the last four years in federal district courts in the United States (Table 6).

TABLE 4. Violations of Penal and Special Laws

			Suspension of Prosecution		Suspension of Disposition
	Dispositions	Prosecution	Susp. of Indictment	Susp. by Other Reasons	
Violations of Penal Code					
Assault	2			2	
Bodily injury/Not intentional	1			1	
Bodily injury/Not intentional/During Work (Non-Traffic Related)	1			1	
Larceny	1			1	
Embezzlement	1			1	
TOTAL of Violations of Penal Code	6			6	
Violations of Special Laws (Non-Penal Code)					
Public Offices Election Law	1			1	
Law on Control and Improvement of Amusement Business	311	186	113	11	1
Antic Dealings Law	7	2	5		
Explosives Control Law	36	24	11	1	
Possession of Firearms and Weapons Law	2	1	1		
Anti-Prostitution Law	36	29	6	1	
Child Welfare Law	10	4	6		
Auto Liability Security Law	2	1	1		
Food and Sanitation Law	9	3	5	1	
Waste Disposal and Public Cleaning Law	322	167	135	12	8
Drugs, Cosmetics, and Medical Instruments Law	34	22	11	1	
Law for Control of Poisonous and Powerful Agents	13	5	8		
Mariners Law	101	55	39	4	3
Labor Standard Law	208	45	145	15	3
Industrial Safety and Health Law	831	472	277	54	28
Income Tax Law	1		1	1	
Corporate Tax Law	83	83			
Customs Law	17	14	4	2	
Law Concerning the Regulation of Receiving of Capital Subscription, Deposits and Interests on Deposits	11	7			
Agriculture Land Law	3	2	1		
Forest Law	2	1	1		
Fishing Vessel Law	3	3			
Fisheries Law	17	17			
Fishing Net Regulations	2	2			
Law Regarding Permit and Control of Regulated Fishing	13	12			
Foreign Exchange and Foreign Trade Law	6	4	2		
Building Lots and Buildings Transaction Business Law	44	27	14	3	1
Water Pollution Control Law	32	26	5	1	

TABLE 4. *(cont'd.)*

| | Dispositions | Prosecution | *Suspension of Prosecution* | | Suspension of Disposition |
			Susp. of Indictment	Susp. by Other Reasons	
Road Freight Law	82	43	39		
Road Trucking Vehicle Law	48	30	16	2	
Law for Safety of Vessels	367	276	72	4	15
Port Regulation Law	109	71	38		
Law for Ship's Officer	87	55	28	2	2
Marine Pollution Prevention Law	249	125	90	6	28
Radio Law	14	6	6	1	1
Gravel Gathering Law	27	23	4		
River Law	2	1	1		
Building Standards Law	10	4	3	3	
Immigration Control and Refugee Recognition Act	13	9	4		
Regulations of Local Public Entity (Covering the protection and care of juveniles)	16	9	7		
Regulations of Local Public Entity (Others)	28	21	6	1	
Rules of Local Public Entity	32	27	4	1	
Other Special Laws	556	277	181	95	3
TOTAL of Violations of Special Laws	3797	2191	1290	223	93
TOTAL of Violations of Penal Code and Special Laws	3803	2191	1290	229	93

TABLE 5.   Dispositions Through Normal Procedure at District Court

	Total Number of Dispositions	Guilty	Fine	Not Guilty	Acquittal Other Than Not Guilty	Not Guilty
Violation of Special Laws (Non-Penal Code)						
Anti-Prostitution Law	21	21	21			
Law on Control and Improvement of Amusement Business	1	1	1			
Copyright Law	3	3	3			
Waste Disposal and Public Cleaning Law	9	8	8		1	
Water Pollution Control Law	1	1	1			
Drugs, Cosmetics, and Medical Instruments Law	2	2	2			1
Industrial Safety and Health Law	1	1	1			
Laws Regarding Dispatching Personnel Business	6	6	6			1
Corporate Tax Law	84	84	84			11
Gasoline Tax Law	1	1	1			1
Sales Tax Law	1	1	1			
Customs Law	3	3	3			
Law Concerning the Regulation of Receiving of Capital Subscription, Deposits and Interests on Deposits	1	1	1			
Trade Mark Law	11	11	11			1
Agriculture Land Law	1	1	1			1
Fisheries Law	3	3	3			
Laws Regarding Permit and Control of Regulated Fishing	1	1	1			
Regulations Regarding Control of Net Fishing for Cuttle Fish	3	3	3			
Building Lots and Buildings Transaction Business Law	4	4	4			
Road Freight Law	2	2	2			
Road Trucking Vehicle Law	2	2	2			
Road Traffic Law	2	1	1	1		
Law for Safety of Vessels	1	1	1			
Immigration-Control and Refugee Recognition Act	1	1	1			1
TOTAL	165	163	163	1	1	17

TABLE 6. Organizational Defendants
by Offense Code Groups
January 1, 1984–December 31, 1987

	Projections	Convictions
Property Crimes	1,076 (68.6%)	842 (69.0%)
Antitrust	322	274
Fraud	578	432
Tax & Customs	113	94
Other Property Offenses	63	42
Regulatory Crimes	367 (23.4%)	313 (25.6%)
Food & Drug	87	76
Motor Carrier Act	62	55
Agriculture	42	35
Firearms	8	6
Others	168	141
Other Crimes	126 (8.0%)	66 (5.4%)
Racketeering, Gambling, & Perjury	28	18
Bribery	24	19
Drug Abuse Control	31	14
Immigration	4	3
All Other Offenses	39	12
TOTALS	1,569 (100%)	1,211 (100%)

SOURCE: Jeffery S. Parker, "Criminal Sentencing Policy for Organizations: The Unifying Approach of Optimal Penalties," *American Criminal Law Review, 26* 513–604 (1989).

A careful examination of the Japanese corporate data, however, suggests that the offenses may not be fully comparable. A significant number of the Japanese statutory offenses appear similar to administrative-law violations in the United States for which civil sanctions apply. This is not particularly surprising, as violations of law in Japan, with few exceptions, are treated as criminal. Japanese courts simply do not have equity powers and, thus, are limited in their ability to enforce administrative orders and fashion creative remedies.[36]

On the other hand, while the offenses may not be entirely comparable, Tables 5 and 6 do show the extent to which Japanese corporations are the objects of criminal prosecution. They reveal, as well, the high rate of suspension and dismissal observed for individuals under the Penal Code. In addition, they suggest that the informal and consensu-

al administrative guidance that forms the basis for much informal social control of organizations is regularly supplemented by more formal criminal prosecution. Perhaps most important, Tables 4 and 5 may say a great deal about the selectivity of enforcement of laws for which corporate criminal liability exists.

Thus, it is worth considering two areas of Japanese statutory law which explicitly provide for corporate criminal liability, but are not represented in Tables 5 and 6: anti-monopolistic measures and insider trading. These two classes of offenses are well reported in the federal organizational data (as antitrust and fraud) in Table 6.

ANTI-MONOPOLISTIC MEASURES

In response to significant pressure from the United States, the Japanese Federal Trade Commission (FTC) filed criminal charges of price-fixing in November 6, 1991 against eight major chemical companies.[37] The companies were considered part of a major industrial group characterized by interlocking share ownership, known in Japan as *keiretsu*. The complaint alleged that members of this *keiretsu* (in 1990) reached two secret agreements which had the effect of increasing the price of plastic wrap by 40 percent. If convicted, the companies could be fined up to $3.8 million.

These recent charges were important for a number of reasons. First, the charges were said to have resulted from pressure by the United States to ensure openness and fairness in the Japanese economy.[38] Second, the charges were described by FTC officials as a sign of a new and more restrictive stance toward monopolistic practices. This stance was reflected in the indictment of both the eight corporations and their respective sales managers. And finally, these were the first criminal charges brought against Japanese corporations for price-fixing since the famous oil-cartel cases nineteen years ago. In the oil-cartel cases of 1973, twelve of the fourteen wholesale oil refining corporations operating in Japan were charged with violating Article 3 of the Anti-Monopoly Law by fixing and controlling oil prices and production volume. Article 3 prohibits unreasonable restraint of trade, such as any agreement to mutually restrict or conduct business so as to fix, maintain, or enhance prices.[39]

The message from the FTC was clear: administrative guidance will be supplemented by the more frequent filing of criminal charges. According to one Japanese monopoly expert, " . . . it will take more to convince people that the Fair Trade Commission will really enforce laws strictly. But most companies are going to realize clearly that they can't continue old practices.[40]

INSIDER TRADING

The transition from an exclusive reliance on administrative guidance to a mix of informal and more formal social control is nowhere more evident than in Japanese securities law. In September of 1987, Tateho Chemical Industries experienced serious losses as a result of speculations in the yen-bond market.[41] Shortly before the company publicly announced losses of ¥28 billion, several of its employees, bankers, and brokers sold their shares in Tateho.[42] Tateho leaked inside information to these parties so that they could benefit from the news before it went public. The insiders promptly sold their shares, but no legal action was taken against them or the company.[43]

Shortly after the Tateho incident, Nippon Steel Company, the world's largest steel manufacturer, was planning to purchase a large equity stake in Sankyo Seiki Manufacturing, a precision machinery concern. Before the announcement of the purchase, the stock price of Sankyo soared. After an investigation by the Tokyo Stock Exchange and the Ministry of Finance (MOF), over one hundred employees of both companies were found to have bought Sankyo stock the week before the announcement of Nippon's acquisition intentions. Again, no administrative action

was taken. The MOF, however, did speed up its plans to revise the Securities and Exchange Law and considered increasing its investigatory efforts.[44]

In 1988, perhaps the most significant securities scandal involving Japanese politicians was made public. A large Japanese publishing conglomerate, Recruit, sold a series of its shares to politicians and business leaders for well below their market value in exchange for favors. Current Japanese Prime Minister Kiichi Miyazawa was forced to resign from his post as Finance Minister in December 1988 for his involvement in the scandal. The bribery scandals also led to the downfall of the former Prime Minister Noboru Takeshita.[45]

These three securities scandals significantly affected both domestic and foreign-investor confidence in the eight Japanese stock exchanges. In order to ensure an equitable and sound market for trading securities, the Securities and Exchange Counsel (SEC) of Japan formed a subcommittee in 1987 to report on fairness in the trading of securities.[46] A report issued by this subcommittee argued in favor of developing a series of measures to prevent insider trading and reestablish the confidence of domestic and foreign investors. This report led to the passage of the 1988 Amendments to the securities laws—laws which specifically prescribed criminal sanctions for individuals and corporations where there is evidence of insider trading in securities (equities and options) on the basis of material non-public information. More thorough public disclosures of company information are also emphasized by the new law. Corporate violators of the amendments are subject to fines totalling ¥500.000.

Loss Compensation

A 1989 MOF directive banned loss-compensating payments to clients. Nonetheless, in Summer 1991, a new wake of securities scandals once again put pressure on the ministry to more effectively monitor the industry. These scandals revealed that between

October 1987 and March 1990 Japan's four largest securities houses (Nomura, Daiwa, Nikko, and Yamaichi) were compensating favored clients for losses incurred in the stock market. The firms saw the practice as a way of ensuring the maintenance of a long-term relationship.

Given the competitive nature of the Japanese brokerage industry over the past decade, it is not surprising that the Big Four firms desperately sought to keep clients in this way. A host of factors made it rather easy to justify the compensation transactions, including the importance of achieving the goals of the firm, the profits-first management style of some of the firms, the bursting of the "bubble economy," the lack of ethical codes and internal controls within the firms, and lax administrative oversight coupled with ineffective laws.

Given that group membership is an essential part of Japanese life, self-identity is dependent upon the identity of the group, in this case a company (*kaisha*), or a division with a company, and one's position within it. Adherence to the group's standards and fulfilling the expectations of the group become overwhelming forms of social control. Failure to conform to the group results in shame. Failure to meet expectations, such as achieving a certain level of profit, results in a deep sense of shame.

The great need to achieve success may explain why securities firms went to such great lengths to retain customers by reimbursing them for losses. An employee of a major Japanese securities firm stated, "[the] Japanese will do anything for their companies, even unfair things."[47] Thus, ethically questionable behavior may be neutralized if it is consistent with the goals of the group. The fierce competition between the securities firms and other financial institutions made client retention a top priority. The firms simply did what they felt was necessary.

In addition, overemphasizing profits at the securities firms may have caused managers and employees to temporarily lose

sight of the importance of ethical conduct. The chairman emeritus of Nomura blames the "'profit-first' expansionist management style" of the firm for the stock scandal. Yoshihisa Tabuchi, president of Nomura during the time of the scandal, is alleged to have created an atmosphere that made commissions and selling the most important aspects of conducting business.[48]

The bubble economy of Japan in the late 1980s also may have been a contributing factor to this scandal. The bubble economy reflected a period of easy monetary policy, when the government lowered the discount rate to 2.5 percent. The low interest rate resulted in significant incentives for investors to speculate, and for banks to fund such speculations.[49] The record high level of investments caused stock and property prices to soar to unprecedented levels. When the bubble burst, stock prices fell dramatically and the brokerage firms ended up covering the losses.

A lack of clear ethical standards within the securities firms may have played a significant role in the scandal, as well. With few internal controls to identify ethically questionable transactions, there were few incentives to question the policy of reimbursing favored clients. In fact, it would have been unusual for employees to raise such ethical issues while their superiors seemed unmoved by the practice.

Of course, the firms cannot shoulder all the blame. MOF supervision over the securities industry had been lax. But the MOF has conflicting responsibilities. While it oversees the securities industry, the MOF also assists firms in improving their competitive position internationally. It is very likely that the MOF knew of the compensation schemes well before their exposure but preferred to keep the scandal private so as not to disrupt the daily activities of the brokerage houses.[50] The MOF, like most administrative agencies, must make ongoing efforts to maintain a cooperative and consensual relationship in order to obtain information necessary to monitor the industry as a whole even if it allows the continuance of undesirable behavior.[51]

This dual role appears to undermine the MOF's ability to bring order to the securities industry. But it is possible—perhaps likely—that administrative guidance in the securities industry must be reinforced or supplemented by more formal social controls. This notion is supported by the fact that while the MOF's December 1989 directive banning compensation was essentially ignored, former Chairman of Nomura, Setsuya Tabuchi, testified that Nomura would never have paid loss compensations if the practice had been specifically prohibited by law.[52]

Taking Responsibility

The resignations of the top officials at Nomura and Nikko following the news release of the scandals suggest that public admissions of guilt and promises not to repeat transgressions are still powerful controls.[53] Normally, the government would not call for further penalties, but the seriousness of Nomura's and Nikko's transgressions led to fines and trading suspensions. The unprecedented severity of these punishments resulted from the companies' dealings with a former crime syndicate boss and the fact that the companies were suspected of manipulating the price of a railway corporation stock.[54]

Soon after the scandals were made public, the MOF ordered the big-four firms to suspend all client transactions for four business days.[55] As the scandals unravelled throughout the summer of 1991 and into September, the possibility of stock manipulations on behalf of Nomura and Nikko became more apparent. In one of the most severe punishments ever to be issued by the MOF against a securities firm, eight Nomura branch operations were suspended from trading for six weeks and 79 of 153 domestic offices were suspended for one month. Not only was Nomura not to purchase for its customers' accounts, but it was suspended from trading on its own account and was forced to close its research division.[56]

Nomura, Nikko, Daiwa, and Yamaichi were all prohibited from underwriting government bonds for the month of October 1991. Nomura's penalty was extended through November. The corporate sales divisions of the four firms were also ordered to close for a period of one to three weeks for violating the MOF directive to discontinue client compensation practices.[57] Nikko's involvement with the crime syndicate, lending a large sum of money to a former gangster boss, as well as its compensation schemes caused the MOF to bar it from a large underwriting of government-held Nippon Telegraph and Telephone Corporation shares.[58]

Nomura and Nikko demonstrated a desire to be absolved of the scandal by taking their own disciplinary actions. The securities firms sent letters of deep regret to their clients. The letters, totaling more than six million, were extremely apologetic and promised that the scandals would not reoccur.[59] Paycuts, forced retirements, and demotions were also effected as an indication of the shame they felt for misconduct.[60]

The Finance Minister, Ryutaro Hashimoto, announced punishments against top ministry officials, including himself, in the form of paycuts to compensate for MOF's failure to effectively supervise the securities industry.[61] Hashimoto eventually resigned because of continuing criticisms of the Ministry's lax administrative guidance. The ministry was also being blamed for an inappropriate licensing system which restricted competition and allowed large firms to amass enormous profits.

The ritual of group leaders resigning to take responsibility for the transgressions of the group (known popularly as *noblesse oblige*) may have at one time been enough to indemnify the group. But now that Japan is a modern society functioning in an international arena, symbolic cultural actions grounded in shame and censure may not be enough.

Changes in Action

The compensation scandal has drawn considerable attention to the need for changes in the way the Japanese define and treat illegal behavior within corporations. Such changes include the creation of a watchdog body with functions similar to the United States Securities and Exchange Commission, revision of the Securities and Exchange Law to be more transparent and include harsher penalties, and changes within corporations to place greater emphasis on ethics and the value of conducting business fairly.[62]

How should the new body be structured? At the time the scandals were made public, Prime Minister Toshiki Kaifu suggested that the watchdog body be independent from the Ministry of Finance and be similar in function to the Securities and Exchange Commission in the United States. Politicians and business leaders also favored the establishment of an independent body. Understandably, the finance minister greatly resisted these suggestions because the creation of an independent agency would take away the ministry's control over the industry. The minister strongly urged parliament to let a new investigative division within the MOF serve the watchdog function.[63] A bill drafted by the MOF calls for the creation of a body within the ministry to monitor the securities market and identify fraud and abusive practices.[64] Although this falls short of demands to create an independent watchdog body, it does represent a significant move in the direction of creating a more soundly operated securities market.

Soon after the scandals became public, the MOF began to investigate ways to change the Securities and Exchange law in order to prevent a reoccurrence of the unfair practice of compensating favored clients. In August 1991, a bill was proposed which included penalties for brokerages of a maximum fine of ¥1 million.[65] The penalties for clients were a six-month maximum prison term or a maximum fine of ¥500.000.[66] The bill also prohibited discretionary accounts where brokerages had complete control over investors' money.[67] These proposed changes in the law were specifically designed to supplement the practice of administrative guidance. The punitive sanctions, although small, indicate a willingness on the part of the MOF to replace infor-

mal, extra-legal controls with codified legislative sanctions.

At the same time, the MOF also issued a new set of directives to the brokerage industry. Included were the following recommendations:

- the firms should establish in-house watchdog bodies to monitor the fairness of the transactions conducted by the firm;
- educational and training sessions should be held for employees to understand the nature of their responsibilities and the types of transactions they conduct;
- the firms should actively seek to learn if an investor is affiliated with a crime syndicate, and if so, sever all ties to the investor; and
- managers of client accounts should not keep any one particular client for more than three years.[68]

Recently, the big-four firms announced voluntary reforms to assure clients that effective internal changes will prevent a reoccurrence of the scandals. A shift away from the profit-first management style that encouraged unethical behavior was promised. Firms also displayed a willingness to consider the priorities of their customers.[69]

CORPORATE SANCTIONS

At first, the move toward more formal sanctions against Japanese corporations in response to anti-monopoly and securities-law violations appears curious. It seems much more curious when one considers the sheer number of corporate prosecutions under regulatory statutes each year. Indeed, it is strange to see the responsibility for organizational crime placed squarely on the shoulders of the Japanese business entity, rather than on its president.

Of course, few observers would be surprised by the prospect of scandals in the United States prompting Congress to pass new and more restrictive legislation. Consider, for example, the effect on Congress of a host of highly publicized insider-trading prosecutions throughout the 1980s.[70] The scandals that brought about these prosecutions convinced Congress that corporate codes of ethics were insufficient, compliance programs were not working, and existing laws were not effective. The House committee that fashioned a legislative response called for an affirmative statutory obligation to prevent insider trading.[71] This affirmative statutory obligation, aimed at corporations and individuals, became the Insider Trading and Securities Fraud Enforcement Act (ITSFEA) of 1988.[72]

ITSFEA was a natural and probable consequence of a long and well-publicized history of trading abuses. Comparable legislation in Japan, such as the 1988 Amendments prohibiting insider trading, seem more like an anomaly. But this anomaly can be explained. It reflects a clash between Japan's communitarian heritage—which it clings to with great fortitude—and the realities and responsibilities of promoting a modern economy. Gregory Clark captured the essence of this clash: "Japan is still a large tribal, village-style society where morality is not decided in terms of principles and absolutes but in terms of how one's actions affect others within one's range of responsibility. But Japan also realizes the need for western style legalism if it is to create the basis for a modern society and economy. So it compromises. It sets up the laws and regulations it thinks it needs, many borrowed directly from the west. But it brings them into force only when traditional morality clearly becomes inadequate."[73]

Thus, there is nothing curious about the transformation of corporate criminal liability in Japan. It is simply a compromise—perhaps even an accommodation of Western interests. This compromise has both practical and theoretical importance. Each scandal that erupts results in the reform of targeted abuses, and allows for self-reflection regarding the limits of administrative guidance. The compromise has theoretical importance as well. The way in which a society controls behavior, sets norms, and ensures conformity reflects the state of social control. The compromise of traditional morality and more formal statutory obligation was envisioned by Ross at the turn

of the century. As noted earlier, he maintained that as society grows more complex, as personal and intimate relations are replaced by impersonal and contractual relations, the natural bonds that derive from the aggregation of individuals in a rural community no longer control and curb self-interest. The transition from a natural community, held together by a traditional morality, to an artificial society characterized by an amalgam of private interests, requires artificial order. Thus, the compromise between the natural order and the artificial order is Japan's compromise between traditional morality and Western style legalism.

The theoretical significance of trying to balance natural and artificial order extends to each of the models of social control described earlier. Those models use law as a locus of control when other less formal controls fail (social control of deviance); the imposition of formal sanctions to control the actions of constituents (social control of power); and relative strength of an individual's attachments, conventional involvements and commitments, and beliefs in the social order (social control of social bonds).

Finally, there may be significant and yet unforeseen costs associated with the clash and resulting compromise. In November of 1991, Prime Minister Kiichi Miyazawa invited into his new cabinet a number of politicians who were involved, to varying degrees, in the Recruit scandal. His decision reflects one of the central themes of punishment in Japan. Western nations punish through finding guilt and ostracizing the offender. The finding of guilt and the process of being an outcast conveys our message of moral condemnation. Japan, by contrast, has a long tradition of relying upon shame. But shaming in Japanese culture entails more than censure and disgrace. Shame felt by an individual is often born by the group, perhaps the family or company. And most important, shame is reintegrative. John Braithwaite has made this distinction clear: "Reintegrative shaming means that expressions of community disapproval, which may range from mild rebuke to degradation ceremonies, are followed by gestures of reacceptance into the community of law-abiding citizens."[74] Reintegrative shaming is tied to the tradition of apology in Japan. It explains corporate *noblesse oblige*, a long standing tradition of presidents and managers of corporations taking full responsibility for the acts of employees. It provides a foundation for the tradition of suspending prosecutions. It goes to the very heart of the conception of Japan as a nation-family. Quite simply, the cost associated with the clash and compromise would be felt were fines for corporate illegality to replace these traditions— were the artificial order to outweigh the natural order.

The protracted debate over fashioning sanctions for organizations in the United States should provide a valuable lesson about the outer boundaries of the artificial order. For several years, members of the United States Sentencing Commission, economists, sociologists, and lawyers sought the optimal monetary penalty in relation to corporate harm. (What price would be too much to pay for a rational corporation considering the commission of a crime?) Initially, proposals expressed little concern with corporate culpability. Fortunately, the final guidelines incorporated provisions which included a "culpability score." This score encourages the immediate acceptance of responsibility and the reporting of illegalities. It allows corporations to mitigate fines by acting responsibly in detecting and reporting illegalities. Culpability also may be assessed by the presence of a corporate ethics code or ongoing compliance program. Corporate culpability? Accepting responsibility? Reporting illegalities? Some novel ideas for American corporations. Perhaps both societies could learn from each other.

NOTES

1. National Police Agency, *White Paper on Police* (Tokyo: Government of Japan, 1990), 132.
2. See, e.g., Freda Adler, *Nations Not Obsessed with Crime* (Littleton, CO: Rothman, 1983); Gideon Fishman and Sy Diniz, "Japan: A Country with Safe Streets," in W.S. Laufer and Freda Adler, eds., *Advances in Criminological Theory* (New Brunswick, NJ: Transaction, 1988).
3. The exception is an interesting article which is restricted to white collar rather than corporate or entity crime by Harold R. Kerbo and Mariko Inoue, "Japanese Social Structure and White Collar Crime: Recruit Cosmos and Beyond," *Deviant Behavior* 11 (1990): 139–54.
4. See, e.g., Donald J. Shoemaker, *Theories of Delinquency: An Examination of Explanations of Delinquent Behavior* (New York: Oxford University Press, 1984); George Vold and Thomas Bernard, *Theoretical Criminology* (New York: Oxford University Press, 1988); Freda Adler, Gerhard O.W. Mueller, and William S. Laufer, *Criminology* (New York: McGraw-Hill, 1991).
5. See, e.g., Robert K. Merton "Social Structure and Anomie," *American Sociological Review* 3, (1938): 672–82; Robert K. Merton, *Social* *Theory and the Social Structure* (New York: Free Press, 1957).
6. Clifford Shaw and Henry D. McKay, *Juvenile Delinquency and Urban Areas* (Chicago: University of Chicago Press, 1942). More recent work includes: Robert J. Sampson and W. Byron Groves, "Community Structure and Crime: Testing Social Disorganization Theory," *American Journal of Sociology* 94, (1989): 774–802; Robert J. Bursik, Jr., "Social Disorganization and Theories of Crime and Delinquency: Problems and Prospects," *Criminology* 26 (1988): 519–51.
7. Edward Alsworth Ross, *Social Control: A Survey of the Foundation of Order* (New York: Macmillan, 1901).
8. C.H. Cooley, *Social Organization* (New York: Scribner, 1909).
9. Ross, 11.
10. Donald Black, *The Behavior of Law* (New York: Academic Press, 1976). See also, Roscoe Pound, *Social Control Through Law* (New Haven: Yale University Press, 1942).
12. See, Nanette J. Davis and Bo Anderson, *Social Control: The Production of Deviance in the Modern State* (New York: Irvingtron, 1983);

S. Cohen and A. Scull, eds., *Social Control and the State* (New York: St. Martins Press, 1983).

13. Albert J. Reiss, "Delinquency as the Failure of Personal and Social Controls," *American Sociological Review* 16 (1951): 206–15.

14. Jackson Toby, "Social Disorganization and Stake in Conformity: Complementary Factors in the Predatory Behavior of Hoodlums" *Journal of Criminal Law, Criminology, and Police Science* 48 (1957): 12–17; Francis Ivan Nye, *Family Relationships and Delinquent Behavior* (New York: Wiley, 1958).

15. Nye.

16. Travis Hirschi, *Cause of Delinquency* (Berkeley: University of California Press, 1969).

17. Our discussion of crime in Japan has been influenced by Ted D. Westerman and James W. Burfeind's excellent text *Crime and Justice in Two Societies: Japan and the United States* (Pacific Grove, CA: Brooks Cole, 1991).

18. John O. Haley, "Introduction: Legal vs. Social Control," *Law in Japan* 17 (1984): 1–6.

19. B.J. George, "Discretionary Authority of Public Prosecutors in Japan," *Law in Japan* 17 (1984): 42–72.

20. Ibid., 58f.

21. Hiroshi Wagatsuma and Arthur Rosett, "The Implications of Apology: Law and Culture in Japan and the United States," *Law and Society Review* 20 (1986): 461–78; John O. Haley, "Comment: The Implications of Apology," *Law and Society Review* 20, 499–507.

22. See, e.g., Mitsuo Matsushita and Thomas J. Schoenbaum, *Japanese International Trade and Investment Law* (Tokyo: University of Tokyo Press, 1989); Wolfgang Pape, "Gyosei Shido and the Antimonopoly Law," *Law in Japan* 15 (1982): 12–23; Lawrence Repeta, "The Limits of Administrative Authority in Japan: The Oil Cartel Criminal Cases and the Reaction of MITI and the FTC," *Law in Japan* 15 (1982): 24–56; Kenji Sanekata, "Administrative Guidance and the Antimonopoly Law—Another View of the Oil Cartel Criminal Decisions," *Law in Japan* 15 (1982): 95–99; Yoriaki Narita, "Administrative Guidance," *Law in Japan* 2 (1968): 45–79.

23. Chie Nakane, *Japanese Society* (Berkeley: University of California Press, 1972); Robert J. Smith, *Japanese Society: Tradition, Self and the Social Order* (Cambridge, UK: Cambridge University Press, 1983).

24. "Japanese Drug Companies Euthanasia," *The Economist*, 11 December 1982; "Total Ban on Drug Making at Chemiphar," *The Financial Times*, 8 December 1982; "Chemiphar Admits False Data on More Drugs," *The Financial Times*, 4 December 1982.

25. See, e.g., John Braithwaite, *Crime, Shame and Reintegration* (Cambridge, UK: Cambridge University Press, 1989).

26. See, e.g., Boye De Mente, *Japanese Etiquette and Ethics in Business* (Lincolnwood, IL: NTC Business Books, 1990).

27. Ibid., 38.

28. See, D.H. Bayley, *Forces of Order: Police Behavior in Japan and the United States* (Berkeley: University of California Press, 1976); W. Clifford, *Crime Control in Japan* (Lexington, MA: Lexington Books, 1976); John Braithwaite, 84–97.

29. Braithwaite, 85-86.

30. See, American Law Institute, *Model Penal Code* (Philadelphia: American Law Institute, 1978); Kathy Brickey, "Rethinking Corporate Liability Under the Model Penal Code," *Rutgers Law Journal* 19 (1988): 593–634.

31. *Model Penal Code*, sec. 2.07 (1)(c) (Proposed Official Draft 1962).

32. *Model Penal Code*, sec. 632.

33. See, sec. 4.02, *Final Report of the National Commission on Reform of Federal Criminal Law* (Washington, DC: U.S. Government Printing Office, 1971).

34. See, Kathy Brickey, *Corporate Criminal Liability: A Treatise on the Criminal Liability of Corporations, Their Officers and Agents* (Deerfield, IL: Callaghan & Co., 1984).

35. For one of the few articles to consider this issue, see Hyoichiro Kusano, "The Punishment of Corporations," *Law in Japan* 5: 83–94.

36. John O. Haney, "Introduction: Legal vs. Social Controls," *Law in Japan* 17 (1984): 1–6.

37. "Japan, in Rare Move, Charges Price-Fixing of Food Wrap," *New York Times*, 7 November 1991, D2.

38. Ibid.

39. See, John O. Haney, "The Oil Cartel Cases: The End of an Era," *Law in Japan* 15 (1982): 1–11.

40. See, "Japan, in Rare Move, Charges Price-Fixing of Food Wrap."

41. "Japanese Insider Trading, New Law for Old," *The Economist*, 1 October 1988, 92.

42. "Control of Insider Trading to Be Tightened" *Kyodo News Service*, 8 January 1988; Pat Widder, "Worldwide Trading, the Sun Never Sets on the Electronic Stockmarket," *Chicago Tribune*, 1 May 1988, 10.

43. Widder, 10.

44. Tetsuo Jimbo, "Japan's Inside-Trading 'Tradition' Under Attack," *Christian Science Monitor*, 13 September 1988, 12.

45. Michael Nol, "Miyazawa Rapped Over Scandal," *United Press International*, 11 November 1991.

46. Chieko Takeshita and Kazumi Okamura, "Japan's Securities Markets: Regulation of Insider Trading," *East Asian Executive Reports*, vol. 12, no. 10, November 15, 1990, 8.

47. Yoshiaki Itoh, "Scandals Spur Debate on Ethics, Business Culture; Consensus Grows for Internal Checks," *The Nikkei Weekly*, 3 August 1991, 1.

48. "Nomura's Plunge from Grace: Tabuchis Drove Company with 'Profits-First' Style—and Now They Are Among the Casualties," *The Nikkei Weekly*, 3 August 1991, 4.

49. "Bubble Economy Comes Under Close Parliamentary Scrutiny," *Kyodo News Service*, 8 August 1991.

50. "Securities Scandal Probe Only Half Finished," *The Nikkei Weekly*, 14 September 1991, 6.

51. "MOF's Punishment Does Not Fit the Crime," *The Nikkei Weekly*, 20 July 1991, p. 6.

52. "Securities Scandal Probe Only Half Finished."

53. Haley, 2; "Nomura's 2 Top Executives Resign Over Stock Scandal," *Kyodo News Service*, 22 July 1991.

54. Robert Thomson, "Japan's Big Four Penalized: Four-Day Ban on Stockbrokers' Trading with Corporate Investors," *Financial Times*, 9 July 1991, 1.

55. "'Big Four' Begin Four-Day Transaction Suspensions," *Kyodo News Service*, 10 July 1991.

56. James Sterngold, "Nomura Gets Big Penalties," *New York Times*, 9 October 1991, D1.

57. Ibid.

58. "Nikko to Be Excluded from NTT Stock Underwriters," *Kyodo News Service*, 27 September 1991.

59. "Nomura, Nikko Send Letters of Apology to clients," *Kyodo News Service*, 8 August 1991.

60. Naoyuki Isono, "Penalties Imposed for Scandal: Big Four Securities Companies, Top Finance Ministry Officials Chastened," *The Nikkei Weekly*, 20 July 1991, 4.

61. Ibid.

62. "Reform Initiatives Will Aim to Clarify Brokerage Licensing Rules," *International Securities Report*, November 18, 1991.

63. Hideteka Tomomatsuand-Yas Idei, "Securities Watchdog: Hunter or House Pet: Debate Centers on Creation of Independent Body or Stricter Ministry Scrutiny," *The Nikkei Weekly*, 10 August 1991, 1.

64. Fumiko Fujisaki, "Japan Panels Rush to Prevent Repeat of Scandals," *Reuter*, 3 December 1991.

65. "Government to Decide on Securities and Exchange Law Revision," *Kyodo News Service*, 21 August 1991.

66. Ibid.

67. Ibid.

68. "MOF Issues Scandal-Prevention Instructions to Brokers," *Kyodo News Service*, 31 July 1991.

69. Kenji Nagano, "Nomura: From 'Profits-First' to 'Deep Regrets'; Scandals Pressure Brokerage to Change," *The Nikkei Weekly*, 12 October 1991, 4.

70. Harvey L. Pitt and Karl A. Groskaufmanis, "Minimizing Corporate Civil and Criminal Liability: A Second Look at Corporate Codes of Conduct," *Georgetown Law Journal* (1990): 1–115.

71. Ibid., 38.

72. Insider Trading and Securities Fraud Enforcement Act of 1988, P.L. 100–704, 102 Stat 4677.

73. Gregory Clark, "Stock Price Manipulation Is the Real Scandal," *The Nikkei Weekly*, 17 August 1991, 6.

74. Braithwaite, 55.

THE PARADOX OF ECONOMIC GLOBALISM

*The myth and reality of the "global village"—
the changing role of multinational corporations*

S. Prakash Sethi, Joel A. Kurtzman, and Bharat B. Bhalla

A vision conceptualized in the oft-quoted phrase "Global Village" suggests that the world is becoming more interdependent economically and more integrated politically.[1] Judging from global trade and investment flows, this notion is not hyperbole; nor is it new. It surfaced in the 1972 Club of Rome Report.[2] However, the speed with which the new world is developing is both exhilarating and frightening. It is full of risks and uncertainties. On the one hand, the future might hold an immense promise of well being for all. Alternately, it might portend a greatly divided world where the haves and the have-nots are bound in a mortal struggle, not of their making, but from which they can not see any escape.

THE OPTIMIST'S VIEW
OF THE "BRAVE NEW WORLD"

At one level, the world indeed is becoming more integrated and economically interdependent. Consider, for example, that 60 percent of the world economy is linked, i.e., more than half of every transaction has an international component. Looking at any personal computer, one finds

> the United Nations at work—chips from California, Malaysia, Korea, [and] Japan based on designs from Switzerland, the United

States, Israel, Japan, and France, executed in exotic materials produced in Germany, the United States, Japan and France from raw materials mined or recycled from who knows where.[3]

The same is true of the Boeing, the symbol of "Made in America" prowess. The new Boeing 767, assembled in the United States, has components from different countries around the world: fuselage parts from South Korea and Japan, wings and landing gear from the United States, wing tips from Spain, rudders from Italy, engines from the United Kingdom and the United States, electronics from Japan, and various sundry parts made in the United Kingdom, Germany, Portugal, Spain and Taiwan.[4]

Since 1970, world trade has grown twice as fast as world GNP, and expansion supported by a 50 percent real increase in foreign direct investment. Global trade in financial instruments is now worth many times more than trade in goods and services.[5] The financial markets and the universe of ideas and information are connected through computers that operate around the clock. This electronic continent is linked together by transnational corporations (TNCs), the primary economic unit, which use nations and their geopolitical boundaries as platforms upon which to arrange and rearrange the building blocks of their economic empires.[6] Another distinguishing characteristic of this electronic continent is the gradual disappearance of the physical, tangible symbols of money consisting of paper notes and metal coins. They are being replaced by "Megabyte Money," a system which operates around the clock on a network of computers "wired together in places as lofty as the Federal Reserve—which settles accounts between banks every night that are worth trillions of dollars."[7]

The new global village of the optimist is primarily personified by the twenty-four industrially advanced countries of the Organization for Economic Cooperation and Development (OECD). It "is united with the speed-of-light electronic network technology, a global jet transportation network and computer linkages that span the globe—making location and distance irrelevant."[8] People are wealthier in the OECD countries, they are healthier, and they live longer. Over 90 percent of households own televisions and radios and 50 percent of the population own cars. Although these countries contain only 15 percent of the world's population, they produce 71 percent of the global GNP, over $19,000 per capita, roughly five times the average per-capita GNP of the world and twenty-four times that of the developing countries. OECD nations consume roughly 85 percent of the world's forest products, 80 percent of its food, 75 percent of its metals, and 70 percent of its energy; produce 75 percent of world's industrial output, absorb 70 percent of the global inflows of foreign direct investment, and buy 75 percent of goods and services traded in the world market. With a 95 percent literacy rate, the OECD has the most productive labor force.[9] Another important element uniting these countries is that they are essentially pluralistic societies in which freedom of faith, speech and ballot box are guaranteed to every citizen.

Three great market regions—Japan, Europe, and the United States—dominate the world of multinational business. The combined gross domestic product (GDP) of Japan and the United States now accounts for 40 per-

cent of the free world's total; add the GDP of the four biggest Western European nations (France, Germany, Italy and the United Kingdom) and the figure reaches 60 percent. Customers in the Japan-Europe-U.S. Triad buy over 85 percent of the world's supply of computers and consumer-electronic products. Germany, Japan, and the United States alone absorb 70 percent of the global production of numerically controlled machine tools.[10]

In the global village,

> Countries are [indeed] bound more closely together than ever before, and they are more aware of each other than ever before. The massive mingling through trade, tourism, television, immigration, and international investments has created superficial similarities and has led to a leveling of living standards. This euphoric vision of the new global village, unfortunately, conceals a great many details . . . [not readily] apparent. Although prosperity has gone "global," statistical differences are ignored in the grand scheme of things.[11]

Economic convergence has failed to bring cultural convergence. The societies of the global village are intent on maintaining their cultural identity in terms of history, language and traditions. The underlying uncertainties and risks portend a sharply divided world where people of different ethnic, religious and political orientations are engaged in a struggle to which there is no apparent end.

THE PESSIMIST'S VIEW OF THE "BRAVE NEW WORLD"

The "facts," the data, of the First-World global village are accurate, but they do not go far enough. Therefore, we cannot accept this vision of the "brave new world." Instead, we suggest a scenario based on a different set of facts and additional data and on an analysis that recognizes these facts in a way that offers more plausible answers to the inconsistencies in the emerging world economic and sociopolitical order. We must focus on how different elements and components enmesh in a great cobweb; we must learn to distinguish between the predators and the victims and between the promises of the brave new world and the miseries of those who, in that world, would be left behind.

The integrated global village of the optimist excludes the highly fragmented Third World—where a majority of the people live. The world they inhabit—their *real* world—does not seem to have much to do with the glitzy brave new world. For them, the meaning of global village is living in poverty and denial. Beyond the sanitized versions that appear in palatable sixty-second segments on their evening newscasts or on "Save the Children" posters, those living on the bright side of the global village have little comprehension of the poverty, deprivation, and ignorance that exists in the Third World. Similarly, the Third World has no concept of how the First World sees, acts, and behaves. Yet these worlds cohabit on the same planet.

More than 50 percent of the world's population lives in economies that border on subsistence. Two-thirds of the people of the world live and die within 100 miles of where they were born. Hardly 15 percent of the people of the world have ever travelled on a plane and even fewer have ever travelled abroad. Less than 1 percent of the population of China, Ghana, India and Kenya have a telephone, whereas there are over eighty telephones per 100 people in Canada, Denmark, Switzerland and the United States.[12] Compared to OECD nations, developing countries on a per-capita basis, have only one-eighth as many newspapers, one-sixth as many radios, one-eighteenth as many telephones and one-twentieth as many computers[13]

People living in the First World may be jetting around the globe, commuting in cars between their homes and workplace, and communicating with each other through electronic networks; but the poor in the Third world still travel on bullock carts, bicycles and man-powered rickshaws. In this latter world, the beast of burden is not a sixteen-wheeler but the stooping back of the peasant woman, the listless young child, the despon-dent old man and the half-starved donkey. Even such basic amenities as electricity and roads are in short supply.

The rural and inward-looking bias of developing countries' economies is evident in the makeup of their population, structure of GDP and merchandise trade. Between 60 to 75 percent of their population still live in rural areas; agro-industry contributes 70 percent to their annual GDP; and natural resources, including primary commodities and minerals, comprise 50 to 73 percent of their merchandise exports.[14] Third World countries have also done poorly in economic growth. While these countries account for 75 percent of the global population (over five times the OECD population), their average per-capita income is roughly 5 percent that of OECD nations.[15]

Developing countries, in an attempt to earn foreign exchange required to service their foreign debt, sell increasing quantities of their primary products in international markets in competition with each other. They are further encouraged to sell these materials in a raw or semi-processed form to industrially advanced countries whose tariff structures favor such imports. They are denied opportunities to diversify their domestic economies; are compelled to sell their goods at depressed prices; are forced to accept marginal returns; suffer persistent deficits in their balance of payments; and continue to wallow in mounting debt burden and poverty.

The latest report on human development by the United Nation's Development Programme (UNDP) sharply focuses on the economic, political, and social challenges that Third World countries face "in removing the immense backlog of human deprivation."[16] The UNDP report discloses that 1.2 billion people, roughly 1.5 times the current population of OECD countries, live in absolute poverty; nearly 1 billion adults are unable to read or write; 2.3 billion people live in unsanitary conditions; 1.5 billion people lack access to health services; and 1.3 billion people are without access to safe drinking water. In addition, about 100 million are completely without shelter, some 800 million remain hungry every day, 180 million children under five (one in three) are malnourished and 14 million children die each year before their fifth birthday.[17]

Nor do a majority of the people of this world have the luxury of democracy, representative government, freedom of choice, or freedom of opportunity. In 1988, the percentage of the world's population classified by Freedom House as living in "free" countries was 38.3 percent.[18] UNDP—basing its conclusion on its 1992 Political Freedom Index (consisting of five variables: personal security, rule of law, freedom of expression, political participation, and equality of opportunity) for 104 countries representing 92 percent of the world population—reported that only 33 percent of all countries have a high degree of freedom.[19] The only government many of these countries know is tyranny, and the only safety net they have is a support system of family and tribe. Those in the West, who have flourished under the aegis of individual rights and representative governments, seem content to live with such as situation so long as it allows them to have stable markets and dependable despots.

CONTRASTING VISIONS OF ECONOMIC GLOBALISM

The modern world has a thin veneer beneath which lies a structure tottering on the brink of collapse. We do not have the building blocks of a happy future; we have, rather, a caldron of frustration and misery ready to explode and engulf us all.

Nonetheless, the OECD nations are optimists about the integrating world. Despite the fact that the original basis for the European Community (EC)—the European Steel and Coal Community—remains unfulfilled, they consider the triad—the European Single Market, the North American Free Trade Agreement (NAFTA) and the Pacific Rim—as the building blocks of the emerging integrated world in which resources will be efficiently utilized for the benefit of all mankind.

The Third World countries, on the other hand, are pessimistic about the global village. While they, themselves, must take a large part of the blame for their predicament, they consider themselves victims of their erstwhile colonial masters and hold the latter responsible for their existing poverty, dependency, and weak bargaining power. Developing countries feel that the neocolonialist powers, through their foreign-aid programs and multilateral financial institutions, have managed to perpetuate the dependency relationship, a relationship that was reinforced by the desire of Western powers to keep these countries in one or the other political bloc during the Cold War.[20]

Even given the end of the Cold War, the argument that the developing countries should follow the route taken by the newly industrializing countries (NICs) is misplaced. Conditions in the two groups of countries are dissimilar, and some respectable economists and social and political scientists seriously question whether the NIC model is indeed replicable in large parts of Africa and Latin America.

Whatever the correctness of these differing views, the economic rationality underlying globalism—i.e., that globalism maximizes output and therefore global wealth—is a mixed blessing. One of the pernicious effects, thus far, of growth in global wealth is the shift in income and wealth distribution it has created and the widening gap between the haves and have-nots that has resulted therefrom. Income disparities are widening both nationally and globally. For example, in Brazil, the richest 20 percent of the population receives twenty-six times the income earned by the poorest 20 percent. The income concentration is more transparent at the global level. During the thirty years (between 1960 and 1989), the countries with the richest 20 percent of the world population increased their share of global GNP from 70.2 percent to 82.7 percent, while the share of the countries with the poorest 20 percent of the population declined from 2.3 percent to 1.4 percent.[21] Measured in absolute (1989 dollar) terms, the disparity in per-capita income of the richest 20 percent and the poorest 20 percent of world population increased from $1,864 in 1960 to $15,149 in 1989.[22]

THE MULTINATIONAL CORPORATION IN THE NEW GLOBAL VILLAGE

A major issue is how to create a village where both worlds can unite and people of all nations may live as a global community. The emergence of the global village will call for a greater and more proactive role for the multinational corporation (MNC). Concomitants of that role will include greater public scrutiny of the MNC and increased sociopolitical accountability regarding MNC behavior in the marketplace and standards of performance. The challenge facing the MNC is profound: will the MNC be an agent of economic growth and human welfare or a harbinger of economic exploitation and sociopolitical conflict? The MNCs' response to this challenge will largely determine economic growth; it may also determine the nature of global economic arrangements, the future of capitalism and democracy, and, indeed, future human welfare.

The past behavior of MNCs offers little guidance because: (a) multinationals operated under different assumptions and rules of the game; (b) nation-states had unrealistic and unsustainable expectations of multinationals; and, (c) Cold-War geopolitics made normal standards of economic performance among nation-states largely irrelevant. Therefore, we must develop a new paradigm to enable MNCs to gain maximum efficiency in the allocation and utilization of global resources and, at the same time, ensure all nation-states a fair and equitable share in the economic wealth created within their borders. To this proposition we now turn our attention.

The accelerating pace of economic globalization has been led by the MNC, the epitome of private enterprise. Furthermore, the collapse of the centralized economies of Russia and its satellite states has put renewed emphasis on the role of private economic institutions in generating economic growth. Nevertheless, a number of factors that have led many developing nations to choose the state-controlled model of growth remain undiminished and may actually have strengthened. Governments and people of developing countries, desperately needing new technologies, fear exploitation because of lack of relative bargaining power and inaccessibility to technical expertise and information. The public-advocacy movement has sought to fill the gap by acting as surrogate for many groups and nations, demanding a "better deal" from the MNCs. In the process, they have thrown new light on the changing role of multinational corporations around the world.

At the aggregate level, the assumption that MNCs serve public interest in host countries through their activities in the private sector is easily defended. We have the example of newly industrializing countries (NICs) such as Hong Kong, South Korea, Singapore and Taiwan. There is also strong evidence that the Third World countries which seem to have made the least progress in the economic and political spheres are also the countries that, relying primarily on state-owned enterprise and government-to-government assistance, have restricted private enterprise.[23]

The munificence of the multinational corporation, however, is not an unmixed blessing. Problems arise because the objectives of private-owned multinational corporations in investing abroad may not always agree with the goals of the host countries, especially the poor and less developed. The host country may have unrealistic hopes of what it can expect or extract from the multinational corporation within its borders. A whole body of scholarly literature and polemical-political publications lists the MNCs' sins of omission and commission.[24]

It is not difficult to see the fallacy of stereotypes of MNCs as economic behemoths whose enormous wealth and economic power make them impervious to the needs of people in countries where they operate and whose governments are afraid and unable to control them. The power of the multinationals, given their goals, must be exercised rationally, i.e., in response to market opportunities. It is unreasonable to blame the multinationals for the economic and social ills of developing countries or to expect MNCs to exercise economic power in a manner that would significantly harm their own self-interest.

We should speak of economic power being abused only when it is exercised irrationally, illegally, or under the aegis of political dictatorships and command economies where people's freedom to assert their economic will is replaced by the dictates of centralized authority. The extent to which a corporation can deviate from this narrow mandate depends on society's changing expectations of the functions and performance of economic institutions. Indeed, democratic societies also impose tremendous constraints on the use of economic power by its holders. Power also imposes its own discipline. If it is not wielded in a restrained manner, the holder loses legitimacy[25]

The challenge for MNCs is to find a role for themselves that would take into consideration the new realities of the world's changing sociopolitical environment. In dealing with the Third World countries, MNCs must develop a broader political perspective regarding the impact of their activities on the long-term prospects for democracy and capitalism in those countries. Too often in the past, this perspective unfortunately, has been ignored.

The conventional wisdom of MNC operations has been rooted in the logic of economic efficiency: MNCs contribute to international economic growth, wealth creation, and human welfare through efficient utilization and distribution of global physical, financial, and human resources. Economic logic suggests that in a world of perfect, or at least effective, competition, distribution of wealth and income would reflect the relative contributions of various factors of production. In the real world, however, global corporations shift resources to maximize their internal

productivity—often at a tremendous cost to the efficiencies and rewards for host countries. For example, developing countries, which have a large reservoir of labor and key natural resources, should be the preferred locations for foreign direct investment by multinational corporations. Instead, over the past two decades the share of developing countries in the global flows of foreign direct investment has steadily declined from 31 percent in 1968 to 17 percent in 1989.[26]

One should also not take too seriously the assertion of globalism on the part of corporate leaders. The economics of the corporation may have become global; its culture certainly has not, irrespectively of whether a corporation is headquartered in the United States, England, Germany, Japan, Switzerland, or some other haven of economic wealth. Multinational corporations have become adept at global manufacturing using local labor, but the locus of power remains essentially ethnocentric. Is it any wonder that most U.S. corporations find the best talent for their top management positions in corporate headquarters among their own people. This situation is even more pervasive, and practiced with less pretense, in the corridors of power in other industrially advanced nations. The world of the global corporation, notwithstanding its international trappings of production and use of local resources, even quite enlightened in itself though it might be, is essentially human, i.e., culturally biased in favor of those who wield power.

Notwithstanding the collapse of the seventy-year old Marxist-socialist experiment in economic development the present world remains divided into two camps based on their level of economic growth. For the first time in history, however, the world has become largely unified in a common belief that the market economy is more efficient in the allocation and utilization of global resources.

In the brave new world, MNCs have a historic opportunity to participate in the economic growth of developing countries and to support in those countries the establishment of democratic regimes which would follow policies favorable to private enterprise. On the other hand, present governments in many developing countries are oppressive and unmindful of democratic institutions and the rights of their subjects. Those countries are witnessing a rise in religious fundamentalism and Liberation Theology against their oppressive regimes and despotic dictatorships. Should MNCs cooperate with governments of such countries which may be endowed with rich natural resources required for maximization of global wealth? In order to meet the challenge, MNCs need to follow a three-pronged strategy to become a positive force for change in creating the global village, i.e., (a) develop a new global approach to harnessing global resources; (b) support the establishment and growth of democratic institutions and nurture and protect basic human rights in all parts of the world; and (c) become good corporate citizens.

Efficient Utilization of Resources for Maximum Global Welfare

MNCs should harness world economic resources using production and process technologies consistent with the environmental and cultural sensitivities of the nations concerned, especially Third world countries; use economic and production arrangements to build alliances among nations for the common good rather than create conflicts for private exploitation; place a higher emphasis on distribution of ownership and control among all participants; and, ensure a more equitable distribution of economic gains among participants.

Efficient utilization of global resources can be achieved by utilizing the latest production and process technologies that are economical in results and have less serious social consequences or externalities. Problems, however, arise at the level of a single company or industry in the Third World as a consequence of MNC operations. These may have to do with the inappropriate or ill-conceived transfer of technology and plant operations. The most recent, and by far the most tragic, example of this kind occurred in December 1984 in Bhopal, India. The specific causes of the accident and Union Carbide's culpability may never be fully known. The important thing, however, is that, given the operating experience of Union Carbide, the Bhopal accident, a man-made disaster, could have been foreseen and prevented.[27] While a multinational corporation may not deliberately violate any laws, its normal business activities may have unintended, undesirable social consequences. Not every individual action, pursued in enlightened self-interest, leads to the collective good. Thus rational individual actions may lead to irrational collective outcomes—which had we anticipated them before the fact we would not have wanted to cause.[28] We become victims of the tragedy of the commons where collective responsibility becomes total irresponsibility.[29]

The efficient utilization of resources can be equally achieved if MNCs foster strategic alliances among themselves and nation-states. Through strategic alliances, MNCs can pool their production, marketing, and technology strengths for the benefit of all. Such alliances would yield efficiencies arising out of economies of scale not possible under current circumstances when MNCs operate individually in search of maximizing their own shareholders' wealth. Moreover, such alliances would also insulate MNCs from being used as a hostage by nation-states interested in creating socialistically oriented economies and/or in perpetuating their nondemocratic regimes. Neighboring nations should also form cooperative alliances for developing infrastructure facilities and some of the key/basic industries for the economic benefit of all the member nations.[30] Such cooperative arrangements among nation-states would also strengthen their bargaining and economic power and would create an environment in which economic gains could be shared justly and equitably with MNCs.

MNCs should also ensure that goods they produce and sell are appropriate to the host-country culture. The logic that what is good for a U.S. consumer is equally good for a Third World consumer is untenable. Alternatively, merely because the sale of a particular product is not restricted in another country (because of either local ignorance or the greed of the local government), that circumstance does not justify the sale or export by the MNC (even though it is abiding by local laws) of a harmful product. Examples include the cases of infant formula, export of pesticides, transportation and dumping of toxic wastes, and operating local plants and exposing local workers to health dangers greater than would be permissible in one's own country. The U.S. tobacco industry, which is finding its domestic market shrinking, is trying to sell increasing quantities of its tobacco products in developing countries. It is encouraging smoking among younger people through aggressive advertising and distribution of free samples—practices banned in the United States—without concern for the negative consequences that increased smoking would have on the health and welfare of the people in those countries.[31]

Finally, there is the question of control and ownership of multinational enterprises and their foreign subsidiaries. In the emerging global village, where all nations are politically and economically interdependent, MNCs will have to reevaluate their operative model. Under such an environment, private investments will have to be justified simultaneously for their economic efficiency, political legitimacy and moral sufficiency.[32] The creation and success of large corporations has been made possible by a careful separation between ownership and control. A similar approach must be used to guarantee the success of the global corporation not merely for what it can do for its immediate owners, but equally important, for the kind of world it can forge—a world that would make possible hitherto unimagined expansion of economic activity, enhancement of human welfare, and its own longevity. This would come about through a process of decentralization during which effective control of local activities would rest with local managers who seek to blend the objectives of national welfare with those of the corporate good.

A system of decentralized local control and international or even centralized ownership is possible—provided both the corporation and the nation-state view the arrangement as a non-zero-sum game in which cooperation and compromises are perceived to be beneficial to all and from which excessive demands by one or the other can lead to justifiable withdrawal with the full knowledge of other global players.

Because the interests of the nation-state are often viewed to be in conflict with those of the corporation, this might seem an impossibility. It need not be so. The modern corporation has lived in harmony with the national state because it has sought legitimacy for its operations and the welfare of its owners within the framework of broader welfare concerns of society. Conflict has arisen when the corporation has sought to insulate itself from the demands of the nation-state by seeking an extra-national character. No nation or people will allow willingly their political destiny to be determined by economic managers who flourish under the political protection offered by the nation-state, but who are reluctant to live by its dictates. The recent actions of the government of Malaysia (similar examples can be found in Singapore, India and other developing nations) provide an example. In response to the many pleas by the Western nations for improvement in its human-rights record, Malaysia has retorted that the Western nations have their own closets full of the skeletons of human-rights violations and degradation in the quality of life of their people and that these nations seek to impose "their" version of human rights while ignoring the host-country's cultural values and practices.[33]

Support of Democratic Institutions

Nonetheless, MNCs should attempt to foster the development of democratic institutions and protection of human rights in all parts of the world even when such a course might adversely affect their short-term economic and financial interests. The trade-off between economic interests and human rights is a critical issue. In the past, private business, both local and foreign, has acted hand-in-glove with authoritarian regimes in Africa and Latin America to profit from the misery of the poor and disenfranchised. It is ironic to see that while the U.S. government is attempting to pressure China to improve its human-rights record, its corporate citizens are urging their government to turn a blind eye to the conditions in China so that the Chinese government would look favorably toward their economic interests.[34] Lost in this race for profits and fortune is the basic question: Economic gain for what? Are economic interests the instruments for sustaining and enhancing human rights and human dignity or should they be sacrificed at the altar of economic growth?

Admittedly, many authoritarian regimes control key domestic resources and provide a stable—albeit repressive and coercive—political environment that appears less risky to the many MNCs which choose to invest in those countries without sufficient regard for the future implications of such an association, should there be a change of government in those countries. If recent history is a guide, this is an extremely shortsighted view. Dictatorships, no matter how violent, have a way of falling when violence, even extreme violence, can no longer sustain a repressive regime. Is it any wonder that the liberated masses view the MNCs as instruments of exploitation associated with the erstwhile regimes and treat them with distrust and contempt?

There is some evidence to suggest that a handful of MNCs are moving toward unilateral action to introduce a higher level of ethical conduct and operational standards in dealing with their overseas workers, local communities, and the environment—even when these actions are viewed with hostility by the host-country governments and may also have an adverse effect on MNCs' competitive position—e.g., the operation of U.S. companies in South Africa under the Sullivan Principles. Companies such as Levi Straus have established worldwide standards for their local suppliers regarding non-abuse of

child labor, minimum-wage laws, and safe work environments. In part, the companies may have been pushed to take these actions under pressure from their home-country governments, social activists, and general public opinion. However, they are also moved by a perspective that a world not safe for democratic values and human dignity is unlikely to be safe for private property and economic freedom. Unfortunately, illustrative cases of proactive, ethical corporate behavior are exceptions rather than the rule of corporate conduct. One has only to peruse the headlines in national newspapers to find examples of corporate indifference—Shell Oil in Nigeria and U.S. tobacco companies in Asia and other emerging economies—to the plight of local people and environment and even collusion with the repressive local governments to ensure the safety and profitability of their foreign operations.[35]

MNCs justify their actions under the guise that they provide jobs and other benefits through their investments even when they occur under these repressive conditions. However, since the benefits are the secondary, not the primary motive for investment, the arguments are at best after-the-fact rationalizations, not highly credible, and are generally dismissed by corporate critics and host-country people whose respect and trust MNCs must eventually gain.

If private enterprise and free markets wish to survive as a desirable form of managing national and international economic activity, they must dissociate themselves from the totalitarian regimes and should not condone state-managed economies in the name of nonintervention, political stability, or national security. Instead, MNCs should pursue policies of supporting only those nations that are attempting to open their economies and that allow their people to live in dignity and to determine their own political destiny.

Good Corporate Citizenship

Within the context of doing whatever they can to foster the development of democracy, good corporate citizenship implies that MNCs obey the laws of host countries, pay their full share of local taxes, use appropriate technologies, avoid pollution of social and physical environments, abstain from interfering in local political affairs, and follow ethical standards in their operational behavior. Nation-states, in cooperation and full consultation with MNCs, should develop policy regimes and international protocols that bind all parties to cooperate in developing and applying uniform standards for business practices. These standards should relate to MNC operations and such critical issues as environmental protection, health and welfare of workers, protection of individual rights and private property, and a system of global monitoring and accounting for commonly agreed standards of good corporate behavior.

MNCs have been criticized for their lack of sensitivity to the laws and needs of host countries and for exploiting local resources in their own self-interest while neglecting the economic goals and objectives of host nations. MNCs have themselves to blame for this criticism. In the past, MNCs have used their bargaining power and operational technologies to maximize their own cash flows. For the past four decades, efforts have been made at national, regional, and international levels to develop either legal or informal systems for controlling MNCs' operations and holding them accountable for their actions. Of all these efforts, only the OECD Guidelines for Multinational Corporations developed voluntarily in joint cooperation with MNCs have enjoyed some success. All other efforts—unilateral, bilateral or collectively by nation-states within the forum of the United Nations—to define the ground rules for MNCs have been made without the participation of MNCs: for fifteen years the U.N. Commission on Transnational Corporations has worked without significant consequence on an acceptable code of conduct.[36]

We do not propose a vast system of supranational institutions responsible for developing a legal framework or a code of conduct for MNCs and for monitoring their behavior. Our experience with the working of such institutions suggests that unless the willing cooperation of all parties involved (including nation-states, corporations, and nongovernmental organizations) is sought in the code-development process, enforcement becomes difficult. Moreover, vast bureaucracies have an innate tendency to become inward-looking, self-protective and often impervious to the needs of a society. The Code on International Marketing of Breast-milk Substitutes (the Infant Formula Code) developed by the World Health Organization (WHO), for example, was passed on May 21, 1981 by a majority of 118 nations in response to the need for preventing high infant mortality in developing countries. Since then only ten countries have taken serious action in implementing the Infant Formula Code and WHO has taken a passive attitude regarding its enforcement and monitoring.[37]

We do not deny the need for creating a "level playing field" applicable both to MNCs and host nations. Such a code of conduct, defining mutual obligations and privileges, would create a stable environment in which MNCs could develop global resources for the benefit of mankind. However, this code-development effort cannot be successful unless all the stakeholders are involved and agree to the ultimate outcome of the deliberative process. An exclusion of any one of the stakeholders would render the process futile. History is replete with examples of such abortive efforts. The Montreal Protocol is an example of a successful multilateral effort in which all the key players including nation-states, business and nongovernmental organizations participated in developing guidelines for environmental protection and accepted its verdict.

We propose an international policy regime that will ensure the creation of the global village of our vision. This policy regime should ensure that MNCs fully participate in the process and perform three specific functions:

- facilitate the efficient allocation of global resources in a manner consistent with the needs of both the rich and the poor countries and protective of the environment;
- facilitate transfer of those technologies that make the most effective use of local-factor endowments, generate higher values on the pro-

duct chain, and provide adequate rewards for the use of intellectual property to the MNC; and,

- allow nations a fair and equitable share in the economic gains resulting from the enhanced level of economic activities.

NOTES

1. Marshall McLuhan was the first to introduce the phrase "Global Village" in the literature. See Marshall McLuhan and Quentin Fiore, "War and Peace in the Global Village" (New York: Bantam, 1968).
2. Donella H. Meadows et al., "The Limits to Growth: A Report for the Club of Romis Project on the Predicament of Mankind" (New York: Universe Books, 1972).
3. Joel Kurtzman, "The Emergence of Economic Globalism," a speech delivered at a conference, "The Keystone Project," Keystone Conference Center, Denver, Colorado, October 3–5, 1990, 10.
4. Kurtzman, "The Emergence of Economic Globalism."
5. Peter Nulty, "How the World Will Change," *Fortune*, 15 January 1990, 44–54.
6. Nulty, 13-14.
7. Joel Kurtzman, "The Death of Money: How the Electronic Economy has Destabilized the World's Markets and Created Financial Chaos" (New York: Simon & Schuster, 1993), 11.
8. Kurtzman, "The Emergence of Economic Globalism," 2.
9. The World Bank, *World Development Report 1991* (New York: Oxford University Press, World Development Indicators, 1991).
10. Kenichi Ohmae, "Becoming a Triad Power: The New Global Competition," *McKinsey Quarterly* (Spring 1985): 2–25.
11. Robert J. Samuelson, "The Global Village Revisited," *The Economist, Book of Vital World Statistics* (New York: Random House, 1993), 8.
12. United Nations, *United Nations Statistical Year Book 1985/86* (New York: United Nations, 1988).
13. United Nations Development Programme (UNDP), *Human Development Report 1992* (New York: Oxford University Press, 1992), 40.
14. *World Development Report 1991*.

15. S. Prakash Sethi and Bharat B. Bhalla, "Free Market Orientation and Economic Growth: Some Lessons for the Developing Countries and Multinational Corporations," *Business in the Contemporary World* 3, no. 2 (Winter 1991): 86– 101. Source: The Economist, Book of Vital World Statistics (New York: Random House, 1990), 34–35.
16. *Human Development Report 1992*, 14.
17. *Human Development Report 1992*, 2.
18. John Naisbitt and Patricia Aburdene, *Megatrends 2000* (New York: William Morrow, 1990).
19. *Human Development Report 1992*, 32.
20. Sethi and Bhalla, "Free Market Orientation and Economic Growth," 86–101.
21. *Human Development Report 1992*, 34.
22. *Human Development Report 1992*, 34, 35.
23. P.T. Bauer, *Equality, the Third World, and Economic Delusion* (Cambridge: Harvard University Press, 1981).
24. Meadows.
25. A large part of the discussion in this discussion is drawn from S. Prakash Sethi, *Multinational Corporations and the Impact of Public Advocacy on Corporate Strategy: Nestle and the Infant Formula Controversy* (Boston: Kluwer, 1994), 355–83.
26. Sethi, *Multinational Corporations and the Impact of Public Advocacy on Corporate Strategy*, 52.
27. S. Prakash Sethi, "The Inhuman Error— Lessons from the Union Carbide Plant Accident in Bhopal, India," *The New Management* (Summer 1985): 41–45.
28. Thomas C. Schelling, "On the Ecology of Micromotives," *The Public Interest* 25 (Fall 1971): 59–98.
29. Garrett Hardin, "The Tragedy of the Commons," *Science*, vol. 162, 13 December 1968, 1103–07.
30. S. Prakash Sethi and Bharat B. Bhalla, "Strategic Economic Alliances: An Approach to

Integrating the Economy of Post-Apartheid South Africa into Sub-Sahara Africa," *Development Southern Africa* 9, no. 3 (1992): 331–45.

31. For a detailed treatment and analysis of the marketing practices of major tobacco companies in developing countries, please see S. Prakash Sethi and Paul Steidlmeier, *Up Against the Corporate Wall*, 5th ed. (Englewood Cliffs, NJ: Prentice Hall, 1991), 355–73.

32. Sethi and Bhalla, "Free Market Orientation and Economic Growth."

33. "Malaysia's Mahathir: Leading a Crusade Against the West," *Business Week*, 25 April 1994, 51.

34. Albert R. Hunt, "Pressure China on Human Rights, But Sever Ties to Trade," *Wall Street Journal*, 5 May 1994, A15.

35. Geraldine Brooks, "Shell's Nigerian Fields Produce Few Benefits for Region's Villagers," *Wall Street Journal*, 6 May 1994, A1, A4.

36. For a history of development of codes of conduct for multinational corporations, please see *Legal Problems of Codes of Conduct for Multinational Enterprises*, Norbert Horn, ed. (Deventer, Netherlands: Kluwer, 1980).

37. S. Prakash Sethi and Bharat B. Bhalla, "A New Perspective on the International Regulation of Business: An Evaluation of the Compliance Status of the International Code of Marketing of Breast-milk Substitutes," *The Journal of Socio-Economics* 22, no. 2 (1993): 141–58.

POLICY REGIMES IN THE INTERNATIONAL BUSINESS ENVIRONMENT

Lee E. Preston

Abstract: As international business and economic activities have expanded in scale and complexity, international policy regimes have come into being to facilitate, regulate and mediate their operations and effects. Such regimes are created by a combination of government, industry and third-sector efforts. This essay examines the nature and characteristics of international policy regimes, and points out some likely directions of future regime development. The concluding section analyses some of the important effects of policy regimes on international business activity.

The growth of international business and economic activities both requires and generates a corresponding growth in the number, variety and strength of international agreements and understandings that facilitate and regulate such activities. Merchandise cannot legitimately be moved from one country to another, nor can currencies be converted, foreign airplanes land, or international investments take place without there being some shared expectations among both the private interests and the governments involved as to the conditions, responsibilities and limitations associated with these contacts.

The complex of understandings and agreements facilitating and governing international contacts are referred to, broadly, as **international policy regimes**. The "regimes" of interest here are **sets of explicit or implicit principles, norms, rules and decision-making procedures around which actor expectations converge with respect to some area of international business and economic activity** (adapted from Krasner, 1983, p. 2).

A recent survey of the wide array of policy regimes affecting international business currently in place or under development shows that they fall into four main categories (see Exhibit 1 for examples):

Global and comprehensive regimes, unrestricted in both their geographic reach and functional scope.
Regional and associative regimes, in which two or more countries agree to special intra-group arrangements different from those prevailing between the individual countries and the rest of the world. The scope of these regimes may be narrow (e.g., free trade in selected lines of merchandise or services) or broad (e.g., monetary union, common market).
Functional business and economic regimes, governing some specific aspect of international activity or commerce, such as currency conversion or air transport
Functional environmental regimes, intended to influence business practices with respect to some aspect of the global environment (e.g., reduce CFC production and use).

This essay is based on material originally presented in Preston and Windsor, 1992.

450

EXHIBIT 1:   Major Policy Regimes and Organizations Affecting International Business.
Although this list contains primarily the names of *organizations*, it is the *regimes*
and not the institutional forms that are of primary interest.

Global and Comprehensive Regimes and Organizations

United Nations regime system, including:
   World Court
   Convention on International Sale of Goods
   Restrictive Business Practices Code
   Codex Alimentarius (WHO and FAO)
   Technology Transfer Code (UNCTAD)
   Code of Conduct on Transnational Corporations (UNCTC—in preparation)
   UN-based Consumer Protection Codes (e.g., Infant Formula)
   UN-based Environmental Regimes (e.g., Moon Treaty)

Regional and Associative Regimes and Organizations

European Community (EC), including:
   European Economic Community
   Euratom
   European Coal and Steel Community
   European Monetary System
US-Canada Free Trade Agreement (North American Free Trade Agreement—pending)
Latin American Free Trade Area, Andean Pact
Organization For Economic Cooperation and Development (OECD)
Council for Mutual Economic Assistance (CMEA, or "COMECON"—dissolved 1991)

Functional Regimes: Economic

Air Transport
   International Air Transport Association (IATA)
   International Civil Aviation Organization (ICAO)
Ocean Shipping
   UNCTAD Liner Conference Code
   International Maritime Organization (IMO)
Telecommunications
   International Telecommunications Union (ITU)
   INTELSAT
Trade
   General Agreement on Tariffs and Trade (GATT)
   Product and commodity agreements, GATT-related and otherwise
Money Exchange and Payments
   International Monetary Fund (IMF)
Investment
   World Bank
   International Finance Corporation (IFC)
   Multilateral Investment Guarantee Agency (MIGA)

Functional Regimes: Environmental

Air Pollution Agreements: Transboundary air pollution, sulfur, nitrogen oxides, chlorofluorocarbons (Vienna/Montreal Protocol)
Law of the Sea Treaty
Moon Treaty
Antarctic Treaty

Source: Preston and Windsor, 1992, p. 9.

It is often convenient to refer to regimes in terms of the organizations associated with them. GATT represents the liberal international trade regime, for example. However, it is important to emphasize that *regimes* consist of the full set of understandings and behaviors involved, and not simply in a particular organizational structure. The gold standard was an effective international monetary regime for several decades, but no corresponding international institution was established to maintain it. Equally relevant, some international organizations—the International Labor Organization (ILO), for example—perform significant functions without creating corresponding regimes of policy and behavior.

The purpose of this essay is to examine the nature and key characteristics of international policy regimes affecting business, and their likely directions of future evolution. In the concluding section we analyze the impact of regimes on both domestic firms engaged in international activities and on multinational enterprises.

CHARACTERISTICS OF REGIMES

The characteristics of regimes may be analyzed according to the following critical features or dimensions (modified from the scheme originally proposed by Haggard and Simmons, 1987).

> **Scope**—The range of business and economic activity over which the regime is intended to have influence (e.g., the international monetary system).
> **Purpose**—The objectives the regime is intended to accomplish, within the given scope (e.g., for the international monetary system, promote foreign exchange stability to facilitate international trade and investment).
> **Organizational form**—The most conspicuous aspect of most regimes, and sometimes of independent significance (e.g., open participation vs. limited membership). The creation of regimes may be easier when it takes place within existing organizations (as in the case of the UNCTAD Line Code); however, the organizational setting may also limit the scope and effectiveness of regimes (OECD codes, for example).
> **Decision and allocation modes**—These include the one participant/one vote option (where the participants may be either governments or enterprises), as well as arrangements in which decision-influencing power is related to size, resource endowments, volume of regime activity, etc. Benefits and costs may also be distributed equally and/or by weighted formula.

> **Strength**—The ability of the regime to influence the behavior of the involved participants (and perhaps of others as well).

CASE STUDY: TELECOMMUNICATIONS

The significance of these characteristics, and the usefulness of an analysis based on them, can be illustrated by a brief case study of the international telecommunications (see Exhibit 2).

The international telecommunications regime is one of the oldest formal multilateral policy systems affecting business; it is also one of the most clearly "global." The International Telegraph Union (ITU) was organized in 1865; in 1932 "Telecommunications" replaced "Telegraph" in the name. ITU became a specialized agency of the UN in 1947. In spite of this long history of formal legitimacy, at the present time there is no set of coherent international policies in place governing inter-connections, access, investment or trade in this important arena of business and technology (Aronson & Cowhey, 1988). A century-old system based on technological standardization, national monopoly and international cartel arrangements is collapsing in the face of technological change, changing national regulatory policies, and the emergence of new forms and forces of competition.

Scope

Telecommunications involves an interwoven system of equipment, services and information content. Two distinct technologies—telephone and broadcast—are utilized, often in combination, to produce both transient contacts (conversations, broadcasts) and permanent records (facsimile copies and data records). And, with a combination of telecommunications and computer services, there are also possibilities for qualitative change (data processing other forms of "value added service" in the transmitted material occurring in the course of the transmission process). International and domestic communications services are indissolubly

EXHIBIT 2: Telecommunications Regime

Description	Cable	Satellite	All Modes
Institutional identification	Joint operating agreements	INTELSAT	ITI/CCITT
Technology	Point-to-point	Network	All technologies
Purpose and Scope Purpose	Market access to monopoly facility	Administer access	Set technical standards; resolve increasingly complex issues
Scope	Entry, rates, technology	Entry, rates, technology	Expanding to include all issues
Organizational Form Structure	Private (no government aspect)	Enterprise-level (US COMSAT and national PTTs) multipartite, under government auspices	Multilateral (governments)
Power/concentration	Companies/countries with critical locations and capabilities	US technology initially assured control	Political; uncertain
Decision and Allocation Modes	Market, with government approval	Administrative	Administrative, negotiated
Strength and Change Peak strength	1800s–present	1965–1980	ITU: 1900s–1960s
Current	High	Medium, declining	ITU/CCITT strong but new institutions emerging (e.g., GATT)
Why change?	Satellite technology did not eliminate cable; new competition is developing in satellites; increasingly complex issues emerging.		

SOURCE: Preston and Windsor, 1992, p. 96.

interlinked, and domestic services are universally regulated and frequently state-owned. Efficient international telecommunications requires technological compatibility among systems; indeed, compatibility, plus the avoidance of interference, was the major principle of the telecommunications policy regime during its first century. However, technological compatibility facilitates contacts that may be in conflict with other national policies—control of national security information, censorship of political and cultural viewpoints, etc. Hence, even at a technical level, the concerns of the international telecommunications regime expand to include issues of system utilization and com-munications content as well as equipment and channels (Dizard, 1988).

Purpose, Form and Allocation Mode

From the beginning, the ITU has been the administrative authority for the "global commons" of worldwide communications space. Its primary focus has been on technological cooperation, including standardization of both procedures and equipment. Compliance with ITU regulations has been very high because of the common interests among the national PTTs, and also because any nation had to conform to international standards in order to participate in the worldwide communication system. However, the circumstances that favored voluntary compliance are now being altered by changes in technology and national policies.

As with air transport at a later date, the North Atlantic region was a major focus of international telecommunications development from the beginning. The first undersea telegraph cable linking North America and Europe was laid in 1866, and the number of cables increased steadily for several decades. These undersea cables were owned and operated by private firms which controlled the entire communications circuit and negotiated connections with domestic carriers at either end. Two-way radio (voice) transmission across the Atlantic was initiated by AT&T in 1915 and offered commercially in 1927. Although this technology ultimately proved unreliable, it introduced a new policy feature of permanent importance. For national security and spectrum scarcity reasons, both the U.S. and European nations were unwilling to grant broadcast licenses to foreign enterprises. Therefore, radio links were based on operating agreements between domestic carriers in each country, with each carrier formally in control of only a "half circuit" of the international communications link. When later technology permitted the laying of transatlantic telephone cables, the principle of half-circuit joint operation was maintained. In contrast to this arrangement, international one-way broadcast communication is limited, of course, only by the power of transmitters and receiver, and by overt interference in broadcast signals ("jamming") to prevent their reception. The right of sovereign governments to engage in such interference is not seriously questioned, although their success is often limited. Hence: telephone communications links were inevitably cooperative, broadcast links essentially independent, except for agreements among the parties to limit interference.

Development of satellite technology in the 1960s opened an entirely new phase of international telecommunications. The vast potential capacity of satellite systems appeared just as increasing world economic integration was greatly increasing the demand for communications services and computerization was generating enormous new collections of material available for transmission. In addition, satellite technology permitted the creation of global networks, within which multiple stations send and receive information simultaneously. However, because satellite communication involves conventional broadcast technology for the up-down links, the issue of national control arose here just as it had with radio a half century earlier.

In the light of all these considerations, during the 1960s a plan was developed for an internationally owned and operated satellite system (INTELSAT) with nationally owned earth stations in each participating country. At that time, it was generally believed that satellite technology would displace cable and that INTELSAT's structure and service capacity would make it the global monopolist of satellite operations; both of these beliefs, however, proved unfounded. Fiber optic technology has revitalized cable operations; and, although considerable excess capacity remains in the INTELSAT system, a number of competitive alternatives and proposals have arisen. Some of these bypass common carrier communications channels entirely. Orion, a private U.S. satellite firm, has established direct linkages among users in various countries (usually units of a single multinational entity) who install their own transponders for direct contact with the satellite; a similar arrangement for a firm specializing in service to international financial institutions has been approved by the FCC. In addition, various groups of nations have proposed new systems targeted toward their special needs—Arabsat (Arab countries consortium); ECS (European Communications System); Palapa-B (Indonesia and neighboring countries).

In the midst of all of these developments, the fundamental jurisdictional concept of international communications law has also been challenged. From the very beginning of international communication among persons (which took place, of course, by post), it has been assumed that each sovereign state had the right to control the flow of communications into and out of its territory, and most states have in fact exercised such control at one time or another. In recent years, however the concept of a basic human right to communicate, including contact across national boundaries, which was enunciated in the 1948 Universal Declaration on Human Rights, has gained a certain amount of general support. The ITU formally recognized such a right in 1973, and comparable ideas are included in numerous bilateral treaties and conventions. Although these declarations are primarily aimed at freedom of personal communication and open access to public news and information, the principle of unrestricted communication almost necessarily implies the disregard of content, particularly since the same facilities and systems are used for all purposes. On the other hand, the concern of various governments and enterprises with the control of trans-border data flows and the maintenance of cultural independence creates a strong set of offsetting pressures.

Both the forces pressing for greater freedom and openness of communications, as well as those pressing for greater control and restriction, increase the pressure for further development of the international telecommunications regime. These issues clearly cannot be resolved by national policies or bilateral agreements alone. The complex inter-linkage of government and business interests and concerns involved in these issues—particularly the functional needs of multinational enterprises and of international financial service firms—demands their resolution through multi-partite negotiations. The likely outcome would seem to be gradual evolution of a communications policy regime of increasing openness (Branscomb, 1986; Noam, 1989).

POLICY REGIMES
FOR MULTINATIONAL ENTERPRISES

The telecommunications regime is only one of many actual and proposed international arrangements with powerful effects, both direct and indirect, on the operations of multinational enterprises. In the case of telecommunications—as with the international monetary regime, air and sea transport, etc. —the focus of regime development is on the functional activity itself, and the impact on MNEs is consequential, rather than intentional. However, other regime initiatives focus directly on the MNE and its relationship to home and host political jurisdictions.

There are two distinct views of the relative strength of MNEs vis-a-vis national and international policies and institutions. One view, succinctly captured in the title of Vernon's classic study *Sovereignty at Bay* (1971), holds that large MNEs are more powerful than the governments of many of the countries within which they operate. By playing one interest off against another, and by optimizing their operations in relation to national and international policies as well as in relation to resources, costs and markets, they may select and control their environments in their own interest. The opposite view, associated with Wallace (1982, 1990) along with many others, holds that MNEs are victims, rather than masters, of national and international policies, and are more likely to suffer than benefit from differences among national policies and objectives. An additional element is added to this debate by the emergence of state-owned and state-sponsored/protected MNEs from both Third World and post-Communist countries in recent years, and by the growth of joint ventures between such enterprises and private-sector MNEs from First World countries.

Whatever the relative balance of power between MNEs and governments, either individually or collectively, MNEs are inevitably socio-political institutions and MNE management conspicuously a problem of *governance* and balance among multiple, and often competing, interests (Bower and Doz, 1979). National states are inevitably "stakeholders" in the enterprises operating within their respective jurisdictions (and particularly so in the case of state-owned or -sponsored enterprises); and the relationship is always symbiotic, that is, MNEs are also "stakeholders" in their host environments. The distinctive feature of MNEs, however, is that they are involved in several, possibly even many, such relationships. And these involvements automatically create new linkages and interactions—and not necessarily welcome or consistent ones—among the various jurisdictions themselves (Fisher and Turner, 1983).

The actual or potential conflict between MNE activities and specific national interests has been a major policy concern in both advanced and developed countries for half a century. MNE "home" countries fear the export of jobs, capital and productive capacity. Host countries fear domination and exploitation. In nearly all host countries, MNEs are encouraged to engage in certain types of activity (e.g., exports), and restricted or entirely foreclosed from others. Behrman and Grosse contend that relationships between MNEs and governments generally follow a "bargaining pattern . . . That is, both government and company seek to pursue their own goals, and each is constrained by the other . . . ; therefore, negotiation is required" (1990, p. 7). In addition, of course, MNEs and governments (both home and host) share many common goals, and the distinction between them may become blurred, either through the "capture" of one side by the other or through the growth of state-owned MNEs, joint ventures and other intermediate arrangements.

Taxation is a particularly important focus of government-MNE conflict, although the net impact of specific tax policies is often unclear. For example: The U.S. is generally perceived to have higher corporate tax rates than Germany; but the U.S. defers taxes on foreign subsidiary income until it is remitted to the U.S. parent. Germany requires consolidation of domestic and foreign earnings and does not permit deferrals. With such differences in both tax rates and methods of tax calculation, it is not clear which country offers greater tax stimulus (or less handicap) to the growth of home-based MNEs. Comparable differences occur in the treatment of MNE subsidiaries in host environments as well; it is widely believed that the U.S. subsidiaries of foreign MNEs do not pay their "fair share" of U.S. taxes (Levinsohn and Slemrod, 1990).

In addition to broad policies, such as taxation, that affect similarly situated MNE units within a particular jurisdiction in a similar manner, governments engage in a wide variety of "micro-interventions" with respect to foreign subsidiaries. Important examples are: (a) reservation of market shares or product lines to "home" country enterprises; (b) domestic content requirements; (c) partial domestic ownership or joint venture requirements; (d) export requirements; and (e) specific activity (e.g., R&D) requirements.

In view of the large volume and great variety of national policy actions directed toward MNEs over the past half century it is not surprising that a number of attempts have been made to establish a broader multinational framework of norms and understandings about the relations among MNEs and their major clients and stakeholders, particularly including national governments. As early as the 1940s, specific MNE Code proposals were offered by the International Chamber of Commerce; and more recent proposals have come from the OECD, ILO, the Committee for Economic Development and other sources as well as the UN (cf. Kline, 1985, for more details).

None of the proposals for comprehensive international surveillance or control of MNEs has achieved the status of a formal regime, and such a development no longer seems likely. In fact, the activities and impacts of MNEs, joint ventures and domestic enterprises are now so closely intertwined that the rationale for developing a special policy framework for MNEs may be gradually disappearing. Most of the critical policy issues of international business arise from the *activities* being carried out, not from the type of enterprise (MNE or other) involved. In addition, both home and host governments have become more sophisticated in their dealings with MNEs, and better able to protect their own interests through domestic policies and specific negotiations. Furthermore, it appears that MNEs themselves have realized that their operations need to be carried out in ways that support and harmonize with, rather than undermine, diverse national cultures and objectives.

THE FUTURE OF INTERNATIONAL POLICY REGIMES

Since policy regimes affecting most areas of international business are already in place, and are continually subject to dynamic change in response to changing circumstances, analysis of the likely direction and speed of regime evolution is a critical aspect of international management. There seems to be general agreement that policy regimes affecting international business are likely to become more numerous, more complex and more important over time. Some view this development with alarm; others see it as desirable, or simply inevitable (cf., the collection of views presented in Adelman, 1988). In any event, the trend toward continued regime development is not likely to be reversed.

In this section we look briefly at the status and evolutionary prospects for regimes of each major type—global, regional, and functional. However, in addition to the specific topics discussed below, there is a general issue to be raised at the outset: Growth in the number, scope and complexity of individual regimes greatly increases the likelihood of inter-regime contact and conflict. In the past, most regimes have operated apart from each other—air transport and sea transport, for example. Some few have been deliberately designed to be mutually supportive—the liberal trade and monetary regimes, for example. The possibilities for inter-regime conflict are well illustrated by recent controversies in both NAFTA and GATT negotiations concerning environmental protection. On one hand, there is strong pressure to use these trade agreements to advance the environmental concerns of some of the contracting parties; at the same time, pressure for strong environmental protocols has threatened to sabotage the trade agreements themselves. Domestic U.S. experience with conflicts among labor union practices, equal employment opportunity goals, environmental concerns, tax policies, etc., gives some idea of the problematic situations that may arise from continued regime expansion.

Global and Comprehensive Regimes. The frontier issue with respect to global/comprehensive regimes remains, as it has for a decade, the refinement and adoption of the UN Code of Conduct for Transnational Corporations, which has been in preparation for almost twenty years. It could well be argued that the actual complex of regimes in place—both within and outside the UN framework—has long since evolved beyond the scope of any such integrative concept or document. Indeed, the environment of international business in the 1990s is quite different from that of the 1970s which gave initial stimulus to the UN proposals, and the proposed content of the Code has changed substantially as a result (UNCTC, 1990). The current draft document, which is addressed to both enterprises and governments, might be more appropriately titled "Statement of Generally Accepted Principles Relating to International Business." The argument favoring formal adoption of this (or some similar) version of the Code is not that such an action will actually change arrangements and behaviors that have become established over the last couple of decades, nor even that there is a great need for change in current practices. Instead, the argument is that a formal Code stands as a summary statement of mutually understood principles. Reference to such a document should encourage anticipatory behavior on the part of both enterprises and governments, and should contribute to the avoidance of future problems and misunderstandings.

Regional Regimes. The single most dramatic current regime developments involve the evolution of regional regimes, particularly the transformation of the European Community (EC) into the European Union (EU), and the creation of the North American Free Trade Area (NAFTA). These two developments, both of which occurred in 1993, reflect widespread belief that such arrangements will yield long-term benefits for their members. In both cases other countries are poised to join the regimes, as soon as detailed arrangements can be worked out. There are, however, several critical questions about the future evolution and impact of these, and perhaps other, regional regimes. These questions involve both (1) their membership structures and geographic scope, and (2) the collaborative or conflictual relationships that may arise between/among them.

Both EU and NAFTA have significant expansion possibilities. The EU is gradually including former EFTA members within its purview, and the emergent states of the former Soviet Bloc are petitioning for some type of associative membership. Similarly, completion of NAFTA as an agreement among Canada, U.S. and Mexico has led directly to proposals for selective immediate expansion (e.g., admission of Chile) and gradual inclusion of most or all of Latin America. Growth of this type would not only increase the number of players to be accommodated within each regime but also would increase their internal diversity, very likely with serious consequences. If there are already important differences of view between, for example, Denmark and Germany about intra-EU relationships, the additional problems that would arise if, say, Bulgaria were brought into the arrangement can scarcely be imagined.

The second main issue involves the ways in which the two major economic blocs, plus any others that may evolve, will relate to each other. Some authorities fear the growth of "Fortress Europe," leading to the counter-development of "Fortress America" and perhaps a "Greater East Asia Prosperity Sphere" centered on Japan. A recent OECD study, however, argues that current regionalization initiatives tend to encourage, rather than dis-

courage, liberal trade policies, and that regional regime developments other than the EC and NAFTA, each with rather limited scope, are unlikely (Fishlow and Haggard, 1992).

Functional Regimes. Functional regimes governing international business are so numerous and varied that no serious survey of their status and potential evolution can be undertaken within a short article. We focus here on three main areas: (1) transport and communications, which have been significantly affected by changes in both demand and technology; (2) the money and trade regimes, with an emphasis on current strains and on critical areas of potential evolution; and (3) recent developments with respect to international environmental protection.

Transport and Communication. International transport cannot take place at all without some kind of mutual understanding between the jurisdiction of origin and destination; in the absence of such understandings, the arrival of foreign vessels constitutes illegal entry, with unfavorable consequences. Hence, it is no surprise that policy regimes for international sea and air transport have been in place for many decades. Technological change in all forms of transportation has given rise to increasing economies of scale; but demand for international transport has grown even more rapidly and therefore the number of market participants has increased as well. National policy interests in transport, particularly in the form of state-owned or subsidized airlines, have also contributed to the increase in numbers and types of firms involved. Although there are some examples of national efforts to protect domestic carriers, the major trend within both air and sea transport regimes has been toward increasing liberalization, both with respect to formal arrangements (so that the regimes themselves become less and less restrictive) and with respect to enterprise-level evolution, so that cooperative agreements, joint ventures, etc., are becoming more numerous. The result is increasing flexibility in rates and fares, inter-carrier links and service performance, which in turn gives increasing importance to the informational and consultative functions (as opposed to market allocation and price setting functions) of the regimes.

The communication industry provides "transport service" for information; and communications contracts are both generators of and substitutes for physical movements of both people and goods. International communications is becoming the "freest" of international business functions, largely because some of the technology in use is simply beyond the control of individual states and even of intergovernmental agencies. For example, it was believed in the early 1960s that international communication by undersea cable would inevitably be replaced by satellite systems, and that satellite operations would involve such economies of scale that a single service provider would be able to handle worldwide demand. Under U.S. leadership, the international consortium INTELSAT was created to be the monopoly service provider in this field. As events unfolded, however, fiber optics revolutionized cable technology and cable capacity expanded substantially; meanwhile, competitive satellite services entered the market under the price umbrella provided by INTELSAT. The interaction of technological change and price competition has moved the entire international communications industry toward increased efficiency and lower prices in spite of restrictive and protective inter-governmental policies.

Money and Trade.   The post-war money and trade regimes centered on the IMF and GATT have undergone substantial changes over the last couple of decades, and continue to experience severe strains. The post-war monetary regime was originally based on fixed, or "pegged," exchange rates among the major currencies. This system was abandoned unilaterally by the U.S. in 1971, and international currency markets have become increasingly turbulent in recent years. Direct consultations among governments of the most advanced industrial countries (G-5, G7, etc.) have become the major means of monetary coordination, and this approach has not proved entirely successful. Correspondingly, the Uruguay Round of GATT negotiations, originally scheduled for completion in 1990, was stalled for four years by disagreements over agricultural subsidies, intellectual property, and other critical issues, some of which were simply put aside in order to reach a final agreement. The new GATT agreement creates a "World Trade Organization," an entity first suggested in the Havana Charter of 1948. However, the role and strength of this new organization cannot be anticipated at the present time. In fact, both the money and trade regimes are devolving more and more into networks of bilateral and sub-global arrangements involving specific trading partners (e.g., U.S.-Israel free trade agreement) or specific lines of business (e.g., the Multifiber Agreement).

In spite of these developments, however, there is almost universal agreement that an international "bank" (like IMF) to handle routine currency exchange problems and an international "forum" (like GATT) for discussion of trade-related issues are essential elements of the global economic framework. Moreover, the IMF has expanded its role considerably by providing consultative services to developing and transitional economies throughout the world, along with its currency exchange functions. Whatever specific rules and practices may be adopted (or NOT adopted) by both GATT and the IMF at any point in time, the continued existence of these institutions reflects an enduring international commitment to a *process* of mutual consultation and collaboration. Evidence of the importance of this commitment is the contemporary effort of the constituent and satellite states of the former USSR to become full participants in these institutions.

One element conspicuously missing from the current money/trade regime is a set of common international understandings concerning foreign investment. In spite of intensive discussion for a couple of decades—and in spite of the creation of the International Finance Corporation (IFC) and the Multilateral Investment Guarantee Agency (MIGA), both World Bank affiliates—it seems unlikely that a comprehensive investment regime will emerge in the near future. The more likely prospect is that broad investment guidelines will gradually evolve out of the activities of these World Bank affiliates and new agreements on capital transfers and related topics within the OECD. Related understandings about enterprise governance and national treatment principles (along with exceptions thereto) may also be guided by the UN Code negotiations (whether or not the Code itself is formally adopted) and regional and bilateral agreements.

Another major gap in the money/trade regime involves international trade in services. Although the total volume of international service business is very difficult to measure, there is little doubt that the relative share of services (vis-a-vis) goods) in both trade and investment is large and rapidly increasing (Feketekuty, 1988). As a result, the need for—and problems and potential of—an international policy regime focused on service industries and activities has been a major subject of discussion throughout the 1980s and a principal focus of the Uruguay Round of GATT negotiations.

As noted above, policy regimes have long since evolved in such basic international service activities as transport and communications. However, international tourism, financial and insurance services, business and professional services, etc., have grown rapidly in recent decades and this growth, along with very imprecise understanding of its exact magnitude and effects, has given rise to considerable concern. Service activities are often invisible, even nebulous, in character. They take place without any direct contact with national borders—by post or through telecommunications, for example; and they may also occur through the movement of *persons* who subsequently *receive* services (e.g., tourism) or *provide* services (e.g., professional work) outside their home jurisdictions. Such activities do not fit easily into conventional concepts of "trade," although they may have substantial effects on the incomes and operations of enterprises and individuals, and on the international accounts of the countries involved.

International service transactions and contacts actually generate at least three different kinds of economic effects. The **trade-like effects** referred to above may be the most obvious, but the role of services as **lubricants** for merchandise trade and foreign investment may actually be more important. Services are also major **vehicles** for the transfer of technology and management processes among countries. A significant problem in the measurement of international service activities is the fact that their value is often embedded in the value of merchandise, equipment, investment or ownership transfers to which the services themselves are applied.

One reason for the widespread concern about international business in service industries is that some of the most important services (financial services and insurance, for example) are tightly regulated within individual countries, and ownership is often restricted to citizens of the particular country. The connection between such national policies and the operations of foreign enterprises performing similar functions is highly problematic, particularly when the magnitude and consequences of the activities involved are imprecisely known. It is also true that service industry activities are intimately linked with the ownership and use of intellectual property, including artistic creations, data collections, operating routines and communications procedures. Enterprises and governments seek to control service activities both to **obtain** access to intellectual property originating elsewhere and to **prevent** or **control** access to their own intellectual property holdings by other interests. For all of these reasons, there is a strong desire to integrate service industries into national development policies and to stimulate/protect nationally-based service activities, particularly financial services.

The complexity of these issues strongly suggests that development of a policy framework for international services is not an easy task. Some authorities (e.g., Feketekuty, 1988), noting that both DFI and the mobility of skilled labor are of unusual importance in the service sector, believe that the key feature of a services regime should be the adaptation and extension of basic GATT principles: most favored national (MFN) status, national treatment, and special consideration for LDCs (the GSP system). The preparation of an international agreement on "telematics"—a combination of telecommunications, data processing and information services—is seen as a critical development which might provide a focus and model for other service industries. However, removal of national protections for financial services (which, combined with insurance, account for by far the largest aggregate value of internationally traded services) may be the more critical, and much more difficult, issue. Dominance of international financial activity by the advanced industrial countries provides the justification for protectionist national policies in other states, and this dominance—and therefore protective counter-action—is likely to persist for a considerable time period in the future.

Environmental Protection. International regime to control and protect the global environment are the newest, most difficult, most controversial, and possibly most important types of prospective regime developments affecting international business. The UN Conference on Environment and Development ("Earth Summit") held in Rio de Janeiro in June 1992 focused worldwide attention on environmental issues and adopted a "Declaration on Environment and Development" that contains 27 principles of good environ-

mental practice, many of which have significant implications for business. Agenda 21, the UNCED document emerging from the conference, emphasized the concept of **sustainable global development**—that is, development levels and trends that could be maintained into the indefinite future—and examined critical problems in three major and inter-related areas: (a) population growth and geographic concentration, (b) conflicting patterns of resource use, and (c) control of hazardous materials and wastes in a global context (United Nations, 1993).

Two factors account for the widespread current acceptance of global perspectives on the environment, which were uncommon only a few decades ago. One is increased knowledge about the characteristics and functions of the earth and its atmosphere. The other is worldwide population growth and economic development which lead to increased overall resource use, involving both the exhaustion of some basic resources and the generation of wastes. These factors and their implications account for a growing perception of the earth as a "global commons," a collection of resources to be shared among earth's inhabitants, both present and future.

The "commons" concept is now being increasingly applied not only to unarguably "common" resources such as the biosphere and the moon, but also to both renewable and nonrenewable resources and to the problem of planetary waste. Regimes concerned with some of these issues, such as the UN-sponsored Moon Treaty, are rather tentative and uncontroversial. Others, such as proposed controls on undersea mining and on forest management, involve sharp differences in scientific judgment and the clash of powerful interests. Environmental regimes enjoying widespread international support include those involving the protection of wildlife (whales, seals, etc.), acid rain (Europe), and the protection of the ozone layer. Many of these regimes are likely to be expanded and refined over the coming decade.

Another important area of interest is the use of outer space, which is unquestionably an element of the "global commons." It seems most likely that space utilization will be governed by **national** and **bilateral** policy development, with leadership by some countries establishing patterns for others (Papp and McIntyre, 1987). This has, of course, been the model followed in the historic cases of air transport and telecommunications.

In the broad context of the Rio "Earth Summit," documents aimed at the establishment of three major new environmental regimes were developed:

> Framework convention on Climate Change—Signed by 153 countries, including the U.S., after all specific targets and timetables for reducing greenhouse gas emissions were removed. The EC and Japan pledged to limit their emissions to 1990 levels by the year 2000; the U.S. called for a follow-up conference for the presentation of detailed national plans.
> Convention on the Protection of Biodiversity—Signed by 154 countries, with the U.S. alone in public opposition. This treaty's objective is to give all parties access to genetic resources and to the technology necessary to exploit them; this latter provision was the focus of U.S. opposition.
> Declaration of Principles on Forests—A weak document reflecting fundamental conflicts between environmental groups (largely supported by advanced countries) favoring strict protection of worldwide forest resources, and governments of less developed countries who saw such proposals as hypocritical infringements on their sovereignty.

In view of the high level of current worldwide interest, the great variety of issues involved, and the critical need for additional knowledge and step-by-step experience in most areas of current environmental concern, it seems most likely that the 1990s will be a period of active experimentation, discussion and debate about international environmental issues, but that few if any major regime-creating developments should be anticipated.

CONCLUSION: IMPLICATIONS FOR INTERNATIONAL MANAGEMENT

Policy regimes are central and critical elements of the international business environment. Some of them provide necessary foundations for international business activity. Basic functions of international trade, currency exchange, investment, transport and communication cannot take place without the existence of supportive agreements and understandings among the parties involved, both enterprises and governments. Some new areas of international concern, such as environmental protection and the use of planetary resources, involve not simply business activity but the quality and sustainability of human life itself.

Policy regimes are intended to influence both the **processes** through which international business contact takes place and the ultimate **outcomes** resulting—e.g., the volume of production, its distribution among users and final disposal. Regime objectives include both (a) **efficiency** in the use of resources, which may involve increasing emphasis on long-run **sustainability** as well as short-run input/output relationships, and (b) **equity**, agreement by involved parties that international business relationships and their outcomes are in some sense "just" and "fair."

Industries and enterprises are critical actors in the formation and functioning of regimes, not simply impacted parties. The oldest regimes—ocean shipping and radio—originated in response to the specific needs of enterprises. Current efforts to regulate international fishing are intended to preserve, not eliminate, the opportunities for fishing enterprises over time. Whatever their original sources, all regimes require collaborative and adaptive behavior on the part of both businesses and governments for their operations and impacts.

Policy regimes are by their very nature dynamic; adaptation and change over time is one of their principal characteristics. Thus, although most important regimes contain significant institutional elements (formal agreements, organizations), the understandings and norms governing the behavior of participants are of primary importance and tend to change in response to changing circumstances. Anticipating and participating in this process of change is the ultimate strategic task for international managers.

REFERENCES

Adelman, Carol C., ed. 1988. *International Regulation*. San Francisco: Institution for Contemporary Studies.

Aronson, J.D., and Peter F. Cowhey. 1988. *When Nations Talk*. Cambridge, MA: Ballinger.

Behrman, Jack N., & Robert E. Grosse. 1990. *International Business and Governments*. Columbia, SC: University of South Carolina Press.

Bower, Joseph, and Yves Doz. 1979. "Strategy Formulation: A Social and Political Process," in Schendel and Hofer, p. 165.

Branscomb, Anne W. 1986. *Toward a Law of Global Communications Networks*. New York: Longman. (See especially articles by Branscomb, Herzstein and Glasner.)

Dizard, Wilson P. 1988. "International Regulation: Telecommunications and Information," in Carol C. Adelman, ed., *International Regulation: New Rules in a Changing World Order*. San Francisco: Institute for Contemporary Studies, pp. 115–136.

Goodrich, John. 1989. *The Commercialization of Outer Space*. Westport, CT: Quorum.

Feketekuty, F. 1988. *International Trade in Services: An Overview and Blueprint for Negotiations*. Cambridge, MA: Ballinger.

Fisher, B.S., and Turner, J. 1983. *Regulating the Multinational Enterprise: National and International Challenges*. New York: Praeger.

Fishlow, A. and S. Haggard. 1992. *The United States and the Regionalization of the World Economy*. Washington, DC: OECD.

Haggard, Stephen, and Beth A. Simmons. 1987. "Theories of International Regimes." *International Organizations*, 41(3), pp. 491–517.

Kline, John M. 1985. *International Codes and Multinational Business*. Westport, CT: Quorum.

Krasner, Stephen D. 1983. *International Regimes*. Ithaca, NY: Cornell University Press.

Levinsohn, J.A., and J.B. Slemrod. 1990. *Taxes, Tariffs, and the Global Corporation*, Working Paper No. 3500. Cambridge, MA: National Bureau of Economic Research.

Noam, Eli M. 1989. "International Telecommunications in Transition," in Robert W. Crandall and Kenneth Flamm, eds., *Changing the Rules: Technological Change, International Competition, and Regulation in Communications*. Washington, DC: Brookings. pp. 257–297.

Papp, D.S., and J.R. McIntyre, eds. 1987. *International Space Policy*. Westport, CT: Quorum.

Preston, L.E., and D. Windsor. 1992. *The Rules of the Game in the Global Economy: Policy Regimes for International Business*. Norwell MA: Kluwer.

United Nations. 1993. *The Global Partnership for Environment and Development*. New York: United Nations.

U.N. Centre on Transnational Corporations. 1990. *The New Code Environment*. New York: UNCTC.

Vernon, Raymond. 1971. *Sovereignty at Bay: The Multinational Spread of U.S. Enterprises*. New York: Basic Books.

Wallace, Cynthia Day. 1982. *Legal Control of the Multinational Enterprise*. The Hague: Martinus Nijhoff.

Wallace, Cynthia Day. 1990. *Foreign Direct Investment in the 1990s*. Dordrecht: Martinus Nijhoff.

A NEW PERSPECTIVE
ON THE INTERNATIONAL SOCIAL
REGULATION OF BUSINESS

*An evaluation of the compliance status of the international
code of the marketing of breast milk substitutes*

S. Prakash Sethi

Bharat B. Bhalla

ABSTRACT: This article uses the case of breast-milk substitutes to study the nature and effectiveness of international regulation of business. The findings are disappointing. An international code adopted by the World Health Organization is found to have had little impact on the signatory nations.

May 21, 1981 was the turning point in the annals of the international regulation of business. On that fateful day, the World Health Assembly (the Assembly) in its 34th session, by its resolution 34.22 adopted an International Code of Marketing of Breast-milk Substitutes (hereinafter referred to as the "WHO Code" or the "Code") with 118 votes in favor, 1 against and 3 abstentions (World Health Organization 1981). The lone negative vote was cast by the United States. With the adoption of the Code, eight years of intense battle between the infant formula industry and the social activists had reached, at least for the time being, a conclusive milestone. The U.S. negative vote was the subject of severe public and governmental criticism in most foreign countries and also at home. The U.S. Congress held hearings on the subject where a majority of law makers voiced their opposi-

tion to the Administration's position which was viewed as an expression of the conservative-doctrinaire position of the Reagan administration (e.g., Chetley, 1986; Johnson, 1986; McComas, Fookes & Taucher, 1982; Muller, 1975; Sethi, forthcoming; U.S. Senate, 1978).

ECONOMIC AND SOCIO-POLITICAL CONTEXT OF INTERNATIONAL REGULATION OF BUSINESS

The passage of the Infant Formula Code was a strong manifestation of the continuing struggle between large multinational corporations (MNCs) and nation states, especially the Third World countries, to secure what each considers a more equitable share of the gains in trade and investment by the multinationals within the latters' jurisdiction. Following the end of World War II and the great wave of decolonization, the economic relationship between MNCs and Third World countries has wavered between intense hostility and cooperation. During this period, both the direction and magnitude of relationship were influenced by (a) emerging political and economic philosophies as to the role of the government in a nation's economic policies, (b) perception of inequities in international trade (See Baer, 1962; Evans, 1984; Prebisch, 1959; Spraos, 1983; United Nations, 1950), and (c) relative bargaining power be-

Acknowledgments: This article is a revision of the unpublished paper, *The righteous and the powerful: Corporations, religious institutions and International social activism—the case of the infant formula controversy and the Nestle boycott*, by S. Prakash Sethi.

tween the nations of the First World and Third World, and the Governments of Third World and MNCs (See Moran, 1985; Smith & Wells, 1975; Vernon, 1971).

At the micro level, we witnessed the rise of national planning and an increased role of the government in the ownership and management of industrial enterprises. At the macro (international) level, relations between the two groups of nations were often seen in terms of "North-South Conflicts" or "Imperialist Modes of Economic Alliances" where former colonies continued to depend on the "mother" country for their economic development. This dependency was further strengthened through foreign and Cold War alliances. More recently, Third World countries have sought to reduce the inequities in wealth and living standards through calls for international sharing of hitherto unexploited global natural resources, and demands on the First World governments to provide them with free technology transfer and systematic preferences in trade.

At the national level, Third World countries, sought to compensate for their weak bargaining position by inducing MNCs with financial and other incentives to make large investment commitments in the expectation that once MNCs have made a sizeable local investment the host country could alter at a later date the terms of relationship to their relative advantage. More often than not, these tactics did not yield the desired benefits to host countries because (a) MNCs, which control technology and international markets, invariably outmaneuvered the host countries which competed among themselves for seeking MNC investments; and (b) host countries were invariably hobbled by internal strife, corruption, and lack of management and negotiating skills to exploit their real or perceived competitive advantage.

The historical context of this conflict has been confounded, during the last 5–10 years, by a series of world events causing a profound change in our perception of a new world political and economic order. The collapse of the Russian Empire and planned economic systems have renewed focus on the role of private enterprise and a democratic system of political governance around the world. Having lost most of their political leverage and economic aid related to the politics of the Cold War era, Third World countries are now dependent on private enterprise and market competition for their economic growth.

Unfortunately, for the Third World nations, there has been another change of major import that has worsened their relative bargaining power vis-a-vis MNCs and industrially advanced countries. The changing nature of industrial processes emphasizes automation and technology-based product values over cheap labor and raw materials. This change has robbed Third World countries of comparative advantage in two of their most important factor endowments, i.e., cheap labor and abundant raw materials. This has thus forced them to become even more dependent on MNCs for domestic economic growth.

The convergence of all these factors has forced Third World countries to put greater reliance on international organizations and negotiating mechanisms to further their goal of economic growth. They have also used these mechanisms to lessen, if not eliminate, the power of MNCs to play them against each other in self-defeating competition for their investment and know-how. Furthermore, in an unusual extension of this approach, Third World nations, in alliance with even many First World countries, have sought to develop international codes of conduct, not for the governments of sovereign states, but for private economic institutions, e.g., multinational corporations. The WHO-Code discussed herein is one of the first and most successful examples of this approach. The second one, still in the process of formulation, is the U.N.'s Code of Conduct for Transnational Corporations.

Another wrinkle in this brave new world of First World-Third World Governments, International Agencies and Multinational Corporations, has been the emergence of

Public Interest Groups, called Non-Governmental Organizations or NGOs in the U.N. parlance. Often rooted in strong religious and ethical concerns to protect the poor, and using techniques of grass-roots mobilization of public opinion, media pressure, and confrontational tactics, NGOs have been successful in pressuring MNCs to change their pattern of behavior.

The confluence of all these forces can best be seen in the passage of the WHO-sponsored Infant Formula Code and its implementation by MNCs and host country governments. The advocates of the Code had argued for its passage in the belief that only an internationally designed Code could strengthen the hands of Third World governments in making major international infant formula producers alter their marketing practices which they felt were injurious to the health and safety of the infants in those countries. Another objective was to force MNCs to make unilateral changes in their marketing practices and thereby reduce their power and influence in Third World countries.

ANTECEDENTS
TO THE DEVELOPMENT
OF THE INFANT FORMULA CODE

The passage of the Code reflected a widespread concern on the part of a multitude of private and public groups over the unbridled promotion and sale of infant formula products, especially in Third World countries. The critics of the industry argued that breast-feeding was the best and most efficacious infant food, and that by encouraging the use of infant formula, the industry caused a decline in breast-feeding. Moreover, the sale of infant formula was particularly inappropriate in Third World countries where most people could not afford it and where appropriate hygienic conditions were largely unavailable thereby making its use unsafe and potentially hazardous. Consequently, its use contributed to infant morbidity and mortality. Infant formula manufacturers, while agree-

ing to the concept that "mother's milk is best," vehemently deny the critics' assertions of existence of scientific proof of a linkage between infant formula consumption and infant morbidity and mortality. The industry also rejects the charge that it systematically uses excessive promotion and high pressure sales tactics. Instead, it argues that it only promotes safe use of its products, where mothers have already decided, for biological, social, or economic reasons, to use infant formula foods (Sethi, in print, p. 728).

In arguing for an international approach to curb the problems of decline in breast-feeding and unneeded and inappropriate use of infant formula, the activists and many Third World countries, along with the scientific and health care professionals on the staff of the WHO and the United Nations Children Fund (UNICEF), argued that:

1. Infant mortality is a global problem, with a greater incidence in the Third World. Governments in poorer countries lack the necessary expertise, administrative capabilities and financial resources to handle the problem by themselves. They are also in a weaker bargaining position in dealing with large and powerful foreign MNCs.
2. An international code would provide member governments with a uniform set of standards and guidelines for developing a legal or administrative response, and suitable monitoring mechanisms, which are in harmony with their own social and cultural norms.
3. The code would help the health ministries and public health officials in Third World countries to pressure their own governments into assigning health issues a higher priority and increased budgetary resources.

From its very inception, the infant formula controversy had been laden with emotional and moral overtones; scientific controversies as to facts, charges and counter-charges among various groups about the veracity of their opponents' statements; the moral authority and concerns for the poor on the part of religious institutions and Third World related public interest groups; and, the right of companies to market what they consider to be a safe and useful product in a manner they assert to be responsible and morally defensible. Starting in the early sixties concerns for the improper use of infant formula were expressed by various Third World health-care professionals and became the focus of enquiry by various U.S. agencies involved with Third World problems. The issue became a matter of public controversy in 1974 with the publication a book *The Baby Killer* by a London group called War on Want. The report, among other things, accused Nestle, the largest marketer of infant formula in the world, of promoting the sale of infant formula among the Third World's poor thereby contributing to their infant morbidity and mortality. The ensuing clash between Nestle and the activists, a worldwide boycott of Nestle products, Congressional hearings in the United States, and confrontations between the activists and infant formula companies eventually culminated in the discussions at the World Health Assembly and the passage of the Code.

At the World Health Assembly, it took almost four years for the Code to be adopted. The Secretariat, supported by the Third World member governments and NGOs, wanted the Assembly to adopt the Code as a regulation in the sense of Articles 21 and 22 of the WHO constitution. However, it became apparent that the Code, in the mandatory form, was unlikely to be supported by industrially advanced countries and was finally approved as a recommendation in the sense of article 23 of the WHO constitution (WHO, 1981). In its recommendatory form, the Code considered its provisions minimum standards to be enforced by member governments while urging the industry to make its marketing practices voluntarily consistent with the Code provisions.

CRITICAL ISSUES FOR ANALYSIS

Prima facie, it would seem that any country that wishes to impose conditions on the promotion and sale of infant formula, or for that matter on any other product, within its borders may easily do so through appropriate laws and regulations. Most countries do indeed regulate a variety of marketing activities without resort to international mechanisms. The interesting question, therefore, is to ascertain the extent to which the expectations of the Code proponents have been met and the degree to which the underlying assumptions of its passage were indeed relevant. The passage of the Code incurred enormous financial costs, time, and professional resources, by all parties concerned. It came into being through a long process of acrimony, boycotts, conflicts, negotiations and interminable meetings of WHO lasting over a period of almost four years. Although, specific cost estimates are unavailable, it is apparent that scores of millions of dollars were spent by all parties involved. Of even greater importance is the issue of the other approaches that were not undertaken and that could have yielded more efficacious solutions.

An analysis of the available literature and activities of the various players since the enactment of the Code in May 1981, indicates that the focus of the monitoring effort on the part of the activists, as well as the WHO, has been primarily, if not exclusively, directed at the infant formula industry. While this effort is highly desirable, and quite legitimate in emphasis and intent, it offer at best, a partial picture of the situation in view of the fact that both the Third World countries and the WHO have an infinitely larger role to play in improving the environment relating to infant health and nutrition. It is, therefore, legitimate to ask what programs and actions have been undertaken by the WHO member governments, especially those in the Third World countries, and WHO itself, in carrying out the mandate of the Code.

The objective of this article is to evaluate the working of the WHO-Code over the last 10 years. Our primary focus will be to analyze and evaluate the efforts made by individual countries, especially in the Third World, to promote the objectives of infant health and nutrition enunciated in the Code and to undertake necessary legislative and administrative actions in compliance with the Code's various provisions. We will examine the actions of the World Health Assembly and the WHO in mobilizing member governments and other interested parties fulfilling the Code's mandate. Finally, we will analyze the Code compliance efforts on the part of the four multinational infant formula manufacturers that account for an overwhelming majority of worldwide infant formula sales.

ESSENTIAL FEATURES OF THE INFANT FORMULA CODE

The aim of the "International Code of Marketing of Breast-milk Substitutes" (the Code) is to provide "safe and adequate nutrition to infants by the protection and promotion of breast-feeding and by ensuring the proper use of breast-milk substitutes when these are necessary on the basis of adequate information and through appropriate marketing and distribution" (WHO, 1981). It attempts to achieve this noble and laudable objective by "codifying" the industry's future "proper" conduct. The Code imposes a number of specific restrictions on the industry's marketing and distribution practices by proclaiming these as the minimum required standards to be accepted by the industry and all member states.

1. *Education and promotion.* The Code prohibits the industry from advertising infant formula products to the general pubic in any form. The industry, however, may provide information and educational materials in written, audio, and visual forms dealing with infant feeding and intended to reach pregnant women and mothers of infants and young children. The Code prohibits the industry from promoting, directly or indirectly, the use of infant formula by offering free samples to pregnant women and mothers of young children and infants [Articles 4, 5, 6, & 8].
2. *Role of health workers.* The Code considers local health workers as the linchpin in the implementation effort. The industry's contact with end-users is to take place only through local health workers. Companies are restricted to providing health workers with only general and actual information about their products. They are to refrain from giving free samples, other materials and financial help for purposes other than the enhancement of their professional capabilities and only with the prior approval of local authorities [Article 7].
3. *Labelling.* The Code requires that labels must state in a clearly understandable local language, the important message that breast-feeding is superior to bottle-feeding. Labels should not imply by any means, written or visual, that the packaged product is as good as mother's milk [Article 9].
4. *Implementation and monitoring.* The Code provides a three-tier system of implementation. The primary responsibility for implementation is assigned to member governments, who are required to take appropriate legal and administrative actions consistent with their social and legislative frameworks. These laws and regulations are required to be applicable equally to both domestic and foreign suppliers of infant formula products. *In developing local laws and regulations, member governments are encouraged to seek help from WHO, UNICEF and other agencies of the UN system and to inform WHO each year of actions taken by them in implementing the Code.* [Emphasis Added] Manufacturers and distributors of infant formula products, irrespective of any action taken by member states, are held responsible for monitoring their own marketing practices in conformity with the principles and aim of the Code and for taking steps to ensure that their conduct at every level conforms to them. And finally, the Code requires WHO to provide technical assistance to member governments in preparing their legal and administrative responses to the Code [Article 11].

Monitoring of the Code was one of the most contentious issues during the code development phase. The Code went through four different drafts before it could be finally adopted. Under Article 7 of the first Draft Code, WHO/UNICEF were to assume the key responsibility for monitoring the Code implementation and for adjudicating disputes over its interpretation. To support these monitoring activities, the Draft Code had provided for the creation of a "Central Office" for WHO/UNICEF for collecting, archiving, analysis and interpretation of the necessary data. However, in the final and fourth draft this provision was dropped in favor of a three-tier monitoring and enforcement system incorporating the member countries, the industry and NGOs.

The inclusion of NGOs in the monitoring process was a tacit recognition of the key role played by the activist groups in the Code's enactment and their growing political power within the UN system. The Code designates NGOs, professional groups, institutions, and concerned individuals as the external watchdogs for monitoring industry's compliance of the Code in different countries and regions.

WHO is charged with the responsibility of informing the Health Assembly, biennially in even years, as to the status of individual country compliance. This report is based on the information received each year from member states [Article 11].

EVALUATION OF THE COMPLIANCE OF INFANT FORMULA CODE

Over ten years have passed since the Code was adopted in May, 1981. It is appropriate that we review the progress made by various parties in implementing the Code, which was considered by the Assembly to be the "expression of the collective will of the membership of the World Health Organization" to eradicate the problem of infant morbidity and mortality in the third world (WHO, 1981).

Code Compliance by Member Countries

From the very beginning, industrially advanced countries had contended that infant mortality was essentially a Third World problem. As a matter of fact, the vote by most of these countries in favor of the WHO Code was widely interpreted as a largely political gesture to demonstrate their solidarity with the Third World countries. Consequently, the advanced countries have developed, in consultation with their own infant formula companies, infant formula marketing codes that are voluntary in character.

Code Compliance by Third World Countries

Our analysis of developing countries covers 123 nations where the problem of infant mortality is acute and whose governments were vociferous in their criticism of infant formula companies' marketing practices, and who actively campaigned for the passage of the WHO Code. The country compliance analysis is limited by the amount and quality of information available from non-governmental sources.

For all importance given to infant health and nutrition, neither the World Health Organization (WHO), nor the member governments have been aggressive in collecting and reporting data on the working of the Code. WHO's efforts in this regard are contained in a biennial report on the Code implementation status to the World Health Assembly (WHA). These reports are based on the information supplied by member states. The role of WHO in this instance is simple that of the collator and disseminator of information. WHO lacks any formal authority over member governments to seek their compliance with the Code provisions. During the World Health Assembly (WHA) deliberations at the time of the passage of the Infant Formula Code, WHO lobbied against receiving such an authority despite the willingness of the WHA to do so.

Even where the information is furnished by the countries themselves, WHO does not make public the Code compliance information on individual countries. It is, therefore, impossible to undertake any independent analysis of the veracity or adequacy of the information furnished by individual country governments to WHO. The data made public by WHO also do not provide any indication as to the consistency of the information so provided and the problems that may have occurred in the process of aggregation of the data. One might glean some indication of the progress made by different countries through the oral statements made by their delegates during the biennial proceedings of the WHA. These statements are quite general and rarely provide specific details.

Another source of corroborating information is provided by the American Public Health Association (APHA), a Washington-based private organization funded by the U.S. Agency for International Development (AID), which collects information on country code compliance. Both these sources follow an identical pattern and a near-common basis in collecting and disseminating information of country compliance with the Code. To wit, neither APHA nor AID make any attempt at verifying the information provided by individual country governments. Thus the best that can be said for the information generated by WHO and APHA is that it is simply a tally sheet or a report card indicating the extent of efforts reportedly being made by individual governments in implementing the Code and not the actual outcome of these efforts.

Wherever possible, we have also made use of information made public by NGOs, mainly the International Baby Food Action Network (IBFAN) and the International Organization of Consumers Union (IOCU), which have a worldwide network. IOCU represents consumers throughout the world and has a membership of 164 consumer organizations in some 60 developing and industrialized countries.

Given the severe imitations and deficiencies of available data, it is not possible to draw any definitive conclusions as to the extent of the effectiveness of the Code in meeting its objectives. However, the paucity of data itself, and the unwillingness of WHO to collect and individual countries to report, more specific information suggests that a large gap exists between the rhetoric of intentions and the reality of implementation.

The following analysis, based as it is on the somewhat superficial nature of country reported data, still strongly indicates that the Third World governments have been grossly negligent in fulfilling their part of the undertaking in implementing the Code. Moreover, we also find that where credit has been taken for Code compliance, more often than not, it refers to the actions that infant formula manufacturers were obligated to take under the provisions of the Code.

The Code compliance has two interrelated aspects: code implementation and code monitoring. The Code implementation demonstrates the steps taken by various countries toward adopting the Infant Formula Code either in toto or partially within their legal and administrative systems, and the progress made by them in this effort since May 21, 1981. These data would indicate the seriousness of purpose or the sense of urgency exhibited by a country in resolving its critical infant health problems. The effort at Code monitoring would suggest the extent to which a country was enforcing the code provisions, after having been enacted in the first place. Furthermore, it would show what local administrative apparatus is in place in each country for monitoring such implementation. This would provide an indication of the extent of resource commitment made by individual countries. The score card of Third World countries is very disappointing on both these counts.

Code Implementation

Our analysis of the Code implementation by Third World countries suggests the following key conclusions:

1. Only 10 countries, i.e., barely 8 percent of those reporting, had adopted the Infant Formula code in toto by the end of 1988, latest year for which the data are available (Table 1). Consider the fact that Third World countries account for about 72 percent of the world population and contribute roughly 16 percent to the world gross national product (GNP). In contrast, the ten countries mentioned in Table 1 represent less than 5 percent of the world population and less than 2 per-

Table 1:   The Code Compliance by Third World Countries: 1981–1988

Number of Countries

Compliance Status	A	B	C	D	E	F
Regions						
Africa	1	12	3	3	22	11
Americas	5	7	0	1	17	3
Asia	4	8	4	4	15	7
Total	10	27	7	8	54	21

Compliance Status Description
A. The total Code in effect as law in the country.
B. Some of the Code provisions in effect as law.
C. Some of the Code provisions in effect on a voluntary basis.
D. Government controls the supply and distribution of breast milk substitutes.
E. The Code being studied by a working group or by a government appointed committee or awaiting legislation.
F. No action at all.

SOURCE: IBFAN/IOCU, Documentation Center, Penang, Malaysia; APHA, Clearinghouse on Infant Feeding & Maternal Nutrition, Washington, D.C.

cent of the world's GNP. Of those, 4 countries enforce the Code on a voluntary basis. There are 343 other countries that claim to have adopted only some provisions of the Code either on a mandatory or a voluntary basis. Unfortunately, these countries also do not provide any details as to the specificity of the Code provisions that they have adopted; the extent to which they have been implemented; and, the resources that have been devoted to their enforcement.

Information from IBFAN/IOCU, APHA and WHO biennial reports reveals that, by and large, countries have zeroed in essentially on two key areas of the Code i.e., Labelling and Promotion and Education. Compliance with the labelling provision is simple because the industry has made these changes voluntarily. IBFAN/IOCU reported in their 1988 survey that the industry had made considerable progress in this area. According to this report, with the exception of five countries in Europe, Japan and Korea, all other companies had complied, either partially or fully, with the Code's labelling provisions. The survey disclosed that Nestle of Switzerland and three major U.S. companies (Ross Laboratories of Abbott Labs, Mead Johnson of Bristol-Myers and Wyeth Laboratories of American Home Products) were in full compliance with Article 9 of the Code (IBFAN/IOCU, 1988).

In the area of Promotion and Education (Articles 4, 5 and 6), these countries have banned mass advertising of breast-milk substitutes to the general public. The potential impact of this activity, however, should not be over estimated. These countries suffer from a very high rate of illiteracy, low per capita income and no nationwide television network. Under these conditions a ban on general advertising is of little significance.

2. Progress in compliance with the Code was also uneven when analyzed region by region. In Africa, where the infant mortality problem is most severe, governments have shown a callous disregard for infant welfare. According to the World Bank, the infant mortality rate (deaths per 1000 live births) averages about 65 in developing countries versus 9 in industrialized countries. The low-income countries in Sub-Saharan Africa have an infant mortality rate of 107, the highest in the world (The World Bank, 1991).

In 1982, the Inter-Parliamentary Conference, attended by delegates from 23 African nations, had urged all regional governments to implement the Code through local legislation. To date, only Kenya has implemented the Code in toto. Thirty-three other countries, representing 43 percent of the region's population, either have taken no action at all or are still reviewing the Code for legislative action.

3. Countries have been equally slow in developing their implementation response to the Code. Kenya, Mexico and the Philippines, which have adopted the Code *in toto*, took between 5 and 6 years to pass the necessary local legislation (Table 2).

In 1982, 17 countries reported for the first time that they were "studying" the feasibility of code implementation. Unfortunately, as of 1988, none of these countries had as yet

Table 2:   Time Progression of the Code Compliance by Third World Countries: 1981–1987

Provisions Compiled	1981	1982	1983	1984	1985	1986	1987
A. The Code as a Law	—	2	3	1	—	1	3
B. Some provisions adopted as law	4	4	6	4	2	5	2
C. Some provisions adopted voluntarily	1	3	—	1	—	—	3
D. The Code under study	2	17	3	3	1	26	6
Total	7	26	12	9	3	32	14

SOURCE: IBFAN/IOCU, ALPHA, and WHO.

crossed that stage. In 1986, 32 countries had disclosed the extent of progress made by them in the Code implementation. Of these, 26 countries had disclosed for the first time, after waiting for 5 to 6 years, that either the Infant Formula Code was under review by a committee or its draft was awaiting legislation.

This sorry state of affairs is confirmed by the report card issued by IBFAN/IOCU. Mrs. A. Allain of IBFAN/IOCU made the following comments at the WHA meeting in May 1988 on the global state of Code implementation (WHO, 1988):

> Only six governments had adopted the entire code as law, 11 had relatively well-monitored voluntary codes, 24 had passed legislation on significant parts of the Code and 33 had drafts awaiting legislation, some of which had waited as long as four or five years. 34 countries had taken no action, 8 had an industry-written code in effect and 23 were still studying the situation seven years after their endorsement of the Code.

Reluctant as it may be, even WHO obliquely acknowledges that developing countries have been negligent in the Infant Formula Code implementation (WHO, 1986).

In 1990, WHO presented to the Assembly a synthesis of its country compliance reports submitted between 1982-1990. The sole basis of this report was the information provided by member states. The tabular summary included in the report indicated the time when a member country informed WHO of its progress on the Code implementation. The report did not distinguish between the countries that intended to take some action and those that had taken specific action toward implementing the Code. The WHO tabular summary leaves one with the impression that "intent to act" tantamounts to action. The best interpretation one can put on the report is to call it an apology for the slow response on the part of Third World countries to the Code (WHO, 1990). As of 1990, nine years after the Code adoption, 75 countries representing 54 percent of the total third world population are still "considering" some suitable action for implementing the Code.

Code Enforcement

Most developing countries have been silent on the issue of the Code enforcement. Even IBFAN/IOCU, APHA and WHO have not released any information in this respect. There is only one inescapable conclusion. Despite all the agitation for the Code's passage and their alleged concern for infant morbidity and mortality, most Third World countries have not taken even the minimal steps that they could have taken even in the absence of any international code to address these problems to the extent that they fall within their purview. The problem of lack of progress is compounded by a number of factors that are inherent in the structure and provisions of the Code. For example:

1. The Code does not provide a specific mechanism for holding member states accountable for its implementation.

2. Most Third World countries, faced with the pressures of maintaining a balance between economic growth and social progress, and between concerns for national security and social welfare, seem to have opted in favor of weapons and economic growth and have given a short shrift to public health and welfare needs.

A number of examples of individual country efforts lend further evidence to this sad state of affairs. According to Health Alert 83, in the Philippines, which had adopted the Code in toto in 1986 (APHA, 1989):

> Almost 2 years after (its) enactment and despite the strong sanctions provisions of the Code, the Department of health, which is responsible for monitoring and enforcement, seems unable to curtail blatant violations by infant formula companies. Also the "dominant method of infant feeding in Metro Manila continues to be bottle-feeding, and the infant formula companies continue to rake in profits.

3. Malaysia, which since 1983 has banned all mass advertising and relies on voluntary code enforcement, monitors industry promotion and distribution activities through the Government Liaison Committee. According to the Consumers Union of Penang (Headquarters of IOCU) "formula companies' promotion in Malaysia continues as aggressively as ever" and the voluntary Code is "weak with many loopholes" (APHA, 1989). Liberia has also banned advertising of breast-milk substitutes via mass media and health institutions. However, the Breast-feeding Advocacy Group (BAG), a private voluntary organization, reports that "substitutes and baby foods are widely available in shops and markets and continue to be imported as essential commodities" (APHA, 1989).

One of the key responsibilities of local governments under the WHO-Code is to ensure that health workers and, through them, pregnant women and young mothers receive "objective and consistent" information on the virtues of breast-feeding and disadvantages of breast-milk substitutes. This is a serious responsibility and its implementation requires

Table 3: Share of Central Government Expenditures on Health: 1972–1987 (by percent)

Countries	1972	1987
Developing Countries:	5.9	4.6
Low-Income Countries	5.4	3.4
High-Debt Countries	8.14	5.9
Upper-Income Countries	6.7	n.a.
Developed Countries:	11.2	12.6

SOURCE: World Bank, *World Development Report, 1989*; Table 11. Central Government Expenditures.

major investments in updating and maintaining the existing administrative infrastructure, including building of additional health care facilities, revamping existing instructional materials, and retraining of existing health care workers. This is a tall order and is difficult and expensive to achieve in most developing countries. For example, between 1972 and 1987, the share of Third World countries' total budget expenditures on health declined from an average of 5.9 percent in 1972 to 4.6 percent in 1987 (Table 3).

Of the 34 countries that claim to have certain provisions of the Infant Formula Code in effect either as a law or on a voluntary basis, all except Bangladesh and Ecuador, experienced a decline in government expenditures on health during this period. For example, the high-debt countries in Latin America and other regions reduced the share of their expenditures on health significantly, from 8.4 percent in 1972 to 5.9 percent in 1987 in order to meet their more urgent economic and debt service needs.

4. In an effort to protect domestic producers of infant formula products, a number of countries have been deliberately slow in implementing the Code. For example, in 1985, the Government of India had adopted a National Code for the Protection and Promotion of Breast-feeding. This National Code barred foreign MNCs from advertising their infant formula to the general public and from direct contact between their marketing personnel and young and pregnant mothers. The National Code, however, exempted the local

infant formula companies from these provisions. Furthermore, in contravention to the WHO-Code provisions, the National Code allows local companies to promote their products through health workers and by handing out free samples (APHA, 1989).

THE ROLE OF THE WORLD HEALTH ORGANIZATION (WHO)

WHO defines its role as being merely a conduit between member states and the World Health Assembly. This may explain why WHO's biennial reports to the Assembly on the Code implementation status are no more than collated and summarized versions of information provided by member nations. This is what the member nations want to make public and WHO is only too happy to oblige. WHO argues that it does not have the authority, which it tried very hard not to have in the first place, either to interpret the code or to judge whether certain industry marketing practices are in violation of the Code. It considers these matters to be the preserve of member states (WHO, 1982). Thus, like all other parties, WHO is equally negligent in this respect.

The World Health Assembly, in its 39th session held in Geneva in 1986, requested WHO "to propose a simplified and standardized form for use by member states to facilitate the monitoring and evaluation by them of their implementation of the Code and reporting thereon to WHO, as well as the preparation by WHO of a consolidated report covering each of the articles of the Code" (WHO, 1986). Even after a passage of four years, WHO's 1990 report failed to respond to the request of the Assembly. It would appear that the WHO is unwilling to assume any responsibility for monitoring the Code implementation and thereby risk the wrath of its political bosses.

CODE COMPLIANCE BY INFANT FORMULA MANUFACTURERS

Although, Nestle was one of the most ardent opponents of the Infant Formula Code during its formulation stages, it was the first one to embrace the Code once it was passed. However, the company conditioned its acceptance only so far as it applied to Third World countries. Most other major international formula manufacturers soon followed with similar announcements. There is, however, no record of announcement of "intention to comply" by any of the major domestic producers of infant formula products in Third World countries. It should be noted here that some of these producers often hold significant shares of their domestic markets, e.g., India (Sethi, in print).

From the very beginning, a major bone of contention between the multinational infant formula manufacturers, WHO and NGOs, in terms of the Code compliance had to do with its "universal coverage." The companies argued that the "alleged" marketing and promotion problems, as well as unhygienic conditions, prevailed only in Third World countries. Furthermore, since the consumer in industrially advanced countries had the means and capabilities to be informed about the product, and the discretionary income to acquire the product, the consumer's right to choose could not be limited without overwhelming evidence of countervailing factors. The regulatory and health authorities in these countries were also considered to be capable of protecting the health and welfare of their citizens. To date, this issue remains unresolved.

The industry compliance efforts can be briefly summarized as follows:

1. The multinational infant formula manufacturers created a new institutional structure called the International Association of Infant Food manufacturers (IFM). It consisted of 33 major national and international manufacturers with the sole exception of the U.S. based Abbott Ross Laboratories. Among IFM's objectives are: development of common industry policies relating to composition, utilization, labelling, packaging and marketing of infant and young children foods; representing industry interests before WHO, FAO and UNICEF; promotion of high ethical standards for the marketing of infant foods; providing

technical and scientific expertise to member companies and industry associations; and, to collect and disseminate information pertaining to IFM members and their activities in the marketing of infant foods. Participation by member companies in any and all of IFM activities, however, is voluntary. IFM has no provisions either to monitor individual member's performance or to persuade member companies to improve their compliance efforts should such actions be called for.

2. Among the major elements of compliance on the part of individual companies have been in the areas of: labelling, consumer advertising, instructional materials, and some of the other marketing activities. Disagreements,however,persist between the companies and the activists as to the degree of compliance of various Code provisions by individual companies.

3. Nestle also took certain additional steps. In an effort to gain public credibility for its actions and as part of its attempt to terminate consumer boycott against its products, the company established an independent commission, called the Nestle Infant Formula Audit Commission (NIFAC), under the chairmanship of former U.S. Senator Edmond Muskie. Under the terms of its charter, NIFAC was free to receive complaints against Nestle, initiate its own investigation, and publish its findings. In all, the Commission published over 15 reports about its actions. The Commission was dissolved in late 1991 as its members felt that the remaining problems can best be resolved through direct discussions among various groups.

4. In 1991, IFM members reached agreement with WHO and UNICEF to cooperate in a new country-by-country initiative aimed at phasing out infant formula donations to maternity hospitals in developing countries by the end of 1992.

CONCLUSION

Our analysis of the impact of the Infant Formula Code is disheartening. The best that can be said is that the Code succeeded in creating public awareness and political interest on the vital public policy issue of infant health in the Third World. There is also evidence to indicate that large multinational infant formula producers have implemented, to a considerable degree, most of the Code provisions within their purview. Unfortunately, neither the industry's claims nor the critics' charges can be verified for the simple fact that at present there is no independent organization in existence which would carry out such a task. The Code provided a framework within which Third World nations and multinational infant formula manufacturers could develop a mutually beneficial relationship. "The modern corporation has lived in relative harmony within the nation-state because the corporation has sought legitimacy for its operations and benefits for its owners within the framework of the broader welfare concerns of society" (Sethi & Bhalla, 1991). The Third World nations, by not implementing the Code, have failed to make use of this framework or to create more appropriate indigenous structures within which mutual cooperation and action would yield their social goal of reducing infant mortality.

The paramount question, however, remains unanswered and is unlikely to be resolved any time soon. To wit, what if any difference has been made in reducing infants' sickness and deaths in Third World countries as a consequence of the Infant Formula Code.

REFERENCES

American Public Health Association (June 1989). *Legislation and policies to support maternal and child nutrition, Report No. 6.* Washington, DC: American Public Health Association.

Baer, W. (1962). The economics of prebisch and ECLA. *Economic Development and Cultural Change* 10(2): 169-182.

Chetley, A. (1986). *The politics of baby foods.* London: Frances Printer.

Evans, D. (1984). A critical assessment of some neo-marxian trade theories. *Economic Development and Cultural Change* 10(2): 11,169–182.

IBFAN/IOCU. (May 1988). *State of the code by country 1988.* Penang Malaysia: IBFAN/IOCU Documentation Center.

Johnson, D.A. (1986). Confronting corporate power: Strategies and phases of the Nestle boycott. Pp. 323–344 in *Research in corporate social performance and policy*, Vol. 8, edited by J.E. Post. Greenwich, CT: JAI Press.

McComas, M., G. Fookes, and G. Taucher. (1982). *The infant formula controversy*. Vevey, Switzerland: Nestle, S.A.

Moran, T.H. (1985). Multinational corporations: The political economy of foreign direct investment. Lexington, MA: DC Heath.

Muller, M. (1975). *The baby killer*, 2nd ed. London: War on Want.

Prebisch, R. (1959). Commercial policy in the underdeveloped countries. *American Economic Review* XLIV: 251–273.

Sethi, S. Prakash. (in print). *Multinational corporations and the impact of public advocacy on corporate strategy: Nestle and the infant formula controversy*. Norwell, MA: Kluwer Academic Press.

Sethi, S. Prakash (1986). New sociopolitical forces: The globalization of conflict. *The Journal of Business Strategy* 6(4): 24–31.

Sethi, S. Prakash and B. Bhalla. (1991). The free market and economic growth. *Business in the contemporary World* Winter: 80–100.

Smith, D.N. and L.T. Wells, Jr. (1975). *Negotiating third world mineral agreements*. Cambridge, MA: Ballinger.

Spraos, J. (1983). *Inequalizing trade?* Oxford: Clarendon Press.

U.S. Congress. Senate. Committee on Human Resources. (May 1978). *Hearings before the subcommittee on health and scientific research on examination of the advertising, marketing, promotion and use of infant formula in developing nations*. Washington, DC: 95th Congress.

United Nations (1950). *The economic development of Latin America and its principal problems*. New York: United Nations.

Vernon, R. (1971). *Sovereignty at bay: The multinational spread of U.S. enterprises*. New York: Basic Books.

The World Bank. (1991). *World development report 1991* New York: Oxford University Press.

WHO. (1981). *WHA resolution 34.22 international code of marketing of breast-milk substitutes*. Geneva, Switzerland: WHO/UNICEF.

WHO, Executive Board Seventy First Session. (November 1982). *Provisional agenda item 13: Infant and young child feeding, report by the director general*. Geneva, Switzerland: WHO.

WHO, Thirty Seventh World Health Assembly. (April 1986). *Provisional agenda item 21-infant and young child nutrition [progress and evaluation report; and status of implementation of the international code of marketing of breast-milk substitutes]*. Geneva, Switzerland: WHO.

WHO, Thirty Ninth World Health Assembly. (1986). *Provisional agenda item 21, infant and young child nutrition [progress and evaluation report; and status of implementation of the international code of marketing of breast-milk substitutes, report by the director general]*. Geneva, Switzerland: WHO.

WHO, Executive Board Eighty First Session. (January 1988). *Resolutions and decisions annexes*. Geneva, Switzerland: WHO.

WHO, Forty First World Health Assembly, Committee A. (May 1988). *Provisional summary report of the second meeting*. Geneva, Switzerland: WHO.

WHO. (1990). *The international code of marketing of breast-milk substitutes: Synthesis of reports on action taken—1981–1990 [WHO/MCH/NUT90.]*. Geneva, Switzerland: WHO.

THE SOCIAL ENVIRONMENT OF BUSINESS IN EUROPE

Peter Curwen

INTRODUCTION

The discussion that follows is concerned with the social environment of business within what used to be know as the European Community, but which is more properly referred to as the European Union (EU) now that the Maastricht Treaty has finally been signed (on 1 November 1993). The EU nevertheless remains a collection of nation states[1] despite the expanding body of supranational rules and laws arising out of the Treaty of Rome, the Single European Act and the Treaty on European Union.

The social environment of business is created via national laws and increasingly via the social policy provisions of the EU. The latter were initially to be found among the provisions of the Treaty of Rome, but were very limited in practice. Title III of Part Three (Articles 117 to 128) referred, under the heading of "social policy," to the need for "close co-operation between member states" in matters relating to employment, labour legislation, occupational training, accidents and diseases and social security. It was clear at the time, however, and indeed subsequently, that no member state had the slightest intention of altering its social provisions in order to bring them into line with some European norm.

The only specific provision of the Treaty applied to the introduction of national rules in relation to equal pay for equal work for males and females (Article 119). Some idea of the lethargic progress characteristic of the Community at that time can be gauged by the fact that this provision was supposed to be implemented by the end of 1961, but could not be said to have been implemented in all member states (and even then in a less than clear cut manner) until 1976. Given that this was the only specific matter referred to in the Treaty, it is hardly surprising that its more general aspirations mostly fell by the wayside.

THE SINGLE EUROPEAN ACT 1986

The passing of the Single European Act (SEA), which came into effect on 1 July 1987, provided a blueprint for the creation of the Single European Market (SEM). The task set out in the SEA was necessarily more ambitious than that envisaged in the Treaty of Rome, if only because Greece, Portugal and Spain had joined the Community by the end of 1986 and their economic and social circumstances were quite different from those of established northern members. The need for unanimity in the creation of supranational laws established under the Treaty of Rome could, therefore, have placed a block on progress as it had done in previous years, but this was prevented by a change in the decision-making procedures of the Council of Ministers.[2]

In respect of social policy, the Treaty of Rome was amended by a newly-added Article 118A of the SEA to provide for qualified majority voting on proposals to encourage **improvements in the working environment**, on proposals in respect of the **health and safety of workers** and in respect of harmonisation of conditions in these areas. This did not, however, remove all barriers to progress since the term "working environment" was something of an ambiguous catch-all, the interpretation of which has remained an ongoing matter of dispute between member states, especially since unanimous voting was retained in the SEA for measures affecting **"the rights and interests of employed persons"**. (Article 100A) (2) and the **free movement of workers.**

The passing of the SEA was seen as potentially threatening to social welfare. According to Rhodes the underlying rationale of the SEA was that:

> market integration was the means by which pressure would be placed on the Member States to sign up for political integration. . . . [This] meant that social affairs were initially marginalized from the integration process and that market oriented forces dominated in defining the shape of the new Europe. For this reason the fight for a social dimension has been very much a rearguard action . . . against the deregulatory threat of the 1992 programme and the market orientation of the SEA.[3]

THE SOCIAL CHARTER

In the period subsequent to the SEA there were extensive discussions concerned with how to take account of the new pressures for social policy convergence. The outcome, in May 1990, was the **European Community Charter of the Fundamental Social Rights of Workers**, usually known as the **Social Charter**. The purpose of the Charter was to guarantee the basic rights of workers in the Community. It was formally adopted by eleven of the twelve member states on 9 December 1989 with the UK unilaterally objecting to a good half of its contents.

For a variety of reasons the Charter started out as a declaration without legal force. However, it contained a mandate allowing the European Commission to set out detailed proposals on workers' rights in the twelve areas set out in Table 1.

For the most part the twelve areas were outlined in very broad terms. Item (2), for example, stated that "all employment shall be fairly remunerated" and that "a decent wage shall be established."[4] This approach recognised that national laws and negotiations between employers and unions within each country would already enshrine workers' rights such that it remained to be discovered to what extent it would be necessary to introduce detailed supranational laws in these areas.

The link between the SEA and the Social Charter was reiterated throughout the latter document. For example, "completion of the single market cannot be regarded as an end in itself; it pursues a much wider objective, namely to ensure the maximum well being of all."[5] Unfortunately, achievement of this objective raised a host of awkward issues, not least those pertaining to **subsidiarity** (discussed below) and **social dumping**.

SOCIAL DUMPING

Those who advocate that supranational rules are necessary in the realm of social policy have recourse to the **social dumping** argument. One variant of this argues that, in the absence of labour market regulation, poorer members of the EU will hold down wages and social benefits in order to control imports from richer members and to create better opportunities to export to them (in effect exporting unemployment). The other variant states that if investment is free to go wherever it wishes within the bounds of the Single European Market, it will end up for the most part in those countries where pay and working conditions are inferior. Hence, it is alleged, northern member states where standards of worker protection are relatively high

TABLE 1: Fundamental Social Rights: Summary of the Contents of the Social Charter

The preamble refers to the importance of the social dimension "particularly in view of the impending completion of the internal market" which "must be accompanied, either at European Community level or at the level of the Member States or of their constituent parts, by a development of the social rights of citizens of the European Community, especially workers and self-employed persons." Such "rights must not, when implemented, provide grounds for any retrogression compared with the situation currently existing in each Member State" (CEC, 1990, pp. 92–3).

Title 1 Fundamental social rights

Right of freedom of movement (paras. 1–8) covers rights to freedom of movement; freedom to pursue any occupation; equal treatment; recognition of qualifications; subcontracted labour; social protection and public works contracts.

Employment and remuneration (paras. 9–11) covers fair remuneration; freedom to pursue an occupation; and access to placement services free of charge.

Improvement of living and working conditions (paras. 12–13) covers working time, especially its maximum duration; contracts of fixed duration; seasonal work; part-time; temporary work; night work; procedures for collective redundancies and bankruptcies.

Right to social protection (paras. 14–15) covers access to social security and minimum income for the unemployed.

Right to freedom of association and collective bargaining (paras. 16–18) covers freedom of association, union recognition; right to strike; settlement of disputes. Para. 18 advocates development of a "social dialogue."

Right to vocational training (paras. 19–20) covers training and retraining opportunities, both national and cross-border.

Right of men and women to equal treatment (para. 21) covers intensification of existing arrangements.

Right of information, consultation and participation of workers (paras. 22–23) to be developed along "appropriate lines," especially in multinationals, in cases of technological change and restructuring and in respect of trans-frontier workers.

Right to health protection and safety at the workplace (para. 24) covers further harmonization with particular regard to public works.

Protection of children and adolescents (paras. 25–27) covers minimum employment age (16), equitable remuneration, training and labour regulations.

The **elderly** (paras. 28–30) covers living standards, minimum income and social protection.

The **disabled** (para. 31) covers integration into working life.

Table II Implementation

(paras. 32–35) Member States to do everything in their power to guarantee these rights either through "legislative measures or by encouraging both sides of industry to conclude collective arrangements." The Commission to draw up an action programme and to report back regularly on implementation to relevant EC bodies.

will be obliged to lower them in order to maintain competitiveness. The purpose of the Social Charter is thus to protect the living standards and working conditions of employees threatened by the move towards the SEM.

There can be no doubt that there are at present large differences between gross wage costs in different member states. Taking salaries/wages together with various social benefits, the labour cost per worker in the former West Germany is five times as high as in Portugal and four times as high as in Greece.[6] Nevertheless, it does not follow as a matter of simple logic that wage differences in a single market will lead to the distortion of competition once adjustments are made for differences in productivity, since in practice wage differences tend to be very closely related to productivity differences.

Furthermore, locational decisions are not driven purely by differences in wage costs. The existence of a pool of trained labour, high quality component suppliers or excellent transport links may have much to do with a preference to locate in a high wage economy. Under such circumstances, relatively underdeveloped countries must rely upon cheap labour in order to compete effectively, and this should not be opposed on "social dumping" grounds.[7]

It may be counter-argued that **deliberate** social dumping is analogous to economic dumping (that is, export prices held below domestic prices). However, there is little evidence to support the idea that this happens in practice. But if social dumping is a naturally occurring phenomenon, upward harmonization of labour regulations may serve only to worsen the position of less-developed member sates. As Rhodes has noted:

Unless the Southern countries are able to upgrade their product quality . . . market integration could well mean further specialization in labour-intensive, low demand growth sectors such as clothing and footwear where fierce competition from the NICs is already occurring. Rather than convergence, this could produce cumulative divergence. For contrary to the fears expressed in the "social dumping" argument (which ignores the dependence of capital productivity on labour quality) a vicious circle could develop in which investment in well-regulated, high wage/high productivity economies offers consistently better returns than the loosely-regulated, low wage/low productivity areas, permitting neither convergence nor social harmonization.[8]

THE SOCIAL ACTION PROGRAMME

It is hardly surprising that organized labour has been anxious to formalise the Social Charter, and the governments of the countries allegedly threatened by social dumping are understandably sympathetic. It is curious, on the face of it, that there is so much support from Spain, Portugal and Greece which seem unlikely to benefit from explicit regulations governing the labour market. A "Eurosceptic" would argue that their support stems from the knowledge that they will anyway be unable to enforce such regulations, and that it represents a trade-off for improved financing via the Cohesion Fund.[9] Nevertheless, it has to be recognized that the Social Charter provided a rallying call for socialists throughout the Community in the face of the increasingly dominant economic doctrine of deregulation in the SEA.

Mrs. Vasso Papandreou, the then Commissioner for Social Affairs,[10] latched upon the apparent widespread enthusiasm (other than in the UK) for the Social Charter to push through a series of draft directives as part of what is known as the **Social Action Programme**. It was quickly appreciated that most of these directives, which when approved by the Council of Ministers must subsequently be converted into national law in each member state within a specified time frame, unless covered by a derogation, needed to be subject to **qualified majority voting** rather than unanimity, given the UK's entrenched position, if they were to have a realistic chance of success.

As of today the Social Action Programme consists of 47 individual measures, of which 27 are in the form of directives or other binding measures.[11] The Programme is to all intents and purposes fully issued, but it is not yet fully enacted. The sections below analyse some of the most contentious directives and provide specific illustrations of the opposing views taken of social legislation.

Working Time

The draft Direct for the **Adaptation of Working Time** was issued on 25 July 1990.[12] This was proposed as a health and safety directive.[13] because such directives can be approved by qualified majority vote, and it was clear from the outset that both the UK government and UNICE, the European employers' federation, would be utterly opposed to the directive. At the time, all member states except the UK and Denmark had laws governing the maximum daily working period, although many exceptions were permitted. The limit to the working week ranged from 39 hours in France to 48 hours in half a dozen states, although in practice only Portugal actually had a working week in excess of 41 hours with all other states falling between 39 and 41 hours. It followed, therefore, that the main impact of the directive was inevitably going to be felt in the UK in respect of aggregate hours worked (although it is interesting to note that workers in relatively poor member states have become much less willing than in the mid-1980s to forgo a nominal rise in income for shorter working hours).[14]

However, the directive was more controversial insofar as it addressed **shift and night work**.[15] On average, 20 percent of EU employees were doing shift work, with the highest rates in the UK and Spain (roughly 30 percent) and the lowest in Germany, Portugal and Denmark (below 15 percent). According to the European Commission, there was an established link between long hours of night work and ill health. On the other hand, several surveys had shown that, given the choice, many workers preferred to work longer shifts over shorter periods, and it was observed that British workers habitually took fewer days off work on average than their counterparts in Germany and the Netherlands.

The prevalence of extended shift work and overtime in the UK meant that it would bear the main brunt of the draft directive, with adjustment costs estimated initially at roughly $3 billion a year. The UK government accordingly fought hard to hold back the directive, but finding itself continually isolated it eventually abstained on 1 June 1993 with the other eleven member states voting in favour. The main provisions of the directive are:

- A minimum daily rest period of 11 consecutive hours.
- At least one day off a week.
- Mandatory daily rest breaks after six hours.
- Four weeks annual paid holiday.
- No more than eight hours per shift for night work averaged over a period to be determined by each member state.
- The reference period within which the working week must not exceed an average of 48 hours will be a minimum of four months and, with union agreement, a maximum of twelve months.
- Equivalent health and safety services must be available for night workers.

The directive was formally adopted in November 1993. All countries bar the UK are required to implement its contents within three years, whereas the UK need only guarantee three weeks holiday for a further six years and has ten years overall for full implementation (a "derogation" which may be extended subject to "review"). There are also exemptions for transport, agriculture, fisheries, all work at sea and doctors in training. UK employees who wish to work more than 48 hours a week will be able to do so; those who do not will have the protection of the law.

Despite alleging that he had drawn most of the directive's teeth, the UK Employment Secretary, David Hunt, nevertheless gave notice that he would appeal against the use of majority voting. He will almost certainly fail in this endeavor.

Part-time and Temporary Work

There are currently three directives under consideration concerned with part-time and temporary work. Because there are so many different contractual forms which fall under this heading the Commission has been driven to refer to contracts and employment relationships "other than full-time open-ended contracts."[16] The Commission justifies the need to legislate in this area on the grounds that:

> Unless safeguards are introduced, there is a danger of seeing the development of terms of employment such as to cause problems of social dumping or even the distortion of competition at Community level.[17]

The intention of the draft directives is to provide the same treatment for part-time and temporary workers as that accorded to "typical" full-time employees (hence the common use of the term "atypical workers" to refer to the former). Given that the discrimination against part-timers comes in many forms, the directive seeks to encompass working conditions, access to training, and social security and other measures of social protection.

The first draft directive is essentially concerned with the harmonization of working conditions.[18] The second concentrates on harmonising the laws on employment relationships, and a key clause requires member states to "ensure that part-time workers are afforded the same entitlements to annual holidays, dismissal allowances and seniority allowances as full-time employees, in proportion to the total hours worked" in the pursuit of the level playing field.[19] The third draft directive extends health and safety protection for temporary workers.[20] A key issue here is the threshold of weekly working hours below which protection will not apply. In the UK this is currently sixteen. It was argued that such a high threshold invites employers to offer sightly lower hours than this figure in order to avoid even the impact of existing UK legislation, and also to roll-over temporary contracts. The draft directives set the threshold at eight hours, thereby encompassing the great majority of part-time workers, and propose that permanent status must be provided once workers have been "temporary" for three years.

The UK, like the USA, has a particularly large proportion of its workforce employed in a part-time capacity, and would be very significantly affected by new legislation in this area.[21] The Confederation of British Industry has gone on record that "the added costs would force employers to reduce the number of part-time and temporary contracts." The UK Department of Employment has calculated that it would cost $1.5 billion, excluding increased social security contributions, to meet the provisions of these directives.

Temporary working is not all that common in the UK, whereas it has become extremely prevalent in countries such as Spain precisely because it is extremely costly there both to hire and fire permanent employees. The opposition to the draft directives has caused them to be held back from consideration by the Council of Members since November 1990.

It is frequently pointed out by critics of the UK government's stance that the great majority of part-time and temporary workers are women and hence that they are, as a group, being actively discriminated against under current practices. As it happens, surveys by the UK Department of Employment and the European Commission have consistently shown that most part-timers prefer to work that way. However, such inconvenient evidence is politely brushed aside, and discrimination is held to be sufficiently pervasive as to warrant remedial legislation.

Protection in Pregnancy

A particularly contentious attempt to improve the position of women workers relates to the provision of maternity leave. It is interesting to note that the USA is the only advanced economy which provides no statutory maternity benefits nor permits job-protection leave of absence. An attempt to introduce this in a draft **Family and Medical Leave Act** was vetoed by President Bush in 1990. Whilst a number of states grant unpaid leave of varying duration, the effect is said to be a dramatic reduction in the pay of full-time female workers with children relative to their male counterparts because of the "lost years" while caring for babies.

The situation in the UK was somewhat better, but was the worst among the member states. Women qualified for maternity leave only if they had two years' continuous service in full-time employment or five years in part-time employment, and had no rights if working fewer than eight hours a week. As a result, almost one half of working women in the UK did not qualify for maternity benefits.

It may be noted that even relatively poor member states such as Portugal and Greece provided much longer periods of leave than the UK, and at full pay. **The draft directive concerning measures to encourage improvements in the safety and health of pregnant workers, women workers who have recently given birth and those who are breastfeeding** originally proposed that all women be granted fourteen weeks' leave at full salary together with a guaranteed return to the job being done prior to going on leave. In addition, women were to be granted two weeks' compulsory rest before birth, whether working full-time or part-time, and prenatal visits to the doctor were to be counted as paid work time. Employers were also expected to improve workplace facilities for pregnant and breastfeeding women.[22]

At a meeting on 14 October 1990 the draft directive was laid before the Council of Ministers concerned with social affairs.[23] It was proposed that maternity benefits (for women who had paid social security contributions for one year) should be set at the same level as sick pay, thereby much reducing the payments made to pregnant women and new mothers in most of the EU. Although there was general support for the draft directive in the Council, there were also substantive disagreements about whether jobs should be protected since there could be legitimate reasons for dismissing workers who happened also to be pregnant and, more significantly, as to whether the draft directives was a health and safety directive and hence subject only to majority vote or concerned with social security provisions requiring unanimity.

The directive was eventually accepted on 19 October 1992 in a watered down version, on a majority vote, with a deadline of 20 October 1994 for introduction in member states as national law.[24] It sets out minimum provisions, leaving it to the member states to decide whether to adopt more favourable arrangements. It also contains a "non-regression clause" to ensure that member states cannot use the directive to lower the level of protection for the workers concerned. Its main provisions are as follows:

- Minimum maternity benefits (which may not be less than those received by a worker stopping work for reasons connected with his or her state of health—thus implying no analogy between pregnancy and sickness).
- At least 14 uninterrupted weeks' maternity leave.
- A ban on dismissal for reasons connected with pregnancy or maternity.
- Maintenance of employment rights.
- Entitlement to ante-natal medical examination during working hours.
- Reduction to one year of the qualifying period for maternity benefits.

Worker Representation

Currently under discussion are draft directives concerned with worker representation which, while they are in many ways the descendants of more ambitious attempts to impose worker representation such as the Vredling directive, are different in certain significant respects. One key difference, for example, relates to the fact that previous directives have been exclusively concerned with national bodies whereas the current directives are essentially transnational in nature.

A draft **directive on informing and consulting employees** was issued in December 1990 which, if implemented, will require worker representation on boards of directors of companies with more than 1,000 employees where at least 100 workers are employed in each of two member states. A further draft directive concerned with the establishment of a **European Works Council**[25] originally set out to require any company with more than 1,000 employees and at least 100 employed in each of two member states to set up a European works council, effectively a consultative council at group level where strategic decisions will be discussed which touch on plant closures, employment contracts, new working practices and the introduction of new technology.

In February 1994, a new draft sought to induce voluntary agreements at company level with unions and employers deciding their own *modus operandi*. Unfortunately, the "social partners"[26] were unable to reach agreement among themselves and the European Commission was obliged to reintroduce a compulsory system. The directive is expected to be passed in October 1994, operative from October 1996 and with a deadline for works councils to be introduced in each member state of October 1998.

It is possible to argue that little more than annual briefings appear to be required. It is equally possible to argue that the entire exercise is anyway pointless because forward-looking companies have already learned from the evidence of Japanese team-working methods that it pays to keep employees informed. The majority of UK employers nevertheless argue strongly that the councils will merely serve to interfere with existing channels of information, and that unlike most social legislation, it creates a high-level corporate structure rather than refining existing systems as in the case of most other directives. They are also very concerned that the enthusiasm shown by the unions reflects the latters' view that councils will promote the introduction of EU-wide collective bargaining systems and provide opportunities to network at employers' expense. It is worthy of note that in 1988, ETUC passed a resolution which called for "the right for workers' representatives to obstruct any decisions which are taken without prior negotiation."

Some 35 European multinationals have already created works councils, but they are mostly operated in a fashion which is insufficiently well-defined to meet the requirements of the directive. Altogether, some 1,000 pan-European companies are expected to be affected by the directive. It may be observed that some 90 UK companies are directly affected through their continental EU subsidiaries despite the "opt-out" secured by the UK from the social provisions of the Maastricht Treaty (see below), and many others may find it expedient to create works councils even if no obligation as such exists.

UK VERSUS THE REST?

Both the Commission and many member states have exerted continuous pressure to subject as much as possible of the Social Action Programme to majority voting, while the UK has grimly held to the view that majority voting should apply only to health and safety legislation, narrowly defined. On many occasions the UK has stood ready to exercise its veto if need be, and as a consequence it has created the image that the UK is wholly antithetical to EU-wide social legislation.

Such a conclusion would nevertheless be quite erroneous. Many of the Social Action Programme measures outlined rights to, for example, a safe working environment, training and trade union representation which already existed under UK law. Such law also covered equal opportunities and the protection of young, disabled and elderly workers.[27] Furthermore, measures designed to enhance the transferability of benefits or pensions, and the mutual recognition of vocational and educational qualifications, are very much in line with the UK government's free-market philosophy. Indeed, it is slightly ironic that the UK was the first member state

to implement at national level all of the eighteen directives on social policy which the European Council had adopted by the end of 1990.

It is of particular interest, given the scale of unemployment throughout the EU, to note the underlying philosophy of the Social Charter:

> In addition, and this is possibly more fundamental than the question of social dumping, the creation of jobs must not be achieved at too high a price (in particular in terms of health and safety and social protection).[28]

By way of contrast, the then UK Employment Secretary stated in June 1991 that "the most important social dimension of the single market is the creation of jobs." This is a view with which the unemployed might well concur even if their governments are obsessed with the level playing field and the avoidance of social dumping, and the view that relative inequality is socially damaging and a cause of labour unrest.

In the latter respect, however, the UK government has arguably been resisting the inevitable because the Social Action Programme can be seen as an attempt to persuade employees that the Single European Market is not simply a charter for capitalists. As the Social Charter stated:

> This is why [the Commission] will continue to take and propose whatever measures are needed to strengthen cohesion between social groups. The Community is concerned to show solidarity.[29]

Nevertheless, the Commission has embarked upon a path which clearly runs the risk of, firstly, making labour markets much more rigid at precisely the time that they need to be made more flexible in order to tackle the problem of unemployment and, secondly, raising labour costs relative to those in Japan and the USA and thereby creating for the EU a competitive disadvantage in world trade at a time of recession.

This does not appear to worry the Commission overmuch. Indeed, they argue that:

Flexibility of employment may be a factor which is detrimental to competitiveness as it acts as a disincentive for workers. For firms too, flexibility may have negative effects in the medium and long term, as it may reduce the motivation to invest in "human capital," which has become one of the factors essential to growth.[30]

Similar sentiments were expressed by the new Commissioner for Social Affairs and Employment, Padraig Flynn, in September 1993. On the other hand, it worries the UK government very deeply that more than a decade spent fostering the deregulation of the labour market has produced results which are incompatible with the Commission's vision of supranational labour market. Politicians in other member states beset by unemployment have become increasingly sympathetic with the views expressed by the UK government, and it must be remembered that whereas they are often constrained from stating this in public, for fear of offending coalition partners, they have found it helpful to treat the UK as a scapegoat when it has delayed measures about which they are themselves unenthusiastic.

As the full programme of directives comes into force, smaller member states will face the realisation that they are no longer able to exploit their comparative advantage in trade. This will probably oblige them either to seek additional EU funds by way of compensation, or alternatively protection against "technological dumping" by northern members.[31] Much the same effect will be felt in individual regions even within northern states. Harmonising social conditions must inevitably assist core regions at the expense of those on the periphery, and this must be viewed as undesirable at a time when relocation decisions are increasingly necessitated by the advent of the Single European Market.

Harmonisation of social standards will anyway come about in the natural course of events as living standards rise in poorer member states. It can therefore be argued that it is unnecessary to enforce it, and indeed that it is inadvisable at this stage. It is also worth observing that once the directives come into force, it will be much more difficult to widen the European Union's membership by the addition of less-developed states such as those from Eastern Europe.

Eurosceptics in the UK are somewhat cynical about the enthusiasm of certain other member states for the Social Action Programme. They note, firstly, that those among them who (unlike the UK) trade comparatively little outside the EU feel little concern about any loss of competitive advantage relative to the USA and the Far East; secondly, that industry in countries such as Germany is already so heavily regulated that the directives will make them more competitive relative to other member states; and thirdly, that some governments, notably Italy, have a patchy record of implementing and enforcing directives, and those they do not really support are rendered *de facto* inoperative.

THE TREATY ON EUROPEAN UNION

When the Inter-Governmental Conference on Economic and Political Union convened at Maastricht in December 1991, it was hoped that social policy would form a Social Chapter within the draft Treaty on European Union. However, a Treaty amendment requires unanimity and, predictably, the UK government rejected outright any such amendment to the Treaty of Rome.[32]

The original five pages in the draft Treaty were reduced to "Present EEC treaty provision unchanged (cf Annex III)." The annex contains a **Protocol on Social Policy** (frequently referred to in practice as the Social Chapter) which as part of the Treaty has been ratified by the UK government. However, annexed to this Protocol is an **Agreement** signed by all member states bar the UK (which "opted-out"). The Protocol contains the agreement of the twelve signatories to authorising the eleven parties to the Agreement to give effect to its contents.

The Protocol is undoubtedly a Treaty amendment. The Agreement may or may not be.[33] Article 1 of the Protocol commits its eleven signatories to:

> the promotion of employment, improved living and working conditions, proper social protection, dialogue between management and labour, the development of human resources with a view to lasting high employment and the combatting of exclusion

In the Council of Ministers, from which the UK will absent itself, there will be qualified majority voting (44 out of 66 votes required) in five areas covered by the Protocol, namely improvement of the working environment to protect workers' health and safety; working conditions; information for and consultation of workers; gender equality; and the integration of persons excluded from the labour market. However, unanimity will be required in respect of employee representation and co-determination, social security and protection against dismissal. In addition, the Protocol excludes consideration of pay, the right of association, the right to strike and the right to impose lock-outs.

No-one is altogether sure how all of this will operate in practice. For example, matters stemming from the Treaty of Rome and the Social Charter prior to the enactment of the new Treaty are unaffected, and hence require the participation of the UK government even if they also form part of the Agreement. Secondly, certain draft directives, such as that on works councils, are now likely to go before the Eleven, acting as the **European Social Community** in order to circumvent a UK veto, whereupon, as noted previously, many UK companies may either compulsorily or voluntarily become subject to their prescriptions. A third complication is that if at some future date the UK government should decide to accept the Agreement, it will have to honour any decisions previously agreed in its absence. Finally, it is possible that where practices in the UK are perceived to provide an "uneven playing field," they will be taken before the European Court of Justice and struck down.

SUBSIDIARITY

It is possible to argue that the extension of the competence of the Commission in the field of social responsibility represents a development which is incompatible with the principle of subsidiarity, itself a recurrent theme in the Social Charter. The Treaty on European Union defined subsidiarity as follows:

> In areas which do not fall within its exclusive competence, the Community shall take action, in accordance with the principle of subsidiarity, only and insofar as the objectives of the proposed action cannot be sufficiently achieved by the Member States and can therefore, by reason of the scale or effects of the proposed action, be better achieved by the Community.

In practice, this can be interpreted in various ways, the UK government's preference being for the view that the EU should only do things which the UK cannot do at all. Clearly, this principle would exclude virtually any attempt by the Commission to introduce new social policy legislation, and the Commission understandably prefers to interpret the concept in a less restrictive manner.

Nevertheless, the initial rejection of the Treaty in Denmark, and the manifest lack of enthusiasm for further supranational control over their lives among the general public in, for example, France as much as in the UK, has induced the Commission to tone down considerably its ambitions for a new improved Social Europe. It is shortly due to publish a Green Paper on social policy which is likely to be less detailed and to introduce "framework directives" which will set binding objectives but leave governments and the "social partners" to decide how they should be met. One area where this could have been applied is that of works councils, but as noted above, a prescriptive solution was not avoided in that case.

CONCLUSIONS

In the end the UK may feel obliged to join in **Social Europe**, although it will take a change of government for this to be a truly voluntary act. If so, Mrs. Thatcher's nightmare of "socialism by the back Delors" may yet come to pass. In the meantime the Social Action Programme will largely come to fruition in the UK, although there may be some dragging of feet in other member states ostensibly more enthusiastic about its content.

It is worth reiterating that, irrespective of the merits of legislation to enforce social responsibility, it cannot be divorced from the economic circumstances of the time, and these have undoubtedly deteriorated badly over the past few years. It is the low-skilled, poorly-paid sections of the workforce who are supposed to be protected by existing and proposed legislation, yet they tend to bear the brunt of a leveling of the playing field, as do small companies which have provided a disproportionate number of new jobs over the past decade.[34]

In refusing to be a party to the Agreement the UK may indeed gain at the expense of other member states, but it also suffers many ongoing disadvantages in respect, for example, of its education and training systems and the relative ease and cheapness when making workers redundant, so it is not unreasonable that it should utilise such comparative advantage as is available. It is easy to level accusations of social irresponsibility at the government, but under present circumstances they are largely wide of the mark.

NOTES

1. Of which there are currently twelve, rising to a maximum of sixteen by the end of 1994.
2. Consists of 12 representatives, one from each member state. The make up of the Council depends upon the subject under discussion —12 social policy ministers if the subject is social policy and so forth. Only the Council has the power to ratify European laws.
3. M. Rhodes, "The Future of the 'Social Dimension': Labour Market Regulation in post-1992 Europe," *Journal of Common Market Studies*, March 1992, p. 25.
4. Commission of the European Communities (CEC) "European Community Charter of the Fundamental Social Rights of Workers," *Social Europe* (No. 1), 1990, p. 94.
5. Ibid, p. 84.
6. Ibid. p. 36.
7. A. Kotios & M. Schafers, "The Social Dimension and Cohesion: Complementary or Contradictory?" *Intereconomics*, May/June 1990, p. 146.
8. Rhodes, op. cit., p. 32.
9. Set up expressly to transfer funds to member states where per capita incomes fall well below the average for the EU.
10. The European Commission comprises 17 members, of whom 1 is President. Commissioners are allocated by member state, with the four largest having 2 and the others one apiece. The Commission is the EU's civil service—it has no direct political power. Its main role is to instigate proposals and to see them through to acceptance or rejection by the Council and, where applicable, the European Parliament.
11. See Table 1 in J. Addison & W. Seibert, *Social Engineering in the European Community: The Social Charter, Maastricht and Beyond*, IEA, (1993).
12. Commission of the European Communities, (CEC), "First Report on the Application of the Community Charter of the Fundamental Social Rights of Workers," *Social Europe*, No. 1), 1992.
13. Under Article 118A.
14. Commission of the European Communities, "Developments in the Labour Market in the Community: Results of a Survey Covering Employers and Employees," *European Economy*, March 1991, p. 18.

15. The references are OJ C254/90 and OJ C214/91, where OJ refers to the Official Journal and C stands for "Communications."

16. CEC (1990) p. 48 and CEC (1992) p. 12.

17. CEC (1990) p. 59.

18. Article 100—see OJ C224/90.

19. Article 100A—see OJ C305/90.

20. Article 118A—see OJ L206/91 where L stands for "Legislation."

21. R. Jackman & M. Rubin, "Should We Be Afraid of the Social Charter?" *Employment Institute Economic Report*, August 1991, Table 3.

22. Article 118A—see OJ L348/92.

23. CEC (1992) p. 124.

24. *Bulletin of the EC*, 10–1992, p. 44.

25. See OJ C39/91 and OJ C336/91.

26. Comprising UNICE, the Union of Industrial and Employers' Confederations of Europe, which is the principal body representing private sector employers at the European level, and ETUC, the European Trade Union Confederation, which consists of 35 affiliated confederations in 21 European countries representing about 45 million workers.

27. CEC (1992) pp. 194–205.

28. CEC (1990) p. 36.

29. Ibid, p. 37.

30. Ibid, p. 40

31. Kotios & Schafers, op. cit., p. 146.

32. For an overview both of the Maastricht negotiations and the prior history of social policy see M. Gold (ed) (1993), *The Social Dimension: Employment Policy in the European Community* (Macmillan), and especially chapter 1.

33. Anyone interested in the legal niceties can consult, for example, E. Whiteford, "Social Policy After Maastricht," *European Law Review*, 1993, vol. 18, pp. 202-222.

34. Addison & Siebert, op. cit., p. 38.

A STAKEHOLDER APPROACH TO THE GLOBALIZATION OF LABOR

Richard Morfopoulos and Cecilia M. Falbe

U.S. manufacturers are increasing their presence in the global marketplace to take advantage of opportunities for growth and profitability. According to a study of the performance of 1250 manufacturers from 1987 to 1991, corporations in every size category involved in global operations grew faster and showed higher profitability in every industry than firms without global activity (Taylor and Fosler, 1994). Global expansion provides great opportunities for firms; however, various stakeholders of these companies, who are concerned with global corporate social responsibility, point to the potential for exploitation of labor that can result from globalization. Exploitation issues include forced labor, employment of children, excessive work hours, safety issues especially fire hazards, wages that are below the minimum of the country or are below a subsistence level, violations of privacy, the harassment of female workers, and restrictions on workers organizing independently. A larger issue is whether it is appropriate for global firms either to operate directly or to subcontract for goods and services in countries that violate human rights.

The perspectives taken by companies and their stakeholders depend on the interests and values of individuals and groups and these perspectives are often in direct conflict. Stakeholders are individuals or groups that directly affect or are affected by a firm (Freeman and Gilbert, 1987). Companies seek the lowest labor costs and they also hope to maintain a favorable corporate image in the press; workers in developing countries seek jobs, regardless of working conditions, in order to survive; government officials in less developed countries often place a higher priority on economic development than on working conditions for their citizens. Other interested parties include U.S. labor organizations which argue for keeping jobs in the U.S., and a number of special interest groups which seek uniform standards of corporate social performance in all geographic locations. In this paper, we elaborate on conflicting perspectives on the globalization of labor by different stakeholders and then compare the corporate social performance of two global firms and their global labor activities. Our research for this paper is based on an analysis of company documents, reports from interest groups, publications in the academic and business literature, media special features, and a number of interviews with corporate executives, government officials and representatives of special interest groups. Our findings indicate that the analysis of globalization of labor is highly charged, is often incomplete and may be biased by the way the issue is framed by the media.

THE CORPORATE POSITION

Firms embrace globalization for a number of reasons. These include obtaining a presence in a new market or gaining proximity to suppliers and customers, but the major attraction is cost reduction. Outsourcing production and moving jobs offshore results in considerable savings from employing a workforce that readily accepts lower wages, poorer working conditions, and fewer benefits than are expected in the U.S. While some groups criticize firms for moving production offshore, others argue that outsourcing manufacturing permits firms to focus on pre- and post-production functions. For Example, Nike outsources much of its production and concentrates on design, advertising, marketing and distribution in the U.S. (Quinn, 1992). The latter functions are identified as providing the greatest value to customers and these functions constitute the core competence of the firms. From a business standpoint, a geographical mix of locations of functions is particularly attractive to firms that have very high marketing and promotion costs and can benefit from low wages. In addition, firms point out that they are providing desperately needed jobs in less developed countries. They also argue that it is difficult to apply U.S. standards in foreign countries and to monitor the performance of subcontractors and suppliers.

Outsourcing production to subcontractors in developing countries has resulted in unexpected costs for some firms. Corporate images and reputations have been damaged by recent feature stories on television and in the press on the exploitation of labor by U.S. firms operating in less developed counties. At an earlier time, firms argued that the abuses came from subcontractors over whom they had little control. This explanation is no longer accepted and public opinion is coalescing around the position that firms have the obligation to monitor closely the employment practices of their contractors (Zachary, 1994).

STAKEHOLDER POSITIONS

Stakeholders are individuals or groups that affect or are affected by the globalization of labor issue. These include stockholders, employees, suppliers, customers, and host country officials. Other special interest groups such as labor organizations and watchdog groups are active in monitoring corporate social performance on a global basis. We confine our discussion to the following stakeholders and their positions on the issue: officials of the host country, laborers in the host country, unions, activist organizations, the media, regulators, and the general public and consumers.

(1) The Host Country: The interests of countries vary widely but the agenda of many officials who are in positions of political and economic power in less developed countries is to promote long term economic development in spite of the short term painful cost to economically and socially disadvantaged laborers in their country. For example, Indonesia is being transformed into one of the fastest-growing economies in the world; however, laborers still work for $1.18 a day in factories under contract by Reebok (Goodman, 1993). The Minister of Manpower in Jakarta explains that wages must stay low if Indonesia is to exploit its competitive advantage over other countries. The Prime Minister of Malaysia recently acknowledged criticism of his country's lax labor regulation and stated that his country has no intention of bowing to Western demands for a minimum wage and recognition of unions (Zachary, 1994).

(2) Laborers of the Host Country.   The term common laborer refers to unskilled labor that is utilized by global firms. The position of a majority of workers is that they need jobs desperately. Workers argue for jobs that provide better opportunities than are otherwise available. Alternative jobs include work in agriculture or jobs that pay based on the minimum physical need standard (MPN). Such standards vary widely from area to area and do not include any benefits. Comparable work is difficult to obtain. Many workers, despite a relatively young age, are the sole support of a family. Workers argue that there

often are no other jobs available and the alternatives to work involve activities such as begging, prostitution or the final alternative of starvation.

(3) Unions. The primary union organizations involved in globalization of labor issues are the AFL-CIO and the International Confederation of Free Trade Unions. Although the AFL-CIO is concerned over the number of U.S. manufacturing jobs lost due to outsourcing production, they claim their position is not limited to protecting the interests of American laborers. By taking part in the ICFTU's international battle for trade union rights, American unions claim the moral high ground by concurrently promoting their own interests and exerting influence on the debate over corporate social performance in the globalization of labor. Enzo Friso, the General Secretary of the ICFTU, takes such a stance in the following statement:

> The battle for trade union rights is undeniably a battle for development and democracy. But it is much more than a political battle. We must never lose sight of the fact that our first aim is to protect our members. The general truth is that without proper respect for trade union rights, societies will tend to be unjust, poor, and unstable. The truth is that people will suffer and die. (ICFTU, 1993)

The official position of the AFL/CIO and the ICFTU is that the treatment of workers in less developed countries falls far below accepted U.S. standards. The agenda of the ICFTU is to protect workers and promote the formation and growth of unions on a global scale. Their activities are often opposed by global firms and host countries that are against extending union rights to their workers. In fact, a number of less developed countries deny workers the right to associate for the purpose of organizing.

(4) Activist Organizations. The term activist refers to stakeholders whose objective is to enhance international human rights by engaging in proactive, investigative, fact-find-

ing activities. A large number of these stakeholder organizations exist. We discuss the primary agenda of one organization in each of three subcategories.

A. *Protection of Political Prisoners.* Amnesty International is a non-profit organization working for human rights with a primary agenda of freeing prisoners of conscience, insuring fair trials for political prisoners, and stopping tortures and executions. They attempt to influence host countries and global firms to respect the most basic human rights. Letter writing is the primary method of influence used by this organization (Amnesty International, 1994).

B. *Religion and Activism.* The Interfaith Center of Corporate Responsibility brings together representatives from a number of religions. The primary agenda of the ICCR is to encourage investments that assist the poor and oppose investments that are harmful. The ICCR coordinates a Clearinghouse on Alternative Investments for church groups seeking to place investments with socially creative organizations working for the poor. The ICCR is also widely recognized for their role in drawing attention to the problems associated with the use of Nestle's infant formula in less developed countries (ICCR, 1994).

C. *Research and Corporate Profiles.* The Council on Economic Priorities (CEP) conducts and disseminates a wide range of research on corporate social performance. CEP monitors and evaluates the global labor activities of firms. Their primary strategy is to reward with favorable publicity companies that are leaders in charitable giving, responsiveness to employees, environmental stewardship, providers of equal opportunity and leaders in community action (Lydenberg, Marlin & Strobb, 1986). A recent issue highlighted the activities of Levi Strauss (Leipziger, 1994). At the same time, CEP publicly identifies firms that fall short in the area of corporate social responsibility (Leipziger, 1994).

Although these stakeholder organizations use different methods in their approaches to human rights, they are in agreement that globalization of labor has the potential to violate the basic rights of workers. The most serious violation is the use of forced labor; other violations include substandard working conditions and the payment of below subsistence wages. The activist organizations counter the position of global firms and host country officials that workers exercise choice in accepting jobs. They argue that choice infers knowledge and freedom. Workers in less developed countries may only understand the short-run benefits of a job and fail to see the long term drawbacks of these jobs such as the effect of working conditions on future health, little opportunity for advancement or further education. Unfortunately, long-run ramifications mean little to a starving or desperate worker.

(5) The Media. Television and the print media have focused on exploitation of workers employed by global firms in less developed countries. The motives of the media organizations are dual; their situation is analogous to that of unions. They express a general interest in the human rights of workers in less developed countries and at the same time their immediate concern is with presenting a steady supply of sensational material that will hold the attention of viewers and increase ratings on which their advertising revenue is based.

Reports of the potential for the media to abuse its watchdog status involve national as well as multinational events. In 1992, "Dateline" reported that GM trucks could be at risk of exploding on impact. In the "Dateline" report this claim was presented by NBC to the public with trucks that had been equipped with explosives. The "Dateline" report is an example of why critics say that such programs are capable of overextending the media's "watchdog" role beyond its legitimate boundaries. Commenting of the "Dateline" segment, Richard Irvine, executive director of Accuracy in Media, added that "'60 Minutes' has been getting away with that kind of 'gotcha' journalism for years."

If we accept the premise that journalists can adversely affect the quality of informa-

tion related to corporate behavior in the U.S., what factors could further complicate the objectivity of mass media as journalists investigate the globalization of labor? David Gergen, one time advisor to Presidents and former editor of *U.S. News and World Report*, states his reservations of television coverage of international affairs (Bloomberg News Service, 1994a):

> By its nature, television is an instrument of simplicity in a world of complexity. In a report of 80 seconds—150 words at most—a television reporter cannot provide context or background. Another limitation is that television cannot and does not provide continuity in its coverage of international affairs. As a medium that depends on drama, it is drawn to conflict and crisis. It shuns the quiet periods in which most people live.

Gergen's critique of the media asserts that the media is more a medium for drama than for objective reporting. Global firms are aware that the media provides an exclusive lens through which the public, activist organizations and unions perceive the intentions and actions of the firms. Immediate detailed responses are not part of the featured stories. Firms continue to sue in response to unfavorable news reports, regardless of the prospects of courtroom victory or the unlikely event of collecting damages. A noted libel lawyer states: "These suits are never without a public relations quotient that is meant to have an impact on regulators and the company's stock price" (Bloomberg New Service, 1994b).

(6) Regulators. Among the efforts that address global labor issues are the President's discussion of human rights under the topic of most favored nation status for U.S. trading partners; the concern of the U.S. State Department with workers rights and the legislative efforts at regulation of labor standards with trading partners as illustrated by the legislation introduced and supported by Congressman Gephardt. We elaborate briefly on the latter initiatives.

The U.S. Department of State (1993) supports five internationally recognized worker rights. These include:

(1) *The right of association* as defined by the International Labor Organization (ILO) as the right of workers and employers to establish and join organizations of their own choosing. The right of association includes the right to strike restricted only to the case of essential services, i.e., those services in the public sector, the interruption of which would endanger the life, personal safety, or health of a significant portion of the population.

(2) *The right to organize and bargain collectively* includes the right of workers to be represented in negotiating the prevention and settlement of disputes with employers; the right to protection against interference; and the right to protection against acts of anti-union discrimination.

(3) A prohibition on the use of *forced or compulsory labor* is defined as work or service exacted from any person under the menace of penalty and for which the person has not volunteered.

(4) A *minimum age for employment of children* concerns the effective abolition of child labor by raising the minimum age for employment to a level consistent with the fullest physical and mental development of young people. In addition, young people should not be employed in hazardous conditions.

(5) *Acceptable conditions of work* refers to the establishment and maintenance of machinery, adapted to national conditions, that provides for minimum working standards, i.e., wages that provide a decent living for workers and their families; working hours that do not exceed 48 hours per week, with a full 24-hour rest day.

The legislation drafted by Congressman Richard Gephardt addresses the concerns of stakeholders of global labor issues. The intention of Congressman Gephardt is to insure that all host countries comply with minimum level standards in relation to worker rights and the environment. The following state-

ment is a synopsis of Gephardt's espoused agenda:

> This is a moral issue. Because if we don't honor the world's workers—if we don't care about them, and invest in them, and empower them—then we're abandoning our highest mission as a government, and as a people . . . Many of these nations do have decent laws on the books—labor laws, anti-pollution laws. But they're not being enforced. So I will soon introduce a new bill, called blue and green 301. This new law would say: if you don't even enforce your own laws—if you abuse your own workers, misuse the environment, and make it hard for nations with a conscience to compete—that's an unfair labor practice, and we're going to call you on the carpet. (Gephardt, 1994)

Congressman Gephardt's stated agenda is further supported by his recent sponsorship and introduction of HR 4375, the *Chile Free Trade Agreement Negotiating Act of 1994*, in which acceleration of the agreement (fast track procedures) is permitted only if the President certifies to the Congress that the trade agreement contains provisions requiring the parties to adhere to internationally recognized worker rights as defined in the Trade Act of 1974 (section 502(a)(4). Senator Harkin has introduced a bill that would ban goods made by foreign child labor. Regulation requiring enforcement of such rights on a worldwide level could have profound ramifications for the entire global labor force. However, assuming eventual passage, implementation is an issue. Who will decide the criteria used to uphold the principles of such legislation? How will regulation be enforced? What will the penalties be for violators? Will a host country found in violation have the chance to appeal the judgments of the "we" to which Congressman Gephardt refers in his testimony? What process would be used to do so? These questions represent only a sample of the complex problems associated with such a broad legislative undertaking. It appears unlikely that legislation alone can remedy global labor abuse.

(6) The American Public and Consumers. At present the American public lacks a compelling enough interest in labor issues in developing countries to persuade firms to act in a socially responsible manner regarding globalization of labor. A number of surveys over the years have shown that the American public's level of global awareness is generally quite poor with little sign of improvement (Gergen, 1990). However, the American public may be motivated to take some action as a result of pressure from the media, activist organizations, and unions. A growing number of people are reluctant to purchase clothing made by children or by forced labor (Goll & Zuckerman, 1993). Possible public actions range from demanding increased regulation to the threat of consumer boycotts. There appears to be increasing support for the notion that firms must take greater responsibility for the actions of their subcontractors. A proactive approach by some global firms, indicating their determination to improve conditions for workers, may counter the threat of regulation and delay future public action.

A review of stakeholders and their positions on the issues demonstrates the complexity of the globalization of labor issue. The criterion for corporate social performance can vary depending upon which stakeholder(s) determines the criterion. In spite of criticisms, many global firms claim to be proactively promoting the welfare of the workers and the environment in less developed countries. Examples include Levi Strauss & Co.'s Country Selection guidelines, Merck's commitments to biodiversity and tropical forest conservation in Costa Rica, and 3M's global environmental impact program (Leipziger, 1993). In some cases, the claims of global firms regarding their social performance are either contested or ignored by other stakeholder groups. A comparison of two global firms, Levi Strauss and Nike, that are frequently spotlighted by the media and other stakeholders, provide some specific exam-

ples of the nature and complexity of stakeholder relations and the role of the media in presenting examples of alleged abuses associated with globalization of labor.

CASE STUDY: LEVI STRAUSS & COMPANY

A recent report from one of the watchdog groups cited Levi Strauss as an example of a firm that promotes ethical practices in developing countries (Leipziger, 1994). Levi Strauss adopted two major codes of conduct, *Guidelines for Country Selection* and *Global Sourcing Guidelines*. The country selection criteria address the following issues: brand image, health and safety, human rights, legal requirements and political or social stability. The sourcing guidelines are directed to company contractors and deal specifically with the following criteria: child labor is prohibited; prison labor is prohibited; the work environment must be safe and healthy; water effluence must be limited to certain prescribed levels; employees cannot work more than sixty hours a week and must be allowed one day off in seven; business partners must comply with legal business requirements. Levi Strauss has also agreed to take local social and cultural customs into account and seeks to balance U.S. values with cultural differences in developing countries. The research by CEP reported that Levi Strauss backed up their written guidelines with an audit of 700 contractor's facilities. The company later announced that they had terminated five percent of their contractors, twenty-five percent needed to make improvements and the remainder were in compliance with the guidelines (Leipziger, 1994).

A recent feature article in the business press identified Levi Strauss as a value driven company with a respect for labor (*Business Week*, 1994). The coverage also noted that the company's value driven strategy is not necessarily one that is shared by all insiders, including some members of the Board who would prefer a purely economic focus rather than include social performance. For example, the decision to withdraw from China was the subject of considerable debate within the company. The feature article as well as other articles highlight the complexity the company finds in implementing its own guidelines (Leipziger, 1994). In another case, children were found to be employed by a Levi Strauss contractor in Bangladesh. A strict interpretation of the guidelines would suggest dismissing the children immediately. Closer examination indicated many of the children were the sole support of their families. Levi Strauss struck a balance between their ethical standards and their concern for the families. The company paid for the children to attend school until they were fourteen; they also paid for tuition, books and uniforms. At the age of fourteen, the children would be free to return and work for Levi Strauss (Haas, 1994).

While Levi Strauss receives high marks for social responsiveness from a number of stakeholders including representatives of the media and watchdog organizations, some negative publicity also appears. They are accused along with Nike and Reebock of searching out cheap labor, free from unions and safety codes (Goodman, 1993). Other reports accuse Levi Strauss of transferring production from U.S. plants to contract plants in the Caribbean where workers are paid less $1.00 per hour (Moskowitz, 1993).

Officials at Levi Strauss respond to these criticisms with the following points.

(1) Wherever Levi Strauss does business, the human rights climate is monitored continuously since this climate is subject to change.
(2) Levi Strauss does source in Indonesia; however, the company meets with contractors on a regular basis to discuss specific guidelines and audits are conducted every three months. Audits are conducted by the company's own employees and their responsibilities include working with the contractors on key safety issues. Contractors have been terminated for not following the guidelines.
(3) In regard to criticisms of the treatment of Costa Rican workers, Levi Strauss pays its workers 20 percent more than minimum wage in Costa Rica; pays its workers 21 percent more than the annual per capita income in Costa Rica and provides its workers an average wage which is 24 percent higher than the wages in the industrial sector of Costa Rica. Audits of contractors are also carried out by Levi Strauss employees.
(4) In the case of a plant closing in San Antonio, Levi Strauss went far beyond what is either required by law or what is customary in the San Antonio plant closing. Workers were provided 90 days advance notice even though the law requires 60; workers were provided one week of severance pay for every year of service; health care benefits were extended for three months; an outplacement service was created and staffed by Levi Strauss for 15 months; and Levi Strauss contributed over $1 million for job training, case management, and emergencies, targeted for their former workers. Laid off workers received preferential treatment at other Levi Strauss facilities and five hundred of these workers eventually were provided jobs at one of the two remaining San Antonio facilities (Samson, 1994).

The guidelines present difficult challenges for Levi Strauss; some of these were discussed in a recent article on the labor practices of the company (Zachary 1994). For example, auditors miss violations and some contractors have been terminated only after complaints were made by workers to local labor boards. Levi Strauss concedes that it can do a better job of evaluating the labor practices of its roughly 700 Indonesian factories; its handful of full-time inspectors and approximately 50 part-time inspectors must continue to improve their methods. The issue of meeting current local standards in developing countries rather than U.S. standards is also a topic of debate among stakeholders. Levi Strauss is not only concerned with ethics in the workplace but, as the world's largest provider of brand name clothing, the company is interested in preserving the positive image of the corporation and the brand and avoiding the risks of a scandal associated with labor abuse. The company equates being socially responsive with good business.

On balance, it seems fair to categorize Levi Strauss as an organization that is generally successful in its sincere effort to behave in a socially responsive manner.

CASE STUDY: NIKE

The Nike Company also receives considerable attention from the media and other stakeholder groups. In contrast to the generally favorable light in which Levi Strauss is portrayed, Nike is characterized most often as the villain of global labor abuse. Many of the critics of Nike rely on two sources for their data base, a news broadcast by CBS focusing on the labor practices of a Nike contractor in Indonesia, (Baker, 1993) and a series of three written accounts of labor practices in the plant of a Nike contractor in Indonesia (Baker, 1993). Both the CBS film crew and the reporter were given permission by Nike to visit the contractor. The CBS report focused on substandard wages and working conditions. The newspaper reporter wrote that in the contractor's plant, 6,700 workers crank out 2,000 pairs of Nike every hour in a plant that "reeks of paints and glue" and where temperatures hovers near 100 degrees and workers are paid less than the minimum wage.[1] No mention was made that the factory also produces for Reebok and Addidas.

Following these news reports, there was widespread criticism of Nike's human rights practices and a number of critiques of Nike appeared from various stakeholders. One analyst noted that the world's leading maker of athletic shoes found itself at the heart of a controversy over whether it was exploiting workers in Asian factories. The AFL-CIO believed the media accounts to be valid and strongly supported a campaign mounted by the Made in the U.S.A. Foundation which wanted Nike to make shoes in the United States (Moskowitz, 1993). Other articles by stakeholders criticized Nike for the labor practices of its subcontractors (Leipziger 1994).

Nike strongly disputes the portrayal of their labor practices by TV and the press. Company representatives point out that Nike was the only American company that agreed to allow CBS in to see its subcontractor operations (Kidd, 1994). Nike claimed that although they pay the minimum wage, they cannot set minimum wage or minimum physical need (MPN) standards in developing countries. Nike asserts that they can and do ensure that factories are certified to meet or exceed all the local government's standards with regard to wages, working conditions, benefits, and treatment of workers (Nike, 1993). The company asserts that Nike subcontractors in Indonesia are obliged by the company to pay workers at or above the minimum wage of the country. Nike provides free housing at the site, a free cafeteria, and a free hospital at the site staffed by four physicians, a mosque on site for devout Muslims to pray five times a day (Kidd, 1994; Knight, 1993). Nike claims that CBS was made aware of the housing and health benefits provided to workers and chose not to acknowledge them. For example, CBS conducted an interview with a Nike official approximately fifty feet from the workers' housing and was invited to film the housing with their standard camera equipment and lights (Kidd, 1994). CBS declined to film at that time. Instead, according to Nike representatives, CBS returned at night with a hidden camera and filmed the housing without light using lens that appeared flawed. Nike officials also perceive that the CBS correspondent did not fully understand some of the basics of Asian life, such as the paternalistic role that the factory often assumes. Nike officials feel that CBS was not interested in comparing the conditions in Nike's subcontractor factories with those of its competitors (Kidd, 1994).[2]

Nike officials assert that the company is guided by their Code of Conduct and they expect all business partners to operate on the principles of trust, teamwork, honesty and mutual respect. Further, the Code affirms an appreciation of individual diversity, a dedication to equal opportunity for each individual, and a commitment to follow, to the extent possible, the three "R"s of environmental action: reduce, reuse and recycle (Nike, 1993). The last two paragraphs of the code state:

> We seek always to be a leader in our quest to enhance people's lives through sports and fitness. That means at every opportunity—whether in the design, manufacturing and marketing of products; in the environment; in the areas of human rights and equal opportunity; or in our relationships in the communities in which we do business—we seek to do not only what is *required*, but whenever possible, what is *expected* of a leader. There is No Finish Line. (Nike, 1993)

In addition to the Code, Nike expects their business partners to sign a memorandum of understanding that, along with other points, includes subcontractor/supplier compliance with all applicable local government regulations regarding child labor laws, wages, leaves and benefits; occupational health and safety; health insurance, life insurance, worker's compensation; and environmental practices. The subcontractor/supplier also agrees not to use forced labor, including prison labor, and must certify that it does not discriminate on the basis of gender, race, religion, age, sexual orientation or ethnic origin. The subcontractor/supplier agrees to maintain necessary documentation to demonstrate compliance with these certifications and agrees to have the documentation ready for inspection by Nike representatives at any time (Nike, 1993). Nike shares with Levi Strauss the situation that meeting current local standards in developing countries, rather than implementing U.S. standards, is a concern of union and watchdog stakeholders.

Nike is cited by an independent source as an example of the new corporation which retains the value added pre- and post-manufacturing functions of design, research and development, advertising and marketing in the U.S., while outsourcing much of their manufacturing (Quinn, 1992). Nike has a three-tier system of outsourcing their offshore manufacturing operations. The highest level is that of *developed partners* who co-develop products and co-invest and produce the most expensive products. These partners produce exclusively for Nike and are located in countries like Korea or Taiwan. In this case, Nike prefers the term partner to that of contractor or supplier since it infers joint responsibilities (Quinn, 1992). *Volume producers* are the second tier; they do no development, and they produce for as many as seven or eight different buyers. *Developing sources* are the lowest cost contractors, they use primitive production methods, the workers are inexperienced and the contractor produces exclusively for Nike. Nike has a tutelage program for developing sources and provides additional training and resources and promotes links between developed partners and developing sources. The objective is to transform sources to partners. Nike reports on policies that support their sourcing system including treating partners as true partners and participation in the manufacturing process with "expatriates" who become permanent personnel in each factory producing for Nike. The latter oversee production and act as a liaison with corporate research and development.[3] This independent account of Nike's operations appears consistent with Nike's discussion of the nature of their association with developing sources.

MEDIA STUDIES

Like Levi Strauss, Nike acknowledges the difficulties of operating with subcontractors in countries in which there is extensive poverty, high unemployment and a standard of living very far below that of the United States or developed countries in East Asia. Striking differences between the reports of the media and the responses of Nike officials—who deny the charges and document flaws in the methods that CBS employed—raise questions concerning the validity of news specials that depend on the sensational to capture viewers' attention. Campbell (1991) in an analysis of CBS's "60 Minutes" devised a number of reporter formulas that are used to manipulate the dramatic appeal of news reports. One such formula has been classified as "the interviewee as the hero or villain." It appears that the villain formula was applied to Nike. The dependence of many of the stakeholder groups on the media for data places a special responsibility on the media to follow the standards to which other researchers adhere. Reporters should have an extensive background of knowledge of the country in which they are filming so that they make informed comparisons. A sample of contractors should be studied using multiple observations. Interviews should be conducted with those on both sides of the issue and the interviews should be conducted by more than one independent interviewer for interrator reliability. A fair evaluation of social performance should not be limited to information obtained solely through the lens of the media. An equitable evaluation of a firm's human rights record requires concurrent critical analysis of both the media's role in reporting the event and the direct responses of representatives of the firms.

One explanation of why the media focuses so much attention on Levi Strauss and Nike is the image each company portrays to the public. Levi Strauss stresses the ethical values that inform their decisions; stakeholders examine the extent to which the company acts as it says it does. On the other hand, Nike, through their advertising, emphasizes high profile, entrepreneurial, fast time, "just do it" image (Katz, 1994). The company's very high profile may provoke the media into focusing attention on them. An observer has to question why alleged labor abuses of competitors (Goodman, 1993) are not subjected to equal scrutiny. A systematic evaluation should be made of the labor practices of the large number of global firms operating in Indonesia.[4] Without adhering to the research standards discussed above, representatives of the media, including CBS, leave themselves open to charges of abuse of power.

CONCLUSION

Levi Strauss takes a more dynamic, proactive stance that is more responsive to addressing the long-term needs of their impoverished laborers from developing countries. Their approach is close to what Sethi (1987) terms *social responsiveness*, that is, going beyond legal and economic requirements, and social norms to take a long term perspective on what their role in a dynamic social system should be. In contrast, the position taken by Nike is in line with Sethi's description of *social obligation*, and to some extent *social responsibility*, meeting both legal and economic requirements of the host country in which they operate as well as providing some additional benefits. Strict adherence to the leadership concept in the Nike Code of Conduct would require proactivity regarding workers that goes beyond the required and accepted.

A stakeholder analysis of the globalization of labor issue illustrates the different, conflicting perspectives of the various groups. The positions of global firms and officials of developing host countries share a perspective in which they are content with taking a long term perspective. That is, higher foreign standards are not to be imposed on developing countries, and in time, economic development will improve the global position of the host country and gradually raise the standard of living for workers. Global firms accept gradual development while at the same time they benefit from the low cost labor that gradualism provides. Other stakeholder groups contend that immediate change is required, arguing that the subcontractors and suppliers of global firms should perform at a much higher standard than what is acceptable in developing countries. Integrating a stakeholder framework with the model for classifying corporate social performance on a three stage continuum of *social obligation*, *social responsibility* and *social responsiveness* shows promise for examining and explaining the basis of conflicting stakeholder perspectives on the globalization of labor.

NOTES

1. According to Baker (1993), the workers are paid $0.15 per hour while Nike pays the factory $16.50 for a pair of Air Pegasus sneakers, which it then sells to retailers for $35, who then offer it to consumers for $70. Baker does not provide an explicit comparison of this factory with other shoe factories in different countries nor provide data on the total number of factories she visited.

2. Discussion of the position of Nike, Inc. is drawn from interviews and correspondence provided by Dusty Kidd, the Director of Communications of Nike International/Asia Pacific.

3. This section is drawn from the arguments supporting the notion of strategic direction of new types of firms, i.e., intelligent enterprises (Quinn, 1992, chapter 2).

4. According to the Directory of American Firms Operating in Foreign Countries (1994), many other MNC's such as Coca-Cola, The Dow Chemical Co., Exxon Corp., General Electric Co., The Gillette Co., The Goodyear Tire and Rubber Co., ITT Corp., Johnson and Johnson, Pfizer Inc., Texaco Inc., Union Carbide Corp., and Xerox Corp. are just some of the other manufacturers in Indonesia.

REFERENCES

Amnesty International USA. 1994. *Human Rights Watch World Report 1994.*

Baker, N. 1993. Three part feature on the operations of a Nike subcontractor in Indonesia. Portland, OR: *The Oregonian.*

Bloomberg News Service. 1994a. Legal Affairs: As TV news magazines proliferate, so do lawsuits. Nashville, TN: *The Tennessean*, (Sunday), 8E.

Bloomberg News Service. 1994b. Quotation from Richard Winfield of the New York law firm of Roger and Wells. Nashville, TN: *The Tennessean*, April 10, (Sunday), 8E.

Business Week. (1994). Managing by Values: Is Levi Strauss' approach visionary—or flaky? New York: McGraw-Hill (Aug. 1) pp. 46–52.

Campbell, R. 1991. Securing the middleground: Reporter formulas in 60 minutes. In R. Avery and D. Eason (Eds.): *Critical Perspectives on the Media and Society.* New York: Guilford Press, chapter 12.

Freeman, R.E. and Gilbert, Jr., D. 1987. Managing stakeholder relationships. In S.P. sethi & C.M. Falbe, (Eds.): *Business and Society: Dimensions of Conflict and Cooperation.* New York: Lexington Books.

Gephardt, R. 1994. *News from the House Majority Leader*, H-148, U.S. Capitol, March 23, page 2.

March 23, 1994 testimony before the subcommittee on International Development, Finance, and Monetary Policy.

Gergen, D. 1990. Diplomacy in a television age: The dangers of teledemocracy. In S. Safety (Ed.), *The Media and Foreign Policy.* New York: St. Martin's Press, pp. 50–51.

Goll, S. and Zuckerman, L. 1993. Levi Strauss, leaving China, passes crowd of firms going the other way. *The Wall Street Journal*, Wednesday, May 5, A18.

Goodman, P. 1993. Slavery plain and simple: Reebok, Nike, and Levi Strauss on the prowl for cheap labor in Indonesia. *The Progressive*, 57: 26–28.

Haas, R. 1994. Ethics in the trenches. 1994. *Across the Board*, 31: 12–13.

Interfaith Center on Corporate Responsibility (ICCR). 1994. Personal Communication.

International Confederation of Free Trade Unions (ICFTU). 1993. Introduction. *Survey of Violations of Trade Union Rights.*

Katz, R. 1994. *Just Do It.* New York: Random House.

Kidd, D. 1994. Written communication from the Director of Communications of Nike International/Asia Pacific.

Knight, P. 1993. Correspondence from Phillip Knight, Chairman and CEO, Nike, Inc. to David Hawkins, Producer, CBS.

Leipziger, D. 1993. The transnational corporation: Global influence, global responsibility. *Research Report.* New York: Council on Economic Priorities (October).

Leipziger, D. 1994. The Denim Revolution: Levi Strauss & Co. *Research Report.* New York: Council on Economic Priorities (February).

Lydenberg, S., Marlin, A., Strub, A. & the Council on Economic Priorities. 1986. *Rating America's Corporate Conscience* New York: Council on Economic Priorities.

Moskowitz, M. 1993. Corporate Performance Roundup. *Business and Society Review*, 84: 72–79.

Nike Inc. 1993. *Nike, Inc.: A Global Company.* Beaverton, OR: Nike, Inc.

Quinn, J.B. 1992. *Intelligent Enterprise.* New York: Free Press.

Samson, D. 1994. Personal communication from the Senior Manager of Corporate Communication, Levi Strauss & Co.

Sethi, S.P. 1987. Models of business and society interaction. In S.P.Sethi & C.M. Falbe, (Eds.). *Business and Society: Dimensions of Conflict and Cooperation.* New York: Lexington Books.

Taylor, C. and Fosler, G. 1994. The necessity of being global. Across the Board, 31: 41–43.

United States Department of State. 1993. *Country reports on human rights: Practices for 1992.* Submitted to the Committee on Foreign Relations-U.S. Senate (February).

Zachary, G. 1994. Levi tries to make sure contract plants in Asia. *The Wall Street Journal*, Thursday, July 28.

AMERICAN ACTIVISTS' ATTEMPTS TO REFORM CHINA AND THE PROSPECTS FOR U.S. BUSINESS

Paul Steidlmeier

I. INTRODUCTION: OF OPEN DOORS AND LIMITED PROSPECTS

The United States has had a tumultuous history with the Peoples Republic of China. All that seemed to change with the advent of "ping pong diplomacy" and the opening of the Nixon administration to China in the early seventies. From that epoch making change, commercial relations steadily improved up until the Tiananmen incident of June 4, 1989, when the Chinese government used the armed forces to quell its opposition. In the four succeeding years relations between the two countries have often been publicly shrill. As a matter of fact, however, commercial relations slowed down only initially following Tiananmen, rather than reversing themselves, and, since 1991, they have vigorously expanded.

In a drama almost as ritualized as Beijing Opera, every June the U.S. has threatened to cancel China's "most favored nation" [MFN] status and every June China has squeaked by. One of the most tense moments came in 1991. On November 26, 1991, the Office of the United States Trade Representative threatened China with severe trade sanctions (to the level of $1.5 billion or 10% of U.S. imports from China) unless the Chinese government significantly opened up its trade and investment policy and met U.S. concerns regarding intellectual property.[1] During the preceding year, the U.S. Congress repeatedly threatened to deprive China of "most favored nation" trading status because of human rights violations and international arms sales policies.[2]

In terms of public anxiety, a turning point was reached in March, 1992, when the House voted on March 11 to override President Bush's veto of a bill (HR2212) to impose trade restrictions on China by a vote of 357–61. The Senate vote on March 18 was 60–38, only seven votes short of the two-thirds majority needed to override the veto.[3] China escaped sanctions, but it still faced considerable negative sentiment as the debate became renewed every year.

Another flashpoint was reached during Secretary of State, Warren Christopher's, visit to China in March of 1994. The U.S. seemed to adopt an inflexible position on human rights and the Chinese, equally inflexible, asserted that they could do well on their own. At the time, the Clinton administration position was widely criticized in the U.S. In the end, as the June decision to renew or cancel MFN approached, both sides wanted to get beyond the annual battle and establish a more stable basis for commercial relations.[4] Although MFN had served as an orchestrating principle for a wide variety of complex negotiations on several issues, both economic and social, the Clinton administration finally changed the policy of ritual annual threat.[5]

The first signs of change actually became apparent in January of 1994, when Treasury Secretary Lloyd Bentsen visited China. On the whole, his trip was far more positive than the subsequent visit of Mr. Christopher. Over the first half of 1994, the Clinton administration was clearly sending mixed signals. The Bentsen visit promised to be a harbinger of a new stability in U.S.-China relations. One sign of this was that the two nations' Joint Economic Committee, founded in 1979 and disbanded in 1989, was reestablished.[6] This alone did not offset the imbroglio over human rights in China. Increasingly, however, it was felt that trade and investment would dominate the real rules of the game.[7] American business lobbied very strongly and successfully to reject a "code of conduct" for doing business in China.[8] This orientation was strengthened even further in August of 1994 when Commerce Secretary Ron Brown led a high level trade delegation to China.[9] By late 1994, it became clear that human rights and social issues were no longer linked to trade and investment in a primary way.

This whole debate on economic openness and human rights has evoked an eerie time warp. At the turn of the century foreign powers were line up demanding that China include a "most favored nation" clause in Sino-foreign treaties, thereby opening its ports to the commerce of all nations, once they were open to one nation. Ironically, the first "open door" policy was put forth by the American government in 1899. It was a policy, which was *imposed upon* China and demanded equal commercial access to China for all nations.[10] The Chinese government sees the present debate within this larger historical context. No surprise then that Premier Li Peng reminded then Secretary State James Baker that for more than 100 years the Chinese people had suffered very much from foreign aggression and humiliation and "Therefore, we cherish our independence and sovereignty."[11]

American business has long been tantalized by the prospect of China's vast consumer market. When President Nixon signed the Shanghai Communique in 1972, the dream of one billion customers seemed about to become a reality.[12] The realization of this dream has been confounded by three factors.

At present, American business is being pressured on three sides. First of all, by the geopolitical interests of the U.S. government. Second, the Chinese government is insisting that American companies go along with government policies or risk being dealt out of the lucrative China business altogether. Third, American activists, bolstered by Chinese dissidents in the U.S., want American business, together with the U.S. Government, to exert pressure upon China to change.

In what follows I first present the leading geopolitical issues which frame the economic dialogue between the U.S. and China. Secondly, I discuss China's development priorities and the pressures the Chinese government places on companies to meet economic goals of China's development and industrial policies and to stay out of politics. Following this I review the principal activist issues and interpret their significance for American business prospects. These issues include China's human rights record as well as other stakeholder issues such as environmental policy, public health and tobacco policies, protection of intellectual property, and labor. Social activists (including organized labor) are exerting tremendous pressures for the United States Government to deny China Most Favored Nation (MFN) trading status and for American business to either take its investments elsewhere or, at least, exert leverage on the Chinese government to change. As noted above, the Bush administration and American business in general continued to be against such a move.

II. THE GEOPOLITICAL FRAMEWORK FOR ECONOMIC DIALOGUE

United States' relations with other countries stand on a triad of political, economic and human rights imperatives. All three are tailored to a pattern of perceived national self-interest. In an article providing an overview of U.S.-China relations, then Secretary of

State James Baker stated the policy toward China as follows:

> We want to protect human rights and advance liberty. We want to counter the threat of nuclear and missile proliferation. We want free and fair trade that benefits both countries.[13] (pp. 15–16)

Playing these three goals off each other in the calculus of national interest has led to paradoxical behavior: the U.S. government argues for non-intervention and yet has a history of intervention, defends human rights and yet allies itself with repressive regimes. The U.S. rarely deals with other countries on simply an economic basis as Japan and the EU are more prone to do. At the same time, its basic principles are frequently applied selectively to different countries. The human rights issue, for example, is frequently brandished against socialist countries but is soft-pedalled against repressive regimes, which are geopolitically significant or open to Western business. In reflecting upon American-Chinese relations from 1941 to 1991, historian Nancy Tucker put it succinctly:

> When their national security is at stake, Americans have been prepared to ally with the devil; in the absence of such a threat they prefer to associate with nations that share their values.[14]

In the case of China, economic and business issues become particularly complex. In Table 1 I summarize the principle factors which affect the status of business and economic relations.

In terms of international trade and investment, China's comeback from its banned status following the Tiananmen incident coincided with the Iraq war, where China's potential veto in the United Nations proved to be of critical importance to U.S. policy. The U.S. Government acquiesced both to Japan resuming loans in September and to the World Bank renewing its operations in December of 1990, while promising to maintain China's MFN status in the United States.[15] China has

TABLE 1   Geopolitical Factors Which Frame China/U.S. Business Prospects

GLOBAL POLITICS	• UN Veto
	• Arm Sales
	• Client States
	• Destabilization
HUMAN RIGHTS	• Western Messianism
	• Prison Labor
ECONOMIC RELATIONS	• Trade Balance
	• Restrictive Trade and Investment Policies
	• Intellectual Property

proven adept at playing its political cards (in terms of international arms sales, nuclear proliferation and policy toward client states such as North Korea and Cambodia) in order to extract economic concessions.[16]

At the same time the U.S. has been alarmed to see its trade deficit with China grow from a surplus in 1980–82 to a mushrooming deficit from 1983 to 1990. The deficit in 1986 was $1.6 billion; it grew to $3.5 billion in 1988 and to $10.4 billion in 1990, with a $15 billion deficit for 1991.[17] In 1993, early estimates project a deficit of around $25 billion. The U.S. clearly wants China to buy more American goods as well as to remove a host of trade and investment barriers.[18] This is the case not only for profits but because of jobs. In 1973 hardly any American earned his or her living from the China trade; today over 200,000 do and this figure will surely grow.[19] Because of geopolitical considerations, however, the U.S. feels it cannot really set rigid demands.

Enter human rights, which serve a dual purpose. Human rights remain a true goal of American policy, but they are also a convenient tool to rally public opinion to exert pressure upon China for economic change. Prison labor, for example, is a valid human rights issue, but also one which directly appeals to an American labor force fearful of losing jobs. American activists, as well as some Chinese dissidents domiciled in the U.S., however, are more single-minded. They are dead serious about human rights and their call for economic sanctions against China. The China human rights lobby fields a diverse array of sponsors: those for whom human rights is the real agenda and those for whom human rights provides cover for other agendas.

For their part, the Chinese are not at all enthused about the U.S. design for the new world order and strenuously object to what they term the imposition of U.S. values.[20] In fact, they view it as hypocritical as seen in a detailed article by a professor at the Foreign Affairs College.[21] In the end, American business prospects are profoundly affected by the kaleidoscopic patterns defined by geopolitical, economic and ideological concerns.

III. CHINESE HOPES FOR DEVELOPMENT AND THE RESULTANT NORMS FOR FOREIGN BUSINESSES' RELATION TO CHINESE SOCIETY

The present Chinese "open door" policy was declared in 1978. Since then the government's position regarding openness to foreign capitalism has been under constant development. Initially, China never opened the major part of the country to foreign investment. Only after some time was most of the country even open to tourism. Up until recently, foreign companies have been primarily confined to some 14 special zones and the principal coastal cities.[22]

One of the principal development issues, which emerged in Deng Xiaoping's opening of China in 1978, was that China was unable to finance the rate and style of development that it desired. Domestically it was not able to generate an adequate surplus for investment and, internationally, it was strapped by a lack of foreign exchange. In addition China was not able to keep developing the technologies it purchased (when, for example, it would buy an entire new plant outright). The result was that, even though the economy showed positive growth, China ended up behind,

both in terms of its own objectives as well as in comparison to other developing countries. To remedy the situation a number of reforms in the domestic economy have been introduced since 1979.[23] China also turned to the outside world.

What China wanted from international business at the time was very straightforward: capital, technology and management skills. By this means the Chinese hoped to initiate new enterprises and renovate old ones.[24] China wanted foreign companies to serve China's development needs. The issues can be summarized as follows:

1. Capital: a foreign company must contribute capital for investment; it may earn profits by exporting part of what it produces in China, but, ideally, it should not drain any foreign exchange out of China
2. Technology: China wants the transfer of up-to-date technology; there are considerable disputes over intellectual property and marketing restrictions
3. Management: China expects training for its managers; most important it wishes its managers to exercise ultimate control in a joint venture enterprise; it is above all the manager who is the agent of China's interests

The hard reality of China's foreign exchange and international debt picture, for example, provided the reason why China insisted throughout the eighties that much of foreign investment should be export-oriented. China explicitly planned on managing foreign investment and trade so that it would produce foreign exchange to fuel development.[25] Furthermore, in stressing "horizontal ties" between the special economic zones and the interior of China's economy, China hoped to use local sourcing as inputs in producing exported products.

In addition to capital and foreign exchange, China is interested in acquiring modern technology and management skills. The previous technology strategy of the early seventies of importing whole plants proved unsustainable in several respects. Modern industry is characterized by both major and rapidly recurring innovations in management and technology. China realized it was not competitive in this area. Even if the Chinese could clone a state of the art plant when they acquired it, they were not in a position to keep developing it. To introduce the continued technological and management innovations which they desired, they needed to have continuing partnerships. A good example of this is provided in the deal China made with McDonnell-Douglass regarding the MD-82. McDonnell-Douglass licensed the technology to China, provided management and labor training, and committed itself to including China in future developments.[26]

In one sense, China viewed the joint venture as an educational process. It carried on negotiations with the aim of securing the highest quality education, while not paying a high tuition. At the same time it recognized that it must offer an attractive deal to foreigners.[27] Joint ventures were attractive to China's leadership, because it liked the accelerated push forward which they could provide in terms of management training and technology transfer. However, China always wanted to control them according to its social priorities.[28]

For all that, by the mid-eighties, China appeared to be a fairly attractive place for investment. The "feeling out period" of 1979 to 1984 was successful. Problems with inflation during 1987/88 and the Tiananmen troubles slowed things down but did not fundamentally alter the business assessment that China was a good investment opportunity. In its 1991 study, *International Country Risk Guide*, International Business Communications Ltd. ranked China in the medium-risk category. Ranked 58th out of 129 countries, China was behind the leading democratic, market oriented countries, but ahead of most developing countries as well as all other socialist and former socialist countries except Czechoslovakia and Poland.[29] Corporations found China fairly attractive nd appeared to be willing to sacrifice short term gains for

long term leverage in Chinese markets. Yet the companies wanted some assurance of a future payoff. They also wanted to hedge against the risk of possible changes in joint venture and other investment policies. They did not want their business venture subject to the roller coaster of domestic Chinese politics.

The result is that, while in the early years potential foreign investors proved to be remarkably cautious, investment has steadily accelerated since 1991. The Chinese have shown themselves to be tough negotiators but flexible and, from a strictly business point of view, the conditions surrounding investment in China have improved over the past decade, and especially so in the past three years.[30] China sees itself as embarking on a new phase in its development; from 1992 on, it has sought an ever fuller integration into global markets. This means that China is beginning to remove the barriers separating its domestic markets from international business; the role for foreign enterprises has been vigorously expanded.

In the past two years, there seems to be an unending list of investment opportunities. The Chinese government, at various levels, sells regularly updated databases in over ten areas, providing a profile of opportunities in different sectors and regions as well as company profiles and other relevant information. The American Journal, *The China Business Review*, provides a regular chronicle of investment activity. The British Journal, *China-Britain Trade Review*, carries a listing at the end of each issue called "Business Opportunities" where projects are listed by sector.[31] While China may still wish to impose several conditions upon foreigners, opportunities are proliferating rather than decreasing.

IV. SOCIAL ACTIVIST ISSUES

The West, and America in particular, has always harbored messianic dreams to reform China. Secretary of State James Baker noted as much in commenting how American views of China have oscillated between fascination and confrontation over the past 150 years:

> When the Chinese seemed to adopt our principles—either religious or secular—we enthusiastically welcomed them into the fold. But when periodic upheavals led to disappointment and frequently bloodshed, Americans felt the anger of rejection— of a *conversion* that failed.[32] [emphasis added]

American fervor to reform China has not abated. Activists have a number of issues on the agenda, the principal one being human rights. At the same time a number of other problems have arisen. I confine myself to four which have garnered the most attention: 1) the environment, 2) public health, 3) intellectual property, and 4) labor.

Human Rights

Under Mao Dzdong the Communist Party always had a clearly repressive if not violent policy for those whom it deemed "enemies of the people."[33] In seizing power in 1949, as well as in purging what the leadership labelled "reactionaries," [notably during the Great Leap Forward (1958-60), the Cultural Revolution (1966-69), and the Post-Tiananmen (1989-present) periods], the Party policy has been clear; "re-education" for those opposed to the Party and, for those impervious to re-education, imprisonment and even death. For all his economic openness, this policy has not changed under Deng Xiaoping. A number of studies, which feature Chinese sources, attest to the gravity of the problem.[34] In terms of Chinese history, the Tiananmen massacre was not an anomaly. In early 1978-79 (as soon as he came to power) Deng moved to crush the "Democracy Wall Movement" (many of its leaders are still imprisoned, although one of the most renowned, Wei Jingsheng, was recently released, but still is harassed by the authorities). Tibet has been brutally controlled by martial law and blatant repression

of human rights. In theory the Communist Party exercises dictatorship on behalf of the people. It has, however, not proven to be a benevolent agent of the people. Rather, the Party has concentrated absolute power in its hands and maintains it by police force. At the same time, its leaders have become ensconced as a privileged class accountable to no one but themselves. The only stakeholders who seem to count seem to be the Party leaders and those who serve their interests. During the spring of 1989, the following "big character poster," addressed to China's leaders, was observed in Tiananmen Square:

> What are you lacking?
> The newspapers are in your hands
> The radio and TV are in your hands
> The guns are in your hands
> The prisons are in your hands
> So, what are you lacking, oh Emperor?
> You lack only the hearts of the people
> You lack only the truth.[35]

The pressure is on. While the Chinese government maintains a very hard line against outside interference, it is also moving to refurbish its image.[36] It is unclear how much real change has actually taken place. China is, however, at least willing to put human rights on the agenda, whereas previously it steadfastly refused to do so.[37] Over the past year the Chinese government has produced a white paper, *Human Rights in China*, summarizing the government's theories and its own report on its practices. These have drawn negative comment from the U.S. Government, to which the Chinese representative to the UN Commission on Human Rights, Zhang Yishan, has retorted:

> A country saddled with human rights violations at home and abroad has no right whatsoever to comment on human rights violations in other countries . . . This is a direct violation of international law and an expression of power politics and hegemony . . . [38]

What is often forgotten in the West, however, is that there is considerable regional diversity in China, where actual practices may widely diverge from official policy. This is particularly true of coastal and Southern China, where enforcement of the politically correct line emanating from Beijing is often attenuated if not ignored.[39]

Environment

China's official policy is to protect the environment.[40] Yet, if an investment project will earn hard currency, the government and local officials are willing to look the other way. This is not unusual for developing countries.[41] In the aftermath of the 1987 Montreal Protocol, an international conference discussing global warming, depletion of the ozone layer and related issues, China has said as much.[42] It has been joined by India, Brazil and a host of developing countries in maintaining that their primary development priority must be to feed the people and raise the standard of living to meet basic needs. If ecological concerns mean lower growth they cannot be accorded priority. Further, China has argued that it is the responsibility of developed countries and their business enterprises to develop technologies which would be in harmony with growth objectives and then to transfer these technologies to developing countries.[43] The environmental problem raises a particular issue of responsibility for foreign business enterprises, which generally do not take special means to control environmental pollution, because they know that it will not be required of them to do so. The question is whether foreign companies have an obligation to go beyond the requirements of Chinese law and practice.

If one adopts a global stakeholder framework (and the question of the ozone and global warming suggests that it is legitimate to do so), then both the foreign company as well as the set of global stakeholders may each have a distinct set of responsibilities. Indeed, the World Ozone Pact, which was reached at the end of June 1990, established a $160 million fund to help developing countries phase out non-ecological practices. Many other issues involving toxic wastes, however (such as the export of old batteries to China), have not been resolved.[44] In China and many other developing countries first world enterprises have shown themselves all to ready to dump their wastes in poor countries which need the scarce foreign exchange.[45] At present there are no effective controls and few companies show evidence of proactive moral restraint. The Chinese position supports solutions such as the Montreal Protocol and goes on to state:

> We also believe that poverty is at the root of the environmental problems of the developing world . . . We re-emphasize that we intend to participate fully in the global effort to protect the environment without hindering the development process and that this can be achieved if the right climate is created for global co-operation by a positive, constructive and practical response on the part of the developed countries . . . [46]

China insists that its domestic environmental problems call for a global framework if they are to be resolved.

Public Health and Tobacco

Tobacco provides another example of social issues which are ignored in China, because of development priorities. In China tobacco is a State monopoly. The tobacco economy is flourishing and is one of the areas of the world about which the American tobacco industry is rhapsodic.[47] While paying lip service to health concerns, the Chinese government follows an unabashedly economic policy, because tobacco accounts for over 8% of the government's total revenue.[48] In the past years China has set aside over $200 million in scarce foreign exchange to update the tobacco industry with state of the art equipment purchased from, among others, the Philip Morris Company and RJR Nabisco.[49] The American cigarette industry itself sees China as an area of tremendous growth potential and lauds the government's open attitude and its provision of special incentives to the industry in terms of high prices, subsidies and low taxes. The principal problem which American companies express regarding China is that the government seems intent on preserving its market monopoly.

For most Chinese stakeholders, the tobacco issue is not on their list of problems. The World Health Organization's worldwide campaign against smoking has had practically no effect on Chinese policy. Furthermore, the United States government and other Western governments, which actively curtail smoking at home, actively promote it in developing countries.[50] What is notable in this problem, as well as in the previous one, is the regional compartmentilization of stakeholder interests on a given issue. Regarding health and tobacco, cigarette companies in China have not concerned themselves with health warning labels, restricting advertising and other measures common in the U.S. The Law of the People's Republic of China on Tobacco Monopoly was adopted on June 29, 1991.[51] This law mandates health warnings, restricts advertising, prohibits smoking in some public places, adopts measures to dissuade youth from smoking and spells out legal liability. So far, however, the manner in which it has been implemented has not dampened the market. Dale Sisel, President and CEO of R.J. Reynolds Tobacco International, remarks:

> RJRTI has put in a request with the government of China to double capacity of its joint-venture Xiamen plant to 5 billion sticks annually. "We're selling everything we can produce," Sisel says, "and there is pent-up demand for our brand Golden Bridge that we haven't been able to supply."[52]

It appears that American companies accord top priority to a narrowly conceived economic approach. In this they are joined by the Chinese government (as well as many other developing countries, Eastern Europe and the Soviet Union). The impetus for reform clearly emanates from global public health activists who, up to now, have little real clout in China.

Intellectual Property

According to the United States International Trade Commission, China is a major violator of intellectual property rights.[53] This issue is promoted primarily by economic activists, led by industry trade groups as well as by labor. Only a few years ago Taiwan, South Korea and Brazil were also on the list until they began to amend their patent, copyright and trademark laws and practices. It is not easy to quantify losses, but most observers think the Chinese government is pretty lax in this area. Cases range from the small—where a Shanghai firm pirated "M&M's" candies and marketed them as "W&W's"—to the pirating of high technology.[54] On June 1, 1991 a new copyright law took effect in China.[55] It is very significant, however, that chapter 6, article 53, of the new law states that "Regulations for the protection of computer software shall be established separately by the State Council." This statement effectively means there is no rigorous regulation of that industry and that the issue is far from being resolved. Although the Chinese Government has promised to take action, the state of its laws and the functioning of the judicial system leave a lot to be desired.[56] The policy of the United States is to apply the sanctions associated with section 301b of the Omnibus Trade Bill of 1988, resurrected by President Clinton in trade disputes with Japan in early 1994. As U.S. trade is so important for China, this may have some results as it did with Taiwan and South Korea. The prognosis is that China will prove flexible in the end; however, one can expect delaying tactics, partial measures, poor enforcement and legal ambiguities in the process.

Labor

Regarding labor, American interests raise two issues: the lack of a free market in labor and the use of prison labor. In China, wages have a productivity component and a social welfare component (which in effect is a tax). Part of worker remuneration is composed of welfare payments to housing and other funds. There is really no market in labor; workers are assigned by the government. Manager's rights to either select workers, provide special incentives or to lay them off are severely restricted by the Chinese side, although   there is some evidence that this is beginning to change. Foreign enterprises do not face many of the regulations which they find in the United States under OSHA (the Occupational Safety and Health Administration established in 1970). However, wage rates in foreign enterprise factories are higher than in ordinary Chinese factories. Typically, the wage levels of the staff and workers of joint ventures are fixed at 120% to 150% of the "real wages" of the staff and workers of state enterprises in the same locality. While an unskilled employee in north china might have a take-home pay of $40, the direct cost to the joint venture would approximate $140.[57] Given China's population pressures, there is a mounting problem of unemployment. Government authorities fear that a true labor market would severely aggravate this situation and they are very reluctant to make changes. The policy seems to be to remain competitive with the Asian labor market but not to drive wages below that.

At the same time, human rights activists as well as American workers fearful of losing their jobs are raising a storm over China's policies regarding prison labor.[58] They are urging the U.S. government to prohibit any imports produced by prison labor. China is pretending to go along, but critics assert that China is actually setting up an obstacle course by separating the trading companies from the factories which supply them with products to sell. The trading company can honestly say it uses no prison labor, while claiming ignorance regarding its suppliers. For the most part, American business is forswearing the use of prison labor.

VI. PUBLIC POLICY RECOMMENDATIONS AND BUSINESS STRATEGIES: AMERICAN INVESTMENT AND MOST FAVORED NATION STATUS

In a manner analogous to the situation in South Africa, corporations are challenged as to whether it is morally justifiable to deal with a repressive and morally illegitimate government.

For most corporations, after June 1989, when things died down a bit and the U.S. became preoccupied with Iraq, it proved to be business as usual. Both Western governments and companies put China on hold for about a year. No one really withdrew, however. Some new investments were delayed, but mainly due to fears of instability. As early as June, 1990, Japan was calling for change and by August it resumed loans to China. By December 1990, the World Bank (with U.S. approval) was resuming loans to the Peoples' Republic.[59] China's leadership is again being clothed in moral respectability. For their part, Western corporations (and governments) basically present an argument of moral leverage: being present in China will be a greater force for good than withdrawing and leaving China isolated. This is increasingly the argument as trade and investment have boomed since 1991.

While the leverage argument is not without merit, the South African experience seems to suggest that sanctions can also bring pressure to bear upon governments so that they yield to leverage. Leverage and judicious choice of sanctions can work in tandem. To this end many continue to campaign for the U.S. to deny China Most Favored Nation (MFN) trading status, or at least threaten it. In 1990 U.S./China merchandise trade totalled some $19.9 billion, with China running a $10.3 billion surplus which, in 1991 topped $15 billion.[60] Since then it has continued to accelerate, approaching $25 billion in 1993. If China were denied MFN status it would suf-

TABLE 2 The Effects on China of non-MFN Tariffs

Item	MFN Tariffs (%) Range	Non-MFN Tariffs (%) Range
rubber manufactures	0–15.0	0–80.0
photographic equipment	0–8.5	0–35.0
organic chemicals	0–20.0	0–149.5
silk	0–7.8	0–90.0
cotton	0–33.0	0–68.5
footwear	2.8–48.0	25–84.0
knitwear/jackets	6–34.6	35–90.0
non-knitwear	3–32.0	35–90.0
toys	10–12.0	0–90.0
dolls	12.0	70.0
electric trains	6.8	70.0
sweaters, vests	6.0	70.0
petroleum	10.5*	21.0
rubber footwear	6.0	35.0
telephones	8.5	35.0
artificial flowers	9.0	71.5
stuffed toys	6.8	70.0
rubber, plastic-soled footwear	10.0	20.0
radio-tape players	3.7	35.0

*cents.bbl

SOURCE: *China Trade Report*, (Hong Kong) v. XXVII, June 1990, p. 1; a similar study based upon U.S. Customs statistics was published in "Letter From the President," *The China Business Review*, May-June, 1990, pp. 6–9.

fer a severe blow to its development plans. However, this could also be a major setback for the reformers and provide the hardliners with an opportunity for a crackdown. The Chinese government remains very sensitive to this issue and, as noted above, has indicated some flexibility, not so much in what it says but in what it actually does.

The move to deny MFN status would clearly hurt China. As illustrated in Table 2, the tariffs on China's major exports would jump dramatically. The U.S. is China's largest market, while China is the fifteenth largest U.S. market accounting for slightly more than 1% of total U.S. trade.

U.S. firms would not emerge unscathed, however. In 1991, U.S. investments in China total some $2 billion, much of which is export oriented. American firms would suffer from the increased tariffs.[61] China would also retaliate. Speaking in May of 1991 Premier Li

Peng asserted that if China lost MFN status, "American industrial and business interests would lose a potential huge market.[62] That point has been reiterated several times since. The Chinese have also pointed out that higher tariffs would hurt American consumers, as China accounts for 33% of the American toy market, 15% of the imported clothing market and 10% of the footwear market.[63] In addition, many U.S. firms doing business in China import a significant portion of parts and raw materials, which would face higher Chinese tariffs.

Denial of MFN status to China is problematic on other grounds as well. It is highly unlikely that either the European Union, Japan or the ASEAN nations would follow suit. As a strategy to pressure China, the denial of MFN status would likely be ineffective, while harming U.S. commercial interests.

Another issue complicates the whole scenario: China's geopolitical power. China possesses nuclear technology, is a major arms exporter (to the Middle East among other places), plays a pivotal role in the future of Kampuchea, the Koreas and Viet Nam, possesses a permanent seat in the U.N. Security Council, and could be a catalyst in mobilizing developing country sentiment against United States interests. In the Iraq war China clearly traded political acquiescence, if not support, for economic favors. It has acted in the same way with respect to proposed UN sanctions against North Korea and Libya. In world politics, China is playing its own "China card" with apparent success. The U.S. Government position that "China not be isolated" is a euphemism for the political hardball that is being played.

Leverage and sanctions are not incompatible strategies. They can well be judiciously combined. I think that the return to business as usual in China in the field on international loans and trade is a moral error. It forgets the big character poster cited above. While the internal affairs of a country are to be respected, a government clique has no moral right to savage its own people in the name of state sovereignty. Pressure must be applied judiciously, however, and with solid hope of success. There is scope, for example, for partial restrictions in areas such as Chinese exports of goods made with inhumane "gulag" prison labor.[64] Other possible areas for restrictions include trade and loan concessions, military goods, high technology, and Chinese investments in the U.S.[65] Continued selective sanctions would serve to keep the issue alive and enable companies present in China to argue with the Chinese for securing broader stakeholder interests so that business could continue unencumbered by mounting U.S. legislation. With the return to business as usual the Chinese leadership, in effect, has paid little for its repression.

With regard to China's own development priorities, I think China's business/society stance is correct in insisting that foreign enterprises be in accord with its development priorities. Companies will have to judge whether China's policies on capital, technology, management and labor provide a strategic fit with the company's mission. If not, a company would be advised to postpone its China involvement. One has to add, however, that human rights violations prevent the Chinese people from freely articulating their own development priorities. That the government's priorities may not be the people's is borne out by the tremendous diversity of policies and practices found in the coastal regions and in South China. American companies should take advantage of the *de facto* situation, while realizing that open confrontation or an open break does not fit Chinese culture and the way of doing things. Even so, the present Chinese government's development plans do possess some economic logic and have produced significant economic results.[66] If Taiwan and South Korea are any guide, internal pressures will continue to build for a more participatory society.

For a corporation to be a "good citizen" in China means adopting a different posture than it would in a developed country. In this context, a proactive social strategy would call for integrating company strategic objectives with China's development priorities, crafting a fit between official policy and *de facto* divergent policies. China's development policies have always exhibited ambiguous characteristics. It is important to remember that ambiguity provides room for maneuver. In terms of stakeholder theory, the Chinese ask that, for a particular investment, the Chinese people (both individually and as a whole) be accorded priority in balancing out the interests of various constituencies. Possible conflicts may arise between stakeholders in an investment project and home country stakeholders in the company in general. The Chinese suggest, that, for a particular project at least, China has priority as the effective home country. The company must consider China and the Chinese as the primary stakeholders.

Regarding issues such as environmental protection and tobacco, I think international accords such as the World Ozone Pact represent the kinds of solutions called for, because they attack the capital problem underlying the issues. China is not unique with respect to these problems. Rather, it presents problems typical of many developing countries.

Regarding intellectual property, it seems that only U.S. 301b trade sanctions will have an immediate effect for American companies. They have proven effective elsewhere. Long term, however, international negotiations regarding patents, copyrights and trademarks will have the most effect if tied to OECD as well as to GATT and IMF policies. American companies should explore many other commercial options at their disposal.

To conclude, the prospects for U.S. business in China are essentially positive, while not optimal. It is important for business to actively lobby both governments to create a more positive business environment. Unless pressure is judiciously applied, little change will take place. For the U.S. government to pursue narrow geopolitical interests without the support of the developed world would only hurt American business; conversely, allowing economic relations to prosper will provide a more solid foundation for geopolitical harmony. In dealing with the Chinese, American companies should take pains to align their strategic objectives with China's development priorities (official and unofficial). With respect to human rights, American business should avoid obvious land mines such as prison labor, at the same time lobbying the Chinese government to the effect that a more favorable social environment will help business relations prosper. Regarding intellectual property, American business should continue to urge the U.S. government to pressure China to change under 301b legislation. At the same time it should pursue a wider variety of intellectual property strategies, including competitive and cooperative market strategies, participating in drafting global standards, settling disputes by way of arbitration as well as legal suits, and supporting

global accords.[67] Finally, issues of the environment and public health are best handled by not causing the harm in the first place. Those problems will not be resolved, however, without solving the capital and fiscal problems, which lie at their base. With respect to tobacco, it is unlikely that it will be banned. The U.S. government and American companies should at least support the public health legislation, which is found in developed countries.

Business support for sensible public policy in these areas will enhance its long-term interests. In the end, American companies cannot completely control either the U.S. government, the Chinese government or activists. It can, however, take a proactive and constructive stance in shaping the future. Prospects will be brighter to the degree it does just that.

NOTES

1. Keith Bradsher, "Chinese Goods Listed for Higher Tariffs in Trade Dispute," *New York Times*, November 28, 1991, p. D10.
   Eduardo Lachica, "U.S. Issues List of Chinese Exports Subject to Tariff," *Wall St. Journal*, November 29, 1991, p. B3.
2. Davis S. Cloud, "Sentiment Grows in Congress to Reject MFN for China," *Congressional Quarterly Weekly*, April 27, 1991, pp. 1044–1046.
3. *Congressional Quarterly Weekly*, "House OKs Override of China MFN," March 14, 1992, p. 608.
   Keith Bradsher, "China Will Keep Trade Privileges," *New York Times*, March 19, 1992, p. A5.
4. *The Economist*, "Colliding with China," March 12, 1994, pp. 37–38.
   Patrick E. Tyler, "Beijing Says It Could Live Well Even if U.S. Trade Was Cut Off," *New York Times*, March 21, 1994, pp. A1, A10.
   Thomas L. Friedman, "U.S. Signals China It May End Annual Trade-Rights Battles," *New York Times*, March 24, 1994, pp. A1, A13.
5. *New York Times*, "Clinton and China: How Promise Self-Destructed," May 29, 1994, pp. A1, A8.

6. Thomas J. Friedman, "Bank Rules Are Eased by China," *New York Times*, January 22, 1994, pp. 37, 49.
7. Thomas L. Friedman, "Trade vs Human Rights," *New York Times*, February 6, 1994, pp. A1, A10.
8. Edward A. Gargan, "Business Objects to a Code in China," *New York Times*, May 24, 1994, p.D2.
9. David Lindorff, "Ron Brown's 'Lovefest' in Beijing," *Business Week*, September 12, 1994, p. 54.
   Thomas L. Friedman, "Clinton Votes for Business," *New York Times*, May 27, 1994, p. A1.
   Douglas Jehl, "U.S. to Maintain Trade Privileges for China's Goods: A Policy Reversal, President Seeking Other Levers to Get Beijing to Improve Human Rights," *New York Times*, May 27, 1994, p. A1.
10. David G. Brown, *Partnership with China: Sino-Foreign Joint Ventures in Historical Perspective*, Boulder, CO, Westview Press, p. 33–35.
11. *Beijing Review*, "Baker's Mission to China Called a Success," November 25–December 1, 1991; p. 7.

12. Christopher Engholm, *The China Venture: America's Corporate Encounter with the People's Republic of China*, Glenview, IL, Scott, Foresman and Co., 1989, pp. 1–3.

13. James A. Baker III, "America in Asia: Emerging Architecture for a Pacific Community," *Foreign Affairs*, v. 70, n. 5, Winter, 1991–1992, pp. 1–18.
    The official Chinese press identifies the same variables. See Gu Dexin, "Three Factors Affecting Sino-US Relations," *Beijing Review*, September 30–October 6, 1991, pp. 30–33; Zhu Qizhen, "China's Foreign Policy: Independent Policy of Peace," *Beijing Review,* April 29–May 5, 1991, pp. 35–39.

14. Nancy Bernkopf Tucker, "China and America: 1941–1991," *Foreign Affairs*, v. 70, n. 5, Winter 1991–1992, pp. 75–92; p. 92.

15. Stephen Labaton, "World Bank Lends China $114 Million," *New York Times*, December 5, 1990, p. A13. Japan moved first. Barely one year after Tiananmen at the G-7 meeting in Houston it sought approval to resume a 810 billion Yen loan which was arranged before the incident. *Japan Economic Institute Report*, "Tokyo Pursues Independent Path on China At Summit," no. 27B, July 13, 1990, pp. 1–3.

16. U.S. Arms Control and Disarmament Agency, *World Military Expenditures and Arms Transfers*, 1990, Washington, DC, U.S. Government Printing, 1991.

17. United States International Trade Commission, *Composition of U.S. Merchandise Trade, 1986–1990*, Washington, DC, U.S. Government Printing Office, 1991, p. 66–69.

18. Central Intelligence Agency, U.S. Government, *The Chinese Economy in 1990 and 1991: Uncertain Recovery*, Washington, DC, U.S. Government Printing Office, 1991. Appendix C of this document, "Measures Adopted to Strengthen Central Control Over China's Trade, 1988–1991," details 59 restrictive trade practices adopted between January 1988 and January 1991.

19. Thomas L. Friedman, "Trade vs Human Rights," *New York Times*, February 6, 1994, pp. A1, A10.

20. Pan Tongwen, "New World Order—According to Mr. Bush," *Beijing Review*, October 28–November 3, 1991, pp. 12–14.

21. Liu Wenzong, "On the Human Rights Diplomacy of the United States," *Guoji Wenti Yanjiu [International Studies]*, July 13, 1993, pp. 28–34; JPRS-CAR-93-067, September 15, 1993, pp. 1–5.

22. Huang Taihe, "Development of China's SEZ," *Beijing Review*, April 8-14, 1991, pp. 20–26.
    Jerome Alan Cohen and Stuart J. Valentine, "Foreign Direct Investment in the People's Republic of China: Progress, Problems and Proposals," *Journal of Chinese Law*, 16, 1, 1987, pp. 161–215.

23. World Bank, *China Between Plan and Market*, Washington, DC, 1990.

24. Li Peng, "Report on the Outline of the Ten-Year Programme and of the Eighth Five-Year Plan for National Economic and Social Development," Address to the Fourth Session of the Seventh Annual People's Congress, March 25, 1991; reprinted in *Beijing Review*, April 15–21, 1991, pp. I–XXIV.
    Chu Baotai, "China—A Major Recipient of International Investment in the 1990s," *Intertrade*, February, 1991, pp. 39–41.

25. Yin Jieyan, "Foreign Exchange Administration," *Intertrade* (Beijing) April, 1991, pp. 28–31.
    Intertrade (Beijing), "China's Policy for Export-Oriented Industries," April, 1990, pp. 60–61.

26. The Chinese provide a glowing account of their dealings with McDonnell-Douglass. See Li Ming, "MD and China Creating a New Tomorrow," *Beijing Review*, July 29–August 4, 1991; pp. 13–15.

27. Chu Baotai, *Foreign Investment in China: Questions an Answers*, Beijing Foreign Languages Press, 1986, p. 34.

28. Xinhua News Agency, "Chen Jinhua on Reform during Eighth Five Year Plan," *Newsletter*, N. 51, October 25, 1990.
    Cheng Sanyan and Nie Haiou, "Laws Related to Foreign Investment in China," *Intertrade* (Beijing), February, 1991, pp. 20–24.

29. Cited in *Wall St. Journal*, "Rating Risk in the Hot Countries," September 20, 1991, p. R4; the article also cites similar results in an Economist Intelligence Unit study.

30. Coopers and Lybrand, *Business Opportunities in the Far East*, Homewood, IL, Dow Jones Irwin, 1990, Part V, China, pp. 507–602.
    Kearney, A.T., Ltd., and International Trade Research Institute of the People's Republic of China, *Managing Equity Joint Ventures in China*, Chicago and London, 1987.
    The Chinese view is presented in Zheng

Baoyin and Han Qi, "Management Problems in Foreign-Invested Enterprises and Their Solutions," *International Trade Journal* (Chinese), February 28, 1991, pp. 8–13; translated by U.S. Government, Joint Publications Research Service, May 22, 1991, CAR-91-028, pp. 54–60.

31. Information of the databases is outlined in Jo Drew, "Chinese Business Information Databases," *China-Britain Trade Review*, November 1993, pp. 7–8.

32. James A. Baker III, "America in Asia: Emerging Architecture for a Pacific Community," *Foreign Affairs*, v. 70, n. 5, Winter, 1991–1992, pp. 1–18; p. 15.

33. Mao Dzdong, *On the Correct Handling of Contradictions Among the People*, Beijing, Foreign Languages Press. 1958.

34. United States Congress, House Foreign Affairs Committee, *Country Reports on Human Rights Practices for 1990*, Washington, DC, U.S. Government Printing Office, 1991.
Amnesty International, *Prisoners of Conscience in the People's Republic of China*, New York, NY, 1987.
Amnesty International, *Preliminary Findings on Killings of Unarmed Civilians Arbitrary Arrests and Summary Executions Since June 3, 1989*, New York, NY, 1989.
Asia Watch, "Two Years After Tiananmen: Political Prisoners in China," New York, NY, May 31, 1991.

35. Hua Sheng, "Big Character Posters in China: A Historical Survey," *Journal of Chinese Law*, v. 4, n. 2, Fall 1990, pp. 233–256; p. 255.

36. Patrick E.Tyler, "China Promises U.S. To Try to Improve Its Human Rights," *New York Times*, January 16, 1994, pp. A1, A9.

37. Guo Jisi, "On Human Rights and Development Right," *Beijing Review*, February 11–17, 1991, pp. 16–18.
Fan Guoxiang, "Thoughts on Human Rights Conference," *Beijing Review*, April 1–7, 1991, pp. 14–15.

38. *Beijing Review*, "U.S. Official's Allegations Refuted," March 2–8, 1992, p. 27.

39. Ezra F. Vogel, *One Step Ahead in China: Guangdong Under Reform*, Cambridge, MA, Harvard University Press, 1989.
Secretary of State Baker, op. cit., cites the growing "integration" of China's coastal provinces with Hong Kong, Taiwan and the global economy (p. 16).

40. Lester Ross and Mitchell A.Silk, "China—Environmental Regulation: Developments and Trends." *East Asian Executive Reports*, v. 10, November 15, 1988, p. 11.
For the Chinese view, see *Beijing Review*, "Beijing Declaration on Environment, Development," July 8-14, 1991, pp. 10–14.

41. Bernhard Glaeser, ed., *Learning from China? Development and Environment in Third World Countries*, London, Allen and Unwin, 1987.

42. Dale S. Bryk, "The Montreal Protocol and Recent Developments to Protect the Ozone Layer," *Harvard Environmental Law Review*, vol. 15, n. 275, pp. 275–298.
See also *Facts on File*, "World Ozone Pact Reached," June 29, 1990, pp. 512–513.

43. Liu Huaqiu, "Environment and Development: Inseparable Issues," *Beijing Review*, March 23–29, 1992, pp. 45–47.

44. Center for Investigative Reporting, *Global Dumping Ground*, San Francisco, CA, 1990.

45. United States Congress, House of Representatives, Committee on Foreign Affairs, Subcommittee on Human Rights and International Organizations, *U.S. Waste Exports*, 101st Cong, 1st session, HR2525, Washington, DC, Government Printing Office, 1989.

46. *Beijing Review*, "Beijing Declaration on Environment, Development," July 8–14, 1991, pp. 12, 14.

47. Coleman, Zimmerman, "Spotlight on China," *Tobacco Reporter*, February 1993, pp. 24–38.

48. International Tobacco Growers' Association, *Tobacco in the Developing World*, West Sussex, England, 1990.

49. Chadha, K.K. and Joe Sokohl, "Spotlight on China; Cautious Optimism in Tobacco Trade," *Tobacco Reporter*, March, 1990, pp. 22–23.

50. Editorial Research Report, *Tobacco Industry: On the Defensive, But Still Strong*, Vol. 1, 35, September 21, 1990, Washington, DC, Congressional Quarterly.

51. Zheng Suping, "Spotlight on China: Monopoly Becomes Law," *Tobacco Reporter*, January 1992, pp. 18–20.

52. David E. Doolittle, "Update: R.J. Reynolds Tobacco International—Major Avenues of Growth," *Tobacco Review*, March 1992, pp. 20–24; quote from p. 24.

53. *Business Week*, "The West's Tough New Line Against China," May 20, 1991, pp. 56–57.

54. Business International, *Business China*, November 12, 1990, pp. 162–168. The Chinese

authorities have stopped the pirating of candies, but have not moved significantly in high technology areas.

55. *Intertrade* (Beijing), "Copyright Law of the People's Republic of China," May/June, 1991, pp. 56–60.

56. Yu Jianyang, "Protect Intellectual Property Rights and Improve the Investment Environment," *Beijing Review*, June 3–9, 1991, pp. 31–33. *Beijing Review* "Remarkable Progress Made in China's Intellectual Property Rights Protection," June 24–30, pp. 32–33.

57. Jerome Alan Cohen and Stuart J. Valentine, "Foreign Direct Investment in the People's Republic of China: Progress, Problems and Proposals," *Journal of Chinese Law*, 1, 1987, p. 196; pp. 162–215.

58. Asia Watch, "Prison Labor in China," April 19, 1991, 244 pp. (photocopy).

59. United States International Trade Commission, "Resumption of Development Loans to China," *International Economic Review*, Washington DC, March 1991, pp. 4–5.

60. United States International Trade Commission, *U.S. Trade Shifts in Selected Commodity Areas*, Washington, DC, 1990, p. 1–4. For Hong Kong figures see *China Trade Report*, v. XXVII, June 1990, p. 1. Official U.S. trade figures include Chinese re-exports through Hong Kong (some $6 billion) while China does not.

61. *The China Business Review*, "MFN: Sorting Out the Issues," July–August, 1991, pp. 12–13.

62. Li Peng, "Continued Calls for Renewal of MFN Status," *Beijing Review*, n. 20, May 20–26, 1991, pp. 6–7. A more detailed Chinese statement of their position, including geopolitical ramifications, is presented in *Beijing Review* "MFN: For a Realistic and Wise Decision," June 17–23, 1991, pp. 31–35.

63. *Beijing Review*, "Bush's Comments on MFN Commented," May 27–June 2, 1991, pp. 9–10.

64. Asia Watch, "Prison Labor in China," New York, NY, April 19, 1991.

65. As of January 1991, China has strategically invested $720 million in 500 enterprises in 79 countries and regions. See Xu Xianquan and Li Gang, "International Operations of Chinese Enterprises," *Intertrade* (Beijing), January, 1991, pp. 7–8.

66. *Beijing Review*, "Statistical Communique of the State Statistical Bureau of the People's Republic of China on 1991 National Economic and Social Development," March 23–29, 1992, pp. 37–44.

67. Paul Steidlmeier, "International Technology Strategies Under Inadequate Protection of Intellectual Property," *Business in the Contemporary World*, v. 3, n. 4, Summer 1991, pp. 83–91.